The Wiley-Blackwell Handbook of Legal and Ethical Aspects of Sex Offender Treatment and Management

The Wiley-Blackwell Handbook of Legal and Ethical Aspects of Sex Offender Treatment and Management

Edited by

Karen Harrison and Bernadette Rainey

A John Wiley & Sons, Ltd., Publication

Library of Congress Cataloging-in-Publication Data
The Wiley-Blackwell handbook of legal and ethical aspects of sex offender treatment and
management / edited by Karen Harrison and Bernadette Rainey.
    p. cm.
  Includes index.
  ISBN 978-1-119-94555-0 (cloth)
  1. Sex offenders.   2. Sex offenders–Rehabilitation.   3. Sex offenders–
Treatment.   4. Sex crimes–Treatment.   5. Sex crimes–Moral and ethical
aspects.   6. Forensic psychology.   I. Harrison, Karen,   1974-   II. Rainey,
Bernadette.   III. Handbook of legal and ethical aspects of sex offender treatment and
management.
  K5194.W55 2013
  364.4'045–dc23
                      2012033915

A catalogue record for this book is available from the British Library.

Cover image: Untitled 35, 2006. © Mario Ayerbe/Getty Images.
Cover design by www/cyandesign.co.uk

Set in 10/12.5 pt Galliard by Toppan Best-set Premedia Limited
Printed and bound in Malaysia by Vivar Printing Sdn Bhd

1   2013

Contents

About the Contributors

Sherry Ashfield joined the Lucy Faithfull Foundation in 2001 and works as a principal practitioner informing its work with female abusers. Sherry provides assessment, intervention, consultancy and training services to many organizations including probation trusts, the prison service, local authorities and the voluntary and community sector.

J.C. Barnes is an Assistant Professor in the Criminology Program at the University of Texas at Dallas. His primary research focus seeks to understand how genetic and environmental factors combine to impact criminological phenomena. His work can be found in journals such as *Aggressive Behavior, Criminology, Intelligence, Journal of Marriage and Family, Justice Quarterly* and *Physiology & Behavior*.

Dr Raphaela Basdekis-Jozsa is a senior physician at the Institute for Sex Research and Forensic Psychiatry. She studied Medicine and Philosophy at the University of Hamburg, graduating in 1999, and received her doctorate in pure research in 2000. Dr Basdekis-Jozsa has been a member of the International Association for the Treatment of Sexual Offenders and the German Association for Sex Research since 2010. She has published pieces on co-morbidity of schizophrenia and addiction, psychoeducation of heroin addicts and sex addiction. Her main research activities include the pharmacological and psychotherapeutic treatment of sexual offenders, hypersexuality, sexual homicide, and new developments in laws on preventive detention and their impact on forensic psychiatric assessments.

Professor (Dr) Peer Briken is the Director of the Institute for Sex Research and Forensic Psychiatry. He studied medicine at the University of Hamburg, graduating in 1998, with further studies in psychiatry, psychotherapy and sexual medicine in 2006. He completed his postdoctoral thesis in 2006 and became a Professor of sex research and forensic psychiatry and Director of the institute in 2010. His main research activities include pharmacological and psychotherapeutic treatment of sexual offenders, sexual homicide, hypersexuality, juvenile sexual offenders and delinquency, and the sexual relationships of juveniles. He is a reviewer for many international journals, an editorial board member of the *Open Forensic Science Journal* and *Sex Offender Treatment* and Editor of the *German Journal of Sex Research*. He is also a member of several societies: the German Association for Psychiatry and Psychotherapy, the German Association for Sex Research and the International Association for the Treatment of Sexual Offenders. Since 2010 he has been the President of the German Association for Sex Research.

Douglas P. Boer, PhD, is an Associate Professor of Clinical Psychology at the University of Waikato. Prior to 2006, he worked for the Correctional Service of Canada. Among other publications, he has co-authored the Sexual Violence Risk – 20 (the SVR-20) and the Assessment of Risk and Manageability of Intellectually Disabled Individuals who Offend – Sexually (the ARMIDILO-S). He is the New Zealand editor of the journal *Sexual Abuse: Australia, New Zealand* and is on several other editorial boards. Dr Boer is also a Research Associate of the Institute of Sex Research and Forensic Psychiatry at the University Medical Center Hamburg-Eppendorf, Germany, a Clinical Advisor to the KAOS program at the Hospital Brøset, Trondheim, Norway, and a Visiting Professor in the Department of Psychiatry of the University of São Paulo, Brazil.

Sheila Brotherston is Criminal Justice Services Director for Women and Young People with the Lucy Faithfull Foundation in the United Kingdom. She currently manages the Lucy Faithfull Foundation's work with female sex offenders.

Peter Brown is a PhD student at the Cardiff School of Journalism, Media and Cultural Studies. His research interests are in media representations of child sexual abuse and his thesis compares the framing of public discourses around online "grooming" in Australia, Canada, the United Kingdom and the United States.

Christmas Covell, PhD, received her doctorate in clinical psychology from the University of Nebraska-Lincoln, specializing in forensic psychology. Her work has focused on performance of psycho-legal evaluations, as well as treatment of individuals with sexual behavior problems across a variety of institutional and community settings. Dr Covell is a licensed psychologist in private practice, and presently provides forensic evaluation, clinical consultation and treatment services in Washington State.

Nora V. Demleitner is the Dean of Washington and Lee University School of Law and Roy L. Steinheimer Professor of Law. Her scholarly work has been in the sentencing field, with an emphasis on collateral sanctions and on the intersection between crime and immigration. She is the lead author of *Sentencing: Law and Policy* (3rd edn., Aspen, 2012). Much of her writing is comparative, and has been published in a host of leading US law reviews. Professor Demleitner has also previously served as Dean at Hofstra University's Maurice A. Deane School of Law. She holds a J.D. from Yale Law School, a B.A. from Bates College, and an LL.M. from the Georgetown University Law Center.

Hilary Eldridge is Chief Executive of the Lucy Faithfull Foundation, a child protection charity preventing and working with child sexual abuse in the United Kingdom.

She co-authors and monitors assessment and treatment programs for adult male offenders, female offenders, young people and their families. She is an honorary lecturer in Forensic Psychology at the University of Birmingham.

Ian Elliott is a research psychologist with the Lucy Faithfull Foundation, where he is engaged in a project relating both to female sexual offending and internet offending. Ian is also a Course Tutor in Forensic Psychology at the University of Birmingham. He has published and presented research findings at both national and international conferences.

Phil Fennell is a Professor of Law at Cardiff University where he teaches Public Law, Mental Health Law and Medical Law. He has written widely on mental health law. His recent books include *Mental Health: Law and Practice* (2nd edn., Jordans, 2011) (with Lawrence Gostin and others) and *Principles of Mental Health Law* (Oxford University Press, 2010).

Dr Bill Glaser has been Consultant Psychiatrist to the Sex Offender Programs run by Corrections Victoria and to the Disability Forensic Assessment and Treatment Service run by the Victorian Department of Human Services. He is a member of the Forensic Leave Panel of Victoria, and a Visiting Fellow at the Consulting and Custom Programs of the University of Melbourne, where he coordinates a course in Forensic Disability. Bill's publications have focused on sex offenders, offenders with an intellectual disability, the assessment of personal injury litigants and the ethics of offender treatment programs.

Stephen Hanvey was appointed as the first CEO to Circles UK, the national organization for Circles of Support and Accountability in England and Wales, in December 2007. Stephen has a professional background in social work and charity management and worked initially in a London authority social services department, and then with various family support organizations, managing a Barnardos community development project in East London for seven years. Stephen has facilitated self-help groups for survivors of sexual abuse. He has written a number of articles on Circles of Support and Accountability and recently co-authored the first book on the subject, *A Community-Based Approach to the Reduction of Sexual Reoffending; Circles of Support and Accountability* (Jessica Kingsley, 2011).

Grant Harris, PhD, is the Director of Research, Waypoint Centre for Mental Health, Associate Professor of Psychology (adjunct) at Queen's University, and Associate Professor of Psychiatry (adjunct) at the University of Toronto. He is also a Fellow of the Canadian Psychological Association. Dr Harris has published extensively in the scientific and academic literature on violence risk assessment, sexual aggression, psychopathy and mental disorder.

Dr Karen Harrison is a Senior Lecturer in the School of Law at the University of Hull. She has research interests in sentencing, the use of community penalties and dangerous offenders; her current research is focused on dangerous offenders, with several articles published on the use of pharmacotherapy with high risk sex offenders. She has recently published her first monograph with Routledge, which is entitled *Dangerousness, Risk and the Governance of Serious Sexual and Violent Offenders*. Karen is an editorial board member of both the *Journal of Sexual Aggression* and the *Prison Service Journal* and is an Associate Editor of *Sexual Offender Treatment*.

Dr Knut Hermstad is a Specialist in Clinical Sexology NACS, and a Senior Adviser at the University Hospital of Trondheim. He is a member of the Scientific Board of the International Association for the Treatment of Sexual Offenders. His field of expertise is the treatment of sexual offenders and he has written several articles and scientific literature.

Mari Hirayama is Associate Professor of Law, Hakuoh University. Her recent research has examined the impact of the Lay Judge System on criminal justice policy for sex crime in Japan. Her publications include (with others) *Introduction to Criminal Procedure* (Yachiyo, 2011) (Japanese) and *Direction of Criminology – Challenge of Legal Criminology* (Horitsu Bunka, 1st edn. 2003, 2nd edn. 2007) (Japanese),

Mechtild Höing has been a lecturer at Avans University of Applied Sciences and Breda School of Social Studies and a researcher at the Avans Centre for Public Safety and Criminal Justice, since 2009. Mechtild has a Master's degree in Sociology and is currently a PhD candidate at Tilburg University, studying Circles of Support and Accountability. Since moving from her birth country of Germany to the Netherlands in 1979, she has assisted in a community development project in Breda for one year, worked as a social worker in a women's shelter for two years, a nurse in a mental health clinic for eight years, and from 2000 to 2009 as a (senior) researcher for Rutgers WPF, a Dutch Centre on Sexology. This involved studying sexual victimization, sexual offending and the effects of preventive programs.

Rebecca L. Jackson, PhD, is a licensed Clinical Psychologist who works exclusively in the field of sex offender civil commitment. She holds a faculty position with Palo Alto University and works with several Sex Offender Civil Commitment programs around the country. She is the current President of the Sex Offender Civil Commitment Programs Network (SOCCPN) and serves on the editorial board of *Psychology, Public Policy, and Law*. In 2008, she received the Theodore Blau Early Career Award from the American Psychological Association and the American Psychological Foundation. Her research and publications are primarily in the field of sex offender civil commitment and psychopathy.

Dr Jann Karp is a lecturer in criminology and holds a PhD in social policy. Having spent 23 years as a serving police officer in New South Wales, Jann's research interests consist of monitoring criminal and deviant behavior within discreet groups. She has written two text books; the first addresses police corruption and the second centers on the professional activities of interstate truck drivers. Jann's current research relates to the evaluation of increasing regulatory oversight and consideration of its effectiveness in crime prevention.

Dr Xanthè Mallett is a lecturer in criminology and practicing forensic anthropologist. Her area of expertise is human identification. She has worked on a collaborative facial recognition project with the FBI, has undertaken casework in the area of child sex abuse, and has co-authored expert witness reports. Her research relates to behavior patterns of sex offenders, and societal, legal and political responses to cases of child sexual abuse on an international scale.

William L. Marshall, OC, FRSC, PhD, C Psych, is Director of Rockwood Psychological Services which provides treatment for sexual offenders in various settings. He has over 380 publications including 20 books, and he has served on the editorial boards of 17 international journals. Bill has received several awards and in 2006 he was appointed an Officer of the Order of Canada, Canada's highest honor for a civilian, which was awarded for Bill's national and international contributions to making societies safer.

Liam E. Marshall, PhD, has been treating and conducting research on offenders for more than 15 years. He has helped design preparatory, regular, denier, low-functioning, maintenance and juvenile sexual offender programs, as well as anger management, domestic violence, gambling, self-esteem and cognitive skills programs. Liam has many publications including three books and more than 50 peer-reviewed journal articles. He has made numerous international conference presentations on sexual offending, sexual addiction, violence, aging and problem gambling issues and has delivered more than 70 trainings for therapists who work with sexual and violent offenders in 15 countries worldwide. Liam is a reviewer and board member for a number of international journals on sexually problematic behavior and gambling problems. He is currently a therapist, and training and research director for Rockwood Psychological Services; he is a consultant to the Royal Ottawa Health Care Group Secure Treatment Unit and to the St Lawrence Youth Association.

Dr Anne-Marie McAlinden is Reader in Law at Queen's University Belfast. Her first book, *The Shaming of Sexual Offenders* (Hart, 2007) was awarded the British Society of Criminology Book Prize 2008. A further monograph, *Grooming: The Familial, Institutional and Internet Abuse of Children*, is to be published by Oxford University Press in 2012 (Clarendon Series).

Sheri Oz, MSc, is a family and marital therapist with expertise in the field of child sexual abuse. In 1999, she founded the first private multidisciplinary clinic in Israel that provides treatment for victims/survivors of abuse and their families and perpetrators of abuse and their families. A respected teacher and supervisor, she has presented workshops and lectures at international conferences and published a book and several articles promoting her approach to clinical work. In 2010, she founded a unique two-year training program for experienced practitioners who want to learn how to conduct therapy with sex trauma survivors and their families.

Daniel Pacheco is a doctoral student in the Criminology Program at the University of Texas at Dallas. He is interested in the way cognitive processes are associated with delinquency as well as how research impacts public policy. His recent work can be found in *Criminal Justice and Behavior*.

Dr Bernadette Rainey is a lecturer at Cardiff Law School and is the Director of the Cardiff Law School Centre for Human Rights and Public Law. Her research interests include human rights and equality law, refugee law and public law. She has published on several areas of human rights law including equality duties and sexual offenders. Her research is primarily focused on "excluded" groups such as refugees and offenders.

Martin Rettenberger, PhD, worked as a psychologist and criminologist at the Federal Evaluation Centre for Violent and Sexual Offenders in the Austrian Prison System in Vienna, Austria. Since August 2010 he has been working as a postdoctoral researcher at the Institute of Sex Research and Forensic Psychiatry at the University Medical Center Hamburg-Eppendorf, Germany.

Marnie Rice, PhD, FRSC, is Research Director Emerita, Waypoint Centre for Mental Health (formerly the Mental Health Centre, Penetanguishene, Ontario, Canada); Professor of Psychiatry and Behavioral Neurosciences (part-time) at McMaster University; Professor of Psychiatry (adjunct) at the University of Toronto; and Associate Professor of Psychology (adjunct) at Queen's University. She is a Fellow of the Royal Society of Canada and of the Canadian Psychological Association. Dr Rice has published extensively in the scientific and academic literature on violence risk assessment, sexual aggression, psychopathy and mental disorder.

Chelsea Rose, BSc (Hons), is a doctoral candidate at Victoria University of Wellington, New Zealand. Her research interests include conspiracy beliefs, animal welfare issues, and all aspects of forensic and correctional psychology.

Jeffrey C. Singer, PhD, is a psychologist in private practice as an Associate at Morris Psychological Group, PA, in Parsippany, New Jersey. There he maintains a forensic and clinical practice and is active in several associations. Since 1995, he has treated and evaluated sex offenders in various settings and has testified numerous times in state and federal court.

Terry Thomas was Professor of Criminal Justice Studies at Leeds Metropolitan University until his retirement in 2011 and is now a Visiting Professor at the University. He is a former senior social worker in a local authority social services department and long-time observer of the registration and monitoring of sexual offenders. In 2002 Professor Thomas spent six months at the University of Minnesota looking at the management of sex offenders in the United States. He is the author of the books *The Registration and Monitoring of Sex Offenders: A Comparative Study* (Routledge, 2011), *Criminal Records: A Database for the Criminal Justice System and Beyond* (Palgrave, 2007) and *Sex Crime: Sex Offending and Society* (Willan Publishing, 2005).

Daniel Turner, Dipl-Psych, is a research assistant at the Institute for Sex Research and Forensic Psychiatry. He studied psychology at the University of Frankfurt/Main and graduated in 2010. He started his medical studies in 2009 at the University of Hamburg and is expecting to graduate in 2015. His special research interests include anti-androgenic sex offender treatment, the ethical aspects of sex offender treatment and child sexual abuse in institutional settings.

Tony Ward (no relation to the other contributor of the same name) is Reader in Law at the University of Hull, where he is also Co-Director of the Centre for Experts and Instructions, and Director of the Criminal Justice Programme at the Institute of Applied Ethics.

Tony Ward, PhD, DipClinPsyc, is Professor of Clinical Psychology at Victoria University of Wellington, New Zealand. He has authored over 315 academic publications. Professor Ward is the developer of the Good Lives Model and has published numerous books, book chapters and academic articles on this model since 2002. His most recent book, *Desistance from Sex Offending: Alternatives to Throwing away the Keys* (2011, Guilford Press) (coauthored with Richard Laws), presents an integration of the Good Lives Model with desistance theory and research.

Professor Daniel T. Wilcox is a Consultant Clinical and Forensic Psychologist who is Chartered with the British Psychological Society (BPS) and Registered with the Health Professions Council (HPC). Prof. Wilcox has a BA and MA in Psychology from the State University of New York and a Doctorate in Clinical Psychology (PsychD) from the University of Surrey. He is also an Associate Fellow of the BPS. Prof. Wilcox has been awarded the title of Registered EuroPsy Psychologist and is qualified to practice throughout the European Union. Further, he is a Chartered Scientist and an assessor with the BPS for the qualification in Forensic Psychology. Prof. Wilcox is an Honorary Associate Professor in the School of Community Health Sciences at the University of Nottingham and an Honorary Research Fellow with the University of Birmingham, School of Psychology. He has provided specialist consultancy to a number of National Probation Service Sex Offender Units since 1994 and contributed to the first Home Office accredited Sex Offender Treatment Programme in the United Kingdom. Prof Wilcox also initiated the first UK National Probation Service based polygraph trials with sex offenders in 1999 and 2000. He is a member of the International Advisory Board for the *Journal of Sexual Aggression* and on the editorial boards of the *Child Abuse Review* and the *European Polygraph Journal*. In addition to managing a busy independent psychology practice in Birmingham, England, Prof. Wilcox has regularly presented at national and international conferences as well as producing many publications in relation to working with sex offenders.

Gwenda Willis, PhD, PGDipCinPsyc, is a research fellow at Deakin University and is working with Tony Ward on a number of offender desistance and reintegration projects. She has published extensively in these areas and was awarded a Fulbright New Zealand Senior Scholars Award in 2011 to examine the degree to which Northern America Sex Offender Programs adhere to the principles of the Good Lives Model.

Preface

Sex offenders and in particular pedophiles have become the "folk devils" of modern society. This depiction of sex offenders is promoted by the media and to a lesser extent by governments and their politicians. As argued by a number of academics, including Chaffin (2008), sex offenders are probably one of the only groups of offenders who it is acceptable to hate. Due to this loathing and also because of the dangers which some sex offenders pose to the public there has been an increased emphasis on populist punitiveness throughout the Western world. This global prominence given to public protection has therefore permeated through the vast majority of state criminal justice legislation and risk management strategies, often culminating in a system that is based on a community protection model (Kemshall and Wood, 2007).

The community protection approach to dealing with high-risk offenders arguably emerged during the early 1990s and, as explained by Vess (2009: 264), "was a response to perceived inadequacies in previous approaches to provide for public safety." The idea behind the model is that it attempts to strike a balance between issues of public safety and the protection of an offender's human rights. Despite the existence of such a balance, Vess argues, however, that:

> in contrast to earlier approaches, the community protection model is less concerned about [the] treatment or rehabilitation of offenders to reduce recidivism or facilitate community reintegration. The primary goal of the community protection model is the incapacitation of sexual offenders for the sake of public safety. (Vess, 2009: 264)

Kemshall and Wood (2007: 204) describe the model as one where the "containment and effective management of high-risk offenders is paramount," with the model being characterized by the use of monitoring and control, compulsory treatment, restriction, surveillance and longer than commensurate sentencing. Other punitive responses include civil commitment, residence restrictions, registration requirements, mandatory polygraph testing and "chemical castration," or, to use its more correct and less emotive term, pharmacotherapy. It would therefore appear that less emphasis is now being placed on the needs of the offender, and the balancing act between public protection and offender rights seems firmly weighted on the side against the offender.

Against this background of public and governmental pressures, there has been a growing engagement with the legality and morality of such practices. The significance of this has always been recognized, but it is increasingly being viewed as fundamentally important by academics, practitioners, policy makers and international advisory bodies such as the International Association for the Treatment of Sexual Offenders (IATSO). This book therefore aims to contribute to this essential debate. It attempts to do this by bringing together a number of well-known international academics and practitioners who are working and writing in this important area. To give the book a truly international flavor there are contributions from four continents, with chapters from Australia, Canada, England and Wales, Germany, Israel, Japan, the Netherlands, New Zealand, Northern Ireland, Norway and the United States. These provide important points of comparison between different state law and policy as well as underlining similarities and differing cultural approaches to offender treatment and management. As Douglas (1992) notes, concepts of risk are "value laden" and a similar argument can be put forward for rights-based approaches to law and policy. The chapters will illustrate how similar issues have triggered greater public protection measures in different states and also affected sex offender treatment and management. Common themes will emerge, such as the influence of risk, the recognition of a rights-based approach and the need for ethically based and legally acceptable responses to sexual offending.

The book is divided into three sections:

- Treating and Managing Sexual Offender Risk in Context: Legal and Ethical Concerns;
- Legal and Ethical Issues in Risk Treatment;
- Legal and Ethical Issues in Risk Management.

While no one section is exclusive, an attempt has been made to group similar chapters and topics/themes together, although cross-references are made throughout the chapters.

The first section, Treating and Managing Sexual Offender Risk in Context: Legal and Ethical Concerns, opens with a chapter by Knut Hermstad. He examines the relationship between legal regulation, moral attitudes and punishment. He questions the effectiveness of legal and moral efforts at regulating offender behavior and examines the influence of morality on attitudes, discussing alternatives to punitive strategies. Bernadette Rainey's chapter then examines the use of a rights-based approach to sex offender issues. Using the United Kingdom as an example, she argues that there is a complex relationship between rights and risk which needs further examination, and that dignity can act as a framework for legal and ethical regulation of sex offender treatment and management. Similarly, Phil Fennell also raises the question of the politics of risk in his chapter on consent to treatment. The chapter concentrates on the mental health system and the interaction between the prison and the psychiatric settings. The chapter gives an insightful analysis of the legal use of consent for mentally disordered offenders. Following from these two chapters, Rainey's chapter on equality and sex offenders considers subgroups of the sex offender population and examines how the application of a legal duty to treat different groups differently would enhance sex offender treatment and management. Legal issues are further explored in Ward's chapter on expert evidence, which gives an account of the ethical responsibilities of experts, judges and lawyers. It stresses the importance of the duty of "transparency" and issues of confidentiality. Chapter 6 follows the discussion of the ethics of expert evidence by discussing the ethical issues in sex offender research, Tony Ward and Gwenda Willis outline some of the issues involved in ethical research and discuss some of the topics mentioned in previous chapters such as dignity and consent. Anne-Marie McAlinden's chapter discusses legal and ethical issues in the context of "reintegrative and disintegrative shaming," contrasting the treatment and management strategies of notification requirements with restorative justice techniques. The chapter again discusses risk and rights in relation to sex offender programs and highlights the legal and ethical considerations of different types of intervention mechanism. Chapter 8 focuses on the media portrayal of sex offenders and how this has helped advance the risk penology. Peter Brown discusses the ethics of media coverage of "chemical castration" by examining the UK press coverage of this treatment area.

Following on from the context chapters, the last four chapters in Part One focus on sentencing issues. The first, by Harrison, looks at sex offender sentencing policy and legislation from an international perspective. In particular it examines legislation and practices in Australia, England and Wales, Germany and South Africa. Policies such as continuing detention, imprisonment for public protection, detention for the purpose of incapacitation and mandatory minimum sentencing are considered and evaluated. It considers whether such methods are being driven by populist punitiveness and an agenda based on public protection or whether welfare goals are also considered. In short, the fundamental aim of the author is to consider first whether such policies are lawful and then, if they are, whether they are also ethically acceptable.

This is followed by Chapter 10, which assesses and evaluates sentencing and criminal justice policy for sexual crimes in Japan and notes the reaction of the state to public protection concerns with the increased use of lay judges in decision making. The penultimate chapter in Part One is by Demleitner, who focuses on Native American crime in the United States, with a special emphasis on sexual offenses. The chapter centers on the federal sentencing of Native sex offenders in light of their unique legal and economic situation and assesses the way in which such offenders are dealt with in the United States. In conclusion the author emphasizes the need for culturally appropriate treatment, on the basis that Canadian and Australian studies have indicated success, by using such techniques, both in decreasing recidivism and increasing community safety.

The final chapter in Part One and in the sentencing block is Chapter 12, which focuses on mandatory reporting requirements in Israel. As explained in the chapter, the law purports to increase child protection by counteracting the tendency for secrecy whereby growing numbers of disclosures equal greater justice for victims and a better chance for therapeutic interventions for victims and perpetrators. Unfortunately, the law in its current form actually prevents some cases from reaching a satisfactory conclusion because (1) families who would otherwise engage actively in therapy do not have the chance to digest the trauma of disclosure before having to contend with the police and the courts; (2) some families avoid therapy altogether in order to avoid reporting; and (3) some victims feel betrayed and harmed by the system that handles the disclosure. The chapter therefore argues that a balance must be achieved between the existence of laws consistent with the seriousness of child sexual abuse and a wise application of such laws to situations characterized by secrecy, fear, horror, guilt, shame and helplessness among victims, non-abusive family members and abusers.

Part Two is entitled Legal and Ethical Issues in Risk Treatment. The first in this collection is by Rice and Harris who question whether or not we should reject the null hypothesis when considering treatment for adult sex offenders. They argue that after more than 50 years of effort, we know too little about whether any form of treatment has ever caused a reduction in the risk of recidivism of adult sex offenders. Throughout the chapter, the authors present examples of medical and psychological treatments for other populations where treatments thought to be beneficial on the basis of weak research evidence were subsequently found to be useless or harmful on the basis of random controlled trials (RCTs). The authors review the sex offender treatment outcome literature and challenge the claim that positive treatment effects have been demonstrated according to generally accepted scientific standards of inference. They reject fallacious arguments against strong inference research based on RCTs, and argue that the field has come as far as it can without RCTs; that RCTs are essential to advancing knowledge about sex offender treatment; and that the costs of not conducting such studies are unacceptable. By way of demonstrating ethically sound practice, the chapter concludes by presenting an example of how an ethically and scientifically acceptable RCT might be accomplished.

In Chapter 14, Marshall and Marshall examine the application of empirically-based process features of treatment delivery and suggest that ethical concerns demand that treatment programs for sexual offenders should adhere to the risk, need and responsivity principles of effective offender treatment. In particular the chapter focuses on the responsivity principle and argues that in order for sex offender treatment programs to be ethically sound, they must not only adhere to the principles of effective treatment, but must also have therapists who are sufficiently well-trained and competent to be able to deliver treatment in the most effective way. In essence the authors argue that it is the quality of the delivery of treatment that accounts for the majority of the observed benefits in programs for all types of clients, including sexual offenders.

Following on from the debate about the efficacy of sex offender treatment, Wilcox in Chapter 15 offers his experiences of working with sex offenders in his role as a psychologist. He sets out his reflections on the development of sex offender treatment during his time in this field. The chapter addresses changes in approaches to assessment, intervention and supervision. The chapter discusses new technology and more recent legislation, and reflects on ethical practice issues, including the balance between individual rights and public protection.

Part Two then turns to a more theoretical discussion, including whether sex offender treatment should be classified as punishment or rehabilitation. Written by

Ward and Rose, Chapter 16 looks at the intersection of the two frameworks of punishment and rehabilitation in the criminal justice system, arguing that it can create ethical flashpoints, which, if ignored, may result in unprofessional and harmful practice. In particular the authors discuss the challenges created by the convergence of punishment and rehabilitation practice with sex offenders and suggest ways of resolving, or at least managing, the inevitable ethical tensions. This is then followed by a discussion of the moral theories often used to justify rehabilitation programs. Specifically, the chapter written by Glaser uses the Good Lives Model (GLM) as an example of how moral and clinical decisions on offender rehabilitation programs may be difficult to distinguish. It therefore provides a brief overview of some of the moral theories commonly used as the ethical bases of human service models, although it is argued that virtue ethics seems to best fit the assumptions and practices of the GLM. The shortcomings of this framework are then described, particularly those which might impact on the decisions made by clinicians using a GLM approach, and some ways of overcoming these, using ethical rather than clinical responses, are suggested. The author concludes that, however difficult they may be to attain, the GLM's aspirations of achieving a meaningful and worthwhile life for even the most despised members of our community may result in policy and attitude changes that will benefit society enormously as a whole.

The last two chapters in Part Two are arguably more specific in nature; with Chapter 18 looking at a specific treatment method and Chapter 19 considering a specific treatment group. The first, written by Basdekis-Jozsa, Turner and Briken, considers the legal and ethical aspects of using pharmacotherapy with sex offenders. The chapter acknowledges that until now very little has been known about the effects of anti-hormonal treatment on the recidivism rates of sexual offenders, mainly because many studies on the effectiveness of such treatment have lacked equivalent control groups. The chapter therefore looks at developments in this area, examining the legal aspects of prescribing anti-androgens in the forensic setting, the ethical aspects of the regime (for example, future and/or irreversible side effects and the question of informed consent in a forensic setting), and the questionable effect of the treatment on recidivism rates. In essence, the authors question whether anti-androgen treatment should be used for sex offenders suffering from non-controllable deviant urges and, if so, what safeguards need to be put into place.

Turning to a specific offender group, the final chapter in this section considers female sex offenders and the need for a gender responsive approach for such offenders. Written by Ashfield, Brotherston, Eldridge and Elliott, the chapter comments on how the empirical information on women who sexually offend indicates that a blanket application of research knowledge based on *male* sexual offenders to understand sexual offending by females is not a viable option. In sexual offending, as in general offending, gender matters. Although women engage in similar acts to men, their pathways to offending remain uniquely female and so demand separate explanations to those of their male counterparts. The authors therefore review the developments in our understanding of female sexual offending and explore how gender responsiveness can inform our understanding of good practice in the assessment and treatment of female sex offenders.

Finally, Part Three focuses on legal and ethical issues in relation to a number of risk management strategies. The choice of strategy to be employed for any given offender is usually determined by means of risk assessment and this is the subject of Chapter 20. Singer, Boer and Rettenberger therefore look at the different models for risk assessment. They discuss actuarial methods and structured professional judgment. The chapter argues that both methods have benefits and that risk assessment can be greatly enhanced by taking a convergent approach and combining both methods.

Following on from risk assessment, the remaining chapters look at specific risk management strategies. Chapter 21, written by Thomas, examines sex offender registration in both the United States and the United Kingdom. It looks at the difficulties experienced in the United States, as states have struggled to comply with the requirements of the federal 2006 Sex Offender Registration and Notification Act and furthermore considers the successful legal challenge in 2010 to the UK register demonstrating that it is not compatible with Article 8 of the European Convention on Human Rights. The chapter also considers the position of young sex offenders who are registered and the continuing problems the police have in monitoring the behavior of adult registered sex offenders. Experienced difficulties of monitoring are evaluated, and the new police child sex offender disclosure schemes are examined.

Next is a chapter looking at the development and efficacy of Circles of Support and Accountability (COSA), with the authors Hanvey and Höing arguing that COSA are a more ethical way of working with sex offenders. The chapter briefly introduces the goals of COSA and the problems which the method is seeking to address before looking at how they operate and have been rolled out across Europe. In particular the authors look at the ethical and theoretical principles of COSA, including restorative as opposed to retributive justice and humanitarian principles. They consider the diverse treatment models used and models of behavior change such as the GLM, desistance, social capital and inclusive community-building, before considering the future potential of Circles, and the possible wider impact they can have across criminal justice provision and services.

Chapter 23, written by Wilcox, then considers the ethical use of polygraphs in working with sex offenders. The chapter begins by looking at a brief background of what the polygraph is and how it works, including a discussion of its strengths and weaknesses. It then explores the developing use of polygraphy in the criminal justice field and specifically in its employment with sex offenders. The author reviews perceptions about the accuracy, reliability and validity of polygraphy and provides a discussion focused on ethical and professional positions concerning the use of the polygraph, generally and within the specific field of sex offender work. Throughout, the chapter directs attention to ethical issues in the employment of polygraphy with sex offenders, including the balance between individual rights and public protection.

This is then followed by an examination of the legal and ethical issues involved in the civil commitment of sex offenders in the United States. Authored by Jackson and Covell, the chapter reviews the historical foundation and constitutional underpinning of sex offender civil commitment in the United States and explains how these controversial statutes, often termed Sexually Violent Predator laws, serve to detain sexual offenders after the expiration of their criminal sentences. The legal criteria necessary for commitment and those elements separating civil commitment from punishment are also helpfully reviewed. Specifically, however, the chapter considers the legal and ethical aspects inherent in the evaluation, commitment, treatment, management and release of these individuals and discusses what can be done to make practice more ethically sound.

Chapter 25, written by Pacheco and Barnes, stays with the United States, this time considering the use of sex offender residence restrictions. Explaining how such restrictions have emerged as one of the most politically popular responses to sex offender crimes, the chapter explains what the restrictions are and how they work (or do not work) in practice. In particular it comments on how the vast majority of efficacy studies on residence restrictions conclude that such requirements are unlikely to reduce sex offender recidivism. Despite the existence of such studies there has been no sustained effort systematically to summarize their results, which is exactly what this chapter does. The authors offer a systematic review of the sex offender residence restriction literature, giving primary consideration to whether residence restrictions are a salient strategy to reducing recidivism and boosting community re-entry likelihood among sex offenders. Whether residence restrictions impact other domains of the re-entry process is also discussed.

The penultimate chapter concerns the traveling sex offender, with an evaluation of how sex offender movements are monitored across international borders. Written by Thomas, Chapter 26 looks at the problems created by sex offenders traveling internationally and considers why such offenders would wish to travel abroad. It critically examines the legal requirements in the United Kingdom and the United States on registered sex offenders to notify the police when they are traveling abroad and how these requirements have been strengthened in recent years. It also examines the orders now available that can prevent people leaving a country for determinate periods of time and the measures that can be applied to newly arrived travelers known to have committed sexual offenses in other countries or to be registered sex offenders in other countries. The chapter ends by looking at arrangements being devised to collect and use personal information on sex offenders and to exchange that information across international borders.

The final chapter written by Mallet and Karp examines the increasing use of GPS tracking as a management tool and considers the influence of risk penology on post-release management of sex offenders. A common theme throughout the collection is highlighted in the chapter: the influence of risk and the public protection agenda in the treatment and management of sex offenders and the need for a legal and ethical response that recognizes the rule of law and the individual.

To conclude, the collection encompasses a wide-ranging and comprehensive critique of ethical and legal issues that arise from sex offender treatment and management. Several themes emerge from the chapters described. First, there is considerable agreement concerning the importance of ethical good practice, even if there may be differences as to how to achieve this; there is debate about what assessment tools to use, whether treatment methods work and where the focus of treatment should be. There is also a consensus concerning the role of penal punitiveness in state policy, not only of the ramifications of these policies for ethical practice but also the legal restraints placed on offenders. Concerns about infringement of dignity and rights of offenders (and in some cases potential victims) are evident throughout the chapters, as is a growing consensus on the responsivity of treatment and a recognition of the adverse differential impact on offender groups where assessment and treatment fails to recognize "difference." The collection provides an important contribution to the growing practitioner and academic concerns surrounding risk penologies in states and underlines the need to research, treat and manage sexual offenders in a humane, ethical and dignified manner.

References

Chaffin, M. (2008) "Our minds are made up – don't confuse use with the facts: commentary on policies concerning children with sexual behavior problems and juvenile sex offenders," *Child Maltreatment* 13, 2, 110–121.

Douglas, M. (1992) *Risk and Blame: Essays in Cultural Theory.* London: Routledge.

Kemshall, H. and Wood, J. (2007) "Beyond public protection: an examination of community protection and public health approaches to high-risk offenders," *Criminology & Criminal Justice* 7, 3, 203–222.

Vess, J. (2009) "Fear and loathing in public policy: ethical issues in law for sex offenders," *Aggression and Violent Behavior* 14, 264–272.

Abbreviations

ACPO	Association of Chief Police Officers
ADT	androgen disrupting therapy
APA	American Psychiatric Association
ARAI	Actuarial Risk Assessment Instrument
ARMIDILO-S	Assessment of Risk and Manageability of Intellectually Disabled Individuals who Offend
ATSA	Association for the Treatment of Sexual Abusers
AWA	Adam Walsh Act
BIA	Bureau of Indian Affairs
BME	Black and Minority Ethnic group
CBT	cognitive behavior therapy
CCSA	clerical child sex abuse
CEOP	Child Exploitation and On-Line Protection Centre
CJA	Criminal Justice Act
CJIA	Criminal Justice and Immigration Act
CLAA	Criminal Law Amendment Act
CODC	Collaborative Outcome Data Committee
COSA	Circles of Support and Accountability
CPA	Cyproterone Acetate
CPS	Child Protection Service
CPW	Child Protection Worker
CRB	Criminal Records Bureau
Crim PR	Criminal Procedure Rules
CSA	child sexual abuse
CTO	Community Treatment Order
DoH	Department of Health
DPSOA	Dangerous Prisoners (Sexual Offenders) Act
DSM	Diagnostic and Statistical Manual of Mental Disorders
DSPD	dangerous severe personality disorder
ECHR	European Convention on Human Rights
ECPAT	End Child Prostitution, Child Pornography and the Trafficking of Children for Sexual Purposes

ECRIS	European Criminal Records Information System
ECtHR	European Court of Human Rights
ECT	electroconvulsive therapy
EHRC	Equality and Human Rights Commission (United Kingdom)
EM	Electronic Monitoring
EMGPS	Electronic Monitoring Global Positioning System
EPPCC	Ethical Principles of Psychologists and Code of Conduct
EQIA	equality impact assessment
EU	European Union
FBI	Federal Bureau of Investigation
FTO	Foreign Travel Order
GCS	Group Climate Scale
GIS	Geographic Information Systems
GLM	Good Lives Model
GnRH	Gonadotropin-Releasing Hormone
GPS	Global Positioning System
IATSO	International Association for the Treatment of Sexual Offenders
ICD	International Classification of Diseases
ICE	Immigration and Customs Enforcement
ID	intellectually disabled
Interpol	International Criminal Police Organization
IOG	Intensive Outpatient Group Therapy
IPP	Imprisonment for Public Protection
LH	luteinizing hormone
MAPPA	Multi-Agency Public Protection Arrangements
MAPPPs	Multi-Agency Public Protection Panels
MATS-1	Multisample Age-stratified Table of Sexual recidivism rates
MHA	Mental Health Act (England and Wales)
MNSOST-3	Minnesota Sex Offender Screening Tool-3
MOJ	Ministry of Justice
MPA	Medroxyprogesterone Acetate
NAMBLA	North American Man–Boy Love Association
NHS	National Health Service (United Kingdom)
NOTA	National Organization for the Treatment of Abusers
NPA	National Police Agency (Japan)
NSPCC	National Society for the Prevention of Cruelty to Children
OCD	Obsessive Compulsive Disorder
PCL-R	Psychopathy Checklist Revised
PCSOT	post-conviction sex offender testing
PD	Parkinson's disease
PNC	Police National Computer
PPG	penile plethysmography
PROTECT	Prosecutorial Remedies and Other Tools to End the Exploitation of Children Today
PTSD	post-traumatic stress disorder
RC	responsible clinician

RCT	randomized controlled trial
RF	radio frequency
RNR	risk, need, responsivity
RSHO	Risk of Sexual Harm Order
RTI	Research and Training Institute
SHDE	Sexual History Disclosure Examinations
SMART	Sex Offender Sentencing, Monitoring, Apprehending, Registering and Tracking
SOAD	second opinion appointed doctor
SOPO	Sexual Offenses Prevention Order
SORAG	Sex Offender Risk Appraisal Guide
SORNA	Sex Offender Registration and Notification Act
SOTP	Sex Offender Treatment Program
SPJ	structured professional judgment
SSRI	selective serotonin reuptake inhibitors
STGB	Strafgesetzbuch (German Criminal Code)
SVP	sexually violent predator
SVR-20	Sexual Violence Risk 20
UCJ	unguided critical judgment
UNCRC	United Nations Convention on the Rights of the Child
UNICEF	United Nations Children's Fund
ViSOR	Violent and Sex Offender Register

Part One

Treating and Managing Sexual Offender Risk in Context:
Legal and Ethical Concerns

1

Sexual Offenses, Law and Morals
Can Behavior and Attitudes Be Changed by Legal and Moral Efforts?
Knut Hermstad

Introduction

There is a general belief that prison sentences are an effective way of reducing the number of sex offenses. This is the reason why sentences in sex offending cases have become stricter in many countries in recent years. In addition to prevention and safety strategies, the penal code is seen as an instrument for expressing the moral values and norms of society. As they become more aware of the problem of sex offenses, authorities and societies are looking for ways to show support and empathy to victims, while morally condemning offenders for their acts.

It is not only in sex offending cases that sentences have become stricter. Over the last 30 years there has been a general shift in criminal justice policy in most Western countries, with interest increasingly being focused on the protection of society, rather than the rehabilitation of the offender.[1] This does not mean that rehabilitation is now out of question; it is more the case that the safety of the public has become the number one priority. An observation from Norway, a traditionally liberal country, illustrates the point: until the 1970s judges had to present good arguments for handing out long prison sentences; they now have to present good arguments for *not* handing out long sentences in cases that the public views as serious (Hauge, 2004; Christie, 2000).[2]

The belief in so-called punitive strategies in criminal justice policy takes it for granted that the move towards stricter penalties is necessary as well as effective. The importance of the prison sentence is regarded as self-evident, sending the message that crime does not pay. This raises the question of the role and effectiveness of punitive strategies: should we assume that the attitudes of sex offenders can be changed and their behavior regulated by use of remedies that have their origins in

The Wiley-Blackwell Handbook of Legal and Ethical Aspects of Sex Offender Treatment and Management,
First Edition. Edited by Karen Harrison and Bernadette Rainey.
© 2013 John Wiley & Sons, Ltd. Published 2013 by John Wiley & Sons, Ltd.

criminal law? And is the handing out of prison sentences the right way to handle the human and moral dilemmas involved in these cases?

This chapter looks at the relationship between offenders' behavior and attitudes on the one hand and punitive strategies on the other, asking whether stricter penalties really do change offenders' behavior and attitudes so that society can be better protected. To answer this question, the chapter draws on Norwegian statistical material, together with the results of a qualitative study of 13 convicted sex offenders. It also examines the effects of a law which makes the buying of sexual services a criminal offense in Sweden and Norway.

Punitive Strategies in Sex Offending Cases

Defining the effectiveness of the law might be difficult but in what follows it can be seen as the ability to make people act, behave and think in accordance with the legislation.

From a psychological point of view, offending behavior can be understood as needs, urges and despair connected to the offenders' inherent problems. Though offenders might be afraid of disclosure and arrest, this usually does not stop them from offending. They are struggling with greater problems than fear of conviction. When comparing the number of sex offenses with the number of cases taken to court, we can see that the legal system plays a marginal role in sex offending cases.[3] The gap between the marginalized role of the legal system on the one hand, and the high numbers of sex offenses on the other, raises the question of whether punitive strategies represent serious attempts at solving the problem, or if they are just intended to meet the demands of politicians and public opinion.

However, the use of prison sentences is about more than regulating behavior. An important purpose of the law is to express messages about morality, solidarity, revenge and other more absolute ideological values. When the aim is to express these sorts of messages, there might be well-founded reasons for supporting a move towards stricter penalties, regardless of what effects the penalties may have on offenders' behavior. In this case the aim is not to regulate behavior but to make some moral statement, which, for instance, could be to tell people that the authorities are aware of the problem of sex offenses and that victims will be supported. On the other hand it is not obvious that morality and punishment are correlated, so that moral values can only be expressed by strict sentences. But in real life situations, people's general feeling of justice tends to be satisfied only when strict sentences are handed out in serious criminal cases such as sex offenses, assaults and so on.

Though it has not been widely discussed, police work is also connected to the communication of messages about morality. By giving priority and resources to an investigation, the police signal that the case is important. It might be the well-being and security of people which is at stake, or perhaps the moral values of society. Police use of resources, and the priority and the quality of the investigation, communicate a moral understanding.

When the aim is to send certain ideological signals, there must be some connection between the acts and the risk of disclosure. If offenders are not caught, no messages will be sent. The question of how moral issues should be handled in criminal justice policy is therefore important. If deprivation of liberty is the only way of showing empathy to those who suffer the pain of sex offenses, the consequence might be that this empathy can only be expressed when there is an offender to prosecute. The moral value of *empathy* is then dependent on the outcome of the criminal case. The risk is that this support and empathy will not be provided for those who do not see their offender sentenced.

Sexual Offenses: Statistics and Legal Aspects

In the period 1991–2009, the number of sex offenses and strategies to combat these rising numbers increased in Norway; new and more punitive strategies were established, and sex offender treatment programs were launched (Hermstad, 2006; Statistisk Sentralbyrå, 1980–2009). Statistics from this period show that the number of sex offenses of all sorts reported to the police increased from 2,348 in 1991 to 4,112 in 2009, which is a growth of 175% in 18 years. Most cases reported to the police were also investigated; the percentage of investigated cases increased from 76% of reported cases in 1991 to 89% in 2009.

With regard to rape, the statistics show that the number of incidents reported and investigated by the police increased from 376 in 1991 to 853 in 2009, a growth of 226%. On the other hand, sex offenses against children, including incest (involving victims aged under 16 years and 14 years) were relatively stable at a level of 500–700 each year in the period.

The growth in the number of cases reported and investigated by the police is slightly lower in the field of sex offending than it is for crime generally, though the differences are not dramatic. More important is that people's attitudes to sex offenses have undergone a considerable change. Thirty years ago sex offenses were denied and underestimated; now they are acknowledged as a problem that needs to be taken seriously by the whole of society.

How are sex offenses handled in the legal system? Ten to twenty percent of reported and investigated cases end in a conviction. Though we do not have sufficiently good figures for the years 1991–1999, it seems that the percentage of convictions is slightly higher at the start of the period than at the end, while the total number of convictions has increased slightly less than the number of reported and investigated offenses. This may show that victims' barriers to reporting incidents to the police have been lowered, and that the police are taking the cases more seriously. But even taking into consideration that the number of convictions nearly doubled during this period, it still remains a fact that most cases are neither reported to the police nor end in a conviction.

The outcome of a conviction is usually a prison sentence, typically ranging from a few months to one year, and more seldom up to 10 or 12 years. After 2003 legislation was changed so that the minimum and maximum penalties have been raised. The total number of convictions (all types of sex offenses included) has been around 400 to 700 each year in the period after 2003.

When comparing the number of sex offenses with developments in violent crime, we can see that reported and investigated incidents of violence of all sorts have increased by nearly 100% in the period, which is slightly more than for reported and investigated sex offenses of all sorts. Normally 20 to 25% of the cases of violence that are reported and investigated end in a conviction. The equivalent percentage in sex offending cases is 10 to 20%, though slightly increasing towards the 20% level at the end of the period. Most of the violence occurs between persons who either live together or know each other well; the majority of cases involve domestic violence, while there are just a few cases of assault. The same can be observed for sexual offenses; in most cases the sex offender and the victim know each other or have some sort of relationship. Public opinion tends to overestimate the general risk of sexual assault, while the risk connected to private homes is underestimated.

The growth in the number of sex offenses reported, investigated and concluded with a conviction could indicate that there has been an increase in the total number of incidents in the period, but this does not seem to be the case. A combination of better policing work and growing public awareness might be reasons for the increase. More offenders are caught. However, it is still the case that more than 90% are never sentenced. As far as we can understand, the numbers of offenses is probably at a stable level.

In Norway three major studies on the occurrence of sex offenses have been carried out, all before 2000 (Schei, Muus and Bendixen, 1994; Tambs, 1994; Sætre, Holter and Jebsen, 1986). Based on these studies and observations in the field, it is agreed that it would be reasonable to assume that at least 4 to 7% of the population have experienced sex offenses, of one kind or another, during their lifetime. Given that the total population of Norway is five million, this means that between 200,000 and 350,000 people have experienced sex offenses. Breaking down this number to provide annual figures, it is reasonable to believe that 12,000 to 24,000 persons experience sexual offenses every year. Approximately 3,500 sex offenses are reported and investigated by the police every year, while 600 to 700 offenders are convicted. Given that the real occurrence of sex offenses is between 12,000 and 24,000, this means that only 2 to 5% of the offenders are convicted. The number of offenders at any given point during the year could then be approximately 14,000.[4]

Thirteen Convicted Sex Offenders: Legal and Moral Understanding

What do offenders who have served prison sentences think about this punitive strategy? Did they stop offending after having served their sentences? And what do they think about the moral aspect of their offenses?

In research carried out in Norway, 13 sex offenders sentenced to prison for one year or more were interviewed on these topics (Hermstad, 2006). These informants belong to the small and select group of convicted offenders.[5] As this was a qualitative study the informants were not recruited by use of randomized methods, but mainly because they fulfilled the inclusion criterion (of being sentenced to one year or more in prison). The study especially focused on the offenders' moral understanding, their view on women's liberation, children's right to be protected against sex offenses and what they thought about sexual rights. They were also asked about their views on the use of prison sentences in sex offending cases.

All the informants agreed that offenders should be punished, but thought that the punishment need not necessarily be a prison sentence. Most of them thought that the offender should take responsibility for his acts, and that the victim should never be blamed or held responsible for what happened. An important aspect of punishment is the moral side of it: the punishment is necessary to re-establish relations between offender and victim; the offender therefore should tell the victim that he is sorry for what he has done.

The informants agreed that sexual relations between adults and children are unacceptable and must be dealt with harshly by society. During the years the offenses took place, the 11 child abusers in the study realized that they should have stopped themselves, but only two of them had managed to do so. The other nine stopped only when the police arrived on their doorstep.

Most informants felt it was a relief to be caught by the police. But the relief turned into a nightmare when they became aware of the realities of the trial and the prison time. However, when considering individual prevention, they confirm that the legal system plays an important role: if they had not been caught most of them would have continued to offend. All of them said that offenders should receive treatment during their time in prison. However, they did not see the treatment as a strategy for relapse prevention; rather, they thought that offenders need treatment because of the emotional and psychological distress they experience. Most of them seemed to think that the best relapse prevention strategy was the prison sentence in itself.[6]

Based on the informants' information it appears that sex offenders have the same moral and ethical standards as most other people in society. They applaud women's liberation, they think that children have the right not to be victims of crime and they support the same moral standards as do the majority of the population. They do not think that sex offenders need the criminal law to learn that sex offending is unacceptable; they already know this and they also knew it when they committed the offenses.

The findings of the study may be summarized in eight points:

1. Sex offenses are not a question of knowledge about right and wrong. It is a question of the ability to do what is right.
2. Sex offenders seem to be highly aware that they are committing illegal acts. Therefore they remove evidence and deny their guilt when they are caught.
3. Denying guilt is a rewarding strategy, but when addressing their own feelings and morality, most offenders have a bad conscience because of what they have done.
4. Sex offenders feel a sort of helplessness about their offending behavior. Often they want to stop but usually they are not able to do so.
5. The idea of prevention is that people are rational beings, and that they can adjust their behavior to rules and legal regulations. But offenders do not commit sex offenses because they think it is right to do so; they do it because they lack the ability to do what they already know is right.
6. We cannot assume that the number of sex offenses will be reduced by the use of more punitive strategies.
7. The large number of sex offenses shows that the legal system lacks the tools necessary to regulate this problem in an effective way. There is a need for better

legal instruments so that the problem-solving methods are fit for the problems they are supposed to solve.

8.   Offenders who have been caught seem to have learnt their lesson; at least many of them think so themselves. They say they will never offend again. Though punished offenders are a minority among all offenders, this could be an argument for supporting traditional, punitive reactions in some of the offending cases.

Legislation, Moral Signals and Behavior

There are no studies on the possible correlations between legislation and offending behavior. But in the field of sexology there is a general assumption that people's sexual behavior is not likely to be regulated by legislation. The most important factor in the regulation of people's sexual practices was the commercial release of the contraceptive pill in the middle of the 1960s. The pill contributed to the so-called "sexual revolution" so that most people after this time could choose their sexual practices regardless of legal authorities, churches and social institutions. This does not mean that regulations and norms from then on became irrelevant; it just means that a person's own autonomy started to play a more important role in matters of sexual behavior. Factors such as social control, religious beliefs and even economic considerations continue to influence sexual practice.

As it is different from sex offenses, general sexual behavior should not be compared when addressing the question of the possibility of legal regulation of behavior. It is legitimate to have consenting sex with an appropriate partner; it is illegal to have sex with a minor or with a partner who is not comfortable with the situation. However, while sexual behavior in general is hard to regulate, it seems to be even more difficult to influence an offender's behavior patterns.

The figures show that twice as many offenders are caught today as were caught 20 years ago. But compared with the total number of offenses, it is still a minority of offenders who end up in prison. As pointed out by researchers, police officers and clinicians in the field find no evidence to show that the number of sex offenses has either increased or decreased in the last 20 years.

If the legal system communicates messages about justice and moral values in this situation, where just a minority of offenders are caught, this might seem to send the message that sex offenses are not particularly serious. This has two consequences. First, it makes victims think that there is only a limited possibility of receiving justice, and that they must seek justice in arenas other than the courtroom. Second, it makes offenders think that denying guilt is a rewarding strategy. Punitive strategies provide offenders with reasons for hiding and denying, which they already have learnt to do successfully.

Attitude-Regulating Laws

There is little evidence for assuming that offending behavior can be regulated by legal and moral efforts; but what about attitudes? Can these be regulated by the criminal law? If the answer is yes, is it then probable that changes in attitude brought about by the influence of the law will result in changed behavior patterns?

To answer these questions it is necessary to look at legislation in the field of prostitution in Norway and Sweden (Hermstad, 2009). It has been illegal to buy sexual services in Sweden since 1999 and in Norway since 2009. Although buying sex is forbidden, it is not illegal for a woman to sell sex. These laws are so-called "attitude-regulating laws" which means that the purpose of the law is to regulate people's attitudes more than it is to regulate their actual behavior. The law states that prostitution is violence against women, regardless of how the partners involved understand the situation themselves. It is the customers' power to buy sex which is defined as violence against women.

During the 10 years of criminalization there seems to have been a small decrease in the total amount of prostitution in Sweden, though we do not know exactly how much. The number of sex-buyers may also have decreased, but probably not that much. However, what really have changed are people's attitudes towards prostitution. In 1999, 61% of the population in Sweden thought it was wrong to buy sex; this percentage increased to 81% in 2009. Given that the group of sex-buyers is stable and that the decrease in prostitution is moderate, one might assume that the change in people's attitudes towards prostitution has not had that much effect on behavior. Those who have changed their minds are those who would not have bought sex in any case.

Since the law in Norway is only two years old, there is little research on its effects. However, reports indicate that there has been a small decrease in the total level of prostitution; at least in street prostitution. Reports also indicate that street prostitution only decreases during times when the police are active in catching customers. The market now seems to have moved from the streets to various indoor facilities. But there is reason to believe that people's attitudes towards prostitution have changed. Since the group of sex-buyers is a very small one, the shift in attitudes will not have that much effect on the total amount of prostitution. As in Sweden, those who have changed their view of prostitution to a negative one are those who would not have bought sexual services anyway.

We can summarize the effects of legislation in the field of prostitution as follows:

1. The criminalization of the buying of sexual services has been a success insofar as it has had an influence on people's attitudes, but the law has had only a limited effect on the way people behave.
2. Depending on conditions and circumstances, it is reasonable to assume that people's attitudes can be changed by use of the penal code.
3. Changing attitudes is not the same as changing behavior. Changes of attitude towards prostitution have little impact on people's behavior, since the majority of people do not buy sexual services in any case.

In the field of sex offending, do most people (including sex offenders) agree upon the legal situation? Sex with children is wrong, as is sex without a partner's consent. Due to stricter legal regulations and a growing public awareness, are people now generally aware of the problem and also willing to do something about it? This might be the reason why more offenders are caught today than 20 years ago.

So far neither the legislation nor the punitive strategies have demonstrated effectiveness in reducing the total number of offenses. Although it is important to target people's attitudes and moral standards, this in itself is not sufficient. Though this does not mean that sex offenses should be legalized, it clearly indicates that the police and the legal system lack the necessary tools to establish effective prevention strategies.

Why Do We Punish?

It is taken for granted that the threat of punishment is necessary to make people comply with law and order. But if sex offenders do not pay very much attention to the criminal law, it is not likely that their behavior would be influenced by the threat of a stricter sentence. So why do we still continue to punish them?

The most obvious reason is the simple one given by the authorities and the representatives of the legal system: to protect society from harm (Andenæs, 1994). But the impact of people's so-called "feeling of justice" should not be overlooked either: offenders must be punished because they deserve it. They have done something wrong. The retributive theory of "just deserts," which has been popular in the United States and other countries for years, claims that justice is a question of the nature of the criminal act and the harm being done (Von Hirsch, 1976). Offenders must be punished regardless of their life situation, motivation or personal reasons for their doings, and the punishment should be proportional to the felony.

Others see the punishment as a *moral obligation*. Punishment is not for the sake of the persons involved, but for the sake of law and order. This is the position of the philosopher Immanuel Kant (1982), whose writings have been highly influential in the criminological field in countries all over the world throughout the last two centuries. According to this view, punishment is a moral obligation whose main purpose is to make clear the moral responsibility of man. Changing offenders' behavior and attitudes may also be important, but not as important as the moral side of it.

A more practical and evidence-based way of arguing is provided by theories of how people's attitudes and behavior can be regulated by use of the penal code. *Crime prevention theories* are popular with the authorities as well as with ordinary people; these theories fall into two categories. The *theory of general prevention* holds that people avoid criminality because they fear punishment. The problem of increasing crime can be met by enforcing stricter penalties. The authorities have to prescribe the correct amount of punishment. The other category is that of *individual prevention strategies*, which hold that the experience of the pain of punishment will prevent perpetrators from carrying out new offenses (Andenæs, 1997).

If imprisonment serves as a practical and rational way of regulating people's behavior, the legal system could be seen as an evidence-based system with its main purpose being to secure law and order. Although there is no doubt that the legal system should secure law and order, the evidence-based aspect also raises moral and ideological questions. The use of prison sentences cannot be understood only as a remedy to be evaluated with regard to its effectiveness; it requires even more thorough evaluation with regard to its ability to communicate moral values. So far little effort has been made to investigate whether sex offenses have been reduced as a result of stricter penalties.

Perhaps the focus has not been on offenses as such but more on making moral statements to show that the authorities take action in these cases. There may be considerable doubt about the quality of the moral signals communicated by the legal system.

The Need for Alternatives to Punitive Strategies

One important reason for stricter sentences in sex offending cases is to make clear the moral values of society and to express support for victims for sex offenses. But as long as cases are rarely taken to court, one might question the value of these messages. Because of the harms being done, it is obvious that the victims need all the support they can get, but declarations of solidarity are of limited value as long as the victims' stories are not believed or are deemed insufficient as evidence in the courtroom. Offenders normally avoid conviction by denying and minimizing guilt.

This raises questions about the role of the legal system in sex offending cases. Though this role is becoming marginalized, there does not seem to be any call to decriminalize sex offenses or to take the cases away from the legal system's responsibility. Nor would it be a good idea to lower the level of penalties in itself. It is obvious that we need new and better remedies in the field that can communicate the severity of sex offenses as well as helping and supporting the victims.

An alternative to punitive strategies is described by the professor of medical law at the University of Edinburgh, Alexander McCall Smith. In his popular books about the female private detective Precious Ramotswe from Botswana in southern Africa, he shows how the philosophy of restoration and mutual understanding between the partners involved in criminal acts might challenge punitive strategies (McCall Smith, 1998, 2001). Precious Ramotswe replaces black-and-white justice with a heart-and-soul justice so that the reader sometimes is confused as to who the good guys are and who the bad guys are. The mission of Precious Ramotswe is to make people talk together regardless of their position as victim, offender, judge, police officer or whoever they might be.

The books of McCall Smith could be seen as representing the criminological movement *restorative justice*, a movement which has become well-known all over the world after the work of the Truth and Reconciliation Committee (TRC) of South Africa in the last decade of the twentieth century. So far the legal system in most Western countries has been working along the two tracks of *punishment* and *treatment* in sex offending cases.[7] Its success in reducing the number of sex offenses is limited. Against this background one must ask whether the legal system needs more remedies than merely the option of sending perpetrators to prison. Could restorative justice be such a remedy, so that the two tracks in future will be *restoration* and *treatment* instead of punishment and treatment (see Chapter 7)?

Restorative Justice as a Challenge to the Traditional Understanding of Justice

The problem in sex offending cases is not so much the punishment of offenders, but rather how victims can live with their painful experiences. In these cases, there are two major concerns about the role of the traditional legal system:

1. *Ownership of the case:* Victims as well as offenders may wish to have a confrontation and perhaps also the possibility of reconciliation. But criminal cases lie in the hands of the state, and not in the hands of victims and offenders. Psychological, emotional and existential needs are of limited interest in the legal part of the process.
2. *The court is not adapted to the problems involved.* The treatment of evidence in court implies that the question of truth primarily is a question of evidence, rather than what really happened between the offender and victim. The protection of the defendant's right to a fair trial is the main reason why most sex offending cases are dismissed by the court.

What, then, are the needs of the partners involved when an offending case is taken to the court? Four major needs may be identified:

1. The truth must be expressed.
2. Guilt and responsibility must be addressed.
3. Victimization must be avoided.
4. Atonement should be made.

The TRC in South Africa provides an interesting and important example of alternative ways of handling severe criminality. The principle of the TRC was: *the truth in return for giving away the demands of punishment of the perpetrators.* The TRC therefore offered "a space for victims to speak and the right for the perpetrator to be heard" (Verwoerd, 2000). Space precludes us from providing a detailed discussion of the TRC, but an important question is: do the legal systems of the Western world's democracies have something to learn from South Africa?

The answer is: yes, definitely. In the field of sex offending we are facing human and moral problems that are too severe to be solved in the courtroom alone. Guilt is about more than questions of evidence and punishment. Guilt is an existential phenomenon, influencing how victims and offenders live their lives when the trial is over. No punishment can undo the pain of the evil act, not even the death penalty.

In therapy we can often observe that victims do not place much emphasis on having the offender punished. Of course many of them want revenge and even more to see the offender suffering severely. But more than that, they struggle to understand how the offenses could happen. Some of them take the responsibility on their own shoulders, thinking that it must have been something wrong with their own behavior. How else could it be that a person they knew or even respected would do such evil and painful acts?

The interviewees from the 2006 Norwegian study, who are mostly child molesters, also struggle to understand how they could do what they did. This may be a surprise to many, but understanding reasons is not just a question of explaining how actions could take place; it is much more a question of exploring the relations between the actions and the person carrying them out: "How could it be that I just did what I have done?" Many of the offenders in the study wanted to tell their victims about their regrets.

From a human and psychological point of view, persons involved in sex offending cases often seem to lack a meeting place where they can talk together and be honest about shame, pain and anger. In an article from 1988 the Norwegian professor of criminology at the University of Oslo, Liv Finstad (1988), asks for a new system in sex offending cases, where telling the truth is not followed by any judicial sanctions. She wants an "*empathetic listening*" where the offender is given the opportunity to confess and to take responsibility for his doings. The crucial question is of course why sex offenders, in contrast to other offenders, should get away with just a confession and no punishment. Finstad's position is that sex offenders are likely to evade punishment anyway. By motivating them to realize what they have done, they will probably experience a pain much more severe than a sentence of some years in prison. It is more valuable for victims to see offenders take responsibility and feel pain than it is to see them behind bars. This was also found to be the case during the process of the TRC of South Africa: telling the truth to the families and friends of the victims could be much harder than standing in front of a judge and getting a verdict.

However, the point is not primarily to make the perpetrator experience pain but to restore relations between the partners involved. Most victims are afraid of meeting their offender, which is likely to happen if the offender and the victim know each other. Date-rape and incest are the most frequent sex offenses and in these cases there are usually many and varied relations between offender and victim. These relations have to be regulated in one way or another. The concept of restorative justice may be helpful to some of the people affected by these issues (see Chapter 22).

Future Directions

What we need in the future is probably a model for combining the concept of restorative justice with the traditional legal system. Perhaps there could be two tracks, so that it would be possible to examine each specific situation while asking: what is the best way of solving this case?

In different countries around the world, including New Zealand, Canada, Norway and others, there is on-going work in the field of restorative justice. The concepts are different from country to country, as are the legal traditions, but a common element is the wish to handle violence and sex offenses in a way that is adapted to the situation of the persons involved.

At the moment a project of restorative justice at the University Hospital of Trondheim, Norway, is in its final planning stages. The project focuses on the situation of young women who have experienced date-rape, primarily incidents where both victim and offender belong to the same college, university or social milieu. Many collaborators are taking part in the project, including the district attorney, the local police of Trondheim, the University Hospital of Trondheim and other partners. This project is mentioned here because the Western world has just a limited experience of the concept of restorative justice; ideas therefore need to be spread.

The majority of rape incidents are date-rapes, though despite being very numerous they are seldom reported or they are dropped by the police. Health professionals report that date-rapes cause severe problems to the partners involved, but in cases where the offenders are not sentenced, neither the victims nor the offenders are offered professional help. Victims of date-rape usually have a social relationship with their offender, and they are likely to meet him again at some point. Many of them feel that next time they meet they are at risk of being raped again. This causes considerable fear. To address this fear, it could be helpful for victims to meet with their offenders in safe and controlled settings. It is likely that they will feel the need to tell the offender about their anger, fear and pain, and the offender will probably tell his victim how sorry he is.

Victims of date-rape share the fear of meeting their offender with most victims of sex offenses. A severe penalty cannot remove this fear. Even when the offender is sent to prison for a long time, the fear will remain. The penalty might correspond with people's feeling of justice, but it does not help the partners involved to solve their psychological problems.

The meeting between the partners in the Trondheim project will be facilitated by professionals in the field; the initiative to meet is to be taken by the victim. Participation by the offenders is voluntary, and the victims give no guarantee that they will not take the case to court. Both the victim and the offender will be supported by a health professional in the preparation process; and they both will be encouraged to be honest when meeting. After the preparation process, which lasts for three to five hours, the partners meet in a Guided Dialogue led by a mediator from the Regional Conflict Council of Trondheim.

The concept of restorative justice may have many weaknesses. One major problem is the asymmetric power in the relation between victim and offender. This has to be balanced by professionals making sure that the risk of a re-offense when the partners meet is minimized. Professionals should also ensure that all partners get the necessary support and help during the process.

The main problem in most sex offending cases is that an attempt is made to deal with the victims' fear using the legal system. As long as no meeting between offender and victim is organized in a safe way for those who want it, the asymmetry of power continues. Today more than 90% of the victims will never experience justice through the legal system. Instead of thinking of moral value as something that has to be expressed in terms of penalties, we should think of it in a relational way. It is more important to show victims that we are willing to help them than to make declarations about moral values. As long as offenders profit from denying and minimizing guilt, victims will not be helped that much by better policing methods or stricter penalties.

The idea of restorative justice is that the partners suffering the pain of an offense should be given the opportunity to experience ownership of the case, and to realize that it does not belong to the state or to others who do not experience their pain. Usually pain cannot be cured by inflicting new pain; but it helps a great deal if the person responsible for the pain takes the responsibility on his own shoulders, and says that he is willing to do something about the situation.

Restorative justice is not an abandonment of the values of the Western world's legal traditions; it is an adaption of the system to some severe problems which are yet to be solved. The asymmetric power between offender and victim continues to be a source of fear as long as the partners are not obliged to meet and talk together.

Maybe the fear will still remain after they have met. Nevertheless, facing the danger is usually a better strategy than running from it.

To advance further across this complex terrain we have to modify or even change the way we understand justice. Traditionally, justice has been understood as providing the right dose of punishment for the felony, taking into consideration the background and situation of the perpetrator. In restorative justice, the term justice is about the responsibility of the person who has done wrong. When taking on his responsibility the offender reveals the truth; the offender, and not the victim, is to be blamed (see Chapter 22). But then we must address the question: what should the price be for causing pain and harm to others?

The TRC of South Africa prescribed some symbolic means of compensation, which were not aimed at paying the real or full price for the damage caused by the felony. However, the amount of compensation is not the most important matter (though it has to be dealt with, of course). The point is to find alternatives that make it possible to help more victims, and offenders. In today's sex offending cases, one priority could be to develop methods that reduce the advantage to the offender of denying guilt and responsibility. Then it is important to handle the cases in public settings so that the principles of legal protection can be maintained. Finally, both the victim and the offender should be offered qualified, sufficient and necessary treatment. Restorative justice is an idea more than a fixed and developed method. This idea will not solve all the problems, but it is still an idea that is open to further development. Maybe the idea is even better – at least to some extent – than the system we have developed so far.

Conclusion

Preventing sex offenses from taking place through the use of legal action has not turned out to be an effective strategy. Nor does it seem that legal action has been particularly successful in individual prevention, though some offenders might be less likely to commit new offenses after having served their prison term.

In this chapter we have seen that the legal system is marginalized in sex offending cases. Though legislation has an impact on people's attitudes and moral understandings, offending behavior is not much affected by legal regulations. It is nearly impossible to reduce the numbers of sex offenses by use of the penal code. On the other hand, this does not mean that the legislation and the legal system do not have a role. Victims must be supported by a society that expresses solidarity with their sufferings. And we need some absolute norms in the field of sexual behavior, so that the individual's right to free sexual choices is protected. Sex offenses are a violation of human freedom.

There is also a need to handle sex offending cases in public settings. Sex offending is everybody's business; everybody has an obligation to promote attitudes and norms that prevent offenses from taking place. The main principle of restorative justice is to involve all persons affected by a criminal case. The ownership of the case must lie with the partners, not with the state alone. The most important aspect of the problem-solving process is to encourage people talk to each other.

But is it reasonable to assume that restorative justice – as opposed to punitive strategies – will reduce the number of sex offenses? We cannot know that. What we know is that the partners receive better care, which gives reason to believe that their long-term suffering will probably be reduced. In the field of sex offending, we are facing severe human tragedies on both sides of the line. This should inspire us to try to find better ways of handling these cases, realizing that so far none of us has got the answers. In the meantime we have to look for the answers and seek possible solutions.

Notes

1   This chapter particularly focuses on democratic nations in Western Europe and the United States. As democracies, these nations support the right of their people to influence the law, though not that the individual should stand above the law. The role of public opinion in criminal cases in recent years is characterized by a growing influence of people's "feeling of justice," which might be complicated in relation to the defendant's right to have a fair and just trial.

2   This is the author's observation from 25 years of clinical work and research in the field, and it is supported by other research.

3   The figures showing the reasons for this will be presented later in the chapter.

4   Some reservations must be expressed concerning these figures. The estimate is based on criminal statistics referred to earlier in this chapter, showing that approximately 700 persons were convicted in Norway in 2009 (Statistisk Sentralbyrå, 1980–2009). If this is 5% of all offenders, the total number of offenders would be 14,000. These figures should be compared with an evaluation presented by a committee appointed by the Ministry of Justice in 2008, concluding that rape incidents alone account for 8,000–16,000 victims each year (Sletner, 2008).

5   As already shown, convicted offenders are a small and select group when compared with the total number of offenders. Knowledge related to such a small group has some inbuilt weaknesses; on the other hand, the high quality of the information compensates for the low numbers.

6   This is not supported by international research showing that the most significant factor predicting behavior in sex offenders is recent convictions. This research indicates that convicted offenders are more likely than others to carry out sex offenses in the future. However, the research findings do not necessarily indicate that the reason for relapse is the former conviction in itself; it just indicates that those who have carried out an offense in the past are more likely to carry out new offenses.

7   This has been the main tendency in Norwegian criminal policy for more than 50 years, and is also the case in most European countries.

References

Andenæs, J. (1994) *Straffen som problem (The Problem of Punishment)* Oslo: Exil Forlag A/S.

Andenæs, J. (1997) *Alminnelig strafferett (Common Criminal Law)* Oslo: Universitetsforlaget.

Christie, N. (2000) "Om straffens hegemoni," *Nordisk tidskrift for Kriminalvidenskab* 91, 4, 316–319.

Finstad, L. (1988) "Sedelighetsforbrytere ut av fengslene: prinsipper for en realistisk utopi," *Materialisten* 3, 1–21.

Hauge, R. (2004) "Kriminalitetsutviklingen i Norge siden 1980," *Nordisk tidsskrift for Kriminalvidenskab* 2–3, 124–131.

Hermstad, K. (2006) Forbrytelse og selvforståelse. Et bidrag til forståelsen av en gruppe menn dømt til fengsel for seksuelle overgrep, i lys av terapi, etikk og strafferett. (Felony and self-understanding. A contribution to the understanding of a group of men sentenced to prison for sexual abuse – an analysis in the light of therapy, ethics and the criminal law.) Doctoral thesis, Norwegian University of Science and Technology, Trondheim.

Hermstad, K. (2009) Regulating sexual behaviour and attitudes by use of the criminal law. Paper presented at the 19th WAS World Congress for Sexual Health, "Sexual Health & Rights: A Global Challenge," Gothenburg, July 21–25.

Hirsch, A. v. (1976) *Doing Justice*. New York: Hill and Wang.

Kant, I. (1982) *Die Methaphysik der Sitten*. Frankfurt a.M.: Suhrkamp.

McCall Smith, A. (1998) *The No.1 Ladies' Detective Agency*. London: Abacus.

McCall Smith, A. (2001) *Morality for Beautiful Girls*. London: Abacus.

Sætre, M., Holter, H. and Jebsen, E. (1986) *Tvang til seksualitet. En undersøkelse av seksuelle overgrep mot barn (Forced into Sex. An Investigation of Sex Offenses Against Children)*. Oslo: Cappelen.

Schei, B., Muus, K.M. and Bendixen, M. (1994) "Forekomsten av seksuelle overgrep blant studenter i Trondheim" ("Prevalence of rape among students in Trondheim") *Tidsskrift for den Norske Lægeforeningen* 118, 21, 2491–2494.

Sletner, R. (2008) *Fra ord til handling. Bekjempelse av voldtekt krever handling (From Words to Actions: Combating Rape Takes Actions)*. Oslo: Justice Department of Norway.

Statistisk Sentralbyrå (1980–2009) *Statistisk årbok, årbøkene for perioden 1980–2010. (Yearbooks of the Statistical Central Agency of Norway for 1980–2010)*. Kongsvinger: Statistisk Sentralbyrå.

Tambs, K. (1994) *Undersøkelse av seksuelle overgrep mot barn (A Survey of Sex Offenses Against Children in Norway)*. Oslo: Statens Institutt for Folkehelse.

Verwoerd, W. (2000) "A space for victims to speak and the right for perpetrators to be heard," in C. Villa-Vicencio and W. Verwoerd (eds), *Looking Back, Reaching Forward. Reflections on the Truth and Reconciliation Commission of South Africa*. Cape Town: University of Cape Town Press, pp. 155–165.

2

Human Rights and Sexual Offenders

Bernadette Rainey

Introduction

The treatment and management of sex offenders both in detention and in the community raises human rights concerns in an era when community protection arguments are increasingly dominant in governmental policy. The right of the individual to a dignified existence is often seen to be outweighed by the state's and the public's desire for "safer communities." This utilitarianism raises concerns for human rights advocates in several areas concerning the treatment and management of sex offenders. The chapter will examine rights concerns with treatment such as drug therapy, with sentencing and detention, and with community measures. (It does not focus on areas such as civil preventative orders and restorative justice, which may give rise to similar debates.)

Rights and Risk

It has been argued that, historically, human rights lawyers in the United Kingdom have not engaged in an analysis of risk and, similarly, criminologists have had a tendency to leave rights issues to the lawyers (Murphy and Whitty, 2007). It is argued that one of the reasons for this is that lawyers see risk as a non-legal area of knowledge to be left to expert evidence and scientific inquiry (Murphy and Whitty, 2007), whereas criminologists are wary of intruding into a legal discourse traditionally dominated by expert lawyers (Valverde, Levi and Moore, 2005). However, the dominance of a risk penology (Kemshall, 2008) means that lawyers can no longer ignore the influence of risk in the protection of individual rights. According to Beck (2007), we

The Wiley-Blackwell Handbook of Legal and Ethical Aspects of Sex Offender Treatment and Management,
First Edition. Edited by Karen Harrison and Bernadette Rainey.
© 2013 John Wiley & Sons, Ltd. Published 2013 by John Wiley & Sons, Ltd.

are living in a risk society, where the precautionary principle dominates. It has been posited that there is a dichotomy between risk penology and rights-based governance, the focus of risk being control, which undermines liberty (Hudson, 2001). Therefore, a rights-based approach can lessen the threat to liberty from policies based on risk by providing a legal framework based on the principle of equality and dignity (Zedner, 2006). However, despite recognizing that the state may be best placed to determine risk, the courts have been willing to weigh the risk against the rights enshrined in the European Convention on Human Rights (ECHR) and enforceable in English law through the Human Rights Act 1998 (HRA) (Rainey, 2010).

However, as Murphy and Whitty (2007) argue, there is a more complex relationship between the two concepts. They argue that Sparks' (2001) analysis of risk as pluralist highlights how risk discourse is contingent on context and is therefore similar to rights discourse as both operate in "different institutional and cultural settings" (Murphy and Whitty, 2007: 805) and both struggle for "influence, credibility and recognition" (Sparks, 2001: 162). It has been noted that both concepts can be analyzed based on a social, contextual construction and there is a recognition of the importance of the interaction of legal and non-legal knowledge in policy making and differing models of regulation (Murphy and Whitty, 2007). The discussion in this chapter will highlight the importance of rights and risk discourse in the treatment and management of sex offenders.

Rights: the protection of dignity and the individual

The public and political debate has focused on dehumanizing the sex offender and removing the offender from the realm of those who deserve protection (see Chapter 8). This reflects a delineation between "deserving" and "undeserving" that is prominent in welfare discourse but is rejected by human rights lawyers. Instead, traditional human rights have been premised on the concept of human dignity and, as noted by Baroness Hale, human rights apply to all, "no matter how unpopular or unworthy she may be" (*R (Adam and Others)* v. *Secretary of State for Home Department* (2005) UKHL 66).

Human dignity is a central tenet of human rights law and flows from natural rights theory and Kant's categorical imperative which states that no person should be used as a means to an end (McCrudden, 2008). Modern thinkers such as Gerwith (1978) have taken this further, basing human rights protection on ideas of human agency. It has been argued that the principle of dignity is the basis for ethical consideration of offender treatment and management (see Chapter 6). In a legal context, the idea of dignity has been described as one of the three adjudicating principles in the application of human rights law (Gearty, 2004: 4). The protection of dignity is explicit in international human rights instruments and various national constitutions (the Constitutions of South Africa, for example) and although there is no codified constitution in the United Kingdom, dignity has become more prominent in English law since the passing of the Human Rights Act in 1998 (Feldman, 2000).

However, dignity is a difficult legal concept to apply in decision making due to its nebulous definition. It has been described as a malleable concept (Feldman, 1999) and is open to cultural reinterpretation (Donnelly, 2003). As noted by McCrudden

(2008: 698), "human dignity . . . is exposed as culturally relative, deeply contingent on local politics and values, resulting in significantly diverging, even conflicting, conceptions." That is not to say that the concept is illusory and unusable. Different conceptions may arise in different legal cultures but there remains a "minimum core" of meaning that is arguably universal (McCrudden, 2008). McCrudden (2008: 679) argues that this minimum core has three elements; the recognition of the intrinsic worth of every human being, that this intrinsic worth is recognized and respected by others and that the state should recognize and exist for the sake of individual worth. Feldman (1999: 686) defines human dignity as "an expression of an attitude to life which we humans should value when we see it in others as an expression of something which gives particular point and poignancy to the human condition." The role of law is to provide a list of rights which reflect at least the "minimum core" and that help preserve the opportunity for a dignified life (Feldman, 2000).

However, Feldman (2000) argues that dignity can be defined as subjective or objective dignity. Subjective dignity focuses on the individual values of autonomy and self-determination. However, this may clash with objective dignity, which focuses on the dignity of humanity as a whole. Hence the state can limit individual autonomy to protect the dignity of the human collective, such as the banning of "dwarf tossing" in France, where the court decided that even if the individual consented, the activity undermined the dignity of humanity as a whole (Feldman, 2000). The culturally relative meanings of dignity and the lack of legal consensus as to how dignity should be used in adjudication (McCrudden, 2008) has not precluded its use to justify decision making. The ECHR does not include dignity explicitly but the European Court of Human Rights (ECtHR) has increasingly used the concept to justify its reasoning (for example, see *Pretty* v. *UK* (2002) 3 EHHR) It is argued that the treatment and management of sex offenders should be premised on the human dignity of the offender, while recognizing the need to protect the dignity of potential victims. The protection agenda should not automatically outweigh the intrinsic worth of the individual; there must be a strong justification for this. In the area of penal policy, this justification is usually premised on risk. However, the permissibility of limitations on rights is dependent on the right involved and the justifications used. Any breach of the right not to be ill-treated (Article 3 ECHR) cannot be justified, whereas the qualified rights, such as the right to private and family life (Article 8 ECHR), allow the state to limit rights as long as any limitation meets a legitimate aim, is in accordance with law and is proportionate. The safety of others is recognized as a legitimate aim of public policy when considering qualified rights. However, a question arises as to the legitimacy of claims of dangerousness and risk when law and policy limit rights.

It should also be noted that risk may be used not just to limit rights but also to place an obligation on the state to protect individuals in the community from "dangerous" offenders. The state is under a positive obligation to protect the rights of all within the community, an obligation that has been recognized by the ECtHR. For example, under Article 2 and Article 3 on the right to life and not to be ill-treated, the state has obligations to provide protection where there is a real and immediate *risk* of death or serious harm that the state knows or ought to know exists and the state can take reasonable steps to protect identifiable individuals (*Osman* v. *UK* (2000) 29 EHRR 245). Similar obligations apply under Article 8. The courts have not given a detailed analysis of risk in these cases, instead reaching conclusions on all the evidence (for example, *Chahal* v. *UK* [1996] ECHR 54). Therefore the concept of risk is clearly interrelated with dignity and the protection of rights.

Risk: the protection of the community

As discussed above, the literature of risk has not traditionally examined rights in detail. However, there has been a growing concern with "legal risk" in regulation studies and in areas such as insurance and tort law (Ewald, 2000; Ericson, 2007; Steele, 2004). As noted by Murphy and Whitty (2007), the relationship between the two concepts is complex and intersecting. Similar to dignity, the concept of risk is open to interpretation across the political, social and legal spectrum as well as between policy makers, practitioners and legal enforcement (Kemshall, 2008). The term "risk" is value-laden (Douglas, 1992). The concept of risk has increasingly been used as a descriptor for the postmodern or late modern age; we are living in a risk society (Beck, 2007). This leads to demands for a risk-averse society driven by the precautionary principle (Beck, 2007). This "precautionary logic" (Hebenton and Seddon, 2009) to risk impacts on legal regulation. "Security is displacing freedom and equality from the highest position on the scale of values. The result is a tightening of laws, a seemingly rational totalitarianism of defence against threats" (Beck, 2007: 8–9). This has led to a shift from welfare to risk, from treating the offender as a moral agent who can be transformed (Garland, 1985) to the management of risk classified by dangerousness (Feely and Simon, 1992). This new risk penology has not only been driven by a focus on risk by policy makers but also by public opinion. Sex offenders are the new "folk devils" and moral panic has heightened the fear of pedophiles following high-profile murders (Kemshall and McIvor, 2004; see Chapter 8). The cultural understanding of risk (Kemshall and McGuire, 2003) has led to legislative and policy changes that focus on regulating the perceived dangerousness of sex offenders.

If risk has become the predominant rationale of penal policy, then there has to be a framework to assess offender risk. Assessment tools have been developed in order to manage and differentiate risk. Different methods have been used, such as clinical assessment tools which focus on the individual and actuarial methods of assessment focusing solely on the context and statistical data available (Grubin, 2004; see Chapter 20). In actuarial risk assessment, there is little focus on individual characteristics. The failure to take individual characteristics into account has been criticized as being flawed (Grubin, 2004) and may compromise the rights protection of the individual. Removing individual characteristics objectifies the offender and undermines his dignity. Recent risk assessment tools use dynamic methods of assessment, which combine actuarial assessment with the individual circumstances and characteristics of the offender. These third-generation tools are arguably more effective and do consider the needs of the offender (Kemshall, 2003). However, there are still difficulties with assessing what is meant by a "high-risk offender" (Kemshall, 2003). The use of risk moves the penal system further from traditional notions of proportionate punishment and deterrence focused on past crime (Von Hirsch, 1985), to prevention of acts that may occur in the future.

Applying Rights Protection to Dangerous Sex Offenders

The adoption of a rights-based approach to the treatment and management of sex offenders involves the application of the concept of dignity to penal policy and community protection. Specific examples will be used to illustrate the application of a rights framework, the use of risk penology and the implications for community protection.

Sentencing and detention

The shift in the criminal justice system from welfarism to risk is illustrated in the increased sentencing schemes for sex offenders. Indeterminate sentencing is increasingly being used to keep dangerous sex offenders in detention and has been introduced in various jurisdictions (Fish, 2008; see Chapter 9). This has been described as the deployment of "counter law" (Ericson, 2007), where new legislation is used to pre-empt the traditional rationale for sentencing, such as just deserts based on proportionality (Von Hirsch, 1985; Hebenton and Seddon, 2009: 347). This has been achieved by the controversial use of differing forms of preventative detention such as civil commitment in the United States (see Chapter 24), the use of preventative detention in the United Kingdom for "mentally disordered" offenders (see Chapter 3) and criminal commitment in Australia and the United Kingdom.

How does this circumvention of traditional sentencing practices impact on the rights of the offender? The main right involved is the right not to be arbitrarily detained (Article 5 of the ECHR). Although Article 5 can be derogated from during a state emergency, the state is limited by the Article as to when it can deprive a person of his or her liberty. The Article states that persons can only be deprived of their liberty for specified reasons such as criminal sanction, health and deportation and any detention must be in accordance with law (Rainey, 2010; Ovey and White, 2010). Article 5 also guarantees that a review of detention has to be held speedily by a judicial body under Article 5(4). The ECtHR has held that indeterminate sentencing schemes are compatible with Article 5 as long as there is a link between the initial sentence passed by the court and the reason for continuing detention (*Weeks* v. *UK* Application no. 9787/82)). The detention cannot be arbitrary under Article 5(1) as long as this link exists and the ECtHR has recognized that the reasons for continuing detention may change (*Stafford* v. *UK* (2002) 35 EHRR 1121). The need for a speedy review under Article 5(4) is important once the minimum tariff for imprisonment is fulfilled to determine if the link between the reason for deprivation of liberty and continuing detention still exists. Two European examples will be examined to illustrate the issues that may be raised with detention for public protection.

Human rights challenges: public protection sentencing in England and Wales

In England and Wales (Scotland and Northern Ireland have separate jurisdiction in this area), the sentencing of offenders beyond determinate, fixed-term sentences is governed by ss225–230 Criminal Justice Act 2003 (as amended by the Criminal Justice and Immigration Act 2008). Under the legislation there are three types of sentences involving detention beyond a determinate sentence: life, imprisonment for public protection (IPP) and extended sentences, with decisions on release made by the Parole Board. Under s225, IPPs *may* be made if there is a "significant risk to members of the public of serious harm" and the offense is a listed serious offense with a determinate sentence of 10 years or the notional minimum term of the offense is two years. Extended sentences under s227 can be given for less serious offenses where there is a similar risk to the public. The rationale for this sentencing structure is dangerousness as set out in s229. When assessing future risk of harm the court *must* take into account the nature and circumstances of the offense and *may* take into account the nature and circumstances of any other offenses of which the offender has been convicted, information on patterns of behavior and any information about the offender before the court. The criteria are interpreted subjectively by the courts. In *R* v. *Lang and Others* ((2005) EWCA Crim 2864), the Court of Appeal adopted the dictionary definition of "significant" as "of considerable importance" (para. 17). The Court stated that it should be guided by the assessment of risk in reports but that it should also consider the circumstances of the offenses, including socio-economic factors, employability, relationships and so on. The reasoning indicated that the judiciary should take a "restrained and careful approach" to sentencing (Thomas, 2006: 179). However, when the 2003 Act provisions came into force in 2005, the number of IPPs increased as judges "loyally followed the unequivocal terms of the statute" (Lord Brown, *Wells* v. *Secretary of State for Justice (Parole Board Intervening)* [2009] UKHL 22 para. 119). The amendments in the 2008 Act reflected judicial concerns over the complexity of the indeterminate sentencing scheme. The presumption of risk for those who had committed a previous offense under s229 was removed and the mandatory nature of sentencing under s225 and s227 was removed to allow more judicial discretion. However, the principles in *Lang* have been reaffirmed in subsequent cases. In *Attorney General's Reference No.5 of 2011) (Troninas)* ([2011] EWCA Crim 1244), the Court of Appeal underlined the nature of an indeterminate sentence as purely about future harm and not the gravity of the offense: "It contained no denunciatory element; it was pure protection" (Thomas, 2011: 371).

The indeterminate sentence scheme has been challenged under the HRA, which incorporated the ECHR rights into English law. The challenges focused on the assessment of risk and the determination of risk when the indeterminate sentence has begun. First, fears have been expressed that assessment tools may be applied arbitrarily, depending on their use by professionals (Kemshall, 2008). Unpredictability may undermine the legal certainty needed to satisfy rights concerns (Rainey, 2010). When applying "in accordance with law" under Article 5, the law must be predictable and foreseeable (Harris, O'Boyle and Warbrick, 2009). As noted, the legislation has laid down criteria which the court should follow when determining dangerousness. In *R* v. *Pedley and Ors* ([2009] EWCA Crim 840), the claimants argued that their IPP sentences violated their ECHR rights based on the vagueness of the assessment of risk. The claimants argued that significant risk should mean more likely than not or should be a numerical possibility (35 to 50%). Without this standard, "significant" has an arbitrary and disproportionate threshold, meaning the legislation would be incompatible with Article 5(1) as any detention would be based on unpredictable grounds. The Court rejected this argument. It affirmed the interpretation given in *Lang* and the limits put on judicial discretion by statute. It rejected the proposition that a numerical value can be put on risk assessment. Given the interpretation of the Courts, "it is unlikely that the significant risk test would be found to violate the convention unless a claimant can clearly demonstrate a judge has failed to apply the statutory scheme" (Rainey, 2010: 277). As noted, the ECtHR has accepted dangerousness and risk as reasons for detention (*Stafford* v. *UK* (2002) 35 EHRR 1121), though there has been no definitive case on how risk should be assessed. The state may be given a discretion known as the margin of appreciation when assessing risk at domestic level. In deportation/removal cases, the ECtHR has found that the real and substantial risk of ill treatment to the claimant could violate the right not to be ill-treated under Article 3. Whether a risk is "real and substantial" is based on all the circumstances of the case and considering all the evidence (*Chahal* v. *UK* [1996] ECHR 54). It is likely that the ECtHR would examine the compliance of a domestic decision with the statutory scheme explained above. It may be prepared to consider the domestic assessment of "real" risk but it is suggested that unless there was evidence of a failure to assess relevant material, the ECtHR would be reluctant to intervene (Rainey, 2010).

Secondly, several cases have challenged indeterminate detention as the offenders had not been provided with the means to demonstrate they were no longer a risk after the end of the determinate part of the sentence. In *Walker* v. *Secretary of State for Home Department* ([2008] 3 All ER 104), the Court of Appeal found that the Secretary of State had failed in his public law duty to provide necessary resources. The Court stated that the subsequent delay before the offender could put his case to the Parole Board would not automatically contravene Article 5 but *may* lead to a violation of Article 5(4) as a review by the Parole Board may become meaningless. This seems to be a conservative approach. The House of Lords (now the Supreme Court) in *Wells* v. *Secretary of State for Justice (Parole Board Intervening)* ([2009] UKHL 22) went further in restricting the application of Article 5. The Court found that there was no violation of Article 5(1) as there was still a link between the reason for the indeterminate sentence and continuing detention. When considering Article 5(4), the Court took a functional, minimalist approach. It noted that although it was difficult for a prisoner to demonstrate that he was no longer a risk, he had access to the review process and the Parole Board had information on which it could base a decision with a further review at *reasonable* intervals. Lord Brown had sympathy for the argument that the review could become an empty exercise but found that Article 5(4) required the procedural obligations to be met and no more. Article 5(4) could in theory be breached by a lack of resources to demonstrate lack of risk, but only in circumstances where the Board could not carry out its functions and any delay was for a lengthy period of time, described as years (para. 126).

Although critical of the IPP scheme before the 2008 amendments, the House of Lords has taken a conservative approach to the application of Article 5. It has shown a reluctance to go beyond present ECtHR jurisprudence and provide substantive protection for offenders' rights while under the indeterminate sentencing regime.

This approach may reflect a judicial reluctance to interfere in state resource allocation and an unwillingness to interfere in substantive penal policy (Londono, 2008) as long as the procedures are compatible. Recently, the ECtHR was critical of the German preventative detention regime because there appeared to be:

> no special measures, instruments or institutions in place, other than those available to ordinary long-term prisoners, directed at persons subject to preventive detention and aimed at reducing the danger they present and thus at limiting the duration of their detention to what is strictly necessary in order to prevent them from committing further offences. (*Grosskopf* v. *Germany* (2010) Application no. 24478/02, para. 52)

However, despite this criticism, it was not a basis for violation of Article 5. It could be argued that the domestic courts and the ECtHR should be more proactive in this area. A failure to provide an opportunity for rehabilitation leading to an indeterminate sentence can undermine the rights and the dignity of the offender. It is also unclear how this promotes public protection as the offender does not get recourse to tools that could prevent him from reoffending (Rainey, 2010).

Along with the judicial concerns surrounding IPPs, Padfield (2011) described the low release rate of post tariff prisoners under the indeterminate scheme as "shocking" and the UK Parliamentary Joint Committee on Human Rights (2011) has expressed similar concerns (see also Chapter 9). Due to these concerns and possibly the desire to cut the prison population, new legislation will replace IPPs in England and Wales. The Legal Aid, Sentencing and Punishment of Offenders Act 2012 will amend the law concerning sentencing of dangerous offenders. When in force,[1] it will abolish IPPs and replace them with mandatory life sentences under certain circumstances. The threshold is high for mandatory life sentencing (s122 which will be new s224A Criminal Justice Act 2003), requiring an offense under new Schedule 15B of the 2003 Act and requiring two conditions to be met: the "seriousness" condition (offense with 10 years or more imprisonment) and "previous offence" condition (previous conviction of an offense under Schedule 15B). A further restriction on the use of mandatory life sentencing is the discretion given to the court not to impose the sentence if there are "particular circumstances" that would make it unjust to impose the sentence in all circumstances. The discretionary life sentence and the extended sentencing provisions remain in the new sentencing scheme.

It is arguable that the use of mandatory life sentences for dangerous sex offenders may be limited given the conditions that must be met (Sentencing Review, 2011). When imposing discretionary life sentences, the Courts have set a high threshold of seriousness before imposing such sentences (*Wilkinson* [2010] 1 Cr App R (S) 100) and it is unlikely that the discretionary life sentences will be used more regularly by the Courts instead of IPPs, despite the optimism of the government that this will be the case (Kenneth Clarke, *Hansard*, HC Deb, November 1, 2011, vol. 534, col. 789). It could also be argued that determinate life sentences are closer to traditional "denunciatory" sentencing, focusing on the gravity of the offense rather than future harm. The abolition of the IPP scheme does meet some of the human rights concerns raised by the case law and has been welcomed by the Parliamentary Joint Committee on Human Rights (2011). The replacement of IPPs may lead to more sex offenders being released into the community under conditions described below. The judicial interpretation of the mandatory scheme will determine whether the new scheme raises further rights concerns.

Human rights challenges and preventative detention in Germany

In Germany, preventative detention is mandated at federal level. Germany has a history of preventative detention laws which co-exist alongside the traditional criminal justice provisions. Until 1998, preventative detention was circumscribed by a number of safeguards (Drenkhahn, Morgenstern and Van Zyl Smit, 2012; see also Chapter 9). These safeguards included a limit of 10 years in the first instance on preventative detention following a fixed term. Certain criteria had to be met, such as a term of imprisonment lasting more than two years, and the proportionality of the preventative detention to the danger posed by the prisoner, and was reviewed every two years (Drenkhahn, Morgenstern and Van Zyl Smit, 2012; see also Chapter 9). These restrictions on the use of preventative detention meant there were few cases of detention under these parts of the penal code (Michaelsen, 2012: 169).

However, following a series of highly publicized sex offender cases (Michaelsen, 2012), the risk penology was illustrated by increasingly draconian legislation. The penal code was amended in 1998 to allow for indefinite preventative detention instead of the 10-year limit and was further widened in 2002 to allow preventative detention to be imposed after the original determinate sentence. In 2004, preventative detention could be imposed retrospectively (Michaelsen, 2012). Challenges to the legislation in the German Federal Constitutional Court failed. The Court underlined the principle in German law that preventative detention was not a penalty and so was not covered by the rule against retrospectivity in the German Constitution (BVG, 2 BvR 2029/01 Feb 2004). Despite the German court upholding the law, the rise in numbers held under the amended legislation was criticized by the Council of Europe's Commissioner for Human Rights (2007a) as well as the Council of Europe Committee for Prevention of Torture (2007b).

The law was further challenged in a series of cases in the ECtHR. In *M* v. *Germany* ((2010) 51 EHRR 41) the ECtHR found the amended preventative scheme to be a violation of Article 5(1). While affirming its previous case law on the permissibility of indeterminate sentencing if linked to the original conviction (see above), the Court found that the German legislation went beyond this. M had been sentenced and given the maximum of 10 years preventative detention under the old law. This was then changed to indefinite detention when the amended law was introduced. This retrospective change to the original sentence was held to break the link between the original sentence and the continuing detention. The Court also found that the preventative detention was a "penalty" and therefore violated Article 7 of the ECHR which protects persons from retrospective law. Similar violations were found in the German cases of *Kallweit* (2011) (Application no. 17792/07), *Mautes* (2011) (Application no. 20008/07), *Schummer* (2011) (Application no. 27360/04), *Jedrowiak* (2011) (Application no. 30060/04) and *Haidn* (2011) (Application no. 6587/04).

In response, the German Constitutional Court revisited the law in cases before it in 2011 (BVG, 2 BvR 2365/09). It found that the amended law violated the German Basic Law on deprivation of liberty and legitimate expectation under the law. In order to be compatible, the code should be "liberty orientated" (Michaelsen, 2012: 163); a concept of preventative detention which focused on therapy. The preventative detention scheme was also closely interrelated with the determinate prison regime and so the "twin track" approach was not clearly exclusive. To avoid being a "penalty" under German law, the preventative detention regime should be clearly separate, with the aim of therapy for mental disorder. In summary, preventative detention would only be ordered if "the required distance from punishment was kept, if a high risk of the most serious crimes . . . could be inferred from the specific circumstances . . . and if the requirements of Article 5(1) were satisfied" (Michaelsen, 2011: 164). However, the German response has been criticized for having a restrictive view of "penalty" and the use of "mental disorder" for preventative detention (Drenkhahn, Morgenstern and Van Zyl Smit, 2012) as well as partial compliance under new legislation (Merkel, 2011).

Both the UK and German indefinite detention schemes are premised on risk and public protection. However, the German changes in response to the ECtHR noted the primacy of "liberty" over public protection (Michaelsen, 2011: 164) and the need for proportionality. Although the English Courts have taken an arguably procedural approach, recent amendments to legislation suggest recognition that the substantive treatment of prisoners on IPPs does not meet the needs of public protection, nor is it beneficial to have prisoners indefinitely held in an overcrowded prison environment. The application of public protection sentencing exemplifies the convergence of rights and risk, the weighing up of liberty and public protection and the use of "counter law" to undermine due process rights (Hebenton and Seddon, 2009: 349).

Community Protection

The public protection agenda based on risk has led to restrictions on sex offenders in the community, usually after a conviction for a sexual offense. Two major issues that affect the rights of the offender will be examined; sex offender registers and the disclosure of information to the public. The focus will be on the law in England and Wales but similar concerns have been raised in other jurisdictions (see Chapter 21).

Human rights challenges and the sex offender register in England and Wales

As Thomas (2010) notes, the use of sex offender registration in the United Kingdom has been influenced by US federal law, premised on public protection and crime prevention. The requirements for the register were first legislated for by the Sex Offenders Act 1997 and later amended by the Sexual Offences Act (SOA) 2003. Thomas (2010) outlines the increasingly draconian additions to the register since 1997. The register requires registration for designated sexual offenses: registration is indefinite for sentences of more than 30 months; for a period of six to 30 months registration is for 10 years; for less than six months registration is for seven years; with a police caution meaning registration for two years (SOA 2003 ss81–82). As well as being on the register, an offender must report to the police station within three days, be photographed, give fingerprints, give notification of travel abroad, and be subject to annual verification visits, powers of forced entry by police into registered sex offenders' premises, and the use of polygraphs (Thomas, 2006). These measures will be further extended under the Sexual Offences Act 2003 (Notification Requirements) England and Wales Regulations 2012. The measures are motivated by public protection arguments (Thomas, 2006; Kemshall, 2008: 115).

However, sex offender rights are engaged under this regime. The main right engaged is the right to private and family life under Article 8 of the ECHR.[2] Article 8 is a qualified right; the state may justify interference if it is in accordance with law, meets a legitimate aim and is necessary in a democratic society.[3] Article 8(1) does not define what private and family life means. Family life covers most familial relationships, while private life has been interpreted widely by the court to include "a person's physical and psychological integrity" for which respect is due in order to "ensure the development, without outside interference, of the personality of each individual in his relations with other human beings" (*Botta* v. *Italy* (1998) 26 EHRR 241).

As a minor intrusion can constitute interference, many cases are decided under Article 8(2). A measure has to be "in accordance with law," meaning that there should be some legislative basis for the treatment (*Malone* v. *UK* (1984) 7 EHHR 14). The state will then have to demonstrate a legitimate aim when implementing the measure. These include public safety, crime prevention and protection of others. The issue upon which most of the jurisprudence on Article 8 is decisive, is that of the necessity for such a measure in a democratic society. For a measure to be necessary it has to be proportionate; does it strike a "fair balance" between the right of the individual and the needs of the community (*Hatton* v. *UK* (2003) ECHR 338)? The decision maker will carry out a balancing exercise where the right of the individual is weighed against the public interest. In this balancing exercise, the clash of the differing forms of dignity discussed above is illustrated.

Article 8 places positive obligations on states to ensure respect of the right to private and family life. Victims of sex offenders potentially have a claim for protection in order to fulfill their rights to protection under Article 8.[4] Where a Court decides the balance should be struck may depend on the margin of appreciation it gives to the states. This is the amount of discretion the ECtHR will give to the states as best placed to decide on certain issues due to "their direct and continuous contact with the vital forces of their countries" (*Handyside* v. *UK* (1976) 1 EHRR 737).

The register itself is an administrative requirement as a result of a criminal sentence rather than a punitive measure and has been recognized as such by the ECtHR. In *Adamson* v. *UK* (Application no. 42293/98), the applicant argued that it was a penalty separate from his conviction and so violated Article 7, as a penalty heavier than the one applicable for his offense. The ECtHR rejected this argument, finding that the requirements at the time of the case were not onerous enough to constitute a penalty. However, the more draconian the requirements of the register, the more likely that it may be seen as a penalty (Home Office/Scottish Executive, 2001: 13).

Adamson v. *UK* did recognize that the register engaged Article 8 in regard to its effects but the measure was not held to be disproportionate. However, the more onerous the interference the less likely that it will be found to be proportionate under Article 8(2). There have been several challenges to the register which until recently were dismissed. However, recent UK case law has challenged the compatibility of the register regime with Convention rights.

A series of cases challenged the automatic nature of the register regime. Those placed on the register indefinitely had no right to seek a review of the decision. In *Re Gallagher* ([2003] NIQB 26), the applicant used Article 8 to challenge the automatic nature of the register requirements which denied him the right to review of the indefinite registration. The judge underlined the need for the state to justify interferences with individual rights (para. 24) but noted that "the gravity of sex offences and the serious harm . . . must weigh heavily in favour of a scheme designed to protect potential victims of such crime" (para. 24); individuals "must be of secondary importance" (para. 23). Dangerousness was placed above individual rights; "the court deferring to parliament and reflecting governmental and public attitudes" (Rainey, 2010: 280). Subsequent case law followed this reasoning (*Forbes* v. *Secretary of State for Home Department* [2006] 1 WLR 3075; *H* v. *The Queen* [2007] EWCA Crim 2622; *A* v. *Scottish Ministers* [2007] CSOH 189). The latter two cases dealt with minors. The argument that as children their circumstances should have been open to greater scrutiny was rejected. However, in both cases the court did consider individual circumstances in finding that the seriousness of the offenses in question meant the indefinite registration period was not disproportionate.

However, the Courts now seem prepared to show less deference to parliament. In *F and Thompson* v. *Secretary of State for Justice* ([2010] UKSC 17), the Supreme Court declared the indefinite nature of registration without review incompatible with Article 8. F was 11 years old when the offense was committed. The Court found that juveniles should have a right to review indefinite registration. A lack of review was disproportionate given that the general approach of the Courts to juvenile sentencing was to consider the maturity of the offender. In Thompson's case, the Court noted that indefinite registration may be necessary but where an offender believes he is no longer a risk, in principle he should be given the opportunity to establish this. As the statutory scheme made no provision for review, it was declared incompatible with Article 8. The Court noted that evidence was inconclusive with regard to the impact on recidivism of indefinite registration. It also noted the negative impact on rehabilitation that indefinite registration can have on those who are no longer a risk (paras. 55, 51). The case may also reflect concerns that the legislation failed to consider juvenile characteristics. The courts have been aware of the necessity of considering maturity and age in sentencing. The Court noted the decision in *S and Marper* v. *UK* ((2008) Application no. 30562/04), in which the ECtHR criticized the UK for a blanket penal policy that failed to consider children. The decision in *F and Thompson* does not go as far as interfering with the actual requirements of the register but lays down a minimum safeguard of access to review. This reflects the emphasis on procedural rather than substantive protection given in IPP cases above, but it also demonstrates that the judiciary is prepared to find that a scheme excluding any consideration of the individual may be incompatible with convention rights.

Despite government rhetoric condemning the decision, claiming it was "disappointed and appalled" and would put public protection first (Theresa May, *Hansard*, HC Deb, February 16, 2011, vol. 523, col. 959), the government has responded to the Court ruling by amending the law and allowing a right to review indefinite registration. When in force,[5] the Sexual Offences Act 2003 (Remedial) Order 2012 will allow for a right to review indefinite registration. Unlike in Scotland, where amended legislation allows for an automatic right of appeal after 15 years (Sexual Offences 2003 (Remedial) (Scotland) Order 2011), the amendments in England and Wales give a more limited right to review which reflects the government's desire to take a minimalist approach and be "tougher" than the Scottish regime (Theresa May, *Hansard*, HC Deb, February 16, 2011, vol. 523, cols. 955, 959; Liberty, 2011). The Order allows for a review of indefinite registration if requested by an adult offender after 15 years and an offender aged under 18 after eight years (s91B 2003 Act). The review will be carried out by a chief police officer. If the police officer decides to keep the offender on the register, then it may be reviewed again in eight years. This further review can be postponed by the police officer until 15 years after the initial review. The test for deciding if the offender is to remain on the register is the "risk of sexual harm" (s91B). This includes psychological as well as physical harm to the community. This definition has been criticized as being too vague (Parliamentary Joint Committee on Human Rights, 2012). Coupled with this, the police officer may contact relevant bodies such as Multi-Agency Public Protection Panels (MAPPPs) for information on risk and so on, but there is no obligation to do so. Therefore the efficacy of decision making on risk is questionable.

In the original draft of the Order, the decision of the police officer was final. This was criticized as failing to comply with the decision in *F and Thompson*, where the Supreme Court explicitly noted the need for an independent tribunal (as underlined in *Bouchacourt* v. *France* ((2009) Application no. 5335/06)). It is questionable that the police are an independent authority for the purposes of review and it was arguable that such a review process was not rights-compliant (Parliamentary Joint Committee on Human Rights, 2012; Liberty, 2011; Howard League for Penal Reform, 2011). In response, the draft Order now includes a right to appeal to a magistrate's court from the review decision of the police officer. This does provide a minimum level of compatibility with Article 8. However, the test of "sexual harm" and the limited examination of risk undermine the review process. As noted by critics of the Order, sex offender registration uses considerable resources so it makes little sense for the government to maintain offenders on the register who are no longer a risk (Liberty, 2011). The statements by the government condemning the Supreme Court decision in terms of victims and public protection may suggest a political reason for the minimalist review allowed under the legislation.

Human rights challenges and disclosure

Following "Megan's law" in the United States, the UK government has resisted the public pressure to introduce a similar regime in the United Kingdom (Thomas, 2010; Kemshall, 2008: 118). There is no general duty on the police to disclose the whereabouts of registered sex offenders, though there has been a discretionary disclosure policy, which is circumscribed (Kemshall, 2008: 119). However, disclosure is now legislated for in limited circumstances. S327A Criminal Justice Act 2003 (as amended by s140 of the Criminal Justice and Immigration Act 2008) allows a public authority to disclose to a relevant member of the public if a sex offender poses a risk of serious harm to a child and it is necessary to protect the child. The authority may impose conditions on the relevant person as to further disclosure. There is a presumption that disclosure should be made.

The case law on public disclosures has tended to uphold the right to disclose in particular circumstances but the courts have been clear that any disclosure engages Article 8(1) and must be justified under Article 8(2). For example, in *Re C* (unreported, February 15, 2002), the Court allowed a disclosure concerning the dangerousness of C. However, it weighed the need to protect others with C's right to private life, the danger to C from vigilantes and dangers in controlling sensitive information (Power, 2003: 84). One of the problems that may arise under the "presumption to disclose" may be the difficulty in restricting information to those considered in need of protection. Based on previous case law, any challenge to a disclosure would lead to careful scrutiny of the necessity of such disclosure. This may be due to the fear of vigilantism or the fear that offenders may be forced into hiding.

There may also be an awareness that the state is under a positive obligation to protect. As noted, the ruling in *Osman* v. *UK* ((2000) 29 EHRR 245) found that the state can be held responsible for a death if it knew or ought to have known of a credible threat and did not take reasonable steps to protect. This applies both to offenders and to the potential victims. An offender could be put in danger if information is made public and measures are not in place to protect him, as noted in *Re C*. However, a potential victim may claim a credible threat against him/her if an offender is in the area. This may be more difficult to argue as the claimant would have to demonstrate he/she was a specific target for the offender and that the register requirements did not provide reasonable protection. In decisions based on *Osman* in other cases, the Courts have shown a reluctance to find against the police (*Van Colle* v. *Chief Constable of Hertfordshire Police* [2008 UKHL 50]) but the potential for challenges still remains. There is also an argument that there may be a positive obligation under Article 8 to provide information where members of the public are at risk. The ECtHR has held that where claimants' health was affected by a failure to disclose information, a state may be liable (*Guerra* v. *Italy* [1998] 26 EHRR 357). However, as Power (2003: 88) notes, register disclosure involves competing rights (of the offender and the potential victim) whereas *Guerra* did not.

Sex Offender Treatment: Pharmacotherapy

Pharmacotherapy is the use of drugs to lower the testosterone levels in male sex offenders. Anti-libidinal suppressants are known as a form of "chemical castration" though the drugs should not cause the permanent castration of the offender (Harrison and Rainey, 2009: 48). Pharmacotherapy has been used in several US states as well as several European countries (Harrison and Rainey, 2009: 49). The type of drug used and the method and length of administration of the drug vary between jurisdictions. In several US states, Medroxyprogesterone Acetate (MPA) is used, often on a mandatory basis as part of a sentence or a condition of prison release. In contrast, European countries administer Cyproterone Acetate (CPA) on a voluntary basis as part of a treatment program (Harrison, 2010: 2007). There is debate on the effectiveness of drug therapy, though the research suggests positive results only on preferential pedophiles (Harrison and Rainey, 2009: 50). MPA has been reported to have caused side effects including blood clotting, serious allergic reactions, diabetes, depression and irreversible feminization (Spalding, 1998). CPA has reportedly less side effects and any effects are reversible (Cooper, 1981). In England and Wales, the government has been trialing the use of pharmacotherapy since 2007 on a voluntary basis following a Home Office review of child protection (Home Office, 2007).

Human rights challenges to pharmacotherapy

The prominent rights that are engaged with the use of pharmacotherapy are Article 3 and Article 8. Article 3 of the ECHR[6] prohibits the use of torture, or inhuman or degrading treatment. The right has been interpreted by the ECtHR as imposing negative and positive obligations on states. The state must not be responsible for, or fail to take measures to prevent, a person within its jurisdiction being ill-treated. The fundamental nature of the right is illustrated by its absolute, non-derogable nature. Ill treatment directly undermines human dignity. The dangerousness of a person is irrelevant to protection under Article 3. The ECtHR has stated that "the Convention prohibits in absolute terms torture or inhuman or degrading treatment or punishment, irrespective of the victim's conduct" (*Chahal* v. *UK* (1997) 23 EHRR 413, para 80). The punishment or treatment has to reach a minimum level of severity for Article 3 to be engaged. It is for the ECtHR to decide whether this threshold has been met. In making its decision the court will assess a number of factors, including the nature and duration of the treatment; the age, sex and health of the victim, and the physical and mental effects (*Ireland* v. *UK* (1979–1980) 2 EHRR 25).

The use of pharmacotherapy has not yet been challenged in the ECtHR. If an offender consents to treatment then it could arguably be difficult to raise objections based on rights arguments. However, the nature of consent is important (see Chapter 3). Consent should be valid and informed. Valid consent consists of understanding the nature and effects of treatment and not being coerced into making decisions he would not otherwise have made. If consent is conditional then it may be difficult to define such consent as free. This is the case when treatment is linked to sentencing or prison release. Although it has been argued that conditional consent can still be a free choice (Miller, 2003: 252), it is arguably still a choice between two evils. The Council of Europe (2006) has emphasized the need for offender treatment to be free and fully informed. A recent case concerning extradition from the United Kingdom to the Czech Republic noted that drug therapy without consent may breach Articles 3 and 8, but when carried out with consent, the Court held that there was no breach of the ECHR despite the fact that a refusal to undergo treatment may lead to extended detention (*Janiga* v. *Usti Nad Labem Regional Court, Czech Republic* (2011) EWHC 553 (Admin)).

Those receiving treatment should also have the capacity to consent. If an offender does not have the competence to consent, then he may be forcibly medicated. One common method of treating sex offenders without consent is under mental health legislation. In England and Wales, the Mental Health Act 1983 (as amended by the Mental Health Act 2007) now includes sexual deviancy in the definition of mental disorder and allows forced medication under s58. The reformed Act has been criticized as being "predicated on social control rather than individual treatment" (Harrison and Rainey, 2009: 62). It raises human rights concerns given the vagueness of the amended definition and the three-month delay before forcible treatment is reviewed under s58 of the Act (see Chapter 3; Harrison and Rainey, 2009: 63).

If consent is free and informed then chemical castration may be rights-compliant, but if this is not the case or the state decides to have a compulsory regime on competent (or incompetent) persons then issues may arise under the ECHR. Would pharmacotherapy meet the threshold necessary for degrading treatment under Article 3? There is no doubt pharmacotherapy is better than surgical castration, which has been found to be cruel and unusual punishment by the US Supreme Court (*State* v. *Brown* 326 SE2d 410). However, the side effects of the drugs may be enough to humiliate an offender and therefore be degrading. The length and appropriateness of the treatment may also be a factor. Some US programs have broad definitions of sex offenders and lack clear procedures for suitability (Spalding, 1998). It should be noted that ECtHR jurisprudence may limit the possibility of finding a breach of the ECHR. The Court has found that severe side effects of coercive drug therapy did not meet the threshold for Article 3 (*Grare* v. *France* (Application no. 18835/91)). Furthermore, in *Herczegfalvy* v. *Austria* ((1992) 15 EHRR 437), the ECtHR held that "as a general rule, a measure which is a therapeutic necessity cannot be regarded as inhuman or degrading" (para. 82). It may be the case that only treatment which is not medically necessary will be considered by the Court. It makes it even more important to ensure that the offender is medically suitable and also that the medication is effective; otherwise it is not therapeutically necessary. Consequently, any excessive use of force or treatment beyond that which is necessary may violate Article 3 (*Jalloh* v. *Germany* (2006) ECHR 721) If the use of drug therapy is primarily to ensure public protection, with the "medical" needs of the offender being secondary, then the ECtHR may find it is not medically necessary. If the use of pharmacotherapy is argued before the Court, the Court would have to consider the seriousness of the side effects and the *Herczegfalvy* test. This might suggest that it would be difficult to find a state in violation of Article 3 unless the side effects were severe and long term (possibly akin to surgical castration), and where the treatment was clearly beyond what was considered to be therapeutically necessary.

It may also be possible to bring a case under Article 8 as any coercive treatment would clearly be an interference with the right to private life. The outcome would depend on whether treatment is justifiable. Any program of drug therapy would have to be in accordance with law. There should be legal guidelines for use that meet a legitimate aim, such as health or public order. Drug therapy should be necessary in a democratic society, which means the use of this kind of treatment would have to be proportionate to the stated aim, such as public protection or health. A court may put great weight in the public interest, given that vulnerable groups may be victims. The court would also consider if there is a less intrusive measure that could be taken to achieve the aim. It could be argued that treatment is actually less intrusive than prison if the drugs were offered in lieu of prison (Harrison and Rainey, 2009: 70). The court will also examine the side effects. It should be noted that when deciding if a measure is proportionate, the Court may consider the concomitant right of the partner of the claimant to a private and family life (*Dickson* v. *UK* (2007) 34 EHRR 21).

If pharmacotherapy is to be used, then it should be operated within a human rights framework so that the dignity of the offender is maintained while meeting policy goals of risk management. It is suggested that all programs should be voluntary, should have procedures which are published and publicly available, should ensure medical suitability and medical necessity of treatment, should monitor for potential negative side effects, should allow for independent reviews of individual treatment and treatment programs and should permit the offender to freeze sperm before program commencement in case of irreversible side effects.

Conclusion: Finding a Balance?

The increasingly transparent role of dignity and rights in law has developed alongside government penal policy based on risk. In recent years, it is apparent that the state has placed community protection above the individual rights of the offender (Kemshall, 2008: 110). There is also an increasing recognition in the literature of the complex relationship between rights and risk and the need to use both legal and non-legal knowledge to determine the "balance" between rights and risk.

However, the idea of "balance" can be misleading when discussing rights protection. In some cases, a balancing act does take place between the rights of the individual and the needs of the community. This is most obvious when discussing Article 8, where there is a balancing of subjective and objective dignity (Feldman, 1999). This allows limitations on an individual's rights, but the essence of the right itself should not be undermined (Fenwick, 2002: 31). The idea of balance is misplaced in relation to due process and ill treatment. The basic procedural rights in the criminal justice system apply to all, irrespective of conduct, in the same way as the right not to be tortured or degraded is universal. Does access to a review procedure mean the offender's rights take precedence over the victim or potential victim? Having access to a review does not mean that sex offenders are more likely to be released or removed from a register. Indeed, it could be argued that the system will be enhanced by review and a continuing examination of risk with the prospect of rehabilitation. As Liberty (2011, para. 13) notes, the system of indefinite registration without review meant control of sex offenders was ineffective and "continued registration by certain ex-offenders may actually undermine public safety by diverting police resources away from those who continue to pose a serious risk."

Case law has provided limited protection for offender rights and legal reasoning suggests that determining risk should be subjective and contextual. The state has a duty to protect all within its jurisdiction and high risk sexual offenders may require treatment and management that may lead to some limitation on individual rights.

However, public protection should not allow the objectification of offenders within the system, which undermines individual and collective dignity.

Notes

1 Not yet in force as of May 1, 2012. Chapter 5 will be brought into force by the Secretary of State by statutory instrument.
2 "(1) everyone has the right to respect for his private and family life, his home and his correspondence."
3 "There shall be no interference by a public authority with the exercise of this right except such as is in accordance with the law and is necessary in a democratic society in the interests of national security, public safety or the economic well-being of the country, for the prevention of disorder or crime for the protection of health or morals, or for the protection of rights and freedoms of others."
4 Where the state fails to prevent a violation of Article 8 either by its own agents or by non-state actors. See *X and Y* v. *Netherlands* (1986) 8 EHRR 235.
5 Not yet in force as of May 30, 2012.
6 "No one shall be subjected to torture or to inhuman or degrading treatment or punishment."

References

Beck, U. (2007) *World at Risk*. Cambridge: Polity Press.

Cooper, A.J. (1981) "A placebo-controlled trial of the antiandrogen Cyproterone Acetate in deviant hypersexuality," *Comprehensive Psychiatry* 22, 5, 458–465.

Council of Europe (2006) *European Committee on Crime Problems, the State of Work on the Text of a Draft Recommendation on the Treatment of Sex Offenders in Penal Institutions and the Community CDPC-BU, 02 E*. Strasbourg: Council of Europe.

Council of Europe (2007a) Report by the Commissioner for Human Rights on His Visit to Germany, CommDH July 2007, https://wcd.coe.int/ViewDoc.jsp?id=1162763 (accessed August 8, 2012).

Council of Europe (2007b) Report to the German Government on the Visit to Germany Carried out by the European Committee for the Prevention of Torture and Inhuman or Degrading Treatment or Punishment (CPT), CPT/Inf(2007)18, http://www.cpt.coe.int/documents/deu/2007-18-inf-eng.htm (accessed September 11, 2012).

Donnelly, J. (2003) *Universal Human Rights in Theory and Practice*, 3rd edn. Cornell: Cornell University Press.

Douglas, M. (1992) *Risk and Blame: Essays in Cultural Theory*. London: Routledge.

Drenkhahn, K., Morgenstern, C. and Van Zyl Smit, D. (2012) "What is in a name? Preventative detention in Germany in the shadow of European human rights law," *Criminal Law Review* 3, 167–187.

Ericson, R.V. (2007) *Crime in an Insecure World*. Cambridge: Polity Press.

Ewald, F. (2000) "Risk in contemporary society," *Connecticut Insurance Law Journal* 6, 365–379.

Feely, M. and Simon, J. (1992) "The new penology: notes on the emerging strategy for corrections," *Criminology* 30, 4, 449–475.

Feldman, D. (1999) "Human dignity as a legal value: part 1," *Public Law*, winter, 682.

Feldman, D. (2000) "Human dignity as a legal value: part 2," *Public Law*, spring, 61.

Fenwick, H. (2002) *Civil Liberties and Human Rights*, 3rd edn. London: Cavendish Publishing,

Fish, M.J. (2008) "Proportionality as a moral principle of punishment." *Oxford Journal of Legal Studies* 28, 1, 57–71.

Garland, D. (1985) *Punishment and Welfare: A History of Penal Strategies*. Aldershot: Gower.

Gearty, C. (2004) *Principles of Human Rights Adjudication*. Oxford: Oxford University Press.

Gerwith, A. (1978) *Reason and Morality*. Chicago: University of Chicago Press.

Grubin, D. (2004) "The risk assessment of sex offenders," in H. Kemshall and G. McIvor (eds), *Managing Sex Offender Risk*. London: Jessica Kingsley Publishers, pp. 91–110.

Harris, D.J., O'Boyle, M. and Warbrick, C. (2009) *Law of the European Convention on Human Rights*, 2nd edn. Oxford: Oxford University Press.

Harrison, K. (2007) "The high-risk sex offender strategy in England and Wales: is chemical castration an option?," *Howard Journal* 46, 1, 16.

Harrison, K. (2010) "The use of pharmacotherapy with high risk sex offenders," in K. Harrison (ed.), *Managing High Risk Sex Offenders in the Community*, Cullompton: Willan Publishing, pp. 105–132.

Harrison, K. and Rainey, B. (2009) "Suppressing human rights? A rights-based approach to the use of pharmacotherapy with sex offenders," *Legal Studies* 29, 1, 47–74.

Hebenton, B. and Seddon, T. (2009) "From dangerousness to precaution: managing sexual and violent offenders in an insecure and uncertain age," *British Journal of Criminology* 49, 3, 343–362.

Home Office (2007) *Review of the Protection of Children from Sex Offenders*. London: Home Office.

Home Office/Scottish Executive (2001) *Consultation Paper on the Review of Part 1 of the Sex Offenders Act 1997* July. London: Home Office/Scottish Executive.

Howard League for Penal Reform (2011) Evidence of the Howard League for Penal Reform to the Joint Committee on Human Rights on review proposals for the Sex Offenders Register, http://d19ylpo4aovc7m.cloudfront.net/fileadmin/howard_league/user/pdf/Consultations/Evidence_to_JCHR_on_review_proposals_for_the_Sex_Offenders_Register_19.07.2011.pdf (accessed September 11, 2012).

Hudson, B. (2001) "Human rights, public safety and the probation service: defending justice in the risk society," *Howard Journal* 40, 103–113.

Kemshall, H. (2003) *Understanding Risk in Criminal Justice*. Maidenhead: Open University Press.

Kemshall, H. (2008) *Understanding the Community Management of High Risk Offenders*. Maidenhead: Open University Press.

Kemshall, H. and McGuire, M. (2003) "Sex offenders, risk penalty and the problem of disclosure in the community," in A. Matravers (ed.), *Sex Offenders in the Community*. Cullompton: Willan Publishing, pp. 102–124.

Kemshall, H. and McIvor, G. (2004) "Sex offenders: policy and legislative developments," in H. Kemshall and G. McIvor (eds), *Managing Sex Offender Risk*. London: Jessica Kingsley Publishers, pp. 7–24.

Liberty (2011) *Liberty's Submission to the Joint Committee on Human Rights Report on the Draft Sexual Offences Act 2003 (Remedial) Order 2011*. London: Liberty.

Londono, P. (2008) "The Executive, the Parole Board and Article 5 ECHR: progress within an 'unhappy state of affairs'?," *Cambridge Law Journal* 67, 2, 230–233.

McCrudden, C. (2008) "Human dignity and judicial interpretation of human rights," *European Journal of International Law* 19, 4, 655–724.

Merkel, G. (2011) "Retrospective preventative detention in Germany: a comment on the ECHR decision *Haidn v Germany* of 13 January 2011," *German Law Journal* 12, 3, 968–977.

Michaelsen, C. (2012) "'From Strasbourg with love' – preventative detention before the German Constitutional Court and the European Court of Human Rights," *Human Rights Law Review* 12, 1, 148–167.

Miller, R. (2003) "Chemical castration of sex offenders: treatment or punishment," in B.J. Winick and J.Q. LaFond (eds), *Protecting Society from Sexually Dangerous Offenders. Law, Justice and Therapy*. Washington, DC: American Psychological Association, pp. 249–263.

Murphy, T. and Whitty, N. (2007) "Risk and human rights in UK prison governance," *British Journal of Criminology* 47, 5, 798–816.

Ovey, C. and White, R. (2010) *The European Convention on Human Rights*, 3rd edn. Oxford: Oxford University Press.

Padfield, N. (2011) "The Green Paper 'Breaking the Cycle: Effective Punishment, Rehabilitation and Sentencing of Offenders'," *Archbold Review* 2, 6–9.

Parliamentary Joint Committee on Human Rights (2011) *Legislative Scrutiny: Legal Aid, Sentencing and Punishment of Offenders Bill 22nd Report*. HL Paper 237/HC Paper 171.

Parliamentary Joint Committee on Human Rights (2012) *Draft Sexual Offences Act 2003 (Remedial) Order: Second Report*. HL Paper 8/HC Paper 165.

Power, H. (2003) "Disclosing information on sex offenders: the human rights implications," in A. Matravers (ed.), *Sex Offenders in the Community*. Cullompton: Willan Publishing, pp. 72–101.

Rainey, B. (2010) "Dignity and dangerousness: sex offenders and the community-human rights in the balance? The use of pharmacotherapy with high risk sex offenders," in K. Harrison (ed.), *Managing High Risk Sex Offenders in the Community*. Cullompton: Willan Publishing, pp. 269–290.

Sentencing Review (2011) *Commentary on Legal Aid, Sentencing and Punishment of Offenders Bill 4 (Dec)*, 6–9.

Spalding, L. (1998) "Florida's 1997 Chemical Castration Law: a return to the Dark Ages," *Florida State University Law Review* 25, 117.

Sparks, R. (2001) "Degrees of estrangement: the cultural theory of risk and comparative penology," *Theoretical Criminology* 5, 159–276.

Steele, J. (2004) *Risks and Legal Theory*. Oxford: Hart Publishing.

Thomas, D. (2006) "Case comment: sentencing dangerous offenders – Criminal Justice Act 2003," *Criminal Law Review* February, 174–179.

Thomas, D. (2011) "Case comment: sentencing: Attorney General's Reference (No 5 of 2011) (Troninas) – dangerous offenders," *Criminal Law Review* 9, 720–732.

Thomas, T. (2010) "The sex offender register, community notification and some reflection on privacy," in K. Harrison (ed.), *Managing High Risk Sex Offenders in the Community*. Cullompton: Willan Publishing, pp. 61–80.

Valverde, M., Levi, R. and Moore, D. (2005) "Legal knowledge's of risk," in Law Commission of Canada (ed.), *Law and Risk*. Vancouver: UBC Press, pp. 86–120.

Von Hirsch, A. (1985) *Past of Future Crimes: Deservedness and Dangerousness in the Sentencing of Criminals*. Manchester: Manchester University Press.

Zedner, L. (2006) "Neither safe nor sound: the perils and possibilities of risk," *Canadian Journal of Criminology and Criminal Justice* 48, 423–434.

3

Sex Offenders, Consent to Treatment and the Politics of Risk

Phil Fennell

Introduction

Sex offenses are often viewed as a consequence of mental disorder. Medical responses to sexual deviance can be traced back to Richard von Krafft-Ebing's *Psychopathia Sexualis* (1886). Oosterhuis (2000: 15) shows how, in the late nineteenth century, sexuality became "an object of medical interference and research in general and psychiatry in particular in central and Western Europe." Moreover, "medical theories entailed a fundamental metamorphosis of the social and psychological reality of sexual deviance from a form of behaviour to a way of being: irregular sexual acts were not just classed as immoral, but as the manifestation of an underlying morbid condition" (Oosterhuis, 2000: 2).

"Treatments" for "sexual disorder" have included surgical and chemical castration, hormone injections, aversion therapy (including by electric shock) and numerous psychological interventions (Shorter, 1997: 303). Chemical castration, psychological interventions and surgical castration remain in use today as treatments of sex offenders. Consent plays a key role in legitimizing these controversial interventions, albeit that consent may be given in order to avoid indeterminate detention in either prison or hospital.

Contemporary "risk society" (Beck, 1992: 120) manifests itself in criminal justice and mental health policy by affording primacy to managing risk from mentally disordered people. Rose (1998: 177) explains how the central professional obligation of assessing and managing risk requires psychologists and psychiatrists to assess individual clients in terms of the risk they represent, to allocate each to a risk level, and make "appropriate administrative arrangements for the management of the individual in the light of the requirement to minimise risk and to take responsibility, indeed blame, if an untoward incident occurs."

The Wiley-Blackwell Handbook of Legal and Ethical Aspects of Sex Offender Treatment and Management,
First Edition. Edited by Karen Harrison and Bernadette Rainey.
© 2013 John Wiley & Sons, Ltd. Published 2013 by John Wiley & Sons, Ltd.

The key prediction and prevention strategy in managing sex offenders is "selective incapacitation," whereby those particularly prone to sexual offending or violence are "selected" and "the offender's capacity to commit new crimes is . . . concretely obstructed or reduced" (Mathiesen, 1998: 455). Medical interventions intended to reduce capacity to offend include psychological treatment and pharmacological interventions with libidinal suppressants or anti-depressant drugs.

This chapter examines treatment of sex offenders and consent in the context of the convergence over the last 30 years between the values and legal structures of the penal and mental health systems, and between the legal status of patients and prisoners (Fennell, 2001: 20, 2002; Fennell and Yeates, 2002: 288; Rutherford and Telford, 2001; Rutherford, 2010). Convergence is driven by the government's desire, compatibly with the European Convention on Human Rights, to manage risk through indeterminate detention and post-release risk management strategies of community control and treatment, backed up by mechanisms allowing ready recall to prison or hospital of those whose conduct gives rise to concern.

The chapter outlines the linkages between the penal system and the psychiatric system in Britain. It then examines the association between mental disorder and sex offending and the 2007 reforms which made it easier to use the Mental Health Act (MHA) 1983 to detain offenders and risky non-offender patients on grounds of sexual deviance and risk. There follows an examination of the law of consent as applied to detained patients, coupled with analysis of the problematic legal concept of treatment for mental disorder, and the boundaries between treatment, punishment and preventive detention. The penultimate section considers consent in relation to those subject to compulsory powers in the community. The chapter concludes by summarizing the role of consent to medical treatment of sex offenders for mental disorder in the psychiatric and penal systems.

Patients and Prisoners and Convergence between the Psychiatric and Penal Systems (England and Wales)

The case law of the European Court of Human Rights (ECtHR) allows indeterminate detention compatibly with Article 5 in a hospital or clinic on grounds of unsoundness of mind (Article 5(1)(e)), or in prison following conviction of a criminal offense on grounds of dangerousness (Article 5(1)(a)) (see Chapter 2). No conviction is necessary for psychiatric detention provided "objective medical evidence of a true mental disorder of a kind or degree warranting confinement" is presented to the detaining authority (*Winterwerp* v. *the Netherlands* 1979 2 EHRR 387). Detention may continue compatibly with Article 5(4) provided the patient has the opportunity at intervals to challenge its lawfulness before a court or tribunal empowered to order discharge if he is no longer suffering from mental disorder of a kind or degree warranting detention (*X* v. *United Kingdom* 1981 4 EHRR 188). This role is exercised by Mental Health Tribunals.

A prisoner may be detained indeterminately on grounds of dangerousness provided he is afforded the right under Article 5(4) to challenge the finding of dangerousness before a court or tribunal with the power to order release (*Thynne, Wilson and*

Gunnell v. *United Kingdom* 1991 13 EHRR 666). This role is exercised by the Parole Board. The composition and powers of the tribunal and the Parole Board panels are "closely analogous" (*R* v. *A* [2005] EWCA Crim 2077 (CA)), and each includes a psychiatrist. Criminal courts may sentence sex offenders to imprisonment or to a hospital disposal under Part III of the MHA 1983. Due to the steady convergence of the penal and psychiatric systems there is little to choose between the different disposals in terms of risk management.

In the penal system convergence is marked by increased use of life sentences for sex offenders (Sexual Offences Act 2003, Part I), indeterminate public protection (IPP) sentences under the Criminal Justice Act 2003, prison-based Sex Offender Treatment Programmes (SOTPs), largely based on psychological treatments, with prisoners' progress being assessed by phallometric monitoring by penile plethysmograph (Barker and Howell, 1992; Launay, 1999), extended periods of license for those released on license (10 years for IPP prisoners, life for lifers), and the use of GPS tracking of offenders in the community.

In the psychiatric system, which once had a near monopoly on indeterminate detention, convergence is evident in the broadening of powers to detain on grounds of risk, introduction of the albeit rarely used hospital direction with its minimum tariff period of detention (MHA 1983 s45A), erosion of confidentiality by the duty to share medical information via Multi-Agency Public Protection Arrangements (MAPPA), and extension of tagging and satellite tracking to psychiatric patients in the community (BBC, 2010).

MAPPA provide the key mechanism of coordination between the psychiatric system and the penal system in managing risky offenders in the community. All registered sex offenders, whether they receive a penal or a psychiatric disposal, are subject to MAPPA (Sexual Offences Act 2003 s80 and Schedule 8). On March 31, 2011 there were 37,225 MAPPA-eligible sex offenders in the community: 35,655 were managed at level 1, 1,467 at level 2, and 93 at level 3 (Ministry of Justice, 2012, Table 1). MAPPA involves an assessment of risk posed by an offender, upon which a risk management plan is subsequently based. This can include setting appropriate license conditions for prisoners, or appropriate conditions for conditionally discharged patients or patients subject to Community Treatment Orders (CTOs) under the MHA 1983. Panels may recommend recall of license prisoners or community patients to detention, and admission of patients to psychiatric hospital under civil powers of detention.

These parallel and interconnected systems of risk management, overseen by the National Offender Management Service (NOMS), operate by moving patients and prisoners from institutional settings to the community (and back) depending on their level of risk, and being able to move them between the penal and the psychiatric system depending on where risk may most appropriately be managed. Foucault's (1977) concept of a "carceral network" of prisons, psychiatric hospitals and clinics, and powers and mechanisms of surveillance in the community, offers an apt summary of the characteristics of this system. Within this network prisoners and patients are supposed to take responsibility for managing their own risk. In criminal justice parlance this is known as "responsibilization" (Kemshall and Maguire, 2003; Harrison and Rainey, 2009, 2011). The equivalent mental health terms are compliance with treatment and possession of "insight." Those who are responsible, who possess insight into their own need for treatment interventions, and who consent to them, can be afforded a greater degree of liberty. Those who refuse and do not cooperate require more intensive control and probably detention.

The MHA 2007 changed the concept of mental disorder used in connection with detention under the MHA 1983, and altered the criteria for detention of both offender and non-offender patients, making it easier to detain not only sex offenders, but also those who suffer from mental disorders which place them in a risk category to offend in the future.

Sex Offending and Mental Disorder

Following the 2007 Act a broad definition of mental disorder has been applied – "any disorder or disability of the mind" (MHA 1983 s1). Three forms of mental disorder may be associated with sex offending: (1) paraphilia (fetishistic disorders) which includes pedophilia; (2) personality disorder or psychopathic disorder; and (3) learning disability. Some offenders may suffer from more than one form of mental disorder, for example, paraphilia in conjunction with one or more forms of personality disorder, and perhaps also a learning disability. Such "co-morbidities" present considerable problems in relation to treatment and management.

The 2007 Act removed obstacles to using the 1983 Act to detain sex offenders assessed as being at high risk of re-offending and who were about to leave prison at the end of determinate sentences. Although mental health legislation is primarily a Department of Health (DoH) responsibility, reform of the 1983 Act was jointly managed by the DoH and the Home Office, the Department then in charge of criminal justice policy. Public protection and managing the risk of offending by mentally disordered people topped the agenda (Fennell, 2001, 2002). The three principal "fault lines" in the 1983 Act were the exclusion that no one could be treated as mentally disordered by reason only of sexual deviancy; the "treatability test," which applied in relation to detention of persons suffering from psychopathic disorder, that no one could be detained unless medical treatment was "likely to alleviate or prevent deterioration in their condition"; and the absence of an effective Community Treatment Order (CTO), to enforce compliance with medication in the community.

The paraphilia manifest themselves in sexual deviancy. The sexual deviancy exclusion was therefore a major obstacle to detention of anyone with this diagnosis. The Explanatory Notes to the 2007 Act make clear the government's intention to enable psychiatric detention of people assessed as high risk to commit sex offenses, whose mental disorder manifested itself only in sexual deviance (Department of Health, Ministry of Justice, Welsh Assembly Government, 2007: para. 24). The new "catch-all" concept of mental disorder – "any disorder or disability of the mind" – clearly includes paraphilia, personality disorder and learning disability, so that any sex offender is detainable under the 1983 Act.

Psychopathic disorder/personality disorder

The legal category "psychopathic disorder" first appeared in the MHA 1959, defined as "a persistent disorder or disability of mind . . . which results in abnormally aggressive or seriously irresponsible conduct." Since there was considerable doubt about the prospect of treatment benefitting patients in this category, a person was only detainable if their condition "required or was susceptible to hospital treatment." During the parliamentary debates, Dr Bennett MP voiced what would become the perennial issue in relation to this group when he said that so far as he could make out the treatment was "custodial." "Perhaps," he said, "the treatment intended for the psychopath is simply ageing in custody, in which case it seems unnecessary to commit him to hospital" (Reginald Bennett, *Hansard*, HC Deb, January 26, 1959, ser. 5, vol. 598, cols. 783–784).

The MHA 1983 retained psychopathic disorder, but introduced a "treatability test" which applied to patients with psychopathic disorder or mental impairment. To detain patients in these categories, medical treatment had to be certified as likely to alleviate or prevent deterioration in the patient's condition, which would be hard to do if a person with a personality disorder refused to engage with cognitive behavior therapy or some other psychological treatment. Treatment was unlikely to make any difference if the patient refused to participate.

However, the breadth of the concept of medical treatment in the 1983 Act, which includes nursing, care, habilitation and rehabilitation, made it difficult for this argument to succeed. In *Reid* v. *Secretary of State for Scotland* ([1999] 2 AC 512 (HL)), the House of Lords held that the applicant was treatable as he was receiving anger management classes and being cared for in a structured environment. As Jones (2011: 44) aptly put it, "the interpretation in case law of the treatability test was so broad that it is difficult to imagine the circumstances which would cause a patient to fail it."

Despite the legal position, there was widespread concern that treatability provided a ground on which psychiatrists justified refusal to detain risky patients. A Department of Health and Home Office Committee (1994) recommended replacement of the stigmatizing term psychopathic disorder with "personality disorder," the diagnostic umbrella term used in international diagnostic manuals (DSM-IV, APA, 1994: 633; see also ICD-10, WHO, 2010, categories F60–69). The term psychopath is still used in clinical practice. Roberts and Coid (2007: 24–25) have observed a strong association between psychopathy and sadistic and violent sex offending, and refer to Hare's Psychopathy Checklist Revised (PCL-R) (Hare, 2003) as the clinical "gold standard" used in mental health and criminal justice settings.

Michael Stone, diagnosed with psychopathic disorder, was convicted in 1997 of murder and attempted murder. This led to calls for removal of the so-called "treatability test" and an Independent Inquiry into Stone's care and treatment (South East Coast Strategic Health Authority, 2006). The Home Secretary, Jack Straw (*Hansard*, HC Deb, February 15, 1999, vol. 325, cols. 601–613), made a statement to Parliament saying:

> society cannot rely on a lottery in which, through no fault of the courts, some dangerous, severely personality disordered people are sent for a limited time to prison or to

hospital, while others remain in the community, or return to it, with no interventions whatever.

The DoH and Home Office published a *Discussion Document: Managing Dangerous People with a Severe Personality Disorder: Proposals for Policy Development* and established four Dangerous Severe Personality Disorder (DSPD) Units (Home Office and Department of Health, 1999). Gunn (2000: 135) criticized this "political use of medical terminology," stating that what Mr Straw may have meant "is patients who give him the biggest political problems, such as persistent sex offenders . . . and those who are sadistically violent and homicidal." It often appears that DSPD has been little more than a coded reference to sex offenders. Burns *et al.* (2011: 411– 412) described the term as an "administrative category . . . a proto diagnosis . . . introduced in response to two pressing problems. The first of these was offenders ending their sentences who still posed a serious risk of violence, and the second was personality disordered individuals whom psychiatrists would not detain." The DSPD program is now being discontinued, and offenders in this category will in future be managed either in hospital or prison, but not in special DSPD units.

The treatability test was removed by the 2007 Act, and replaced by the requirement that appropriate treatment must be available, "appropriate treatment" meaning "medical treatment which is appropriate in his case, taking into account the nature and degree of the mental disorder and all other circumstances of his case." The government's intention was "to remove ground for argument about the efficacy or likely efficacy of a treatment, which can be used to prevent detention of people who present a risk to themselves or others" (Joint Committee on Human Rights, 2007: 45).

The government's position that abolishing treatability did not infringe the European Convention was based on *Reid* v. *United Kingdom* (2003 37 EHRR 9) where the ECtHR said that Article 5(1)(e) imposed no requirement that detention in a mental hospital was conditional on the illness or condition being of a nature or degree amenable to medical treatment. The Joint Committee on Human Rights accepted that there was nothing in the European Convention to prevent abolition of the treatability test. They also noted Article 17(1)(iii) of Council of Europe (2004) Recommendation No. (2004)10 on the human rights of persons with mental disorder, which requires that detention must have a "therapeutic purpose." This is broadly defined (in Article 2(3)) as "including prevention, diagnosis, *control*, cure or treatment" (emphasis added).

Learning disability

Some sex offenders suffer from learning disability, defined in the MHA 1983 s1(4) as "a state of arrested or incomplete development of the mind which includes significant impairment of intelligence and social functioning." A person with a learning disability cannot be placed under guardianship (or detained for longer than 28 days under the MHA) unless their learning disability is associated with abnormally aggressive or seriously irresponsible conduct on their part ("the conduct requirement") (MHA 1983 s1(2A)). A sex offense would meet the conduct requirement for detention.

The 2007 Act reforms have made it easier to detain sex offenders and potential sex offenders under the MHA 1983. The abolition of the treatability test and its replacement with the availability of appropriate treatment test has further marginalized the issue of consent in relation to psychological treatments, and blurred the boundary between therapy and preventive detention.

Detention under the Mental Health Act 1983

Both the psychiatric and prison systems now offer extensive possibilities for indeterminate detention. Part II of the MHA 1983 provides procedures for compulsory admission of non-offender patients and CTOs, and Part III contains a regime of powers for courts to sentence offenders to psychiatric detention and for ministers to issue warrants transferring prisoners to hospital. From a risk management point of view, disposal under the MHA 1983 offers a number of advantages.

"Civil" admission under Part II

A patient may be detained under Part II without the need for conviction of any offense (MHA 1983 ss2 and 3). These may be used where there is mental disorder and risk, but insufficient evidence to convict a person of a criminal offense, or when a sex offender is coming to the end of a determinate prison sentence. In the latter case the prisoner may be transferred to hospital under s47, but due to case law on the use of s47 (discussed below), civil commitment is now seen by the Ministry of Justice as offering an important alternative.

A patient may be admitted for treatment under s3 of the 1983 Act if suffering from mental disorder of a nature or degree which makes it appropriate for him to receive treatment in a hospital. Such treatment must be necessary for the health or safety of the patient or for the protection of other persons and it must be the case that the treatment cannot be provided unless he is detained. Finally, appropriate treatment must be available for the patient (MHA 1983 ss1(2) and 3(2)).

Each detained patient has a responsible clinician (RC) who need not be a doctor, but has overall responsibility for the patient's case. The RC has the power to renew detention (for a further six months, and thereafter at yearly intervals), to grant leave, to discharge, and to apply for a CTO. The CTO, introduced by the 2007 Act, allows controls to be imposed on the patient in the community. Hence the RC, usually the treating psychiatrist, has immense power to influence the patient's situation, and patients generally know that greater freedom will depend on cooperation. Patients may appeal against detention or a CTO to the Mental Health Tribunal which must direct discharge if not satisfied that any of the criteria for compulsion are met.

Hospital orders

An offender who has committed an imprisonable offense may be sentenced to a hospital order by a court, allowing indeterminate detention for as long as he continues to suffer from mental disorder of a kind or degree warranting confinement (MHA

1983 s37). The court must be satisfied (a) that the offender is suffering from mental disorder of a nature or degree making detention in hospital for medical treatment appropriate and (b) that appropriate treatment is available for him. A hospital order must be the most suitable method of disposing of the case.

Detention is for up to six months, renewable by the RC for a further six months, and then at yearly intervals. The RC may discharge a hospital order patient without recourse to higher authority, and may renew detention, grant leave, discharge, and apply for a CTO. The risk management advantage of a hospital order is that potentially indeterminate detention may be authorized in a case where the offender would not be eligible for an indeterminate sentence for public protection because of restrictions on these in the Criminal Justice and Immigration Act (CJIA) 2008. Patients may appeal against detention to the Mental Health Tribunal which must direct discharge if not satisfied that any of the criteria for detention are met.

Hospital orders with restrictions

The "top of the range" risk management power is the hospital order with restrictions. Where a hospital order has been made, a Court may impose a restriction order where necessary to protect the public from serious harm. This is not limited to personal injury, nor need it relate to the public in general, as long as the potential harm is serious (*R* v. *Birch* (1989) 11 Cr App R (S) 202). Sex offenses will generally warrant a restriction order. Since the 2007 reforms restriction orders are automatically without limit of time, and so offer indeterminate detention. The patient's RC cannot grant leave of absence, transfer or discharge the patient without the consent of the Secretary of State for Justice (MHA 1983 ss41–42). Only the Secretary of State for Justice or the Mental Health Tribunal may direct discharge.

The rationale for the Secretary of State's powers is that "the control of patients who have been found to be dangerous and who are not being punished, should be vested in an authority which would have special regard to the protection of the public" (Ministry of Justice, 2010: 160). Restriction order patients are usually only discharged subject to conditions, and remain liable to recall by the Ministry of Justice Mental Health Casework Unit (MHCU). Re-offending rates in terms of serious sexual offenses or violent offenses of the 1,500 patients conditionally discharged between 1999 and 2006 averaged 1% for grave offenses and 7% for all offenses (Ministry of Justice, 2010: Table 7). This success rate has been a major factor in the transplantation of the restriction order model into the prison and probation systems evidenced in the sentencing reforms of the past 20 years. The conditional discharge model has also influenced the CTO introduced in 2008, which applies both to non-offender patients and offenders who are not subject to Ministry of Justice restrictions.

Transfer from prison to psychiatric hospital

A sentenced prisoner may be transferred to hospital by direction of the Secretary of State for Justice, and a restriction direction may be attached, imposing restrictions on discharge (MHA 1983 ss47 and 49). The Secretary of State must be satisfied on medical evidence of two doctors that the prisoner is suffering from mental disorder of a nature or degree which makes hospital detention for medical treatment appropriate, and that appropriate medical treatment is available for him.

A life sentence or IPP prisoner may be detained in hospital irrespective of his tariff for as long as his RC believes it necessary to give him medical treatment. The person has the right to apply to the Mental Health Tribunal, which may find that the criteria for his detention in hospital are no longer met. The Ministry of Justice National Offender Management Service *Guidance on MAPPA* states that:

> Where that happens, he will be remitted to prison unless the Tribunal additionally recommends that he remain in hospital. If he has passed his tariff date he will have automatic access to the Parole Board, whether he remains in hospital or is remitted to prison. His release can only be ordered by the Parole Board and will be on life licence subject to probation supervision. The life sentence prisoner will be on licence for life, whereas the IPP prisoner, whilst his sentence is technically indefinite, may apply to the Parole Board after ten years on licence for the lifting of the licence. (Ministry of Justice National Offender Management Service, 2010, para. 3.4)

If a restriction direction is made in the case of a determinate sentence prisoner, the restrictions expire on the offender's earliest release date. Thereafter, the patient is detained as if under an s37 hospital order without restrictions (a "notional s37 patient"). Detention may then be renewed by the RC, and the RC or the Mental Health Tribunal may discharge without recourse to the Ministry of Justice.

There has been a long-standing concern about the transfer of patients nearing the end of a determinate sentence as a means of public protection (Grounds, 1990, 1991). The Mental Health Act Commission (2007: 382–383) said this was "distorting mental health law by using it for primarily public protection purposes, and that transfer should take place as soon as is therapeutically indicated rather than being delayed until risk is the primary factor." When a patient is transferred to hospital near the end of their sentence the hospital authorities must carefully scrutinize the medical reports to ensure that they provide a sound basis for transfer.

In *R (TF)* v. *Secretary of State for Justice* ([2008] EWCA Civ 1457, para. 31) Waller LJ expressed the hope that s47 would only be used at the end of the sentence in "very exceptional cases" and placed the onus on the Secretary of State "to show that the mind of the decision-maker has focused on each of the criteria which it is necessary to satisfy if there is to be power to issue a warrant directing transfer to a hospital."

Both the *MAPPA Guidance* (2010) and the Department of Health *Good Practice Procedure Guide on Transfer of Prisoners* take the consequences of the *TF* ruling and advise that if transfer at the end of sentence is necessary on clinical grounds (Ministry of Justice, 2010: para. 5.8; Department of Health, 2011: paras. 3.10–3.16):

> Assessment and admission under civil powers is to be preferred, a procedure which demonstrates that the decision is clinically-led, and is not a misuse of the powers of the Mental Health Act to extend the sentence of the Court.

Hence detention under the Mental Health Act remains a very important technique of risk management. Even if transfer under s47 is not appropriate, civil commitment powers may effectively be used in relation to sex offenders coming to the end of a determinate sentence, especially since the broadening of the definition of mental disorder, the removal of the sexual deviance exclusion, and the new test of availability of appropriate treatment. Whether transferred under s47 without restrictions or detained under s3, patients are eligible for a CTO and therefore may subsequently be subject to control and treatment in the community.

Hybrid orders

Section 45A of the 1983 Act provides a "hybrid order" whereby a mentally disordered offender may be given a sentence of imprisonment coupled with an immediate direction to hospital. The risk management advantage is that the offender must serve a minimum tariff period in detention, and thereafter their detention is potentially indeterminate. Initially confined to people with a personality disorder diagnosis, this is now available for offenders with any mental disorder of a nature or degree making detention in hospital for treatment appropriate, as long as appropriate treatment is available to him. Although directed initially to hospital, the offender has the legal status of prisoner rather than patient. In the event of the mental disorder being successfully treated before the expiry of the prison sentence, the offender can be returned to prison for the remainder of the tariff sentence. Only one hybrid order was made in 2010–2011 (NHS Information Centre, 2011: Table 2a), and in 2009 there were only 16 such patients resident in hospitals (Ministry of Justice, 2010: 163).

In summary, the position of offender patients is that the RC and, in the case of restricted patients, the MHCU in the Ministry of Justice, exercise effective control over the situation of patients detained under the 1983 Act, subject only to a patient's right to challenge detention or a CTO before a Mental Health Tribunal. In the psychiatric system the RC has considerable power to influence the patient's situation and prospects of discharge, and indeed has the power to discharge a non-restricted patient. Compliance with treatment is seen as a mark of insight, and refusal a sign that it is lacking. The presence of insight is more likely to lead to a finding that a mental disorder is not of a nature or degree warranting detention. A patient who complies with medication will therefore be more likely to be discharged by the RC or the Mental Health Tribunal.

Consent to Treatment and Detained Patients

The European Committee for the Prevention of Torture and Inhuman or Degrading Treatment (CPT) "CPT standards" establish the principle that even though a person is detained, they must still as a matter of principle be placed in a position to give "free and informed" consent to treatment:

> The admission of a person to a psychiatric establishment on an involuntary basis should not be construed as authorising treatment without his consent. It follows that every

competent patient, whether voluntary or involuntary, should be given the opportunity
to refuse treatment or other medical intervention. (European Committee for the Prevention
of Torture and Inhuman or Degrading Treatment, 2006: Ch VI para. 41)

Any derogation from this fundamental principle should be based upon law and only
relate to clearly defined exceptional circumstances. Detained patients and CTO
patients are subject to special rules in relation to consent set out in Parts IV and IVA
of the 1983 Act.

English law refers to the existence of valid or real consent rather than the CPT
terminology of "free and informed consent." The existence of consent is a question
of fact to be determined by the doctor or the court, taking into account all the circumstances of the case (*Freeman* v. *Home Office (No. 2)* [1984] QB 524 (CA)).
Freeman was a prisoner who had been injected with anti-psychotic drugs. The Home
Office asserted that he had consented and reiterated its position that "doctors
working in prisons have no statutory authority to administer treatment against the
wishes of their patients." Freeman contended that the components of valid consent
(capacity, knowledge and voluntariness) set out by the Nuremberg court in *United
States* v. *Karl Brandt* (1948; Katz, 1972) and endorsed in *Kaimowitz* v. *Department
of Mental Health for the State of Michigan* ((1973) No. 73·19434·AW 42 USLW
2063 (Mich. Cir. Ct., Wayne County, July 10, 1973) 1 Mental Disability L. Rep.
150 (1976–1977), 147–154) could not be met in his case, because his doctor exerted
control over him, being "part doctor, part turnkey."

The Court of Appeal held that a prisoner was not under a legal inability to consent,
and where, in a prison, a doctor had the power to influence a prisoner's situation and
prospects, the court must be alive to the risk that what might appear, on the face of
it, to be a real consent was not so. On the facts Freeman had been informed in broad
terms of the nature of the treatment and had given valid consent (*Freeman* v. *Home
Office* 1984, 556).

Consent to treatment under Part IV of the Mental Health Act 1983

Part IV of the MHA 1983 establishes powers to administer treatment for mental
disorder without consent, subject to a system of second opinion safeguards. The
procedures were introduced in 1983 to clarify that there was a power to treat detained
patients compulsorily if they refused treatment, or if they lacked capacity to understand its nature, purpose and likely effects. The 1983 Act also introduced statutory
second opinion safeguards in relation to certain treatments.

Section 63 provides that a detained patient's consent is "not required for any
medical treatment given to him for the mental disorder from which he is suffering . . . if it is given by or under the direction of the approved clinician in charge of
the treatment." Three groups of treatment are excepted from s63, each subject to a
different form of second opinion. Two of these are particularly relevant to sex offenders: (1) the surgical implantation of hormones to reduce male sex drive (s57); and
(2) medicines for mental disorder which may be given without consent to a detained
patient (s58).

Surgical implantation of sexual suppressants

Section 57 prohibits these treatments without consent, which must be certified as valid by an independent three-person panel appointed by the Care Quality Commission. The medical member of that panel must then certify that it is appropriate for the treatment to be given. These procedures apply whether or not the patient is detained under the Act, and were applied to surgical implants of hormones because in the 1980s sex offenders detained in Broadmoor Hospital had been given implants by a trocar and cannula of estradiol, a synthetic equivalent to estrogen (no longer in use) which produced distressing side effects. The men contended that they had only accepted the drug to increase their chances of release.

Section 57 has only been used once in relation to libidinal suppressants. It was in relation to the administration to a sex offender by trocar and cannula of a cancer drug Goserelin, a hormone analogue, which was not licensed for use as a sexual suppressant (Hamilton, 1988; Fennell, 1988). The second opinion team decided that the patient had not truly consented, since he had adopted a "cavalier" attitude to the risk. The medical member of the team decided that there was no basis on which to say that the drug was likely to alleviate or prevent deterioration in the patient's condition, since using it as a sexual suppressant was experimental. The patient's application for judicial review was granted, the court holding that the Commission did not have jurisdiction under s57. The drug was not a hormone, but a hormone analogue, and the procedure by which it was administered was not surgical (*R v. Mental Health Act Commission ex parte W* The Times 28 May 1988 reported sub nomine *R v. Mental Health Act Commission ex parte X* (1988) 9 BMLR 77).

As to the test of consent for the purposes of Part IV, Stuart-Smith LJ applied *Freeman* and held that on the facts W had consented:

> No doubt the consent had to be an informed consent in that he knows the nature and likely effect of the treatment. There can be no doubt that the applicant knew this. So too in the case where treatment was not routinely used for control of sexual urges . . . it was important that the applicant should realise that the use on him was a novel one and the full implications with use on young men had not been studied . . . Again it is perfectly clear that the applicant knew this.

Despite his "cavalier attitude" to the risks, W had given true consent (*R v. Mental Health Act Commission ex parte W* 1988; Fennell, 1988). The drug did not produce the desired effect. Its use on W was discontinued.

Androcur (cyproterone acetate) is the sexual suppressant most frequently used in the United Kingdom to achieve "chemical castration" of sex offenders. It is never surgically implanted. In the United Kingdom it is usually given orally. Elsewhere in Europe a depot injection version is licensed which is available in the United Kingdom on a named-patient basis (Gordon and Grubin, 2004: 78). Beech and Grubin (2010: 433) argue that treatment directed towards the biological drive is clinically indicated "When the intensity or ability to control sexual arousal is the presenting feature – whether it manifests as frequent rumination and fantasy or strong and recurrent urges." They report that:

> When drugs work the clinical effect is often dramatic, with offenders reporting great benefit from no longer being preoccupied by sexual thoughts or dominated by sexual drive. These drugs can also allow offenders to participate in psychological treatment programmes where previously they may have been too distracted to take part. (Beech and Grubin, 2010: 434)

Side effects of Androcur include breast growth, lactation, and in some cases liver damage, cardiovascular disease, metabolic abnormalities, osteoporosis or depression. Rates of withdrawal from treatment are high. The consensus is that the drug should therefore almost always be prescribed in combination with psychological treatment, either individual or group-based.

The court in *R* v. *Mental Health Act Commission ex parte W* (1988) accepted that treatment by sexual suppressants was "treatment for mental disorder." Treatment for the sexual problem was "inextricably linked with the mental disorder." The implication was that sexual suppressants are medicines for mental disorder, and consequently might lawfully be administered without consent, subject to the second opinion procedure in s58. Whatever may have been the position in 1988, since the Human Rights Act 1998 this is now open to significant doubt.

Medicines for mental disorder

Section 58 allows drugs to be given without consent for up to three months from the first time drugs were given in that period of detention, and thereafter only if authorized by a second opinion appointed doctor (SOAD) appointed by the Care Quality Commission, who must certify that the treatment is appropriate. The absence of consent may arise because the patient refuses treatment, or because they lack capacity to understand its nature, purpose and likely effects. The Mental Health Act Code of Practice states that for detained and community patients:

> The patient's consent should be sought for all proposed treatments, even if they may lawfully be given under the Act without consent. It is the personal responsibility of the person in charge of the treatment to ensure that valid consent has been sought. The interview at which such consent was sought should be properly recorded in the patient's notes. (Department of Health, 2008: para. 23.37)

This complies with the principle in the CPT Standards (European Committee for the Prevention of Torture and Inhuman or Degrading Treatment, 2006: para. 41) that even though a person is detained, they must still be placed in a position to give or withhold consent to treatment.

Following *R* v. *Mental Health Act Commission ex parte W* (1988) it was clear that although most psychiatrists would say that the use of libidinal suppressants should be "voluntary and extremely carefully considered" (Gelder, Lopez Ibor and Andreasen, 2000: 129), as a matter of law "chemical castration" by depot injection of Androcur was medicine for mental disorder which could be given without consent to a detained patient under s58 of the 1983 Act. In *B v Croydon Health Authority* ([1995] 1 All ER 683 (CA)), treatment for mental disorder was held to apply to treatment directed at the "symptoms or sequelae" of mental disorder just as much as to treatment directed at the core disorder. The MHA 2007 reaffirmed this, introducing a new s145(4) into the 1983 Act, which states that "Any reference . . . to medical treatment, in relation to mental disorder, shall be construed as a reference to medical treatment the purpose of which is to alleviate, or prevent a worsening of, the disorder or one or more of its symptoms or manifestations." As Baroness Royall put it: "'Symptoms' is intended to cover the consequences of which patients themselves complain while 'manifestations' more obviously covers the evidence of the disorder as seen by other people" (*Hansard*, HL Deb, July 2, 2007, vol. 693, col. 835).

A manifestation could be violent conduct, sex offending, or self-harming. Treatment must have the *purpose* of alleviating or preventing "a worsening of the disorder or one or more of its symptoms or manifestations." Hence libidinal suppressants could be drug treatment for mental disorder, given without consent under s58 with the purpose of preventing a worsening of the manifestations of the disorder.

However, *Janiga* v. *Usti Nad Labem Regional Court, Czech Republic* (2011) indicates that chemical castration applied without consent could amount to a breach of the prohibition against degrading treatment in Article 3 of the Convention, but if there is full and informed consent, there is no breach. The Divisional Court held that while non-consensual administration of libidinal suppressants will potentially breach Article 3, consent would be viewed as free and informed, even though it is given in the knowledge that refusal will lead to prolonged incarceration.

Sexual suppressants may also be given with consent to prisoners and offenders on license. In 2007 the government issued Probation Circular 35/2007 which states that "Whilst psychological intervention will remain the preferred method of treatment for most sex offenders, in certain cases this could usefully be supplemented by medical treatment." Bradford and Kaye (1999: 17) have suggested that the paraphilia are types of Obsessive Compulsive Disorder (OCD) and therefore treatment with anti-depressant specific serotonin re-uptake inhibitors (SSRIs) such as sertraline may be clinically indicated. Beech and Grubin (2010: 433) have also found the SSRIs effective, particularly when sexual rumination is the presenting problem. SSRIs have a strong libidinal suppressant effect, and this does not necessarily resolve after discontinuation (Taylor, Rudkin and Hawton, 2005; Bahrick, 2006; Balon, 2006; Czoka, Bahrick, and Mehtonen, 2008; Kennedy and Rizvi, 2009). SSRIs, being treatments for depression or OCD, can more readily be seen as drugs for mental disorder, and therefore falling squarely within s58, with much less likelihood that their administration might breach Article 3 or Article 8.

Other treatment for mental disorder

Section 63 allows treatments other than those subject to the second opinion procedures to be given without consent to detained patients. The definition of medical treatment in s145(1) of the 1983 Act is a non-exhaustive list and now "includes nursing and also psychological intervention and specialist mental health habilitation, rehabilitation and care." This means that other treatments not on the list may be given without consent or a second opinion. Introducing psychological interventions in 2007 is significant since these are the main treatments used for people with personality disorders.

This prompts two questions: (1) the extent to which removing the treatability test further obscures the distinction between therapy and selective incapacitation by preventive detention; and (2) whether, given the non-exhaustive definition of treatment, surgical castration may be viewed as a treatment for mental disorder which could be given without consent or a second opinion.

Appropriate treatment and preventive detention

Removing the treatability test and replacing it with the requirement that appropriate treatment must be available was intended to ensure that refusal to accept psychological treatment can no longer be an obstacle to detention, as long as the treatment is available. The Minister of State said she had been informed that "lawyers have advised their patients not to engage with treatment because if it can be proved that they are not treatable they have to be released" (Public Bill Committee, Parliament, 2007: cols. 121–122). This argument is eliminated. As long as appropriate treatment is available, whether the patient accepts is now immaterial.

The key issue remains the extent to which therapeutic interventions are required which go beyond presence in what is sometimes referred to as "a structured environment," or even "milieu therapy." The Department of Health Code of Practice distinguishes between nursing and specialist care and mere preventive detention:

> Appropriate medical treatment does not have to involve medication or individual or group psychological therapy – although it very often will. There may be patients whose particular circumstances mean that treatment may be appropriate even though it consists only of nursing and specialist day-to-day care . . . in a safe and secure therapeutic environment.

> Simply detaining someone – even in a hospital – does not constitute medical treatment. (Department of Health, 2008: paras. 6.16–6.17)

The line between preventive detention and treatment was raised in two cases involving patients with personality disorder who appealed against tribunal decisions refusing discharge. In *MD* v. *Nottinghamshire Health Care NHS Trust* ([2010] UKUT 59 (AAC)), MD refused to engage in psychotherapy, and argued that he was entitled to discharge in that one of the conditions of detention (the availability of appropriate treatment) was no longer met. The tribunal declined to discharge because MD had a psychopathic personality disorder, was at risk of violent re-offending, and, taking a long-term view, "appropriate positive psychotherapeutic treatment is available here." Alternatively, the tribunal concluded that the patient had been:

> Engaging in and benefiting from the specialist nursing care and "milieu" therapy on the ward . . . nursing and specialist day to day care under clinical supervision of an approved clinician, in a safe and secure therapeutic environment with a structured regime . . . the language of Code paragraph 6.16. (paras. 25–26)

MD had the potential to benefit from the milieu of the ward, both for its short-term effects and for the possibility that it would break through his defense mechanisms and allow him later to engage. Judge Jacobs held that the distinction between containment and treatment and the definition of "available" and "appropriate" were "matters of fact and judgment for the tribunal . . . [which] is an expert body and . . . has to use that expertise to make its findings and exercise its judgment" (para. 48).

The line between treatment and containment would be crossed (para. 35) "if there was no prospect of the patient progressing beyond milieu" and then treatment would no longer be appropriate, but the facts found by the tribunal showed that the patient had not reached that position as there was the potential for the milieu to benefit the patient in both the short and longer term. To say the least this is not a rigorous standard. Despite Judge Jacobs's protestations about the words "appropriate" and "available" not being mere verbiage, in reality, where there is continued risk, a tribunal is likely to find that the line between appropriate treatment being available and mere containment will not be crossed as long as they can find as a matter of "fact" that there is some potential for milieu therapy to benefit the patient in the long term. In any event, for the purposes of s145, nursing and care are as much treatment as is psychological intervention.

In *DL-H* v. *Devon Partnership NHS Trust* v. *Secretary of State for Justice* ([2010] UKUT 102 (AAC)), the patient also refused to engage. Judge Jacobs acknowledged that since attempts to get the patient to engage can be treatment under s145(1), there is "a danger that a patient for whom no appropriate treatment is available may be contained for public safety rather than detained for treatment" (para. 42). The solution lay in the tribunal's duty to "investigate behind assertions, generalisations and standard phrases," to address the question of whether the patient could be persuaded to engage, and to make an individualized assessment of the precise treatment that can be provided. However, as long as the tribunal goes through a thorough inquisitorial process and gives adequate reasons for its findings, it would seem to be open to the tribunal to find that, even if the only present treatment is "milieu" nursing and care, as long as they can find some prospect that the patient may progress beyond milieu and engage with other therapies, then appropriate treatment will be available.

The question raised by Dr Bennett in 1959, whether treatment merely means "growing old in custody," is reiterated in the concerns raised by Tyrer *et al.* (2010: 97) about patients being "warehoused," that is "'parked' for long periods, thereby preventing them from being released from custody and reoffending in society." Research on the effectiveness of the DSPD program does little to dispel this worry. Burns *et al.* (2011: 413) found difficulty distinguishing between "treatments" and "care," but decided that "the distinction was best anchored in the idea of the 'personal contract,' [where] treatments were defined as interventions with a specific agreement between therapist and patient to work together with an agreed process and goal, with a predicted duration and frequency." The researchers found that the average weekly time in treatment was less than two hours per week, which varied across four units and across individual patients within units (Burns *et al.*, 2011: 421). Approximately 10% of patients received no formal treatment in each year. The authors found the reasons for this non-compliance hard to determine but noted that:

> For several patients it reflected a long term pattern of non-engagement and resentment. For a number of patients, however, for some of the time at least, it was a conscious decision not to take part in treatment in order to "prove" that they were not treatable and pre-cipitate their return to prison care. Some insisted that they were doing so on the advice of their solicitor. (Burns *et al.*, 2011: 421)

After the abolition of the treatability test this argument would have made little dif-ference to their situation.

The authors state that "Whether two hours of formal treatment is right for this group requires careful consideration. At first sight it appears very little for the levels of investment, particularly when patients have their liberty denied on the basis of needing this type of treatment" (Burns *et al.*, 2011: 422). However, they also note the observation of staff that many patients have low IQs and "hence traditional psy-chotherapies require considerable time for reflection" (Burns *et al.*, 2011: 422).

Barret and Byford's (2012) cost benefit analysis of the DSPD program estimates the cost per serious offense prevented at over £2 million. They suggest that carrying the program out in a lower-cost prison could be cost-effective, concluding that, despite frequent calls for mentally disordered offenders to be detained in secure hospitals rather than prisons, "if reoffending remains the outcome of interest for policy makers, it is likely that the costs of detention in hospital will remain greater than the benefits for dangerous offenders with a personality disorder" (Barret and Byford, 2012: 341).

Some patients are reluctant to engage with psychotherapy because they fear it is primarily an exercise in gathering information about their risk. If they refuse psycho-therapy they risk prolonged detention with the appropriate treatment requirement being satisfied by milieu therapy – nursing and care and efforts to persuade them to engage.

Surgical castration

Surgical castration was widespread in Europe in the early part of the twentieth century but is not now practiced in any European country except for the Czech Republic. Its decline was due to conflicting results, but also to ethical objections (Gunn, 2000: 790). Helm and Hursch's (1979: 281) literature review concluded that "there is no scientific or ethical basis for castration in the treatment of sex offenders."

In 2010 the CPT reported on the Czech Republic where in 2008 and 2009 at least six detained sex offenders had undergone surgical castration. The CPT found this to be degrading treatment contrary to Article 3 and called upon the Czech gov-ernment, pending abolition, to impose a moratorium on castration of sex offenders (European Committee for the Prevention of Torture and Inhuman or Degrading Treatment or Punishment, 2010: paras. 9 and 10).

The Czech government denied that castration could be degrading treatment as it was a medical procedure performed at the request of patients who were fully informed of the nature and consequences of the operation and is "a measure which facilitates the reintegration of the people concerned into society" (European Committee for the Prevention of Torture and Inhuman or Degrading Treatment or Punishment, 2010a:

5–6). It declined to abolish the practice, but instead announced that it was "seeking to strengthen the existing legal guarantees ensuring informed consent and to create more detailed regulation of the procedure for surgical castration" (European Committee for the Prevention of Torture and Inhuman or Degrading Treatment or Punishment, 2010a: 6).

The Czech government placed strong reliance on the existence of consent in transforming what might otherwise be a breach of Article 3 or Article 8 into an acceptable medical procedure. We have already seen how the Divisional Court in *Janiga* v. *Usti Nad Labem Regional Court, Czech Republic* (2011) considered that consent had this transformative power in relation to Article 3. Whether the European Court of Human Rights would take a similar view in relation to a case alleging breach of Article 3 in respect of surgical castration of a sex offender is most doubtful.

In *Herczegfalvy* v. *Austria* (1992 15 EHRR 437, para. 82) the ECtHR held that medical treatment which is a therapeutic necessity in accordance with accepted principles of medicine cannot be inhuman or degrading treatment, but "The Court must nevertheless satisfy itself that the medical necessity has been convincingly shown to exist." The consensus of medical opinion in Europe has moved away from the use of surgical castration as a treatment of sex offenders, and even Czech sexologists dispute the therapeutic efficacy and ethical acceptability of the practice.

The ECtHR is likely to accept the CPT's finding. If treatment has reached the threshold of severity to amount to inhuman or degrading treatment, the consent of the individual is unlikely to prove effective in negating the breach of Article 3. In *HL* v. *United Kingdom* (2004 40 EHRR 761) the European Court held that the absence of objection on the part of the patient was not decisive in determining whether Article 5 was engaged, and that:

> The right to liberty in a democratic society is too important for a person to lose the benefit of Convention protection simply because he has given himself up to detention, especially when it is not disputed that that person is legally incapable of consenting to, or disagreeing with, the proposed action. (para. 90)

The same principle must surely apply to the absolute prohibition on inhuman and degrading treatment in Article 3. Consequently we should treat with extra caution Beech and Grubin's (2010: 434) tentative view that:

> Physical castration as part of a rehabilitative strategy may even have a place, although the observations of the Council of Europe's Committee for the Prevention of Torture . . . should not be overlooked given the significant risk of human rights abuses, with individuals acquiescing rather than consenting in the belief that it is the only way to avoid indefinite confinement.

Consent to treatment on the part of those subject to detention must always be open to question, since it will very often be given in the hope that it will result in earlier release. However, where there is increased risk if treatment is not accepted, the courts will invariably accept consent as valid. Both the penal and the psychiatric system offer extensive possibilities to exercise control over community patients and prisoners on license. In these circumstances consent will often be given in the knowledge that refusal will in all probability lead to recall to prison or hospital. Here too such consent is invariably accepted as valid.

Control and Treatment in the Community under the Mental Health Act

Patients detained under the provisions discussed above may be made subject to compulsory supervision in the community, the therapeutic equivalent to being released from prison on license. Registered sex offenders are subject to supervision via the MAPPA arrangements. Patients subject to Ministry of Justice restrictions will be conditionally discharged, viewed as the most effective means of risk management because of the supervision by the Ministry of Justice MHCU. The 2007 Act introduced a CTO, available for all non-restricted patients detained under s3 or subject to a hospital order, a hospital direction, or a transfer direction. Restricted patients are not eligible.

One of the main differences between conditional discharge and the CTO is that a CTO patient's RC has the power of discharge. With a conditionally discharged restricted patient the permission of the Ministry of Justice MHCU is required. The other is that a system of statutory second opinions applies to treatment under a CTO (MHA 1983 Part IVA).

Conditional discharge

A restriction order patient may be conditionally discharged by the Secretary of State for Justice or by a Mental Health Tribunal. Conditional discharge means that a patient may be directed to live in a specified place, to attend for treatment, and to accept treatment by or under the direction of the RC. Because it may be a condition that conditionally discharged patients must accept treatment for mental disorder, they are not eligible for a second opinion under Part IV of the 1983 Act.

In *R (SH)* v. *Mental Health Review Tribunal* ([2007] EWHC 884 (Admin), para. 2) SH was required by a tribunal to "comply with prescribed medication, which is likely to be by depot for several years." He argued that this condition was unlawful since it deprived him of his right to choose whether to accept treatment. Holman J refused to quash the condition (2007: para. 35) holding that, despite the existence of the condition,

> on each occasion that SH attends, or should attend, for his fortnightly depot injection he has an absolute right to choose whether to consent to it or not. The treating doctor or nurse must, on each occasion, satisfy himself that the apparent consent is a real consent and that the independence of the patient's decision or his will has not been overborne.

Although in deciding whether to consent SH may take into account the condition (2007: para. 37), "[it] must be read as respecting and being subject to his own final choice, which must be his real or true choice."

The judge recommended that tribunals should in future add to a condition that the patient accept medication that this was "subject always to his right to give or withhold consent to treatment or medication on any given occasion" (2007: para. 42). The existence of consent is a question of fact. The fact that consent is given in the knowledge that refusal will most probably lead to recall to hospital does not render it invalid.

The Ministry of Justice *Guidance* (2009) states that the MHCU should be notified by the RC of a conditionally discharged patient in any case where there appears to be a risk to the public, the patient is unwilling to cooperate with supervision, or the patient needs further in-patient treatment. Non-compliance with medication would amount to non-cooperation with supervision. A conditionally discharged patient may be recalled to hospital by the Minister of Justice or by the RC at any time while the restriction order is in force but, unless it is an emergency recall, in order to comply with Article 5, there must be medical evidence of mental disorder warranting confinement (*Kay* v. *United Kingdom* (1994 40 BMLR 20)).

In *R(MM)* v. *Secretary of State for the Home Department* ([2007] EWCA Civ 687) the Court of Appeal held that breach of a condition was not a free-standing ground for ordering recall. The question was whether the breach enables the Secretary of State to form a proper judgment on the medical evidence that the statutory criteria for detention are established (mental disorder of a kind or degree warranting detention). Nevertheless, the Court of Appeal held that there do not have to be psychotic symptoms or the certainty of psychotic symptoms in the near future before detention for treatment could be authorized. The case of a conditionally discharged patient who is recalled to hospital must be referred by the Minister of Justice to a MHT within a month of his return to hospital.

Despite these safeguards, and Holman J's view in *HS* (2007: para. 37) that a conditionally discharged patient should take into account the fact that refusal would breach a condition "just as he might take into account strong medical advice or the persuasion of a relative," the fact that refusal would lead to notification of the MHCU and possible recall means that the "right" of a conditionally discharged patient to refuse treatment is largely illusory.

Community Treatment Orders (CTOs)

CTOs have been available since 2008. To be eligible the patient must be liable to be detained under s3 or, if a Part III patient, be subject to a hospital order, a hospital direction, or a transfer direction without restrictions. The patient's RC makes a CTO by furnishing a report to the hospital managers to the effect that (MHA 1983 s17A) the patient suffers from mental disorder of a nature or degree which makes it appropriate for him to receive medical treatment which is necessary for his health or safety or for the protection of other persons. The RC must report that subject to his being liable to be recalled, such treatment can be provided without the patient continuing to be detained in a hospital, that it is necessary that the RC should have the power to recall the patient to hospital, and that appropriate medical treatment is available for him.

In determining whether the power of recall is necessary the RC must:

in particular, consider, having regard to the patient's history of mental disorder and any other relevant factors, what risk there would be of a deterioration of the patient's condition if he were not detained in a hospital (as a result, for example, of his refusing or neglecting to receive the medical treatment he requires for his mental disorder). (MHA 1983 s17A(6))

A Mental Health Tribunal must consider the same issue in deciding whether a patient is entitled to discharge from a CTO (MHA 1983 s72 (1A)). Hence in order to secure release on a CTO a non-restricted patient will generally need to agree to accept treatment in the community.

Conditions may be imposed which are "necessary or appropriate" for:

(a) ensuring that the patient receives medical treatment;
(b) preventing risk of harm to the patient's health or safety;
(c) protecting other persons.

(MHA 1983 s17B)

A CTO patient may be recalled to any hospital if in the RC's opinion:

(a) the patient requires medical treatment in hospital for his mental disorder; and
(b) without recall there would be a risk of harm to the health or safety of the patient or to other persons.

(MHA 1983 s17E)

Failure to comply with a condition may be "taken into account" by the RC in deciding whether to recall, but (Department of Health, Ministry of Justice, Welsh Assembly Government, 2007: para. 113) provided the recall criteria are met, the patient may still be recalled even if he or she is complying with the conditions (MHA 1983 s17B(7)).

A recalled patient may be held in hospital for up to 72 hours. If the patient does not agree to comply within that period, and the conditions for detention under s3 are met, the CTO may be revoked and the person will resume status as a detained patient (MHA 1983 s17G).

Part IVA of the MHA 1983 (ss64A–64K) regulates giving medicines for mental disorder to community patients while in the community. Within one month of the CTO being made, a SOAD must visit and issue a certificate that it is appropriate for the treatment to be given. The certificate can specify treatment which may be given without consent on recall of the patient (MHA 1983 s62A). A patient with capacity may only be given drug treatment for mental disorder in the community if they consent and the treatment is authorized in the second opinion certificate. This again is consent in the shadow of compulsion, since the patient will know that a likely consequence of refusal will be recall to hospital and possible revocation of the CTO. If the patient is capable and refusing, treatment may be given without consent by recalling the patient and treating under s62A of the 1983 Act.

Conclusion

Prisoners and patients are subject to an interconnected and legally constituted system of what Castel (1976) describes as "tutelary relationships." extending from detention in conditions of high security to surveillance in the community, where decision-making power over the affairs of an adult is conferred on others. Law confers clinical authority to extend detention and to discharge on RCs and, in the case of restricted patients, on the MHCU. In certain cases drug treatment for mental disorder prescribed by the RC may be given without consent, subject to second opinion safeguards. In other cases consent may be required. In each case the patient's or prisoner's progress to a less restrictive environment, and ability to remain there, will be conditional on consent and compliance with treatment. The community has been institutionalized by the extension of powers of supervision and treatment, with continued consent and compliance anchored by the threat of return to detention (Fennell, 2010).

Treatment and consent play key roles in the developing apparatus of risk management which over the past 30 years has brought about a near merger of the penal and psychiatric systems. Each allows indeterminate detention. Each allows conditional release which may be extended indefinitely. Each allows recall from the community to detention, whether on the basis of risk or mental disorder, or both. The concept of treatment is itself highly problematic. Nursing and care in a structured environment under medical supervision can be medical treatment, blurring the boundary between preventive detention and therapy, which is a question of fact to be determined by the court or tribunal taking into account all relevant circumstances.

Consent in medical law and ethics is seen as protecting the patient's physical integrity and autonomous right to choose. In relation to prisoners and detained patients it is also something else – it is a sign, a token of good faith, that the person is taking responsibility for managing their own risk by complying with prescribed treatment. Prisoners and detained patients often consent to quite drastic interventions carried out in the name of treatment in the hope that they will be released from detention, usually on a register and under strict medical or probation supervision. Once in the community and subject to such supervision, continued consent is the price of freedom. The right to refuse remains, but its exercise will put in jeopardy the patient's right to liberty. In the United Kingdom, whether there has been valid consent is a question of fact (*Freeman* v. *Home Office*, 2004), and both law and psychiatric ethics accept such circumscribed consent as valid, even when given in the knowledge that the likely consequence of refusal is indeterminate detention.

Valid consent is a transformative concept, capable of legitimizing as treatment what might otherwise be viewed as assaults, inhuman or degrading treatment or punishment, or breaches of the right to physical integrity (*Janiga* v. *Usti Nad Labem Regional Court, Czech Republic*, [2011] EWHC 553 (Admin)). It is suggested here that there are limits to that transformative power, and in line with the CPT Report on the Czech Republic, that these apply to surgical castration. The difficulty here is that, given the existence of consent, and the fact that offenders who have been castrated may view it as an acceptable price for freedom from indeterminate detention, it is less likely that a challenge will reach the Strasbourg Court.

References

APA (American Psychiatric Association) (1994) *Diagnostic and Statistical Manual of Mental Disorders (Fourth Edition) (DSM-IV-TR)*. Washington: APA.

Bahrick, A. (2006) "Post SSRI sexual dysfunction," *Tablet (American Society for the Advancement of Pharmacotherapy)* 7, 3, 2–10.

Balon, R. (2006) "SSRI associated sexual dysfunction," *American Journal of Psychiatry* 163, 1504–1509.

Barker, J.G. and Howell, R.J. (1992) "The plethysmograph: a review of recent literature," *Bulletin of the American Academy of Psychiatry and Law* 20, 13–25.

Barret, B. and Byford, S. (2012) "Costs and outcomes of a programme for offenders with personality disorders," *British Journal of Psychiatry* 200, 336–341.

BBC (2010) Dangerous psychiatric patients tracked with GPS, http://www.bbc.co.uk/news/10245086 (accessed August 25, 2012).

Beck, U. (1992) "From industrial society to risk society: questions of survival, social structure and ecological enlightenment," *Theory, Culture and Society* 9, 91–123.

Beech, A. and Grubin, D. (2010) "Chemical castration doctors should avoid becoming agents of social control," *British Medical Journal* 340, 433–434.

Bradford, J.M.W. and Kaye, N.S. (1999) "Pharmacological treatment of sexual offenders," *American Academy of Psychiatry and Law Newsletter* 24, 16–17.

Burns, T., Yiend, J., Fahey, T. *et al.* (2011) "Treatments for dangerous severe personality disorder," *Journal of Forensic Psychiatry and Psychology* 22, 3, 411–426.

Castel, R. (1976) *L'Ordre Psychiatrique: l'age d'or de l'alienisme.* Paris: Editions de Minuit.

Council of Europe (2004) *Recommendation No (2004)10 of the Committee of Ministers to Member States Concerning the Human Rights and Dignity of Persons with Mental Disorder.* Strasbourg: Council of Europe.

Czoka, A., Bahrick, A. and Mehtonen, O.-P. (2008) "Persistent sexual dysfunction after discontinuation of selective serotonin reuptake inhibitors," *Journal of Sexual Medicine* 5, 227–233.

Department of Health and Home Office (1994) *Report of the Department of Health and Home Office Working Group on Psychopathic Disorder.* London: HMSO.

Department of Health, Ministry of Justice, Welsh Assembly Government (2007) *Mental Health Act 2007 Explanatory Notes.* London and Cardiff: Department of Health, Ministry of Justice, Welsh Assembly Government.

Department of Health (2008) *Mental Health Act 1983 Code of Practice.* London: TSO.

Department of Health (2011) *Good Practice Procedure Guide: The Transfer and Remission of Adult Prisoners under s 47 and 48 of the Mental Health Act.* London: Department of Health.

European Committee for the Prevention of Torture and Inhuman or Degrading Treatment (2006) *The CPT Standards.* Strasbourg: Council of Europe CPT/Inf/E (2002) 1 – Rev. 2006.

European Committee for the Prevention of Torture and Inhuman or Degrading Treatment or Punishment (CPT) (2010) *Report to the Czech Government on the Visit to the Czech Republic from 21 to 23 October 2009.* Strasbourg: CPT/Inf (2010) 22.

European Committee for the Prevention of Torture and Inhuman or Degrading Treatment or Punishment (CPT) (2010a) *Response of the Czech Government to the Report of the European Committee for the Prevention of Torture and Inhuman or Degrading Treatment or Punishment (CPT) on its Visit to the Czech Republic.* Strasbourg: CPT/Inf (2010) 23.

Fennell, P. (1988) "Sexual suppressants and the Mental Health Act," *Criminal Law Review* 660–676.

Fennell, P. (2001) "Reforming the Mental Health Act 1983, joined up compulsion," *Journal of Mental Health Law* June, 3–20.

Fennell, P. (2002) "Radical risk management, mental health and criminal justice," in N. Gray, J. Laing and L. Noakes (eds), *Criminal Justice, Mental Health and the Politics of Risk.* London: Cavendish pp. 69–97.

Fennell, P. (2010) "Institutionalising the community: the codification of clinical authority and the limits of rights-based approaches," in B. McSherry and P. Weller (eds), *Rethinking Rights-Based Mental Health Laws*. Oxford: Hart Publishing, pp. 13–49.

Fennell, P. and Yeates, V. (2002) "To serve which master? Criminal justice policy, community care and the mentally disordered offender," in A. Buchanan (ed.), *Community Care and the Mentally Disordered Offender*. Oxford: Oxford University Press, pp. 288–234.

Foucault, M. (1977) *Discipline and Punish: The Birth of the Prison*, trans. A. Sheridan. New York: Pantheon Books.

Gelder, M., Lopez Ibor, J. and Andreasen, N. (eds) (2000) *New Oxford Textbook of Psychiatry*. Oxford: Oxford University Press.

Gordon, H. and Grubin, D. (2004) "Psychiatric aspects of the assessment and treatment of sex offenders," *Advances in Psychiatric Treatment* 10, 73–80.

Grounds, A. (1990) "Transfers of sentenced prisoners to hospital," *Criminal Law Review* 544–551.

Grounds, A. (1991) "The transfer of sentenced prisoners to hospital 1960–1983: a study in one special hospital," *British Journal of Criminology* 31, 54–71.

Gunn, J. (2000) "Future directions for treatment in forensic psychiatry," *British Journal of Psychiatry* 176, 132–138.

Hamilton, J. (1988) "Chemical castration and consent to treatment," *Psychiatric Bulletin* 12, 493–494.

Hare, R.D. (2003) *Hare Psychopathy Checklist – Revised 2nd Edition Technical Manual*. North Tonawanda, NY: Multi Health Systems.

Harrison, K. and Rainey, B. (2009) "Suppressing human rights – a rights-based approach to the use of pharmacotherapy with sex offenders," *Legal Studies* 29, 47–74.

Harrison, K. and Rainey, B. (2011) "Morality and legality in the use of anti-androgenic pharmacotherapy with sexual offenders," in D. Boer and R. Eher (eds), *International Perspectives on the Assessment and Treatment of Sexual Offenders. Theory, Practice, and Policy*. Oxford: Wiley-Blackwell, pp. 627–651.

Helm, N. and Hursch, C. (1979) "Castration for sex offenders: treatment or punishment? A review and critique of recent European literature," *Archives of Sexual Behavior* 8, 281–305.

Home Office and Department of Health (1999) *Discussion Document: Managing Dangerous People with a Severe Personality Disorder: Proposals for Policy Development*. London: Home Office and Department of Health.

Joint Committee on Human Rights (2007) *Legislative Scrutiny: Mental Health Bill Fourth Report of Session 2006–07*. 4 February. HL Paper 40, HC Paper 288.

Jones, R. (2011) *Mental Health Act Manual*, 14th edn. London: Sweet and Maxwell.

Katz, J. (1972) *Experimentation with Human Beings*. New York: Russell Sage Foundation.

Kemshall, H. and Maguire, M. (2003) "Sex offenders, risk penalty, and the problem of disclosure to the community," in A. Matravers (ed.), *Sex Offenders in the Community: Managing and Reducing the Risks*. Cullompton: Willan Publishing, pp. 102–124.

Kennedy, S. and Rizvi, S. (2009) "Sexual dysfunction, depression, and the impact of antidepressants," *Journal of Clinical Psychopharmacology* 29, 2, 157–164.

Launay, G. (1999) "The phallometric assessment of sex offenders: an update," *Criminal Behaviour and Mental Health* 9, 254–274.

Mathiesen, T. (1998) "Selective incapacitation revisited," *Law and Human Behaviour* 22, 4, 455–469.

Mental Health Act Commission (2007) *Placed Among Strangers* (Thirteenth Biennial Report 2005–2007). London: TSO.

Ministry of Justice (2009) *Guidance on Recall of Conditionally Discharged Restricted Patients*. London: Ministry of Justice.

Ministry of Justice (2010) *Statistics of Mentally Disordered Offenders 2008 England and Wales*. London: Ministry of Justice.

Ministry of Justice National Offender Management Service (2010) *Guidance for Working with MAPPA and Mentally Disordered Offenders*, http://www.justice.gov.uk/downloads/offenders/mentally-disordered-offenders/mappa-mental.pdf (accessed August 25, 2012).

Ministry of Justice (2010) *Statistics Bulletin: Offender Management Caseload Statistics Bulletin*. July 22. London: Ministry of Justice.

Ministry of Justice (2012) *Multi Agency Public Protection Arrangements Annual Report 2010/2011*, http://www.justice.gov.uk/downloads/statistics/mojstats/mappa-annual-report-2010-11.pdf (accessed August 25, 2012).

NHS Information Centre (2011) *In-Patients Formally Detained under the Mental Health Act 1983 and Patients Subject to Supervised Community Treatment: England 2009–2010*. London: Health and Social Care Information Centre.

Oosterhuis, H. (2000) *Stepchildren of Nature: Kraft Ebing, Psychiatry and the Making of Sexual Identity*. Chicago: University of Chicago Press.

Parliament (2007) Public Bill Committee on the Mental Health Bill, http://www.publications.parliament.uk/pa/cm200607/cmpublic/mental/070424/pm/70424s02.htm (accessed August 25, 2012).

Roberts, A. and Coid, J. (2007) "Psychopathy and offending behaviour: findings from the national survey of prisoners in England and Wales," *Journal of Forensic Psychiatry and Psychology* 18, 1, 23–43.

Rose, N. (1998) "Governing risky individuals: the role of psychiatry in new regimes of control," *Psychiatry, Psychology and Law* 5, 177–195.

Rutherford, A. and Telford, M. (2001) "Dealing with people with severe personality disorders," *Future Governance: Lessons from Comparative Public Policy*. Hull: Future Governance Programme, Economic and Social Research Council.

Rutherford, M. (2010) *Blurring the Boundaries: The Convergence of Mental Health and Criminal Justice Policy, Legislation, Systems and Practice*. London: Sainsbury Centre.

Shorter, E. (1997) *A History of Psychiatry: From the Era of the Asylum to the Age of Prozac*. New York: John Wiley & Sons, Inc.

South East Coast Strategic Health Authority (2006) *Report into the Care and Treatment of Michael Stone*. Maidstone: South East Coast Strategic Health Authority.

Taylor, M., Rudkin, L. and Hawton, K. (2005) "Strategies for managing antidepressant-induced sexual dysfunction: systematic review of randomised controlled trials," *Journal of Affective Disorders* 88, 241–254.

Tyrer, P., Duggan, C., Cooper, S., *et al.* (2010) "The successes and failures of the DSPD experiment: the assessment and management of severe personality disorder," *Medicine, Science and the Law* 50, 95–99.

United States v. *Karl Brandt* (1948) *Trial of War Criminals before the Nuremberg Military Tribunals. Volume 1 and 2*, "The Medical Case." Washington, DC: US Government Printing Office, http://www.loc.gov/rr/frd/Military_Law/pdf/NT_war-criminals_Vol-I.pdf (accessed September 20, 2012).

Von Krafft-Ebing, R. (1886) *Psychopathia Sexualis: Eine Klinisch-Forensische Studie*. Stuttgart: Verlag von Ferdinand Enke.

WHO (World Health Organization) (2010) *International Classification of Diseases (ICD-10)*. Geneva: WHO.

4

Special Offender Groups and Equality
A Duty to Treat Differently?
Bernadette Rainey

Introduction

The treatment and management of sex offenders has ethical and legal implications encompassing issues of equal treatment and non-discrimination concerning offenders. Equality considerations and legal obligations may be placed on those treating and managing sex offenders both in private and public institutional and community settings. The literature and research on sex offenders has increasingly underlined the fact that offenders are not a homogenous group and comprise several sub-categories or "special offender" groups including women, minorities, juveniles and the disabled (Harrison, 2010). This chapter will examine the meaning of equality as a legal concept as it applies in this area and the differing needs of these groups of offenders as identified by research studies. Using the example of equality law in the United Kingdom, the chapter will examine the application of legal regulation to sex offender treatment by discussing the equality duty on public bodies.

The Concept of Equality and the Law

It can be argued that equality is one of the basic values of a liberal, democratic society. However, the concept of equality is philosophically and legally open to interpretation and is contested (McCrudden and Prechal, 2009). Equality "appears to be an open-ended and indeterminate concept, capable of giving rise to multiple and often conflicting accounts of its 'proper' meaning" (O'Cinneide, 2008: 78). There is considerable debate surrounding the scope and societal guarantees that equality can provide and equality is often "fragmented into distinct and often rival concepts" (Fredman, 2008: 176).

The Wiley-Blackwell Handbook of Legal and Ethical Aspects of Sex Offender Treatment and Management,
First Edition. Edited by Karen Harrison and Bernadette Rainey.
© 2013 John Wiley & Sons, Ltd. Published 2013 by John Wiley & Sons, Ltd.

Equality is often divided into concepts of formal equality and substantive equality. Formal equality as endorsed by libertarians such as Hayek (O'Cinneide, 2008: 93) advocates the negative aspect of equality; the non-interference with personal autonomy that may lead to inequality. Other philosophers such as Rawls argue for some form of substantive equality, where steps are taken to enhance equality through opportunities with fair competition (Mason, 2006). Others go further, arguing for policies that lead to equality of outcomes (O'Cinneide, 2008: 94). Legal approaches to equality have reflected these conceptual differences.

The emergence of equality as a principle value in legal discourse has relatively modern foundations (Fredman, 2011). The twentieth century witnessed a rapid expansion of legal rules aimed at tackling some of the inequalities within society. Anti-discrimination law developed at international and national level as a tool to tackle discrimination based on personal characteristics. Following the mass discrimination and genocide of the Second World War, the United Nations (UN) placed non-discrimination as a foundational principle in the Universal Declaration of Human Rights in 1948, as well as formulating several specific treaties to prevent discrimination based on specific characteristics (Rainey, 2012). The codification of equality was further endorsed in other international instruments such as the European Convention on Human Rights (ECHR) and in domestic constitutions. In Europe, the European Union has been proactive in developing non-discrimination policies in employment which have now been expanded to goods and services (McCrudden and Prechal, 2009).

Formal equality in law

Most international and domestic law on equality deals with non-discrimination. This is the unjustified, less favorable treatment of a person because of a personal characteristic or because they belong to a particular social group. Formal equality is reactive; the law acts to compensate a person after past discriminatory practice and guarantees equal treatment before the law (for example, the fourteenth amendment to the US Constitution). This form of discrimination law is embodied in the idea of direct discrimination where it is clear that a person has been treated unequally. However, this cannot happen in a vacuum and there must be someone that the person can be compared to in order to demonstrate unequal treatment. In direct discrimination cases, the treatment is intended by the discriminator. Non-discrimination is not a value in itself but a "characteristic of a society based on the value of equality" (Bell, 2004: 245). It is not an end in itself but a means of furthering the equality ideal by removing the most egregious forms of direct discrimination. Different forms of anti-discrimination law have been used as tools in an attempt to achieve equality. This can include the two forms of the Aristotelian concept of equality. Aristotle argued that like cases should be treated alike. This reflects a minimalist view of protection from discrimination under which every person is treated similarly under the law. However, Aristotle argued that the corollary to this concept is that in some cases, inequality can arise from an attempt to make unequal things equal (McCrudden and Prechal, 2009; see also *Thlimmenos* v. *Greece* (2001) 31 EHRR 411; the European Court of Human Rights (ECtHR) found that difference of treatment can result from the state's failure to treat two different situations differently). Therefore, difference and diversity need to be recognized in order to achieve equal treatment.

Substantive equality in law

However, although non-discrimination law can redress individual discrimination and provide a remedy, it has been argued that a different approach is needed as this negative aspect of equality fails to remove the underlying barriers to equality that are pervasive in society. As noted above, equality advocates argue than in order to effect societal change and remove inequality it is necessary to have substantive equality provisions. The recognition of difference can not only remove individual direct discriminatory practice but can also lead to the recognition of indirect discrimination: where a legal rule, policy or practice can apply equally to all under the law (treating everyone the same), but can have an adverse impact on a particular group. In this scenario, intent to discriminate is irrelevant as it is the effect that is important. A good example of this was established in *Brown* v. *Board of Education* (347 U.S. 483 (1954)), where racial segregation in schools in US states was held to be indirectly discriminatory due to the impact of segregation on black children even though the state involved had provided education as required under the law and segregation was allowed under previous judicial interpretation of the equal treatment amendment in the US Constitution which endorsed the "separate but equal" doctrine (*Plessy* v. *Ferguson* 163 U.S. 537 (1896)). Indirect discrimination has been important in recognizing the impact of law and policy on groups as well as individuals.

A focus on group protection has also led to the development of the idea of equality of opportunity. This term is also contested (Mason, 2006), but, put simply, involves the attempt to create a "level playing field" based on fair competition. This may lead to "positive discrimination" policies, where a disadvantaged group is given preferential treatment in order to "level" the field and redress a history of discriminatory practice (Rainey, 2012; Fredman, 2011). The most substantive attempt to achieve equality is the desire for "equality of outcome." This is the most controversial area of legal intervention, with differing claims concerning the use of law to "socially engineer" society and the relationship between equality and liberty (O'Cinneide, 2008). A concept which is increasingly being used to achieve equality of outcome in the long term is the "mainstreaming" of equality into law and policy, meaning the state is placed under a duty to promote and progressively achieve equality.

Mainstreaming and equality duties

Since the mid-1980s mainstreaming has emerged in various areas of law and policy. It was identified by women's rights organizations as an effective way of going further than formal legal methods of tackling discrimination and instead actively promoting gender issues. This idea has since permeated into other areas of law and policy including the environment, regulation, human rights, development and equality. It has been defined differently for different concepts. With regard to equality, the Council of Europe (1998: 12) defined it as:

the reorganisation, improvement, development and evaluation of policy processes, so
that an equality perspective is incorporated in all policies at all levels and at all stages,
by the actors normally involved in policy making.

Mainstreaming is an effort to move equality from the margins of policy formulation
into a central decision-making role in government. It is aimed at tackling problems
with present-day policy making. However, it is anticipatory in that it identifies where
issues and problems may arise in the future. It is also participatory in that it encourages a proactive approach by both policy makers and those directly affected by the
decisions made in government (Rainey and Jenkins, 2007).

The mainstreaming of equality in the United Kingdom has led to the development
of equality duties. These are legal duties placed on public bodies to have due regard
to equality and adverse impact on protected groups when formulating and implementing policies. Section 75 of the Northern Ireland Act 1998 introduced the legal
duty in Northern Ireland and this was followed in the rest of the United Kingdom
under non-discrimination legislation (Rainey and Jenkins, 2007). Disparate legislation covering differing protected groups were combined in the Equality Act 2010
in the United Kingdom (not including Northern Ireland), which now contains
the general legal equality duty to have due regard to equality of the groups protected
by the Act (see below). The duty does not guarantee equality of outcome in the
short term but develops recognition of differential impacts and a duty to take steps
to mitigate any impact. Research on the use of the equality duty in Northern Ireland
has highlighted the importance of the political context for achieving the aims
of mainstreaming (Fredman, 2008) and other issues such as problems with consultation, a lack of substantive engagement with the process as well as issues with measuring impact given the contested meaning of equality (Rainey and Jenkins, 2007;
McLaughlin and Faris, 2004). However, there is recognition that there has been
an improvement in participation of civil society in the development of government
policies (Donaghy, 2004). The duties also allow an individual to mount a legal challenge against the public bodies for a failure to fulfill the duty under the legislation.
It can be argued that the equality duties in UK legislation encompass a duty on
the state to recognize difference and under certain circumstances to modify or commit
resources to mitigate differential impact; in other words, to treat certain groups
differently.

Equality, rights and risk

Equality is a central tenet of human rights discourse as discrimination undermines
human dignity and the rights guaranteed in international and domestic law (see
Chapter 2). As noted above, international human rights instruments either have a
non-discrimination clause or have been formulated to deal specifically with certain
groups (for example, the UN Convention on the Elimination of All Forms of Racial
Discrimination, 1966; the UN Convention on the Elimination of All Forms
of Discrimination Against Women, 1979; the UN Convention on the Rights of the
Child, 1989; the UN Convention on the Rights of Persons with Disabilities, 2008).

The ECHR also contains a non-discrimination clause in Article 14.[1] However, this clause is limited as it cannot be raised as a stand-alone right. It can only be engaged if another right in the Convention is arguable before the Court (Ovey and White, 2010; McColgan, 2003). Protocol 12 to the ECHR has now allowed discrimination to be raised as a stand-alone right although it has rarely been used (Rainey, 2012). The limitation on the use of Article 14 is restrictive as it ties discrimination to civil and political rights, which are the rights enshrined in the ECHR (Ovey and White, 2010). These "first generation" rights are traditionally viewed as negative rights. They require non-interference of the state with personal autonomy and require little state intervention (Moeckli *et al.*, 2010). This is arguably a limitation on the application of substantive equality as it focuses on the protection of the individual from discrimination rather than the protection and promotion of equality for groups (Rainey, 2012; Fredman, 2008).

In contrast, substantive equality, including indirect discrimination, encompasses economic and social concerns and rights such as education, housing, employment and so on. As noted above, positive duties such as the equality duty are designed to promote societal change in the long term and address structural discrimination. As noted by Fredman (2008: 175) this distinction between negative and positive aspects of rights and equality is increasingly being recognized as artificial and "without a positive duty to promote equality, patterns of discrimination and social exclusion will remain unchanged." This reflects a growing recognition in human rights law generally that civil/political and economic/social rights are indivisible and interrelated (UN, 1993). Group protection is increasingly being recognized as necessary to achieve effective protection of rights as well as substantive equality.

At the same time as the right to non-discrimination has been expanded, risk penology has been used as justification to restrict offender rights (see Chapter 2). As will be discussed below, the focus on risk assessment has led to the development of tools of assessment to categorize sex offenders' level of risk and suitability for treatment programs. Different methods have been developed, such as clinical assessment tools, which focus on the individual and actuarial methods of assessment, concentrating solely on the context and statistical data available (Grubin, 2004; see Chapter 20). In actuarial risk assessment, there is little focus on individual characteristics. The failure to take individual characteristics into account has been criticized as being flawed (Grubin, 2004). This may compromise individual rights by removing individual characteristics and objectifying the offender. Actuarial assessment may also have a negative impact on particular groups whose social and cultural circumstances are not taken into account or they are treated as a homogenous sub-category (Hudson and Bramhall, 2005; Martel, Brassard and Mylene, 2011). In terms of discrimination, one of the justifications for the development of these tools is that they use risk markers with no variance for gender or ethnicity and therefore are universally applicable (Martel, Brassard and Mylene, 2011). Thus, scientific methods are neutral and it has been argued that they reduce discrimination by removing bias that may be found in clinical assessment tools (Cheliotis, 2006). However, actuarial tools fail to recognize that different groups may need to be treated differently and so violate Aristotle's second precept of equality (see above).

Recent risk assessment tools use dynamic methods of assessment, which combine actuarial assessment with the individual circumstances and characteristics of the offender (see Chapter 20). These third-generation tools are arguably more effective and do consider the needs of the offender (Kemshall, 2003). However, there are still difficulties with assessing what is meant by a high risk offender (Kemshall, 2003). It has also been argued that dynamic assessment tools have been used to the detriment of ethnic groups (Martel, Brassard and Mylene, 2011; see below). As noted by Douglas (1992), the concept of risk is "value laden," and like equality, is open to interpretation by both policy makers and practitioners (Kemshall, 2008). Dynamic risk assessments may be open to the same criticism of earlier assessment tools, where discretion given to decision makers and practitioners may allow bias into the process. It may be that assessment methods would benefit from the continual monitoring and standards that an equality duty in the public sector can provide.

Special Offender Groups

Given the legal framework that operates both to prevent discrimination and in some cases to promote equality, the treatment and management of sex offenders should recognize common risk factors but also identify how different characteristics may impact on offending and rehabilitation. Research has increasingly highlighted the need to move away from treating sex offenders as a homogenous group of white, adult, male offenders (Duncan, 2006). As case examples, several groups have been identified from the research. However, this is not an exhaustive list and it should be remembered that an offender may possess more than one characteristic that affects offending and treatment.

Ethnic minority/indigenous sex offenders

As noted above, one of the problems that have been highlighted concerning risk assessment is the lack of sensitivity to ethnicity in assessment tools such as the Static-99 or SVR-20 (Tamatea, Webb and Boer, 2011). Tamatea, Webb and Boer (2011: 314) noted that although historically, treatment has been concerned with risk and need, the responsivity principle (delivery and suitability) of treatment "has become increasingly prominent as a heuristic to inform treatment suitability and a range of offender variables" which include cultural identity.

While research on indigenous offenders is scant in some areas (see Chapter 11), research has highlighted problematic areas that have arisen when treating minority groups, as well as recognizing differential needs and culturally specific assessment that may benefit the offender. It should be noted that the studies suggest that across different ethnic groups in different states, ethnic groups tend to be over-represented in the prison population (Hudson and Bramhall, 2005 (UK); Martel, Brassard and Mylene, 2011 (Canada); Chapter 11 (USA); Tamatea, Webb and Boer, 2011 (New Zealand)).

Dynamic risk and bias As noted above, one issue that has arisen is the perceived influence of bias or stereotyping on dynamic risk assessments. In a study of Asian offenders (which, it should be noted, deals generally with offenders rather than specifically with sex offenders), Hudson and Bramhall (2005: 737) concluded that the:

> alchemy of "race" and risk is producing a construction of the Pakistani/Muslim as criminalized Other, which is leading to unintended but demonstrable criminal justice disadvantage for this group of offenders.

The research noted that the stereotyping of Asian men by the probation service was not necessarily deliberate. Similar findings were found in a study of Black and Minority Ethnic (BME) sex offenders on sex offender treatment programs (SOTPs) in England and Wales between1989 and 2007 (Cowburn, Lavis and Walker, 2008). However, as noted above, misunderstanding of ethnicity can lead to a differential impact. The findings correlate with the description of risk as "value laden" (Douglas, 1992) rather than neutral, and with Kemshall's (2003) identification of the role practitioners play in the construction of risk. It also underlines the need to recognize indirect discrimination and to take steps to promote equality through training cultural change, using equality duties and culture-appropriate tools. Equality impact assessment (EQIA) can play an important role in identifying training needs for staff. An equality impact assessment of SOTPs by Her Majesty's Prison Service identified the need for staff training in diversity awareness (Cowburn, Lavis and Walker, 2008).

Responsivity: delivery The renewed focus on the delivery and suitability of SOTPs (see Chapter 14) has helped to demonstrate the need for a culturally sensitive and responsive program if recidivism is to be reduced. The study of BMEs in England noted that the SOTP used an essentially Western, individualized perspective for its cognitive behavioral program, which was criticized by those on the program who felt it failed to recognize their different needs in a family and community setting (Cowburn, Lavis and Walker, 2008). These findings are reflected in other studies of ethnic or indigenous groups (Martel, Brassard and Mylene, 2011 (Canada); Chapter 11 (USA)).

In response, some states have developed culturally sensitive and appropriate programs that recognize specific issues faced by these groups, and these programs have attempted to address the issues by involving the communities that the offenders come from. Tamatea, Webb and Boer (2011: 315) report that New Zealand has attempted to address a lack of response to Maori and Pacific people's needs by combining traditional and mainstream therapeutic methods and an emphasis on reintegration into family and communities. Similarly in Canada, the criminal justice system has developed partnerships with aboriginal communities to create culturally specific programs. These types of programs would address the concerns expressed in the findings on the use of SOTPs in England and Wales.

The use of minority communities in the criminal justice system in order to address the problems noted has been criticized. Martel, Brassard and Mylene (2011) are critical of the coopting of aboriginal culture into the Canadian criminal justice system as a form of responsibilization for aboriginal offenders and the community. It is argued this perpetuates myths about a homogenous aboriginal community and ignores possible marginalization within differing community settings. Responsibilization also distances the state from being the provider of security, and places that burden on the indigenous community; a community where there are underlying structural problems of poverty and "challenging life circumstances" (Martel, Brassard and Mylene, 2011: 248). The coopting of indigenous culture into the dominant criminal justice model may lead to assimilation rather than a shift of power to indigenous groups (Sutherland, 2002).

The criticisms of the Canadian experience may be valid in some respects. However, from the perspective of "equality of outcomes," the "coopting" of Aboriginal and other cultural knowledge may have a long term positive impact on the development of risk assessment programs as diversity is "mainstreamed" into the prison and assessment regime. However, this mainstreaming must be grounded in "structures and organisational culture for them to be of practical relevance" (Escott and Whitfield, 2002: 38). As noted by Martel, Brassard and Mylene (2011), shifting responsibility from the criminal justice system to the communities may not help to change the culture within the dominant system.

As more research is carried out in the area of ethnicity and sex offending, it may become clearer how guidelines can be established that will improve the treatment of diverse ethnic groups. Tamatea, Webb and Boer (2011) offer some guidelines based on the New Zealand experience, including pre-therapy intervention, appropriate cultural supervision, integrated risk assessment, and enhanced service delivery by engaging the offender's family and a cultural advisor in therapeutic planning, cultural matching and training.

Female sex offenders

Similar issues have arisen with the treatment and management of female sex offenders and in recent years research has begun to focus on the treatment and management of female sex offenders, with arguments being put forward for a gendered response to female issues.

It has been argued by Londono (2007) that the ECHR can provide protection for women in the penal system under Article 3 governing the right not to be ill-treated and Article 8 guaranteeing private and family life alongside Article 14. Under Article 3, sex is a factor to be taken into account when the Court decides if the suffering is severe enough to be ill treatment under the ECHR (*Ireland* v. *UK* (1978) 2 EHRR 25) and will also be considered when weighing the proportionality of a restriction on private or family life under Article 8. The Commission on Human Rights[2] has held that a sentencing policy which affects individuals in a discriminatory way may give rise to a violation under Article 14 (Londono, 2007; *Nelson* v. *UK* (1986) 49 DR 170).

Duncan (2006) has argued that research itself demonstrates a lack of sensitivity to female issues, and that gender tended to be missing from research on juvenile and other groups of offenders. The dearth of research into female sex offenders has been noted. However, this seems to be improving with increasing amounts of research being carried out on female offenders (see Chapter 19; Cortoni, 2010; Gannon and Rose, 2008). The percentage of sex offenders who are female is debated.

However, recent research puts the number at between 1% (Berner, Briken and Hill, 2009) and 5% (Cortoni and Hanson, 2005). This is a small group but significant enough to suggest that female needs should be addressed.

Risk assessment   Although male and female sexual offenders may share characteristics that relate to risk, research has noted that there are differences between them, including how sexual offenses are defined (Cortoni and Gannon, 2010). Rates of recidivism are an important factor in evaluating risk. Research has demonstrated that rates of sexual recidivism for women are lower than for men (Cortoni and Gannon, 2010: 41). Therefore, the use of risk assessment tools for women based on male recidivism rates would arguably not be suitable for female offenders, For example, the "what works" agenda in the UK has been criticized for using actuarial risk assessment tools that are based on a single model of assessment for men and women (Martin, Kautt and Gelsthorpe, 2009). Research has also increasingly identified a difference in risk factors between men and women that should be addressed, such as the influence of prior child abuse, rates of co-offending, prior sexual and criminal history and problematic relationships (Cortoni, 2010; Cortoni and Gannon, 2010). Risk assessment tools that do not address gender-specific factors can be in danger of treating women as "correctional afterthoughts" (Ross and Fabiano, 1986).

Responsivity: delivery   Similar issues that were identified above with ethnic minorities have been highlighted in regard to female sex offenders. The delivery of programs necessary to respond to offenders' criminogenic needs should be suitable and effective. It has been argued that there has been a failure to provide a gender-responsive approach to treatment. Research by Martin, Kautt and Gelsthorpe (2009) concluded that the General Offending Behavior Programs used in England and Wales often failed to recognize gender issues in design and delivery and the need for gender-specific interventions. Similarly Cortoni (2010) and Cortoni and Gannon (2011) have noted various factors that differentiate treatment needs between men and women that affect the efficacy of treatment. They note that although similar characteristics affecting treatment needs may arise in male and female offenders, these can manifest in gender-specific ways that need to be considered (Cortoni and Gannon, 2010: 44).

Female sex offenders face gender bias within the criminal process and there has been a gap in the development of guidelines for treatment that focus on female sex offenders (Duncan, 2006). Duncan (2006) suggests some guidelines for a gender-responsive treatment program which could include a pre-treatment evaluation, individual treatment, community management and specific group work for women and the provision of gender-specific services. These are similar to those suggested for ethnicity but are tailored for gender-specific needs. Gender guidelines have been developed for public decision making in other areas of the law, such as refugee determination (see UK gender guidelines, Immigration Appellate Authority, 2000). Similar guidelines should be available to prison and probation staff as well as to practitioners who deal with female sex offenders. A legal duty to promote gender equality could require the use of good practice guidelines as well as training in female-specific issues and monitoring/mitigating of adverse impact on female offenders. This would address the issues raised by the research and address the concerns expressed that assessment tools and treatment methods used for female offenders simply reflect male offender risk and need.

Juvenile sex offenders

In recent years, there has been increasing legal intervention to prevent discrimination based on age. In the European Union and in the United Kingdom age is now a protected characteristic in equality legislation (Equality Act 2010). It should also be noted that the UN Convention on the Rights of the Child (1989) is applicable to juvenile offenders. This includes Article 2 which protects children from discrimination, Article 3 which guarantees the best interests of the child and Article 12 which states that the views of the child should be given due weight, given the child's age and maturity.

There has also been increasing research into the specific characteristics of juveniles in the criminal justice system. The term "juvenile" is used here, though some researchers prefer "sexually abusive youth" or adolescent to avoid labeling young people as sex offenders, as this may be counterproductive in attempting to treat these offenders (Metzner, Humphreys and Ryan, 2009).

Risk assessment   The research suggests that the issues raised with other subgroups apply to juveniles. Applying predictions of recidivism based on risk factors attributable to adults may not be appropriate for juveniles and there is a lack of knowledge and research into sexually deviant behavior in juveniles (Hendricks and Bijleveld, 2008). Research suggests that the juvenile subgroup is not homogenous and that a significant portion of offenders in this group have co-occurring development disabilities, suffer from family breakdown and have poor social skills (Schladale, 2010), thus underlining the need to consider specific criteria when assessing risk. It has been noted that as children, these offenders are continuing to develop cognitively and this needs to be recognized (Poortinga *et al.*, 2009). Research has identified possible juvenile-specific risk factors that should be taken into account (Schladale, 2010; Poortinga *et al.*, 2009). As noted by Poortinga *et al.* (2009), evidence-based research focused on the characteristics of juveniles is needed to ensure the efficacy of treatment.

Responsivity: delivery   Given the specific issues relating to juveniles, it is necessary to respond to variant risk factors with suitable and effective treatment and management. Research has highlighted the need for tailored programs for juveniles. It has been suggested that successful treatment requires a "holistic, individualised approach based upon empirically driven practices for youth prevention" (Schladale, 2010: 182). Without this, the efficacy of treatment can be questioned. The need for a responsive treatment program is mirrored in the criminal justice system and the management of juvenile sex offenders. There are issues that arise concerning consent to treatment, age-appropriate interviews for treatment and management, the use of polygraphy on juveniles and the use of drug therapy (Scott, 2009). The UK Supreme Court has also noted that sex offender registration rules should consider the age of the offender and that the right to review registration should be age-appropriate (*F and Thompson* v. *Secretary of State for Justice* [2010] UKSC 17; see Chapter 2). It has been argued that registers are not appropriate for juvenile offenders and can have potentially harmful effects (Miner *et al.*, 2006).

As above, clear guidelines for treatment and management of juvenile sex offenders would enhance successful treatment and may help reduce recidivism. The International Association for the Treatment of Sexual Offenders (IATSO) has developed standards of care for juvenile treatment that could be a useful measurement tool to evaluate a public body's legal duty to take into account age in policy and decision making. The standards outline juvenile-specific factors to be taken into account, including consideration of the family context, sensitivity to development change in juveniles, and heterogeneity of juvenile offenders. The standards indicate that juvenile offenders should be treated with respect and dignity, that sex offender notification should not be used against juveniles, and that research should be based on specialized clinical experience (Miner *et al.*, 2006).

Disability: intellectually disabled sex offenders

It has been recognized by practitioners that intellectually disabled (ID) sex offenders are a specific subgroup within sexual offenders (Lindsay, 2011). An intellectual disability is usually measured by an examination of cognitive functioning (such as IQ scores) but adaptive and social functioning can also be used (Van Horn, Mulder and Kusters, 2010). It is often unclear how many offenders with ID are within the criminal justice system (Van Horn, Mulder and Kusters, 2010). However, research into ID offending has found high recidivism rates among this subgroup of offenders. Given the re-offending rates of this subgroup, it is important to establish if there are specific factors related to ID offenders.

Risk assessment Research has identified specific factors that may lead to sex offenders with ID having high recidivism rates. One reason put forward is a bias against those with ID by the police, who treat their behavior as more serious than that of other offenders. ID offenders may also fail to grasp the seriousness of their actions and so are not able to take responsibility for their actions, which undermines the availability of treatment. It has also been argued that ID offenders are more visible and more likely to get caught (Craig, Stringer and Moss, 2006). Recognition of these specific characteristics and the bias within the system can lead to a more directed intervention program for these offenders.

Responsivity: delivery As noted above, recognition of specific risk and needs of a subgroup should lead to responsive treatment and management programs. Programs have already been put in place that are designed to meet the needs of ID sex offenders. It has been noted that programs targeted at the general population fail to consider the problems ID offenders have with understanding the cognitive behavioral programs, as well as problems with reintegrating into a community setting (Van Horn, Mulder and Kusters 2010). Several models of treatment programs have been used to develop specific pathways to treat ID offenders (Lindsay, 2011). These require funding and a recognition of the specific treatment needs of ID offenders. As Van Horn, Mulder and Kusters (2010: 222) note in their study of an intensive program for sex offenders with ID in the Netherlands, improvements can be made to programs to be sure that "intervention is tuned to their low level of intellectual functioning."

An Equality Duty: United Kingdom

The above discussion has outlined examples of subgroups within the general population of sex offenders. Research has demonstrated the specific needs of each group and the need for the treatment and management of sex offenders to be responsive to different groups. Practitioners have noted the ethical need for specific programs. The guidelines put forward for different groups could be used to guide a legal duty on public bodies to have due regard to equality when devising policies and programs within a prison or community setting.

Recent legislation in the United Kingdom has developed an equality duty to promote equality for the protected groups. In England, Wales and Scotland the Equality Act 2010 brought together the previously separate legislation on non-discrimination against different groups and now includes several protected characteristics: sex, race, disability, religion or belief, sexual orientation, age, gender reassignment, pregnancy and maternity. (Northern Ireland has a separate and more detailed equality duty under s75 of the Northern Ireland Act.) The previous legislation required equality schemes to be drawn up by public bodies. This has now been consolidated into a general public duty.

Section 149 of the Equality Act sets out the public sector equality duty. It places on public bodies an obligation to have due regard to the need to:

- eliminate unlawful discrimination, harassment and victimization and other conduct prohibited by the Act (s149(1) (a));
- advance equality of opportunity between people who share a protected characteristic and those who do not (s149(1) (b));
- foster good relations between people who share a protected characteristic and those who do not (s149(1) (c)).

The section goes on to explain that having due regard for advancing equality involves removing or minimizing disadvantages, taking steps to meet the needs of people from protected groups where these are *different* from the needs of others, and encouraging people from protected groups to participate in public life (s149(3)).

This general duty is supplemented by specific duties made under regulations for each jurisdiction. The regulations for England (the Equality Act 2010 (Specific Duties) Regulations) are arguably less onerous than in Wales, as in England public bodies are required to publish information on how the equality duty has been fulfilled but they are under no obligation to carry out equality impact assessments. In contrast, the Welsh and Scottish Regulations are more prescriptive and include the need for equality plans and assessments to be published (Equality Act 2010 (Statutory Duties) (Wales) Regulations 2011; Equality Act 2010 (Specific Duties) (Scotland) Regulations 2012). The Equality and Human Rights Commission (EHRC) is responsible for monitoring and enforcing compliance with the equality duty and issues guidance to public bodies (EHRC, 2012).

Possible impact on sexual offender treatment and management

The public sector equality duty recognizes difference and acknowledges the importance of this for the advancement of equality (EHRC, 2012). Public bodies responsible for the treatment and management of sex offenders are under a duty to ensure policies and programs do not discriminate against one of the protected groups *and* recognize difference in order to further substantive equality. In doing so, a public body should establish monitoring and training schemes to address the differential needs of the protected groups and to mitigate adverse impact on these groups.

An example of the equality duty in practice is the recent review of indeterminate sentencing for sexual and violent offenders in England and Wales (see Chapter 2). An equality impact assessment was carried out by the Ministry of Justice (2011) on the proposals to amend the sentencing structure for sex offenders. The assessment identified potential differential impact on age (those aged under 21 are less likely to be released), disability (due to mental disorder), and gender (as men are more likely to get an IPP than women), In mitigation, the assessment noted the plans to have better and more individualized rehabilitation programs in prison to negate adverse impact, including new pathways for IPP prisoners with a mental disorder. The assessment also noted that these new rehabilitation programs would have a positive impact on equality, therefore meeting the obligation to advance equality and recognize difference. The assessment also noted the positive impact on potential victims of the proposed sentencing scheme. There would be monitoring in place to establish the impact of the sentencing scheme on the protected groups. However, the assessment stated the opinion of the Ministry that any negative impact would be proportionate in relation to the changes as, overall, they will improve the protection of victims and potentially aid prisoners.

The equality impact assessment may have accepted that some negative impact may occur, but it can be argued that the benefit of the legal duty to have due regard to equality has forced the public body to engage with the differences between groups of offenders. The assessment produced statistics on different groups, and this kind of information gathering is important as it provides evidence of differential impact. It also is participatory as it is part of the consultation process of policy change. It is important for anticipating differential impact and what the consequences might be. As illustrated above, a failure to address the different needs of subgroups of offenders may lead to recidivism. Examining assessment tools or penal policies before they are implemented may help to ensure appropriate measures are taken that can be successful in preventing further offending.

However, if there is a lack of engagement by public bodies and they do the minimum to fulfill their obligations, then the goal of the duty may be undermined. For example, in Northern Ireland, the Department of Justice (NI) carried out equality assessment of the proposed changes to the sex offender notification scheme (Department of Justice, 2011). Under s75 of the Northern Ireland Act 1998, all policies have to be screened to determine if an equality impact assessment is necessary. The screening form for the notification scheme gives little information as to why it was decided that an equality impact assessment was not necessary. Despite the criticisms of notification requirements on juveniles (see above), the screening paper simply states there is no impact on juveniles, fails to note impact on disability despite more draconian limitations on sex offenders that may have an adverse impact on physically and mentally disabled offenders, and when addressing men and women simply states the vast majority of sexual offenders are men without explaining the relevance of that statement. The form does note the potential positive impact on vulnerable groups of victims but little else. It also notes that the only adverse impact on any group would be where a member of that group committed a sexual crime. Overall, it could be argued that the scant information given as to why the decision was taken not to assess equality impact suggests a lack of engagement with the process and possibly a failure to recognize the importance of difference in the treatment and management of sex offenders which might have a negative impact on potential victims.

Legal challenge

If a public body fails in its duty to have due regard to equality, there is the possibility of judicial redress. The goals of the public duty include cooperation and cultural change, so recourse to the courts should only be needed where there is a lack of cooperation or where an individual feels a failure to comply needs a remedy from the Courts. There have been several cases brought against the government under the equality duties (under previous legislation) on areas such as education and social services. There have also been challenges made to the prison service involving the treatment of prisoners. Some of these cases have been brought by the Equality and Human Rights Commission on behalf of an individual(s).

In *R (on the application of Equality and Human Rights Commission)* v. *Secretary of State for Justice* ([2010] EWHC 147), the court found that the National Offender Management Service (NOMS) and the UK Border Agency failed to fulfill their statutory duty under disability and race legislation to have due regard to the equality of these groups. The bodies had decided to remove foreign prisoners to different prisons without any evidence that the policy had been assessed for differential impact. The lack of evidence of an assessment of the impact of the policies was compounded by a response from the defendant body in correspondence with the applicants, asserting that as the policy does not discriminate then their obligations were limited. As noted by the judge, this did not inspire confidence that the duty was taken seriously.

Another example of a failure to fulfill the statutory duty can be found in *R (on the application of Gill)* v. *Secretary of State for Justice* ([2010] EWHC 364). The applicant was a violent offender with a learning disability who was unable to access the offender rehabilitation programs he needed in order to demonstrate he no longer posed a risk and therefore served more than double his minimum sentence tariff. The reason he was unable to access these programs was his low IQ. It was decided that a person with his intellectual capability would not benefit from the programs. Despite the fact that several versions of NOMS policies stated that offender programs should be responsive to the individual needs of the offender, the applicant was excluded from the offender programs deemed necessary by the Parole Board if he was to be released. The prison also failed to offer effective alternative help. The prison had a disabled prisoners' policy with a list of specialist organizations, but these were not used. The judge also dismissed any argument of excessive cost in providing tailored programs for ID prisoners (para. 75).

The impact assessment schemes described are examples of good and bad practice. The assessment of IPPs has provided data and detail that at least aids transparency and notes group-specific characteristics, whereas the screening of changes to sex offender notification is limited and demonstrates little appreciation of difference. Where a public body does fail to engage or propagates a policy that clearly has negative impact, then the court can be used as a method of enforcement. The case law demonstrates that group-specific considerations need to be taken into account when devising and applying penal policy which may impact on subgroups of sex offenders. The UK public sector duty demonstrates some potential benefits for recognizing difference in sex offender policies which include: training, monitoring, impact data and group-specific criteria to measure compliance with the duty.

Conclusion

There is an increasing literature on sex offender treatment and management which identifies the lack of homogeneity in offenders. Organizations such as IATSO are developing guidelines for practitioners to ensure both ethical and appropriate treatment is used. There is also a recognition that research into sex offending should highlight the need to identify diversity in offender groups and conduct research accordingly (see Chapter 6). Alongside the need for ethical treatment, legal duties can play a role both in promoting greater equality among different offender groups and in enforcing legal obligations on public bodies. It should also be noted that "protected" groups are not homogenous as groups. Duncan (2006) notes that research on groups such as juveniles are usually male juveniles and there is a lack of literature on offenders who are juvenile *and* female. McColgan (2005) notes the difficulties adjudicating on multiple discrimination, although a single equality act such as the Equality Act 2010 helps to overcome these issues. Hannett (2003) identifies different forms of multiple discrimination: additive discrimination involving two or more personal characteristics, and intersectional discrimination where having two or more characteristics (as in the case of Black lesbian women, for example) lead to a particular form of discrimination. The latter category cannot be addressed properly through formal equality. The focus should be on difference *and* disadvantage; economic and social causes that need to be tackled through structural change in society. Offenders belonging to multiple groups should have the impact of these differing characteristics taken into account during risk assessment and treatment, with guidelines in place for the particular subgroups and a more nuanced approach to those with multiple characteristics.

The development of substantive equality has furthered the equality debate and moved it away from formal equality which secures equal protection before the law, treats all persons the same and guarantees non-interference with civil and political rights. Substantive equality attempts to tackle the structural and organizational inequality inherent in society by placing positive duties on states to take steps to achieve a more equal society. Thus, equality duties may encompass economic and social rights. This has been illustrated above, as treatment and management programs increasingly recognize the specific needs of differing groups. Responses to offender risk and need must take into account a myriad of factors influenced by diverse backgrounds. It has also been noted that developing equality compliant schemes costs money (Duncan, 2006) and may be more expensive than homogeneous policies and tools that can be used across the different groups. However, in making an argument for "mainstreaming" equality into public decision making and policies, it should be noted that the cost both in monetary terms and to society in the long term may be much greater if re-offending occurs due to the unsuitability of schemes (Duncan, 2006).

Although equality duties and equality impact assessments have been criticized as being bureaucratic and failing to create meaningful change, it may be too early to tell what long-term differences such policies have made in the United Kingdom. Tentative progress has arguably been made in Northern Ireland, albeit with criticisms. What has been flagged as a possible early success is a greater participation in policy making through consultation with interested groups and civil society. Equality duties are a shift from the "command and control" measures of achieving equality through non-discrimination law to deliberative democratic methods (Rainey and Jenkins, 2007; McCrudden, 2001). Similarly, the use of equality impact assessments when introducing penal policies or treatment and management tools may allow for greater participation of government, practitioners, community and offenders as to the most appropriate methods. This may not only reduce recidivism but it may also enhance awareness and properly informed debate on sex offender treatment, acting as a counterpoint to the media portrayal of sex offenders (see Chapter 8; Kemshall, 2008).

However, as noted by Martel, Brassard and Mylene (2011), participation should not lead to a shift of responsibility for the treatment and management of sex offenders from government to the community. Involving ethnic minority and other groups in an attempt to address specific criminogenic needs of offenders should not lead to a withdrawal of state intervention, especially if structural inequalities afflicting those communities are not addressed. In an age of austerity, the present government in the United Kingdom has championed a "Big Society" where communities take responsibility for public goods, while at the same time implementing cuts in welfare, social services, policing, prisons and so on (NEF, 2010). The UK equality duties obligate the government at least to consult and consider the protected groups before making policy decisions. The rationale of equality duties is one of participation, not abdication. However, equality advocates are concerned that the UK government is now trying to limit the equality duty under the 2010 Act (Employment Lawyers Association, 2012). If this is indeed the case, it may in fact be a step backwards on the road to a more equal society. Equality duties are not a panacea for an unequal society. However, this chapter has illustrated that practitioners in sex offender treatment and management are responding to the ethical challenge of recognizing differential impact between groups of sex offenders. A legal public sector duty to assess and monitor this impact further underlines the Aristotelian maxim that equality also involves a duty to treat different things differently.

Notes

1 Article 14 of the ECHR: "The enjoyment of the rights and freedoms set forth in this Convention shall be secured without discrimination on any ground such as sex, race, colour, language, religion, political or other opinion, national or social origin, association with a national minority, property, birth or other status."
2 Part of the Council of Europe adjudication system before 1998.

References

Bell, M. (2004) "Equality and the European Union Constitution," *Industrial Law Journal* 33, 242–260.

Berner, W., Briken, P. and Hill, A. (2009) "Female sexual offenders," in F.M. Saleh, A.J. Grudzinskas, J.M. Bradford and D.J. Brodsky (eds), *Sex Offenders: Identification, Risk Assessment, Treatment and Legal Issues.* Oxford: Oxford University Press, pp. 276–285.

Cheliotis, L.K. (2006) "How iron is the iron cage of new penology? The role of human agency in the implementation of criminal justice policy," *Punishment and Society* 8, 313–340.

Cortoni, F. (2010) "The assessment of female sexual offenders," in T.A. Gannon and F. Cortoni (eds), *Female Sex Offenders: Theory: Assessment and Treatment.* Oxford: Wiley-Blackwell, pp. 87–100.

Cortoni, F. and Gannon, T.A. (2010) "Female sexual offenders," in D.P. Boer, R. Eher, L.A. Craig, *et al.* (eds), *International Perspectives on the Assessment and Treatment of Sexual Offenders.* Oxford: Wiley-Blackwell, pp. 35–49.

Cortoni, F. and Hanson, R.H. (2005) *A Review of the Recidivism Rates of Adult Female Sex Offenders. Research Report R-169.* Ottowa: Correctional Services Canada.

Council of Europe (1998) *Gender Mainstreaming. Conceptual Framework, Methodology and Presentation of Good Practices.* Strasbourg: Council of Europe.

Cowburn, M., Lavis, V. and Walker, T. (2008) "BME sex offenders in prison: the problem of participation in offending behaviour groupwork programmes – a tripartite model of understanding," *British Journal of Community Justice* 6, 1, 19–34.

Craig, L.A., Stringer, I. and Moss, T. (2006) "Treating sexual offenders with learning disabilities in the community," *International Journal of Offender Therapy and Comparative Criminology* 50, 4, 360–390.

Department of Justice (NI) (2011) S75 Equality Screening Form: Sex Offender Notification, Department of Justice (NI), Belfast, at http://www.dojni.gov.uk/index/public-consultations/archive-consultations/sex-offender-notification-screening-document.pdf (accessed September 12, 2012).

Donaghy, T.B. (2004) "Mainstreaming: Northern Ireland's participative-democratic approach," *Policy and Politics* 32, 1, 48–62.

Douglas, M. (1992) *Risk and Blame: Essays in Cultural Theory.* London: Routledge.

Duncan, J. (2006) "Gender equity in the field of child sexual abuse: does gender matter in sexual offense treatment for females and their victims?," adapted from paper presented at the Association for the Treatment of Sexual Abusers Conference in Chicago, Illinois, September, originally titled "Does Gender Matter: Female Sex Offender," http://www.theright2besafe.org/articles/Gender%20Equity%20in%20Sexual%20Abuse%20-%20Duncan%202006.pdf (accessed August 25, 2012).

Employment Lawyers Association (2012) "Reforms to Equality Act 2010 and Equality and Human Right Commission announced," *ELA Newsletter* May 2012, http://www.elaweb.org.uk/ (accessed May 20, 2012).

Equality and Human Rights Commission (EHRC) (2012) The Essential Guide to the Public Sector Equality Duty (England and Non-devolved Public Authorities in Scotland and Wales), http://www.equalityhumanrights.com/uploaded_files/EqualityAct/PSED/essential_guide_update.doc (accessed August 25, 2012).

Escott, K. and Whitfield, D. (2002) *Promoting Equality in the Public Sector*. Manchester: Equal Opportunities Commission.

Fredman, S. (2008) *Human Rights Transformed*. Oxford: Oxford University Press.

Fredman, S. (2011) *Discrimination Law*, 2nd edn. Oxford: Clarendon Press.

Gannon, T.A. and Rose, M.R. (2008) "Female child sexual abusers: towards integrating theory and practice," *Aggression and Violent Behaviour* 21, 194–207.

Grubin, D. (2004) "The risk assessment of sex offenders," in H. Kemshall and G. McIvor (eds), *Managing Sex Offender Risk*. London: Jessica Kingsley Publishers, pp. 91–110.

Hannett, S. (2003) "Equality at the intersections: the legislative and judicial failure to tackle multiple discrimination," *Oxford Journal of Legal Studies* 23, 65–86.

Harrison, K. (2010) "The use of pharmacotherapy with high risk sex offenders," in K. Harrison (ed.), *Managing High Risk Sex Offenders in the Community*. Cullompton: Willan Publishing, pp. 105–132.

Hendricks, J. and Bijleveld, C. (2008) "Recidivism among juvenile sex offenders after residential treatment," *Journal of Sexual Aggression* 14, 1, 19–32.

Hudson, B. and Bramhall, G. (2005) "Assessing the 'other': constructions of Asianness in risk assessments by probation officers," *British Journal of Criminology* 45, 5, 721–740.

Immigration Appellate Authority (2000) Asylum Gender Guidelines, http://www.unhcr.org/refworld/docid/3ae6b3414.html (accessed August 25, 2012).

Kemshall, H. (2003) *Understanding Risk in Criminal Justice*. Maidenhead: Open University Press.

Kemshall, H. (2008) *Understanding the Community Management of High Risk Offenders*. Maidenhead: Open University Press.

Lindsay, W.R. (2011) "Theoretical perspectives and their practical application for assessment and treatment of sexual offenders with an intellectual disability," in D.P. Boer, R. Eher, L.A. Craig *et al.* (eds), *International Perspectives on the Assessment and Treatment of Sexual Offenders*. Oxford: Wiley-Blackwell, pp. 215–234.

Londono, P. (2007) "Applying convention jurisprudence to the needs of women prisoners," *Public Law*, Summer, 198–208.

Martel, J., Brassard, R. and Mylene, J. (2011) "When two worlds collide: aboriginal risk management in Canadian Corrections," *British Journal of Criminology* 51, 2, 235–255.

Martin, J., Kautt, P. and Gelsthorpe, L. (2009) "What works for women? A comparison of community-based general offending programme completion," *British Journal of Criminology* 49, 6, 879–899.

Mason, A. (2006) *Levelling the Playing Field: The Idea of Equal Opportunity and Its Place in Egalitarian Thought*. Oxford: Oxford University Press.

McColgan, A. (2003) "Principles of equality and protection from discrimination in International Human Rights Law," *European Human Rights Law Review* 2, 157–175.

McColgan, A. (2005) *Discrimination Law: Text. Cases and Materials*, 2nd edn. Oxford: Hart.

McCrudden, C. (2001) "Equality," in C. Harvey (ed.), *Human Rights, Equality and Democratic Renewal in Northern Ireland*. Oxford: Hart Publishing, pp. 75–113.

McCrudden, C. and Prechal, S. (2009) "The concepts of equality and non-discrimination in Europe." European Legal Network in the Field of Gender Equality, European Commission, Directorate-General for Employment, Social Affairs and Equal Opportunities Unit, Strasbourg, http://webcache.googleusercontent.com/search?hl=en&q=cache:VR5n9YlGPE0J:http://ec.europa.eu/social/BlobServlet%3FdocId%3D4553%26langId%3Den%2Bmccrudden+equality&ct=clnk (accessed August 25, 2012).

McLaughlin, E. and Faris, N. (2004) *The Section 75 Equality Duty – An Operational Review Vol. 1.* Belfast: Northern Ireland Office.

Metzner, J.L., Humphreys, S. and Ryan, G. (2009) "Juveniles who sexually offend: psychosocial intervention and treatment," in F.M. Saleh, A.J. Grudzinskas, J.M. Bradford and D.J. Brodsky (eds), *Sex Offenders: Identification, Risk Assessment, Treatment and Legal Issues.* Oxford: Oxford University Press, pp. 241–253.

Miner, M., Borduin, C., Prescott, D., *et al.* (2006) "Standards of care for juvenile sexual offenders of the International Association for the Treatment of Sexual Offenders" *Sexual Offender Treatment* 1, 3, 1–7.

Ministry of Justice (2011) Review of Indeterminate Sentences for Public Protection (IPPs) – Equality Impact Assessment, http://www.justice.gov.uk/downloads/legislation/bills-acts/legal-aid-sentencing/ipp-review-equality-impact-assessment.pdf (accessed August 25, 2012).

Moeckli, D., Shah, S., Sivakumaram, S. and Harris, D. (2010) *International Human Rights Law.* Oxford: Oxford University Press.

NEF (New Economics Foundation) (2010) Cutting it: The Big Society and the New Austerity, http://www.neweconomics.org/sites/neweconomics.org/files/Cutting_it.pdf (accessed September 11, 2012).

O'Cinneide, C. (2008) "The right to equality: a substantive legal norm or vacuous rhetoric?," *UCL Human Rights Review* 1, 1, 78–101.

Ovey, C. and White, R. (2010) *The European Convention on Human Rights*, 3rd edn. Oxford: Oxford University Press.

Poortinga, E., Newman S.S., Negendank, C.F. and Benedeck, E.P. (2009) "Juvenile sexual offenders: epidemiology, risk assessment, and treatment," in F.M. Saleh, A.J. Grudzinskas, J.M. Bradford and D.J. Brodsky (eds), *Sex Offenders: Identification, Risk Assessment, Treatment and Legal Issues.* Oxford: Oxford University Press, pp. 241–261.

Rainey, B. (2012) *Human Rights Law Concentrate.* Oxford: Oxford University Press.

Rainey, B. and Jenkins, V. (2007) "Moving into the mainstream: an analysis of regulatory responses to impact assessment in equality and sustainable development," *Northern Ireland Legal Quarterly* 58, 1, 78–107.

Ross, R. and Fabiano, E. (1986) *Female Offenders: Correctional Afterthoughts.* Jefferson: McFarland.

Schladale, J. (2010) "Enhancing community collaboration to stop sexual harm by youth," in K. Harrison (ed.), *Managing High Risk Sex Offenders in the Community.* Cullompton: Willan Publishing, pp. 174–192.

Scott, C. (2009) "Forensic evaluations of juvenile sex offenders," in F.M. Saleh, A.J. Grudzinskas, J.M. Bradford and D.J. Brodsky (eds), *Sex Offenders: Identification, Risk Assessment, Treatment and Legal Issues.* Oxford: Oxford University Press, pp. 211–240.

Sutherland, J. (2002) "Colonialism, crime and dispute resolution: a critical analysis of Canada's Aboriginal Justice Strategy," *James Boskey ADR Writing Competition*, http://www.mediate.com/articles/sutherlandJ.cfm (accessed August 25, 2012).

Tamatea, A.J., Webb, M. and Boer, D.P. (2011) "The role of culture in sexual offender rehabilitation: a New Zealand perspective," in D.P. Boer, R. Eher, L.A. Craig, *et al.* (eds), *International Perspectives on the Assessment and Treatment of Sexual Offenders.* Oxford: Wiley-Blackwell, pp. 314–329.

UN (United Nations) (1993) *Vienna Declaration and Programme of Action*, World Conference on Human Rights, Vienna 14–15 June 1993, A/CONF.157/23, http://www.unhchr.ch/huridocda/huridoca.nsf/(symbol)/a.conf.157.23.en (accessed August 25, 2012).

Van Horn, J., Mulder, J. and Kusters, I. (2010) "Intellectually disabled sexual offenders: subgroup profiling and recidivism after outpatient treatment," in K. Harrison (ed.), *Managing High Risk Sex Offenders in the Community.* Cullompton: Willan Publishing, pp. 209–225.

5

Expert Evidence, Ethics and the Law

Tony Ward

Introduction

The first and most fundamental decision that has to be taken about the management of a sex offender is that the individual in question has in fact committed a sexual offense. This decision may be taken by a criminal court, where the matter has to be proved beyond reasonable doubt, or by a family court, where the standard of proof is the balance of probabilities. In both civil and criminal courts, expert evidence in fields ranging from DNA analysis to social work plays a vital role; but as Wall J (later to become President of the Family Division) pointed out in *Re M (Application for Care Order)* ([1995] 3 FCR 611: 629–630):

> Clinicians must . . . remember that . . . a disputed question of whether or not a child has been sexually abused is a matter which Parliament has decreed should be decided by the court . . . The clinical assessment by a doctor or other suitably qualified expert is an important part of this process, and one on which the court often places great weight. The clinician's task therefore in my judgment carries a corresponding responsibility to ensure that the clinical judgment is soundly based and can be objectively justified.

In law, expert evidence is distinguished from non-expert evidence by the greater latitude given to experts to state their opinions. Opinions are conventionally defined as inferences drawn from facts observed by the witness or reported to the witness by others; these can range from a scientist's interpretation of a DNA profile to a social worker's assessment of a child's behavior. The scope for experts to give opinion evidence, and the weight that is often attached to that evidence by the courts, places them, in the eyes of the judiciary, in a "privileged position" which carries special

The Wiley-Blackwell Handbook of Legal and Ethical Aspects of Sex Offender Treatment and Management,
First Edition. Edited by Karen Harrison and Bernadette Rainey.
© 2013 John Wiley & Sons, Ltd. Published 2013 by John Wiley & Sons, Ltd.

responsibilities (*Re J* [1991] FCR 193: 225). Commentators on the ethics of expert evidence agree with the judges that the central duties of experts are to give opinions that are both sincerely held and rationally justifiable, to be open about the limitations of their expertise, and not to encroach upon the roles constitutionally allocated to judges and juries (Melton and Limber, 1989; Hardwig, 1994; Lavin and Sales, 1998; Sanders, 2007). The law of evidence and the ethics of expertise are complementary and closely related attempts to define the proper relationship between experts and the courts. Much of the law contained in judicial decisions, rules of procedure and practice directions is designed to remind experts of their ethical obligations (as interpreted by the judiciary) rather than to restrict their evidence by rigid rules, and where relatively rigid limits are set on what experts can say (particularly in the criminal courts) these too are intended to prevent experts from exceeding their ethically appropriate role. Accordingly, this chapter does not make a sharp distinction between law and ethics but treats both together as a single body of (sometimes conflicting) guidance for experts and the courts. Although the law discussed is that of England and Wales the ethical dimension of the discussion will, it is hoped, be of interest to readers from other jurisdictions. (For an excellent comparative study of some of these issues in common-law jurisdictions, see Hoyano and Keenan, 2007.)

The first part of the chapter discusses the admissibility of expert evidence, focusing particularly on an issue of particular relevance to sexual offenses, that of expert evidence of the credibility of witnesses. The second part discusses the ethical duties of expert witnesses and the way in which these are instantiated in the procedural rules of the English and Welsh courts. Finally, the chapter discusses the tensions that may exist between the duties of experts as witnesses and their duties to their patients or clients.

Admissibility of Expert Evidence

The basic principle that decisions about legally significant facts are for judges and juries rather than experts is reflected, particularly in the criminal courts, in a fear that letting experts give certain kinds of evidence will lead to their "usurping the role of the jury" – or more accurately to the jury abdicating their proper role by uncritically deferring to the experts. As Lord Justice Lawton put it in the leading case of *R* v. *Turner* ([1975] QB 834: 842), "trial by psychiatrists" must not be allowed "to take the place of trial by jury and magistrates."

In *R* v. *Ugoh* ([2001] EWCA Crim 1381), the three defendants were charged with the rape of a woman who was very drunk; their defense was that she consented to intercourse, or alternatively that they believed she consented. A psychopharmacologist gave evidence that her level of intoxication was such that she would not have been able to give informed consent, and it would have been obvious to anyone that she was too confused to consent. On the defendants' appeal against conviction, the Court of Appeal held that it was not inherently objectionable for the expert to testify to the so-called "ultimate issue," that is, to say that one of the elements of the offense of rape, lack of consent, had been present. He ought not, however, to have testified about what "anyone who was with her" would have been able to judge about her mental state. That was a matter for the jury to assess, taking into account what the expert could tell them about her likely behavior. (Today, under the Sexual Offences Act 2003, s1(1)(c), the question is whether the defendant *reasonably* believed the complainant consented, which is even more clearly a question for the jury rather than the expert.) Moreover, where expert testimony on an "ultimate issue" was admitted, it was vital for the judge to make clear to the jury that they were not bound by the expert's opinion, and it was primarily the judge's failure to do this that led the Court of Appeal to quash the conviction.

Expert evidence of witness credibility

The criminal courts' anxiety to shield juries from the temptation to let experts decide key issues for them is particularly evident in respect of questions of credibility, that is, the likelihood that a witness's evidence is a true account of events. The defendant in the leading case of *R v. Robinson* ((1994) 98 Cr App R 370) was charged with rape and indecent assault on a "very backward" 15-year-old girl. An educational psychologist who had administered IQ tests to the girl testified that she "remembers important matters quite well . . . She could not adopt ideas from someone else. She would have difficulties taking them on board and relating them . . . She is not suggestible . . . Her imagination is limited" (373). The Court of Appeal held that this evidence ought not to have been admitted: "the Crown cannot call a witness of fact and then, without more, call a psychologist or psychiatrist to give reasons why the jury should regard that witness as reliable" (374). Such evidence was admissible only to rebut a defense case that the witness was unreliable owing to some mental or physical abnormality.

Though the Court of Appeal did not explain its decision very clearly, it appears quite justifiable on its particular facts. So far as one can tell from the report, the psychologist had tested the complainant for her IQ, not for suggestibility. It is not easy to discern from the report what the basis for her opinion was, and it would probably not have been easy for the jury to assess the reliability of her evidence either. Rather than helping the jury, such evidence complicates their task. Not only do they have to assess the credibility of a girl with a severe learning disability, they also have to assess the credibility of a psychologist's assessment of her credibility (Ward, 2009). In other cases, however, expert evidence may be more helpful.

For example, in *R v. S (VJ)* ([2006] EWCA Crim 2389) the defendant was charged with a number of sexual offenses against a 13-year-old autistic girl. The prosecution called an expert in the treatment of autism who said that her behavior and demeanor during her videotaped police interview:

> was by no means unusual or surprising and it must be regarded against the background of her autistic condition. Further, the doctor was invited to give the jury some general information about autism, which included her view that somebody who functioned at the level of N would find it difficult to invent a story such as had been given by her to the police and eventually had been filmed on video, and if she had been able to invent it, to be able to retain it in her memory for any significant period of time. (para. 9)

Although this evidence was quite similar to that given in *Robinson,* the Court of Appeal held that the trial judge had been right to admit it. Again, the reasoning behind the decision is not very clear, but the decision seems a sensible one on its facts. Unlike *Robinson,* the basis of the expert's opinion is relatively easy to discern – namely, the body of psychological knowledge of autism together with an assessment of the child's condition. For a jury unfamiliar with autism this would have been important information, even though by talking about "a child who functioned at the level of N" the expert clearly indicated her opinion of N's own credibility. If the decision about admissibility is seen as a balancing exercise between the reliability of the expert evidence and its helpfulness to the jury on the one hand, and the risk of unwarranted deference by the jury on the other, it is easy to understand why the balance came down differently in the two superficially similar cases (Ward, 2009).

It has been suggested that expert evidence might help juries to understand the reasons for delay in reporting sexual offenses to the police and disabuse them of other "rape myths" (Office for Criminal Justice Reform, 2006: 16–21; Temkin and Krahé, 2008). The Court of Appeal has, however, preferred to rely on judicial directions on these matters (*R* v. *Doody* [2008] EWCA Crim 2394). In a recent unreported decision dealing with historic allegations of sexual assault, Hughes LJ said unless there was "something very unusual" about the case, "expert evidence of this kind is simply unnecessary" (*R* v. *ER* 2010, quoted by Rook and Ward, 2010: 882, para. 20.19). Research with mock jurors in child sexual assault cases indicates that both jury directions and expert evidence can be effective in countering misconceptions (Goodman-Delahunty, Cossins and O'Brien, 2011), but whether the present model directions (Judicial Studies Board, 2010: 357–362) will have this effect seems doubtful. They tell the jury that they should put "aside any view as to what [they] might or might not have expected to hear"; that "demeanour in court is not necessarily a clue to the truth of the witness's account"; and that consistent accounts are not necessarily true or inconsistent accounts untrue – in short, that nothing a jury might traditionally have been expected to rely on in deciding which of two conflicting accounts to believe can be relied on at all. Though the intention appears to be to make juries more willing to convict, the effect of taking this advice seriously could well be the very opposite. More case-specific insights from an expert witness might be more helpful, but would carry the risk of undue deference.

Another issue in cases of historic sexual abuse is the reliability of adults' recall of abuse they claim to have experienced as children many years earlier. As it is usually the defense that wants to call expert evidence on this point, *Robinson*'s strictures about calling an expert to bolster the credibility of one's own witness do not apply. The question here is whether the accuracy of apparently vivid memories of childhood experiences long ago is a matter that juries are able to assess for themselves, or whether they need the assistance of an expert.

In *R* v. *H (Childhood Amnesia)* ([2005] EWCA Crim 1828, [2006] 1 Cr App R 10), the Court of Appeal accepted that expert evidence was admissible "in those rare cases in which the complainant provides a description of very early events which appears to contain an unrealistic amount of detail" (para. 47). In *R* v. *S (Jonathan)* ([2006] EWCA Crim 1404) the Court emphasized that "save where there is evidence of mental disability or learning difficulties, attempts to persuade the court to admit such evidence should be scrutinised with very great care" (para. 26). Expert evidence was held inadmissible where an adult was recalling events that had occurred between the ages of six and eight and where the memories were characterized by a lack of detail rather than an excessive amount of it, and where another complainant was recalling a history of abuse throughout her childhood that had started earlier than she could remember. The evidence of the expert (Professor Martin Conway, who also testified in *R* v. *H*) troubled the Court because it raised doubts about the accuracy of memory *in general*, while at the same time acknowledging the limited ability of memory research in its current state to help courts with the "very practical issue" of sorting out true from false memories (quoted at para. 17). Such evidence is difficult for the legal system to accept, since it can only operate on the assumption that past events can be ascertained "beyond reasonable doubt" on the basis of memories narrated by witnesses. Professor Conway's skepticism may well have been overstated (Brewin, 2006: 102); but in rejecting expert evidence in all but exceptional cases, the Court of Appeal comes close to the dangerously complacent attitude voiced by Judge Keith Cutler in a radio documentary on historic sexual abuse trials:

> You have twelve people there [the jurors], brought from all walks of life. They know about memory, about what one can remember back ten, twenty years and what one can't, and if twelve of them believe that what a witness is saying is accurate and is honest and they can rely on it, then they will go forward from there. If they don't believe that that's the case, then they'll dismiss it. It's the jury who are, in many ways, the experts of memory. (*File on 4*, 2011: 15)

Taken at face value, this claim about jurors' expertise is quite implausible. It assumes not only that jurors know what they or others can *seem* to remember from childhood, but that they know whether those memories are accurate. They could know that only if they had checked a reasonably large sample of such memories against a reliable independent source. Such a body of experience of demonstrably true or false long-term memories must be rare indeed.

A more realistic view is that most people tend to treat their own memories and the testimony of others as "innocent until proven guilty" (Brandom, 1994: 177) – to assume that apparently sincere accounts of vivid memories are true until they are given reason to doubt them. But particularly in historic abuse cases, this metaphorical presumption of innocence clashes with the legal presumption of innocence on the part of the person whose misdeeds are supposedly being remembered. A defendant ought to be able to adduce any evidence that is capable of rationally persuading a jury to entertain a reasonable doubt of his guilt. It is vital, however, that such evidence has a rational basis and, particularly in such an uncertain and controversial area as memory research, acknowledges the range of scholarly views and the limitations of current knowledge (Brewin, 2006: 101–103). We return to these issues below.

The recent case of *R* v. *Eden* ([2011] EWCA Crim 1690) appears to open up a way around the restriction on evidence of credibility in some cases. A girl referred to as "C" alleged that she had been repeatedly sexual abused by the defendant between the age of 10 and 15. A clinical psychologist who examined C reported that "although she does not meet the criteria of PTSD in response to a single event, the presentation is consistent with a PTSD reaction called type two trauma" (quoted at para. 11). Eden appealed against his conviction on the ground that this was evidence of credibility that infringed the *Robinson* ruling. The Court of Appeal decided, however, that, "although the learned judge did not approach the matter in this way in his ruling, admissibility could have been . . . justified on the grounds that it provided evidence of psychological injury in exactly the same way as any doctor might give evidence of physical injury consistent with a particular allegation" (para. 14). It was then for the jury to decide whether the "injury" in question was caused by prolonged abuse or whether it could be explained as a reaction to marital disharmony between Mr Eden and C's mother.

This distinction between "credibility" and "psychological injury" would not have been so easy to draw if the psychologist had diagnosed PTSD in response to a single event of abuse, with the flashbacks or other intrusive recollections characteristic of PTSD. Such a diagnosis would strongly imply that she really had experienced an event similar to the one she described. Would it thereby infringe the *Robinson* principle?

The "psychological injury" theory advanced in *Eden* is correct in the sense that evidence of PTSD is directly probative of abuse in a way the kind of evidence given in *Robinson* is not. If the scientific basis of the diagnosis is sound, then a real traumatic experience provides the best explanation of the symptoms, and the symptoms are more likely to occur if the patient experienced that event than if she did not. The probative value of the evidence must, however, be balanced against the risk that the jury will focus on the psychologist's assessment of C's account as truthful, rather than on their own assessment of C's evidence in court and its testing by cross-examination. To assess where the balance lies requires an assessment of the probative value of the psychologist's method of diagnosis and the theory underlying it. We shall return to this point below.

The contrast between the criminal and family courts in their attitude to evidence of credibility is striking. In *Re M and R* ([1996] 4 All ER 239) the Court of Appeal (Civil Division) decided that there was no objection to such evidence in the civil courts. In *Re R (Children) (Sexual Abuse: Standard of Proof)* ([1990] 1 FCR 86), Thorpe LJ said that such evidence was "invariably . . . accorded great respect and weight" (para. 19), but that the trial judge had accorded it insufficient weight in accepting that a child's complaint proved on the balance of probabilities that abuse had occurred, despite a child psychiatrist's estimate that there was only a 25% chance that the child's account was accurate. Thorpe LJ gave no reason other than "respect" for the psychiatrist for believing that she could reliably estimate the probability that the child's account was true. By contrast, Baker J in *A London Borough Council* v. *K* ([2009] EWHC 850) observed:

> veracity or validity assessments have a limited role to play in family proceedings. They are, so far as I am aware, unused in criminal proceedings in this country, and I see strong arguments for imposing restrictions on their use in family cases as well . . . [T]here is a danger that some courts, faced with these difficult decisions, will subconsciously defer to the apparent expert . . . The ultimate judge of veracity, i.e. where the truth lies, is the judge and the judge alone. He cannot delegate that decision to any expert. I

acknowledge that a child psychiatrist . . . may be able to point out some features of a
child's account that add or detract from authenticity . . . But, in my experience, many
of these features should be obvious to judges in any event. (para. 162)

This suggests that the gulf between the civil and criminal courts' views of credibility
evidence may be narrowing.

Reliability of expert evidence

English judges do not, in general, scrutinize the basis of expert evidence closely
to determine whether it should be admitted. There is no equivalent of the "gatekeeping" role propounded by the US Supreme Court in *Daubert* v. *Merrell Dow
Pharmaceuticals* (509 S.Ct. 2786 (1993)) requiring the judge to examine such
matters as whether the theory on which an expert relies has been subjected to testing
and peer review. This can result in convictions being based on untested and controversial theories. For example, in *R* v. *A (Michael David)* ([2006] EWCA Crim 905)
the prosecution relied upon the evidence of a colorectal surgeon as to various abnormalities of the complainant's anus and rectal area, which he construed as indicative
of anal penetration. In a subsequent family case where the same surgeon gave similar
evidence, the judge commented that the connections he drew between rectal findings
were made "without any peer review or testing whatever . . . To accept . . . evidence . . . based on his opinions developed by him in entire isolation from the pae-
diatric community and quite unconsidered by them would, in my judgment, be to
border on the reckless" (quoted in *R* v. *A* (2006), para. 11). In the light of this and
other evidence casting doubt on the surgeon's methods, Michael A's conviction was
quashed.

In a recent report, the Law Commission (2010) proposes a new statutory test
of whether expert evidence is sufficiently reliable to be admitted in criminal proceedings. Whether the expert's theory had been adequately tested and subjected to peer
review would be among the matters judges were required to take into account. For
the time being, however, the law remains that above the low threshold required to
establish that the evidence is relevant, its reliability is a matter of weight (*R* v. *Luttrell*
[2004] EWCA Crim 1344, [2004] 2 Cr App R 31). It is for the jury in a criminal
trial, or the judge in civil proceedings, to decide the extent to which any weaknesses
in the expert evidence identified by cross-examination or by other witnesses reduced the
reliance that can be placed upon it.

The concern that we noted in relation to credibility evidence, that juries might be
unduly deferential to expert testimony, is much less apparent in decisions on medical
and forensic science evidence. Here, considerable faith is placed in the ability of juries,
with appropriate guidance from the judge (*R* v. *Henderson* [2010] EWCA Crim
1269, [2010] 2 Cr App R 24) to reach rational conclusions about the reliance to be
placed on expert evidence. The contrasting treatment of the two types of expert
evidence makes sense if the overriding aim of the law is to preserve the jury's role as
decision maker. In the case of credibility evidence, the perceived danger is that the
expert will become the effective decision maker as to whether the complainant is
credible. In the case of scientific or medical evidence, an enhanced "gatekeeping"

role would give the judge, rather than the jury, the power to decide whether the expert is credible – and, where expert evidence is crucial to the prosecution, whether the defendant should be acquitted. In principle there is a good deal to be said for the view that the weight of expert evidence should be assessed by the jury, but it places a heavy responsibility on both the lawyers and the experts to ensure that the jury is fully informed about the strengths and weaknesses of the grounds on which the expert's opinion is based. In this context the ethics of expert witnessing assume crucial importance.

Ethical and Legal Duties of Expert Witnesses

It is uncontroversial that the first duty of a witness is to tell the truth, although a professional's duty as a witness may clash with her other obligations, for example, as a doctor or simply as a caring human being. Telling "the whole truth" is not such a simple matter in the case of an expert witness as it might appear to be for an ordinary witness of fact. Witnesses of fact state what they remember having seen or heard. They may also draw certain inferences, for example, about a person's identity or emotional state, using methods that any judge or juror is presumably able to understand. The distinguishing feature of expert evidence is that the expert draws inferences using methods with which judges and jurors are not assumed to be familiar. The expert puts these forward as sound inferences that the judge or jury may rely upon. The expert's duty is not simply to say what she sincerely believes, but to put forward only inferences that are justified by the relevant data and the state of knowledge in her field (Lavin and Sales, 1998). Given the reliance that others will place on their testimony, it "is unethical for expert witnesses to hold or express unjustified beliefs" (Sanders, 2007: 1542).

English law now provides considerable guidance for experts within the Civil, Criminal and Family Procedure Rules and accompanying practice directions. These rules and directions, which draw on pronouncements from case law, codify the ethical duties of experts to ensure that their opinions are justified, and to provide the court with the information it needs in order to assess whether they are justified. No specific penalty is attached to breach of these rules. A "reckless" disregard of them may lead to an expert being held liable for costs incurred as a result (*Phillips* v. *Symes* [2004] EWHC 2330 (Ch), [2005] 1 WLR 2043), but the main sanction for breach of an expert's duties is censure by the judge, which if it becomes known in the legal world will damage the expert's credibility in any future case.

Objectivity

Rule 33.2 of the Criminal Procedure Rules (Crim PR) sets out the first duty of the expert:

> An expert must help the court to achieve the overriding objective [of dealing with cases justly] by giving objective, unbiased opinion on matters within his expertise.

What does it mean for expert evidence to be "objective"? Kramer (2007: 2, 46–7) distinguishes two aspects of epistemic objectivity: "transindividual discernibility" and impartiality. In the first sense, an expert's evidence is objective if it reports what any competent expert would be likely to report – or if it does not, it explains the divergence in a way with which all competent experts could agree. In the second sense, objectivity or impartiality requires that experts' evidence should not be colored by anything that is at stake for them in the proceedings. There is a tension between this demand for impartiality and the compassion that any decent person is likely to feel for the apparent victim of a serious sexual offense, or for someone they believe to be falsely accused. Compassion, as Nussbaum (2001: 319) argues, involves a judgment that another person's suffering is significant in relation to one's own goals and ends; it affords a motive to do what one can to alleviate the other's suffering. Compassionate experts, then, do have something at stake in proceedings which they take to involve victims of abuse or falsely accused defendants or parents. Particularly in the case of children, Ryder J has acknowledged "the inevitable partiality of social and health care witnesses towards a child who is in their professional care" (*Oldham MBC* v. *GW* [2007] 2 FLR 597, para. 97). It may be for this reason that the Family Proceedings Rules, despite their exacting requirements of expert witnesses (discussed below), do not explicitly demand that their evidence be "objective."

What experts undoubtedly should do, as far as possible, is to exclude their desire for a particular outcome of the case from influencing their evidence. It is certainly unethical, for example, knowingly to make exaggerated statements about the symptoms suffered by (supposed) victims of sexual abuse in order to gain for them the compensation one believes they deserve (*Lillie and Reed* v. *Newcastle City Council* [2002] EWHC 1600 (QB), paras. 73, 392–394). But more is demanded of experts than merely stating what they believe to be true; they must also be open about any factors that count against those beliefs (*Re R (Expert's Evidence)* [1991] 1 FLR 291). In other words they must tell the court of the reasons favoring what they believe to be the wrong conclusion as well as the right one. This is part of what Candilis, Weinstock and Martinez (2007: 21) call the duty of transparency.

Transparency

Expert witnesses have a duty not only to state opinions that are justified but to state the basis of those opinions in a way that enables the court to make its own assessment of the reliance it can place on them. The ethical duty of transparency has three aspects, all of which are reflected in the rules of the English courts.

The first aspect is *transparency as to the basis of the expert's evidence*. Crim PR r. 33.3 requires an expert's report to:

(a) give details of any literature or other information which the expert has relied on in making the report;
(b) contain a statement setting out the substance of all facts given to the expert which are material to the opinions expressed in the report, or upon which those opinions are based;

(c) make clear which of the facts stated in the report are within the expert's own knowledge.

These requirements reflect the logic of appeals to expert opinion (Hardwig, 1994; Ward, 2006).

When an expert is testifying about matters beyond the knowledge of the court, the court may have to accept the expert's conclusions without independently evaluating the reasoning on which it is based. In this situation it must rely on factors such as the expert's skill and experience and the existence of an accepted body of knowledge to infer that the expert probably does have good reasons for what she asserts, even if the court does not fully understand what the reasons are. Where the expert is relying not on specialized observations but on matters that the court is equally, or more, competent to assess, this kind of deference to expert authority has no place. The expert must make it clear when this is the case, not only so that the court can avoid unwarranted deference but also so that it can avoid, in effect, taking account of the same evidence twice. For example, it is dangerously misleading to put forward physical findings as independent confirmation of allegations or behavioral signs of abuse when in fact a doctor is interpreting ambiguous physical findings in light of those very allegations or signs (*Lillie and Reed* v. *Newcastle City Council* [2002] EWHC 1600 (QB), paras. 395–396).

The second aspect is *transparency as to disagreement within the expert community*. One of the reasons that may induce a court to accept an inference drawn by an expert is that it derives from premises that the whole community of experts accepts. If a community of experts reaches consensus or near-consensus on certain matters, this is an indicator, albeit not an infallible one, that belief in those matters is warranted (Haack, 2007: 251). One of the problems facing the court is that it will usually be dependent on the expert witnesses themselves to tell it whether a consensus exists: so it is important that experts do not give a misleading impression on this point. One of Hardwig's (1994: 92) ethical "maxims for experts" is that "When the community of expert opinion is divided, there is an obligation to say that it is." Or as the Crim PR r. 33.3(1)(f) puts it:

where there is a range of opinion on the matters dealt with in the report, [the report must] –

summarise the range of opinion, and

give reasons for his own opinion.

The third aspect is *transparency as to areas of uncertainty and conflicting evidence*. The Practice Direction on expert evidence in the family courts states that an expert report should, in addition to summarizing the range of opinions:

(ii) identify and explain, within the range of opinions, any "unknown cause," whether arising from the facts of the case (for example, because there is too little information to form a scientific opinion) or from limited experience or lack of research, peer review or support in the relevant field of expertise;

(iii) give reasons for any opinion expressed: the use of a balance sheet approach to the factors that support or undermine an opinion can be of great assistance to the court. (Practice Direction 25A, 2011: para. 3.3(f))

The Criminal Procedure Rules are less explicit about the duty to inform the court about limitations of research and factors that undermine the expert's own opinion, saying only that "if the expert is not able to give his opinion without qualification, [his report must] state the qualification" (Crim PR r. 33.3(1)(g)). But there can be no doubt of the ethical importance of this duty in the criminal context, particularly where the limitations of research may afford grounds for reasonable doubt – even if the experts personally have no doubt about their conclusions. Failure to mention such factors may be harmful to the complainant as well as the defendant, if it ultimately leads to a conviction being quashed and a retrial ordered. In *R v. T (Martin)* ([2008] EWCA Crim 3229), experts instructed by the prosecution and defense prepared a joint report confidently asserting that the appearance of a girl's vagina and hymen "show that the vagina has been penetrated by an object the size of an erect penis on a number of occasions" (quoted at para. 10), but failed to mention that very little was known about the frequency of similar characteristics in non-abused pre-pubertal girls. The court was reluctant to put the girl through the ordeal of testifying again, and decided that she had been such an impressive witness at the trial that the conviction could be considered safe despite the unduly "dogmatic" expert evidence.

Conflicts of Duty: "Wearing Two Hats"

The expert witness's duties of objectivity and transparency are not easy to reconcile with the role of therapist. The ethical objections to a therapist appearing as an expert witness in a case involving her patient are threefold. First, it may be difficult to combine the objectivity of a witness with the empathy of a therapist:

> treatment in psychotherapy is brought about through an empathic relationship that has no place in, and is unlikely to survive, the questioning and public reporting of a forensic evaluation. To assume either role in a particular case is to compromise one's capacity to fulfil the other. (Strasburger, Gutheil and Brodsky, 1997: 449)

Secondly, a therapist's primary duty is to the interests of the patient, a witness's is to the court, and these duties are liable to collide (Pruett and Solnit, 1998). In particular, where the client is present in court, the witness may have to give evidence that is harmful or traumatic to the client (Berger, 1979; Strasburger, Gutheil and Brodsky, 1997), or damaging to the therapeutic relationship (Bond, 2002). Thirdly, giving evidence may conflict with the duty of confidentiality.

In *Re B (Sexual Abuse: Expert's Report)* ([2000] 1 FLR 871: 872), Thorpe LJ observed that it "ought to be elementary for any professional working in the family justice system that the role of the expert to treat is not to be muddled with the role of the expert to report." The particular problem in *Re B* was that the therapist had obtained details of the alleged abuse through methods of interviewing that might have been appropriate for therapeutic purposes but flagrantly contravened the guidelines for interviewing witnesses in a criminal investigation. She was an inappropriate expert witness because her report was based on unreliable hearsay evidence and because, at the point where the solicitor acting for the mother of the allegedly abused child instructed her to prepare a report for the court, she had already made up her mind.

These are important considerations in relation to psychiatric or psychological evidence, but they do not apply to every expert who has treated an alleged victim or offender. In *Oldham MBC* v. *GW* ([2007] 2 FLR 597), which concerned an allegation of non-accidental injury, both Wall LJ in the Court of Appeal (*W* v. *Oldham MBC* [2006] 1 FLR 543) and Ryder J in the subsequent rehearing in the High Court, rejected the proposition that it was generally inappropriate for treating clinicians giving evidence. It was in this context that Ryder J made the remark quoted above about the "inevitable partiality" of experts with responsibility for children. He went on to say that such partiality was not a matter for criticism, but simply a factor for the judge to consider in weighing the expert's evidence. The distinction between treatment and therapy was, he suggested, particularly important in the field of mental health because of the complex nature of the doctor–patient relationship in areas such as treatment for sexual abuse, but treating experts could often provide valuable evidence and the courts should not discourage them from giving it (*Oldham MBC* v. *GW* [2007] 2 FLR 597: paras. 97–8).

It seems that from a legal point of view what is objectionable is not "wearing two hats" *per se,* but rather giving expert evidence that is based on unreliable hearsay, or biased in ways that are concealed from the court. From an ethical point of view what is important is whether giving the most honest and objective possible evidence is compatible with the therapeutic interests of a particular patient and with maintaining confidentiality. The courts will very rarely compel anyone to give expert evidence (*Seyfang* v. *Searle* [1973] QB 148), but declining to testify as an expert witness does not guarantee that a doctor or therapist will be able to maintain confidentiality. Although not strictly a matter of expert evidence this is such an important legal and ethical issue related to sexual offenses that it merits consideration here.

Confidentiality and patient records

Doctors and therapists should be aware that even if they do not give expert evidence, their notes of confidential information given by patients may find their way to court as a result of disclosure in criminal proceedings. According to Bond (2002: 138), clients often sign a form authorizing release of records after a prolonged period of interviews and medical examinations, and having been told that no prosecution will be considered unless they do consent. The records may be used by the prosecution as evidence of a complaint, or by the defense in order to discredit the complainant.

As a result of an amendment to the Criminal Justice Act 2003 s120, by the Coroners and Justice Act 2009, evidence of a complaint by the victim of any offense is now admissible regardless of how long after the alleged offense the complaint was made. Moreover, s120(8) of the 2003 Act expressly provides that "the fact that the complaint was elicited (for example, by a leading question) is irrelevant [to its admissibility] unless a threat or a promise was involved." The intention behind this provision was to narrow the common law rule that an alleged victim's previous complaint was admissible only if it was "spontaneous" (Durston, 2005: 212–213), but it also appears to render admissible statements obtained by the sort of therapeutic interviewing techniques that would not be an acceptable basis for expert evidence. Such a statement is admissible under s120 only if the complainant gives evidence that to the best of her belief the statement is true (s120(4)(b)). The fact that the complainant's present account was first elicited by a therapist's leading questions may be more helpful to the defense than to the prosecution; but the judge has power to exclude the evidence on grounds of unfairness to the defendant under the Police and Criminal Evidence Act 1984 s78.

The second use of confidential records is by the defense to discredit the complainant. This may be on the basis that the complainant's statements to a doctor or therapist are inconsistent with her current evidence, or it may be sought to admit them as "sexual history" evidence under one of the exceptions to the general bar on such evidence in the Youth Justice and Criminal Evidence Act 1999 s41, for example, to explain a young witness's knowledge of sexual matters or to provide an alternative explanation for physical findings (see Hoyano and Keenan, 2007).

Although English law does not afford doctor-patient or psychotherapist-patient communications any privilege against disclosure in court, the courts are obliged to respect patients' and clients' rights to privacy under Article 8 of the European Convention on Human Rights. This is recognized in the Disclosure Protocol:

> Victims do not waive the confidentiality of their medical records, or their right to privacy under article 8 of the ECHR, by the mere fact of making a complaint against the accused. Judges should be alert to balance the rights of victims against the real and proven needs of the defence. The court, as a public authority, must ensure that any interference with the article 8 rights of those entitled to privacy is in accordance with the law and necessary in pursuit of a legitimate public interest. (Court of Appeal, 2006: para. 62)

In addition, it has long been recognized that social services records about children are covered by public interest immunity, and any disclosure of them requires careful balancing of the interests of social services, the child and the defense (*Re M (A Minor) (Disclosure of Material)* [1990] 2 FLR 36; *R v. J (DC)* [2010] EWCA Crim 385, [2010] 2 Cr App R 2).

Issues of privacy do not arise in the same way when an interview is being conducted for the purposes of preparing a report for the court. In *R v. Elleray* ([2003] EWCA Crim 553, [2003] 2 Cr App R 11) the defendant had pleaded guilty to indecent assault on a woman but in interviews with probation officers he admitted that he had in fact raped the same woman several times when she was drunk. He was convicted of rape solely on the basis of these admissions. Lord Woolf CJ pointed out that it was the probation officers' duty to give a full and frank assessment of the risk posed by the defendant and they could not do this without mentioning the other offenses to which he had admitted; but he went on to say that in such cases the prosecution should carefully consider whether it was in the public interest to prosecute the defendant and the judge should consider whether to exclude the evidence under the Police and Criminal Evidence Act 1984 s78, bearing in mind the need to promote openness between probation officers and their clients and the fact that interviews with probation officers were not attended with the same safeguards as those with police.

Conclusion

English law in both the criminal and family courts puts its faith in juries and judges to determine whether a sexual offense has taken place, and in so doing to decide for themselves what weight to place on expert evidence. This makes it essential that expert witnesses state opinions that can be rationally justified and are open with the court about the limitations of their expertise and about any factors that could support a different conclusion. The ethical demands that the law makes on expert witnesses are quite onerous, both because objectivity in such an emotive area as sexual offending is hard to achieve, and because experts' duties to the court may conflict with their duties to clients or with their desire to achieve what they believe is a just outcome. Ultimately, however, it is the courts rather than the experts that are the arbiters of justice.

Acknowledgment

Thanks to Paul Roberts for his comments on a draft of this chapter.

References

Berger, L.S. (1979) "Expert clinical testimony and professional ethics," *Journal of Psychiatry and Law* 7, 347–357.

Bond, T. (2002) "The law of confidentiality – a solution or part of the problem?," in P. Jenkins (ed.), *Legal Issues in Counselling and Psychotherapy*. London: Sage, pp. 123–143.

Brandom, R. (1994) *Making it Explicit: Reasoning, Representation and Discursive Commitment.* Cambridge, MA: Harvard University Press.

Brewin, C. (2006) "Recovered memory and false memory," in A. Heaton-Armstrong, E. Shepherd, G. Gudjonsson and D. Wolchover (eds), *Witness Testimony: Psychological, Investigative and Evidential Perspectives.* Oxford: Oxford University Press, pp. 89–104.

Candilis, P.J., Weinstock, R.L. and Martinez, R. (2007) *Forensic Ethics and the Expert Witness.* New York: Springer.

Court of Appeal (2006) Disclosure: A Protocol for the Control and Management of Unused Material in the Crown Court, http://www.judiciary.gov.uk/Resources/JCO/Documents/Protocols/crown_courts_disclosure.pdf (accessed August 25, 2012).

Durston, G. (2005) "Previous (in)consistent statements after the Criminal Justice Act 2003," *Criminal Law Review* March, 206–214.

File on 4 (2011) Memory on Trial, broadcast 29 March, transcript available at http://news.bbc.co.uk/1/shared/bsp/hi/pdfs/29_03_11_fo4_memory.pdf (accessed August 25, 2012).

Goodman-Delahunty, J., Cossins, A. and O'Brien, K. (2011) "A comparison of expert evidence and judicial directions to counter misconceptions in child sexual abuse trials," *Australian & New Zealand Journal of Criminology* 44, 2, 196–217.

Haack, S. (2007) *Defending Science – Within Reason.* Amherst, NY: Prometheus.

Hardwig, J. (1994) "Toward an ethics of expertise," in D. Wueste (ed.), *Professional Ethics and Social Responsibility.* Lanham, MD: Rowman & Littlefield, pp. 83–102.

Hoyano, L. and Keenan, C. (2007) *Child Abuse: Law and Policy across Boundaries.* Oxford: Oxford University Press.

Judicial Studies Board (2010) Crown Court Bench Book: Directing the Jury, http://www.judiciary.gov.uk/publications-and-reports/judicial-college/Pre+2011/crown-court-bench-book-directing-the-jury (accessed August 25, 2012).

Kramer, M. (2007) *Objectivity and the Rule of Law.* Cambridge: Cambridge University Press.

Lavin, M. and Sales, B.D. (1998) "Moral justifications for limits on expert testimony," in S.J. Ceci and H. Hembrooke (eds), *Expert Witnesses in Child Abuse Cases: What Can and Should be Said in Court.* Washington, DC: American Psychological Association, pp. 59–81.

Law Commission (2010) Expert Evidence in Criminal Proceedings (Law Com no. 325), http://www.justice.gov.uk/lawcommission/docs/lc325_Expert_Evidence_Report.pdf (accessed August 25, 2012).

Melton, G.B. and Limber, S. (1989) "Psychologists' involvement in cases of child maltreatment: limits of role and expertise," *American Psychologist* 44, 9, 1225–1233.

Nussbaum, M.C. (2001) *Upheavals of Thought: The Intelligence of Emotions.* Cambridge: Cambridge University Press.

Office for Criminal Justice Reform (2006) *Convicting Rapists and Protecting Victims – Justice for Victims of Rape.* London: Author.

Practice Direction 25A – Experts and Assessors in Family Proceedings (2011) http://www.justice.gov.uk/guidance/courts-and-tribunals/courts/procedure-rules/family/practice_directions/pd_part_25a (accessed August 25, 2012).

Pruett, K.D. and Solnit, A.J. (1998) "Psychological and ethical considerations in the preparation of the mental health professional as expert witness," in S.J. Ceci and H. Hembrooke (eds), *Expert Witnesses in Child Abuse Cases: What Can and Should be Said in Court.* Washington, DC: American Psychological Association, pp. 123–135.

Rook, P. and Ward, R. (2010) *Sexual Offences: Law and Practice,* 4th edn. London: Sweet & Maxwell.

Sanders, J. (2007) "Expert witness ethics," *Fordham Law Review* 76, 1535–1584.

Strasburger, L.H., Gutheil, T.D. and Brodsky, A. (1997) "On wearing two hats: role conflict in serving as both psychotherapist and expert witness," *American Journal of Psychiatry* 154, 4, 448–456.

Temkin, J. and Krahé, B. (2008) *Sexual Assault and the Justice Gap.* Oxford: Hart.

Ward, T. (2006) "English law's epistemology of expert testimony," *Journal of Law and Society* 33, 4, 572–595.

Ward, T. (2009) "Usurping the role of the jury? Expert evidence and witness credibility in English criminal trials," *International Journal of Evidence and Proof* 13, 83–101.

6

Ethical Issues in Sex Offender Research

Tony Ward and Gwenda Willis

Introduction

Forensic and correctional practitioners are typically well aware of ethical problems emerging from their work with offenders, and are equipped with an array of strategies to deal with them effectively (Bush, Connell and Denny, 2006; Haag, 2006). Although it is possible to question the depth of ethical reflection engaged in by clinicians, there is no question that they are familiar with issues such as dual relationships, problems of consent, limits of confidentiality, and duty to warn (Ward and Syversen, 2009; see Chapter 16). However, when it comes to the ethical dimension of forensic and correctional *research* the silence is almost deafening. There is almost a complete lack of sustained analysis and debate concerning the common and unique ethical challenges facing researchers in these domains. The relative invisibility of ethical matters in this arena is well illustrated by the fact that an otherwise excellent recent text by Rosenfeld and Penrod (2011) on research in forensic contexts does not contain a separate chapter on ethical issues. Similarly, a useful paper overviewing the difficulties of conducting research in correctional contexts does not deal with the attendant ethical problems in any meaningful sense at all (Waki *et al.*, 2009). In fact, aside from the edited text by Adshead and Brown (2003) on ethical topics in forensic mental health research, and our own chapter and paper on correctional and forensic research (Ward and Willis, 2010, 2012), we are not aware of any substantive, recent treatment of the subject. This is somewhat astonishing given the importance of such a topic and raises the obvious question, why is there such a poverty of empirical and theoretical work? Perhaps theorists do not believe there are any essential differences between social science, medical and forensic/correctional research, and therefore there is little point in providing specialist analyses, or perhaps it is because the status

The Wiley-Blackwell Handbook of Legal and Ethical Aspects of Sex Offender Treatment and Management, First Edition. Edited by Karen Harrison and Bernadette Rainey.
© 2013 John Wiley & Sons, Ltd. Published 2013 by John Wiley & Sons, Ltd.

of offenders is so low that their interests are viewed as being of lower priority that those of the people research is intended to benefit.

Whatever the reasons for the comparative absence of commentary, it is apparent that the topic is an important one and merits serious discussion. Offenders are a vulnerable population who struggle to have their voices heard by policy makers and the public. There are legitimate concerns that they are subject to human rights violations and that their location within the criminal justice system may blind people to their justified ethical claims (Ward and Birgden, 2007). Individuals convicted of serious crimes are frequently incarcerated and subject to severe curtailment, even forfeiture of their freedom and welfare entitlements. To make matters worse, the harsh conditions encountered in prisons may make it more difficult for individuals competently to evaluate the risks and benefits of participating in research projects.

In this chapter we will discuss a number of pressing ethical issues confronting researchers in the forensic and correctional domains. First, we will present a set of ethical ideas on which we rely in the subsequent analysis of the research problems. Second, we examine a number of difficulties associated with the design, collection, analysis and reporting of data in forensic and correctional research. Third, our focus will be on features of offenders as research participants and researchers in their role as investigators. Finally, we conclude the chapter with some general comments concerning ethics and research.

Dignity and Ethical Justification

We draw upon two ethical concepts in our subsequent exploration of ethical problems in forensic and correctional research, namely dignity and justification. The two ideas are closely linked here and constitute an ethical framework that can assist in the clarification of puzzles confronting researchers. In addition, they can identify issues that are not explicitly stated in codes of practice or in the rules of criminal justice agencies. The conceptual limitations of ethical resources, including professional codes, may result in a failure to *recognize* ethical problems that are intrinsic to practice purely because they are not covered by the code (Ward and Syversen, 2009). The term "ethical blindness" has been used to refer to the risk of overlooking important clinical matters because they are not noticed (Ward and Syversen, 2009). Ethical dilemmas, conflicts, gaps and so on are simply not identified because the typical ethical framework (that is, the code of ethics) utilized by clinicians does not contain the general theoretical resources, or specific standards, that flag them as issues to be noted and responded to. The foundational concept of human dignity and the process of ethical justification can increase the "acuity" of individuals' ethical perception and prompt them to consider factors overlooked in professional codes. Dignity denotes the equal and high value of all human beings, including offenders, and functions as an anchor point for any subsequent ethical reasoning within research contexts. The concept of justification spells out the formal properties ethical decision making ought to possess, that of universality (generalizability) and impartiality.

The concept of dignity

The concept of human dignity is concerned with the intrinsic, as opposed to the extrinsic (externally determined), value of human beings (Beyleveld and Brownsword, 2001). Initially, it was accepted that individuals' level of dignity varied according to their social status, with peasants considered inferior to nobles or clergy. However, during the Enlightenment in the seventeenth century, the scope of the term was extended to include all human beings. This shift in the meaning of the term dignity in modern times is well captured in the following quotation from Waldron (2009: 2):

> Dignity, we are told, was once tied up with rank: the dignity of a king was not the same as the dignity of a bishop and neither of them was the same as the dignity of a professor. If our modern conception of human dignity retains any scintilla of its ancient and historical connection with rank – and I think it does: I think it expresses the idea of the high and equal rank of every human person.

But what properties give people high status? Is it simply a question of social conferral or are there properties that, if present, are markers of great intrinsic value or dignity? Efforts to analyze the features that bestow dignity on individuals have yielded a number of possible candidates: agency, certain standards of living, living in accordance with community norms, flourishing as a human being, and living without unjustified, *external* interference or coercion (Beyleveld and Brownsword, 2001). In our view the key properties of dignity are those of agency and freedom. The other features either provide the external conditions required for individuals to be self-governing persons or reflect this status in some way. In brief, persons possess dignity because of their ability to act on the basis of reasons that are arrived at through a process of critical reflection and instantiated in plans for living that are subsequently implemented. Failure to respond to individuals in ways that reflect their status as self-governing persons amounts to a denial of their dignity, and thus a failure to respond to their high intrinsic value.

Because of their inherent dignity, human beings are assumed to possess equal moral status and therefore are expected to receive due consideration in matters that directly affect their core interests (see Chapter 2). If we all matter equally, it is incumbent on each of us to think about how our actions are likely to affect the people around us, both close and distant. The possibility of their experiencing unjustified harm as a consequence of our actions should function as a red flag and prompt us to reflect on how or whether we should proceed with our planned course of action. Furthermore, the equal moral standing of each person within a community means that every person is entitled to make specific claims against other members of the moral community and, in turn, is expected to acknowledge his or her obligations to others' respective legitimate claims. These claims will concern the goods they are entitled to as members of the community, especially ones that are regarded as essential for securing their core interests and needs. The proper response to the high value of human beings is that of respect (Wood, 2008). Imposing sanctions on individuals is not necessarily a violation of their dignity because the norms that regulate a community, derived from this foundational value, require everyone to act in ways that acknowledge the agency rights of others. If a person commits a serious crime then she or he has failed to act as required, and therefore is obligated to make amends, which may involve criminal sanctions (see Ward and Salmon, 2009). However, any punishment should be undertaken in ways that are respectful of and not demeaning to the offender. It does not take much reflection to realize this is far from the case in most Western criminal justice jurisdictions (see Chapter 2).

Ethical justification

In our view, the concept of dignity provides a foundational ethical value that can be summarized in the following principle formulated by Kant (cited in Wood, 2008: 60):

> So act that you use humanity, as much in your own person as in the person of every other, as always at the same time as an end and never merely as a means.

The notion of an end in itself stipulates that each person is a (self-generating) source of great worth and this intrinsic value ought to be reflected in our dealings with each other. But how should the process of ethical reasoning based upon the concept of human dignity unfold in research contexts? According to Becker (1986), all moral practice is underpinned by two core justificatory assumptions, those of generalizability (universality) and equality or impartiality. Thus, when faced with the inevitable dilemmas generated by research, any solutions should: (a) generalize to other persons in similar situations, and (b) treat every person involved as someone of equal moral status (that is, as possessing inherent dignity) and therefore ensure you are impartial. The latter constraint means that unless there are good reasons it is presumed that the interests of all individuals will be equally considered and any decision should result in outcomes that are judged as fair. It refers back to the high value of every human being referred to earlier. The key point is that during the process of ethical reflection the researcher should inquire what action(s) will take into account the interest of all the parties involved (see Chapter 4).

We accept that the concepts of dignity and justification will not provide a comprehensive account of ethical reflection and it is likely they will need to be supplemented by additional resources, such as codes of ethics and ethical theories which include virtue ethics or the ethics of care (Driver, 2006). However, orienting inquiry by reference to the equal value of all individuals involved, and ensuring that any solution is impartial and generalizable to other, relevantly similar situations, should provide valuable guidance (for more comprehensive models of ethical reasoning, see Cooper, 2004; Kitchener, 2000; Koocher and Keith-Spiegel, 2009; Ward and Syversen, 2009). At the very least, principles regulating ethical reasoning, such as the concept of justification outlined earlier, require anchoring in a foundational value or set of values, one(s) that acknowledges the importance of all persons and therefore presupposes the existence of a moral community in which each individual is highly prized and where norms are arrived at in a way that takes into account the interests of everyone concerned.

Research Design, Data Collection, Analysis and Reporting

The five ethical problems in this section are centered on the design of studies and the ways in which data are collected, analyzed and presented in journals or reports. The various issues group into the following subjects: (a) research aims, (b) research design, (c) data presentation, (d) negative results and finally (e) participants and data ownership.

Research aims

The design of a study and methods of data collection depend on the reasons for undertaking it and also arguably on who is likely to benefit from the findings. For example, if members of the public have a strong interest in ensuring that sexual violence towards women and children is reduced then research priorities in the area of sexual violence are likely to reflect this concern. A difficulty may be that research into other, equally important, correctional and forensic issues is neglected or that there is pressure to develop programs without the basic science being in place. More seriously, it could be the case that a moral agenda that has not been explicitly stated is actually driving the research. An example of this type of undeclared ethical goal could be to protect society by establishing techniques or strategies that ensure moderate-to-high risk offenders remain institutionalized. Sometimes claims to effectiveness can be overstated or public fears are allowed to override norms of good science. In order to acquire funding researchers may prematurely accept clinically derived theory and treatment programs based on this theory as warranted knowledge and proceed to design program evaluation studies. An example of this is arguably the treatment of men who are violent towards their partners, which is based on very little research evidence and surprisingly weak theory (Langlands, Ward and Gilchrist, 2009). It would not be hard to find examples in other areas of forensic and correctional psychology. The key point is that researchers ought to reflect critically on the reasons why they want to proceed with a study and whether there is sufficient justification to do so. The adverse ethical implications of proceeding with research projects based on insufficient grounds is that: (a) it could mislead people, (b) it confers inappropriate authority on a program or research findings, and (c) it may divert precious resources from possibly more valuable projects. The politics of research funding can sometimes distort researchers' judgments and there is a risk that wasted research efforts may damage the chances of further research funding and ultimately the reduction of re-offending rates and human misery. The justificatory assumptions of universality and equality should encourage researchers to think systematically about the benefits and burdens of research from the perspectives of all stakeholders and hopefully lead them to balance any competing interests carefully. Another strand to the question of the underlying aims that motivate research in forensic and correctional contexts is the matter of whose interests are taken into account in the inquiry process. It is arguably unethical without further analysis to disregard the possible risks and benefits to offenders.

Selection of research designs

An ethical problem relates to decisions concerning the kind of research designs and analytical methods employed in a project. The choice between the use of ethnographic, interview-based or experimental research designs is a crucial one and has ethical dimensions alongside epistemic considerations such as the degree to which causal inferences are facilitated or natural social processes respected. A useful example of how disagreement over design issues can erupt into ethical debates is the recent interchange between Marshall and Marshall (2007) and Seto *et al.* (2007) over whether or not the randomized controlled trial (RCT) should be the gold standard for research into the effectiveness of sexual offending treatment. Marshall and Marshall argued that RCT designs lack validity and also raised serious ethical concerns about allocating offenders to non-treatment conditions, thereby possibly placing future members of the community at risk from untreated men. In their view, RCTs are not necessary for treatment evaluation research in the sexual offending arena and they suggested that alternative research designs such as incidental designs or actuarially based evaluations may be better options (see Chapter 14). Seto *et al.* took issue with Marshall and Marshall's contentions and argued strongly for the value of RCT designs (suitably implemented) in providing robust evidence for treatment effectiveness. They commented that proceeding with treatments when there is insufficient evidence for their utility is unethical and also that there may be further unintended (ethical and psychological) consequences that have not been detected; for example, embellishing deviant sexual fantasies in individuals following their exposure to the fantasies of others in groups.

What does research theory have to say about this dispute? Mark and Gamble (2009) assert that, despite constituting an extremely powerful research design, sometimes RCT designs should not necessarily be the design of choice if reasonable evidence already exists that certain treatment approaches are likely to be useful. In fact, evidence from correctional research indicates that sex offender programs that use cognitive behavioral techniques (CBT) that target dynamic risk factors, and that follow the principles of risk, need and responsivity (which most cutting-edge programs do) are likely to result in reduced re-offending rates (Hanson *et al.*, 2009). Thus, if a CBT treatment program for sex offenders follows the principles of risk, need and responsivity, it is possible that a quasi-experimental design of some kind is scientifically acceptable, and ethically supported. In fact, it is reasonable to conclude that the weight of the ethical reasons could favor such designs in view of their practicality and avoidance of the ethical problems associated with RCT designs with a sex offender population.

The issue we would like to highlight is that there are important ethical arguments at work in this dispute alongside the scientific one; claims that ought to be critically evaluated. In this example, the treatment needs of sex offenders as well as the interests of research funders (resource considerations) and the public (safety) should all be considered. The reasons for doing so include considerations of equality and universality, themselves designed to reflect the common dignity of every person.

Data presentation

An important ethical issue relates to the concerns about the way research-generated data are presented in academic and non-academic forums. Researchers should be careful to take note of accepted findings that are relevant for their research questions and ensure that data are analyzed in ways that reflect these distinctions, and that they are presented accordingly. For example, research on sex offenders that fails to distinguish between risk levels and variables that are known to effect outcomes such as age, sexual deviancy, emotional regulation and so on is misleading and ethically unacceptable (Craig, Beech and Harkins, 2009). It may result in clinical and research decisions that unfairly disadvantage offenders, such as unnecessarily long parole periods or intrusive parole conditions. This problem is particularly pertinent to research on risk assessment. An associated issue is the need to examine results closely and not to rely on simple group effects. Bersoff *et al.* (2003) emphasize the importance of acknowledging limitations of empirically derived predictions in practice given their use in court proceedings such as those involving the possible use of preventive detention. They assert that dichotomous judgments are unethical but that class-based judgments (provided the limitations of such judgments are acknowledged) are ethical – that is, those that carefully state the specified risk of re-offending for particular groups. Omitting details of sample characteristics could lead to risk assessment instruments being used with individuals for which the instrument has not been validated. Similarly, Vess (2008) highlights the profound impact risk assessment outcomes can have on (denying) the human rights of sex offenders, and moreover the limitations of current instruments in accurately predicting recidivism. These, in effect, constitute violations of the justificatory assumptions of equality and universality (see Chapter 2). Accordingly, he advocates for careful communication of risk assessment research data, especially acknowledgement of the limitations of interpreting risk assessment findings with respect to individual offenders.

In light of the above debate, it is prudent for researchers when using risk bands for research purposes or conducting research on risk to take great care to communicate the extent and limitations of their findings. The implications of the results and the way they are expressed should be considered from the viewpoints of all the relevant stakeholders, not simply those of the researchers, the public and the relevant funding bodies. It should be assumed from the outset that sex offenders' interests ought to be taken into account in any decisions that are likely to involve them. Failure to do this constitutes a violation of their dignity and runs dangerously close to using them as simply means to reduce the anxiety, and possibly exaggerated fears, of the rest of the community.

Negative results

An associated issue concerns the failure to publish negative study findings, whether they arise from assessment, etiological or program evaluation research projects. This matter is as much the responsibility of journal editors and reviewers as individual researchers. For example, it is a well-established recommendation that real efforts should be made to include both published and unpublished studies in meta-analysis in order to avoid the file drawer problem, where studies with negative effects are not published (Crombie and Davis, 2009). A difficulty in neglecting to make negative findings public is that erroneous conclusions about a measure or intervention program's effectiveness may unduly influence subsequent funding decisions and possibly disadvantage offenders and community members. It goes without saying that such a situation could result in withdrawal of good programs or the continuation of weak ones. The lack of consultation points to a failure to consider the entitlements of all individuals affected, and therefore effectively constitutes a denial of their status as rational agents; that is, they are denied a say in what programs are or are not available, based on the best available evidence. Second, there is little justification for programs that *are funded* because of the unavailability of any negative results. It is reasonable to assume that if the key stakeholders (offenders, members of the public, criminal justice agencies and so on) were aware of the lack of support they might make different decisions. This is both an epistemic (knowledge-related) and an ethical violation – epistemic, because failure to disclose may result in poorly grounded inferences about treatment efficacy, and an ethical violation because it denies individuals the best chance to improve their personal well-being and, furthermore, to create a safer society.

Participants and Data

For both ethical and methodological reasons it could be argued that because research participants consent to become involved in a project they have a claim on the data yielded and therefore should be entitled to co-ownership of the data (Ntseane, 2009). This conclusion is partly a function of regarding participants as equal moral agents and also recognition of the fact that agreement (effort) related to a research project confers an entitlement to a full report on its outcomes, and possibly a say in how the data are used – based on equality and universality considerations. If the data are viewed as partly owned by the participants it follows that the publication of the results ought to appear in forms that they are likely to read and understand, and not simply appear in specialized academic journals. Indigenous offenders may have a particularly strong claim for co-ownership and control, especially when the research touches upon their cultural beliefs and practices (LaFrance and Bull, 2009). In forensic and correctional contexts this ethical concern is pressing because of the power imbalances that exist and apparent widespread reluctance to consider offenders as moral equals and potential research partners (Ward and Salmon, 2009). From a dignity perspective, it is easier to appreciate the force of participant claims to data ownership and to negotiate these complex matters in a fairer way. For example, it seems to us to be reasonable that participants who have contributed significantly to a project should receive a full report on the findings. Furthermore, if their involvement is considerable, as it inevitably is in some types of ethnographic or interview-based research, claims for access to data and some say on where and how they are reported have, at least, *prima facie* validity. An important question is: what are the wishes of the research participants and why would not they be respected?

Offenders and Researchers

The five key issues associated with this category spring directly from the face to face nature of researcher–participant relationships and essentially revolve around the themes of (a) ethical blindness, (b) offenders' moral status, (c) offenders' vulnerability, (d) cultural/social differences and (e) assumptions about disorders and offender treatability.

Ethical blindness

Although professional codes offer important guidelines, several writers have commented on their limitations. Lavin (2004: 51) asserts that ethical codes are opaque in their wording, contain inclusions and exclusions that do little "moral work," and "invite psychologists to forget to look long and hard at controversial areas of practice." Lavin posits that reliance on professional ethical codes is not enough to guide forensic and correctional practice or research and recommends that additional ethical concepts and theory be used to enrich ethical awareness and decision making. Other writers have commented on the limitations of ethical codes with respect to their scope and depth (Ward, 2011). Ethical dilemmas, conflicts, gaps and so on are simply not identified because the ethical framework relied on by clinicians does not contain the general theoretical resources, or specific standards, that flag them as issues to be noted and responded to.

Clearly, there are a number of potentially serious problems that can arise from ethical blindness. Clinicians may fail to act when they should do, or alternatively, they may act in ways that reflect their personal biases and philosophies without applying the careful reflection that they typically give to suitably acknowledged ethical concerns (Kitchener, 2000). For example, unexamined assumptions about patients' lifestyles and culture and the nature of their offending can have a profound effect on clinicians' attitudes to, and engagement with, them. Ethical blindness may also result in clinicians' unquestioned adherence to organizational philosophies, practices and rules that may be unjust or demeaning to patients under their care.

A similar type of problem can occur in forensic and correctional research domains. Certain issues are simply not flagged as ethical ones because codes of ethics that oversee research activities do not signal them as relevant. In a nutshell, they are overlooked. A good example of this is the allocation of offenders into treatment bands according to their assessed level of risk, often defended by reference to the Risk–Need–Responsivity model of offender rehabilitation (RNR; Andrews and Bonta, 2006). The problem with restricting research and treatment in these ways is that offenders can be denied legitimate access to treatment, access that they are ethically entitled to receive according to human rights declarations, and, more fundamentally, their moral equality. In some instances, lower risk offenders in prison or on community orders might have their ability to function effectively seriously compromised by their problems and therefore urgently require help to address the causes of these difficulties (Ward and Maruna, 2007). The worry is that the problems they do experience could impair their agency and, therefore, result in lowered levels of living, hence constituting significant threats to their dignity (as evidenced in adverse life circumstances). Forensic researchers and practitioners often simply assume that the allocation of psychological and social resources is best based on risk level and most sensibly directed at the causes of offending. However, research that proceeds on the basis of risk band allocation, especially research that promises to benefit the offender as well as the community, may result in the neglect of problems experienced by moderate-to-lower risk sex offenders.

An advantage of orienting research from the ethical lens of dignity and the justification model outlined earlier, is that these individuals' interests are automatically factored in and considered. While it makes sense to focus interventions where they are likely to be cost-effective, failure to consider the wishes and needs of lower risk groups (or those suffering from problems such as personality disorder that are considered to be untreatable – see below) is that they are being unfairly neglected and their claims to scarce research, and ultimately therapy resources, overlooked.

The moral status of offenders

The above issue of moral blindness places the question of offenders' moral status directly into center stage: do offenders possess the inherent dignity and hence value of the other members of the community (that is, equality and universality concerns)? If so, does the fact they have received punishment erode their moral status? This is a thorny issue but to cut a complex and long story short we answer these questions in the following way: yes and no (for a detailed discussion of punishment and offender rehabilitation, see Ward and Salmon, 2009; Chapter 16).

Offenders possess the inherent dignity of all members of the community because they are fellow human beings. This dignity is acknowledged and protected by human rights treaties and protocols and applies to offenders and non-offenders alike (Ward and Birgden, 2007; see Chapter 2). Second, because of offenders' inherent dignity, punishment is arguably only ethically justifiable if it is administered in a way that is respectful and proportionate, and allows for the prospects of repentance and reconciliation (Duff, 2001). In effect, this means that research with offenders should proceed in accordance with their equal moral status. The harsh conditions of imprisonment and neglect of offenders' welfare apparent in many correctional jurisdictions throughout the Western world implies a lack of acknowledgement of this inherent dignity (Lazarus, 2004). Poor living conditions, harsh punishment, lack of adequate medical care, isolation from other offenders, lack of sufficient contact with family members, minimal opportunity to acquire useful employment skills and a hostile and unforgiving community all imply a fundamental lack of recognition of offenders' basic human rights and inherent dignity (Lazarus, 2004; Ward and Birgden, 2007). A lack of dignity recognition creates problems for researchers, as such conditions render subsequent research with vulnerable individuals problematic (see below).

The matter of informed consent with prisoners does raise the question as to whether it is ever appropriate to use prisoners as research participants. Perez and Treadwell (2009) cite recent research showing that biomedical researchers in the United States having difficulty recruiting volunteers for clinical trials (for example, Hoffman, 2000) are pushing for access to prisoners as participants in clinical trials (this was common practice as late as 1969, but not currently). The authors discuss ethical issues surrounding prisoners as participants in clinical trials, and argue that "until the question of adequate health care for prisoners is resolved, human experimentation should not be allowed" (Perez and Treadwell, 2009: 201). They go on to assert that "for research in prisons to be ethical, it must be interested in upholding prisoners' constitutional right to appropriate quality care while in prison and ensure a stronger and more effective safety net for them when they return home" (Perez and Treadwell, 2009: 201). The authors therefore advocate for research with prisoners, but only when its focus is on the advancement of prisoners' welfare. It is possible, however, that sometimes the pendulum may swing too far in the other direction and correctional officials could be overly paternalistic and deny offenders the opportunity to decide for themselves whether or not to take part in research projects (Overholser, 1987).

Issues related to informed consent and competency are to the forefront when prisoners are involved in research projects, and there is a heavy burden of proof on researchers to establish that in forensic and correctional settings offenders were under no pressure to consent, and were indeed psychologically competent to do so. Accepting that any decisions arrived at should reflect the equality of all individuals concerned, and that any solutions should generalize to similar contexts, ought to assist researchers in arriving at ethically sound options. Extreme paternalism and coercion represent extremes of a continuum, poles that point to a disregard of offenders' agency and therefore a lack of acknowledgment of their dignity as fellow human beings. Asking whether any decisions (and their underlying norms or principles) concerning research could be ethically generalized and whether a community of moral equals would agree that they were reasonable should counteract the temptation to engage in facile or self-serving projects.

The vulnerability of offenders

Offenders are a vulnerable population because of the fact that their core well-being and freedom interests are often neglected or put at risk when living within correctional and forensic institutions (Overholser, 1987; Regehr, Edwardh and Bradford, 2000). These interests are essential preconditions of effective agency. An Institute of Medicine (2006) report highlights the degree to which prisoners are a vulnerable population and outlines specific ethical considerations that are required for research involving prisoners as participants. For example, potentially inadequate physical and mental healthcare in prisons presents a barrier to ethical research, as research participation might reflect a desperate attempt on the part of prisoners to obtain treatment. The resulting list of recommendations is intended to ensure that any research should benefit prisoners and also ensure universal ethical protection. A particularly noteworthy feature for forensic and correctional research is the requirement that all stakeholders (for example, prisoners, correctional officers, medical staff, administrators) should have input into research design, planning and implementation. This requirement clearly reflects a commitment to moral equality, fairness and impartiality.

The vulnerability of offenders should be taken into account when it comes to research into mandated treatment programs for offenders as well as ones where there is evidence of more subtle types of coercion (see Day, Tucker and Howells, 2004). The fact that offenders who are coerced into treatment may demonstrate favorable outcomes does not necessarily support such interventions because of the violation of offenders' autonomy and ultimately their dignity as human beings.

For example, McSweeney *et al.* (2007) recently conducted a quasi-experimental study investigating outcomes for offenders who volunteered for drug treatment compared to offenders who were coerced (that is, court mandated) into treatment. They found that coerced offenders reported significant and sustained reductions in illicit drug use and offending behaviors, as well as improvements in other areas of social functioning. Findings were similar for the voluntarily treated offenders, and there were no significant differences on outcome variables between both groups. The authors stated that the message "is not that coercion works, but that treatment can be an effective alternative to imprisonment" (McSweeney *et al.*, 2007: 486). Moreover, they emphasized that a large proportion of dependent users do not fund their drug use through crime, and that these individuals should equally have access to good quality drug treatment.

Despite these qualifications, we have grave concerns about such research and it seems apparent that in the design of this study the potential benefits for the community and participants (well-being, risk reduction) were thought to outweigh the autonomy of the participants. Such paternalism is hard to justify ethically unless the autonomy of the participants was severely impaired by drug use and therefore their competence to consent to treatment, or not, was severely undermined. There is no evidence in this study that this was the case. Ethically, much hangs on demonstrating that a person's capacity for autonomous functioning is so impaired that he or she is unable to deliberate effectively about what options to pursue. In other words, we should ask the following question: is the treatment and associated research really in the interests of the offender (equality, dignity) and is my answer generalizable to similar situations involving non-offenders (universality)?

Cultural differences

An examination of the proportion of indigenous prisoners around the world indicates that they are overrepresented in prison rates. To illustrate, as of March 21, 2010, Maori offenders comprised 50.68% of the New Zealand prison population (Department of Corrections, personal communication, March 24, 2010) compared to 14.6% of the general population (Statistics New Zealand, 2006). Irrespective of the actual number of offenders from minority ethnic groups, the key point is that such offenders are currently incarcerated or placed on community orders and that there are cultural differences between such offenders and those belonging to the majority ethnic group. These differences revolve around issues such as informed consent or confidentiality of which researchers need to be aware. A key issue when examining the implications of cultural diversity is to ascertain the particular level at which it is evident within a country, as well as contemplating differences between cultures located in different countries (Parekh, 2006). It is typically the cultural challenges within a given society that are likely to prove most taxing for researchers and practitioners in the course of their day-to-day duties. Under such circumstances, it is imperative to keep in mind the common needs and interests of all individuals and their equal status and value (LaFrance and Bull, 2009; see Chapter 4). The fact of cultural diversity creates problems for researchers. For example, in some cultures the right to make decisions extends to family and even group members and therefore an offender is unlikely to want to make a decision about research participation unless he or she can consult with family and cultural representatives (Ntseane, 2009). In many prison environments this is likely to prove problematic and there is a danger that offenders' wishes may be ignored and they may consent to research because they feel pressured or undermined. Similar points hold for issues related to privacy of research data and their uses (see above). The problem for researchers is that existing codes of ethics do not really help to address such culturally based consent, competency or privacy questions. However, starting with the assumption all individuals possess equal dignity and that their interests should be given equal consideration in matters that affect them is likely to offset this tendency. In addition, it should help researchers to guard against prematurely dismissing claims to knowledge from other cultures because they do not conform to the Western conception of science, or that prioritize experimental methods and quantitative methods of analysis over qualitative and interpretive approaches (Denzin and Lincoln, 2005).

Assumptions about disorders

A final ethical difficulty concerns assumptions made about disorders and offender treatability (Howells and Day, 2007). Every research project is necessarily underpinned by core assumptions about the nature of the problems and the participants being investigated. In the forensic and correctional arena there is the added complication of a strong ethical overlay, that is, offenders have frequently inflicted serious harm on members of the community and are being punished as well as researched or treated. In light of what is at stake for both offenders and the wider community, it is incumbent on researchers and practitioners to examine their ethical and epistemic assumptions about offenders and their problems carefully (Ward and Maruna, 2007). For example, psychopathy has been long regarded by researchers to be virtually untreatable and, as a consequence of this viewpoint, there has been little sustained research into the development and evaluation of suitable programs for individuals diagnosed as psychopathic (Howells and Day, 2007). The worry is that these assumptions may be incorrect or premature, and may instead simply express moral condemnation towards habitually violent and callous individuals masquerading as informed scientific opinion. Similar concerns could be raised about other types of offenders, such as sex offenders with high levels of sexual deviancy or individuals with other types of personality disorder. In our view this point highlights the dependence of scientific research on (but not its reduction to) broader social and cultural variables and reminds researchers always to critically review aims and reasons for their projects prior to proceeding. This includes a careful analysis of researchers' and funding bodies' ethical reasoning, and checks being made to ensure that research opportunities are not overlooked because of incorrect empirical (and ethical) assumptions. It could be argued that prematurely concluding that violent sex offenders with psychopathic traits are untreatable has huge adverse implications for the people themselves as well as the community. It effectively consigns offenders to a second-class status and denies the community their potentially valuable contributions in the future.

Conclusions

In this chapter we have identified a number of ethical issues associated with research with offenders. Our ethical starting point is that offenders have the same intrinsic value – human dignity – as other members of the community and have a right to have their core interests considered in any research that directly or indirectly involves them. This could involve having offenders on research review boards in order that their viewpoints can be heard and respected. Research with offenders is an ethical minefield because of the fact that they are contained within the criminal justice system. By definition, they have committed unethical actions and their punishment reflects their wrongdoing. However, those subject to punishment retain their inherent value, and their status as equal members of the moral community should not be neglected. Codes of ethics are insufficient to ensure that research activities in the criminal justice domain are ethically justified. In our view, an enriched framework based on human dignity and the norms of universality, equality and impartiality is necessary to ensure that valuable and morally acceptable work is undertaken with this vulnerable and maligned population.

Acknowledgment

Parts of this chapter have been published previously in T. Ward and G. Willis (2010) "Ethical issues in forensic and correctional research." *Aggression and Violent Behavior*, 15, 399–409.We would like to thank Elsevier Science for permission to use this material.

References

Adshead, G. and Brown, C. (eds) (2003) *Ethical Issues in Forensic Mental Health Research*. London: Jessica Kingsley.

Andrews, D.A. and Bonta, J. (2006) *The Psychology of Criminal Conduct*, 4th edn. Cincinnati, OH: Anderson Publishing.

Becker, L.C. (1986) *Reciprocity*. Chicago, IL: University of Chicago Press.

Bersoff, D.N., Faust, D., Sales, B.D., *et al.* (2003) "Forensic settings," in D.N. Bersoff (ed.), *Ethical Conflicts in Psychology*. Washington, DC: American Psychological Association, pp. 443–514.

Beyleveld, D. and Brownsword, R. (2001) *Human Dignity in Bioethics and Law*. New York, NY: Oxford University Press.

Bush, S.S., Connell, M.A. and Denny, R.L. (2006) *Ethical Practice in Forensic Psychology: A Systematic Model for Decision Making*. Washington, DC: American Psychological Association.

Cooper, D.E. (2004) *Ethics for Professionals in a Multicultural World*. Upper Saddle River, NJ: Pearson Prentice Hall.

Craig, L.A., Beech, A.R. and Harkins, L. (2009) "The predictive accuracy of risk factors and frameworks," in A.R. Beech, L.A. Craig, and K.D. Browne (eds), *Assessment and Treatment of Sex Offenders*. Oxford: Wiley-Blackwell, pp. 53–74.

Crombie, I.K. and Davis, H.T. (2009) *What Is Meta-analysis? Evidence-based Medicine*, 2nd edn, http://www.whatisseries.co.uk/whatis/pdfs/What_is_meta_analy.pdf (accessed August 25, 2012).

Day, A., Tucker, K. and Howells, K. (2004) "Coerced offender rehabilitation – a defensible practice?," *Psychology, Crime and Law* 10, 259–269.

Denzin, N.K. and Lincoln, Y.S. (2005) *The Sage Handbook of Qualitative Research*, 3rd edn. Thousand Oaks, CA: Sage.

Driver, J. (2006) *Ethics: The Fundamentals*. Oxford: Blackwell Publishing.

Duff, R.A. (2001) *Punishment, Communication, and Community*. New York: Oxford University Press.

Haag, A.D. (2006) "Ethical dilemmas faced by correctional psychologists in Canada," *Criminal Justice and Behavior* 33, 93–109.

Hanson, R.K., Bourgon, G., Helmus, L. and Hodgson, S. (2009) "The principles of effective correctional treatment also apply to sexual offenders: a meta-analysis," *Criminal Justice and Behavior* 36, 865–891.

Hoffman, S. (2000) "Beneficial and unusual punishment: an argument in support of prisoner participation in clinical trials," *Indiana Law Review* 33, 475–513.

Howells, K. and Day, A. (2007) "Readiness for treatment in high risk offenders with personality disorders," *Psychology, Crime and Law. Special Issue: Personality Disorder and Offending* 13, 47–56.

Institute of Medicine (2006) *Ethical Considerations for Research Involving Prisoners*. Washington, DC: National Academies Press.

Kitchener, K.S. (2000) *Foundations of Clinical Practice, Research, and Teaching in Psychology*. Mahwah, NJ: Lawrence Erlbaum.

Koocher, G.P. and Keith-Spiegel, P. (2009) *Ethics in Psychology: Professional Standards and Cases*, 3rd edn. New York: Oxford University Press.

LaFrance, J. and Bull, C.C. (2009) "Researching ourselves back to life: taking control of the research agenda in Indian country," in D.M. Mertens and P.E. Ginsberg (eds), *The Handbook of Social Research Ethics*. Thousand Oaks, CA: Sage Publications, pp. 135–149.

Langlands, R.L., Ward, T. and Gilchrist, E. (2009) "Applying the good lives model to male perpetrators of domestic violence," *Behaviour Change* 26, 113–129.

Lavin, M. (2004) "Ethical issues in forensic psychology," in W.T. O'Donohue and E. Levensky (eds), *Handbook of Forensic Psychology: Resources for Mental Health and Legal Professionals*. New York: Elsevier Science, pp. 46–63.

Lazarus, L. (2004) *Contrasting Prisoners' Rights: A Comparative Examination of England and Germany*. New York: Oxford University Press.

Mark, M.M. and Gamble, C. (2009) "Experiments, quasi-experiments, and ethics," in D.M. Mertens and P.E. Ginsberg (eds), *The Handbook of Social Research Ethics*. Thousand Oaks, CA: Sage, pp. 198–213.

Marshall, W.L. and Marshall, L.E. (2007) "The utility of the random controlled trial for evaluating sexual offender treatment: the gold standard or an inappropriate strategy?," *Sexual Abuse: A Journal of Research and Treatment* 19, 175–191.

McSweeney, T., Stevens, A., Hunt, N. and Turnbull, P.J. (2007) "Twisting arms or helping treatment options," *British Journal of Criminology* 47, 470–490.

Ntseane, P.G. (2009) "The ethics of the researcher-subject relationship," in D.M. Mertens and P.E. Ginsberg (eds), *The Handbook of Social Research Ethics*. Thousand Oaks, CA: Sage, pp. 295–307.

Overholser, J. (1987) "Ethical issues in prison research: a risk/benefit analysis," *Behavioral Sciences and the Law* 5, 187–202.

Parekh, B. (2006) *Rethinking Multiculturalism: Cultural Diversity and Political Theory*, 2nd edn. Basingstoke: Palgrave Macmillan.

Perez, L.M. and Treadwell, H.M. (2009) "Determining what we stand for will guide what we do: community priorities, ethical research paradigms, and research with vulnerable populations," *American Journal of Public Health* 99, 201–204.

Regehr, C., Edwardh, M. and Bradford, J. (2000) "Research ethics and forensic patients," *Canadian Journal of Psychiatry/La Revue Canadienne de Psychiatrie* 45, 892–898.

Rosenfeld, B. and Penrod, S.D. (eds) (2011) *Research Methods in Forensic Psychology*. Chichester: John Wiley & Sons, Ltd.

Seto, M., Marques, J.K., Harris, G.T. *et al.* (2007) "Good science and progress in sex offender treatment are intertwined: a response to Marshall and Marshall (2007)," *Sexual Abuse: A Journal of Research and Treatment*, 19, 175–191.

Statistics New Zealand (2006) 2006 Census Data, http://www.stats.govt.nz/Census/2006CensusHomePage.aspx (accessed September 11, 2012).

Vess, J. (2008) "Sex offender risk assessment: consideration of human rights in community protection legislation," *Legal and Criminological Psychology* 13, 245–256.

Waki, S., Shelton, D., Trestman, R.L. and Kesten, K. (2009) "Conducting research in corrections: challenges and solutions," *Behavioral Sciences and the Law* 27, 743–752.

Waldron, J. (2009) *Dignity, Rank, and Rights: The 2009 Tanner Lectures at UC Berkeley*. New York: New York University of Law.

Ward, T. (2011) "Human rights and dignity in offender rehabilitation," *Journal of Forensic Psychology Practice* 11, 103–123.

Ward, T. and Birgden, A. (2007) "Human rights and correctional clinical practice," *Aggression and Violent Behavior* 12, 628–643.

Ward, T. and Maruna, S. (2007) *Rehabilitation: Beyond the Risk Paradigm*. London: Routledge.

Ward, T. and Salmon, K. (2009) "The ethics of punishment: correctional practice implications," *Aggression and Violent Behavior* 14, 239–247.

Ward, T. and Syversen, K. (2009) "Vulnerable agency and human dignity: an ethical framework for forensic practice," *Aggression and Violent Behavior* 14, 94–105.

Ward, T. and Willis, G. (2010) "Ethical issues in forensic and correctional research," *Aggression and Violent Behavior* 15, 399–409.

Ward, T. and Willis, G. (2012) "Ethical problems arising from forensic and correctional research," in K. Howells, K. Sheldon and J. Davis (eds), *Research in Practice for Forensic Professionals*. Cullompton: Willan Publishing, pp. 16–34.

Wood, A.W. (2008) *Kantian Ethics*. New York: Cambridge University Press.

7

Reintegrative and Disintegrative Shaming
Legal and Ethical Issues
Anne-Marie McAlinden

Introduction

Formal legal measures for reintegrating and managing offenders are heavily premised on public protection and risk management, often to the detriment of offender rights. Community notification in particular gives rise to concerns about placing a potentially lifelong stigma on the offender or exposing them to risk of personal harm. Situational measures such as sexual offenses prevention orders may impose severe restrictions on the movement, behavior and rights of offenders against whom they are obtained. Equally, within the context of reintegrative shaming measures, while such schemes remove the stigma associated with sex offending by informally sanctioning deviance, there may be concerns relating to due process, and the accountability and legitimacy of the process. It will be argued that there are a range of interests and rights implicit in the sex offender problem that have not always been clearly articulated – that of communities to assurances of public safety, of victims to future protection from harm, and of offenders to rehabilitation within civil society. In the current rights-based legal framework, legislators and policy makers need to pay greater attention to these underlying tensions and to achieving a more effective balance between the freedom and control of offenders.

The first part of the chapter will examine the range of legislative and policy measures which have been put in place within the United Kingdom in particular to control the behavior and whereabouts of sex offenders in the community. The second will look at restorative and reintegrative measures with sex offenders which have emerged as an alternative to more punitive discourses. Given the legal and ethical issues which underpin each of these largely dichotomous pathways, the conclusion of the chapter will seek to draw out the fundamental tensions between them and endeavor to

The Wiley-Blackwell Handbook of Legal and Ethical Aspects of Sex Offender Treatment and Management,
First Edition. Edited by Karen Harrison and Bernadette Rainey.
© 2013 John Wiley & Sons, Ltd. Published 2013 by John Wiley & Sons, Ltd.

provide a blueprint for achieving a better balance between the multiple interests at stake in the sex offender problem – communities, victims and potential victims, as well as the offender, and the state.

Part I: Control in the Community and "Disintegrative Shaming"

Public protection, risk management and "crime control"

Wider concerns with "risk" (Beck, 1992; Ericson and Haggerty, 1997), security (Christie, 2000; Loader and Walker, 2007) and preventative governance (Shearing, 2000; Crawford, 2003) within criminal justice discourses more broadly have also manifested themselves in specifically targeted regulatory policies for "at risk" groups such as sexual offenders (Simon, 1998; Kemshall and Maguire, 2001). "Public protection" and "risk management" in particular have become the bywords of sex offender assessment and management (Kemshall and Maguire, 2001) as well as child protection (Parton, Thorpe and Wattam, 1997). In the United Kingdom, from the late 1990s onwards, a range of legislative and policy measures were introduced in order to enhance supervisory methods and increase controls on released sex offenders in the community. These have included most notably sex offender notification and related orders. These measures were founded on the basic premise that the most effective way to protect the public was through increased surveillance and monitoring of released sex offenders in the community (Kemshall, 2001). Indeed, the ethos of situational crime prevention (Wortley and Smallbone, 2006) seeks to locate, manage and respond proactively to crime by putting in place restrictive measures on freedom of movement and often daily activities of known offenders. However, such "transcarceration of the offender" (McAlinden, 2000: 87), may operate with scant regard for the rights of the offender.

Notification and related orders

Sex offender notification was first enacted by Part I of the Sex Offenders Act 1997 (see Chapter 21). This measure required certain categories of sex offender to notify their name and address, and any changes to these details to the police. The conditions and requirements attached to notification for the offender and the degree of disclosure to the local community vary depending on the assessed level of risk. Throughout the United Kingdom, there are Multi-Agency Public Protection Panels (MAPPPs), or equivalents, comprising representatives from the police, probation, social services and other agencies, to coordinate sex offender risk assessment and management (Maguire *et al.*, 2001). Part I of the 1997 Act, however, was replaced with a much broader and enhanced regulatory framework contained in Part 2 of the Sexual Offences Act 2003. Key changes within the 2003 Act included, for example, the requirement that offenders notify their details within three days and in person and not 14 days and by post respectively as was previously the case. Moreover, proposed amendments to the legislative framework, including requiring offenders to provide additional information to the police such as bank account details, as well as increasing the scope of sexual offenses prevention orders, which will be discussed further below, also raises further rights implications.

In the pursuit of efficient knowledge production and effective risk management (Hebenton and Thomas, 1996), the offender's rights, are displaced because of the special risk such offenders are seen as presenting. At the time of the implementation of the 1997 Act concerns were raised about notification operating as an additional form of punishment (Lieb, 1996; Soothill and Francis, 1998) and in particular that the notification requirement would curtail the offender's freedom and a possible notification of this information to the local community would breach his right to privacy (Hebenton and Thomas, 1997; Karp, 1998). The offender's rights, however, under Article 8 of the European Convention on Human Rights (ECHR) which provides for respect for private and family life, are not absolute. The potential adverse consequences for vulnerable groups, including children, may justify interference with such rights on the grounds, inter alia, of public safety and the prevention of crime and disorder (Power, 2003). In practice, as will be discussed further below, "[t]he task then becomes one of minimising whatever harmful effects the offender may experience" (McAlinden, 2007: 115). In this respect, the UK Supreme Court has recently declared lifetime registration, without periodic review, incompatible with the privacy rights under Article 8 of the ECHR[1] (see Chapter 2).

Indeed, the public disclosure of such information may present a particular range of legal and ethical issues, both for law enforcement and for offenders themselves (Power, 2003). Until fairly recently, the extent to which the police or local authorities could publicly identify sex offenders was on a "need to know basis" (Rutherford, 2000; Thomas, 2001).[2] The campaign for enhanced arrangements for public disclosure was given impetus by the death of Sarah Payne.[3] In the aftermath of this case, the *News of the World* tabloid newspaper began what became known as the "Name and Shame" campaign – where it sought to publish the names, photographs and offending histories of all known sex offenders, particularly those against children (Silverman and Wilson, 2002: 146–66). In the aftermath of this case, however, there was a concentration of violent protests and vigilante activity in Portsmouth against suspected "pedophiles" which had a range of negative consequences for offender management and reintegration (Ashenden, 2002; Williams and Thompson, 2004).

At the same time, there were attendant calls for a formal "Sarah's Law," to be the broad equivalent of "Megan's Law" in the United States which provides for a much greater degree of community notification (McAlinden, 1999). A community disclosure scheme allowing parents to check the backgrounds of those with unsupervised access to their children was piloted in four areas in England (Kemshall *et al.*, 2010) with a parallel pilot in the Tayside area in Scotland (Chan *et al.*, 2010). Following the pilots such schemes are likely to be extended throughout the United Kingdom, bringing policies on notification even more closely in line with those in the United States and with them the "latent consequences" of community notification (Edwards and Hensley, 2001) in the form of disintegrative shame penalties. It has also been argued that where public disclosure may have an impact on an offender's rights under Articles 2 (right to life), 3 (prohibition on inhumane or degrading treatment) or 8 of the ECHR, the state must take positive steps to ensure that third parties do not breach these rights (Mullender, 1998; Power, 2003). Acts of disclosure by the police or other agencies may also give rise to challenge under Article 5: the right to liberty and security of person (Barber, 1998). As noted above, public dissemination of personal information about offenders through disintegrative shaming measures like notification or "name and shame" campaigns may place offenders at increased risk of personal harm (McAlinden, 2007: 115–116). Moreover, they may also force offenders into hiding which may increase their risk of offending and displace efforts at reintegration.

The 2003 Act introduced a range of other regulatory measures which place increased requirements on sex offenders and which may also represent a significant curtailment of the civil liberties and rights of the offender (Power, 1999; Shute, 2004). Notification orders require those who have received convictions for sexual offenses abroad to comply with the legislation,[4] while foreign travel orders prevent those offenders with convictions involving children from traveling abroad and targeting children in other countries.[5] Risk of sexual harm orders (RSHOs)[6] and sexual offenses prevention orders (SOPOs)[7] were introduced as civil orders further designed to protect children from the risk of sexual harm (Shute, 2004). The former can be used to prohibit specified behaviors, including the grooming of children and, somewhat controversially, can be used whether or not the individual has a prior record of offending. The latter can be used as a variant on an exclusion order to prohibit the offender from frequenting places where there might be children. Such draconian and retributive measures harness the need to publicly identify and control the whereabouts and behavior of sex offenders in the community to public protection. As a result, however, the civil liberties of the offender together with their chances of rehabilitation may be seriously undermined (McAlinden, 2007).

In this respect, it has been argued that such preventive orders may give rise to a number of ethical and legal concerns by the imposition of acute restrictions on the rights and movements of offenders against whom they are obtained (Shute, 2004: 438–439). These measures, although less overtly premised on "disintegrative shaming" than, for example, public disclosure schemes, may also carry "a strong stigmatising force (Shute, 2004: 439), and with it "the associated dangers of ostracism or vigilante abuse" (McAlinden, 2007: 137). As a further situational attempt to control the behavior of sex offenders, they may also be open to challenge under Article 5. These exclusionary measures, in tandem with inherently restrictive license conditions, may increase the barriers to employment or accommodation for sex offenders (Brown, Spencer and Deakin, 2007). Community safety issues may also require constant supervision of a high risk offender including approved travel mode, route and time between work and home (Seleznow, 2002). The civil liberties implications of such orders mean that the right to apply for variation or discharge becomes highly important (Cleland, 2005: 204).

Sex offenders can also be subjected to a wide range of conditions as part of a SOPO in particular. This may include, for example, prohibitions or restrictions on accessing the internet. Given the centrality of the internet to our contemporary lives, the enforcement of such conditions can be very limiting (Walden and Wasik, 2011). As such, they may involve a breach of privacy rights under Article 8 and the right to freedom of expression under Article 10 of the ECHR (Walden and Wasik, 2011:

379). In this respect, the English Court of Appeal has outlawed outright prohibition of a person's access to the internet on the grounds that it was disproportionate and oppressive as well as virtually impossible to police (Walden and Wasik, 2011). There is, it seems, therefore, "a difficult balance to be struck between the effective monitoring of a preventive order such as a SOPO, and unacceptable intrusion into the defendant's life and the lives of his family and others" (Walden and Wasik, 2011: 386).

In the United States, developments have gone further still. Widespread public disclosure under "Megan's Law" can include, for example, mandatory self-identification by the sex offender, discretionary or mandatory police identification, public access to a police book, and public access by telephone (Bedarf, 1995: 903–906; see Chapter 21). This can include specific information about offenders such as their home address or place of employment (Zevitz and Farkas, 2000). In some states, citizens can search for details of local sex offenders using a map of their area and can sign up for e-mail notifications of changes to this information.[8] In addition, many states subject sex offenders to residence or employment restrictions as part of the conditions attached to community notification or criminal justice supervision (see Chapter 25). These will operate, for example, in terms of avoiding placing a sex offender in housing or employment which is in close proximity to schools or children's playgrounds (Mustaine, Tewksbury and Stengel, 2006; Walker, 2007). Such restrictions also give rise to legal and ethical concerns.

In this context, "Megan's Law" has been challenged under the US Constitution on a number of grounds, including due process concerns and the prohibition on cruel and unusual punishment (Earl-Hubbard, 1996; Logan, 1999). Research has also confirmed the effects of community notification may operate as structural obstacles to the employment, housing and reintegration of sex offenders (Mustaine, Tewksbury and Stengel, 2006; Levenson, 2008). These restrictions may create a shortage of housing options for sex offenders and in turn force them into rural areas where they may be further isolated with reduced opportunities for employment (Levenson and Cotter, 2005; Lester, 2006; Brown, Spencer and Deakin, 2007). Loss of employment and living arrangements were often cited by sex offenders as direct consequences of enhanced community notification as well as the related negative publicity and social stigmatization (Tewksbury, 2005; Zevitz, 2006; Robbers, 2009).

"Shame penalties"

A minority of US judges have begun to use "shame penalties," in the form of "signs" and "apologies," as part of modern probation conditions for sex offenders (Massaro, 1991: 1886–1890; Karp, 1998: 281–283). In one case,[9] the court placed a convicted child molester on probation for five years subject to a requirement that he place a sign on both sides of his car and on the door of his home in large lettering which read: "Dangerous Sex Offender – No Children Allowed" (Kelley, 1989: 760; Massaro, 1991: 1887–1888). Similarly, courts have also required sex offenders to place ads in the local newspaper publicizing their offenses or urging others to seek treatment (Massaro, 1991: 1880). These "scarlet letter" measures (Brilliant, 1989; Earl-Hubbard, 1996) appeal to judges and a concerned public because they satisfy punitive retributive impulses (Karp, 1998: 277–278). Their central component is public exposure – to bring the crime to the community's attention so that it may respond with shaming (Karp, 1998: 281). Their primary purpose is to protect potential victims by warning them of the danger these offenders pose. The risk of stigmatization and social exclusion, however, attaches to those who are subject to such penalties (Kelley, 1989: 775).

A further measure which has been used to control sex offenders in the community and which may also operate as a means of disintegrative shaming is electronic tagging. The possible benefits of electronic monitoring for managing sex offenders in the community, as with all such measures, can be framed in terms of deterrence and prevention. Although not used widely in the UK, in some American states such as Florida, offenders can be "tracked" via second generation systems known as "Ground Position by Satellite" (GPS) (Whitfield, 1997: 112–113). The system has pre-programmed rules which control both where and when offenders are permitted to be away from home, so that in addition to the traditional curfew, permitted or prohibited areas can also be specified. Electronic monitoring has arrived at a time when the pressure to become more tough, controlling and restrictive has affected the whole of the criminal justice system (Whitfield, 1997: 54), not least in relation to sex offenders. Tagging has both punishment and control features – it may not only constrain patterns of behavior, but may also reinforce the consequences of particular actions. In common with "shame penalties," it is this punitive element which may give the measure populist appeal.

Electronic monitoring, however, raises a number of difficult issues, such as the ethics of this type of coercive surveillance, the extension of social control, the intrusiveness of equipment and whether its embarrassing and degrading aspects amount to an infringement of basic civil liberties (Whitfield, 1997: 79). Home detention schemes, in particular, may have a negative impact on the offender's family (Gibbs, 2003). Enforced curfew hours may mean that domestic and family pressures increase and that lifestyles change. This may drive some offenders to sedentary and escapist activities at home, including domestic violence (Walter, Sugg and Moore, 2001). The constitutionality of electronic monitoring has never been successfully challenged in the United States, where the courts have generally viewed the measure as an enhancement of supervision (McAlinden, 2007: 142). The measure, however, may also be susceptible to challenge under Article 5 of the ECHR. Article 5, however, is also a limited right which may be discounted in a limited range of circumstances.[10]

At the time of the enactment of the original sex offender orders, a predecessor of RSHOs and SOPOs, such human rights considerations prompted the UK Labour government to resist a further opposition amendment which would have enabled magistrates to impose positive obligations on sex offenders, namely electronic tagging and a requirement that the offender be forced to remain in a given place for a specified period.[11] However, the European Court of Human Rights has generally held that a person who is prevented from leaving a particular area by a curfew or order has not been deprived of his liberty but merely suffered only a "restriction of liberty."[12] It may be that there is a fine line between deprivation of liberty, as specifically prohibited by Article 5, and restrictions on freedom of movement. The distinction, in fact, is by no means clear cut and remains one of degree rather than substance (Murdoch, 1993). Whether a deprivation of liberty has occurred in a particular case within the scope of Article 5 will depend on the individual situation of the person as well as on the circumstances in which they have been placed, including the type, duration, effects and manner of implementation of the measure in question[13] (see Chapter 2). Such restrictions, for example, are likely to be more severe for high risk sex offenders who have been released into the community.

Part II: Restorative Justice and "Reintegrative Shaming"

Reintegration through safety and support

In contrast to retributive measures which are heavily premised on risk management and formal modes of social control, restorative frameworks aim to reintegrate and rehabilitate offenders by informally sanctioning deviance through measures of safety and support. Restorative justice views crime not as a violation of a legal category which demands punishment but as harm to people and relationships and seeks to redress or restore that harm (Van Ness and Strong, 1997). The key values of restorative justice are said to comprise a number of principles, including inclusivity and the balance of interests of all the parties affected by the offense, consensual non-coercive participation and decision making, and a problem-solving orientation (Crawford and Goodey, 2000). Additionally, restorative or reintegrative approaches are usually based on the following core aims: engaging with offenders to help them appreciate the consequences of their actions; encouraging appropriate forms of reparation by offenders towards their victim or the wider community; seeking reconciliation between the victim and offender where this is desirable; and the reintegration of the offender (Zehr, 1990; Braithwaite, 1999). Restorative justice is in one sense an umbrella term which has been use to cover an increasingly wide range of schemes that seek to respond to crime in a more constructive way than through the use of formal legal methods (Galaway and Hudson, 1996). Restorative justice has three basic models: mediation, conferencing and circles, all three of which have been used to a greater or lesser extent as a response to sexual crime.

In the United States, for example, victim–offender mediation has been used with homicide and sexual assault (Umbreit, Bradshaw and Coates, 1999). Similarly, intimate abuse circles have also been used as a response to gendered and sexualized violence, in particular domestic violence (Mills, 2003). In such a context it provides a forum for addressing the abusive dynamic and may involve both parties and a "care community," comprised of family, friends or the clergy, who work collectively to promote recognition, responsibility and change. The main variants, however, as used with sexual offenders, are conferencing and circles of support and accountability. Restorative justice has been used as a response to some very serious social problems and human rights abuses such as the Truth and Reconciliation Commissions of South Africa (Villa Vincenzo, 1999) and Rwanda (Drumbl, 2000) in relation to genocide, mass torture and rape, and with respect to paramilitary violence in Northern Ireland (McEvoy and Mika, 2001). It is the extension of the restorative paradigm to sexual offending, however, and to sexual offenses involving children in particular, which remains the most controversial and which generates complex legal and ethical issues.

Conferencing and circles

The use of restorative or reintegrative schemes with sexual offenders has developed very much on an ad hoc basis. In South Australia, for example, young people charged with sexual offenses, who admit their behavior, are diverted from court processes and participate in a family conference (Daly, 2006). In Australia and North Carolina the "family decision making model" has also used a conference-style process with children and families affected by child sexual abuse and domestic violence, although usually the offender is excluded from this process (Pennell and Burford, 2000). In Arizona, the RESTORE program uses restorative justice as a response to date and acquaintance rape by first-time adult offenders and those charged with misdemeanor sexual offenses in a collaborative program between Pima County Attorney's Office, the Southern Arizona Center Against Sexual Assault, and the College of Public Health, University of Arizona (Koss, Bachar and Hopkins, 2003).

One of the most established and well-known programs, however, is circles of support and accountability. Circle programs have been used in Canada for more than 10 years to reintegrate selected high risk sex offenders at the end of their custodial sentence (Cesaroni, 2001; Wilson, Huculak and McWhinnie, 2002). At a broad level, these schemes are premised on "reintegrative shaming" (Braithwaite, 1989) and involve the development of restorative support and treatment networks for sex offenders where the community works in partnership with the offender and professional agencies. They are based on the twin philosophies of safety and support; they seek to address public concerns about public protection but, at the same time, meet the offender's needs in terms of reintegration. The circle is individually tailored around the offender, the core member, involving the wider community in tandem with state and voluntary agencies. The offender and other members of the circle enter into a signed covenant which specifies each member's area of assistance. The scheme provides high levels of support, guidance and supervision for the offender, which can mediate between the police, media and the local community to minimize risk and assist with reintegration. The offender agrees to relate to the circle of support, to pursue treatment and to act responsibly in the community. Circles aim to allay the fears of the local community as well as to reduce the likelihood of further offending by holding the offender accountable to their commitment not to re-offend. To this end, early evaluations have produced positive results (Bates, Saunders and Wilson, 2007; Wilson *et al.*, 2007).

Circles have also been extended to other jurisdictions, including Northern Ireland, England and Wales and Scotland, on a pilot basis. Within the United Kingdom they have been used to support the work of the police, the probation service and other agencies in the multi-agency approach to sex offender risk management (see Chapter 22). Indeed, a broad difference between the two dominant models which exist in Canada and the United Kingdom respectively is that while the former model is organic, the latter is systemic. That is, the Canadian model grew out of the need of a faith community to support individual offender reintegration, while the UK model is centrally concerned with the core business of information and offender management and as such remains harnessed to the priorities and interests of the state. These differences, particularly in relation to the nature and degree of the role of the state may also have varying legal and ethical implications.

Due process, legitimacy, accountability and adequate safeguards

Opponents of restorative justice have pointed out the general dangers inherent in a communitarian approach to justice, principally the need to ensure legitimacy (Paternoster *et al.*, 1997), accountability (Roche, 2003) and adequate safeguards (Van Ness, 1999; Ashworth, 2002; Wright, 2002). Paternoster *et al.* (1997) identify several elements which provide legitimacy. These include: representation, in the sense of playing a part in decision making; consistency; impartiality; accuracy; the competency of the legal authority; correctability, as the scope for appeal; and ethicality, treating people with dignity and respect.

Restorative justice embodies some of these elements, particularly with regard to representation of and respect for victims and offenders. It does not meet others since they relate primarily to expectations of "legal authority" derived principally from traditional justice values (Morris and Gelsthorpe, 2000: 421). Restorative justice involves somewhat different values and its legitimacy derives from these. Important ingredients underlying the legitimacy of restorative justice are the inclusion of the key parties, and enhanced understanding of the offense and its impact (Morris and Gelsthorpe, 2000: 421), as embodied in its key principles as outlined above.

Critics also argue that the lack of procedural rules and structure and the absence of recorded precedent make the modes of operation and decision making arbitrary and unpredictable (McAlinden, 2007: 198). There may be little to distinguish voluntarily agreed measures and community-based schemes which, while they are not based on fact-finding or the determination of guilt, may nonetheless impose sanctions. There may also be concerns about double jeopardy if individuals find themselves involved in a community-based scheme and yet also face the threat of simultaneous or subsequent formal legal sanctions. The majority of these objections have been founded on the basic premise that restorative justice aims to replace the formal administration of state justice and the consequent dangers associated with a non-legal community response (Ashworth, 2002). Restorative justice, however, may operate within or outwith the criminal justice system as an alternative, diversionary process.

In this respect, removing the state completely from the process introduces concerns about due process and adequate procedural safeguards, and in particular, how to ensure accountability and the legitimacy of the process (Van Ness, 1999; Braithwaite, 1999). There are particular concerns, for example, in relation to proportionality. There should not be a disproportionate burden placed on the offender, and equally the victims or the wider community should not be allowed to have undue influence on the process which could lead to inconsistency and injustice (Zedner, 1994; Ashworth, 2002). Care also needs to be taken to avoid vengeful or disruptive communities from taking over the process.

At the same time, if the state is to be involved there are also a range of concerns about the extent and nature of its role (Hoyle and Young, 2002: 540–547). Key questions include, first, who should facilitate the programs? Possibilities include the police, social workers or other state or voluntary agencies or neutral facilitators in the form of an entirely independent agency (Maxwell and Morris, 2001; Young, 2001). Secondly, should legal advice or representation should be made available. This is in recognition of the fact that the offender may effectively confess to the commission of an offense (Meier, 1998; Young, 2001) and is regarded as perhaps the most important due process check on the process and outcomes (Warner, 1994). There are others, however, who question the necessity or appropriateness of involving lawyers in the restorative process, pointing chiefly to the need to safeguard against partisan, advisory and representative roles which may monopolize the process and reduce the offender's involvement and the opportunity to confront their offending and take responsibility for their actions (Ball, 1999; Crawford, 2002). Thirdly, what if the influence of the state controls the agenda and consequently limits community involvement? A legitimate and accountable process would properly protect the rights of all participants and this is part of the state's mandate. As will be discussed in the conclusion, however, schemes which work in partnership with, take referrals from, and are subject to accreditation and monitoring by the criminal justice system may negate both sets of concerns.

The concerns of critics are heightened when restorative schemes are applied to sexual crime, particularly those relating to child sexual abuse. In this respect, there are a number of arguments traditionally put forward by opponents of restorative justice as applied to sexual crime. In essence, for these critics, sexual offending is considered an inappropriate or unsuitable area within which to use a restorative response. In the main, it has been suggested that restorative justice trivializes what are very serious criminal offenses, particularly where children and the vulnerable are concerned; it fails to promote offender accountability and allows the offender to reject responsibility for the offense; it reproduces and reinforces the power imbalance entrenched in abusive relationships, which are heightened between adult perpetrators and child victims, and leads to possible re-victimization; and it encourages vigilantism.

Proponents have addressed these critiques concerning "hard" cases and how they can be overcome (Hudson, 1998; Daly, 2002; Morris and Gelsthorpe, 2000; Morris, 2002; McAlinden, 2005, 2007). They counter that even though the criminal law remains as a symbolic signifier and denouncer, restorative processes which involve the abuser's family and the community can meet the affective or expressive need for censure in sexual offenses cases; that while the criminal justice system does little to hold offenders accountable and address entrenched forms of offending behavior, restorative justice seeks genuine engagement with offenders to help them acknowledge the consequences of their actions; it focuses on the empowerment of victims in a supportive environment in which the victim can make clear to the offender the effects of the abuse on them; that by offering constructive rather than purely penal solutions, it may be invoked at an earlier stage in the victim's experience of abuse; and finally, that distortions of power, including abuse of community control, are addressed when programs adhere closely to restorative principles.

Conclusion: The Balance of Rights

This chapter has outlined the range of possible legal and ethical implications of disintegrative shaming measures such as notification which are aimed at controlling the whereabouts and behavior of sex offenders in the community. Public concern and political pressures about the perceived risk posed by sex offenders have combined to enshrine retributive regulatory responses with scant regard for efficacy both in terms of offender reintegration as well as an appropriate balance in terms of rights (Erooga, 2008). Such measures have "forced restrictions and inroads on traditional rights of privacy, freedom of movement and standardised punishment" (McAlinden, 2007: 116) and have created possible risks to the personal safety of offenders arising from the stigma associated with sex offending behavior.

This singling out of the offender via shaming sanctions may also have a number of other negative effects, beyond the physical (McAlinden, 2007: 130–131). It may impede the successful reintegration of the offender into the community, his ability to get a job or accommodation and therefore, ultimately, his rehabilitation. Heightening the offender's sense of isolation may ultimately increase the chance of subsequent delinquent behavior as a coping mechanism. Moreover, if an offender becomes known or ostracized in the area where he lives he will not be deterred from future crime. The offender may simply go underground where he could be of even greater danger and commit crime elsewhere. In sum, the legal and ethical issues which arise from "disintegrative shaming" are encapsulated in the core argument of the appellant in *State* v. *Bateman*: "The defendant will be at best shunned from society and at worst subjected to physical harassment and abuse."[14]

At the other end of the intervention spectrum, the operation of reintegrative shaming measures such as conferencing with young sexual offenders or circles of support with high risk sex offenders also gives rise to a range of procedural issues such as legitimacy, accountability and adequate safeguards. Such concerns are particularly potent where child victims are concerned and when schemes take place outwith the involvement of the state or state agencies where there will always be a risk of vengeful community members taking over the process. At the same time, however, the community has the right to feel safe and secure in the knowledge that sex offenders, particularly high risk or dangerous ones, are being effectively managed. Victims or potential victims also have the right to protection from harm. Offenders themselves have the often overlooked rights to rehabilitation and reintegration, to be supported in their efforts to change, and to remain free from harmful inference in their daily lives.

In this respect, it seems that a concerted effort on the part of policy makers to move from regulation to the reintegration of sexual offenders would offer a more viable means of achieving a better balance between the multiple interests at stake in the sex offender problem – communities, victims and offenders as well as the state. In particular, the fuller implementation of circles of support and accountability, which allow for a measure of community involvement, would strengthen the decision-making process of the state in relation to resettlement of the offender and also help to improve the accountability of both sectors. Moreover, such a seismic shift in public policy would also improve the effective management of risk and dispense with many of the legal and ethical concerns outlined above which currently underpin dichotomous regulatory and reintegrative regimes. Measures such as circles of support, which harness community involvement in sex offender reintegration to statutory schemes and processes, offer a more effective means of achieving a rights-based approach to sex offender reintegration than either regulatory or reintegrative measures on their own currently do. As Erooga (2008) also argues, ultimately a rights-based approach should be applied in terms of public protection policy on sex offending in order to develop more effective approaches to public protection.

Notes

1   See *R (on the application of F and Thompson)* v. *Secretary of State for the Home Department* [2010] UKSC 17.
2   The Court of Appeal in *R* v. *Chief Constable of North Wales Police, ex parte Thorpe* [1999] QB 396, held that although there should never be a policy of blanket disclosure, the police had a right to notify immediate neighbors that two individuals had moved in with a criminal record of child abuse since there was a specific risk of re-offending.
3   Sarah Payne was abducted from near her grandparents' home in Sussex in July 2000 and was molested and murdered by known "pedophile" Roy Whiting.
4   ss97–103.
5   ss114–122, as amended by the Policing and Crime Act 2009, ss23–25.
6   ss123–129.
7   ss104–113.
8   "The town that puts sex offenders on the map," *Sunday Telegraph*, January 29, 2006.
9   *State* v. *Bateman* 95 Or. Ct. App. 456, 771 P.2d 314 (1989).
10 Art 5(1) (a)–(f).
11 See, for example, Mr Alun Michael, HC *Standing Committee on the Crime and Disorder Bill*, 5 May 1998.
12 *Raimondo* v. *Italy* (1994) 18 EHRR 237.
13 *Guzzardi* v. *Italy* (1980) 3 EHRR 333, para. 92, adopting the language of *Engel and others* v. *Netherlands (No 1)* (1976) 1 EHRR 647, para 59.
14 Brief for Appellant, *State* v. *Bateman*, see n. 9 above, at A-2.

References

Ashenden, S. (2002) "Policing perversion: the contemporary governance of paedophilia," *Cultural Values* 6, 197–222.
Ashworth, A. (2002) "Responsibilities, rights and restorative justice," *British Journal of Criminology* 42, 578–595.
Ball, C. (1999) "The Youth Justice and Criminal Evidence Act 1999 – Part I: a significant move towards restorative justice, or a recipe for unintended consequences?," *Criminal Law Review* 211–222.
Barber, N.W. (1998) "Privacy and the police: private right, public right or human right?," *Public Law* 19–24.
Bates, A., Saunders, R. and Wilson, C. (2007) "Doing something about it: a follow-up study of sex offenders participating in Thames Valley Circles of Support and Accountability," *British Journal of Community Justice* 5, 19–42.
Beck, U. (1992) *Risk Society: Towards a New Modernity*. London: Sage.
Bedarf, A. (1995) "Examining sex offender community notification laws," *California Law Review* 83, 885–937.
Braithwaite, J. (1989) *Crime, Shame and Reintegration*. Sydney: Cambridge University Press.

Braithwaite, J. (1999) "Restorative justice: assessing optimistic and pessimistic accounts," in M. Tonry (ed.), *Crime and Justice: A Review of Research, Vol. 25.* Chicago, University of Chicago Press, pp. 1–127.

Brilliant, J.A. (1989) "The modern day scarlet letter: a critical analysis of modern probation conditions," *Duke Law Journal* 5, 1357–1385.

Brown, K., Spencer, J. and Deakin, J. (2007) "The reintegration of sex offenders: barriers and opportunities for employment," *Howard Journal* 46, 32–42.

Cesaroni, C. (2001) "Releasing sex offenders into the community through 'circles of support' – a means of reintegrating the 'worst of the worst'," *Journal of Offender Rehabilitation* 34, 85–98.

Chan, V., Homes, A., Murray, L. *et al.* (2010) *Evaluation of the Sex Offender Community Disclosure Pilot.* Edinburgh: Scottish Government Social Research Series.

Christie, N. (2000) *Crime Control as Industry,* 3rd edn. London: Routledge.

Cleland, A. (2005) "Protection is better than cure," *Scots Law Times* 36, 201.

Crawford, A. (2002) "The prospects for restorative justice in England and Wales: a tale of two acts," in K. McEvoy and T. Newburn (eds), *Criminology and Conflict Resolution.* London: Palgrave, pp. 171–207.

Crawford, A. (2003) "Contractual governance of deviant behaviour," *Journal of Law and Society* 30, 479–505.

Crawford, A. and Goodey, J. (eds) (2000) *Integrating a Victim Perspective Within Criminal Justice.* Aldershot: Ashgate.

Daly, K. (2002) "Restorative justice: the real story," *Punishment and Society* 4, 55–79.

Daly, K. (2006) "Restorative justice and sexual assault: an archival study of court and conference cases," *British Journal of Criminology* 46, 334–356.

Drumbl, M. (2000) "Sclerosis: retributive justice and the Rwandan genocide," *Punishment and Society* 2, 287–308.

Earl-Hubbard, M. (1996) "The child sex offender registration laws: the punishment, liberty, deprivation and unintended results associated with the Scarlet Letter Laws of the 1990s," *North Western Law Review* 90,788.

Edwards, W. and Hensley, C. (2001) "Contextualising sex offender management legislation and policy: evaluating the problem of latent consequences in community notification laws," *International Journal of Offender Therapy and Comparative Criminology* 45, 83–101.

Ericson, R.V. and Haggerty, K.D. (1997) *Policing the Risk Society.* Oxford: Clarendon Press.

Erooga, E. (2008) "A human rights-based approach to sex offender management: the key to effective public protection?," *Journal of Sexual Aggression* 14, 171–183.

Galaway, B. and Hudson, B. (1996) *Restorative Justice: International Perspectives.* Monsey, NY: Criminal Justice Press.

Gibbs, A. (2003) "Home detention with electronic monitoring: the New Zealand experience," *Criminal Justice* 3, 199–211.

Hebenton, B. and Thomas, T. (1996) "Sexual offenders in the community: reflections on problems of law, community and risk management in the USA and England and Wales," *International Journal of the Sociology of Law* 24, 427–443.

Hebenton, B. and Thomas, T. (1997) "Paedophiles, privacy and protecting the public," *Criminal Lawyer* 7–8.

Hoyle, C. and Young, R. (2002) "Restorative justice: assessing the prospects and pitfalls," in M. McConville and G. Wilson (eds), *The Handbook of The Criminal Justice Process.* Oxford: Oxford University Press, pp. 525–548.

Hudson, B. (1998) "Restorative justice: the challenge of sexual and racial violence," *Journal of Law and Society* 25, 237–256.

Karp, D.R. (1998) "The judicial and the judicious use of shame penalties," *Crime and Delinquency* 44, 277–294.

Kelley, R.K. (1989) (Comment) "Sentenced to wear the scarlet letter: judicial innovations in sentencing," *Dickinson Law Review* 93, 759–788.

Kemshall, H. (2001) *Risk Assessment and Management of Known Sexual and Violent Offenders: A Review of Current Issues*, Police Research Series Paper No. 140. London: Home Office.

Kemshall, H. and Maguire, M. (2001) "Public protection, partnership and risk penalty: the multi-agency risk management of sexual and violent offenders," *Punishment and Society* 3, 237–264.

Kemshall, H., Wood, J., Westwood, S., *et al.* (2010) *Child Sex Offender Review (CSOR) Public Disclosure Pilots: A Process Evaluation*, 4th edn. London: Home Office.

Koss, M.P., Bachar, K.J. and Hopkins, C.Q. (2003) "Restorative justice for sexual violence: repairing victims, building community, and holding offenders accountable," *Annals New York Academy of Sciences* 989, 364–477.

Lester, J.L. (2006) "Off to Elba: the legitimacy of sex offender residence and employment restrictions," *Berkeley Electronic Press*, http://law.bepress.com/expresso/eps/1818 (accessed August 25, 2012).

Levenson, J.S. (2008) "Collateral consequences of sex offender residence restrictions," *Criminal Justice Studies* 2, 153–166.

Levenson, J.S. and Cotter, L.P. (2005) "The effect of Megan's Law on sex offender reintegration," *Journal of Contemporary Criminal Justice* 21, 49–66.

Lieb, R. (1996) "Community notification laws: a step towards more effective solutions," *Journal of Interpersonal Violence* 11, 298–300.

Loader, I. and Walker, N. (2007) *Civilizing Security*. Cambridge: Cambridge University Press.

Logan, W. (1999) "Liberty interests in The Preventive State: Procedural Due Process and Sex Offender Community Notification Laws," *Journal of Criminal Law and Criminology* 89, 1167–1232.

Maguire, M., Kemshall, H., Noakes, L., *et al.* (2001) *Risk Management of Sexual and Violent Offenders: The Work of Public Protection Panels*, Police Research Series Paper No. 13. London: Home Office.

Massaro, T.M. (1991) "Shame culture and American criminal law," *Michigan Law Review* 89, 1880–1903.

Maxwell, G. and Morris, A. (2001) "Family group conferences and reoffending," in A. Morris and G. Maxwell (eds), *Restorative Justice for Juveniles: Conferencing, Mediation and Circles*. Oxford: Hart Publishing, pp. 243–263.

McAlinden, A. (1999) "Sex offender registration: some observations on 'Megan's Law' and the Sex Offenders Act 1997," *Crime Prevention and Community Safety: An International Journal* 1, 41–53.

McAlinden, A. (2000) "Sex offender registration: implications and difficulties for Ireland," *Irish Journal of Sociology* (Special Issue: Crime and Policing) 10, 75–102.

McAlinden, A. (2005) "The use of 'shame' with sexual offenders," *British Journal of Criminology* 45, 373–394.

McAlinden, A. (2007) *The Shaming of Sexual Offenders: Risk, Retribution and Reintegration*. Oxford: Hart Publishing.

McEvoy, K. and Mika, H. (2001) "Policing, punishment and praxis: restorative justice and non-violent alternatives to paramilitary punishments in Northern Ireland," *Policing and Society* 11, 259–382.

Meier, B. (1998) "Restorative justice: a new paradigm in criminal law?," *European Journal of Crime, Criminal Law and Criminal Justice* 6, 125–139.

Mills, L.G. (2003) *Insult to Injury: Rethinking Our Responses to Intimate Abuse*. Princeton, Princeton University Press.

Morris, A. (2002) "Critiquing the critics: a brief response to critics of restorative justice," *British Journal of Criminology* 42, 596–615.

Morris, A. and Gelsthorpe, L. (2000) "Re-visioning men's violence against female partners," *Howard Journal* 39, 412–428.

Mullender, R. (1998) "Privacy, paedophilia and the European Convention on Human Rights: a deontological approach," *Public Law* 384–388.

Murdoch, J. (1993) "Safeguarding the liberty of the person: recent Strasbourg jurisprudence," *International Comparative Law Quarterly* 42, 494–522.

Mustaine, E., Tewksbury, R. and Stengel, K. (2006) "Residential location and mobility of registered sex offenders," *American Journal of Criminal Justice* 30, 177–192.

Parton, N., Thorpe, D. and Wattam, C. (1997) *Child Protection: Risk and the Moral Order.* Hampshire: Macmillan.

Paternoster, R., Backman, R., Brame, R. and Sherman, L. (1997) "Do fair procedures matter? The effect of procedural justice on spousal assault," *Law and Society Review* 31, 163–204.

Pennell, J. and Burford, G. (2000) "Family group decision making and family violence," in G. Burford and J. Hudson (eds), *Family Group Conferencing: New Directions in Community-centered Child and Family Practice.* Hawthorne, NY: Aldine de Gruyter, pp. 171–185.

Power, H. (1999) "The Crime and Disorder Act 1998: (1) sex offenders, privacy and the police," *Criminal Law Review* 3.

Power, H. (2003) "Disclosing information on sex offenders: the human rights implications," in A. Matravers (ed.), *Sex Offenders in the Community: Managing and Reducing the Risks.* Devon: Willan Publishing.

Robbers, M.L.P. (2009) "Lifers on the outside: sex offenders and disintegrative shaming," *International Journal of Offender Therapy and Comparative Criminology* 53, 5.

Roche, D. (2003) *Accountability in Restorative Justice.* Oxford: Oxford University Press.

Rutherford, A. (2000) "Holding the line on sex offender notification," *New Law Journal* 150, 1359.

Seleznow, E. (2002) "Time to work: managing the employment of sex offenders under community supervision," Center for Sex Offender Management http://www.csom.org/pubs/timetowork.pdf (accessed August 25, 2012).

Shearing, C. (2000) "Punishment and the changing face of governance," *Punishment and Society* 3, 203–220.

Shute, S. (2004) "The Sexual Offences Act 2003: (4) new civil preventative orders – sexual offences prevention orders; foreign travel orders; risk of sexual harm orders," *Criminal Law Review* 417–440.

Silverman, J. and Wilson, D. (2002) *Innocence Betrayed: Paedophilia, the Media and Society.* Cambridge: Polity Press.

Simon, J. (1998) "Managing the monstrous: sex offenders and the new penology," *Psychology, Public Policy and Law* 4, 452–467.

Soothill, K. and Francis, B. (1998) "Poisoned chalice or just deserts? (The Sex Offenders Act 1997)," *Journal of Forensic Psychiatry* 9, 281–293.

Tewksbury, R. (2005) "Collateral consequences of sex offender registration," *Journal of Contemporary Criminal Justice* 21, 67–81.

Thomas, T. (2001) "Sex offenders, the Home Office and the Sunday papers," *Journal of Social Welfare and Family Law* 23, 103–108.

Umbreit, M., Bradshaw, W. and Coates, R.B. (1999) "Victims of severe violence meet the offender: restorative justice through dialogue," *International Review of Victimology* 6, 321–343.

Van Ness, D. (1999) "Legal Issues of Restorative Justice," in G. Bazemore and L. Walgrave (eds), *Restoring Juvenile Justice: Repairing the Harm of Youth Crime.* Monsey, NY: Criminal Justice Press, pp. 263–284.

Van Ness, D. and Strong, K.H. (1997) *Restoring Justice*. Cincinnati, OH: Anderson Publishing Co.

Villa Vincenzo, C. (1999) "A different kind of justice: the South African Truth and Reconciliation Commission," *Contemporary Justice Review* 1, 403–428.

Walden, I. and Wasik, M. (2011) "The internet: access controlled!," *Criminal Law Review* 377–387.

Walker, J.T. (2007) "Eliminate residency restrictions for sex offenders," *Criminology & Public Policy* 6, 863–870.

Walter, I., Sugg, S. and Moore, L. (2001) *A Year on the Tag: Interviews with Criminal Justice Practitioners and Electronic Monitoring Staff about Curfew Orders*. Home Office Research Findings No. 140. London: Home Office.

Warner, K. (1994) "Family group conferences and the rights of the offender," in C. Alder and J. Wundersitz (eds), *Family Conferencing and Juvenile Justice: The Way Forward or Misplaced Optimism?* Canberra: Australian Institute of Criminology, pp. 141–152.

Whitfield, D. (1997) *Tackling the Tag*. Winchester: Waterside Press.

Williams, A. and Thompson, B. (2004) "Vigilance or vigilantes: the Paulsgrove Riots and policing paedophiles in the community: part 1: the long slow fuse" and "Part 2: the lessons of Paulsgrove," *Police Journal* 77, 99–119 and 193–205.

Wilson, R.J., Huculak, B. and McWhinnie, A. (2002) "Restorative justice innovations in Canada," *Behavioural Sciences and the Law* 20, 363–380.

Wilson, R.J., McWhinnie, A., Picheca, J.E., *et al.* (2007) "Circles of support and accountability: engaging community volunteers in the management of high-risk sexual offenders," *Howard Journal* 46, 1–15.

Wortley, R. and Smallbone, S. (2006) *Situational Prevention of Child Sexual Abuse*, Crime Prevention Studies, Vol. 19. Monsey, NY: Criminal Justice Press, and Devon: Willan Publishing.

Wright, M. (2002) "The court as last resort," *British Journal of Criminology* 42, 654–667.

Young, R. (2001) "Just cops doing 'shameful' business? Police-led restorative justice and the lessons of research," in A. Morris and G. Maxwell (eds), *Restorative Justice for Juveniles: Conferencing, Mediation and Circle*. Oxford: Hart Publishing, pp. 195–226.

Zedner, L. (1994) "Reparation and retribution: are they reconcilable?," *Modern Law Review* 57, 228–250.

Zehr, H. (1990) *Changing Lenses: A New Focus for Crime and Justice*. Scottdale, PA: Herald Press.

Zevitz, R.G. (2006) "Sex offender community notification: its' role in recidivism and offender reintegration," *Criminal Justice Studies* 19, 193–208.

Zevitz, R.G. and Farkas, M.A. (2000) "Sex offender community notification: managing high risk criminals or exacting further vengeance?," *Behavioral Sciences and the Law* 18, 375–391.

8

"Castrate 'Em!"
Treatments, Cures and Ethical Considerations in UK Press Coverage of "Chemical Castration"
Peter Brown

Introduction

Child sexual abuse is a high-profile social problem with a long and varied history (for example, Critcher, 2003; Jenkins, 1998; Kitzinger, 2004; Smart, 1999, 2000). However, it was not until its "discovery" by the media in the mid-1980s that child sexual abuse was first treated as a matter of serious importance by policy makers, educators, journalists and the wider public. In the intervening years, considerable concern has been raised by a wide range of issues concerning the sexual abuse of children, including incest, child pornography, pedophile rings, satanic abuse, pedophile priests, stranger danger and community notification (Ashenden, 2002; Critcher, 2003; Jenkins, 1998; Kitzinger, 1999; Pratt, 2009). Many of these issues – particularly those framed through the latter-day figure of "the pedophile" – have been said to constitute a "moral panic" (Critcher, 2003), although this suggestion has been challenged (Kitzinger, 1999). Regardless, in spite of vastly increased attention from policy makers, educational bodies, citizens and the media, child sexual abuse, it has been argued, "remains an apparently insurmountable problem in Western developed societies" (Smart, 2000: 55). In the news media, this intermittently leads to desperate newspaper headlines such as, "What can we do to beat the menace of child abusers?" (*Daily Express*, August 20, 2008), "Counselling fails to 'cure' paedophile" (*Daily Telegraph*, August 24, 2011), and "The sorry truth is many sex offenders can't be rehabilitated" (*Daily Mail*, March 10, 2010).

The chapter examines the role of the media in shaping and responding to debates around the treatment of child sex offenders, paying particular attention to the issue of "chemical castration." It will by presenting an overview of scholarship around the social construction of "the pedophile," outlining dominant media representations and their implications for how we understand and conceptualize child sexual abuse

The Wiley-Blackwell Handbook of Legal and Ethical Aspects of Sex Offender Treatment and Management, First Edition. Edited by Karen Harrison and Bernadette Rainey.
© 2013 John Wiley & Sons, Ltd. Published 2013 by John Wiley & Sons, Ltd.

as a social problem. Here it will be argued that a disproportionate focus on the individualized "pedophile" has restricted thinking to a limited and constrictive understanding of the problem, which has, in turn, led to equally limited thinking about "solutions" or "cures." Having presented this overview, the chapter will then explore newspaper coverage of debates around chemical castration from the UK national press. This analysis follows two strands. First, it will unpack the manner in which journalists frame "pedophilia" through a medical discourse when discussing the use of chemical castration as a means for treating sex offenders. It will demonstrate how this discourse helps to construct "pedophilia" (and "pedophiles") in one of three ways: (1) entirely curable; (2) treatable; or (3) entirely incurable. This is followed by an examination of some of the discursive strategies used to frame ethical issues relating to the use of chemical castration. To conclude, the chapter will explore readers' letters to the British tabloid newspaper the *Sun* and demonstrate the ways in which they reflect and build upon many of the discourses identified in the earlier parts of the chapter.

Through the course of this discussion of chemical castration the chapter will highlight the importance of lexical choices and rhetoric when constructing "pedophilia" and "the pedophile." It will demonstrate how journalists, expert sources and letter writers routinely manipulate elements of these discourses in order to suit their objectives. Thus, it will be argued that public debates around "chemical castration," as conducted through the national press, demonstrate the vague, inconsistent and ambiguous ways in which the concepts of "pedophilia" and "the pedophile" are used.

The Rise of the Pedophile Problem: A Brief Modern History

Concern about the sexual exploitation of children in the United Kingdom can be traced back over many decades. Jackson (2000a, 2000b) has looked at how child sexual abuse was dealt with during the Victorian and Edwardian eras, while Jeffreys' (1985) account highlights the role early UK feminists and "social purity" activists played in attempting to highlight the plight of young, working-class girls who were trapped into prostitution during the late nineteenth century. However, despite this attention, it is only in the relatively recent past that child sexual abuse has been treated as an issue of serious public concern and debate. Indeed, Smart (1999: 407) calls it "shocking and depressing" that "feminist campaigners in the 1910s and 1920s knew what we think we discovered in the 1970s."

Central to the recognition of child sexual abuse as a serious and widespread social problem was the awareness-raising role of feminist activists, professionals and researchers. These groups played a key part in elevating child sexual abuse onto the public agenda in Australia, Canada, the United Kingdom, the United States and beyond. In so doing, feminists challenged a number of normative assumptions about the nature and extent of child sexual abuse as a social problem. First, they highlighted that, like sexual violence against adult women, child sexual abuse is a gendered crime: the vast majority is perpetrated by men. As Kitzinger (2004: 126) notes, "one of the few things that distinguish people who commit sexual violence from people who don't, is that the former are usually male." From this perspective, child sexual abuse is not an issue of individual pathology, but an issue of gender. Thus, feminists focused attention on the social construction of gender within patriarchal society, specifically, the "problem of masculinity" (McLeod and Saraga, 1988: 43) and the disproportionate power men have in society and institutions within it (the family, the home and so on). Without such a focus, Kelly (1996) argues, attention shifts away from the centrality of male power and control, and defaults back to individualized, medical "explanations" that foreground notions of sexual deviance, obsession and "addiction."

Second, feminists challenged the myth that child sexual abuse was restricted to a narrow band of abnormal, psychotic or sick predators preying on children. They highlighted the fact that, not only is child sexual abuse a widespread problem, but that it is typically perpetrated by "normal," well-adjusted individuals who are known to and trusted by their victims – often family members, and often with the "safe haven" of the family home. During the initial flurry of coverage there was a dramatic shift in public perceptions which saw child sexual abuse become synonymous with incest (Kelly, 1988).

However, while feminist analyses were pivotal in informing early definitions of child sexual abuse, in subsequent years the issue has been at the center of a series of transformations and retransformations, as various stakeholders have sought to define and redefine the terms of the issue. Consequently, the feminist argument that once dominated has been systematically sidelined and focus has reverted to an issue of dangerous strangers – or, more specifically, a certain "type" of dangerous stranger: "the pedophile." As Kitzinger (2004: 155) notes, "the pedophile" "has become the dominant way through which sexual threats to children are conceptualised and articulated." This is nowhere more apparent than in media discourse.

Child sexual abuse as it is understood today was "discovered" by the UK media between the late 1970s and mid-1980s (Critcher, 2003; Jenkins, 1992; Kitzinger, 1999). Following an exposé in a 1986 television broadcast called *Childwatch* – an event which led to the launch of the telephone counseling service Childline – child sexual abuse, hitherto uncovered, became the topic of countless newspaper articles, television documentaries, chat shows, drama programs and soap operas (see Kitzinger, 1999). A series of peaks and troughs ensued before an "explosion of interest" (Soothill, Francis and Ackerley, 1998: 882) in the 1990s led to a substantial increase in coverage of child sexual abuse across the news media.

Across the media, child sexual abuse often tends to be constructed through the all-encompassing umbrella term "pedophilia." This term is used variously, and often uncritically, to frame topics such as child pornography, sex tourism, attacks by strangers, abuse in children's homes, child abductions and, more recently, internet predators. Comparing media coverage of pedophilia to that of other high-profile social problems such as AIDS, ecstasy and raves, "video nasties" and child abuse in families, Critcher (2003: 111) argues that "[n]o other issue . . . [has] provoked such intensive and extensive concern."

Central to media representations of "pedophilia" is the figure of "the pedophile." Both terms are dynamic and problematic, but it should be noted that they are distinct concepts. Although there is no consistency in the way "pedophilia" is defined, it typically refers to a sexual desire directed towards children, whether as a sexual preference or as an exclusive sexual attraction to children as opposed to adults. The term "pedophile," then, refers to a being, a figure who embodies the characteristics of "pedophilia."

Collier (2001: 242) describes the "category of the paedophile" as "a sociocultural phenomenon." According to Jenkins (1992: 73), "[t]he current image (and term) of the pedophile can be dated back with some precision to debates that occurred in 1977 and 1978." However, it was not until around a decade later that it really rose to prominence. Having extended established media images of the "sex fiend" (Soothill and Walby, 1991), Jenkins (1992: 99) argues that by the late 1980s, "[t]he figure of the pedophile had become one of the most terrifying folk-devils imagined in recent British history." This dynamic term has endured (and evolved) through time and continues to dominate popular discourse around child sexual abuse, prompting Silverman and Wilson (2002: 1) to argue that "the very word itself has become a conduit for fear and public loathing, often beyond all moderation."

Critcher (2003: 110) argues that within media discourse the pedophile is "an unequivocal folk devil: inherently evil and incapable of reform; cunning and devious; operating on secret networks; posing a constant threat to all children." Collier (2001) terms the pedophile discourse a "discourse of dangerousness." Meyer (2007: 69) has identified four major discourses used to construct pedophiles in the UK press: (1) evil, (2) perversion/pathology, (3) violence/destruction and (4) cunningness. She argues that through categorization and demonization, "[p]aedophiles are not only portrayed as marginal, evil 'Others' or persons but excluded from the category of humanity by being associated with and placed in the realm of the satanic" (Meyer, 2007: 70). Critcher (2003: 111) concurs, stating that, as far as the media are concerned, "pedophiles" are "sub-humans, [who] should be permanently removed from society."

Journalists often use pedophiles' physical appearance as a vehicle for foregrounding their supposed "difference." The construction of "the pedophile" as an "easily identifiable misfit" (Kitzinger, 2004: 125) suggests that their otherness is written all over their face. This discursive device, together with the wider discourse foregrounding pedophiles' supposed inhumanity and/or inherent evil, encourages the view that, once these individuals have been identified, the problem of child sexual abuse can be "solved" by removing them from society. In short, the simplistic construction of "the pedophile" facilitates the promotion of equally simplistic "common sense" solutions. Indeed, this is a view endorsed by many sections of the news media:

> The problem of sexual violence [is] represented by the newspaper image of the man with staring eyes or the evil smirk, the "beast" and "fiend" who [can] be singled out, electronically tagged, exposed and expelled. If paedophiles are literally "evil personified," then such evil can be exorcised by exclusion of these individuals from society. (Kitzinger, 1999: 218)

The concept of "the pedophile" has been criticized for positioning child sexual abuse "outside" the bounds of "normality." As Kelly (1996: 45) notes:

Immediately the word paedophile appears we have moved away from recognition of abusers as "ordinary men" – fathers, brothers, uncles, colleagues – and are returned to the more comfortable view of them as "other," a small minority who are fundamentally different from most men.

This discursive device is central to any debates around "solutions" to the problem of child sexual abuse because, as Meyer (2007: 74) notes, such terminology "produces knowledge of paedophiles as inhuman and this understanding translates into and legitimises demands for inhuman treatments." In this respect, this dominant construction of "the pedophile" promotes and/or legitimizes "simplistic explanations" (Soothill and Walby, 1991: 149) and, by association, simplistic solutions, for child sexual abuse.

Framing "Chemical Castration"

In June 2006, John Reid, the then newly appointed Home Secretary, found himself at the center of a growing political row about the protection of children from sex offenders. An investigation by the *News of the World* had uncovered 60 known child sex offenders living in government-approved probation hostels located near to schools. The paper was demanding action and stepped up its long-standing campaign for Britain to adopt a community notification system akin to the one employed in many American states (known as Megan's Law) which would allow parents to check if known sex offenders are living in their neighborhood (see Chapter 21).

Reid ordered that the sex offenders identified by the *News of the World* be moved to alternative hostels further away from schools, and news quickly emerged of high-level talks to introduce a raft of other measures aimed at dealing with the pedophile problem. Discussed as part of these proposals was the possibility of offering libido-suppressing drugs, including the anti-depressant drug Fluoxetine (better known as Prozac), to convicted child sex offenders.

Drug treatments for sex offenders were already available and prescribed in the United Kingdom, but Reid's proposals represented an expansion of the existing program. However, these developments led to a flurry of headlines across the national press, with many newspapers framing the move as a step towards a policy of "chemical castration." This led to headlines such as: "Jailed sex offenders to get anti-depressants in controversial treatment approved by ministers" (*Independent on Sunday*, June 25, 2006), "Reid's secret talks on plan to 'castrate' paedophiles" (*Daily Mail*, June 25, 2006) and "Castrate 'em: child sex pervs face shock drug treatment" (*Daily Star*, June 26, 2006).

The legislation was introduced a year later, in June 2007. In addition to stepping up voluntary drug treatment programs (including the use of hormonal medication and anti-depressant drugs), the final legislation took steps towards allowing restricted access to information about possible sex offenders, as well as making wider use of lie detector tests and satellite tracking technology to monitor a minority of offenders after their release from prison. Despite drug therapy remaining voluntary, it was the notion of "chemical castration" that continued to captivate much of the news media

Central to the public debates of 2006/2007 were the concepts of "pedophilia" and "the pedophile." The perceived effectiveness or acceptability of using "chemical castration" as a means for tackling child sexual abuse is partly determined by the discursive means though which these concepts are constructed. The next section will examine some of the foremost ways in which debates around chemical castration utilize a *medical* discourse to construct "pedophilia" (and, by extension, pedophiles) as curable, treatable or incurable.

Medical Discourse

When covering the subject of "chemical castration" journalists frequently construct pedophilia through a *medical* discourse. In this discourse, pedophilia is constructed as an illness – a medical affliction or disorder – which is either (1) curable, (2) controllable, or (3) incurable. As will be demonstrated, the specific terms of the "illness" vary, but the notion at the core of the discourse remains the same: pedophilia is a biological (that is, physical, psychological, genetic) abnormality that afflicts child sex offenders and marks their difference from "normal," "healthy" folk.

Medical discourse of curability

During the debate around John Reid's proposed expansion of the program of chemical castration, journalists in parts of the tabloid press drew upon a medical discourse to construct pedophilia as a "killable" or "stoppable" disorder. For example, an article in the *Sun* began: "Paedophiles may be chemically castrated to *kill off* their evil urges, it was revealed yesterday" ("Chemical castration 'planned for paedophiles'.," *Sun*, June 26, 2006). Another headline on the same day declared: "Drug cuts hormone and *ends* vile urges" (*Sun*, June 26, 2006). A similar approach was in evidence when Reid unveiled the final legislation. A front page headline in the *Daily Mirror* identified a "jab" that could "stop" offenders' "desires": "Paedos to be chemically castrated: Reid plans to give perverts jabs that *stop* sick desires" (*Mirror*, June 13, 2007). Similarly, the *Sun* carried a quotation from John O'Flaherty, described as a "serial child rapist," which framed pedophilia as a disease with which offenders are afflicted and require a cure: "Paedophilia is *a disease* and needs to be cured. Only then should they let me back into society. I am entitled to help" ("Perverts are castrated abroad . . . and it works," *Sun*, June 14, 2007).

Such medicalized discourses of pedophilia have become a staple of news coverage, with questions regarding the curability (or otherwise) of pedophiles frequently occurring during high-profile cases of child sexual abuse. In October 2011, an article in the *Sun* attributed "paedophile behaviour" to a "faulty gene" which could be "cured" through pharmacotherapy (*Sun*, October 22, 2011). The author of the study, Professor Lawrence Pinessi, who was said to have "carried out tests on a dad with abnormal feelings for his nine-year-old daughter," was quoted as saying: "After several weeks of treatment with neuroleptic drugs and anti-depressants the patient has *ceased* his paedophile behaviour." A similar discourse was evidenced when the press covered the return to Britain of disgraced musician Gary Glitter, who had served almost two-and-a-half years in a Vietnamese prison for sexual offenses against under-age girls. The headline of a *Scottish Sun* commentary piece demanded: "Volunteer to be castrated, Gary." Despite carrying sub-headlines of "Beasts" and "Predators," two of the nouns most commonly used to dehumanize sex offenders and depict them as animals, the article claimed that: "Whether in tablet form or as an injection, chemical castration is a way of rebalancing hormones, of *taking away* the urges that make these men a menace to society" (*Scottish Sun*, August 28, 2008).

From these initial examples we can observe that when journalists adopt the medical discourse of *curability*, pedophilia is framed as a fixable illness or disorder: "faulty" genes can be corrected; hormone imbalances can be corrected with tablets or injec-tions; "urges" can be killed off or taken away; desires can be stopped by a jab. The supposed success of such treatments are then intermittently celebrated through head-lines such as the *Daily Mirror*'s "Jab done: hormone injection for paedophiles cuts re-offending from 43% to 5%" (*Daily Mirror*, June 13, 2007).

Medical discourse of controllability

Although popular, the medical discourse of curability is far from omnipresent. During the chemical castration debate of 2006/2007, many journalists were more restrained in their use of the medical discourse, tending not to construct pedophilia as a *curable* disorder but as an "urge" that can be *treated* or *controlled* to some degree. For example, a report in the *Daily Star* began: "Paedophiles and rapists may be chemi-cally castrated to *control* their sick urges" ("Castrate 'em: child sex pervs face shock drug treatment," *Daily Star*, June 26, 2006). Similarly, an article in the *Daily Mail* initially employed rhetoric that implied chemical castration was an absolute solution, but stopped short of framing pedophilia as entirely curable, opting instead to frame it as an "urge" that can be curbed: "Paedophiles are to be offered 'chemical castra-tion' to *stop* them re-offending, John Reid will announce today. The sex offenders will be given injections of drugs to *curb* their urges to assault young children" ("'Castration' for sex offenders: convicted paedophiles will be offered chemical jabs, says Reid," *Daily Mail*, June 13, 2007). The following day an article in the same newspaper again drew upon a discourse of controllability when asserting that: "The attraction to children will return if they stop taking the medication" ("Shop a pae-dophile to your neighbours and risk jail," *Daily Mail*, June 14, 2007), implicit in which is the notion that if medication is *not* stopped then the "attraction to children" will stay away.

As with the medical discourse of curability, the discourse of controllability is fre-quently mobilized in media coverage of high-profile cases of child sexual abuse. During the furor over Gary Glitter's return to the United Kingdom, Bill Leckie, of the *Scottish Sun*, explicitly framed pedophilia as an illness which can be controlled through continued pharmacotherapy. Citing the case of Joseph Smith, a convicted child sex offender who *"cleaned up his act* after chemical castration in the early 80s, but stopped his treatment in 1989 and was jailed in 1999 for assaulting a five-year-old girl," Leckie stated: "like so many other medicines designed to *control illnesses,* not cure them, his symptoms returned once he stopped taking it" ("Volunteer to be castrated, Gary," *Scottish Sun*, August 28, 2008). A year later the same commentator returned to the issue of chemical castration, stating: "With any other *illness*, the offending organs have to be treated. Paedophilia is surely no different. It's time to make tough decisions" ("Time to get real," *Scottish Sun*, July 7, 2009). A similar frame was adopted in a *Sunday Mirror* article about the chemical castration of "paedophile priests" (a mainstay of media coverage of child sexual abuse; see Jenkins, 1992, 1998) which reported that pharmacotherapy was to be adopted as a long-term form of treatment: "Church bosses have started chemically castrating paedophile priests to *curb* their sick urges. The pervert priests are being injected with special hormones to *stop* them reoffending" ("Chemical chop for the pervert priests: sex offender clergy castrated at clinic," *Sunday Mirror*, July 8, 2007).

The discourse of controllability shares similarities with the discourse of curability. As the above examples demonstrate, while they may stop short of forwarding the notion that "pedophilia" is curable, journalists frequently construct it as a medical disorder that can be managed (that is, controlled or curbed) through the application of long-term medication. A breakdown of some of the framing devices used to construct pedophilia and the effect of "chemical castration" through the medical discourses of curability and controllability are presented in Table 8.1.

It is worth noting that even in instances where journalists reject the notion of pedophilia being treatable, some continue to frame it through a medicalized discourse. For example, in an extensive *Sunday Times* feature on Gary Glitter, journalist Minette Marrin described pedophilia as a chronic disorder: "The only point upon which most experts seem to agree is that there is no treatment which can cure paedophilia. The *disorder* is chronic and lifelong" ("Gary Glitter – mad, bad or just dangerous to know?," *Sunday Times*, August 24, 2008). Thus, biological abnormality continues to abound in the form of a chronic condition, although in this instance one that is entirely untreatable.

Table 8.1 Framing devices used to construct pedophilia as a curable or controllable disorder.

Curable		Controllable	
Attraction to children	*Stopped*	Illness	*Controlled Treated*
Chemical imbalance	*Cured*	Sick urge	*Controlled Curbed*
Desire	*Stopped*	Urge to assault young children	*Curbed*
Faulty gene	*Cured*		
Hormone imbalance	*Rebalanced*		
Urge	*Killed off Taken away*		

Medical discourse of incurability

As we have seen, in parts of the news media a medical discourse of pedophilia is used to frame pedophilia as a curable or controllable disorder. In the case of the former, it is variously put down to a faulty gene that can be corrected and cured, a hormone imbalance that can be rectified through pharmacotherapy, or a desire that can be stopped by a jab. For the latter, it is more typically framed as an urge that can be curbed or controlled, or an illness that can be treated. At times, however, journalists also draw upon a medical discourse to frame pedophilia as entirely *incurable*, a discourse that manifests in headlines such as: "The sorry truth is many sex offenders can't be rehabilitated" (*Daily Mail*, March 10, 2010).

In instances where journalists draw upon the discourse of incurability, the *inability* to "cure" or "treat" pedophiles is frequently used to advocate alternative, typically more draconian, forms of punishment. This discourse is particularly pervasive in the right-wing tabloid press. It typically draws upon the image of "the pedophile" as inherently evil and frames abusers as undeserving of help and incapable of, and/or resistant to, rehabilitation or reform. At best, preventative measures such as "chemical castration" are presented as a bare minimum; at worst, they are futile and inadequate steps that are insufficient for tackling the ubiquitous evil of the pedophile problem. In light of the apparent inadequacy of such proposals, journalists and other stakeholders typically offer one of two alternative "solutions": (1) significantly longer or permanent (that is "real" life) prison sentences, or (2) capital punishment. Examples of the rhetoric used to forward these "solutions" are presented below.

Longer prison sentences

The first way in which the discourse of incurability is mobilized is to support calls for longer or indefinite periods of incarceration. Following the announcement that convicted sex offenders would be offered anti-depressant drugs as part of a program of pharmacotherapy, the *Daily Mail* quoted Norman Brennan, of the Victims of Crime Trust, as saying: "There is no medical cure for paedophiles, so what are we doing giving them Prozac? The *only* way to *protect children 100 per cent* is for paedophiles to remain locked-up until they no longer pose a danger" ("Paedophiles will be offered Prozac," *Daily Mail*, November 13, 2007). A similar discursive strategy was utilized in a *Daily Express* leader headlined "*Only* by locking up the paedophiles will we *safeguard our children*." In this article, which drew upon animal terminology to place pedophiles outside the category of humanity, it was asserted that: "Antidepressants and chemical treatments are just the weapons of appeasement. *Only* when these monsters are behind bars can children *really be safe*" (*Daily Express*, June 14, 2007). In both of these examples, permanent incarceration is not merely preferable to treatment-based alternatives, it is the *only* way of ensuring children are protected from the threats posed by pedophiles. In other words, alternative (for example, treatment-based) approaches are inadequate. The *Daily Express* leader column asserts that only by adopting a policy of "real" life sentences will children "really be safe," while the *Daily Mail*'s expert source goes as far as to say that such a policy would "protect children 100 per cent" (in other words, it is an incontrovertible *solution*).

Likewise, the *Sun*'s political editor, George Pascoe-Watson, made reference to unidentified "experts" when furthering the discourse of the incurable pedophile in order to support a policy of permanent incarceration: "Many experts on paedophilia argue child sex offenders can never be cured or helped. They say they should be locked up for life to *protect* children – or undergo castration" ("Three crimes and they're off, pervs," *Sun*, June 26, 2006).

Capital punishment

Other journalists and commentators use the discourse of incurability to make the case for capital punishment. *Sun* columnist Jon Gaunt dismissed John Reid's proposed plans for chemical castration as "just a load of balls," arguing that "what is clearly needed is LIFE meaning LIFE and the restoration of the death penalty for serial predatory paedophiles" ("John Reid," *Sun*, June 27, 2006). A year later, when Reid's proposals were formally announced, Gaunt dismissed the measures as "completely impotent," arguing that longer prison sentences were a *minimum* requirement and capital punishment remained the most appropriate penal response: "The only fair sentence for abusers is death. If we can't have capital punishment because of the human rights of perverts let's have much longer sentences where they can be both punished and treated" ("Longer time for paedos," *Sun*, June 19, 2007), a statement which is also notable for presenting human rights as a hindrance to "fairness." In making the case for capital punishment, Gaunt also used the same discursive strategy as that observed in the *Daily Express* leader column, positioning sex offenders outside the category of humanity by aligning them with feral animals: "I don't want paedophiles chemically castrated and left free to *roam*. I want them *put down* like the *dangerous dogs* they are."

It is also worth noting that mentions of capital punishment are not consigned to the tabloid press. Writing in the *Sunday Telegraph*, for example, Joan Collins, while less hostile towards "chemical castration" than the likes of Jon Gaunt, also endorsed the notion of punishing child sex offenders with the death penalty. In a commentary piece headlined "Extreme measures for the *ultimate evil*," Collins argued: "There's no choice to be made – chemical castration should be instituted, as well as any other means available to stop paedophilia. Hell, bring back the garrote if it helps too" ("Extreme measures for the ultimate evil," *Sunday Telegraph*, October 19, 2008).

Throughout these latter examples of the discourse of incurability we can see the power of the "pedophile" discourse in structuring and shaping discussions about child sexual abuse/"pedophilia" more broadly. In these instances, pedophiles are typically constructed as a homogenized group who are beyond treatment or cure: their "sickness," "evil" or "perversion" is inherent, essential, biologically determined and irreversible. It is therefore only by applying strict, draconian forms of punishment to individual convicted pedo*philes* (be it permanent incarceration or capital punishment) that the problem of pedo*philia* can be "solved" and children can be protected from the prospect of sexual abuse. For this discursive strategy to function, a key criterion must be met: "pedophilia" – the umbrella term used to cover every action or behavior – must be framed as a permanent biological state that cannot be treated.

This serves to position "pedophiles" as abnormal or subhuman, outside the boundaries of humanity. From this perspective, they are too inherently sick to warrant, deserve or desire help, and thus permanent incarceration or death are the *only* plausible solutions.

Chemical Castration: Voluntary Treatment or Enforced Punishment?

Central to any debate about the treatment of sex offenders – whether through pharmacotherapy, surgery or other means – is the issue of ethics. Who should decide on the most appropriate form(s) of treatment? Should treatment be voluntary or mandatory? Should treatment be used as an alternative to incarceration? Assessing the possibility of using chemical castration to treat high risk sex offenders in England and Wales, Harrison has argued that the process developed in Texas represents one of the more ethically sound approaches. This is:

> A process which is voluntary and is not connected with release from, or an attempt to avoid, a prison sentence. A process that is, rather, centred on helping and treating the offender as part of, or separate to, the sentencing package, rather than being at the core of punishment. The only change which the author would advocate is that the process is solely by means of drug therapy rather than by irreversible surgical means. (Harrison, 2007: 23)

Contrary to this, however, many journalists – particularly those from the right-wing press –advocate a rather different approach. In such cases pedophiles are frequently framed as a "special case," beyond the pale, a unique (that is, the "worst") category of criminal who are devoid of rights and to whom ethical questions do not apply. In many regards, this constitutes a discourse of extreme otherness. Especially prominent is the view that castration is *deserved*, and that, far from being voluntary, it should be a mandatory punishment. In some instances, journalists explicitly advocated barbaric forms of physical punishment. In order to further this discourse of extreme otherness, journalists and other stakeholders frequently seek to discredit or denigrate individuals or groups who advocate a human rights approach, characterizing them as a deluded group of "do-gooders" or as a misguided minority who are out of touch.

Castration as enforced punishment

During the debates of 2006/2007, some newspapers highlighted the voluntary nature of the measures through headlines such as: " 'Chemical castration' option for sex crimes" (*The Times*, June 13, 2007). Others, though, were less forward in this regard, reporting developments as if chemical castration was – or should be – a mandatory requirement for convicted offenders. A headline in the *Daily Star* screamed "Castrate 'em: child sex pervs face shock drug treatment" (*Daily Star*, June 26,

2006). The *Sun* announced: "Paedo fiends to get chop" (*Sun*, June 13, 2007), while a corresponding letters page (discussed below) ran under the headline: "Force paedos to have 'chop'" (*Sun*, June 18, 2007). A *Sunday Mirror* headline, following routine practice of privileging elite sources, implicitly advocated mandatory castration in announcing: "Top government adviser: sex perverts *should be* 'chemically castrated'" (*Sunday Mirror*, October 15, 2006).

One newspaper that was particularly critical of the measures introduced by John Reid was the right-leaning, mid-market tabloid the *Daily Express*. In a leader published to coincide with John Reid's formal announcement to MPs, Leo McKinstry argued that, far from being voluntary and treatment-based, measures for convicted child sex offenders would only be effective if they were mandatory and punitive. As such, the measures announced by the Home Office were deemed entirely inadequate: "[t]he voluntary nature of the plan renders it all but meaningless" ("Only by locking up the paedophiles will we safeguard our children," *Daily Express*, June 14, 2007). In making his case for tougher measures, McKinstry constructed pedophiles as a special case, a "breed apart," a unique category of criminal for whom standard forms of retribution were insufficient. For him: "paedophiles deserve the most severe possible punishment. [...] [N]o amount of incarceration is too long for them, no indignity too cruel" (*Daily Express*, June 14, 2007). A year later, Michael Dobbs, a columnist for the same newspaper, revisited the topic in a commentary piece entitled: "Paedophiles *deserve* chemical castration" (*Daily Express*, August 23, 2008). Throughout piece, which focused on the Gary Glitter case, Dobbs disregarded any element of autonomy or choice and asserted that chemical castration should be a mandatory requirement regardless of whether it was to be used as a punishment or a treatment: "If paedophiles are criminals, they *deserve* such treatment. If they are ill, then they *deserve* it, too" (*Daily Express*, August 23, 2008).

Implicit in the view that castration should be mandatory is the assumption that it functions as a form of punishment or retribution. Harrison (2007: 28) has argued that lexical choices are important in framing debates around pharmacotherapy and "[a]s long as the term 'castration' is used, it is always going to summon up images of pain and suffering." In parts of the press, however, such images of pain and suffering were explicitly evoked during the debate about John Reid's plans. The headline of the *Sun*'s report, for example, used an informal slang term for castration – "the chop," a term that evokes imagery of physical cutting – in declaring: "Paedo fiends to get chop" (*Sun*, June 13, 2007). Indeed, within the tabloid press, numerous columnists and commentators were forthright in suggesting that convicted child sex offenders should be subjected to violent, painful forms of *physical* castration. For example, *Sunday Mirror* columnist Anna Smith was supportive of chemical castration, but asked: "why waste cash on the drugs when a couple of half bricks would be cheaper and just as effective?" ("Reid and his plans to chemically castrate," *Sunday Mirror*, June 17, 2007). A similar view was expressed in Donald MacLeod's opinion piece in the *Sun*, which carried the headline "Get knife out for perverts" (*Sun*, June 16, 2007). In the course of his piece, MacLeod welcomed chemical castration as "a punishment," but encouraged a much harsher, intentionally painful and damaging alternative, suggesting that: "[a] butcher's knife with no anesthetic [*sic*] would be more economical" ("Get knife out for perverts," *Sun*, June 16, 2007).

Addressing the human rights issue

During the debate around chemical castration some parts of the national press actively sought to engage with some of the more problematic aspects of treating sex offenders through pharmacotherapy. The *Guardian*, for example, informed readers of unpleasant potential side effects, such as "the irreversible growth of breasts" ("The question: what's chemical castration?," *Guardian*, June 14, 2007), while the *Independent* produced a substantial (largely skeptical) piece addressing the pros and cons of the treatment ("The big question: how do you deal with sex offenders, and does 'chemical castration' work?," *Independent*, June 14, 2007). Other newspapers used their editorial pages – the space "where journalists are authorised to express opinion, often guided by the political leanings of the newspaper . . . [and where] newspapers speak both for and to their audience" (Wahl-Jorgensen, 2008: 71) – to address the issue of ethics. An editorial in the *Daily Mirror*, for example, was tentatively supportive, asserting that: "adopting drug-induced treatments used in Scandinavia could work. [...] [T]he extraordinary new measures . . . might, just might, offer a safe way forward" ("Voice of the Daily Mirror: cutting edge," *Daily Mirror*, June 13, 2007). Notably, though, the paper urged caution with regard to the moral implications of introducing such measures, asserting: "Chemical castration must be voluntary and never imposed against the will of a prisoner."

Such concern for the trickier ethical questions were, however, difficult to find. On the contrary, there were numerous instances of journalists or their sources deliberately seeking to discredit or denigrate groups aiming to uphold sex offenders' human rights. One discursive strategy used to discredit or weaken the arguments of those advocating a human rights approach involved juxtaposing the rights of sex offenders (framed as evil, monstrous, unrepentant) with those of child victims (framed as innocent, vulnerable, damaged). Consequently, individuals or groups seeking to defend sex offenders' human rights were framed as a "soft" or "politically correct" minority of do-gooders who were seeking to "defend the indefensible" (this was particularly evident in readers' letters to the *Sun*, discussed below). Take, for example, another quote from Norman Brennan, of the Victims of Crime Trust, published in the *Daily Mirror*. Through repeated use of pronouns such as "we" and "ourselves," Brennan presented his pro-chemical castration argument as "common sense," utilizing rhetoric that enacted ingroup–outgroup imagery between "us" (right-thinking citizens with a commitment to protecting society's vulnerable young) and "them" (the arrogant, tribal "civil rights brigade" defending criminals who perpetrate "vile and appalling crimes"). He argued:

> The *civil rights brigade* will no doubt start banging *their* chests. But *we* have to ask *ourselves* what *our* priorities are – protecting children from these predators or looking after the human rights of those who've committed the most vile and appalling crimes. *We* live in a world where the rights of the criminal come before those of the victim. *We* need to turn that around. ("Jab done: hormone injection for paedophiles cuts re-offending from 43% to 5%," *Daily Mirror*, June 13, 2007)

A similar strategy was used in the *Sun* when reporting a paper produced by the Council of Europe – described as "Europe's leading human rights body" – which stated: "Surgical castration is a mutilating, irreversible intervention and cannot be considered as a medical necessity in the treatment of sex offenders" ("Paedo beasts should be castrated . . . like us," *Sun*, May 19, 2009). However, far from using this report as a cue to urge caution or advocate a policy of voluntary treatment, this view was immediately juxtaposed against the words of a man whose nine-year-old child had been raped and murdered by a repeat sex offender. He was, the article stated, "furious human rights groups are putting the rights of criminals ahead of victims."

In another article, the same newspaper sought to weaken the case for voluntary treatment by arguing that offenders would themselves be in favor of compulsory treatment if it were used as an incentive for a reduced period of incarceration. Beneath a headline that boldly declared "Drug cuts hormone and ends vile urges," it was stated: "Civil liberties campaigners and left-wingers argue that compulsory treatment for convicted paedophiles is 'medieval' or barbaric. Yet a string of sex offenders wanted castration in exchange for shorter prison terms" (*Sun*, June 26, 2006). Thus, groups seeking to defend convicted offenders' human rights were not only minoritized (identified only as "civil liberties campaigners and left-wingers," evoking classic media images of "the loopy left"), they were also framed as misguided, seemingly acting against the interests of many ("a string") of the very people whose rights they were seeking to protect.

Popular Discourse in Readers' Letters to the *Sun*

To conclude the chapter we will outline some of the ways in which the discourses identified in the earlier parts of the chapter were used to frame readers' letters sent to the *Sun* on the subject of "chemical castration." Readers' letters are important because they are broadly indicative of a newspaper's "pursuit of shared understanding and empathy" between its editorial line and its audience (Wahl-Jorgensen, 2002: 75). As Richardson (2008: 65) notes, "the vast majority of letters to the editor are argumentative, designed to convince an audience of the acceptability of a point of view and to provoke them into an immediate or future course of action." In the following examples, the subject upon which letter writers were attempting to persuade their audience was the acceptability (or otherwise) of using chemical castration as a means for tackling pedophiles/pedophilia.

The *Sun* is the United Kingdom's top-selling daily newspaper. As sister paper to the *News of the World* – a Sunday tabloid with a long and largely successful history of anti-pedophile campaigning prior to its closure in 2011 (see Silverman and Wilson, 2002) – the *Sun* has played a key role in influencing central policy on child sex offenders, particularly through the two papers' shared campaign for Sarah's Law. Indeed, in announcing the legislation of which voluntary "chemical castration" formed a part, John Reid was quoted as saying: "If someone wants to call this Sarah's Law, then I'd be delighted if that's the case" ("Reid's law for Sarah," *Sun*, June 24, 2007).

During the period of heightened coverage in 2006–2007, the *Sun* twice dedicated the entirety of its letters page to the issue of chemical castration, both times under the banner "The big issue." The first, published in June 2006, when it first emerged that John Reid was considering offering chemical castration to convicted sex offenders, was titled "Castration is best solution." The second, published a year later, when the legislation was formally announced, was titled "Force paedos to have 'chop'."

Chemical castration as punishment

In the letters pages of the *Sun*, many readers welcomed chemical castration as a form of punishment (as opposed to help or treatment), variously describing it as evidence that the government was finally making an effort to "seriously tackl[e] the problems with sex offenders and paedophiles" (*Scottish Sun*, June 18, 2007), "a proper deterrent" and an improvement on the previous "softly-softly approach with the emphasis on rehabilitation [which] didn't work" (*Scottish Sun*, June 18, 2007).

When advocating chemical castration as a form of punishment, one of the foremost ways in which *Sun* readers framed pedophiles was through dehumanizing animal terminology. Through the course of the letters, pedophiles were variously described as "vile creatures," "depraved monsters," "(sick) beasts" and "vicious predators." This dehumanizing, animalistic discourse was also utilized in more explicit ways, typically when arguing that if castration (chemical or otherwise) is deemed suitable for animals – or, more specifically, dogs – then it is equally appropriate for convicted child sex offenders. In one example, a reader wrote: "At last, a sensible idea has emerged. Animals are castrated so why not these evil people who *prey* on young children?" (*Sun*, June 29, 2006). Similar rhetoric was deployed in a letter to the Scottish edition, where it was reasoned: "If you have a dog which can't control its sexual urges, you get it castrated – why should it be any different for a human?" (*Scottish Sun*, June 29, 2006). In this latter example, the letter writer also draws upon an element of the medicalized discourse, making reference to uncontrollable "urges" (that is, "urges" that "normal," properly adjusted folk – humans – do not have or are capable of controlling). This discourse was also mobilized in more implicit terms, such as when readers suggested that, rather than being "chemically castrated," convicted sex offenders should be subjected to surgical castration, as is the case with animals in veterinary practice. For example, one argued that "Hardcore offenders should be subject to surgical castration" (*Sun*, June 29, 2006), while another wrote: "I totally agree with castration, but why bother with chemicals?" (*Sun*, June 18, 2007).

Medical discourse

All three strands of the medicalized discourse were evidenced at various times. In terms of framing pedophilia as a curable or treatable disease, one reader enthused: "There is a great deal of evidence to suggest pedophiles *can* be 'cured.' This [chemical castration] is one way to make sure they *can't* re-offend" (*Scottish Sun*, June 29, 2006). In another letter, a reader drew a direct parallel between using chemical castration to treat pedophilia and the treatment of mental illness through pharmacotherapy, stating: "Chemical castration is *no different* to *controlling* mentally ill patients with drugs. The prime concern should be the potential victims" (*Sun*, June 29, 2006).

Concurrently, however, letters printed on the same day also drew upon the medical discourse of *incurability*. For example, one reader stated: "I am fully behind chemically castrating paedophiles but why wait until they have offended three times? A paedophile can *never be cured or rehabilitated* so why delay?" (*Sun*, June 29, 2006). Another reader drew upon discourses of sickness and perversion to dismiss the possibility of redemption (the implicit assumption being that pedophiles are either beyond or undeserving of rehabilitation) and echoed some commentators' calls for convicted sex offenders to be subjected to capital punishment: "Why give *sick* child *perverts* a chemical castration if they commit three strikes? The only injection these vile individuals need is a lethal one" (*Sun*, June 29, 2006).

Ethical considerations and the human rights issue

Almost all published letters were supportive of John Reid's proposals. However, many argued that they did not go far enough; that they were too "soft." Prevalent across these letters was the issue of "choice"; specifically, the question of whether chemical castration should be offered to convicted sex offenders on a voluntary basis (as was proposed by the Home Secretary) or whether it should be a mandatory requirement.

On the subject of chemical castration, it has been argued that:

> the state is under obligations both at a domestic and international level to consider the rights of sex offenders when introducing such measures. These obligations are premised on the protection of all within a state's jurisdiction, regardless of conduct or risk. (Harrison and Rainey, 2009: 72)

However, such consideration for offenders' rights were rarely expressed in readers' letters to the *Sun*. For example, the correspondence chosen as letter of the week by the *Scottish Sun* asserted: "There should be no choice in the matter. If you are caught abusing a child, you should be castrated. [...] This should be the law – like it or lump it" (*Scottish Sun*, June 18, 2007). From a legal perspective, Harrison and Rainey (2009: 72) argue that the "use of chemical castration should be placed within a human rights framework which is compatible with state obligations under the Human Rights Act." This view, however, was actively dismissed in many letters in the *Sun*. For example, one stated: "Paedophiles are a serious threat to society. Chemical castration should be compulsory after their first conviction. *I am not interested in their rights*" (*Sun*, June 29, 2006). Similarly, letters to the *Scottish Sun* argued that offenders relinquished all legal rights by committed their crime: "[T]here must be no choice in the matter. Once they committed the crime, perverts gave up their right to a choice. It should be an automatic sentence" (*Scottish Sun*, June 18, 2007). One reader went further, arguing that by assaulting a child, offenders effectively relinquished themselves from the category of humanity: "My view has always been that anyone who sexually abuses a child automatically gives up their human rights – therefore we should treat them like animals" (*Scottish Sun*, June 29, 2006). Framing castration as a deterrent/punishment (permanent "damage") to be imposed in accordance with the degree of "evil" displayed by individual pedophiles, another letter writer argued that, like other forms of criminal punishment, it was "surely" the role of judges, rather than offenders, to decide whether castration should be implemented:

> Why is there an element of choice? Surely the courts should decide whether a paedophile is evil enough to be castrated. Only then will it be a proper deterrent. Only then will a serious message be sent out to perverts that, if they are caught, they will be seriously damaged forever. (*Scottish Sun*, June 18, 2007)

Throughout these letters, ethical issues and the rights of child sex offenders were disregarded by *Sun* readers. Castration, it was argued, should be an automatic penalty after the first offense. For some it is a criminal punishment and so rightful retribution for pedophiles' inherent evil; for others it should act as a deterrent, to deter other pedophiles and warn them of the consequences of succumbing to their "urges." As in the news pages of many right-wing newspapers, readers' letters to the *Sun* frequently sought to minoritize and dismiss individuals or groups objecting to such a hard line approach. In the *Scottish Sun* one reader partly celebrated the proposed measures on the grounds that they would antagonize proponents of human rights, declaring: "It is great news that Home Secretary John Reid is prepared to think about such extreme measures for paedophiles – especially as he must know the *human rights do-gooders* will be bitterly against it" ("Castration is best solution," *Scottish Sun*, June 29, 2006). Another bemoaned: "No doubt the *PC brigade* will leap to the defence of these vile creatures, and scupper any plans for the only punishment that would guarantee they couldn't re-offend" (*Scottish Sun*, June 29, 2006). In the second series of letters, a reader declared "there should be no door left open for the *woolly minded liberals* to launch a human rights defence" ("Force paedos to have 'chop'," *Scottish Sun*, June 18, 2007).

Only alternative to life sentences

As noted, a common theme throughout the letters was that the Home Secretary's proposals regarding non-compulsory chemical castration were insufficient, that they were too "soft." A common discourse recurrent throughout the tabloid media dictates that "[i]f paedophiles are literally 'evil personified,' then such evil can be exorcised by exclusion of these individuals from society" (Kitzinger, 1999: 218). This typically manifests in calls for "tougher" (that is, longer or indefinite) prison sentences for convicted child sex offenders. This discourse was recurrent throughout the letters, wherein chemical castration and the issue of longer or indefinite prison sentences were often discussed concurrently. For some readers, "real" life sentences remained the most appealing "solution" to the pedophile problem. One letter to the *Scottish Sun* argued that in the absence of a policy of permanent incarceration, chemical castration represented an acceptable compromise, even framing it is a solution of sorts: "If they are not going to lock paedophiles up and throw away the key, castration is the *only answer*" (*Scottish Sun*, June 18, 2007). For another reader, the only way to protect children was to castrate *and* imprison offenders: "All paedophiles should be castrated and locked up. Don't give them a chance to hurt a young child" (*Sun*, June 29, 2006).

Regardless of the degree of enthusiasm expressed towards chemical castration, the notion running through these letters was that the only way of tackling the pedophile problem is through measures that are "*tough,*" *permanent* and *mandatory.* Those suggested in letters to the *Sun* were: (1) mandatory castration, (2) permanent incarceration (for offenders who refuse castration), (3) mandatory castration *and* incarceration, or (4) capital punishment. Implicit in this is the belief that, depending on the frame adopted, pedophiles' affliction – their "sickness" – is permanent and/or their "evil" is inherent and irreversible. Either way, permanent, irreversible responses are required. In the case of the former, mandatory castration is framed as a possible "answer"; for the latter, mandatory castration and imprisonment are required to rid society of this "evil." Regardless, chemical castration is presented as a bare minimum.

Discussion and Conclusions

This chapter has explored the role of the UK national press in shaping and responding to public debates around the "chemical castration" of convicted child sex abusers. It has demonstrated how debates about child sexual abuse are frequently framed through the concepts of "pedophilia" and, in particular, "the pedophile." More pertinently, the examples presented herein have illustrated the vague and ambiguous ways in which these nebulous, socially constructed terms are used. They mean different things to different people at different times. This is an important point because the ways in which journalists (and other stakeholders) construct "the pedophile" and "pedophilia" are pivotal. They have ramifications for how solutions and the associated ethical issues are conceived and framed in terms of their viability, appropriateness and effectiveness. In other words, particular constructions of these concepts feed into and legitimize particular remedies. Constructions of both "pedophilia" and "pedophiles" feed into ethical debates about solutions or cures.

The case studies presented in this chapter have demonstrated how journalists frequently frame pedophilia through a medical discourse, constructing it is an illness or disorder. This medical discourse is typically used to frame the "illness" of pedophilia (and the pedophiles who embody it) in one of three ways: (1) entirely curable (for example, through pharmacotherapy or surgical castration); (2) treatable or manageable, but not necessarily curable; (3) an inherent evil that is entirely incurable.

Such a discourse is unhelpful. It limits thinking about the cause(s) of child sexual abuse to a very narrow focus. Consequently it limits thinking about ways of tackling the problem. The medical discourse (re)imagines child sexual abuse as an issue of individual pathology. It legitimizes the view that the problem of child sexual abuse can be "solved" through relatively straightforward measures. "Pedophiles" – that is, individuals who display or act upon "symptoms" of "pedophilia" – can be identified and dealt with, be it through a "cure" (such as chemical or surgical castration), ongoing treatments to "curb" their "urges," or permanent incarceration. At the most draconian end of the scale, some commentators demanded capital punishment for convicted offenders.

This chapter has also highlighted the selectiveness with which journalists manipulate certain aspects of the pedophile framework according to the nature of the story. Thus the pedophile framework is perhaps not as rigid and inflexible as has previously been claimed. It is not necessarily a universal discourse of inherent evil, or a universal discourse of sickness. These discourses remain very powerful, but this chapter has demonstrated how they were foregrounded (or backgrounded) to varying degrees in coverage of chemical castration. The pedophile discourse is, therefore, perhaps better viewed as a universal discourse of otherness – the terms of that otherness being dynamic and varying according to the socio-political context in which they are being discussed. For example, when advocating pharmacotherapy as a suitable solution to the pedophile problem, journalists *did* utilize the discourse of sickness, but, crucially, they framed pedophilia as a sickness that can be cured or treated. In such instances, other popular discourses, such as the discourse of inherent evil, tended to be sidelined or ignored as they did not fit into the dominant frames of curability or treatability. By contrast, when journalists – typically those from right-leaning tabloids – were advocating more draconian responses, such as permanent incarceration or capital punishment, the discourse of monstrous, inherent evil tended to be very much foregrounded due to their compatibility with the frame of *in*curability.

Animal terminology, a popular discursive strategy in media constructions of pedophiles, was adopted to varying degrees in every instance of the medical discourse. This strategy was often implicitly tied to ethical issues, particularly the question of whether chemical castration should be voluntary – as was suggested and implemented in policy – or mandatory. In this context, the appeal of such an approach is obvious. After all, medical decisions (such as castration) are taken on behalf of animals, either by owners or veterinary professionals; therefore, by placing convicted sex offenders into the same category, journalists afford them the same level of autonomy and legitimize the view that decisions regarding their treatment (for example, chemical castration), rather than being voluntary, can be made on their behalf.

In the right-wing press (including readers' letters to the *Sun*) ethical concerns regarding the treatment of child sex offenders, particularly the issue of their human rights, were often either ignored or dismissed. From this perspective chemical castration is framed as a rightful punishment, something that pedophiles *deserve* (and therefore should have no choice in receiving). At times, journalists, readers and other commentators actively endorsed the use of barbaric forms of physical castration (such as using a butcher's knife without anesthetic). Accordingly, individuals or groups seeking to defend offenders' human rights were minoritized, denigrated as "soft" and caricatured through pejorative labels such as "human rights do-gooders," "woolly minded liberals" or members of the "PC brigade."

Framing child sexual abuse through a medical discourse is appealing to journalists as it simplifies a complicated and nuanced social problem. It reduces child sexual abuse to an issue of individual cases of (among other things) heightened libido, imbalanced hormones, faulty genes or plain evil. Whether framing perpetrators as curable, controllable or incurable, journalists and other stakeholders are able to offer quick-fix solutions that will supposedly address the "pedophile problem." Consequently, they are able to avoid the need to engage with the bigger, more deep-seated issues. While measures such as chemical castration may have a degree of success in treating known offenders and reducing their chances of re-offending, they do nothing to address the broader, institutional or structural factors that facilitate – and, some might argue, encourage – sexual abuse (DeYoung, 1988). Measures such as chemical castration do not, for example, address culturally-engrained power disparities (and abuse) between adults and young people, parents (particularly fathers) and children, or, indeed, males and females. While such complexities continue to be denied, whether through the uncritical adoption of a medical discourse or the ongoing tendency to frame all aspects of the issue through the concepts of "pedophilia" and "the pedophile," any discussion of child sexual abuse – its causes and responses – will continue to do little more than scratch the surface.

References

Ashenden, S. (2002) "Policing perversion: the contemporary governance of paedophilia," *Cultural Values 6*, 1–2, 197–222.

Collier, I. (2001) "Dangerousness, popular knowledge and the criminal law: a case study of the paedophile as socio-cultural phenomenon," in P. Alldridge and C. Brants (eds), *Personal Autonomy, the Private Sphere and the Criminal Law: A Comparative Study.* Oxford and Portland, Oregon: Hart Publishing, pp. 223–245.

Critcher, C. (2003) *Moral Panics and the Media.* Buckingham: Open University Press.

DeYoung, M. (1988) "The good touch/bad touch dilemma," *Child Welfare* LXVII, *1*, 61–68.

Harrison, K. (2007) "The high-risk sex offender strategy in England and Wales: is chemical castration an option?," *Howard Journal of Criminal Justice 46*, 1, 16–31.

Harrison, K. and Rainey, B. (2009) "Suppressing human rights? A rights-based approach to the use of pharmacotherapy with sex offenders," *Legal Studies 29*, 1, 47–74.

Jackson, L.A. (2000a) *Child Sexual Abuse in Victorian England.* London: Routledge.

Jackson, L.A. (2000b) "'Singing birds as well as soap suds': the Salvation Army's work with sexually abused girls in Edwardian England," *Gender and History 12*, 1, 107–126.

Jeffreys, S. (1985) *The Spinster and her Enemies: Feminism and Sexuality 1880–1930.* London: Pandora.

Jenkins, P. (1992) *Intimate Enemies: Moral Panics in Contemporary Great Britain.* New York: Alpine de Gruyere.

Jenkins, P. (1998) *Moral Panic: Changing Concepts of the Child Molester in Modern America.* New Haven, CT: Yale University Press.

Kelly, L. (1988) "What's in a name?: defining child sexual abuse," *Feminist Review 28* (Spring), 65–73.

Kelly, L. (1996) "Weasel words: paedophiles and the cycle of abuse," *Trouble & Strife 33*, 44–49.

Kitzinger, J. (1999) "The ultimate neighbour from hell? Stranger danger and the media framing of paedophiles," in B. Franklin (ed.), *Social Policy, the Media and Misrepresentation.* London: Routledge, pp. 207–221.

Kitzinger, J. (2004) *Framing Abuse: Media Influence and Public Understanding of Sexual Violence Against Children.* London: Pluto Press.

McLeod, M. and Saraga, E. (1988) "Challenging the orthodoxy: towards a feminist theory and practice," *Feminist Review 28* (Spring 1988), 16–55.

Meyer, A. (2007) *The Child at Risk: Paedophiles, Media Responses and Public Opinion.* Manchester: Manchester University Press.

Pratt, J. (2009) "From abusive families to internet predators?: The rise, retraction and reconfiguration of sexual abuse as a social problem in Canada," *Current Sociology 57*, 1, 69–88.

Richardson, J. (2008) "Readers' letters," in B. Franklin (ed.), *Pulling Newspapers Apart: Analysing Print Journalism.* London and New York: Routledge, pp. 56–66.

Silverman, J. and Wilson, D. (2002) *Innocence Betrayed: Paedophilia, the Media and Society.* Cambridge: Polity Press.

Smart, C. (1999) "A history of ambivalence and conflict in the discursive construction of the 'child victim' of sexual abuse," *Social & Legal Studies 8*, 3, 391–409.

Smart, C. (2000) "Reconsidering the recent history of child sexual abuse, 1910–1960," *Journal of Social Policy 29*, 1, 55–71.

Soothill, K., Francis, B.J. and Ackerley, E. (1998) "Paedophilia and paedophiles," *New Law Journal 148* (6844), 882–892.

Soothill, K. and Walby, S. (1991) *Sex Crime in the News.* London: Routledge.

Wahl-Jorgensen, K. (2002) "Understanding the conditions for public discourse: four rules for selecting letters to the editor," *Journalism Studies 3*, 1, 69–81.

Wahl-Jorgensen, K. (2008) "Op-ed pages," in B. Franklin (ed.), *Pulling Newspapers Apart.* Oxford: Routledge, pp. 67–74.

9

Sentencing Sex Offenders
An International Comparison of Sentencing Policy and Legislation
Karen Harrison

Introduction

The sentencing and incapacitation of dangerous sex offenders is an important concern, shared by the vast majority of countries around the globe. While many would agree that the public need protecting from predatory offenders, governments are still obliged to try and attain the correct balance between the rights of the offender and the need to protect society from him. Although just deserts and proportionality are used in the sentencing of many "normal" prisoners, longer than commensurate sentences or even post-conviction orders are commonplace for those classified as sexual offenders. This chapter therefore looks at the sentencing policies and legislation for sex offenders across a number of countries, including Australia, England and Wales, Germany and South Africa. Other chapters in this volume deal with the United States, Israel and Japan. Due to reasons of space, this chapter does not look at those policies designed specifically for those classified as mentally disordered. In short, the fundamental question is whether the balance between offenders' rights and public protection has been legally and ethically achieved.

Australia

The Commonwealth of Australia is made up of six states and 10 territories. Each state has its own state Constitution and is thus permitted to pass laws related to any matter not controlled by the Commonwealth (Australian Government, 2011). This therefore results in a variety of Australian provisions when dealing with sex offenders. For example, Queensland has the Dangerous Prisoners (Sexual Offenders) Act 2003 (Queensland); New South Wales the Crimes (Serious Sex Offenders) Act 2006 NSW;

The Wiley-Blackwell Handbook of Legal and Ethical Aspects of Sex Offender Treatment and Management, First Edition. Edited by Karen Harrison and Bernadette Rainey.
© 2013 John Wiley & Sons, Ltd. Published 2013 by John Wiley & Sons, Ltd.

Western Australia the Dangerous Sexual Offenders Act 2006 (WA); and Victoria the Serious Sex Offenders (Detention and Supervision) Act 2009 (Vic). Despite this variety, all statutes allow for the preventive detention of those classified as serious sexual offenders.

Similar to the United States (see Chapter 24), but dissimilar to England and Wales, preventive detention provisions in Australia are activated *after* the original sentence has lapsed, making it a form of civil rather than continued criminal detention (McSherry, 2010). For example, in Victoria, this extended sentence can take the form of either a detention order or a supervision order. If continued detention is thought appropriate, an application for the order must be made to the Director of Public Prosecutions prior to completion of the original criminal sentence. The application is determined by the Supreme Court of Victoria and can be made for a period of up to three years. The necessity of the order must be reviewed by the Supreme Court on an annual basis, but on its expiry, can be renewed for further periods of three years (Department of Justice, Victoria, 2011), thus enabling detention for life.

Queensland's legislation is similar and provides "for the continued detention in custody or supervised release of a particular class of prisoner to ensure adequate protection of the community" (Dangerous Prisoners (Sexual Offenders) Act (DPSOA) 2003 s3). This particular class relates to sex offenders. An application for such an order is made to the Attorney General and should be completed during the last six months of the prisoner's sentence (DPSOA 2003 s5(2)). In this context a "prisoner" is defined as someone who has been detained in custody for a serious sexual offense (DPSOA 2003 s5(6)). This is defined as an offense, which is sexual in nature, involving violence or against children (Schedule to the DPSOA 2003). The applicability test is whether or not there exist "reasonable grounds for believing that the prisoner is a serious danger to the community" (DPSOA 2003 s 5(3)). In an attempt to determine this, the court can make a "risk assessment order" and/or "an interim detention order"; where the prisoner's sentence is likely to expire prior to the application being decided. As part of the risk assessment order, the offender will be seen by two psychiatrists who must assess the "level of risk that the prisoner will commit another serious sexual offence" (DPSOA 2003s11(2)). In addition to this professional advice, the court will also take into account the views of the victim (DPSOA 2003 s9AA). If the court determines that the risk of serious danger is at an "unacceptable" level it can make either an indefinite "continuing detention order" or a "supervision order" (DPSOA 2003 s13). It is worth noting that there is no definition of what is meant by unacceptable risk. This is particularly worrying when it is now widely accepted that the assessment of risk is difficult to predict (see Chapter 20).

Interestingly, the legislation has retrospective effect and so will apply even if the prisoner received his sentence prior to the commencement of the DPSOA 2003 s5(6). The legislation is viewed as civil commitment, although the prisoner, if continually detained, will remain within a penal institution (Gray, 2005), with the purpose of the detention being one of "control, care *or* treatment" (DPSOA 2003 s13(5), emphasis added). The sole justifier of control is also seen in Western Australia's legislation (Dangerous Sexual Offenders Act 2006 (WA) s3(b)). The decision whether to continue with detention in Queensland is reviewed on a regular basis with completion of a sex offender treatment program (SOTP), often seen as evidence of a lowering of risk. There are, however, two problems with this. The first relates to review, with the DPSOA stating that the first review must be completed within two years but that subsequent reviews must be *started* by the Attorney General within a year of the last order (DPSOA 2003 s27), meaning that in practice by the time the application is considered the prisoner has been detained for 18 rather than 12 months (McSherry and Keyzer, 2009). Worryingly, the Queensland Government has recommended that this be extended to two years, which would effectively mean two-and-a-half years, although this is not yet in force (Keyzer and Coyle, 2009). One advantage of review in this way, however, is that at each review stage it is for the government to prove that the offender still needs to be detained. This was highlighted in *Attorney General* v. *Francis* ([2005] QSC 381) where both the Supreme Court and the Court of Appeal held that it was difficult to justify the continued detention of a man where the corrective services had failed to implement a rehabilitation plan. This links to the second criticism which relates to an offender's eligibility for the SOTP. It is standard practice once a prisoner has been approved for continuing detention that he will be reclassified as having a "high security" status. This will occur even if prior to the order the offender was classified as either "low" or even "open" status. Not only does this reclassification make the task of showing a lowering of risk hard, high security offenders are often not deemed suitable for SOTPs, making release even more difficult to achieve (McSherry and Keyzer, 2009).

The constitutionality of Queensland's post-sentence detention provisions has been challenged in the High Court of Australia in *Fardon* v. *Attorney-General for the State of Queensland* ([2004] HCA 46), with the appellant arguing that section 13 of the Act was beyond the legislative power of the State of Queensland by conferring non-judicial powers on a judicial tribunal. In essence the DPSOA 2003 allows a court to sentence an offender to containment in a prison without a fresh offense, trial or conviction. Despite a similar case in New South Wales (see *Kable* v. *Director of Public Prosecutions (NSW)* (1996) 189 CLR 51) the Court, in a 6:1 majority verdict, denied the appeal with part of the reasoning behind this decision being premised on the fact that the aim of the continuing detention was not to punish, but to protect the public (Gray, 2005). Relating to the balancing act mentioned in the introduction, it is clear here that the court favored public protection over the rights of the offender. Justices Ian Callinan and Dyson Heydon stated that the Act:

> is intended to protect the community from predatory sexual offenders. It is a protective law authorising involuntary detention in the interests of public safety. Its proper characterisation is as a protective rather than a punitive enactment. (*Fardon* v. *Attorney-General for the State of Queensland* [2004] HCA 46, para. 217)

Despite this majority view, Kirby J, in dissent, argued that the DPSOA 2003 breached one of Australia's fundamental legal principles; namely that an individual should not be detained for what they *might* do in the future. Indeed in *Veen* v. *The Queen (no. 2)*((1988) 164 CLR 465), the High Court of Australia held that a sentence could not be lengthened for the purposes of preventive detention. Although Kirby J conceded that the Act had been dressed up to look civil in nature and to be for the protection of the public, he stated that in reality it was punitive and thus criminal:

An order of imprisonment as punishment can only be made by a court following proof of the commission of a criminal offence, established beyond reasonable doubt where the charge is contested, in a fair trial at which the accused is found guilty by an independent court of the offence charged. Here there has been no offence; no charge; no trial. Effectively, the presumption of innocence has been removed. Instead, because of a prisoner's antecedents and criminal history, provision is made for a new form of additional punishment utilising the courts and the corrective services system in a way that stands outside the judicial process hitherto observed in Australia. Civil commitment to prison of persons who have not been convicted of a crime is inconsistent with, and repugnant to, the exercise of the judicial power as envisaged by the Constitution. (*Fardon* v. *Attorney-General for the State of Queensland* [2004] HCA 46, para. 162)

Following this judgment, Fardon made a petition to the Human Rights Committee of the United Nations under the First Optional Protocol to the International Covenant on Civil and Political Rights. In March 2010, the Human Rights Committee found that legislation in Queensland (and in New South Wales) which allowed for the post-sentence detention of serious sexual offenders breached Article 9(1)[1] of the Covenant (McSherry, 2010). In particular 11 out of the 13 members of the Committee thought that the legislation:

1. imposed an additional term of imprisonment, which was not permissible without an additional criminal conviction;
2. subjected Fardon to a heavier sentence than that which was applicable at the time of his sentencing;
3. did not provide adequate due process guarantees, due to the fact that the procedures under the DPSOA were civil in nature; and,
4. did not require the state to prove that rehabilitation could not be achieved through less intrusive means such as supervision within the community (McSherry, 2010).

Such decisions are not, however, legally binding and so the effect of the case on Australian sex offender legislation is debatable; although such judgments are often taken seriously by state governments and have been implemented in some instances (McSherry and Keyzer, 2009). McSherry (2010: 7) therefore argues that it is likely that *Fardon* "will reinforce supervision in the community as the 'default setting' for preventive detention schemes in Australia," and indeed this has been seen in practice. In *R* v. *Francis* ([2006] QCA 324), for example, the Court of Appeal argued that supervision orders, rather than continuing detention, should be used where it was thought that these were adequate to protect the public; with the Attorney General having the burden to prove that risk of re-offending would remain at an unacceptable level if supervision was preferred (McSherry and Keyzer, 2009).

England and Wales

Preventive detention in England and Wales is found in sections 224–229 of the Criminal Justice Act (CJA) 2003 (as amended by the Criminal Justice and Immigration Act (CJIA) 2008) and applies to offenses committed on or after April 4, 2005.[2]

Following previous legislation such as the CJA 1991 and the Powers of Courts (Sentencing) Act 2000, the CJA 2003 works primarily on the basis of commensurate sentencing, following a just deserts model of penal policy. Sentences are therefore only justified if the offense before the court is serious enough to justify the severity of the measure. However, also following on from previous Acts, the CJA 2003 provides provision for the sentencing of offenders to lengths of imprisonment and/or supervision within the community which, while deemed to be incommensurate to the offense, are justified on the basis of the "serious harm" which the offender is likely to cause in the future, and hence defensible under public protection and crime prevention rationales. England and Wales can thus be said to have a bifurcated system.

For sentencing purposes, CJA 2003 s224(3) defines "serious harm" as "death or serious personal injury, whether physical or psychological." The legislation applies to all those who have committed either a "specified violent or sexual offence," which are listed in Schedule 15 of the Act,[3] or a "serious specified offence" which are specified violent or sexual offenses punishable either by life imprisonment or by a custodial sentence of 10 years or more. If an offender is 18 or over, and has been convicted of a serious specified offense and "the court is of the opinion that there is a significant risk to members of the public of serious harm occasioned by the commission by him of further specified offences" (CJA 2003 s225(1)(b)), he will receive either a discretionary life sentence or a sentence of imprisonment for public protection (IPP). For a life sentence, the offense must be punishable by life and the court must be of the opinion "that the seriousness of the offence, or of the offence and one or more offences associated with it, is such as to justify the imposition of a sentence of imprisonment for life" (CJA 2003 s225(2)(b)). If the offense is not punishable by life or does not warrant a life sentence, but is punishable by 10 years or more (and there are 95 offenses which fall into this category) the court, as long as two statutory conditions are met, has the option of a sentence of IPP. The conditions are *either* that the offender has a previous conviction for an offense specified in Schedule 15A of the Act (such as murder, manslaughter, rape, and intercourse with a girl under 13) *or* that the notional determinate term, if the offender was not classified as dangerous, is at least four years.

For this dangerousness legislation to apply, the offender has to satisfy a number of criteria. The first is that the offender must have been "assessed as dangerous." Section 229 helps to define this by providing a list of factors for the court to take into consideration when making its decision. The court "must [therefore] take into account all such information as is available to it about the nature and circumstances of the offence" (CJA 2003 s229(2)(a)); "may take into account all such information as is available to it about the nature and circumstances of any other offences of which the offender has been convicted" (CJA 2003 s229(2)(aa)); "may take into account any information . . . about any pattern of behaviour" (CJA 2003 s229(2)(b)); and "may take into account any information about the offender which is before it" (CJA 2003 s229(2)(c)). This latter proviso allows the court to take into account presentence reports from the Probation Service, psychiatric reports and any other expert opinion which can inform its decision. The test therefore allows an assessment of dangerousness to be made both where the offender has previous convictions and where he is a first-time offender.

When deciding on whether the offender presents a significant risk of causing serious harm through further offending, the court must apply a two-stage test, asking first whether there is a significant risk that the offender will commit further specified offenses (whether serious or not) and if so, whether there is a significant risk that a future victim would suffer serious harm. When assessing significant risk the sentencing judge, following *R* v. *Lang and Others* ([2006] 2 Cr App R (S) 3) should take into account the following,

- The risk identified must be significant. This is a higher threshold than mere possibility and could be taken to mean noteworthy.
- The nature and circumstances of the current offense including the offender's history of offending, together with previous sentences; whether the offending indicated a particular pattern; his attitude to offending, supervision and emotional state; and other social and economic issues such as relationship with alcohol and/or drugs, employment and accommodation.
- A further offense may be serious, but that does not automatically mean that it will necessarily result in a significant risk of serious harm to the public. Indeed persistent offending at a relatively low level which does not cause serious harm does not in itself suggest there is a significant risk of serious future harm.

On release an offender will be subject to a period of supervision of at least 10 years and furthermore subject to recall to prison if he breaches any license conditions. The license can be terminated by the Parole Board, if it thinks it is appropriate to do so, but if it does not, the license can run indefinitely.

The sentence has been heavily criticized. Such criticisms have focused on how dangerousness is assessed; the lack of rehabilitation programs which are needed to effect release; and how the sentence disproportionately contributes to an ever-increasing prison population. The Howard League for Penal Reform, for example, was heavily critical of the sentence in its report on IPPs in 2007. Describing the sentence as "ill-conceived and . . . ultimately flawed" (Howard League for Penal Reform, 2007: 3), they argued that it was misguided, unworkable in the long term and prevented offenders from proving their suitability for release. As a result they recommended that the court should be provided with more discretion when imposing the sentence, changing the situation to one where the court could impose a sentence of IPP rather than it being mandatory. They also recommended that there should be a consistent and effective assessment process so that dangerousness could be accurately assessed; and that the minimum tariff should not be so low so that there is insufficient time for an offender to show a reduction in risk before parole is considered. Other criticisms have focused on the number of prisoners being held past their minimum tariffs because they have not shown a reduction in risk. This is generally because of the unavailability of accredited SOTP programs. At the end of March 2011, there were 3,500 prisoners who were in custody but who had passed their tariff expiry. At the time there were only a further 3,000 offenders on IPPs so over 50% were past tariff expiry (Ministry of Justice, 2011). Between 2006 and 2010 only 202 offenders serving sentences of IPP had been released (*Hansard*, HC Deb, June 15, 2011, vol. 529, col. 842W).

Such criticisms led to a government review, in particular the way in which the sentence was being excessively used. Proposals to reduce its use and therefore to ensure that it was only being used for those offenders who were truly dangerous were enacted through the CJIA 2008. While such amendments have been described as "a vast improvement on the 2003 scheme" (Thomas, 2008: 8), there are still concerns regarding the minimum custodial term for IPP sentences. Courts will have to pay particular attention to the length of the notional determinate sentence to ensure that a length of four years can actually be justified, which can become more complicated if mitigating factors and/or a guilty plea need to be taken into account. The court also has to decide how best public protection can be achieved; that is, whether it is through commensurate sentencing or through the use of dangerousness legislation. Furthermore, how the sentencing court should make these choices is also arguably unclear. Thomas (2008) argues that the overriding principle should be that the court should choose the less onerous option which will provide public protection, but also acknowledges that it is a matter which requires Court of Appeal guidance.

Despite these amendments and the obvious limits which they have imposed, total abolition of the sentence was considered by the House of Lords in October 2009. For this reason, the House debated the insertion of a new clause into the Coroners and Justice Bill (Amendment 90) which would not only have brought to an end the imposition of future indeterminate sentences (where life imprisonment was not a statutory option) but would have secured the release of all offenders serving a sentence of IPP, if this had not already occurred, once the minimum term of imprisonment had been served. The amendment, supported "on grounds of certainty, rehabilitation and resettlement" (*Hansard*, HL Deb, October 28, 2009, vol. 713, col. 1251), was not included in the Bill, although Lord Hunt of Wirral did acknowledge that, while he did not support the amendment:

> We [do] need a fundamental reform of sentencing. If there is to be a Conservative Government – which I strongly believe there will be – I hope that that Government will deliver fundamental reform by introducing honest sentences that spell out minimum and maximum terms. (*Hansard*, HL Deb, October 28, 2009, vol. 713, col. 1251)

In furtherance of this, a review of indeterminate sentencing was announced by David Cameron, leader of the Coalition Government, on 21 June 2011. Proposed changes are currently being debated through the Legal Aid, Sentencing and Punishment of Offenders Bill, with Part 3, Chapter 5 of the Bill dealing with dangerous offenders. The proposal is to abolish the IPP sentence, replacing it with a life sentence where a person has committed a second listed offense. This will apply where the offender is 18 or over and meets a "seriousness condition":

> The seriousness condition is that the court considers that the seriousness of the offence, or of the offence and one or more offences associated with it, is such as to justify the imposition of a sentence of imprisonment for 10 years or more. (Clause 114, Legal Aid, Sentencing and Punishment of Offenders Bill)

As with mandatory minimum sentencing in South Africa (see below) the sentence can be avoided if it would appear "unjust" to impose it. At the time of writing

(January 2012) the Bill was being debated in the House of Lords, so it is presently unclear whether it will be passed and if so whether the above will remain or be amended. While indeterminate IPP sentences may therefore be abolished, they are in all likelihood being replaced with indeterminate life sentences. While it is too early to say if this is the future course of action, the author therefore wonders whether, in practice, this will make any real difference.

Germany

On first appearance Germany appears to have, like England and Wales, a bifurcated sentencing system: one based on proportionality and one based on public protection. "Normal" offenders are sentenced according to commensurability, with a balancing act taking place between the seriousness of the offense and the level of the punishment. "Dangerous" offenders, however, can be given an indeterminate sentence, justified on criminal habit and dangerousness, which must be established on the basis of a high probability (Dunkel and van Zyl Smit, 2004). Found in Section 66 of the German Criminal Code (Strafgesetzbuch (StGB)), Sicherungsverwahrung (preventive detention) is known as detention for the purpose of incapacitation. The section has seen a number of significant changes since 1998 and, as with many other countries, shows an increasingly punitive stance towards the sentencing of sexual offenders.

An incapacitation sentence is available where a person has been found guilty of an intentional offense, which would normally merit a custodial term of at least two years, if:

1. the convicted person has already been sentenced twice, each time to a term of imprisonment of not less than one year for intentional offenses which he committed prior to the offense now at trial;
2. as a result of one or more of these prior offenses he has served a term of imprisonment or detention under a measure of rehabilitation and incapacitation for a total term of not less than two years; and
3. a comprehensive evaluation of the convicted person and his offenses reveals that, due to his propensity to commit serious offenses, particularly of a kind resulting in serious emotional trauma or physical injury to the victim or serious economic damage, he poses a danger to the general public (StGB s66(1); see Bundesministerium der Justiz, 2010).

Under StGB s66(2), prior detention is not needed where the person has committed three intentional offenses and the court gave at least one year imprisonment for each offense and for at least one of the offenses gave a sentence of at least three years. In this circumstance an indeterminate sentence can be given where the person is considered to be a "danger to the general public" as outlined above. If either criterion applies, the prisoner will be given an incapacitative sentence in *addition* to the proportionate term of imprisonment. In essence, therefore, the indeterminate part of the sentence does not take effect until *after* the determinate and punitive element has been served. The purpose of the order is for rehabilitation and incapacitation and as such is independent of guilt (Dessecker, 2009). This bifurcated system is therefore unlike that seen in England and Wales, where proportionate *or* indeterminate sentences are used. Where the determinate part of the sentence is for more than two years and the offense was violent and sexual, the prisoner is obliged to undertake treatment, where it is considered appropriate.

Also dissimilar to England and Wales is the ability to make conditional and/or subsequent incapacitation orders. Conditional orders are found in StGB s66a and have been available since 2002 (Dunkel and van Zyl Smit, 2004). They are used when at the time of sentencing, dangerousness or a criminal habit cannot be established. As long as the other criteria in s66 are fulfilled, the court will decide later, that is, at the point of parole for the determinate sentence, whether the prisoner, at that stage, poses a serious risk to the public. Furthermore, under StGB s66, if a prisoner is nearing the end of a determinate sentence for "a felony against life and limb, personal freedom or sexual self-determination" and it is thought he "presents a significant danger to the general public" an incapacitation order can be made if an evaluation of the prisoner shows "a high likelihood of his committing serious offences resulting in seriously emotional trauma or physical injury to the victim" and the other conditions in s66 are present (StGB s66b(1); see Bundesministerium der Justiz, 2010). This is so even if at the time of sentencing the offender did not fulfill any of the conditions laid down in either s66 or s66a of the StGB. Furthermore, the subsequent conditions in s66 do not need to be met if the original determinate sentence was for five years or more (StGB s66b(2)). This has been in force since July 2004 and is said to fill the gap where previous offending only comes to light after conviction or dangerousness is determined solely on behavior while in prison. It is also worth noting that in 2007, such policies were further extended to include juveniles (aged 14 to 18) and young adults (aged 18 to 20). In many respects, on the basis that this is post-conviction sentencing, subsequent incapacitation orders are similar to the system in Australia, as described above; with conditional orders being a mixture of Anglo and Australian systems.

If an incapacitation order is imposed, whether this takes place at the time of conviction or post-conviction, it will be court reviewed every two years, to ensure that the dangerousness criterion still applies. This can amount to life imprisonment, which has been held by the German courts to be both constitutional and justified (Albrecht, 2004). Prisoners detained under incapacitation orders are held within high security prisons, although they have a different legal status to other "normal" prisoners. This is because, as mentioned above, the incapacitated offender is deemed to be an innocent person; being held not for past crimes but for the prevention of future crimes. The differences between the two classes can be seen by the fact that an indeterminate prisoner cannot be required to wear prison clothing or work (Albrecht, 2004). Despite this, however, there are no other substantial differences between the actual regimes under which incapacitation offenders are kept (*M* v. *Germany* (2009) ECHR, Application No. 19359/04). Release from an incapacitation order is also difficult to achieve. Prior to 1998, the test was the likelihood of further offenses; with a residual risk of failure being considered by the court as acceptable (Dunkel and van Zyl Smit, 2004). This has now been made much stricter and is decided on the basis of whether or not "there is *no* danger that the person under placement will, due to his propensity, commit serious offences resulting in serious emotional trauma or physical injury to the victims" (StGB s67d(3); see Bundesministerium der Justiz, 2010, emphasis added).

Another criticism relates to the fact that historically an incapacitation order could not last for more than 10 years. This, however, changed in 1998 and, controversially, applied retrospectively (Albrecht, 2004). This retroactive implementation has been challenged in the European Court of Human Rights (ECtHR), which in December 2009 ruled in *M* v. *Germany* (Application No. 19359/04) that it was a violation of Article 7[4] of the European Convention on Human Rights (ECHR). Furthermore, the Court unanimously concluded that the applicant's preventive detention beyond the 10-year period additionally amounted to a violation of Article 5(1) of the Convention on the basis that a person can only be lawfully detained where he has been convicted of an offense by a competent court. This subsequently means that post-conviction conditional and subsequent incapacitation orders are also in breach of the ECHR, as they too are made without an additional conviction. In particular, they are not foreseeable as the prisoner does not know at the time of sentencing whether or not he will later be detained under an incapacitation order. According to the ECtHR, this makes the orders arbitrary and in violation of the ECHR. The argument that the detention is preventive rather than punitive makes no difference as continuing detention must remain linked to the original reason for the detention (*Stafford* v. *UK* (2002) 35 EHRR 1121) and the ECtHR in M's case held that there was not a sufficient causal connection between conviction and continuing detention. *M* v. *Germany* has recently been affirmed in three further ECtHR decisions made in January 2011 (*Kallweit* v. *Germany* (Application No. 17792/07), *Mautes* v. *Germany* (Application No. 20008/07) and *Schummer* v. *Germany* (Application Nos. 27360/04 and 42225/07)), largely because Germany had not altered its legislation in response to the 2009 case. In reaction to the more recent cases, in May 2011, Germany's Federal Constitutional Court held that post-conviction incapacitation orders were unconstitutional. The German Parliament now has until 2013 to reform its sentencing policy (Deutsche Welle, 2011). While it is currently unclear what this new legislation will entail, it would seem likely that either courts will be encouraged to make the finding of dangerousness at the sentencing stage so that retroactive orders are not needed, or more offenders will be found to be mentally ill at the parole stage and will be transferred to mental institutions rather than being further detained in custodial settings, a situation which is allowed by Article 5(1)(e) of the ECHR.

South Africa

Unlike the other countries considered thus far, preventive detention does not routinely exist in South Africa, or certainly does not exist in the same way as considered above. Under section 286A-B of the Criminal Procedure Act 51 of 1977 imprisonment for an indefinite period applies to those classified as dangerous criminals, but in the main these provisions are directed at those suffering from psychopathy and other related anti-social disorders. For "sane" serious offenders in South Africa, there is a system of mandatory minimum sentencing. This was first set out in the Criminal Law Amendment Act 105 of 1997 (CLAA) which in addition to the provision of minimum sentencing for certain serious offenses also abolished the use of the death penalty for these said crimes. The Act has been amended several times, although has been fairly static since 2008, with the last major amendment occurring in 2007 (Criminal Law (Sex Offences and Related Matters) Amendment Act 32 of 2007). The relevant offenses include murder, rape, compelled rape (where the offender compels a third person to commit rape), human trafficking for sexual purposes, certain terrorism-related crimes, crimes against humanity and genocide. For all of these offenses certain aggravating factors must apply (CLAA 1997 Schedule 2 Part 1). For the offense of rape this includes when it was committed:

i. in circumstances where the victim was raped more than once whether by the accused or by any co-perpetrator or accomplice;

ii. by more than one person, where such persons acted in the execution or futherance of a common purpose or conspiracy;

iii. by a person who has been convicted of two or more offenses of rape or compelled rape, but has not yet been sentenced in respect of such convictions; or,

iv. by a person, knowing that he has the acquired immune deficiency syndrome or the human immunodeficiency virus (CLAA 1997 Schedule 2 Part 1);

or where the victim:

i. is a person under the age of 16 years;

ii. is a physically disabled person who, due to his or her physical disability, is rendered particularly vulnerable; or

iii. is a person who is mentally disabled (CLAA 1997 Schedule 2 Part 1).

For such an offense the minimum sentence is life imprisonment (CLAA 1997 s51(1)). Where such factors do not exist, minimum sentencing still applies to rape, compelled rape, sexual exploitation of a child, sexual exploitation of a person who is mentally disabled, using a child for child pornography or using a person who is mentally disabled for pornographic purposes (CLAA 1997 Schedule 2 Part 3). Here sentencing lengths depend on previous convictions whereby:

i. a first offender, [is sentenced] to imprisonment for a period not less than 10 years;

ii. a second offender of any such offence, to imprisonment for a period not less than 15 years; and

iii. a third or subsequent offender of any such offence, to imprisonment for a period not less than 20 years (CLAA 1997 s51(2)(b));

as long as the maximum possible term the court can give does not exceed the minimum term imposed here by more than five years. The court is able, however, to deliver a lesser sentence where "it is satisfied that substantial and compelling circumstances exist which justify the imposition of a lesser sentence" (CLAA 1997 s51(3)).

In the case of Schedule 2 Part 1 offenses the court can impose sentences of up to 30 years. It is also worth noting that the legislation does not apply to those aged under 16 at the time the offense was committed (CLAA 1997 s51(6)).

The key factor in this legislation, in relation to sexual offenses, is therefore whether the offense is categorized as either a Part 1 or a Part 3 offense. For example, the rape of a child of 15 could amount to life imprisonment, while of a 16-year-old (for a first-time offender) would amount to 10 years. This is vastly different and arguably arbitrary, especially when there are no statutory gradations between 10 years and life (Baehr, 2008). The sentence of life imprisonment also appears to be somewhat harsh, when compared to the median custodial sentences given for rape prior to the original 1997 Act coming into force. This was 17.5 years in the High Court (Baehr, 2008) but only eight to nine years in the regional Magistrate's Court (D. van Zyl Smit, personal communication, January 30, 2012). Similar to the experiences of other countries, this legislation therefore appears to show a punitive response to the sentencing of sex offenders and perhaps is not unexpected in a country which has high rates of sexual offenses.

As mentioned above, however, deviation from the minimum sentences can occur if there are "substantial and compelling" reasons. The legislation does not define this, although since 2007 it cannot include "the complainant's previous sexual history; an apparent lack of physical injury to the complainant; an accused person's cultural or religious beliefs about rape; or any relationship between the accused person and the complainant prior to the offence being committed" (CLAA 1997 s51(3)). While this list helps to overcome some rape myths prevalent in sentencing courts prior to the 2007 amendment (see *S* v. *Ntuli* [2005] JOL 12442 (ECLD)), it would be more valuable if examples of what amounts to substantial and compelling were also included. Some guidance has been given by the South African Constitutional Court in *S* v. *Malgas* (2001 (2) SA 1222 (A) (S. Afr)), when it held that if "the prescribed sentence would be unjust, as it would be disproportionate to the crime, the criminal and the needs of society, the court may impose a lesser sentence" (*S* v. *Malgas* (2001 (2) SA 1234–25 (A) (S. Afr)). As Baehr (2008) argues, however, this has been interpreted by many sentencing judges to mean that they have substantial levels of discretion when it comes to sentencing rape and other sexual offenses cases, especially as the case gave no guidance on how great these deviations could be. The apparent harshness of the legislation would therefore appear to be somewhat lacking in reality. The reason that the government included this exception clause is arguably because of concerns surrounding proportionality. As stated in *S* v. *Dodo* (2001 (5) BCLR 423 (CC0 (S. Afr)) if a sentence of life did not reflect the gravity of the offense then it was to be seen as an affront to human dignity. The clause therefore keeps the Act within the country's constitution (see Article 10[5] of the Constitution of the Republic of South Africa No. 108 of 1996), but also appears to make the provision somewhat ineffective. It is therefore unusual and perhaps surprising, when bearing in mind the policies outlined above, that South Africa has not opted for a bifurcated system whereby proportionality can be sidelined when dealing with serious offenses. As argued by Paschke and Sherwin (2000) it has resulted in the situation where judges and magistrates feel that they should impose less than the minimum sentence, because giving the minimum would suggest that there are no substantial and compelling circumstances. When these can arguably be found in the vast majority of cases, "the minimum is in effect operating as a maximum" (Paschke and Sherwin, 2000: 9). The legislation is therefore useless. Its practical effect suggests leniency in the courts, yet has created a situation whereby a judge can give a sentence of 40 years for a Part 1 offense, but still has to find some substantial and compelling reasons why he has not imposed life.

What is therefore desperately needed in South Africa is some guidance on how CLAA s51 should be interpreted. Some effort towards this goal was begun in 2000 when the Sentencing Council produced a Sentencing Framework Bill, but this too uses the words "substantial and compelling," explaining that they were used "deliberately, as they allow some flexibility while limiting departures to cases where there is very strong, if not exceptional, justification for it" (South African Law Commission, 2000: 3.1.11). Examples of this justification are not, however, given. Even if more guidance had been given by the Sentencing Council the Bill is not in force (D. van Zyl Smit, personal communication, January 9, 2012) and even though it was commissioned by the government has largely been ignored by it (D. van Zyl Smith, personal communication, January 30, 2012). Unlike the other countries noted above, South Africa has not experienced protracted court cases looking at the balance between the rights of the offender and the need to protect the public. However, the real consequence of this is arguably that it has a piece of legislation which is worthless and which may be seen to be imbalanced – but this time in favor of the offender rather than the public.

Discussion

Although the fundamental aim of preventive detention schemes is one of public protection, it can be argued that the schemes operational in Australia, the United States and the conditional and subsequent elements of the German scheme breach human rights. This is because, as mentioned above, they are contrary to the principle of finality as the prisoner will initially believe that he will be released at the end of a determinate sentence and thus in effect they work by doubly punishing the offender for what he *might* do in the future. In the *Fardon* case, in Australia, this was argued to be contrary to the rule of law and offensive to the principle of the separation of powers, as the DPSOA 2003 effectively allows the court to treat an individual as a criminal and impose a sentence when he has not actually committed a further criminal offense (Gray, 2004). The ECtHR, in respect of similar German provisions, held a comparable view. The argument that this is civil rather than criminal detention makes no difference to legality either, with Williams explaining how,

> The argument that if the system of incarceration can be classified as civil and non-punitive in nature, then the legal and ethical objections to detention based other than on desert are removed . . . seems mistaken. The essence of incarceration from a punitive point of view is the deprivation of liberty, and this is in no way lessened by claiming the incarceration is civil . . . such (preventive) incarceration is . . . properly classified as a form of preventive detention akin to imprisonment. To make use of less harsh sounding

labels is merely to seek to escape from the gravity of the issues inevitably involved in arguing in support of preventive detention. (Williams, 1990, cited in Gray, 2004: 258)

This concern is perhaps alleviated by the system seen in England and Wales where preventive detention forms part of the *original* sentencing process, although even here the use of such a system is not without its critics. Indeed Lord Justice Denning has stated that it "would be contrary to all principle for a man to be punished, not for what he has already done but for what he may hereafter do" (*Everett* v. *Ribbands* [1952] 2 QB 198, at 206). If an offender is placed into the dangerous offender category then arguably a preventive sentence is being imposed because of who the offender is rather than based on what he has done. Furthermore, while it can be argued that IPP/life prisoners at least know of this indeterminacy at the sentencing stage, they are not provided with any greater certainty as to when their actual release date will be. In fact they may be at an even greater disadvantage when compared to their Australian counterparts on the basis that continuing detention there has to be proven by the government; whereas in England and Wales it is for the prisoner to show that his risk has reduced and thus that he is safe to be released back into the community. The one system which can perhaps be seen to work, on a practical basis, in favor of the offender is that seen in South Africa; but arguably this too can be criticized for using inappropriate proportionality principles for serious sexual offenders.

Another criticism with sex offender legislation of the aforementioned countries is the burden of proof which is needed to continually detain. In Queensland and Germany it is only necessary to prove the perceived risk or danger on the basis of a high probability, with this often being recognized as the civil burden of proof. This test of probability is also seen in other Australian sex offender preventive detention legislation (Doyle and Ogloff, 2009) and is unethical when we are talking about the criminal detention of "innocent" beings. This blurring between criminal and civil is not seen in England and Wales where there is a need to prove dangerousness beyond all reasonable doubt; although even here there are other problems with the system, including how dangerousness is actually assessed.

Another issue relates to the status of the prisoner who is being held for preventive purposes, with this being more pertinent when the individual is supposedly being held under civil rather than criminal procedures. In Queensland, for example, where the system is said to be civil in nature, post-conviction detainees remain within the prison system which arguably raises human rights implications because of the punitive nature of the regime (McSherry and Keyzer, 2009). This is the same in Germany, although *in theory* here at least they do have a different legal status, in recognition of their "innocent" standing, and do not have to work or wear prison uniforms. In England and Wales IPP/life prisoners are also held within the prison regime, as are serious sexual offenders detained in South Africa. In comparison, however, the United States has special commitment centers, suggesting that this is the only country which deals with its preventive detention prisoners within a separate regime.

It can be argued, however, that if public protection is truly the aim of indeterminate sentencing rather than more sinister punitive goals, then once the retributive element of the custodial sentence has been completed – that is, the minimum period in the case of an IPP, or the determinate phase in other countries – and the offender either enters into the public protection phase of his sentence, or he is continually detained, he should be moved to a less punitive regime. While it is accepted that modern imprisonment works on the basis that it is the lack of liberty which is the punishment and that the prison regime should not be such as to contribute to this, in reality the vast majority of prison regimes around the world are punitive and detrimental. Following history and the rationale for different regimes in the early twentieth century (see Radzinowicz and Hood, 1980), separate prisons or wings of prisons could be created which foster a more rehabilitative way of life, including a greater focus on education and the learning of life skills. This would support the argument made by Ashworth (1989: 342) that "public protection requires public policies aimed specifically at crime prevention and generally at reducing criminogenic circumstances" to make them work. If offenders remain within the normal prison estate, which for all those within it is for punishment purposes, than the rationality of preventive detention not being about punishment does not stack up. While open prisons may offer this less punitive and rigid way of life, it is unlikely that many offenders being held under preventive sentences will find themselves in such environments, especially as in some countries continued detention results in their risk level being raised. The vast majority of offenders are therefore being held in punitive closed prison conditions, providing support for the belief that they are being detained for punitive rather than for public protection purposes.

Another difference between Australia, England and Wales, Germany and the United States, and linked to the above argument, is the identification of the primary aim of continuing detention. In the former countries prisoners on the whole are detained for reasons of public protection and control. This was emphasized in 2007 by the Queensland Minister for Corrective Services when he explained that the supervision of sex offenders in the community costs more than detention under the DPSOA 2003 (Ronken, 2008), suggesting that continuing detention is about the warehousing of offenders rather than a method of treatment and risk reduction. In the United States, however, the primary aim is supposed to be one of treatment. However, despite these criticisms, it is worth noting that the vast majority of sex offenders held on a continuing detention order in Queensland are released (McSherry and Keyzer, 2009), while a very different experience is shared by those detained in England and Wales and the United States.

The final issue on which this chapter comments is the effect of preventive detention laws on sexual offending rates. The most credible argument for having dangerousness legislation would obviously be that it worked, that is, that it prevented future crime and hence kept the public protected. A number of research studies focused on this issue have, however, reported rather cautious and unimpressive findings. For example, *Taking Offenders out of Circulation* concluded that regarding preventive detention, "it seems safe to say that the effect on the recorded crime rate would be negligible" (Brody and Tarling, 1980: 35). This has also been asserted by van Dine, Dinitz and Conrad (1977: 22) who found in the United States that the effectiveness of its incapacitation strategy "would have prevented no more than 4.0 per cent of the violent crimes in Franklin County in 1973." Furthermore, the Carter Review, in England and Wales, stated that while "prison does reduce crime . . . there is no convincing evidence that further increases in the use of custody would significantly reduce crime" (Carter, 2003: 15). So while it is true to say that preventive detention prevents the individual from offending, there is no reliable evidence to suggest that its deterrent effect works adequately to protect the public from other offenders within society. Such findings are therefore why Ashworth (2004: 521) concludes that, "even in official circles, there is no confidence that the increased use of prison sentences has had a substantial impact on crime rates, let alone on public protection from serious offences." Doyle and Ogloff (2009) additionally explain how a lot of sexual crimes are carried out by offenders who have not previously been convicted of similar offenses; many offenses against both children and adults are undertaken by family acquaintances and thus are never reported to the criminal justice agencies; sex offenders do not re-offend as a matter of course; and, of those sex offenders who do re-offend, many carry out crimes of a non-sexual nature. Post-conviction, mandatory minimum and longer than commensurate sentencing schemes are therefore unlikely to affect the sexual offense rates of such offenders. If public protection is the overall justifying aim of continuing detention, incapacitation orders and IPPs, but the legislation behind such policies ignores the "empirical realities of sexual offending" (Doyle and Ogloff, 2009: 185), this is surely yet another reason for legal and ethical concern. The fact that governments around the globe continually persist in their endeavors to create and update dangerousness legislation would therefore appear to be a waste of time, although being cynical their endeavors are not just to incapacitate the "dangerous" but are largely borne out of a desire to please their ever-increasingly punitive voting public.

Notes

1   This provides that "Everyone has the right to liberty and security of person. No one shall be subjected to arbitrary arrest or detention. No one shall be deprived of his liberty except on such grounds and in accordance with such procedure as are established by law."
2   Although the amendments made by the CJIA 2008 only apply to those offenses committed after July 14, 2008.
3   These include sexual, violent and – since January 12, 2010 (Coroners and Justice Act 2009 s138) – terrorism offenses.
4   This provides that "No one shall be held guilty of any criminal offence on account of any act or omission which did not constitute a criminal offence under national or international law at the time when it was committed. Nor shall a heavier penalty be imposed than the one that was applicable at the time the criminal offence was committed."
5   This provides that "Everyone has inherent dignity and the right to have their dignity respected and protected."

References

Albrecht, H-J. (2004) "Security gaps: responding to dangerous sex offenders in the Federal Republic of Germany," *Federal Sentencing Reporter* 16, 3, 200–207.

Ashworth, A. (1989) "Criminal justice and deserved sentences," *Criminal Law Review*, May, 340–355.

Ashworth, A. (2004) "Criminal Justice Act 2002: Part 2: criminal justice reform – principles, human rights and public protection," *Criminal Law Review*, July, 516–532.

Australian Government (2011) State and Territory Government, http://australia.gov.au/about-australia/our-government/state-and-territory-government (accessed August 25, 2012).

Baehr, K.S. (2008) "Mandatory minimums making minimal difference: ten years of sentencing sex offenders in South Africa," *Yale Journal of Law and Feminism* 20, 213–246.

Brody, S. and Tarling, R. (1980) *Taking Offenders out of Circulation. Home Office Research Study No. 64.* London: Home Office.

Bundesministerium der Justiz (2010) Translation of the German Criminal Code Provided by Prof. Dr. Michael Bohlander, http://www.gesetze-im-internet.de/englisch_stgb/englisch_stgb.html#StGBengl_000P66 (accessed August 25, 2012).

Carter, P. (2003) *Managing Offenders, Reducing Crime. A New Approach.* London: Her Majesty's Stationery Office.

Department of Justice, Victoria (2011) Serious Sex Offenders, http://www.justice.vic.gov.au/home/sentencing/serious+sex+offenders/ (accessed August 25, 2012).

Dessecker, A. (2009) "Dangerousness, long prison terms and preventive measures in Germany," Champ penal, vol. *VI*, http://champpenal.revues.org/7508 (accessed August 25, 2012).

Deutsche Welle (2011) German Court Rules Preventive Detention Unconstitutional, http://www.dw-world.de/dw/article/0,,15046630,00.html (accessed August 25, 2012).

Doyle, D. and Ogloff, J. (2009) "Calling the tune without the music: a psycho-legal analysis of Australia's post-sentence legislation," *Australian & New Zealand Journal of Criminology* 42, 179–203.

Dunkel, F. and van Zyl Smit, D. (2004) "Preventive detention of dangerous offenders re-examined," *German Law Journal* 5, 6, 619–637.

Gray, A. (2004) "Detaining future dangerous offenders: dangerous law," *Deakin Law Review* 9, 243–259.

Gray, A. (2005) "Preventive detention laws. High Court validates Queensland's Dangerous Prisoners Act 2003," *Alternative Law Journal* 30, 2, 75–79.

Howard League for Penal Reform (2007) *Indeterminate Sentences for Public Protection*. Prison Information Bulletin 3. London: Howard League for Penal Reform.

Keyzer, P. and Coyle, I. (2009) "Reintegrating sex offenders into the community. Queensland's proposed reforms," *Alternative Law Journal* 34, 1, 27–31.

McSherry, B. (2010) Preventive Detention of Sex Offenders: Recent Trends. Paper presented at the Professional Legal Education Seminar, Victoria Legal Aid, Melbourne, July 14, 2010, http://www.law.monash.edu.au/centres/calmh/rmhl/docs/p-bmcs-vic-legal-aid.pdf (accessed August 25, 2012).

McSherry, B. and Keyzer, P. (2009) *Sex Offenders and Preventive Detention. Politics, Policy and Practice.* Sydney: Federation Press.

Ministry of Justice (2011) *Provisional Figures Relating to Offenders Serving Indeterminate Sentences of Imprisonment for Public Protection (IPPS)*. London: Ministry of Justice.

Paschke, R. and Sherwin, H. (2000) *Quantitative Research Report on Sentencing 10-11.* Pretoria: South African Law Commission.

Radzinowicz, L. and Hood, R. (1980) "Incapacitating the habitual criminal: the English experience," *Michigan Law Review* 78, 1305–1389.

Ronken, C. (2008) Balancing rights: arguments for indefinite detention for dangerous sex offenders. Paper presented at the Sentencing Conference, National Judicial College of Australia/ANU College of Law, February 8–10, 2008, http://njca.anu.edu.au/

Professional%20Development/programs%20by%20year/2008/Sentencing%20
Conference%202008/papers/Ronken%20Johnson.pdf (accessed August 25, 2012).

South African Law Commission (2000) *The Sentencing Framework Bill.* Pretoria: South African
Law Commission.

Thomas, D. (2008) "IPP amended," *Archbold News* 5, 7–9.

van Dine, S., Dinitz, S. and Conrad, J. (1977) "The incapacitation of the dangerous offender:
a statistical experiment," *Journal of Research in Crime and Delinquency* 14, 1, 22–34.

10

Sentencing and Crime Policy for Sex Offenders in Japan
The Possible Impact of the Lay Judge System
Mari Hirayama

Introduction

Crime involving innocent children as victims always attracts great attention, sometimes causing criminal justice policy to become very radical, to the point where it even seems to become irrational. This is certainly the case in Japan, where a single case in 2004 had a huge impact on criminal justice policy on sex crimes. The other major change relating to sex crimes in Japan has been in sentencing. Since the introduction of the lay judge system in May 2009, sentences for sex crime cases have been rising. Also, it seems that lay people have a great interest in what happens to offenders after their release, which may have some impact on the supervision of sex offenders in the future. This chapter focuses on these recent revolutions in sentencing and criminal justice policy for sex offenders in Japan.

A Single Case Changed the Whole System

A single case sometimes changes the whole criminal justice policy, as we can see in the *Megan Kanka* case in 1994 in New Jersey. That single case forced the United States to enact sex offender registration and community notification laws, widely known as Megan's Law (Koenig, 1998). This movement towards more draconian laws has never slowed down in the United States: now all 50 states and Washington DC have their own version of Megan's Law, and after the enactment of the Adam Walsh Child Protection and Safety Act in 2006, the laws on sex offenders became more consistent and much tougher (David, 2008).

In Japan, there was a case very similar to that of *Megan*. The tragedy happened on November 11, 2004, in Nara prefecture, which is a suburban prefecture in the western part of Japan (hereafter referred to as the *Nara* case) (*Asahi* newspaper,

The Wiley-Blackwell Handbook of Legal and Ethical Aspects of Sex Offender Treatment and Management, First Edition. Edited by Karen Harrison and Bernadette Rainey.

2004). On that day, a seven-year-old girl had gone missing. Her family received e-mails containing photos depicting the girl's dead body, and the body was discovered the next day. The evidence showed that she had been molested and a number of her teeth had been pulled out. For a while, the police investigation did not yield any results. Even worse, the victim's family was blackmailed by threats that the girl's younger sister would be targeted next. At the end of December, more than a month after the kidnapping, a 36-year-old newspaper delivery man, who lived in the same prefecture as the victim, was arrested and confessed to the murder.

After the arrest, it turned out that the man had a record of multiple sex offenses. He had been arrested several times for committing sex crimes, and for the last crime he had served a three-year prison sentence. After his parole in 1995, he was put under probation, but his probation ended eight years before the *Nara* case. Only a few months before the *Nara* case, he committed a lascivious act against a six-year-old girl in Nara prefecture and was prosecuted for this crime. As can be seen he repeatedly committed sex crimes against children, and in the end even killed a little girl.

The whole nation was in a state of fear, and people began to question the justice system and the correctional system. The offender in question had been convicted twice before. So what exactly did the prison and probation office do in order to prevent recidivism? In particular, parents of small children feared that their children could become victims of a sex crime.

Since the *Nara* case, the word "Fu-Shin-Sya" has become very popular among the Japanese people. "Fu-Shin-Sya" means "strange person" or "person who does not seem to be all right." As we can see, the meaning of this word is very ambiguous; however, since the *Nara* case, Japan has been under pressure to ensure a safe and secure community, and in doing so Japanese society has become more and more inclined to exclude those who appear to be different (in many senses of the word) from the majority. Many prefectural police have even established an "Alerting Mailing List for Parents." If a citizen informs the police that he or she saw a Fu-Shin-Sya somewhere, an alerting mail is sent to parents on the mailing list who want this information.

Many researchers and legal professionals in Japan had heard about Megan's Law even before the *Nara* case, but at that time most people in Japan had never heard of Megan's Law. Right after the *Nara* case, some television programs were aired in which Megan's Law was discussed. While some media were in favor of Megan's Law, the majority, especially the newspapers, expressed quite a negative attitude to it, nor was there much popular demand for an equivalent law for Japan. These points will be analyzed later in this chapter.

The *Nara* case had a major impact on sex crime policy in Japan. Its impact can be seen in three different arenas: sex offenders' treatment programs in prison; sex offenders' treatment programs when they are on probation; and the tracking system for sex offenders' residences. These changes will be discussed below.

Sex Offenders' Treatment Programs in Prisons

The *Nara* case made Japanese society realize that there were no effective treatment programs for sex offenders in prison. What was worse, before the *Nara* case, these programs had not been mandatory for sex offenders in prison. Also, surprisingly, the Ministry of Justice (MOJ) and the police did not have sufficient statistics on recidivism by sex offenders. In response to the public outcry, the Research and Training Institute (RTI) of the MOJ launched a special analysis of the nature of sex crimes and recidivism rates (Ministry of Justice, 2006a). They started categorizing sex crimes according to type of offense, age of victim and so on, and reviewed sex offender characteristics (Ministry of Justice, 2006a), In April 2005, the MOJ launched the "Taskforce for Sex Offenders' Treatment Programs" and started to explore programs for sex offenders. The Taskforce comprised not only professionals from within the MOJ, but also researchers working in psychiatry, psychology, criminology and other fields. Sex offenders' treatment programs in prison became mandatory under the Criminal Incarceration Institution and Treatment of Prisoners Act 2006 (hereafter referred to as the Act 2006).[1] Under Article 82.2 of the Act, sex offenders are categorized as "prisoners who need special reform instruction" (Natori, 2006).[2]

Sex Offenders' Treatment Programs at Probation Stage

Referrals

In 2005, the probation system in Japan was strongly condemned by society. It was not only because the offender in the *Nara* case had been under probation but also because other related tragedies occurred,[3] which highlighted that the probation system did not seem to be at all effective in preventing recidivism. Along with the setting up of treatment programs in prison, the MOJ instituted treatment programs for probationers who committed sex crimes from May 2006 onwards (hereafter referred to as the probation program). The program targeted sex offenders on probation (those who are on parole and those who are given suspended sentences with probation). The type of crimes which are referred to the probation programs are those for which the motives are somehow related to sex (Ministry of Justice, 2006b).

As for released sex offenders, the parole committee in each district reviews and decides on whether referral to the probation programs is necessary (Takujima, 2006). Assessments of prisoners in treatment programs in prison are used to assess the prisoners when they are released and put on the probation program (Takujima, 2006). As for sex offenders given a suspended sentence with probation, probation officers review and decide on referrals (Takujima, 2006).

Nature of programs

In the probation program, both through "one on one" counseling with a probation officer and through group meetings, sex offenders are required to realize their own problems and learn ways of controlling their behavior (Ministry of Justice, 2006b). It is very important for them to know what their own triggers are (Ministry of Justice, 2006b). Probation officers set up the program so that offenders must realize their cycle of offending, correct their cognitive misunderstandings, learn self-management and communication skills, express empathy for victims, and make plans to avoid re-offending in the future (Ministry of Justice, 2006b). Each step has five classes, and normally sex offenders finish each step in two weeks (Ministry of Justice, 2006b). These programs are, of course, mandatory for sex offenders, and if they fail to participate they may be sent back to prison.

The tracking system for sex offenders

The tracking system for sex offenders was set up in June 2005 (Hirayama, 2007). When offenders who have committed sex crimes against children aged 13 or younger are released from prison, their data – such as their name, address and workplace – are recorded in a database by the National Police Agency (NPA) in Tokyo. The NPA sends this information on offenders to the police headquarters of the prefecture in which they live. Then, the prefectural police headquarters relay the information to those local police stations that are located closest to the residences of the offenders. At the local police stations, recidivism-preventing officers are assigned to check the residences of the released offenders on a regular basis. Recidivism-preventing officers are selected from officers with a rank higher than inspector. If they find that a released sex offender cannot be located, they will try to find the offender in cooperation with other police stations and will update the database once the offender is relocated (see Figure 10.1). Offenders are tracked for at least five years if they have committed a sex crime only once, and for at least 10 years if they have a record of multiple sex crimes.

When this system was introduced, at the press conference the NPA explained that they would try to preserve offenders' privacy, and therefore would not give information to neighbors or colleagues of the offender. They even said they would check the offenders "over the wall" (that is, without anyone knowing that the checks were being carried out). From the outset, it sounded as if the system would not be very effective in tracking sex offenders. In fact, many sex offenders have gone missing after being released. According to a report by the Community Safety Bureau (CSB) of the NPA in 2010 (NPA, 2010), 740 released sex offenders were tracked by this system for a five-year period (that is, from June 2005 to May 2010). Of these 740, 200 (about 27%) could not be tracked by May 2010. As for recidivism rates, 170 of them had been re-arrested for another crime by May 2010 (NPA, 2010). Of those 170, 105 had been arrested for sex crimes. Furthermore, 49 of those 105 re-arrested sex offenders had committed violent sex crimes against victims under 13 years of age (NPA, 2010).

Though the tracking system did prevent several sex crimes and contributed to the re-arresting of repeat offenders at an early stage (Harada, 2011), there was widespread dissatisfaction with the high percentage of released sex offenders who had gone missing, and with the high rates of recidivism. Therefore, the NPA had to establish a more thorough system for supervising offenders, and a reformed tracking system was set up in April 2011 (Harada, 2011). Under the reformed system, the NPA required the local police to change their method of checking offenders' places of residence (Harada, 2011: 15). They now had to check the whereabouts of offenders by meeting them directly (face to face). Also, they began to hold regular meetings with offenders who were considered to present a high risk for re-offending (those

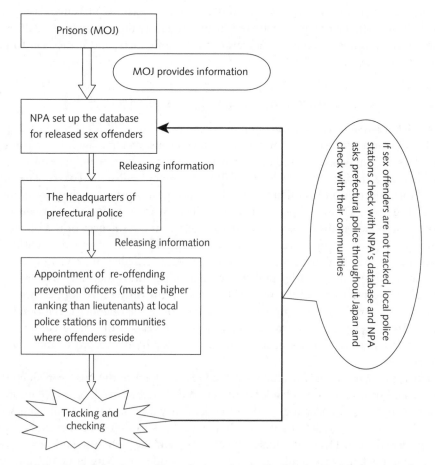

Figure 10.1 System for the tracking of released sex offenders by local police, launched June 2005.

who are younger than 50, have multiple conviction histories for sexually violent crime, or show any inappropriate behavior toward children), with the offenders' permission (Harada, 2011). After these meetings, the police can refer the offenders to counseling agencies if necessary (Harada, 2011). Also, under the reformed system, the MOJ decided to release information held by the police, evaluating how the offenders performed in prison treatment programs (Harada, 2011). We still do not know whether the reformed system will be effective in providing proper supervision and preventing new crimes, but there is great public demand for the police to track released sex offenders closely and effectively.

Did Japan Want Megan's Law after the Nara Case?

Although Japan and the United States experienced quite similar sex crimes (the *Nara* case and the *Megan* case), Japanese policy on sex offenders appears to be heading

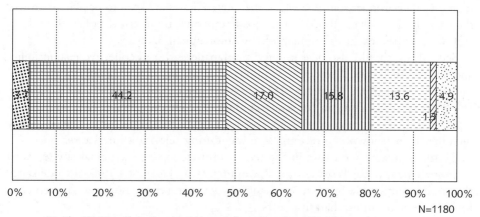

The Ministry of Justice should keep information about the release of people with a history of sex crime offenses to itself. The information should not be provided to police.

Police should share the information. Support the Ministry of Justice's decision.

The information should also be disclosed to parties concerned with public security in communities, such as municipal government and school officials.

The information should be disclosed to community residents upon request.

The information should be disclosed for access via the Internet.

Others

Don't know

Figure 10.2 Public attitude to safety, survey by the Nomura Research Institute, March 15, 2005–March 16, 2005. Source: "Survey of Attitude on Public Safety" page #19 "Disclosure of Information of People with a History of Sex Offenses" (With Permission from Nomura Research Institute, Ltd).

in a different direction from US policy. There are interesting data on whether the Japanese people think information on sex offenders should be released in order to protect the public, according to a survey carried out by the Nomura Research Institute in March 2005, a few months after the *Nara* tragedy (see Figure 10.2).

The institute asked 1,180 members of the public about the degree of disclosure of information that was needed for people with a history of sex offenses. Figure 10.2 shows that only 3.7% of the respondents said that this information should be kept within the MOJ, meaning that over 90% of the respondents believe that the information should be disclosed by the MOJ in some way. The Nomura Research Institute noted that many people now desire more information to be disclosed.

However, what was surprising in the figures was that 44.2% of the respondents said they support the tracking system of sex offenders' residences and they do not object to the police having exclusive access to the information. It seems that many people want the authorities to be the sole force in dealing with crime. So, the question arises, why did they not want Megan's Law?

First of all, I believe the Japanese people put a lot of trust in the authorities. This may be compared to the right to bear arms in the United States, which is strongly related to their frontier spirit; people in the United States are keen to be able to protect their family themselves. By contrast, Japanese people think crime policy should be, and must be, the exclusive domain of law enforcement agencies.

Second, we should also bear in mind the Japanese idea of collective responsibility and shame. In Japan, if someone commits a crime, his or her family members are informally condemned (Suzuki, 2011). In most cases, it becomes impossible for the family to keep on living in the same community. This tendency is far stronger in Japan than in Western countries. In Japan, it is extremely rare for criminals' family members to be shown in a recognizable way during television interviews.

Third, compared with laws in Western countries, Japanese criminal law tends to be more lenient towards sex crimes. For example, the Japanese Criminal Code states that rape is punishable by no more than three years in prison; however, the sentence for robbery is no more than five years.

Fourth, conviction history is strictly confidential in Japan. In 1981, the Japanese Supreme Court ruled that, bar exceptional circumstances, a person's conviction history must be restricted to the relevant government agencies. On the other hand, in the United States, conviction histories, not only of sex offenders but also of criminals who have committed other kinds of felony, are publicly accessible.

The Impact of the Saiban-in System

Impact on sentencing

In May 2009, Japan introduced the new Saiban-in System (the lay judge system), which may change criminal trial drastically. The Japanese lay judge system is quite different from the jury system in the United States and the United Kingdom. The lay judge system only applies to severe criminal cases (not civil cases). Under this system, six lay people and three professional judges try the case together. Along with the professional judges, the lay people are asked to make decisions not only on fact-finding but also on sentencing (Ministry of Justice, 2012).

Before the introduction of the system, one of the biggest concerns was whether Japanese people would cooperate with this new system. Many polls showed negative reactions (*Asahi Shinbun*, 2009), which meant that many Japanese people were reluctant to serve as lay judges. Contrary to these concerns, lay people have seemed to be quite cooperative with the system. When courts summoned candidate lay judges, in most districts high percentages turned up (61 to 91% even in serious cases). Also, what was most surprising was that many lay judges agreed to answer questions from the press, and some of them even agreed to release their names and photographs to the newspapers. In May 2010, exactly one year after the introduction of the system, the Shinbun Kyokai (the Newspaper Association in Japan) reported that lay judges had agreed to participate in press conferences in 95% of all lay judge trials (*Ji-ji Tsushinsya*, May 21, 2010).

One of the biggest concerns about the Saiban-in system was its impact on sentencing, that is, whether lay people could decide cases rationally or not. In considering the factors that could have an emotional impact on lay judges, we should also think about other new systems in criminal cases. The Victims Participation System (Criminal Procedure Code 316-33~), in which victims of crime (including bereaved families) can directly participate in criminal trials, and even influence sentencing, was introduced six months before the introduction of the Saiban-in System. The impact of the Victims Participation System on lay people has also been a major concern. However, in most cases, there has not been evidence of particularly great changes in sentencing due to victim participation.

But when we examine the sentencing carefully, we can see polarization. At one end of the scale, there are homicide cases related to family issues. In these cases defendants receive more lenient sentences. However, the opposite effect has been seen in sex crime cases. In sex crime cases tried by lay judge trials, sentences have been increasing in length. Therefore, it is quite important to examine the impact of the lay judge system on the criminal justice system for sex offenders (Hirayama, 2010; Hirai, 2010).

I have collected and analyzed all sex crime cases[4] tried by lay judge trials (N=208) for two years (from May 21, 2009 to May 20, 2011). In some cases there was more than one defendant, so there were 212 defendants for sex crimes tried during these two years. Of these 212 defendants, 177 received sentences without suspension. Two of these 177 defendants received a 30-year sentence where an indefinite sentence was demanded by the victims, so I calculated the sentencing ratio (sentence/demanded sentence) for 175 defendants. The average sentencing ratio in all cases is 75.95% (up to the end of January 2010). On the other hand, the sentencing ratio for sex crimes, for the two-year period, is 82.17%, which is more than 5% higher than average. If we focus only on cases of "rape resulting in injury," the ratio goes up even higher, to 86.54%. It is quite clear that the involvement of lay people has led to an increase in sentences for sex crimes.

Differences of opinion between lay people and professional judges

Therefore the question arises: why is there such a gap between lay people and professional judges on what they think are proper sentences for sex crimes? First, the male-dominated culture in the legal profession, especially among professional judges, has played a major role in Japan. In this culture, there is a tendency to "blame victims" and underestimate their sufferings. It eventually leads to lenient sentencing guidelines for sex crimes compared with the suffering of victims. These sentencing guidelines have become precedent, and professional judges feel very reluctant to deviate from them. When I reviewed comments by chief judges in sentencing, they seemed to take advantage of lay judges in order to give harsher punishments in sex crime cases (Hirayama, 2010).

Secondly, "Jidan" (settlement out of court) has played an important role in sex crime cases in Japan. It is not difficult to imagine that the reasons why sex crime victims agree to sign Jidan are not because they forgive their offender (Kazue, 1998). Some victims have no choice but to sign Jidan because they fear a "second rape" through the stress of a trial. Others may desperately need the compensation, because they had to leave a job as a result of suffering from victimization. These "hidden reasons" have not, however, been carefully considered by professional judges in some cases. Professional judges have quite automatically interpreted the signing of Jidan as indicating forgiveness from victims, which eventually leads to lenient sentences for offenders. Again, the male-dominated culture of professional judges has played a major role here. On the other hand, lay people seem to pay little attention to Jidan. They seem to know that they still need to consider the sufferings of victims in cases where Jidan has been established.

Future implications of the lay judge system for criminal justice policy on sex offenders

This chapter has discussed the major changes in sentencing for sex crimes brought about by the introduction of the lay judge system. Judging by the comments of lay judges who served in sex crime trials, it seems that many people now realize that sentencing for sex crimes has been quite lenient, and that support systems for victims of sexual crime are still poor. These "realizations" may lead to amendment of the Japanese Penal Code, toughening sentences for sex crimes. We might also wonder whether the lay judge system has brought about any change in people's attitudes toward crime policy. It seems that, after the introduction of the lay judge system, many people are now interested in playing a more active role in crime policy.

As mentioned above, Japanese society did not have much interest in a Japanese version of Megan's Law in 2005. However, this attitude may have changed since then, if people have become more interested in crime policy as a result of the introduction of the lay judge system. An interesting survey on this topic was carried out recently. The Syakai Anzen Zaidan (2011) (the Japanese Research Institute on Safe Society) carried out surveys in 2007 and 2010 on people's opinions on community notification of sex offenders. In these surveys, the Institute asked people if a sex offender moves into their community, which course of action they agreed with: notifying people about this sex offender in order to ensure safety and security, or not notifying anyone in order to respect the offender's privacy. It is quite interesting to see that 44.6% of those surveyed supported community notification in 2007, and 38.4% in 2010 (see Figure 10.3). It seems that people's attitude and opinions may be changing compared with the data seen in Figure 10.2. It will be interesting to see how further experience of the lay judge system impacts on public opinion.

Conclusion

It can be said that sex offenders are "the most difficult group" of offenders to reintegrate into the community. Even if researchers succeed in persuading society that sex offenders do not have the highest rates of recidivism among all criminals, most people may still be strongly opposed to their reintegration. Sex offenders are often regarded as the most "disgusting" of criminals. This intense aversion is understandable, as sex offenders often take advantage of the most vulnerable people in society, such as children, women and the elderly. However, we should be aware of the fact that criminal justice policy for sex offenders can become radical and irrational because of this aversion. There are many types of sex offenders, with different rates of recidivism,

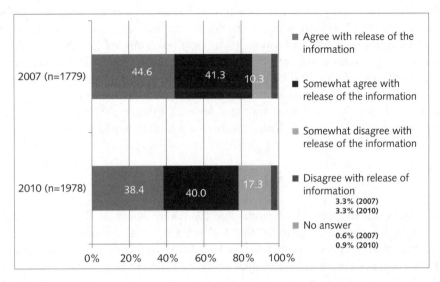

Figure 10.3   Do Japanese people want notification of sex offenders in the community? Note: Respondents were answering the question: "If a sex offender moves into your community, which option do you prefer?: Agree to the release of information on these sex offenders in order to protect the safety and security of your community, or: Disagree with the release of the information in order to respect the offender's privacy." Source: Research Foundation for Safe Society (2011: 80) (With kind permission from Masami Yajima).

and each type of crime needs different approaches. If we are just concerned about excluding sex offenders from society, this may lead to a dangerous situation where rational and appropriate approaches cannot be taken (Someda, 2006). Also, there is a danger that the criminal justice policy could introduce a wider trend for tough approaches for every crime. The Japanese criminal justice system was once criticized as a "Silent Pyramid." There had been very few changes for quite a long time. It has not effectively responded to changes in the needs of victims, offenders and society. The lay judge system could be a good bridge to effect change. In May 2010, one of the major newspapers in Japan, *Yomiuri Shinbun Newspaper* (2010), carried out a survey on those who had participated in trials with lay judges. What they found was that the greatest concern of 60% of the respondents (N=252), was "rehabilitation of defendants."

This raises the question: what did they mean by "rehabilitation of defendants?" If they were mainly concerned with strict supervision and relapse prevention aspects of "rehabilitation of defendants," then society may be starting to display a different attitude towards the provision of information on sex offenders in the community in the near future. This would lay the foundations for a Japanese version of Megan's Law. On the other hand, this could be interpreted in a completely different way, as indicating a more inclusive attitude. If people are also concerned with support for and reintegration of offenders in the community when they emphasize the "rehabilitation of offenders," there may be new trends in criminal justice policy for sex offenders. These new trends will lead to various support programs for sex offenders to help them not only to refrain from re-offending, but also to be situated in the community. A good example of this kind of program is Circles of Support and Accountability (COSA) in Canada. Research has shown that COSA have dramatically reduced recidivism (see Chapter 22). We must wait and see which direction the lay judge system will help to push the criminal justice system for sex offenders in Japan.

Acknowledgments

This chapter was supported by Grant in Aid for Young Scientists (B) "Present Status and Issues for Criminal Justice Policy for Sex Crime: Comparative Research on Integrative and Exclusive Approaches" (April 2008 to March 2011) and Grant in Aid for Young Scientists (B) "Research on Sex Crime and Lay Judge Trials: Issues in Trials, Impact on Sentencing, Corrections and the Criminal Justice Policy for Sex Crime" (April 2011 to March 2014).

Notes

1 The former Prison Law ("Kangoku Ho") was enacted 1910 and it had not been amended for nearly 100 years. In 2000, however, there were several cases where prisoners were fatally abused in Nagoya Prisons, which eventually led the new Prison Law to be enacted.
2 Other special reform instructions are programs for offenders with drug abuse problems, separation from gangs, victims empathy groups, traffic safety education groups and job assistance programs.
3 In February 2005, a 34-year-old man killed a baby in a supermarket in Aichi Prefecture. He had just been released from prison and lived in a halfway house. In 2005, a 24-year-old man was arrested for confining women in his apartment. He repeatedly committed these crimes for several years. Though he was under probation, the probation office could not supervise him properly.
4 Not every sex crime is tried using the lay judge system. The lay judge system deals with crimes which carry the death penalty or indefinite imprisonment. If a perpetrator intentionally commits a crime which results in the death of a victim, that is also tried by a lay judge trial. Over two thousand cases have been tried so far using the lay judge system.

References

Asahi Newspaper (2004) "Nara slaying/caught," December 31, http://www.asahi.com/english/nation/TKY200412310078.html (accessed August 25, 2012).
Asahi Shinbun (2009) "Low interest in participation," March 27, p. 55.
David, J. (2008) "The national pulse, crime registries under fire: Adam Walsh Act mandates sex offender lists, but some say it's unconstitutional," *American Bar Association Journal* 94, 22.

Harada, M. (2011) *Kodomo Taisyo Bouryokuteki Seihanzai Syussyosya ni Taisuru Saihan Boushi Seido no Minaoshi no gaiyou Tou [Reform for the Relapse Prevention System for Sexually Violent Offenders Against Children]*. Osaka: Keisatu Koron.

Hirai, S. (2010) "Sexually violent crime and lay judge trials – cases in 2009 [Sei Bouryoku Hanzai to Saiban-in Saiban-2009 nen no Jirei kara]," *Seinal University Law Review* 225–243.

Hirayama, M. (2007) "Waga Kuni ni Okeru Kodomo wo Taisyotoshita Seihanzai no Genjyo to Sono Saihanboushi Taisaku ni Tsuite [Sex crime against children and relapse prevention scheme in Japan]," *Kwansei Gakuin University Law and Politics Review* 58, 1–3.

Hirayama, M. (2010) "Saiban-in Saiban to Sei Hanzai [Lay judge trials for sex crimes]," *Ritsumeikan Law Review* 323/328, 668–691.

Kazue, A. (1998) "Tatoe Jidan demo Yurusarenai. Teikyo Dai Rugby Buin Rape Jiken [Even if the jidan is settled, the offender must not be forgiven. A rape committed by a student in Teikyo University rugby sport team]," *Monthly Magazine POST* 30, 8, 46–47.

Koenig, W.P. (1998) "Does congress abuse its spending clause power by attaching conditions on the receipt of federal law enforcement funds to a state's compliance with 'Megan's Law?'," *Journal of Criminal Law & Criminology* 88, 2, 721–765.

Ministry of Justice (2006a) "*Actual condition and countermeasure,*" Research and Training Institute, White Paper on Crime, Chapter 4. Tokyo: Ministry of Justice.

Ministry of Justice (2006b) *Taskforce Report on Sex Offenders Program*. Tokyo: Ministry of Justice.

Ministry of Justice (2012) Saiban-in (lay judge) system, http://www.moj.go.jp/ENGLISH/issues/issues03.html (accessed August 25, 2012).

Natori, M. (2006) "Keiji Shisetsu ni Okeru Kaizen Shido no Unyo ni Tsuite – Kihonteki na Wakugumi to Syogu Program no sakutei [Special reform instructions in prisons – basic scheme and plan for treatment programs]," *Crime & Punishment* 43, 3, 24–25.

NPA (National Police Agency) (2010) *Kodomo Taisho Bouryokuteki Seihanzai no Syussyo-Sya no Saihan tou no Kansuru Bunseki [Analysis on Recidivism of Sexually Violent Offenders against Children after their being Released]*. Tokyo: NPA.

Research Foundation for Safe Society (2011) The 4th Report on Fear of Crime in Japan, March, http://www.syaanken.or.jp/wp-content/uploads/2012/05/23031bouhan23_03.pdf (accessed September 15, 2012).

Someda, K. (2006) *Hanzaisya no Syakainai Syogu no Tankyu- Syogu no Tayouka to Syuhuku Teki Shiho [Exploration on Treatment of Offenders in Society – Variation of Treatment and Restorative Justice]*. Tokyo: Seibundo Press.

Suzuki, T. (2011) *Kagaisya Kazoku [Family of Offenders]*.

Syakai Anzen Zaidan (2011) The 4th Report on Fear of Crime in Japan, http://www.syaanken.or.jp/02_goannai/01_bouhan?bouhan23_03/pdf/bouhan23_03.pdf (accessed April 30, 2012).

Takujima, A. (2006) "Hogo Kansatu Syo ni Okeru Seihanzaisya Syoguu Program ni Tsuite [The probation programs for sex offenders]," *Crime & Delinquency* 149, 63.

Yomiuri Shinbun Newspaper (2010) Survey, May.

11

Unique Disadvantages, Unique Needs
Native American Sex Offenders
Nora V. Demleitner

Introduction

In most parts of the United States, Native Americans are an invisible minority.[1] Indian Country encompasses approximately 56 million acres in the Continental United States,[2] located largely in mid-Western and Western states, usually far from major metropolitan centers (Goldberg and Singleton, 1997). Approximately one-third of all American Indians and Alaska Natives, about 1.4 million people, live on tribal lands (Ogunwole, 2006). The largest percentage of Native Americans in any state's population lives in Alaska, with 16% of its population identifying as solely Alaska Native. In absolute numbers, however, California has the largest Native population, on and off Indian lands, constituting approximately 1% of its population (Perry, 2004). While the Native population had been relatively stable for decades, since the 1970s it has grown dramatically due to a substantial increase in the Native birth rate.

Native Americans are substantially overrepresented in US prisons compared to their percentage in the population (Carrington and Pereira, 2009). In 2008 the rate of American Indians and Alaska Natives held in tribal, state and federal jails and prisons was "about 21% higher than the overall national incarceration rate" (Minton, 2009: 2) excluding these two population groups. Nevertheless, relatively little criminological, sociological and legal research exists about Native Americans in the criminal justice system (Wilmot and DeLone, 2010; Nielsen, 1996a). This may be surprising as substantial academic attention is being focused on other racial groups that are overrepresented in the US criminal justice system. Compared with other countries that have substantial Aboriginal populations, such as Australia, New Zealand and Canada, the dearth of research and analysis is even more striking. It may be explicable, though, by the stark black–white disparity in the United States, which has focused research agendas and policy so heavily on African Americans.

The Wiley-Blackwell Handbook of Legal and Ethical Aspects of Sex Offender Treatment and Management, First Edition. Edited by Karen Harrison and Bernadette Rainey.
© 2013 John Wiley & Sons, Ltd. Published 2013 by John Wiley & Sons, Ltd.

This chapter highlights a specific offender group in the Native American community: sex offenders. The Model Tribal Sex Offender Registration Code/Ordinance notes the high level of violent crime and of sex offenses in Indian land. In hyperbolically dire language, the Model Code's Section 1.03 emphasizes that the conduct and presence of convicted (Indian and non-Indian) sex offenders in Indian Country threatens the political integrity, economic security, health and welfare of tribal nations even to the point of imperiling the subsistence of tribal communities. Such commentary reflects the social hysteria surrounding sex offenses, making sex offenders the moral equivalent of terrorists. The fallout for Native Americans, victims, offenders, and community, has been often unforeseen and unconsidered, especially in the federal system. The chapter will delineate the special circumstances of Native Americans, particularly those living on tribal lands. Next it will highlight the distinctive jurisdictional situation, which leads to unique dislocations in the criminal justice system. The following section will focus on sentencing and potential treatment options for Native offenders. The chapter will emphasize the need for culturally appropriate treatment, as Canadian and Australian studies indicate its success in decreasing recidivism and increasing community safety (see Chapter 4).

Native Americans: Offenders and Victims in Indian Country and Beyond

The reported crime rate in Indian Country has been very high compared to the rest of the United States. Between 1992 and 2002 it included a violent crime rate that was twice that for the US population (Perry, 2004). Murder and suicide rates are substantially above national averages (Bachman, 1992). A joint executive committee of the Federal Departments of Justice and Interior and tribal nations found in 1997 that serious violent crime, including child sex abuse, had been rising substantially in Indian Country, contrary to the overall national trend (Baca, 2001). However, in the last few years, crime data indicate a precipitous and largely unexplained drop in Indian Country.

How reliable are crime data on Native Americans?

These data points merit careful analysis. First, not all Native Americans live on reservations though the data collected on Native Americans largely focus on those living in Indian Country rather than on all Native Americans. That form of data distortion may not be problematic since earlier studies have indicated that urban Native Americans have at least the same arrest rate as rural Native Americans (Harring, 1982). Nevertheless, the lack of a distinction between Native Americans on reservations and those living off Indian Country remains jarring. On the other hand, Indian Country data should not be equated with Indian criminality as non-Native offenders commit much of the crime on reservations (Steele, Damon and Denman, 2004). Some researchers have also voiced concern that reservation-based crime data are folded into national race-based data so as to cause inherent confusion about the amount of crime actually occurring on Indian land and the perpetrators (Goldberg and Singleton, 1997).[3] Sole focus on reservation-based data may underestimate the victimization of Native Americans. The overall rate of rural crime is substantially less than for American Indians in rural communities, indicating perhaps that off-reservation crime is more problematic for Indians than crime in Indian Country (Braunstein and Feimer, 2003).

Second, reported crimes may still understate the crime problem in Indian Country as the Department of Justice has found on numerous occasions that crime statistics from Indian Country remain unreliable (Goldberg and Singleton, 1997). This may be particularly true for intra-family offenses, such as child sex abuse and domestic violence. While underreporting remains nationally true for select offenses, certain conditions in Indian Country likely contribute to such underreporting. Among them is an inherent distrust of non-tribal law enforcement authorities; widespread knowledge of the inability of police to provide effective victim protection because they are under-resourced and geographically dispersed; or concern for family harmony if the offender were reported. In addition, family members may rally to the defense of the accused, largely because they perceive the dispute as one between one of their own and the federal government (Williams, Vallee and Staubi, 1997; Goldberg and Singleton, 2007). This dynamic harms the victim, often frustrates prosecution and ultimately may lead to further underreporting (Washburn, 2006).

Third, crime rates vary substantially between Native American tribes and even between geographically separate reservations for the same tribe (Harring, 1982). While some of this difference appears to be related to differential economic development for tribes, poverty levels and the existence of functioning institutions on tribal land, it is unclear whether all the differences can be explained in this way (Ward, 2003).

Fourth, homicides, gang violence, domestic violence and child abuse increased in Indian Country throughout the 1990s while violent crime decreased in the rest of the country. Because of this startling gap, since the mid-1990s the federal government has focused more on the crime problem in Indian Country (Goldberg and Singleton, 1997). This emphasis also correlates with a growing national pre-occupation with domestic violence and especially with sex offenses. By the late 1990s, however, the annual American Indian violent crime rate and murder rate both decreased dramatically (Perry, 2004). Concomitantly, the arrests of American Indians for violent crime went down. No explanation appears to exist for this development unless the same multiplicity of causes responsible for the national decline also applies to Native Americans.

Alternatively, in the absence of a sufficient explanation for such precipitous decline over a relatively short period of time, the question arises whether earlier findings of a high crime rate had been accurate. At least one commentator challenges those claims, arguing that the crime rate was inflated as the census data on Native Americans stemming from pre-2000 census counts were faulty, which created a highly unreliable count of Native Americans in the country (Silverman, 1996). Other commentators have stated that the data may be accurate but the high crime rates are due to extensive surveillance of Indian Country, which may have been triggered by the perception of the crime-prone Indian, which is then confirmed and creates a continuous vicious loop (Harjo, 2006). To sum up, Native Americans seem to be disproportionately the victims of (violent) crime and also appear to offend more than Whites. How accurate the offense and victimization data are, however, remains unresolved.

Domestic violence, sex offenses and crimes against children

Among the most disturbing patterns of Native American criminality and victimization are data on domestic violence, sex offenses and crimes against children, which ravage many Native communities. Some studies indicate that child abuse rates in Indian Country are twice as high as in the rest of the nation. Between 1993 and 1995 the Bureau of Indian Affairs (BIA) reports that child abuse, physical and/or sexual, is among the top three crimes reported in Indian Country. A joint federal-tribal task force established within the Navajo Nation has faced such a substantial child abuse caseload that the Federal Bureau of Investigation (FBI) has had to restrict its investigations to child sexual abuse cases pertaining only to children under 12 (Goldberg and Singleton, 1997). For people older than 12, the rape/sexual assault victimization rate is two-and-a-half times higher for Native Americans than for any other racial group, including African-Americans (Perry, 2004). Other studies demonstrate, however, that the child sexual abuse rate is virtually identical to national numbers, though it varies between tribes (Steele, Damon and Denman, 2004).

As is true nationally, family members, acquaintances or authority figures commit most of the child abuse (Goldberg and Singleton, 1997). For Native Americans, extended family members appear to be more involved in abuse than is true for other racial groups perhaps because extended family plays a substantially more important role in the daily lives of American Indians. The same offender pattern does not apply to rape and sexual assault offenses against Native Americans where victim studies indicate that strangers commit over 40% of those offenses (Perry, 2004). Because of the high incidence of domestic violence and child abuse, under the Violence Against Women Act of 1995, the federal government, together with tribal governments, has put together a number of initiatives to combat these problems. Later projects and legislation have focused on public safety on tribal land in general.

Findings of disproportionate sexual victimization and offense rates for Aboriginals are not unique to the United States: "Indigenous Australians are vastly over-represented as both victims and perpetrators of family violence, violent crime and child abuse" (Carrington and Pereira, 2009: 93). Of Canadian Aboriginal offenders, over a quarter are sex offenders; a pattern not replicated in the general population. Overall, Canadian Aboriginal offenders are more likely to commit violent offenses and violent sexual offenses than non-native offenders (Williams, Vallee and Staubi, 1997). The consequences of the high sexual and violent crime rates are troubling not only immediately for the victim but also because of their long-term ramifications. "[G]eneral research on domestic violence has demonstrated the link between child sexual and physical abuse and substance abuse, psychological disorders, school dropout and childhood delinquency" (Stewart *et al.*, 2009: 2). Canadian research in Aboriginal communities has confirmed that the vast majority of domestic violence perpetrators and sex offenders had themselves been victims of some type of abuse (Stewart *et al.*, 2009). Indigenous communities have long been concerned about the intergenerational nature of such crime.

Explanations for Native American crime

The high crime rate in Indian Country may be closely connected to a host of demographic factors.[4] The American Indian population has a higher percentage of those under 18 than the US population as a whole, with the median age on average running six years below the national median, though the specific age distribution varies between tribal groups.[5] On average, Indian Americans living on tribal lands are the youngest (Ogunwole, 2006).

While the educational attainment of all American Indians lags behind that of the general population, this holds particularly true in Indian Country (Ogunwole, 2006). The labor force participation of American Indians is generally lower than for the population as a whole (Ogunwole, 2006), with staggering unemployment rates on some tribal lands (US Department of the Interior, Bureau of Indian Affairs, 2005). Earnings are substantially lower even for full-time, year-round workers. In light of these data points, it might not be surprising that a 2000 Census Special Report concluded that the average poverty rate among Native Americans was double the rate for the entire population, though tribal differences were again dramatic (Ogunwole, 2006). To sum up, despite stark differences between tribes, overall Native Americans "remain the poorest minority in the United States" (Wakeling *et al.*, 2001: 5).[6]

Poverty, educational deficits, unemployment and a high youth rate may not provide the entire explanation for Native American crime and victimization rates, though Canadian government reports have documented a close relationship between Aboriginals' socio-economic background and their criminal behavior (Williams, Vallee and Staubi, 1997). Historic trauma, displacement and the destruction of Native cultures have also contributed to community dysfunction and other serious dislocations, which may now manifest themselves through crime.

Much of the crime problem in Indian Country is ascribed to substance abuse,[7] largely alcohol but increasingly also illicit drugs, especially marijuana and methamphetamine (Melton, 2006). Despite the long-standing portrayal of the "inebriated Indian," which has historically been very damaging to Native Americans,[8] recent studies indicate that on the whole Native Americans drink less than the average American but display higher rates of binge or heavy drinking (Wood, 2009). Often such episodes lead to violent crime. Violent assaults and sexual offenses seem generally linked to excessive alcohol consumption (Perry, 2004; Goldberg and Singleton, 1997; Williams, Vallee and Staubi, 1997; Wood, 2009). For some families alcohol appears to have become "a way of life . . . resulting in severe and permanent family disintegration and chaos" (Robin *et al.*. 1998: 782). Even though there is no biological basis to assume that Native Americans may be more heavily or more easily addicted to alcohol, some have argued that Aboriginals are more susceptible to substance abuse because of their shyness, which in turn may be a function of the use of shaming as a form of social control (Brant, 1993). Alcohol (ab)use may allow them to release repressed hostility, which results from suppressed conflict, through violent crime (Brant, 1993; Williams, Vallee and Staubi, 1997). Whatever the underlying causes may be, tribes are well aware of the problems resulting from excessive alcohol use and have devoted substantial resources to culturally specific treatment programs, to the creation of drug courts, and to family support mechanisms (Fletcher and Vicaire, 2011). Nevertheless, especially for offenders, treatment programs are frequently insufficient or unavailable on or near Indian Country.

In addition to these types of deeply ingrained issues that may help explain the underlying causes of crime on Indian land, the particular legal situation and the resource constraints of law enforcement agencies may further compound the crime problem in Native American communities.

Prosecution and Sentencing of Native American Sex Offenders

The division of jurisdiction between the tribes, state and local authorities and the federal government substantially burdens the prosecution of offenses in Indian Country. The nature of the offense, the status of the victim and of the offender as Indian (or not) and the existence of legislation conferring state jurisdiction determine which authority can exercise jurisdiction (Adams *et al.*, 2011).[9]

The jurisdictional structure

Under the Assimilative Crimes Act, which is made applicable to reservations through the General Crimes Act, crimes between Indians and non-Indians committed in Indian Country are subject to federal jurisdiction, with the federal courts applying state criminal law when no federal statute is otherwise available (18 USC. § 13). Since passage of that legislation in 1825, Native American tribes have lacked authority to commence criminal prosecutions against non-Indians. The Major Crimes Act, passed in 1885, gave the federal government jurisdiction over an expanding number of serious crimes when committed in Indian Country by a Native American against another Native person.

Tribal jurisdiction runs concurrent to federal jurisdiction. In 1968, Congress restricted tribal jurisdiction to crimes that carry no more than a one-year prison term, thereby effectively granting itself jurisdiction over all felony offenses (Indian Civil Rights Act, 25 USC. § 1302(7)). Tribes, therefore, have had only misdemeanor jurisdiction when Native Americans commit crimes against other Natives in Indian Country. This jurisdictional change reflected a larger policy shift in the federal government's approach at the time to demand greater tribal accountability by granting select protections of the Bill of Rights to Native Americans against tribal governments.

Today's emphasis, however, is on increased tribal independence, a goal that is reflected in a number of criminal justice policy initiatives (Eid and Doyle, 2010). The Tribal Law and Order Act 2010 grants tribal courts the authority to impose up to 36 months of incarceration. The impact of this development will remain unclear until Congress allocates funding to implement the legislation. The distribution of imprisonment is reflective of the limited jurisdiction and sentencing power of tribal courts. In 2008, more than four times as many Native Americans were held in jails outside of Indian Country as on reservations. About 10% of all incarcerated Native Americans are held in federal prisons (Minton, 2009).

In 1953 Congress passed Public Law 280 that confers upon six states criminal jurisdiction over most of the Indian Country within their boundaries. It also allowed other states to accept such jurisdiction, and 10 of them consented to doing so. This action brought almost a quarter of today's Native Americans on Indian land under state jurisdiction (Goldberg and Singleton, 2007). In Public Law 280 states, all those who commit sex offenses that do not include a basis for federal jurisdiction, such as transportation across state lines, will be adjudicated in state courts. Since Public Law 280 changed in 1968 to mandate tribal consent to state jurisdiction, no further state has taken on jurisdiction over Indian Country. Indeed some states have returned jurisdiction to the federal government (Goldberg and Singleton, 2007). In 2007, 93 state prosecutors had at least partial jurisdiction over Indian country under Public Law 280.[10] Over half of these offices prosecuted domestic violence or aggravated assault cases, with about 20% of the offices prosecuting at least one rape case (Perry, Malega and Banks, 2011). Despite the widespread applicability of Public Law 280, research on crime rates and law enforcement effectiveness in such reservations had been scant until 2007 when the National Institute of Justice issued a major research report (Goldberg and Singleton, 2007).

The perceptions of reservation residents differ dramatically between Public Law 280 jurisdictions and those in which the federal government prosecutes serious offenses. Generally Native Americans deem the quality of federal police services superior, including the thoroughness of investigations, and perceive greater understanding of and respect for tribal authority and tribal cultures (Goldberg and Singleton, 2007). Because of the amount of crime occurring in Indian Country and otherwise committed by Native Americans, it may not be surprising to see Native Americans disproportionately represented in many state criminal justice systems. The level of disproportion has nevertheless raised questions about discrimination against Native Americans. Among the reasons tribal leaders gave when lobbying state officials to retrocede jurisdiction under Public Law 280 are "failure of the county to provide for the cultural and rehabilitative needs of Indian arrestees; tribal concerns about disparate and retaliatory treatment of Indians with respect to [sentencing] . . ." (Goldberg and Singleton, 2007: 20).

A 1974 state study indicated that Native Americans were more likely to be sentenced to prison and to receive convictions labeling them as "felony offenders" (Pommersheim and Wise, 1989; Feimer, Pommersheim and Wise, 1990).[11] A later South Dakota study, however, could not replicate this result and found no significant difference with respect to incarceration upon felony conviction. It cannot be ruled out that earlier decisions in the criminal justice system account for disparate incarceration figures (Pommersheim and Wise, 1989).

Discretionary decisions in state criminal justice systems seem infused with nonjustifiable racial disparity. Sentencing studies in guideline states or about guideline-driven decisions, however, indicate a substantial decrease in discrimination (Lee and Vukich, 2001). A change to non-discretionary release decisions in North Dakota, for example, eliminated racial disparity (Braunstein and Feimer, 2003). Racial discrimination may play out in some counterintuitive ways. An Arizona study indicates that

Whites receive substantially higher sentences for violent crime than Native offenders, while the latter were more seriously penalized for property crime, such as robbery and burglary. These findings may demonstrate discrimination with respect to the victim's race. While violent crime is usually intra-racial, property offenses may threaten White high-status individuals more (Alvarez and Bachman, 1996). If discrimination plays a role in the overrepresentation of Native Americans in prison, it does not solely operate against Native offenders but in some cases may curiously favor them (Bachman, Alvarez and Perkins, 1996).

The exercise of federal jurisdiction: difficulties and challenges

Because of the unique jurisdictional structure, generally about 2% of federal suspects are investigated annually for offenses occurring in Indian country (Perry, 2007). Only about 1,000 of all the cases brought in federal court hail from Indian Country. Between one-fifth and a quarter of all defendants charged with violent offenses, however, come from Indian Country, though that does not imply that all of them are Native Americans (Perry, 2007). Three-quarters of investigations of federal crimes occurring in Indian Country involve violent offenses but generally only 5% of all federal crimes are violent offenses (Perry, 2007). These data indicate that the particular make-up of offenses in Indian Country is unique to the federal system, implying that many prosecutors, federal defenders and judges are less familiar with the evaluation of such crimes and offenders. Throughout the 1990s, on average, about 750 American Indians entered federal prisons annually upon conviction of a violent crime. While the proportion of Native Americans in federal prisons convicted of violent crimes has remained steady, the absolute numbers of all violent federal offenders and of Native Americans convicted of violent crimes have increased (Perry, 2007).

Among the legal issues that make federal prosecutions in Indian Country challenging are difficulties in determining jurisdiction as a result of overlapping jurisdictional powers, with federal jurisdiction a function of the location of the crime, the type of crime committed, or the race of the alleged perpetrator or the victim (Office of Justice Programs, Office for Victims of Crime, 1999). Resource constraints magnify these legal problems. In light of the crime rates and the amount of territory to be covered, Indian Country law enforcement remains understaffed and under-resourced (Goldberg and Singleton, 1997; Eid and Doyle, 2010). The level of police coverage in Indian Country, for example, is substantially lower than in other parts of the country, especially when compared to locales with similar crime volume (Wakeling *et al.*, 2001). Because federal law enforcement and US attorneys lack sufficient resources in Indian Country, federal prosecutors appear to decline to prosecute a very substantial number of cases, including relatively serious violent crimes and sexual abuse cases (Eid and Doyle, 2010). Whether these declinations result from a lack of resources or an inability to understand the culture and values of the communities they are charged to represent remains an open question. Among the difficulties federal prosecutors encounter is poor preservation of evidence, especially when sexual offenses are alleged. Among the complaints about the criminal justice system is, for example, the failure of the Indian Health Service to cooperate with law enforcement officials as well as the restricted number of sexual assault nurse examiners available. The combination of these factors often delays investigation so that US Attorneys' offices ultimately decline prosecution (Southwest Center for Law and Policy, 2008).

As indicated earlier, traditional native values, historical experience with law enforcement authorities, and practical considerations may also contribute to the underreporting of intra-family sexual offenses, thereby delaying or thwarting any potential for a criminal investigation.[12] In the end, offenders may benefit from the lack of trust between the Native community and law enforcement authorities as "it provides assurance to them that they will not be punished" (Deer *et al.*, 2007: 10). To address some of the problems caused by overlapping jurisdiction and resource constraints, the federal government has established multidisciplinary child abuse teams in Indian Country and reached agreement with other law enforcement agencies to coordinate investigations and prosecutions (Office of Justice Programs, Office for Victims of Crime, 1999; Victims of Child Abuse Act of 1990 s225(g)). In the absence of more successful cooperation, evidence-gathering and resource allocation, tribal authorities have prosecuted cases that should have fallen under federal jurisdiction because of their severity. In 2008, 15% of inmates in Indian Country jails were held for domestic violence or assault, respectively. Only 2% were detained for rape or sexual assault (Minton, 2009). Because of the limited sentencing power of tribal courts, if serious crime ends up in tribal court when federal prosecutors do not proceed, such offenders will receive sentences disproportionately low compared to the severity of the offense and to the potential sentence exposure in federal court (Washburn, 2004).

The Federal Sentencing Guidelines and Native American Sex Offenders

The federal sentencing guidelines focus most heavily on the severity of the crime and the offender's prior criminal history in determining the sentence range. In limited cases judges may depart, upward or downward, from the otherwise prescribed range. When the US Supreme Court declared the federal guidelines advisory, rather than mandatory, as had been the case in the preceding 17 years, trial court judges regained some sentencing discretion (*United States* v. *Booker*, 543 US 220 (2005)). While they still have to compute the applicable guideline sentence, they may now impose a so-called *Booker* variance that complies with the statutory mandate of adhering to the different principles of punishment, including retribution, restitution, deterrence, public protection and rehabilitation.[13] Nevertheless, for Native American offenders, federal courts rarely diverge from suggested guideline sentences even though federal sentences tend to be substantially longer than comparable state sanctions.

Discrimination at sentencing?

A third of the reservation population perceive even federal courts as discriminatory towards Indians, with even more criminal justice personnel believing that federal judges and juries treat Native Americans differently and unfairly (Goldberg and Singleton, 2007). This attitude may be nursed by the fact that Native Americans generally have difficulty accessing federal courts, as not one is located in Indian

Country and some are hundreds of miles from the center of the reservation. The perception is that cases with Indian victims lead to more lenient sentencing while Indian defendants receive harsher sentences (Goldberg and Singleton, 2007). Some studies indicate that there might be some truth in that belief, at least in select jurisdictions.[14]

Rigorous criminal justice research acknowledges some level of discrimination against Native Americans but solely in particular geographic regions and for select types of offenses (Wilmot and DeLone, 2010). While generally any form of discrimination is lessened in guided sentencing jurisdictions, even guidelines jurisdictions are not immune from extralegal, race-based influence, as a study of sentencing decisions under Minnesota's guidelines indicated. Generally Native Americans received harsher sentencing decisions than Whites, which may either mean that the prison sentence imposed or served is shorter or that diversion from prison is more likely for a comparable offender of a different race. While racial disparity may not always be apparent at sentencing, many studies have indicated discrimination at some point within the criminal justice spectrum (Bynum and Paternoster, 1984; Goldberg and Singleton, 2007; Washburn, 2006; Echohawk, 2001–2002). To what extent such discrimination is apparent with respect to sexual offenses is unclear as comparisons are difficult with small numbers of offenders, especially when they are relatively unique in the federal system. Nevertheless, even the federal guideline system appears to discriminate against Native Americans convicted of violent crimes as offense-related factors cannot fully explain the harshness of sanctions against them (Everett and Wojtkiewicz, 2002).

Violent sex offenders: rejecting leniency

Under violent sex offenses in the federal sentencing guidelines, the "other" racial category, which encompasses everyone not White, Black or Hispanic, has traditionally been represented heavily, consisting of Native American offenders who have committed sex abuse, rape and sexual assault offenses on reservations. Prison sentences imposed on (adult) federal sex offenders are long, as compared to those for comparable state offenders. In 2003 the US Sentencing Commission's Ad Hoc Advisory Group on Native American Sentencing Issues issued a report recommending a number of changes to the guidelines. In the case of sexual offenses, the Group noted the stark federal–state disparity but "elected not to recommend any specific changes to the Guidelines that would directly reduce or eliminate the sentencing disparity identified" (US Sentencing Commission, 2003: 25). One of the reasons for this limited recommendation was the perceived congressional intent to increase the sentences to respond to the seriousness of the offenses and to create deterrent sanctions.

As the jurisdictional structure of the sentencing regime provides a curious ratification of racial bias even though the Guidelines aspire to race neutrality, deterrence concerns ultimately appear to have led to an acceptance of the status quo (Smith, 2004).[15] Some have argued that long-standing fears about sex between people of different races and assumptions about pathology and inability of child rearing by Native Americans have dominated sex crime prosecutions and sentencing and ultimately allow for the greater detention and incarceration of native youths and adults

(Carrington and Pereira, 2009). The Ad Hoc Advisory Group did offer two specific recommendations designed to help some Native American sex offenders. It urged the creation of a new guideline to separate those sex offenses that involve travel or transportation of a minor to engage in prohibited sexual abuse from the "heartland" of Native American sex crimes, which the Commission later implemented. In addition, it suggested expanding the sex offender treatment program and offering sentence reductions of up to 12 months for those who successfully completed such a program. The proposed program would be akin to the drug and alcohol abuse treatment program in federal prisons that leads to a one-year sentence decrease for non-violent offenders upon successful completion (Demleitner, 2009). While the drug and alcohol program now enables federal child pornography offenders to reduce their sentence through successful participation, there is no sentence reduction for other sex offenders. Even though the Ad Hoc Advisory Group chose not to engage the issue of sentence length systemically, federal judges may impose a decreased sentence upon individual offenders. Many have done so extensively in the sentencing of internet child pornography offenders so that the child pornography guideline has become the most departed-from guideline in the entire federal sentencing regime (Basbaum, 2010; Exum, 2010).

Under the guidelines, race, socio-economic factors and religion are prohibited factors for a downward departure; many others that may apply to Native Americans are strongly discouraged. Before the guidelines became advisory, the US Court of Appeals for the Eighth Circuit upheld three district court decisions in which the court had departed downward when a Native American offender was involved. In all three cases the offenders had led exemplary lives and overcome substantial deprivation prevalent on the reservation (Smith, 2004). Unless Native Americans are truly singular role models on their reservations, however, courts seem reluctant to provide for a downward departure. This reluctance has not been restricted to federal courts. Washington State offers diversion into a special alternative sex offender program to select sex offenders. In 2007 out of 11 Native Americans eligible for such alternative, not one received it (Sentencing Guidelines Commission, Washington State, 2008). Under advisory guidelines, some commentators have urged that sentencing judges depart in the case of Native American offenders for cultural reasons (Dearth, 2011), as presumably they had done before the guidelines went into effect (Sands, 1996). Cultural arguments, however, are often under attack and may not constitute a viable ground for a more lenient sentence, especially when sex crimes are involved.

The length of sentences for non-violent sex offenses under the federal guidelines appears to justify the yet greater severity of sanctions for violent sex crimes, as it is indisputable that they inflict greater and more direct harm on the victim. However, most violent sex crime prosecutions are against Native Americans who committed the offense in Indian Country. Only for jurisdictional reason will they be sentenced in a federal system that imposes substantially longer sentences than the state courts would for a comparable offense committed off the reservation. For that reason, some have argued that federal judges use their power to diverge from the guidelines to account for the state/federal disparity in the sentencing of Native Americans (Droske, 2008). Many of the arguments focus on the jurisdictional curiosity that leads to heavy penalties for Native Americans, in violation of the sentencing factors outlined in

3553(a)(2).[16] While state/federal disparity may counsel in this direction, many of the considerations outlined under 3553(a)(2) may lead a court to impose a harsher rather than a more lenient sentence on a Native American sex offender (see, for example, *United States* v. *Plumman*, 188 F. App'x 529 (8th Cir. 2006)), especially when it considers the impact of sex offenses on Indian Country. Generally, state and federal courts are more likely to hold the instability of reservation life against Native American offenders, and therefore are reluctant to divert them from prison or decrease the presumptive prison sentence (Lujan, 2006).

Sentencing of Aboriginal sex offenders outside the United States

Similar to Native American offenders in the United States, Canadian Aboriginal offenders are more likely to commit violent offenses and to commit violent sexual offenses than non-Native offenders. Of Aboriginal offenders, over a quarter are sex offenders, a pattern not typical for the general population, with Aboriginal sex offenders constituting almost 20% of the incarcerated population (Williams, Vallee and Staubi, 1997). In Australia and New Zealand, indigenous populations are also incarcerated at a substantially higher rate than their percentage in the population would indicate (Anthony, 2010; Trevethan, Moore and Allegri, 2005). Australia, New Zealand and Canada have officially recognized the disproportionate crime and imprisonment rate as a priority issue for sentencing and treatment. In three Australian jurisdictions and in New Zealand, legislation mandates that the sentencing judge consider the potential relevance of the offender's cultural background.[17] Courts explicitly consider Aboriginality, including the offender's personal factors and history, in assessing punishment. Courts have found important, among other factors, "the severe social and economic disadvantage, accompanied by endemic alcohol abuse that exists in some Indigenous communities . . . rather than mere aboriginal status of an offender" (Anthony, 2010: 2–3). Some have even put it more pointedly:

> One explanation for the predominance of boys from lower socioeconomic backgrounds among the sex offending population is that young men who are marginalized, displaced and undergoing a crisis in establishing dominance and social status lash out against the women and children they can no longer support economically nor control patriarchally. (Carrington and Pereira, 2009: 108)

However, a recent counter-movement has emerged in Australia. In recent years Australian courts have limited the use of such mitigating factors to allow for greater emphasis to be put on the harm inflicted on the victims of crime and the need for a strong deterrent message, similar to the argument of the US Sentencing Commission's Ad Hoc Advisory Group (Anthony, 2010). In addition, concerns about equality are being raised in conjunction with culturally based sentencing leniency (Hands, 2007). Even if agreement exists on harsh sentences, all systems have to ask themselves how they prepare sex offenders for the inevitable return to their communities and families, especially when many of these crimes were committed against (extended) family or other members of the tribal community.

Sentencing, Treatment and Rehabilitation

While some of the offenders who appear in federal court may be so violent and dangerous that the community and the victim are relieved to see them shipped off to a federal prison for long periods of time, indigenous women have generally opted for alternatives to the criminal justice system to restore their families. Non-indigenous women, on the other hand, have demanded the further criminalization and sanctioning of offenses directed against women and more frequent interventions through the formal criminal justice system (Nancarrow, 2010). Research in Australia has indicated that in many intra-family violence situations indigenous women do not want to see their sons, husbands or fathers go to jail. They just want the violence to stop and be secure in the knowledge that mechanisms are being developed to protect them and their children (Atkinson, 2007). Neither the considerations of the community nor the special situation of Native American offenders, however, appear to factor strongly into criminal justice decisions in the United States.

Retributive versus restorative justice

The American concept of justice is based on notions of written law, proceduralism, adversarial battle and retributive punishment. Ultimately, the assumptions underlying it focus on making society whole by exacting punishment from a bad person. In contrast, Native populations hold a holistic philosophy that focuses on resolving the underlying problem, which includes the restoration of relationships between offender and victim and within the community. The offender has to take deliberate acts to regain face and his own mental and emotional balance that will include apologies and restitution, for example (French, 1982). While many Western countries have rejected restorative principles when so-called dangerous offenders are at issue, UK research indicates that "restorative interventions can be useful with high-risk offenders" (Harrison, 2011: 124). For serious sex offenses, restorative interventions should not be used as diversionary tactics but rather as complementary to the mainstream criminal justice process. Examples of applicable restorative methods are Circles of Support and Accountability, victim/offender mediation and family group conferencing (Harrison, 2011). Early Canadian research has provided positive feedback on the use of Support Circles in particular (see Chapter 22).

Difficulties of treatment

Finding the appropriate form of treatment may be more challenging for Native offenders because of the problems encountered by mental health professionals in assessing them. Canadian research indicates that "the principle of non-interference and emotional restraint" (Williams, Vallee and Staubi, 1997: II. 4–5) impacts the assessment of Aboriginal offenders that can lead to errors in evaluations and then treatment. Officials at Federal Correctional Institution Butler in North Carolina, the Federal Bureau of Prison's preeminent sex offender treatment facility, have indicated that Native Americans are often less likely to participate in sex offender treatment because of "a general distrust of government, a strong sense of self-reliance, and the shame and embarrassment associated with a conviction for a sexual abuse offense" (US Sentencing Commission, 2003: 29).

Among other substantial challenges to preventative and rehabilitative treatment programs for Native American offenders is the dramatic disconnect between the great developmental needs of these offenders, the number of offenders and the restricted opportunities available near reservations. The Bureau of Prisons requires contract facilities, which tend to be located more closely to Indian Country than federal prisons, to provide a minimum of 50 hours of programming a week, which includes cultural activities (Adams *et al.*, 2011), a goal often honored in breach. Native communities do not have staff skilled in providing alcohol and/or sex abuse treatment programs (Macgregor, 2008) or in traditional practices. Lack of financial resources, of facilities and of service support networks further aggravate the situation (Nielsen, 1996b). In some cases it has been possible to make federal funding available to allow for important programming near reservations. Substance abuse treatment is particularly crucial as many of the offenders struggle with addiction, as do their families, who have generally experienced violence or sexual abuse as well (Adams *et al.*, 2011).

One of the most difficult aspects of incarceration for Native Americans is the physical distance between Indian Country and federal prisons, which restricts the continuation of family ties, especially in light of the economic challenges most Native people experience, leads to less community support, and may hamper the offenders' reintegration (Adams *et al.*, 2011; Stewart *et al.*, 2009). There is no consensus whether the separation from family and community is more harmful than treatment options are beneficial (Adams *et al.*, 2011). Studies in Australia and New Zealand, however, have found that for successful treatment, it is important to involve the offender's family. Family involvement is also viewed as helpful to both offender and victim when the offense occurred intra-family (Macgregor, 2008).

Generally, the recidivism rates for Native Americans are similar to those of all offenders (Perry, Malega and Banks, 2011). Evaluations of sex offender treatment specifically tend to be difficult in light of the comparatively small number of offenders at issue. They also require a relatively long follow-up period to document an actual decrease in recidivism. Upon release of a sex offender from federal custody, the Bureau of Prisons is charged with informing the state and the tribe to which the offender will return. Notification of the tribe, however, occurs only rarely, endangering the community and likely impeding further rehabilitation and reintegration of the offender (Southwest Center for Law and Policy, 2008). Federal sex offenders are subject to a supervised release period of at least five years. The US Sentencing Guidelines recommend imposition of the maximum period, which is life. A lengthy supervision period makes it more likely, however, that the ex-offender will return to federal prison, not necessarily upon commission of a new offense but for violation of the terms of supervised release.

The treatment of sex offenders in the United States indicates a heavy focus on incapacitation. While the need for treatment is obvious, especially for Native American offenders, the reality is disappointing. These offenders appear to be more warehoused than prepared for release even though substantial research from Canada and Australia provides a path for the treatment of Native sex offenders. The underlying sentencing philosophy and the lack of imagination in the federal system may prevent us from finding a path forward.

Culturally appropriate treatment: what the United States can learn from Canada and Australia

To achieve the twin goals of decreasing the imprisonment of Aboriginal offenders and reducing recidivism, Canada has combined Western approaches to treatment of violent offenders with traditional Aboriginal spirituality (Stewart *et al.*, 2009). Research conducted in Canada and in Western Australia has found that treatment without culturally appropriate programming led to more rather than less recidivism. "[T]he incorporation of traditional and holistic forms of treatment is more effective for reducing sexual recidivism amongst Indigenous offenders" (Macgregor, 2008: 7). The same also holds true for substance abuse treatment programs, where:

> programs and interventions that are grounded in Aboriginal traditions, spirituality and culture that strive to heal the individual in holistic terms, will facilitate rehabilitation efforts and enhance engagement and participation of the offender in treatment. (Kunic and Varis, 2009: 36)

The programs integrate mental, spiritual, physical and emotional elements, as Aborigines favor holistic approaches. In addition, they take a more family-focused and community-focused approach than merely centering on the individual (Williams, Vallee and Staubi, 1997). One such program, which also included sexual assault offenders, indicated an early positive impact on recidivism (Trevethan, Crutcher and Rastin, 2007).

Even though most Aboriginal offenders are brought up "without Aboriginal language, culture, teachings or ceremonies . . . these core aspects of Aboriginal identity appear critical to the healing process" (Trevethan, Moore and Allegri, 2005: 2). Research has confirmed that some programs tend to be "more effective in reducing recidivism if they are Aboriginal-specific" (Trevethan, Moore and Allegri, 2005: 3). Healing lodges are another example of culturally appropriate programming in a holistic setting. These are designed to prepare the offenders for their release while involving the community to which they will return in their reintegration (Trevethan, Crutcher and Rastin, 2007). In many respects they appear to fulfill the function of a halfway house, as they are close to Aboriginal communities so as to facilitate the involvement of community leaders and preparing inmates for their release.

Some of these Canadian culturally specific sex offender treatment programs have shown remarkable success despite overall offenders' negative demographic factors for successful reintegration. They have successfully engaged Aboriginal convicts to complete the programs and reduce recidivism (Stewart *et al.*, 2009). Culturally specific programs are often more expensive than others (Stewart *et al.*, 2009). It may be easier to overcome concerns about upfront expenses, however, if programs can demonstrate a reduction in recidivism. This is frequently difficult as the number of Aboriginal sex offenders is generally small, however, and the number of those who enter such programs is yet smaller (Stewart *et al.*, 2009). Nevertheless, a research review carried out on New Zealand and Australian sex offender treatment studies indicated that treatment decreases the re-offense rate. Furthermore, "[W]hen the design and implementation [of sex offender treatment programs] are attuned to the cultural background of offenders" (Macgregor, 2008: 4), they are yet more likely to decrease recidivism rates.

As Australia and Canada have increasingly opted for treatment that is culturally specific, in the United States the diversity of recognized tribes makes this potentially more difficult. There are about 565 tribes, all with a distinct history, culture, language, size and geographic location (Perry, Malega and Banks, 2011; Adams *et al.*, 2011). Because of this diversity, federal facilities which house a relatively small number of Native offenders. several states removed from the reservation(s), are particularly challenged to provide culturally appropriate experiences (Adams *et al.*, 2011).

Conclusion

In contrast to Canada and Australia, research on Native American offenders, and especially sex offenders, remains scant in the United States. Nevertheless existing research allows for the following conclusions. Improvements in the overall socio-economic situation of Native Americans are crucial for the reduction of crime in Indian Country and beyond. In addition, meaningful sex education and appropriate and high-quality spare time activities for young people could assist in preventing sex crimes from occurring (Williams, Vallee and Staubi, 1997). As Native populations are growing in the United States and Canada (Kunic and Varis, 2009), the reduction of crime rates is crucial, especially for offenses that leave a long-term negative impact on families and communities. Incarceration merely addresses a symptom of larger underlying pathology caused by US society, which may be addressed through cultural approaches. A positive side benefit of the use of culturally appropriate techniques in treating (sex) offenders may be the restoration of culture-based approaches to combat offending in Native American communities (Lujan, 2006). While the small number and the diversity of Native American sex offenders in federal prisons may make this more challenging than in Canada or Australia, opportunities to create such programs exist Since the criminal justice system is capable of considering and implementing non-US research in program building, we may have to face the reality that the differences between the US and Canadian approaches derive from distinct views of the humanity, dignity, importance, and ultimately dispensability of offenders generally or of Native Americans specifically.

Acknowledgments

I am grateful for the assistance of my research assistant Jenelle DeVits, Hofstra Law, Class of 2013, and my outstanding reference librarian Patricia Kasting in putting together the background material for this chapter. In addition, I acknowledge, with appreciation, all the helpful comments and feedback on this chapter I received from Professor Deborah Denno and her seminar students. All errors are, of course, solely mine.

Notes

1   For purposes of this chapter, "Native American" encompasses American Indians and Alaska Natives. Americans tend to use the terms Native Americans, Indians or Native Americans to describe Native people. Canadians and Australians, on the other hand, frequently refer to their Native peoples as Aboriginal, Native or Indigenous peoples, or alternatively as First Nations (Nielsen, 1996a). In the 2000 census 2.5 million Americans indicated that they were American Indian or Alaska Native, 0.9% of the US population, with an additional 1.6 million noting American Indian/Alaska Native in conjunction with one or more other race(s) (Perry, 2004).

2   18 USC. § 1151 defines "Indian country."

3   For a study reflecting concern about the data that indicate substantially higher crimes rate in Indian Country, see Peak (1994).

4   For an explanation of the high Native American crime rate in light of criminological theories and factual evidence, such as cultural conflict, anomie, economic determinism and alcohol usage, see Flowers (1990).

5   While young, unmarried men commit most crimes, sex offenders are usually in their thirties when convicted.

6   Generally, the economic success of tribes has been tied to them increasing their control over governing institutions. Crucial has been "[a] consonance between present and pre-reservation institutional forms [that] confers legitimacy on the methods and outcomes of government decision making and channels political energies in productive directions" (Wakeling *et al.*, 2001: 5–6).

7   A study of Tupiq sex offenders in Canada showed that almost every participant in a sex offender treatment program had substance abuse problems, with 80% of the participants being diagnosed as having "'some' or 'a lot' of problems with alcohol" (Stewart *et al.*, 2009: 14).

8   For a discussion of the stereotype of the Native American alcoholic, see Lujan (2006).

9   Adams *et al.* (2011: 11–14) discuss the division of jurisdiction and the policies underlying it, which range from "termination and assimilation of tribes on the one end [to] self-determination by the tribes on the other."

10   For a jurisdictional chart, see US Department of Justice, Criminal Resource Manual 689, available at http://www.justice.gov/usao/eousa/foia_reading_room/usam/title9/crm00689.htm (accessed September 18, 2012).

11   For arrest rates in the 1980s that indicate a disproportionate federal arrest rate for Native Americans, especially for sex offenses and substance-abuse-related crimes, see Flowers (1990: 106–111, Tables 7.1 and 7.2).

12   For a discussion of the difficulties state authorities encounter in Public Law 280 jurisdictions, especially in sexual assault cases, see Deer *et al.* (2007: 6–10).

13   18 USC. § 3553(a). For an in-depth discussion of the sentencing of Native American sex offenders under the pre-*Booker* guidelines, much of which remains relevant, see Demleitner (2002).

14   Studies in Washington State indicate that Native offenders receive both aggravated exceptional sentences and mitigated exceptional sentences more than most other offender groups (Crutchfield, 2005).

15   To reduce racial disparity, Smith (2004) suggests adjudicating Native American offenders in federal court but under state criminal and sentencing laws.

16   3553(a)(2) demands that a judge consider the following when imposing a sentence:

(2) the need for the sentence imposed –

    (A)   to reflect the seriousness of the offense, to promote respect for the law, and to provide just punishment for the offense:

    (B)   to afford adequate deterrence to criminal conduct;

    (C)   to protect the public from further crimes of the defendant; and

    (D)   to provide the defendant with needed educational or vocational training, medical care or other correctional treatment in the most effective manner.

17   Available at www.indigenousjustice.gov.au (accessed September 18, 2012).

References

Adams, W., Samuels, J., Willison, J.B. *et al.* (2011) *Tribal Youth in the Federal Justice System, Final Report (Revised)*. Washington: Urban Institute – Justice Policy Center.

Alvarez, A. and Bachman, R.D. (1996) "American Indians and sentencing disparity: an Arizona test," *Journal of Criminal Justice* 24, 549–561.

Anthony, T. (2010) *Sentencing Indigenous Offenders*. New South Wales: Indigenous Justice Clearinghouse.

Atkinson, J. (2007) "Violence against Aboriginal women: reconstitution of community law – the way forward," *Indigenous Law Bulletin* 6, 13–17.

Baca, K. (2001) "The changing federal role in Indian Country," *National Institute of Justice Journal* 247, 8–13.

Bachman, R. (1992) *Death and Violence on the Reservation*. New York: Auburn House.

Bachman, R., Alvarez, A. and Perkins, C. (1996) "Discriminatory imposition of the law: does it affect sentencing outcomes for American Indians?," in M.O. Nielsen and R.A. Silverman (eds), *Native Americans, Crime, and Justice*. Colorado: Westview Press, pp. 10–20.

Basbaum, J.P. (2010) "Inequitable sentencing for possession of child pornography: a failure to distinguish voyeurs from pederasts," *Hastings Law Journal* 61, 1281–1306.

Brant, C. (1993) "Communication patterns in Indians: verbal and non-verbal," *Annals of Sex Research* 6, 259–269.

Braunstein, R. and Feimer, S. (2003) "South Dakota criminal justice: a study of racial disparities," *South Dakota Law Review* 48, 171–207.

Bynum, T.S. and Paternoster, R. (1984) "Discrimination revisited: an exploration of frontstage and backstage criminal justice decision making," *Sociology and Social Research: An International Journal* 69, 90–108.

Carrington, K. and Pereira, M. (2009) *Offending Youth: Sex, Crime and Justice*. Sydney: Federation Press.

Crutchfield, R.D. (2005) "Expert report: racial disparity in the Washington State criminal justice system," in *Farrakhan v. Gregoire*, Exhibit, http://moritzlaw.osu.edu/electionlaw/litigation/documents/exhibitsstatementofmaterialfactspart3.pdf (accessed September 15, 2012).

Dearth, M. (2011) "Defending the 'indefensible': replacing ethnocentrism with a Native American cultural defense," *American Indian Law Review* 35, 621–660.

Deer, S., Goldberg, C., Valdez Singleton, H. and White Eagle, M. (2007) *Final Report: Focus Group on Public Law 280 and the Sexual Assault of Native Women*, December 31. California: Tribal Law and Policy Institute.

Demleitner, N. (2002) "First peoples, first principles: the sentencing commission's obligation to reject false images of criminal offenders," *Iowa Law Review* 87, 563.

Demleitner, N. (2009) "Terms of imprisonment: treating the noncitizen offender equally," *Federal Sentencing Reporter* 21, 174–178.

Droske, T.J. (2008) "Correcting Native American sentencing disparity post-Booker," *Marquette Law Review* 91, 723–813.

Echohawk, L. (2001–2002) "Child sexual abuse in Indian Country: is the guardian keeping in mind the seventh generation?," *New York University Journal of Legislation and Public Policy* 5, 83–128.

Eid, T.A. and Doyle, C.C. (2010) "Separate but unequal: the federal criminal justice system in Indian Country," *University of Colorado Law Review* 81, 1067–1118.

Everett, R.S. and Wojtkiewicz, R.A. (2002) "Difference, disparity, and race/ethnic bias in federal sentencing," *Journal of Quantitative Criminology* 18, 189–211.

Exum, J.J. (2010) "Making the punishment fit the (computer) crime: rebooting notions of possession for the federal sentencing of child pornography offenses," *Richmond Journal of Law and Technology* 16, 8.

Feimer, S., Pommersheim, F. and Wise, S. (1990) "Marking time: does race make a difference? A study of disparate sentencing in South Dakota," *Journal of Crime and Justice*, 13, 86–102.

Fletcher, M.L.M. and Vicaire, P.S. (2011) "Indian wars: old and new," *Journal of Gender, Race and Justice*, http://papers.ssrn.com/sol3/papers.cfm?abstract_id=1832523 (accessed August 25, 2012).

Flowers, R.B. (1990) "Native American criminality," in R.B. Flowers (ed.), *Minorities and Criminality*. Westport: Greenwood Press, pp. 113–117.

French, L. (1982) "Counseling Native Americans," in L. French (ed.), *Indians and Criminal Justice*. New Jersey: Allanheld, Osmun and Co. Publishers Inc., pp. 197–208.

Goldberg, C. and Valdez Singleton, H. (1997) *Final Report of the Executive Committee for Indian Country Law Enforcement Improvements*. Washington: US Department of Justice, Criminal Division.

Goldberg, C. and Valdez Singleton, H. (2007) *Final Report: Law Enforcement and Criminal Justice under Public Law 280*. Washington: National Institute of Justice.

Hands, T. (2007) "Aboriginal Customary Law: the challenge of recognition," *Alternative Law Journal* 32, 42–43.

Harjo, S.S. (2006) "Redskins, savages and other Indian enemies: a historical overview of American media coverage of native peoples," in C.R. Mann, M.S. Zatz and R. Rodriguez (eds), *Images of Color, Images of Crime: Readings*, 3rd edn. California: Roxbury Publishing Company, pp. 62–78.

Harring, S. (1982) "Native American crime in the United States," in L. French (ed.), *Indians and Criminal Justice*. New Jersey: Allanheld, Osmun and Co. Publishers Inc., pp. 93–108.

Harrison, K. (2011) *Dangerousness, Risk and the Governance of Serious Sexual and Violent Offenders*. New York: Routledge.

Kunic, D. and Varis, D.D. (2009) *Research Reports: The Aboriginal Offender Substance Abuse Program (AOSAP): Examining the Effects of Successful Completion on Post-release Outcomes*. Correctional Service of Canada.

Lee, N. and Vukich, E.M. (2001) *Representation and Equity in Washington State: An Assessment of Disproportionality and Disparity in Adult Felony Sentencing – Fiscal Year 2000*. Washington: Washington State Guidelines Commission.

Lujan, C.C. (2006) "American Indians: US politicians and the prevalent stereotyping of American Indian and Alaska Native nations and peoples," in C.R. Mann, M.S. Zatz and R. Rodriguez (eds), *Images of Color, Images of Crime: Readings*, 3rd edn. California: Roxbury Publishing Company, pp. 130–140.

Macgregor, S. (2008) "Sex offender treatment programs: effectiveness of prison and community based programs in Australia and New Zealand," *Indigenous Justice Clearinghouse*, Research Brief 3.

Melton, A.P. (2006) "American Indians: traditional and contemporary tribal justice," in C.R. Mann, M.S. Zatz and R. Rodriguez (eds), *Images of Color, Images of Crime: Readings*, 3rd edn. California: Roxbury Publishing Company, pp. 180–197.

Minton, T. (2009) *Jails in Indian Country, 2008*. Washington: Bureau of Justice Statistics.

Nancarrow, H. (2010) "Restorative justice for domestic and family violence," in J. Ptacez (ed.), *Restorative Justice and Violence against Women*. New York: Oxford University Press, pp. 123–150.

Nielsen, M.O. (1996a) "Contextualization for Native American crime and criminal justice involvement," in M.O. Nielsen and R.A. Silverman (eds), *Native Americans, Crime, and Justice*. Colorado: Westview Press, pp. 10–20.

Nielsen, M.O. (1996b) "Major issues in Native American involvement in the criminal justice system," in M.O. Nielsen and R.A. Silverman (eds), *Native Americans, Crime, and Justice*. Colorado: Westview Press, pp. 293–302.

Office of Justice Programs, Office for Victims of Crime (1999) *Improving Tribal/Federal Prosecution of Child Sexual Abuse Cases through Agency Cooperation*. Washington: US Department of Justice.

Ogunwole, S.U. (2006) *We the People: American Indians and Alaska Natives in the United States – Census 2000 Special Reports*. Washington: US Census Bureau.

Peak, K. (1994) "Policing and crime in Indian Country: history, issues, and challenges," *Journal of Contemporary Criminal Justice* 10, 79–94.

Perry, S.W. (2004) *A BJS Statistical Profile, 1992–2002: American Indians and Crime*. Washington: Bureau of Justice Statistics.

Perry, S.W. (2007) *Improving Criminal History Records in Indian Country, 2004–2006*. Washington: Bureau of Justice Statistics.

Perry, S.W., Malega, R. and Banks, D. (2011) *State Prosecutors' Offices with Jurisdiction in Indian Country*, 2007. Washington: Bureau of Justice Statistics.

Pommersheim, F. and Wise, S. (1989) "Going to the penitentiary: a study of disparate sentencing in South Dakota," *Criminal Justice and Behavior* 16, 155–165.

Robin, R.W., Long, J.C., Rasmussen, J.K. *et al.* (1998) "Relationship of binge drinking to alcohol dependence, other psychiatric disorders, and behavioral problems in an American Indian tribe," *Alcoholism: Clinical and Experimental Research* 22, 2, 518–523.

Sands, J. (1996) "Departure reform and Indian crimes: reading the commission's staff paper with reservations," *Federal Sentencing Reporter* 9, 144.

Sentencing Guidelines Commission, Washington State (2008) *Disproportionality and Disparity in Adult Felony Sentencing – Fiscal Year 2007*. Olympia: Sentencing Guidelines Commission.

Silverman, R.A. (1996) "Patterns of Native American crime," in M.O. Nielsen and R.A. Silverman (eds), *Native Americans, Crime, and Justice*. Colorado: Westview Press, pp. 58–74.

Smith, G. (2004) "Disparate impact of the federal sentencing guidelines on Indians in Indian Country: why Congress should run the Erie Railroad into the Major Crimes Act," *Hamline Law Review* 27, 483–533.

Southwest Center for Law and Policy (2008) *Sex Offender Registration and Notification in Indian Country*. Tucson, AZ: National Roundtable on Sex Offender Registration and Notification in Indian Country.

Steele, P.D., Damon, N. and Denman, K. (2004) *Child Sexual Abuse on New Mexico Tribal Land: 1999–2004*. New Mexico Criminal Justice Analysis Center – Institute for Social Research – University of New Mexico.

Stewart, L., Hamilton, E., Wilton, G. *et al.* (2009) *An Examination of the Effectiveness of Tupiq: A Culturally Specific Program for Inuit Sex Offenders.* Ottawa: Correctional Service of Canada.

Trevethan, S., Crutcher, N. and Rastin, C. (2007) *Pê Sâkâstêw Centre: An In-Depth Examination of a Healing Lodge for Federal Incarcerated Offenders.* Ottawa: Research Branch – Correctional Service of Canada.

Trevethan, S., Moore, J-P. and Allegri, N. (2005) *The "In Search of Your Warrior" Program for Aboriginal Offenders: A Preliminary Evaluation.* Ottawa: Research Brand – Correctional Service of Canada.

US Department of the Interior, Bureau of Indian Affairs (2005) *American Indian Population and Labor Force Report.* Washington: US Department of the Interior, Bureau of Indian Affairs.

US Sentencing Commission, Ad Hoc Advisory Group on Native American Sentencing Issues (2003) *Report of the Ad Hoc Advisory Group on Native American Sentencing Issues – November 4, 2003.* Washington: US Sentencing Commission.

Wakeling, S., Jorgensen, M., Michaelson, S. and Begay, M. (2001) *Policing on American Indian Reservations.* Washington: US Department of Justice.

Ward, J. (2003) "Snapshots: holistic images of female offenders in the criminal justice system," *Fordham Urban Law Journal* 30, 723–749.

Washburn, K. (2004) "Tribal courts and federal sentencing," *Arizona State Law Journal* 36, 403–449.

Washburn, K. (2006) "American Indians, crime, and the law," *Michigan Law Review* 104, 709–777.

Williams, S., Vallee, S. and Staubi, B. (1997) *Aboriginal Sex Offenders: Melding Spiritual Healing with Cognitive-Behavioural Treatment.* Ottawa: Correctional Service Canada.

Wilmot, K.A. and DeLone, M.A. (2010) "Sentencing of Native Americans: a multistage analysis under the Minnesota Sentencing Guidelines," *Journal of Ethnicity in Criminal Justice* 8, 151–180.

Wood, D.S. (2009) *A Review of Research on Alcohol and Drug Use, Criminal Behavior, and the Criminal Justice System Response in American Indian and Alaska Native Communities.* Rockville: National Institute of Justice.

12

Mandated Reporting Laws: Experiences from Israel

Sheri Oz

Introduction

Apparently it is human nature to avoid entering the private realm of other people's homes even when we see that someone is in serious need of rescue. But in 1989, when a three-year-old was killed by her uncle in Tiberias in northern Israel as a result of chronic physical abuse that was no secret to family or neighbors, the Israeli Knesset (Parliament) passed a law stipulating that everyone has the obligation to report to the authorities suspected abuse of minors or legally dependent persons. This law is not contested in principle by anyone in the country; however, there are many problems concerning how and when reports are supposed to be made and the aftermath of the report. This chapter is restricted to a discussion of the law as it concerns sexual abuse.

Over the years, individuals have raised concerns about the negative impact of the law and its reporting requirement. Some have discussed the law's inattention to cultural differences among the various sectors of the Israeli population. Others point to the way investigations may leave some families devastated with no clear way to repair the damage when, perhaps, less invasive methods may have been applied in the search for admissible evidence that would warrant laying charges. Oz and Balshan (2007) suggest that the problem is not with the law but with the fact that the law does not stipulate proper procedure following a report.

Until a short while ago, these individual voices sometimes resulted in highly conflictual personal relations between the group of professionals defensive of the law as it stands and those who take issue with the law. More recently, those in the latter group began meeting and working to present a unified and well-reasoned thesis for change.

The Wiley-Blackwell Handbook of Legal and Ethical Aspects of Sex Offender Treatment and Management, First Edition. Edited by Karen Harrison and Bernadette Rainey.
© 2013 John Wiley & Sons, Ltd. Published 2013 by John Wiley & Sons, Ltd.

The Mandated Reporting Law in Israel
in an International Context

With its basic laws being of British origin, its close relationship with the United States and its isolation within its own neighborhood, Israel is very much interested in and affected by what happens around the world in most spheres. Approaches to the identification and treatment of child abuse victims are no exception. It is within this international context, that I will begin an examination of Israel's means of coping with the problems of child sexual abuse and mandated reporting.

Approaches to effective intervention in child abuse cases differ around the world but one common thread is the move toward mandatory reporting of suspected cases. One of the first books published on the topic focuses on the international scene (Gilbert, 1997). In Belgium (Marneffe and Broos, 1997) and Finland (Poso, 1997), for example, child abuse is regarded as symptomatic of family dysfunction, and family services and therapy are offered. Parents are regarded as partners who can be helped. The Netherlands treats physical abuse and neglect as a family problem; however, reports of sexual abuse are handled through the courts (Roelofs and Baartman, 1997). The situation is similar in Canada (Swift, 1997) and the United States (Levine and Doueck, 1995) and alleged abusers are potentially subject to both criminal and civil prosecution, each bearing different standards of proof and legal considerations (an alleged abuser may be found "not guilty" of sexual abuse in criminal court, but yet have a child "in need of protection" regarding that same sexual abuse, resulting in severance of the parent–child relationship). Civil child protection cases have generally been adversarial in nature, a fact that may pose impediments to the maintenance of a productive therapeutic relationship between the alleged abuser and social workers (D. Sandor, personal communication, 2005).

Interestingly, orientation toward either punishment or therapy does not correspond to the existence or absence of mandated reporting. Gilbert (1997) concludes that the feature distinguishing countries with mandated reporting laws and those without is that the latter apparently have a greater degree of integration and cooperation among medical, educational and social service personnel. Such cooperation ensures that children are protected by the many professionals with whom they have contact (Feng *et al.*, 2010). Israel can be characterized by an attitude that encourages interagency cooperation. However, it cannot be assumed that the various agencies will, in fact, coordinate their work (Bell, 2001).

India, Pakistan and Korea instituted laws defining abuse in 2000 and, while it is expected that professionals working with children will report suspected cases to the police, the issue is regarded more as a private one with little legitimacy afforded to outside invention. It is interesting to note that in Korea, for example, after the legislation went into effect, 17 treatment centers and a hot-line for abused children and their families were established around the country (S.M. Park, personal communication, 2003). In the Philippines the law clearly prohibits child abuse, and section 27 of Act 7610 defines who *may* file a complaint; in other words, reporting is not mandatory and perhaps there is no expectation that one would report. Hong Kong, once under British rule but culturally Asian, has clear guidelines for intervention and no mandated reporting law. Even so, cultural attitudes may prohibit interventions that would be deemed appropriate in Europe and North America (Park, 2005). It remains questionable whether or not services available in one country are transferable to another. A paper discussing the handling of sex abuse disclosures in the Israeli Arab Muslim community (Abu Baker and Dwairy, 2003) provides guidelines for taking cultural and political context into account for that population.

Even where the law mandates reporting suspected cases of child abuse, many professionals who are bound by this do not do so (Alvarex *et al.*, 2004; Forman and Bernet, 2000). One problem commonly discussed is the fear therapists have of betrayal of the client's trust and damage to the therapeutic relationship should they have to break confidentiality (Levine *et al.*, 1998). Some note that the reporting itself may actually hurt the victim rather than solve the problem (Kenny, 2001). Melton (2005: 14) decries the impact on society of a situation in which "rampant civil disobedience of mandated reporting laws" is deemed necessary by professionals who make an ethical decision to break the law in order not to hurt their clients.

School teachers and principals may feel they have insufficient training to report responsibly and fear making unfounded accusations (Greytak, 2009; Walsh *et al.*, 2011) that would then cause problems between the school and the family. They seem to prefer to handle within the school system anything but unquestionable cases of abuse (Tite, 1993). Such "underreporting" is facilitated by the fact that the laws often do not clearly define the specific indicators behind the terminology "reasonable cause to suspect abuse" (Forman and Bernet, 2000) and do not ensure that professionals are fully informed on the proper procedures (Kenny, 2001; Walsh *et al.*, 2011). In Israel, a handbook was prepared specifically for schools in order to combat insufficient training and unclear definitions. In spite of the fact that every school has the handbook and workshops and lectures are offered at education conferences, it is the experience of this author that many school staff feel unclear, to this day, regarding their duty to report and the appropriate measures to take when sexual abuse is suspected.

While some professionals may neglect to report cases of abuse, others may "overreport" (Forman and Bernet, 2000) in order not to risk legal sanctions or in wanting to make every effort to protect children. It seems that well over 50% of all reported abuse remains unsubstantiated in legal terms (Gilbert, 1997; Levine *et al.*, 1998). Clearly, however, this does not mean that none of these 50% merited reporting, just that the evidence that would have proved their merit was not found.

If there is insufficient evidence for litigation, then the file may be closed, if opened in the first place, and the child and his or her family may receive no more help or attention (Melton, 2005) even when professionals are certain that there has been abuse. Thus the victim's distress is painfully compounded both by the investigation process (Eastwood and Patton, 2002) and the ultimately unsupportive adult response to many victims' disclosures of abuse (Paine and Hansen, 2002) by whatever verbal or nonverbal means that the victim was able to use to communicate his or her distress. This point is, in large part, the basis of the outcry of professionals in the field in Israel.

The Clinician's Ethical Dilemma

It is interesting that around the world, in spite of the variety of cultural and political realities, professionals' experience with and attitudes toward mandated reporting are similar. It is, fundamentally, an ethical question. Clearly therapists cannot claim ignorance of the law, nor can they transgress and simply not report when they have reason to believe that a child is being sexually abused. However, compelling a therapist to report when there is reasonable suspicion that the report itself will be somehow damaging to the client creates a clinical and ethical dilemma for the practitioner.

Childhood sexual abuse entails manipulation, trickery, lies, secrets, guilt, shame, boundary violations and crime (Oz, 2005). I suggest that the mandated reporting law, as it stands in Israel today, puts ethical therapists into the position where they may feel it necessary to use a form of manipulation, trickery, lies and secrets in order to protect clients from premature legal intervention by delaying the report in some fashion. If therapists do delay reporting, even to the Child Protection Service (CPS) that is supposed to help in these matters (but often does not), then surely they feel guilt and shame for participating in what the law defines as a crime. Furthermore, they are not able to avail themselves of the professional guidance that should be available to all practitioners.

As a recognized expert in the field of child sexual abuse, I am invited to teach in courses and training programs around the country; I always raise the issue of mandatory reporting for class discussion. The question arose in one class (as it always does) regarding how to respond to a phone call from a parent who asks if the therapist must report the case if a minor sibling sexually abused a younger sibling even if they are coming to therapy. To answer in the affirmative in most cases means the parent ends the phone call without making an appointment. An experienced child protection worker (CPW) taking the course suggested telling the parent that this issue will be discussed in the first session. However, without giving a clear answer, the therapist is giving the impression that the issue is not clear-cut and that there is room for maneuvering. There is not. Inviting the family to a session, breaking their anonymity and then announcing that a report must be made is not ethical behavior even if done with the best of intentions.

The Mandated Reporting Law in Israel

The Criminal Code clearly defines abuse against minors and those adults deemed legally incapable of giving informed consent. An amendment to the law in 1980 expands the definition of those legally responsible for the child to mean not only parents and guardians, but also other adults who play a role in supervising or caring for the child; babysitters, youth group leaders, and so on, are included. The law specifically states that anyone who has a reasonable suspicion that a child is being abused by a responsible party is required to report the case as soon as possible to either the police or a CPW. In 2007, another amendment added minor cousins and siblings to the list of responsible parties, thereby requiring reporting of suspected abuse even in cases in which the one suspected of perpetrating the abuse is also a minor family member.

If the report is made to the police, they may consult with social services and this usually happens where good working relationships have been forged. Whether in coordination with social services or independently, the police refer the case to a child or adolescent forensic investigator and the legal process is underway. If the report is made to a CPW first, and if it is seen to be in the best interests of the child, a special committee can be consulted for permission to delay reporting to the police. However, this is a delay only and all but exceptional cases or those seen as clearly unfounded are eventually reported to the police. On the other hand, if the perpetrator admits to his or her guilt and collaborates with therapy, a police report and legal intervention may be avoided entirely and the family mandated into therapy (B. Reicher, personal communication, 2011). This happens only rarely.

Failure to report can result in six months imprisonment for a professional (that is, doctor, therapist, teacher, and so on), while a nonprofessional citizen can be jailed for three months. However, charges have not yet been brought against laypersons or professionals under this law.

Strengths of the mandatory reporting law

It is important to have laws in effect which help bring cases of sexual abuse to the attention of the authorities. Children often feel too guilty to disclose, blaming themselves for the abuse having happened, or too frightened to disclose as a result of manipulative threats made by the abuser. Furthermore, as dependents they have limited access to resources which would allow them to free themselves from abusive environments (Taylor-Browne, 1997). Therefore, it remains the responsibility of society to declare openly that abuse of children is not permitted; the mandatory reporting law does just that.

Some researchers (for example, Besharov and Laumann, 1996) argue that untrained citizens may be overreporting based on misunderstanding the nature of abuse and this overreporting may tax the ability of social workers to handle the volume of cases that come their way. However, it is more advantageous in the long run to have citizens accept responsibility for the children in their environs than to feel that other people's children are only other people's responsibility.

Over time, laws mandating reporting of suspected cases of child abuse are becoming clearer, with more precise definitions of abuse, responsibility, negligence, reasonable suspicion and other salient terms. Through public service announcements, documentary television programs and community workshops, the public is gaining greater understanding of the salient issue and it may be anticipated that the reporting of suspected cases of abuse will become more precise in time.

Problems with the mandatory reporting law in Israel

One main drawback of the law in Israel relates to the fact that it falls under the Criminal Code rather than under the umbrella of laws that specifically relate to young people, such as the Youth (Supervision and Care) Law or Family Court Law. What this means is that non-reporters risk being prosecuted as criminals if they do not file a report either with the CPS or the police and this sets up an adversarial atmosphere rather than a cooperative one. In addition, if a request is made to delay reporting for clinically significant reasons, the committee considering these requests is headed by a representative of the public prosecution, a professional with legal rather than clinical expertise. This representative has the power to veto any decision and push for prosecution against the advice of social work or psychology professionals. While some clinicians have had positive experiences with these committees, others have had very negative experiences; in other words, there is a degree of inconsistency in the way the committees operate around the country.

Interestingly, this law does not distinguish between ongoing abuse and "old" abuse. Therefore, if it is discovered that a minor was abused by a responsible party, even if that abuse ended many years earlier, that case must be reported as soon as possible. There is no consideration for the impact of this on the young person, whether or not they feel ready to deal with the issue, their current level of safety, the relative probabilities concerning whether the family would rally around the survivor or the abuser, and so on.

Another major problem with the law is that it does not clearly define "suspicion" of abuse. It should not be assumed that all professionals will define this in the same way (Levi and Portwood, 2011). Among other factors, whether clinicians are more motivated to protect their clients from the possible harm of a premature disclosure or to protect themselves from possible prosecution for not reporting may affect how they define "reasonable suspicion."

The third difficulty with the law is that no guidelines for post-report intervention are delineated (Oz and Balshan, 2007). This lack of standardization leaves the field open for interpretation by local social work agencies, which may, and in some cases does, lead to inconsistent treatment of victims and their families around the country. Codification of the post-report procedures would increase the ability of school counselors, therapists in private practice and public agencies, and other professionals to be better prepared to help their clients understand what has happened and why, and what will happen and why. It establishes a firmer basis for interagency understanding and cooperation. The Welfare Ministry has established public child sex abuse centers that handle reporting, investigation and intervention for victims and their families and this should reduce inconsistencies from one agency to another. However, many suspicions arise in the private sector and the ethical therapist will continue to face, alone, reporting dilemmas unless there is a mandate to consult rather than a mandate to report. One recent example should serve to illustrate these points.

Consultation by parents after daughter disclosed abuse by her uncle

It is human nature not to pay attention to things that seem irrelevant to one's life. Although the mandated reporting law has been talked about in the media, until an individual personally faces a relevant situation, it is as if they had no idea this law exists. When a newly disclosed case of ongoing abuse hits the papers or the evening news, one common outcry is: charge the mother with not reporting the abuse under the mandatory reporting law! Yet, as quickly as water drains through sand on a beach, many people forget about this case and this law.

A mother and father were sent to me for consultation after they told a colleague that they had learned that the father's brother had abused their eight-year-old daughter. Upon disclosure of the abuse, they immediately closed ranks and the uncle had no more access to any of their children. They were concerned about whether or not their daughter needed professional help and whether or not to inform the rest of the extended family. They described how the disclosure was made and showed me a videotape of a discussion the father held with his daughter that he had discretely recorded using his mobile phone; in the tape she clearly stated that her uncle had touched her inappropriately.

With that evidence, this case was not one of reasonable suspicion but clearly a reportable crime. The first order of the day was to inform them that according to the law their situation demanded a report to the CPS or the police as soon as possible, an expression that usually means "now" to both the CPS and the police. Their first reaction was one of shock. They could not understand how they could be compelled by law to let authorities intrude into their family unit and make decisions affecting their family and their child when they had done nothing wrong. After all, their child told *them* about the abuse and not a teacher or friend; their child trusted them to protect her. And they were fulfilling their parental duties to the utmost.

The law in Israel leaves no room for parental discretion. In Ontario, Canada, on the other hand, when non-abusive parents take clear steps to ensure the safety of the child after learning of the abuse, they are not compelled by law to file a report and may be helped to make decisions that are right for their particular family (D. Sandor, personal communication, 2006). It seems unreasonable that just because a child fell victim to abuse the state can over-ride parental authority without regard to whether or not they are acting in their child's best interests.

In the case under discussion here, certainly not a unique one, the parents were loath to report a loved brother and uncle who was a main axis around which the family was organized. They needed time to digest what had happened and they needed guidance and support while doing so. Had they reported this case to the CPS, it would have gone on immediately to the police because there were no extenuating circumstances under which to request a delay.[1] To be forced to report to the authorities before having had time to come to terms with the situation would have meant adding trauma upon trauma for these parents.

It is important to recognize that, while sexual abuse is traumatic for the child in most cases,[2] the disclosure is traumatic for the parent (Oz, in press a). We should not belittle the shock, horror and guilt that accompany a disclosure of abuse and its effect on the non-abusive parent(s). Their whole world collapses and the family they thought they had suddenly disintegrates; the normal world they thought they lived in suddenly becomes a monstrous and dirty world. Before they can make any decisions, they need help absorbing what they have just learned. By forcing a report to the authorities before they are ready to deal with the fallout in their extended as well as their nuclear family, the couple's emotional resources are taxed to the limit.

At this first session, we discussed the likely implications for their daughter's healthy development in view of the fact that she was able to tell them about the abuse after only two incidences, together with their immediate protective stance. We discussed the process of reporting and what they could expect following the report. I advised them to keep the issue between themselves and raised the possibility that the abuser would sense he was found out by their changed way of relating with him. I shared with them some ideas related to abuser manipulation of victims and abuser denial. Naively, they believed that he would admit to the abuse if confronted. I gave them two weeks and said that I would help them prepare for making a report. I also told them that if they did not feel capable of making the report themselves, I would do that for them at the end of the two weeks. I do not generally make this kind of declaration; however, I found myself in an uncomfortable position. I did not have a "reasonable suspicion" that there was abuse, I *knew* there was abuse. I felt the judge's mallet above my head and the best thing for me would have been to report in their stead the next morning. However, I had before me a mother and father who came together to take responsibility for their daughter and do what was best for her. They did not know before this moment that that came apparently at the expense of the entire family.[3]

I would have preferred either to involve the CPW without giving their names and work as a team until the couple was ready to disclose their identity or to send the couple to her for them to work as a team. However, the CPW would have been bound to report this case to the police as there was no basis upon which to request a delay. I regarded them as allies in their daughter's protection and not as antagonists. Yet the law makes no allowances for that possibility. Forcing a report, acting *in loco parentis* where there was no clinical reason for doing so, would have undermined the parents' position in their nuclear family and may have caused familial and marital damage that would have been both uncalled for and difficult to repair.

As in most cases with which I have been involved, they were fearful that the report would tear their family apart and were sure other family members would find it hard to believe the disclosure. Repeatedly, I tried to impress upon them that the person tearing the family apart is the abuser; at the same time, I knew it would take time until they would be able to feel that way. I had no way of knowing that the abuser himself would make that a non-issue. Within a few days, the abuser must have sensed that something was wrong. He cleared out the joint bank account he shared with his wife and disappeared, possibly leaving the country. Israel is too small a country to hide here for very long. That shocked the couple into understanding that the real threat to the family was the abuser and not the story. They went to the CPS and reported the abuse.

The CPW's response clearly points out the problem with the current form of the mandatory reporting law. In a conversation with me, she expressed being upset about two things: first, that the father had asked his daughter questions about the abuse and taped the conversation, thus possibly tainting the quality of the forensic investigation; and second, that they had not come earlier because now the abuser had run off and may have been beyond the court's reach.

The most natural response for the concerned parent of a child disclosing abuse is to want to understand exactly what happened. The parent is reeling from the news and needs to come down on one side or the other: was this abuse or is my child misunderstanding something that may have been perfectly innocent? Therefore, the parent will ask questions, trying to get a clear story, before being willing to call a loved family member a criminal. We can train professionals, teachers, counselors, therapists, doctors and nurses not to question a child when a hint of possible abuse arises. We cannot train parents not to do so with their own children, nor should we want to. Caring parents are concerned about their child and whether or not their child was abused. They are not concerned at this point about whether or not the alleged abuser will abuse other children in the future nor about the quality of the forensic evidence that can be gathered from the child. They are concerned about their family falling apart; they are not at this point concerned about another family that may fall apart in the future.

The parents in the case under discussion here are angry that the abuser ran off before he could be brought to justice. At the same time, they are relieved that his escape proved to the entire family that he is, in fact, guilty. In retrospect, they agree that theoretically it would have been better to have filed a report immediately and yet they are grateful that I did not push them into doing so. They understand now that he would have denied having abused his niece, perhaps convincingly so, and they would have been angry at me for having "caused" the stalemate and for having disrespected their parental authority. Instead, the entire family is coming together, opening old wounds that need healing, and providing mutual support.

Through this example, it becomes clear that the law that was established to protect abused children became a law that puts the CPS in conflict with their very clients. Because the law is in the Criminal Code, the focus of the report is on the apprehension and prosecution of a criminal. The social worker becomes an agent of the law, an agent of the courts, an agent of the community, a task that rightly belongs with police and policy makers. The CPW operating under this law is no longer free to represent the rights and the needs of the particular victim before him or her and those who should be given all the resources necessary to shelter and nurture the victim, the parents or guardians.

Social service agencies and the community are concerned that a potentially dangerous person is free to hurt more children. However, that is not the concern of the caring parent at early stages of coping with a disclosure of abuse. Parents are worried about how reporting and giving evidence will affect their child, themselves and the rest of their family; they do not see at first how empowering it can be to young people to stand up to their abusers in a court of law.[4] They do not yet see how opening up the secret promotes healthy relationships for the entire family. Each new family is beginning the journey from the starting point and will have to "re-invent the wheel."

The CPW should be an ally of the protective non-abusive parent and of other professionals perhaps involved in the case. Had I, or better yet the parents, had the freedom to consult with her without her necessarily reporting the case to the police, there would have been a basis for ongoing cooperation and consultation. The social worker would have been regarded as a family-team-member and not as a patronizing agent of society. The mandatory reporting law as it stands today puts her in the latter position.

Addressing Problems with the Law

There are several problems that need to be addressed regarding mandatory reporting of suspected child abuse in Israel. First, there are some differences between sexual abuse and other forms of abuse that need to be considered. It has been suggested that far fewer allegations of sexual abuse are substantiated in a court of law than physical abuse or neglect (Levine *et al.*, 1998). Therefore the tendency of some countries to advocate legal interventions for sexual abuse and therapeutic interventions for other forms of abuse (for example, the Netherlands; see Roelofs and Baartman, 1997) may be more related to the disgust elicited by sexual abuse than to the effectiveness of the legal approach. There may be a need to deal with sexual abuse in a separate law geared to the special nature of sexual abuse that warrants special expertise on the part of the professionals involved.

Related to the suggestion of creating a separate law for sexual abuse, and perhaps the simplest problem to correct, is the oversight of restricting mandatory reporting to cases in which the perpetrator of the abuse is in a position of responsibility over the victim. Oz and Balshan (2007) recommended an amendment to the law that requires the reporting of *all* cases of suspected sexual abuse regardless of the age of the abuser and his/her relationship with the victim. If we combine this with a removal of the law from the Criminal Code and mandating consultation rather than reporting, we may be able to achieve the most desirable results.

First, the CPS would once more be an agent of its clients, providing guidance and support for individuals and families. By emphasizing consultation rather than reporting to the police, the CPW becomes an ally, someone who works with families and other professionals in the search for solutions rather than in the search for trial and conviction. The pace and direction for interventions would then be back in the hands of those with expertise in the psychological impact of abuse and its disclosure.

Second, for some minors who commit sexual offenses and certainly for adults who do so, legal intervention is often an important part of rehabilitation. However, the initiation of police proceedings, if coordinated with a systemic approach to the victim/survivor and the family, stands a better chance of true rehabilitation than today's situation in Israel that prohibits therapy before completion of the forensic investigations. If the forensic stage lasts for months, we are leaving traumatized individuals and families without the means to begin healing. Moreover, offenders of all ages cannot receive any form of treatment before being found guilty in a court of law, thus losing the opportunity to exploit to therapeutic advantage the opportunity afforded by the upset equilibrium. Compliance with therapy may mean that fewer offenders will receive a prison sentence, thus providing a continuity of service that may benefit the victim/survivor, other family members and the community as a whole.

Third, the CPS does not give up its supervisory capacity nor its authority and recourse to legal avenues should cooperation not be forthcoming in a reasonable period of time or according to a positive process of change identified by clinicians working with the family.

Fourth, where the abuse is in the past, there would be clinical follow-up and promotion of current survivor safety, with no threat of filing charges until the survivor himself or herself is ready to do so. It is my experience that survivors grow ready to press charges after two or more years of therapy (after they understand the impact of the abuse on their lives and feel strong enough to cope with the ramifications of a trial). If charges are pressed by the state before the survivor is ready to testify to all that happened, it is likely that the perpetrator will stand trial for only a small part of the abuse, denying the survivor the right to pursue justice later for the entirety of what the abuser did. At present, it might be to the survivor's advantage to not cooperate with an investigation and not provide evidence for any charges, thereby leaving open the option of filing suit in the future. I cannot ethically recommend such an action and I cannot prevent myself from hoping that this is what will happen if I think my client is not yet ready.

Fifth, according to the law today, suspected victims of abuse can be interviewed by a forensic investigator without parental knowledge or consent. Surprisingly, the same is not true for minors under the age of criminal responsibility (12) who are suspected of having abused another minor; parents can prohibit questioning. We should consider minors who commit sexual offenses as minors "in need" since a healthy and secure child or teen would not abuse another; this new law would provide for proper supervision and intervention in the relevant families. At the same time, with the case being under the umbrella of Family or Youth laws rather than the Criminal Code, it would somewhat destigmatize parents and raise the potential for their cooperation with treatment (Oz, in press b). Furthermore, it may prove to be a more humane treatment framework for families in which there has been sibling abuse.

Sixth, Oz and Balshan (2007) recommend that provision be made so that the mandatory reporting law can actually be an instrument of change by suggesting an amendment to the law clearly stipulating the procedures to be followed after the report. This would change the sometimes arbitrary and inconsistent nature of response as it occurs in Israel today. The advisability of such a team approach is not new (see, for example, Coulson, Wallis and Clark, 1994; Somer and Szwarcberg, 2001) and the United Kingdom, for example, has a clearly defined protocol (Department of Health, Home Office and Department for Education and Employment, 1999), but the idea of having the post-report protocol legislated into law is new.

A Brief History of Attempts to Effect Change in Israel

In 2003, Abu Baker and Dwairy published an important paper that challenged the mandated reporting law as culturally irrelevant in the Arab community in Israel. They suggested an alternative approach to intervention and for the promotion of offender acceptance of responsibility for the crimes. It took a few years for this paper to begin to make an impact on discussion of mandated reporting and culturally sensitive interventions in this country.

As director of a private multidisciplinary clinic treating sex trauma victims/survivors and their families, I was struck by the inconsistencies among CPS agencies and CPWs in response to my queries concerning abuse or suspected abuse. In 2005, under the auspices of my private clinic, I organized a nationwide study day on the subject of mandatory reporting of child sexual abuse for the purpose of opening channels for communication and clarification among clinicians in the field and social services agencies. The response was greater than expected; 115 professionals in public or private clinics attended, some flying in for the day from Eilat and Kiryat Shmona.

Unfortunately, the director of Youth Services in the Department of Social Welfare rejected my invitation to speak to the convention. Some local agencies expressed anger that such a day was organized by a private clinic and not the Ministry. For some reason, it was untruthfully claimed that I was against the mandatory reporting law and I was regarded with suspicion.

In an attempt to cultivate a more positive exchange of ideas with CPS, a relationship was forged between a local CPW and me when we worked together on a number of cases in her region. She was equally concerned about the inconsistencies she had observed concerning response to sex abuse disclosures and together we wrote a paper (Oz and Balshan, 2007) in order to continue dialogue among professionals and recommend changes to the law. Since then, other professionals have begun, independently, to express concerns with the law, especially after the law was expanded to include mandated reporting of minor brothers or cousins suspected of abusive behaviors. This meant that families who wanted to help both their children were forced either to stay away from therapy altogether or to see one of their children taken down a road of criminal prosecution before any therapeutic help was forthcoming. Legal experts are, at the same time, providing clarification of the relevant issues that within the law itself remain ambiguously worded (for example, Shmueli, 2009) and showing the way for a balanced approach whereby some cases can be referred to social services and community intervention rather than the police and courts (Shmueli, 2010). The Knesset Law Committee is reviewing the issues.

By 2010, the subject of the negative aspects of the mandatory reporting law became more widely and openly discussed. Doron Agassi, founder and director of a clinic for the treatment of sex offenders and sex trauma victims/survivors in the Ultra-Orthodox community in Israel, took up the banner in the fight for amending the law and updating it for today's reality. Agassi's argument is that the law that was passed in 1989 was appropriate for the legal and social context of that time. There have been many changes since then and the law should reflect the level of expertise available in the country today, the level of awareness among the general population, and the growing willingness of individuals and families in all sectors of the population to engage in therapy. Agassi is forging relationships with Members of the Israeli Knesset, with legal and therapy professionals around the country and with various organizations working with sex trauma victims/survivors. He is continuing to press for open debate, reducing the personal attacks leveled against those who challenge the form of the law, and campaigning for the law to become an instrument promoting clinically significant changes and not criminal charges.

Conclusions

It is, in my opinion, unethical to place therapists in an untenable dilemma, a conflict that in some situations forces them to choose between the fear of transgressing a law that contradicts their clinical knowledge on the one hand and the obligation to consider first and foremost the needs of their clients on the other. Even with almost 30 years of experience in the field of sex trauma therapy in Israel, I do not want to deal alone with the issues that arise around mandatory reporting of suspected cases of sexual abuse. I want to work with a team of professionals who are as concerned as I am with victims/survivors and their families. I want to be able to do so without fear of losing control over the pace and direction of the work with the family to a system that talks in terms of admissible evidence and criminal charges rather than in terms of psychological symptoms and impact and family systems. It is also unethical to place CPWs in the position of being agents of the legal system rather than agents of their clients, to compel these social workers to be more concerned with helping the police gather evidence to prosecute a criminal than with helping therapists and families deal with the trauma of sexual abuse.

By changing the mandated reporting law, removing it from the Criminal Code and placing it within the Welfare Laws, by mandating consultation and intervention rather than mandating police reports, and by stipulating the exact procedures that follow disclosure, we would be providing a public response to the problem of sexual abuse of minors in accordance with contemporary professional expertise. We are not making sex abuse legal; we are changing the legal treatment of the disclosure of the abuse alone. The appropriate changes will allow therapists and other professionals and social workers in the social services agencies to behave both ethically and within the bounds of the law.

Notes

1   A delay may be requested if the child threatens suicide if forced to give evidence, or if there is serious illness in the family or another equally compelling reason.
2   There may be situations in which the child was not threatened or physically hurt and when the abuse was not a frightening experience for the child. In such cases, the abuse may never be considered traumatic or may come to be traumatic at a later age when he or she understands the nature of sex and that what happened was "sexual."
3   In less obvious cases, where there is no actual verbalization of an abusive act by the victim or other clear evidence, it is more responsible to take longer and to examine the situation from many angles, to explore whether or not their suspicion is a reasonable one, at the same time ensuring the child is safe and gently and in step-wise fashion raising the issue of mandatory reporting.
4   In Israel, children under the age of 14 do not themselves testify in court. Specially trained forensic interviewers take children's recorded statements to court and are cross-examined in their stead.

References

Abu Baker, K. and Dwairy, M. (2003) "Cultural norms versus state law in treating incest: a suggested model for Arab families," *Child Abuse and Neglect* 27, 109–123.

Alvarex, K.M., Kenny, M.C., Donohue, B. and Carpin, K.M. (2004) "Why are professionals failing to initiate mandated reports of child maltreatment, and are there any empirically based training programs to assist professionals in the reporting process?," *Aggression and Violent Behavior* 9, 563–578.

Bell, L. (2001) "Patterns of interaction in multidisciplinary child protection teams in New Jersey," *Child Abuse and Neglect* 25, 65–80.

Besharov, D. and Laumann, L. (1996) "Child abuse reporting," *Society* 33, 40–46.

Coulson, K.W., Wallis, S. and Clark, H. (1994) "The diversified team approach in the treatment of incest families," *Psychotherapy in Private Practice* 13, 19–43.

Department of Health, Home Office and Department for Education and Employment (1999) *Working Together to Safeguard Children.* London: The Stationery Office.

Eastwood, C. and Patton, W. (2002) The Experiences of Child Complainants of Sexual Abuse in the Criminal Justice System. Australian Institute of Criminology, http://www.aic.gov.au/documents/1/8/F/%7B18FF5A71-2773-4BC8-BC93-933DD57A5BDD%7Dti250.pdf (accessed August 25, 2012).

Feng, J.Y., Fetzer, S., Chen, Y.W., *et al.* (2010) "Multidisciplinary collaboration reporting child abuse: a grounded theory study," *International Journal of Nursing Studies* 47, 1483–1490.

Forman, T. and Bernet, W. (2000) "A misunderstanding regarding the duty to report suspected abuse," *Child Maltreatment* 5, 190–196.

Gilbert, N. (ed.) (1997) *Combating Child Abuse: International Perspectives and Trends.* Oxford: Oxford University Press.

Greytak, E.A. (2009) "Are teachers prepared? Predictors of teachers' readiness to serve as mandated reporters of child abuse," *Publicly Accessible Penn Dissertations*, Paper 57, http://repository.upenn.edu/edissertations/57 (accessed August 25, 2012).

Kenny, M.C. (2001) "Child abuse reporting: teachers' perceived deterrents," *Child Abuse and Neglect* 25, 81–92.

Levi, B.H. and Portwood, S.G. (2011) "Reasonable suspicion of child abuse: finding a common language," *Journal of Law, Medicine and Ethics* 39, 62–69.

Levine, M. and Doueck, H.J. (1995) *The Impact of Mandated Reporting on the Therapeutic Process: Picking Up the Pieces.* Thousand Oaks, CA: Sage.

Levine, M., Doueck, H.J., Freeman, J.B. and Compaan, C. (1998) "Rush to judgment? Child protective services and allegations of sexual abuse," *American Journal of Orthopsychiatry* 68, 101–107.

Marneffe, C. and Broos, P. (1997) "Belgium: an alternative approach to child abuse reporting and treatment," in N. Gilbert (ed.), *Combating Child Abuse, International Perspectives and Trends.* New York: Oxford University Press, pp. 167–191.

Melton, G.B. (2005) "Mandated reporting: a policy without reason," *Child Abuse and Neglect* 29, 9–18.

Oz, S. (2005) "The 'Wall of Fear': the bridge between the traumatic event and trauma resolution therapy for childhood sexual abuse survivors," *Journal of Child Sexual Abuse* 14, 3, 23–47.

Oz, S. (in press a) "Interventions with non-abusing parents after one of their children discloses a secret of sexual abuse," in R. Regulant-Levy and A. Goldstein (eds), *"Patching the Pieces Together": Ashalim Forum for Child Sex Abuse Treatment Programme Directors 2000–2010. A Collection of Essays.* Jerusalem: Ashalim [in Hebrew].

Oz, S. (in press b) "Parents of children and adolescents who have sexually abused: questions of legal liability and clinical interventions," *Journal of Child Sexual Abuse.*

Oz, S. and Balshan, D. (2007) "Mandatory reporting of childhood sexual abuse in Israel: what happens to the kids after the report has been filed?," *Journal of Child Sexual Abuse* 16, 1–22.

Paine, M.L. and Hansen, D.J. (2002) "Factors influencing children to self-disclose sexual abuse," *Clinical Psychology Review* 22, 271–295.

Park, M.S. (2005) "The application of CPS in Korea," *Journal of Aggression, Maltreatment and Trauma* 11, 4, 117–131.

Poso, T. (1997) "Finland: child abuse as a family problem," in N. Gilbert (ed.), *Combating Child Abuse, International Perspectives and Trends.* New York: Oxford University Press, pp. 143–166.

Roelofs, M.A.S. and Baartman, H.E.M. (1997) "The Netherlands. Responding to abuse – compassion or control?," in N. Gilbert (ed.), *Combating Child Abuse, International Perspectives and Trends.* New York: Oxford University Press, pp. 192–211.

Shmueli, B. (2009) "Between assault, abuse and corporal punishment," in T. Morag (ed.), *Children's Rights and the Israeli Law.* Tel Aviv: Ramot Publishing, pp. 63–100 [in Hebrew], abstract in English available at http://papers.ssrn.com/sol3/papers.cfm?abstract_id=1796126 (accessed August 25, 2012).

Shmueli, B. (2010) "Mandated reporting on child abuse in Jewish Law and Israeli Law," *Family in Law Review* 3, 279–301 [in Hebrew], abstract in English available at http://papers.ssrn.com/sol3/papers.cfm?abstract_id=1514380 (accessed August 25, 2012).

Somer, E. and Szwarcberg, S. (2001) "Variables in delayed disclosure of childhood sexual abuse," *American Journal of Orthopsychiatry* 71, 332–341.

Swift, K.J. (1997) "Canada: trends and issues in child welfare," in N. Gilbert (ed.), *Combating Child Abuse, International Perspectives and Trends.* New York: Oxford University Press, pp. 38–71.

Taylor-Browne, J. (1997) "Obfuscating child sexual abuse II: listening to survivors," *Child Abuse Review* 6, 118–127.

Tite, R. (1993) "How teachers define and respond to child abuse: the distinction between theoretical and reportable cases," *Child Abuse and Neglect* 17, 591–603.

Walsh, K., Laskey, L., McInnes, E. *et al.* (2011) "Locating child protection in teacher education," *Australian Journal of Teacher Education* 36, 7, 1–20.

Part Two

Legal and Ethical Issues in Risk Treatment

13

Treatment for Adult Sex Offenders
May We Reject the Null Hypothesis?
Marnie E. Rice and Grant T. Harris

Introduction

Scientific progress, especially in psychology, has been achieved by means of general principles put into research practice. Among these is the minimization of various forms of bias. Nothing guarantees the absence of all bias and the best any field can do is explicitly recognize sources of undesirable bias and adhere to practices to counteract them. There are also some appropriate "biases." For example, there is an obligation for parsimony, known as Occam's razor, that is, unless evidence compels otherwise, the simplest explanations or models are accepted. Regarding interventions of all kinds, the default, parsimonious (null) hypothesis is that an intervention has no effect unless the evidence forces a conclusion otherwise. In accepting the existence of effects, decisions are conservative, hypothesized effects must be quite likely to be true, given available data, and obtained results should be unlikely, given null hypotheses. And such latter likelihoods must be low (hence the customary alpha = 0.05; Balluerka, Gomez and Hidalgo, 2005).

An important empirical and policy-related matter over the past six decades concerns the evidence that interventions deliberately applied by practitioners have caused reductions in adult sex offenders' risk. In comparing sex offenders exposed to different treatments (including no treatment), if differences in subsequent offending were attributable to known differences in risk measured before treatment occurred, the parsimonious account would proscribe assuming any additional effect of treatment. In the context of sex offender intervention, clearly specifying and evaluating null and alternate hypotheses has been a challenge.

The Wiley-Blackwell Handbook of Legal and Ethical Aspects of Sex Offender Treatment and Management,
First Edition. Edited by Karen Harrison and Bernadette Rainey.
© 2013 John Wiley & Sons, Ltd. Published 2013 by John Wiley & Sons, Ltd.

What Do the Authorities Say about Treatment Efficacy?

Reading summaries in books and chapters, statements by the Association for the Treatment of Sexual Abusers (ATSA), and even meta-analyses on the sex offender treatment literature, one would conclude that the effectiveness of treatment had been conclusively demonstrated and the null hypotheses definitively rejected. Consider the following from ATSA public statements: "Research has shown that well-designed sex offender treatment can reduce the recidivism of sex offenders" (ATSA, 2011a), and "studies conducted since [the 1980s] have examined programs using more 'state-of-the-art' treatment techniques and results are indicative of some reduction in recidivism for the groups of offenders receiving treatment" (ATSA, 2012). The following quotation comes from a recent book chapter: "There is an impressive body of evidence indicating that sexual and non-sexual offenders can be effectively reintegrated into the community provided they participate in specific types of programmes" (Ward, Collie and Bourke, 2009: 308). The following come from a meta-analysis: "Despite a wide range of positive and negative effect sizes, the majority confirmed the benefits of treatment" (Lösel and Schmucker, 2005: 117), and:

> The average effect of physical treatment is much larger than that of psychosocial programs. The main source for this difference is a very strong effect of surgical castration, although hormonal medication also shows a relatively good outcome. (Lösel and Schmucker, 2005: 135)

Furthermore, the following come from narrative reviews:

> Long-acting GnRh agonists, together with psychotherapy, are highly effective in controlling selected paraphilias (pedophilia, exhibitionism, and voyeurism) and are the most promising mode of therapy in the next millennium. (Rösler and Witztum, 2000: 43)

> In light of the high effectiveness and low recidivism rate, it will not be surprising if a "comeback" to surgical castration will occur. (Rösler and Witztum, 2000: 52)

> The treatment of paraphilias using pharmacological agents . . . is effective in all types of sexual deviations, including the simultaneous presence of multiple deviations. In addition, it is the treatment of choice for the most serious sexual deviations . . . (Bradford, 2000: 249)

In each case, readers are assured that treatment has been demonstrated to cause lowered recidivism among adult sex offenders, and that the demonstration has met accepted criteria for the rejection of the relevant null hypothesis.

Why Should We Not Accept All This?

The purpose of this chapter is to ask whether, according to the principles outlined in the first paragraph, the available evidence warrants accepting these firm conclusions, specifically as they apply to adult sex offenders. Early in our careers, we conducted a treatment evaluation that reinforced the importance of empirical evaluations of treatment effectiveness. Between 1968 and 1978, the "social Therapy Unit" of our institution, the Waypoint Centre for Mental Health Care, gained international recognition as a model program for the treatment of serious offenders, especially psychopaths. This maximum security therapeutic community was modeled after programs in England by Maxwell Jones (Jones, 1956, 1968). Our hospital's program has been described at length elsewhere (see, for example, Barker, 1980; Weisman, 1995) and was primarily peer-operated intensive group therapy to promote empathy and responsibility. Visitors came from around the world and, according to available reports, were unanimously impressed. A review commissioned by the Ombudsman of Ontario (Butler, Long and Rowsell, 1977), subsequently presented to a parliamentary subcommittee of the Government of Canada, stated: "This is an exciting program which has the hallmark of being right . . . as the final model of the DNA molecule looked right to Watson and Crick" (Canada, 1977: 45). Furthermore:

> We were satisfied that the patients benefited greatly from the Social Therapy Unit experience. We are quite sure that the program itself is of considerably benefit not only to the patients but to the hospital as a whole and the country . . . We were satisfied that the program [has] . . . a very low recidivism rate . . . [The developers of this program have] . . . developed the techniques that . . . are the most fruitful anywhere in the universe at the present time. (Canada, 1977: 45)

We were eager to carry out empirical measurement of the value of this program. We could not conduct a random assignment study because the program had been discontinued (for reasons having nothing to do with efficacy), but a quasi-experimental design matched treated participants to comparison cases from the penitentiaries on a number of relevant characteristics. Disappointingly, the results showed no overall group difference (therapeutic community versus prison) on recidivism (Rice, Harris and Cormier, 1992). Surprisingly, given the goal of positive change in psychopathic personality, psychopaths who participated in the program had higher rates of violent recidivism than psychopaths who did not. The opposite was observed among non-psychopaths. This study provided an important lesson in the requirement that treatment effects be empirically demonstrated. It also illustrated the possibility that "treatment," even when it is based on solid theoretical foundations, can actually do harm.

Since the publication of this evaluation of the Social Therapy Unit, randomized controlled trials (RCTs) have become the "gold standard" for the evaluation of treatment effectiveness in medicine and related fields. For example, the Cochrane Library is an internationally renowned database containing hundreds of thousands of RCTs (see www.thecochranelibrary.com). RCTs compare participants assigned at random to one of at least two treatments. Typically, participants are assigned either to an active treatment under investigation or to a control condition which can be no treatment, a placebo, an alternate treatment, or some combination of these. The best RCTs are "double-blind" in which neither participants nor clinicians know who receives which treatment. Although common in medical trials, they are much more difficult, if not impossible, for evaluations of psychological treatments. For psychological treatments, single-blind studies, in which therapists are aware whether the treatment is the one expected to do best, but the participant is not, are much more feasible.

Although they are the best designs available, RCTs are not without shortcomings (Berk, 2005), especially related to implementation. Commonly, for various practical reasons, random assignment is not actually implemented. It can be difficult to obtain sufficiently large samples to attain satisfactory statistical power. Often, there is considerable attrition, that is, participants drop out of treatment before completion. Because those who drop out are very likely to be different from those who do not in ways related to the outcomes, analyses must consider treatment as assigned. It is clear that adult sex offenders who quit treatment have worse criminal and socio-demographic histories than completers, and thus their higher rates of recidivism can, in the absence of convincing evidence to the contrary, be attributed to differences that existed before treatment occurred (Nunes and Cortoni, 2008; Olver and Wong, 2009; Seager, Jellicoe and Dhaliwal, 2004).

How Persuasive Is the Adult Sex Offender Treatment Literature?

Among outcome studies for sex offenders, weak designs are the norm. Hanson *et al.* (2009) used guidelines by the Collaborative Outcome Data Committee (CODC) (2007b) to rate the quality of all 129 sex offender treatment outcome studies they could find.[1] Of these, 105 were rejected as too weak to be informative, 19 more were rated as weak, five were rated good, and none as strong. All of the surgery and drug studies were rejected as uninformative by the CODC guidelines. Most troubling is that many of the rejected studies had been published in the peer-reviewed literature.

One study rated "good" examined multi-systemic therapy for adolescents (with a mean age of 14). Although this excellent study showed promise for juvenile sex offenders, it is unclear how this treatment could be applied to adult sex offenders; thus, efficacy of adolescent offender treatment is not addressed here. Of the four studies of adult sex offenders rated "good" by Hanson *et al.* (2009), two were RCTs, and neither showed any positive effect of treatment (Marques *et al.*, 2005; Romero and Williams, 1985). Only one of the four showed any indication of positive treatment effects (McGrath, Hoke and Vojtisek, 1998). In that study, cognitive-behavioral treatment was compared to non-specialized services, and the treatment group exhibited a significantly lower rate of sexual recidivism in a five-year follow-up. However, Hanson *et al.* (2009: 870) called this a "need, volunteer, and dropout" design in which "the factors that excluded offenders from the treatment group were not fully known, but could reasonably be expected to have involved decisions made by the offenders and treatment providers." McGrath, Hoke and Vojtisek (1998) stated that the comparison participants specifically selected non-specialized services and included one offender who had dropped out of cognitive-behavioral treatment. Given that the entire goal of the CODC guidelines was to rate the likelihood of bias, it is clear this study could not warrant a rating of "good."

Another aspect of Hanson *et al.*'s (2009) meta-analysis was examining adherence to the principles of risk, need and responsivity (RNR; Bonta and Andrews, 2007), shown to be important for rehabilitation among criminal offenders generally. According to the risk principle, programs are effective to the extent they apportion services in accordance with actuarially measured risk of recidivism. The need principle mandates targeting personal characteristics or circumstances empirically related to recidivism. The responsivity principle requires that services match the participants' learning styles. For adult offenders, cognitive-behavioral programs most commonly adhere to this principle. Hanson *et al.* (2009) reported an association between the number of RNR principles followed in treatment and the size of treatment effects. However, it is important to note that among the four adult studies rated "good," only two were rated as following any of the RNR principles: Marques *et al.* (2005) and McGrath, Hoke and Vojtisek (1998) were each rated as following two of the three RNR principles.

After more than a half-century of effort, an exhaustive search yielded an impressive population of 129 empirical studies of sex offender treatment from which an unimpressive 81% had to be rejected as uninformative (Hanson *et al.*, 2009). No studies were "strong" and four remaining studies rated as "good" afforded no evidence to reject the null hypothesis. Thus, the authoritative claims of effectiveness cited at the start of this chapter rest entirely on research rated as "weak" or "rejected." A very well recognized but thorny bias has plagued efforts to evaluate sex offender interventions; those who volunteer for and complete treatment are different (in risk-related ways) from those who do not. In all studies in which treated and untreated sex offenders have exhibited differences in recidivism, the most parsimonious explanation of the results is that pre-existing differences between the groups can account for differences in outcomes reported. These biases are classic confounds in observational research and there are commonly accepted statistical methods to provide some control for them. However, the credibility afforded the results of such non-experimental tests depends on a number of other issues, the most important of which is the data from whatever experimental research is available (in this context, RCTs). Because the few available RCTs of adult sex offender interventions have indicated no specific positive effects of treatment, we conclude that the non-experimental evaluations cannot trigger rejection of the null hypothesis (according to the agreed-upon principles discussed in the first paragraph).

We suggest disinterested examination of the entire literature on adult sex offender intervention reveals inappropriate biases on the part of practitioners and researchers. We cite here the very large number of peer-reviewed, published studies with designs so weak they are rejected as uninformative by meta-analysts and others employing objective criteria; and, even among published studies considered informative, anomalies in methods and results that more often favored the alternate hypothesis. We suggest a relevant null sub-hypothesis is that such anomalies are randomly related to study conclusions while an alternate sub-hypothesis is that anomalies are more likely to pass unnoticed when authors purport evidence of treatment effects. We suggest the available evidence supports the latter. Inadvertent and unrecognized biases on the part of practitioners, evaluators, journal reviewers, editors and meta-analysts have instantiated a general *de facto* practice that interventions have positive effects unless it can be demonstrated that such is unlikely given the evidence. We suggest that, in this context of a general inappropriate bias, a few apparently positive results from non-experimental studies cannot legitimately support rejection of the appropriate null hypothesis. Similarly, meta-analysis of an empirical literature this weak cannot reduce uncertainty as to the direction or size of hypothesized specific intervention effects.

Would Bayesian Reasoning Mean the Rejection of the Null Hypothesis?

The discussion in this chapter is based mostly on frequentist statistical reasoning that entails the traditional methodologies of hypothesis testing and confidence intervals. However, some scholars have recently criticized frequentist methods as irrational (for example, Dienes, 2011), and have proposed fundamental changes in the ways researchers draw conclusions from data. Most relevant here is the suggestion that statistical inference concentrate on estimating the probability that a theory (or hypothesis) is true, given available data. This is in contrast to estimating the probability that one would obtain the data given a particular theory, which is the information provided by orthodox null hypothesis significance testing. Standard null hypothesis significance testing usually does not permit acceptance of the null hypothesis even when an alternative hypothesis may also not be accepted.

At first glance, one might hope that Bayesian reasoning would permit some progress away from this uninformative situation. Bayesian reasoning often begins with the prior plausibility of a theory, and extremely plausible theories might require less evidence to support their truth value. Specifically in this context, it might seem that the efficacy of chemical or surgical castration would have high prior plausibility. Indeed, it seems that is the reasoning informally applied by some authorities. Elsewhere, we addressed the plausibility and evidence for this theory and concluded the plausibility is lower and evidence weaker than many suppose (Rice and Harris, 2011). This exposes a weakness in Bayesian advice; agreement on prior plausibility can be difficult to achieve. In the field of research on crime, the lack of a general theory of criminal behavior known to be true (for example, Kanazawa, 2003) suggests that agreement on priors pertaining to the effects of sex offender interventions on recidivism will be elusive.

Other features of Bayesian reasoning also decrease the likelihood that it can presently rescue the theory that treatment for adult sex offenders has lowered their risk of recidivism. It is especially necessary to be clear about just what a theory says. In this context, it matters whether the alternate theory (hypothesis) is that treatment for adult sex offenders has caused any decrease in officially detected violent recidivism; or whether the size of the treatment effect is at least moderate. The theory that treatment causes any effect, no matter how small, is not consistent with the assertions offered by authorities cited at the beginning of this chapter.[2] Bayesian hypothesis testing would require that, in a field of non-experimental studies, the sizes of uncontrolled factors be specified. Our position in this chapter is that disinterested evaluation of the known predictors of recidivism among adult sex offenders (for example, Hanson and Bussière, 1998; Quinsey, Rice and Harris, 1995) and the predictors of treatment non-completion indicates that those who volunteer for and complete psychosocial treatment would, on average, exhibit a moderate to large difference in recidivism compared to those not offered treatment, even if treatment had no effect. It is to be expected that pharmacological treatment would be associated with a larger selection bias, and surgical castration with a very large one. The effects of other, as yet unidentified, pre-treatment factors could be expected to add to these, but by unknown amounts. Bayesian reasoning would permit others to ascribe smaller effects to uncontrolled variables; there is nothing to prevent that, but we suggest that disinterested reading of all the research makes this implausible.

Nothing about Bayesian methods allows for decreased theoretical and methodological rigor. In fact, Bayesian reasoning may only be feasibly applied in a world of well-conducted studies and well-specified theories (Dienes, 2011). The few well-conducted experiments (that is, RCTs) in this domain would, we contend, support Bayesian acceptance of the null hypothesis. For example, a well-conducted experiment yielding a small effect size at a traditional p value of 0.05 could, according to Bayesian reasoning, actually afford more support for the null hypothesis than for the alternate (Wetzels *et al.*, 2011). It is entirely appropriate for investigators to debate the hypothesized size of treatment and selection effects and the relative value of treatment effect sizes (hence our agreement to write this chapter). On the other hand, we suggest that this ongoing debate (lasting in our cases for two decades), based as it is on an empirically weak intervention literature, has reached the end of its value. Both Bayesian and frequentist reasoning require stronger inference designs if progress is to be made.

Why Not Just Accept the Alternate Hypothesis Anyway?

Perhaps generally accepted scientific standards should be jettisoned in this instance. After all, sex offenders cause much harm and incarceration alone is unlikely to be a solution. At least some of the evidence seems promising. Surely some skilled clinicians somewhere have achieved true reductions in risk. Maintaining (however legitimately by rigid scientific standards) that treatment efficacy has not been demonstrated must erode support by offenders, therapists, criminal justice officials, policy makers, politicians and citizens for interventions that might work. Why not drop this issue of the scientific basis for the rejection of the null hypothesis in favor of building support for that which has at least some prospect of efficacy? Of course, the answer is the lesson of the Social Therapy Unit; the reliance on weak evidence entails the risk that interventions have actually increased the risk of sex offenders compared to doing nothing.[3] Consider several examples from criminal justice, psychology and medicine where treatments believed to be effective based on weak evidence were discovered to be harmful when evaluated using strong RCT methods.

At least until 1950, conventional wisdom among those who worked with youth was that affectionate guidance from parents and other sources would prevent delinquency, and an ambitious empirical demonstration, an RCT known as the Cambridge-Somerville Youth Study, was undertaken (McCord, 1978). The 506 boys (with a median age of 10.5), recruited from working-class neighborhoods, included both those labeled "average" and those labeled "difficult." After matching pairs of boys on age, family background, home environment, and ratings of delinquency-proneness, one member of each pair was assigned at random to treatment, while the other was a no-treatment control. The treatment lasted an average of five years, and involved having counselors visit each family twice per month, tutoring in academic subjects, medical or psychiatric attention if indicated, attendance at summer camps, and contact with organizations such as the Boy Scouts and the YMCA. Follow-up measurements were conducted at the end of the intervention, and when participants were in their 40s. By the end of the program, almost equal proportions of the treated and control groups had official and unofficial records of juvenile crime. However, the evaluators retained a firm conviction in the value of the treatment and hypothesized that benefits would emerge over the longer term. No such benefits were found even in participants' fifth decades. In fact, the only significant difference on long-term follow-up of criminality was that treated participants were more likely to have committed more than one offense. Furthermore, treated participants died younger, were more often alcoholic, and had more serious mental disorders. On no measures did treated participants fare better than controls, despite the fact that most reported that the treatment had been helpful. McCord (2002) reported that so unwelcome were these results to criminal justice practitioners she once had tomatoes thrown at her when she presented them. Nevertheless, this research is a criminological classic (Gottfredson, 2010) for its demonstration that even the most well-intentioned and well-implemented interventions can do harm. McCord, after a lifetime reviewing evaluations, argued that studies should employ random assignment whenever possible (Weisburd, 2010).

Lilienfeld (2007) reviewed several psychological treatments thought to be effective based on weak evidence that RCTs later showed to be harmful. These treatments included critical incident stress debriefing, "Scared Straight" programs, expressive-experiential therapies, and drug abuse and resistance (DARE) programs. Consider one example. Critical incident stress debriefing is meant to prevent post-traumatic stress among those exposed to extreme stressors. The treatment is usually provided 24 to 72 hours after the event. A review of uncontrolled studies by Everly, Flannery and Mitchell (2000) claimed it was effective and training in this became popular among psychologists and other professionals; it was eligible for continuing education credits from the American Psychological Association, for example. Meta-analyses of RCTs (Litz *et al.*, 2002; Rose *et al.*, 2002) showed critical incident stress debriefing to have no positive effect on symptoms of post-traumatic stress, despite the fact that recipients usually reported it had been helpful. Moreover, at least two of the RCTs reported long-term harmful effects (Lilienfeld, 2007).

Some evaluation research in medicine shows that strong RCTs can be conducted even when placebo treatment might seem hard to arrange. Arthroscopic surgery is commonly used when less invasive treatments fail to relieve the pain of osteoarthritis of the knee. Over a dozen uncontrolled studies of arthroscopy for osteoarthritis showed that approximately 50% of the patients report pain relief (Moseley *et al.*, 2002). Over half a million such procedures occur annually in the United States at an approximate cost of $5,000 each. Moseley *et al.* (2002) conducted an RCT in which patients were assigned at random to one of three groups, all of whom were treated by a respected and experienced orthopedic surgeon. Two of the groups received procedures reported to be effective in uncontrolled studies: lavage (therapeutic irrigation) alone or débridement (clean up) plus lavage. Control patients received simulated surgery involving simulated anesthetic with short-term tranquilizing effects. The surgeon prepped the knee as for actual arthroscopy, made incisions in the skin, manipulated the knee as in actual arthroscopy, simulated the sounds of actual arthroscopy, and kept the patients in hospital overnight where they were cared for by nurses unaware of group assignment. The authors concluded:

> This study provided strong evidence that arthroscopic lavage with or without débridement is not better than and appears to be equivalent to a placebo procedure in improving knee pain and self-reported function. Indeed, at some points during follow-up, objective function was significantly worse in the débridement group than in the placebo group. (Moseley *et al.*, 2002: 85)

Furthermore, "the billions of dollars spent on such procedures annually might be put to better use" (Moseley *et al.*, 2002: 87).

For Parkinson's disease (PD), transplantation of fetal nigral dopamine neurons has been associated with clinically meaningful improvement in several non-RCT studies (Olanow *et al.*, 2003). Olanow *et al.* (2003) reported the transplantation treatment was offered to many patients in many places throughout the world *before* two double-blind RCTs showed it to have no overall positive effect. In the context of evaluating sex offender treatments, consider the second of these (Olanow *et al.*, 2003), a prospective, two-year, multi-dose, placebo-controlled, double-blind trial of fetal nigral transplantation in patients with advanced PD. The study was approved by the research ethics board of each participating center and by the United States National Institute of Health. Thirty-four patients were assigned at random to one of two treatments, both involving bilateral transplantation of fetal brain tissue, or a control. One treatment group received fetal material from just one donor per side, while the other received material from four donors per side. The control treatment comprised bilateral placebo surgery. Placebo patients were treated identically to patients in the other two groups except they received partial burr holes that did not penetrate the inner table of the skull, needles were not inserted into the brain, and no tissue was transplanted. Like the participants in the other two groups, however, they received a general anesthetic, immunosuppressant drugs before and for six months after surgery, and renal monitoring throughout. All surgeries were by the same neurosurgeon who was the only non-blinded clinician involved. Results showed no overall treatment effect, but more adverse events among treated patients. The authors concluded:

> This study illustrates the importance of performing placebo-controlled, double-blind trials for assessing new treatments and demonstrates the feasibility of using this type of study design even with surgical therapies. This study did not confirm the clinical benefits reported in open-label trials and we cannot recommend fetal nigral transplantation as a therapy for PD at this time. (Olanow *et al.*, 2003: 413)

Sham surgical placebos similar to that used in the Olanow *et al.* (2003) study have become common in PD research, but not without controversy (Kim *et al.*, 2005).

Kim *et al.* (2005) undertook a survey of over 100 clinical researchers' opinions as to the science and ethics of sham surgery controls to test novel therapies for PD. A large majority reported that the sham surgery control condition is ethically permissible and evinced considerable concern about false-positive results that come from weaker designs. Respondents generally agreed that sham surgery conditions are essential to demonstrate conclusively that interventions are effective. Kim *et al.* (2005) suggested their findings represented a shift in thinking over the previous decade due at least in part to strong RCTs that demonstrated interventions to be ineffective or harmful after weaker designs falsely indicated benefits.

Why Then Are RCTs for Adult Sex Offender Treatment So Uncommon?

Weisburd (2010) challenged several "folklores" used to eschew RCTs in the field of crime and justice. We summarize some here because they are so similar to those advanced against RCTs for the evaluation of treatment for adult sex offenders specifically (Marshall and Marshall, 2007). One folklore can be expressed as, "We don't need RCTs because we know the most important causes of recidivism, so we can control for them." Weisburd argued this is very unlikely to be true in crime and justice research given the small fraction of variance in outcomes currently attributable to hypothesized causal variables. Among sex offenders, even the best available actuarial tools (which include variables that cannot be causal) account for less than a quarter of the variance in outcome (Hanson and Morton-Bourgon, 2009). A second folklore discussed by Weisburd was that, when treatment effects are large, uncontrolled confounds are unimportant. Weisburd countered, however, that without full knowledge of causes, there is no way to be certain results will replicate even if they appear to be robust in any single study. Moreover, among sex offenders, no one has seriously argued that the effects of treatment are large. A third folklore discussed by Weisburd was that, after factors known to affect recidivism are controlled, it can be assumed that all other biases are balanced. In fact, Weisburd countered there is strong reason to believe that exclusion of variables is systematic. This is demonstrably the case in sex offender treatment research, where most studies included in meta-analyses compared those who completed treatment to a control group that included many who would have refused or dropped out had treatment been offered. As mentioned earlier in this chapter, this design incorporates a known bias in favor of the treatment group. Weisburd stated that, although RCTs yield results similar to those of propensity matching and regression discontinuity designs in other fields, that is not true in crime and justice research. Without RCTs, systematic biases cannot be identified. In addition, Shadish *et al.* (2011) compared RCTs with regression discontinuity designs, concluding that, although estimates from the latter approximate those from RCTs reasonably well, RCTs are preferred because they require fewer assumptions and have greater power.

Weisburd (2010) discussed other invalid folklores against RCTs relevant to sex offender treatment (Marshall and Marshall, 2007). Among these were that RCTs are not ethical and cannot be implemented in the real world. In fact, however, RCTs have been found to be ethical by research ethics boards (also see Seto *et al.*, 2008) and have been implemented even when they involved procedures as invasive as drilling the skulls of placebo participants. Weisburd pointed out that many would consider it unethical not to use RCTs and thereby risk providing incorrect answers to important societal issues and cause harm and waste limited resources. There were 267 RCTs in the field of crime and justice available in the English language as of 1993 (Petrosino *et al.*, 2003), and 87 RCTs in correctional research as of 2005 (Farrington and Welsh, 2005). Lastly here, the argument that RCTs are unfeasible for adult sex offenders is further undermined by the fact that there have been several RCTs of adolescent sex offenders and younger children with sexual behavior problems (Berliner and Saunders, 1996; Bonder, Walker and Berliner, 1999; Borduin *et al.*, 1990; Borduin, Schaeffer and Heilblum, 2009; Cohen *et al.*, 2004; Cohen and Mannarino, 1996, 1998; Collaborative Outcome Data Committee, 2007a, 2007b; Deblinger, Stauffer and Steer, 2001; Letourneau *et al.*, 2009). It is abundantly clear that RCTs are feasible both ethically and practically in crime and justice fields in general, and in corrections specifically.

Why Is It So Difficult to Change the Beliefs of Sex Offender Researchers and Practitioners?

Next, consider problems that researchers encounter when they find evidence running counter to the beliefs of other researchers, practitioners, the public and (sometimes, at least) even themselves. For example, ultra-long-distance runners commonly use ibuprofen to reduce pain and inflammation. However, a study comparing runners who took the drug to those who did not unequivocally showed ibuprofen failed to reduce muscle pain and blood tests showed the drug actually increased inflammation. Furthermore, ibuprofen use during a long run entails serious risks including gastrointestinal bleeding and acute kidney failure. The study's author stated, "There is absolutely no reason for runners to be using ibuprofen" (David Nieman, cited in Aschwanden, 2010). When these findings were presented to ultra-long-distance marathoners, most said it would not change their habits because they believed ibuprofen worked, data notwithstanding (Aschwanden, 2010).

Unfortunately, as many researchers have learned, evidence is sometimes met with disdain or anger when the findings are counter to popular beliefs or expediency. Social psychologists have shown that when the results of studies on topics such as gun control, the death penalty, and medical marijuana are described to volunteers, results tend to be accepted as unbiased and correct when they match existing beliefs. However, when results are counter to existing beliefs, they and the researcher are dismissed as biased (Robert MacCoun, cited in Aschwanden, 2010). Even researchers fall prey to this bias. Aschwanden (2010) reported a classic 1977 study in which experts were asked to perform a peer review of technical manuscripts which were identical except for the results sections. Reviewers gave more favorable reviews to papers that confirmed their views. Unfortunately, studies show that evidence alone is unlikely to change minds. People tend to believe that which they want to believe. Beliefs about what is true are very difficult to change, especially among those with a vested interest in the conclusions. In the case of sex offender treatment, those with vested interests include researchers who have published pro-treatment findings, sex offender treatment providers, treated sex offenders themselves, and often, in our experience, those charged with making release decisions about sex offenders.

One way evidence might overcome popular myths is through the personal stories of respected experts who acknowledge a change of mind. With respect to RCTs for sex offender treatment, Karl Hanson is probably the best known researcher to have concluded that sex offender treatment has been shown to be effective, for example. He recently stated:

> I, for one, have done enough meta-analyses of barely acceptable studies. It is time to counter the political resistance to random assignment studies by getting ATSA to endorse a position statement supporting their use. (K. Hanson, personal communication, 2010)

Hanson later followed this up by initiating a Task Force of the ATSA Research Committee recommending RCTs. In strongly supporting RCTs, the ATSA board then stated, "After 50 years of research, the field of sex offender treatment cannot, using generally accepted scientific standards, demonstrate conclusively that effective treatments are available for adult sex offenders" (ATSA, 2011b).

The ongoing reliance on weak inference in evaluating the effects of sex offender intervention entails unacceptable risks; interventions might actually have caused an increase in the risk of sex offenders compared to doing nothing. Because practitioners and the public have been prematurely assured that interventions have specific risk reduction effects, vigilance might be inappropriately relaxed. Interventions might have specific risk reduction effects so small (or null or inverse) that their cost cannot be justified, given the agreed-upon requirement that public funds be expended to achieve measureable benefit. There exists a further risk; that to the credibility of the sex offender treatment field. This credibility problem has been exacerbated by authorities urging, given the current evidence, rejection of the null hypothesis because strong evaluation involving experimental methods (that is, RCTs) is too difficult or uninformative, the effects of uncontrolled confounds cannot possibly be large enough to be problematic, relevant targets and effective techniques for intervention have already been identified, similar interventions are efficacious with other populations, other fields are just as bad, researchers never change their minds so that strong methods are pointless anyway, or those who advocate RCTs have not conducted one themselves and thus may be ignored. Disinterested observers will properly regard these as unpersuasive (see Lilienfeld, Lynn and Lohr, 2004, for cautionary demonstrations that rejecting strong evaluation research leads directly to the "pseudoscience" epithet).

How Could an RCT of Adult Sex Offender Treatment be Conducted?

In the last section of this chapter, we outline an RCT we believe is ethical and feasible for the evaluation of androgen disrupting therapy (ADT). Briefly, an intervention should be clearly based on an explicit, disconfirmable hypothesis about the causes of sex offender recidivism. An RCT comparing such an intervention to no treatment will be possible in some jurisdictions and should be undertaken there. An RCT comparing such an intervention to an alternative (treatment as usual, an equally intensive intervention clearly not implied by the causal hypothesis under evaluation) should be undertaken in other jurisdictions. Measurement of intermediate intervention targets expected, and not expected, to affect recidivism should be included. We readily acknowledge this work is more difficult than that appearing in our literature. Unfortunately, the quality (but by no means the quantity) of that work has been so low that no valid conclusions about treatment efficacy may be drawn; stronger methods are the only way forward. As discussed earlier, RCTs have been conducted with adolescent sex offenders and children with problem sexual behaviors. Such strong inference research must be conducted with adult sex offenders.

Incarcerated sex offenders deemed medically suitable ADT candidates would be invited to participate. Consenting candidates would be assigned at random to one of two groups. The treatment group would receive ADT (the particular form and drug to be determined before the study began) and be released earlier than they otherwise would. The control group would not receive ADT and be subject to ordinary release policies as usual. It has been argued by others that there is no ethical problem with offering a volunteering offender a choice between a longer sentence and a shorter sentence with ADT (Bailey and Greenberg, 1998) and we agree. To maximize the likelihood of detecting a treatment effect and to compare the long-term health outcomes, volunteering would include consent to long-term follow-up supervision. It is difficult to imagine how such a study could be double-blind. However, we suggest members of the control group be prescribed a non-ADT drug that has noticeable, but innocuous, effects. Additionally, the study would be strengthened if the effect of expectancy was examined by telling a random half of the offenders (but not their supervising parole officials) in each group that they were receiving a drug known scientifically to reduce severely or eliminate sex drive and thus is very likely to greatly reduce the probability of sexual recidivism, while the other half would be told that no one knows for sure the effect of the drug on recidivism.

Summary and Conclusions

Despite a large literature of individual studies, meta-analyses and commentaries saying that treatments have been shown to reduce risk among adult sex offenders, the currently available evidence is too weak to reject appropriate null hypotheses that such treatments have caused no reductions in recidivism. The findings from the strongest studies (a few RCTs) provide no evidence of treatment effectiveness. The most parsimonious interpretation of findings from weaker designs is that pre-treatment differences and other forms of selection bias are responsible for apparent treatment effects. Other fields have shown that RCTs have demonstrated harmful effects of treatments erroneously thought to be beneficial based on weaker evaluation designs. Various fallacious arguments against conducting RCTs should be rejected. RCTs evaluating the effectiveness of treatment for adult sex offenders can be practically and ethically feasible. Over the past 60 years, the field of sex offender intervention exhibits change where there should be stability; instead of a well-established foundation of effective therapeutic techniques, particular treatments go in and out of fashion in the absence of acceptable evidence as to efficacy. Moreover, the field exhibits stasis where progress should have occurred; the empirical basis underpinning the effectiveness of sex offender intervention, while more voluminous, is negligibly more informative or persuasive now than it was many decades ago. Hypotheses, suggestions and advice aside, essentially nothing is known (in the sense of empirically verified) about which therapeutic or supervisory techniques are effective for which targets in which types of sex offenders. These ongoing failures carry the risk of avoidable harm in the form of inadvertently increasing recidivism and wasting resources. There is the additional risk of harm to the credibility of the field in general; hostile observers may find sufficient basis to label the field of sex offender treatment as pseudoscience. Credibility, once lost, will be difficult to regain. Research entailing strong inference methods entails the field's only chance for progress where such has been absent. We provide an example of a study consistent with such an approach. Until better research is conducted, however, scientific principles do not entitle researchers and clinicians, fervent desires for the possibility of effective treatment notwithstanding, to assume it either in the aggregate for sex offenders or in the case of any individual offender.

Notes

1 Hanson *et al.* (2009) performed a great service to the field in ensuring that essentially no relevant studies were overlooked, hence our focus on this invaluable systematic review.
2 Nothing about Bayesian reasoning makes it impermissible to say that any positive effect size, no matter how small, is worthwhile. But, given that public resources are limited, it probably makes little sense to expend vast sums to achieve tiny positive effects on public safety when much larger effects are available (for example, Lipsey, Landenberger and Wilson, 2007).
3 We acknowledge here that the Social Therapy Unit study was not an RCT, and thus could be classified as a "weak" design similar to those we criticize here. Nevertheless, it was at least an empirical attempt to evaluate the program compared to the completely non-empirical evaluations conducted by others. Had the results been positive (as we had expected), it would have been relatively easy for critics to argue that the results were due to uncontrolled differences between the groups. However, it is more difficult to argue that the crossover results obtained masked a true positive effect for psychopaths because of uncontrolled factors.

References

Aschwanden, C. (2010) "Convincing the public to accept new medical guidelines," *Miller-McCune*, http://miller-mccune.com/health/convincing-the-public-to-accept-new-medical-guidelines-11422 (accessed August 25, 2012).

ATSA (Association for the Treatment of Sexual Abusers) (2011a) Ten Things You Should Know about Sex Offenders and Treatment, http://www.atsa.com/ten-things-you-should-know-about-sex-offenders-and-treatment (accessed August 25, 2012).

ATSA (Association for the Treatment of Sexual Abusers) (2011b) Statement Supporting the Use of Randomized Control Trials for the Evaluation of Sexual Offender Treatment, http://www.atsa.com/statement-supporting-use-randomized-control-trials-evaluation-sexual-offender-treatment (accessed August 25, 2012).

ATSA (Association for the Treatment of Sexual Abusers) (2012) Reducing Sexual Abuse Through Treatment and Intervention with Abusers, http://www.atsa.com/reducing-sexual-abuse-through-treatment-and-intervention-abusers (accessed August 25, 2012).

Bailey, M. and Greenberg, A.S. (1998) "The science and ethics of castration: lessons from the Morse case," *Northwestern University Law Review* 92, 1225–1246.

Balluerka, N., Gomez, J. and Hidalgo, D. (2005) "The controversy over null hypothesis significance testing revisited," *Methodology* 1, 55–70.

Barker, E.T. (1980) "The Penetanguishene program: a personal review," in H. Toch (ed.), *Therapeutic Communities in Corrections.* New York: Praeger, pp. 73–81.

Berk, R.A. (2005) "Randomized experiments as the bronze standard," *Journal of Experimental Criminology* 1, 417–433.

Berliner, S. and Saunders, B.E. (1996) "Treating fear and anxiety in sexually abused children: results of a controlled 2-year follow-up study," *Child Maltreatment* 1, 294–309.

Bonder, B.L., Walker, C.E. and Berliner, L. (1999) *Children with Sexual Behavior Problems: Assessment and Treatment – Final Report* (Grant No. 90-CA-1469). Washington, DC: Department of Health and Human Services, National Clearinghouse on Child Abuse and Neglect.

Bonta, J. and Andrews, D.A. (2007) *Risk-Need-Responsivity Model for Offender Assessment and Rehabilitation. Report No. 2007-06.* Ottawa: Public Safety Canada.

Borduin, C.M., Henggeler, S.W., Blaske, D.M. and Stein, R. (1990) "Multisystemic treatment of adolescent sexual offenders," *International Journal of Offender Therapy and Comparative Criminology* 34, 105–113.

Borduin, C.M., Schaeffer, C.M. and Heilblum, N. (2009) "A randomized clinical trial of multisystemic therapy with juvenile sex offenders: effects on youth social ecology and criminal activity," *Journal of Consulting and Clinical Psychology* 77, 26–37.

Bradford, J.M. (2000) "The treatment of sexual deviation using a pharmacological approach," *Journal of Sex Research* 37, 248–257.

Butler, B., Long, J. and Rowsell, P. (1977) "Evaluative study of the social therapy unit." Unpublished report to the Ombudsman of Ontario.

Canada (1977) *Proceedings of the Subcommittee on the Penitentiary System in Canada. Standing Committee on Justice and Legal Affairs. House of Commons, Second Session of the Thirtieth Parliament.* March 8.

Cohen, J.A., Deblinger, E., Mannarino, A.P. and Steer, R.A. (2004) "Multisite, randomized controlled trial for children with sexual-abuse related PTSD symptoms," *Journal of the American Academy of Child and Adolescent Psychiatry* 43, 393–402.

Cohen, J.A. and Mannarino, A.P. (1996) "Treatment outcome study for sexually abused preschool children: initial findings," *Journal of the American Academy of Child and Adolescent Psychiatry* 35, 42–50.

Cohen, J.A. and Mannarino, A.P. (1998) "Interventions for sexually abused children: initial treatment outcome findings," *Child Maltreatment* 3, 17–26.

Collaborative Outcome Data Committee (2007a) *Sexual Offender Treatment Outcome Research: CODC Guidelines for Evaluation. Part 1: Introduction and Overview.* Ottawa: Public Safety Canada, http://www.publicsafety.gc.ca/res/cor/rep/_fl/CODC_07_e.pdf (accessed August 25, 2012).

Collaborative Outcome Data Committee (2007b) *Sexual Offender Treatment Outcome Research: CODC Guidelines for Evaluation. Part 2: CODC Guidelines.* Ottawa: Public Safety Canada, http://www.publicsafety.gc.ca/res/cor/rep/codc_200703-eng.aspx (accessed August 25, 2012).

Deblinger, E., Stauffer, L.B. and Steer, R.A. (2001) "Comparative efficacies of supportive and cognitive behavioral group therapies for young children who have been sexually abused and their nonoffending mothers," *Child Maltreatment* 6, 332–343.

Dienes, Z. (2011) "Bayesian versus orthodox statistics: which side are you on?," *Perspectives on Psychological Science* 6, 274–290.

Everly, G.S., Flannery, R.B. and Mitchell, J.T. (2000) "Critical incident stress management (CISM): a review of the literature," *Aggression and Violent Behavior* 5, 23–40.

Farrington, D.P. and Welsh, B.C. (2005) "Randomized experiments in criminology, what have we learned in the last two decades?," *Journal of Experimental Criminology* 1, 9–38.

Gottfredson, D.C. (2010) "Deviancy training: understanding how preventive interventions harm," *Journal of Experimental Criminology* 6, 229–243.

Hanson, R.K., Bourgon, G., Helmus, L. and Hodgson, S. (2009) "The principles of effective correctional treatment also apply to sexual offenders," *Criminal Justice and Behavior* 36, 865–891.

Hanson, R.K. and Bussière, M.T. (1998) "Predicting relapse: a meta-analysis of sexual offender recidivism studies," *Journal of Consulting and Clinical Psychology* 66, 348–362.

Hanson, R.K. and Morton-Bourgon, K.E. (2009) "The accuracy of recidivism risk assessments for sexual offenders: a meta-analysis of 118 prediction studies," *Psychological Assessment* 1, 1–21.

Jones, M. (1956) "The concept of a therapeutic community," *American Journal of Psychiatry* 112, 647–650.

Jones, M. (1968) *Social Psychiatry in Practice*. Harmondsworth: Penguin.

Kanazawa, S. (2003) "Why productivity fades with age: the crime-genius connection," *Journal of Research in Personality* 37, 257–272.

Kim, S.Y., Frank, S., Holloway, R., et al. (2005) "Science and ethics of sham surgery," *Archive of Neurology* 62, 1357–1360.

Letourneau, E.J., Henggeler, S.W., Borduin, C.M., et al. (2009) "Multisystemic therapy for juvenile sexual offenders: 1-year results from a randomized effectiveness trial," *Journal of Family Psychology* 23, 89–102.

Lilienfeld, S.O. (2007) "Psychological treatments that cause harm," *Perspectives on Psychological Science* 2, 53–70.

Lilienfeld, S.O., Lynn, S.J. and Lohr, S.M. (2004) *Science and Pseudoscience in Clinical Psychology*. New York: Guilford Press.

Lipsey, M.W., Landenberger, N.A. and Wilson, S.J. (2007) "Effects of cognitive-behavioral programs for criminal offenders," *Campbell Systematic Reviews* 6, 1–27.

Litz, B.T., Gray, M.J., Bryant, R.A. and Adler, A.B. (2002) "Early intervention or trauma: current status and future directions," *Clinical Psychology Science Practice* 9, 112–134.

Lösel, F. and Schmucker, M. (2005) "The effectiveness of treatment for sexual offenders: a comprehensive meta-analysis," *Journal of Experimental Criminology* 1, 117–146.

Marques, J.K., Wiederanders, M., Day, D.M., et al. (2005) "Effects of a relapse prevention program on sexual recidivism: final results from California's sex offender treatment and evaluation project (SOTEP)," *Sexual Abuse: A Journal of Research and Treatment* 17, 79–107.

Marshall, W.L. and Marshall, L.E. (2007) "The utility of the random controlled trial for evaluating sexual offender treatment: the gold standard or an inappropriate strategy?," *Sexual Abuse: A Journal of Research and Treatment* 19, 175–191.

McCord, J. (1978) "A thirty-year follow-up of treatment effects," *American Psychologist* 33, 284–289.

McCord, J. (2002) *Precursors of Violence*. Toronto: University of Toronto.

McGrath, R.J., Hoke, S.E. and Vojtisek, J.E. (1998) "Cognitive-behavioral treatment of sex offenders," *Criminal Justice and Behavior* 25, 203–225.

Moseley, J.B., O'Malley, K., Peterson, N.J., *et al.* (2002) "A controlled trial for arthroscopic surgery for osteoarthritis of the knee," *New England Journal of Medicine* 347, 81–88.

Nunes, K.L. and Cortoni, F. (2008) "Dropout from sex-offender treatment and dimensions of risk of sexual recidivism," *Criminal Justice and Behavior* 35, 24–33.

Olanow, C.W., Goetz, C.G., Kordower, J.H., *et al.* (2003) "A double-blind controlled trial of bilateral fetal nigral transplantation in Parkinson's disease," *Annals of Neurology* 54, 403–414.

Olver, M.E. and Wong, S.C.P. (2009) "Therapeutic responses of psychopathic sexual offenders: treatment attrition, therapeutic change, and long-term recidivism," *Journal of Consulting and Clinical Psychology* 77, 328–336.

Petrosino, A.J., Boruch, R.F., Farrington, D.P., *et al.* (2003) "Toward evidence-based criminology and criminal justice: systematic reviews, the Campbell Collaboration, and the Crime and Justice Group," *International Journal of Comparative Criminology* 3, 42–61.

Quinsey, V.L., Rice, M.E. and Harris, G.T. (1995) "The actuarial prediction of sexual recidivism," *Journal of Interpersonal Violence* 10, 85–105.

Rice, M.E. and Harris, G.T. (2011) "Is androgen deprivation therapy effective in the treatment of sex offenders?," *Psychology, Public Policy, and Law* 17, 315–332.

Rice, M.E., Harris, G.T. and Cormier, C.A. (1992) "An evaluation of a maximum security therapeutic community for psychopaths and other mentally disordered offenders," *Law and Human Behavior* 6, 399–412.

Romero, J.J. and Williams, L.M. (1985) "Recidivism among convicted sex offenders: a 10-year follow-up study," *Federal Probation* 49, 58–64.

Rose, S.C., Bisson, J., Churchill, R. and Wessely, S. (2002) "Psychological debriefing for preventing post-traumatic stress disorder (PTSD)," *Cochrane Database of Systematic Reviews* 2002, 2, Art. No.: CD000560.

Rösler, A. and Witztum, E. (2000) "Pharmacotherapy of paraphilias in the next millennium," *Behavioral Sciences and the Law* 18, 43–56.

Seager, J.A., Jellicoe, D. and Dhaliwal, G.K. (2004) "Refusers, dropouts, and completers: measuring sex offender treatment efficacy," *International Journal of Offender Therapy and Comparative Criminology* 48, 600–612.

Seto, M.C., Marques, J.K., Harris, G.T. *et al.*(2008) "Good science and progress in sex offender treatment are intertwined: a response to Marshall and Marshall (2007)," *Sexual Abuse: A Journal of Research and Treatment* 20, 247–255.

Shadish, W.R., Galindo, R., Wong, V.C., *et al.* (2011) "A randomized experiment comparing random and cutoff-based assignment," *Psychological Methods* 16, 179–191.

Ward, T., Collie, R. and Bourke, P. (2009) "Models of offender rehabilitation: the good lives model and the risk-need-responsivity model," in T. Ward, R.M. Collie and P. Bourke, *Assessment and Treatment of Sex Offenders: A Handbook*. Chichester: John Wiley & Sons, Ltd, pp. 293–310.

Weisburd, D. (2010) "Justifying the use of non-experimental methods and disqualifying the use of randomized controlled trials: challenging folklore in evaluation research in crime and justice," *Journal of Experimental Criminology* 6, 209–227.

Weisman, R. (1995) "Reflections on the Oak Ridge experiment with mentally disordered offenders, 1965–1968," *International Journal of Law and Psychiatry* 18, 265–290.

Wetzels, R., Matzke, D., Lee, M.D., *et al.* (2011) "Statistical evidence in experimental psychology: an empirical comparison using 855 t tests," *Perspectives on Psychological Science* 6, 291–298.

14

Ethical Issues in Treating Sexual Offenders

Applying Empirically Based Process Features of Treatment Delivery

W.L. Marshall and L.E. Marshall

Introduction

One of the most important ethical issues involved in providing treatment for sexual offenders is the requirement that the treatment be state-of-the-art, meaning that treatment must be based on what current evidence indicates is the most effective approach. This is particularly important not only in terms of therapists' responsibility to the offenders but also given the often devastating effects on the victims of these crimes (Conte and Schuerman, 1987; Koss and Harvey, 1991). Among other things programs must adhere to the empirically derived principles of effective offender treatment (Andrews, 2001; Andrews and Bonta, 2006). These principles are described as: risk, needs and responsivity. The *risk principle* demands that more intensive treatment should be employed with the highest risk offenders. The *needs principle* requires treatment to address criminogenic needs (that is, those deficits shown by research to predict re-offending). The *responsivity principle* has a "general" and a "specific" application. The general principle demands that treatment should be an application of the most effective model of therapy but also that treatment should be delivered by skilled and trained therapists (Andrews and Bonta, 2006). The specific principle requires therapists to adjust their delivery to the unique features of each client (for example, his learning ability, his personality style, and his socio-economic perspective).

Evidence suggests that some form of cognitive behavior therapy (CBT) conducted in groups is the most effective approach (Hanson *et al.*, 2002; Lösel and Schmucker, 2005), although variable results are evident across CBT programs for sexual offenders. Some of this variability can be attributed to the differences across programs in the targets that are addressed, which are not always criminogenic, and in the procedures used to modify treatment targets, which are not always evidence-based.

The Wiley-Blackwell Handbook of Legal and Ethical Aspects of Sex Offender Treatment and Management, First Edition. Edited by Karen Harrison and Bernadette Rainey.
© 2013 John Wiley & Sons, Ltd. Published 2013 by John Wiley & Sons, Ltd.

However, the evidence indicates that the critical factors influencing the effectiveness of treatment concern the way in which it is delivered. No matter how well the treatment targets and procedures are supported by evidence, unless therapists display the appropriate characteristics, form the appropriate alliance with the clients, and establish the appropriate group climate, treatment is unlikely to be effective.

For treatment programs targeting sexual offenders to be ethically sound, they must not only adhere to the principles of effective treatment they must also have therapists who are sufficiently well-trained and competent, to be able to deliver treatment in the most effective way. Andrews and Bonta (2006) have shown that treatment will be ineffective unless therapists delivering programs for offenders are well-trained and have the necessary skills. As will be shown, it is the quality of the delivery of treatment that accounts for the majority of the observed benefits in programs for all types of clients including sexual offenders.

Factors in the Delivery of Treatment

Clinicians have long held that the way treatment for any psychological disorder is delivered is far more important than the procedures used to address the problem. Indeed, as early as the 1930s it was claimed that the interaction between the therapist and the client was the critical factor in treatment (Sterba, 1934). Over the years a variety of eminent clinicians have stressed the importance of the therapeutic alliance in achieving the goals of treatment while assigning a minor role to procedures (Frank, 1971; Frankl, 1978; Kohut, 1990; Rogers, 1961; Strupp and Hadley, 1979; Yalom, 1980).

Contrary to this view the nascent behavior therapists of the 1960s and early 1970s seemed to suggest that so long as empirically based procedures were employed, treatment would be effective (Ullmann and Krasner, 1965). Even the evolution of behavior therapy into CBT did not immediately alter this point of view (Kazdin, 1978). Much of the literature on CBT, as applied to a variety of disorders, continued to focus on the detailed description of procedures and their effects. This continues to the present day, although there is a growing body of evidence generated by CBT therapists and researchers demonstrating the powerful influence of what are called process features of treatment (Burns and Auerback, 1996; Keijsers, Schaap and Hoogduin, 2000). These process issues cover three aspects of the delivery of treatment: first, characteristics of the therapist; second, the therapeutic alliance; and third, the therapeutic climate of group treatment.

From the early days of modern interventions, numerous non-behavioral therapists claimed that for treatment to be effective the person delivering the program had to display certain characteristics. Rogers (1957), in particular, held that to be effective, therapists had to display genuineness, warmth and empathy toward the clients. In fact, he declared that these characteristics, along with unconditional regard for the patient, were the exclusive means by which benefits were generated. Other early clinicians (for example, Frank, 1973; Frankl, 1978; Strupp, 1982; Yalom, 1980) pointed to the importance of the quality of the alliance between the therapist and client, indicating that it was the critical factor. Presumably these two factors are linked. It seems unlikely that the appropriate alliance will develop unless the client trusts the therapist and client trust is most likely to be engendered by a therapist who is genuine, warm and empathic.

More recent research indicates that the formation of an effective bond between the client and therapist is the critical factor, rather than simply the presence of good therapist qualities (Kanfer and Goldstein, 1991; Luborsky, Barber and Crits-Christoph, 1990; Marziali and Alexander, 1991). In fact, therapists often judge themselves to have displayed qualities that are not confirmed by their clients' judgments (Free *et al.*, 1985), and it is the clients' judgments that predict successful outcome (Orlinsky, Grawe and Parks, 1994). Thus, in evaluating therapists' characteristics we might sensibly ask the clients for their appraisals or have an independent judge determine the presence of the desired features of the therapist. As we will see, both these approaches have been utilized in the examination of the critically effective features of sexual offender therapists.

Group climate refers to various aspects of the way in which the clients (and the therapist) in group therapy function as a unit. Moos (1986) has developed, based on extensive research, a measure of group climate that appraises several features and his scale has been used quite extensively in evaluating various types of groups (for example, therapy groups and other types of training groups). Moos's measure evaluates 10 features of groups: cohesiveness, expressiveness, leader support, leader control, independence, task-oriented, self-discovery, anger and aggression, order and organization, and innovation. He provides normative data for each of these features.

In this chapter we will first briefly survey the findings on these process variables in the general clinical literature where treatment aims at modifying various non-offending Axis 1 and Axis 2 disorders. We will then describe in some detail the findings relevant to sexual offender treatment.

Results from the General Literature

Much of this literature has focused on treatment delivered by single therapists for individual clients (that is, one-on-one therapy). While this tells us important things relevant to our present concerns, particularly about the important characteristics of the therapist and the formation of an effective alliance, it obviously does not address those features of groups that influence change. There are, however, some studies of group processes in the general literature that are informative and it is clear that the quality of the group climate is dependent upon the characteristics of the therapist. Since sexual offender treatment is typically delivered in groups, observations indicating how to maximize the effectiveness of group therapy are particularly relevant.

Therapist characteristics

Researchers have examined the role of therapist characteristics in producing treatment benefits across various disorders and across various approaches to therapy. The bulk of these research findings began to emerge from the 1970s onward (see Marshall *et al.*,

2003a) with a more recent focus on these issues in CBT treatment (see Schaap *et al.*, 1993). Orlinsky and his colleagues (Orlinsky, Grawe and Parks, 1994; Orlinsky and Howard, 1986) demonstrated the importance of the therapist qualities of empathy and warmth. Just as Rogers (1957) had suggested, the presence of these two qualities powerfully predicted the benefits derived from treatment. Similarly Egan (1998) showed that another of Rogers's (1957) proposed factors, therapist genuineness, was vital to achieving benefits from treatment. Other reports reveal the importance of a variety of therapist characteristics, including: displays of interest in the client (Lambert, 1983), support (Elliott, 1985), therapist confidence (McGuff, Gitlin and Enderlin, 1996) and respect (Strupp, 1980). Features more typical of behavior therapists and CBT therapists have also been shown to be important characteristics of effective therapists. For example, an encouraging or rewarding style (de Ruiter *et al.*, 1989) and some degree of directiveness (Alexander *et al.*, 1976; Mintz, Luborsky and Auerbach, 1971) have been shown to produce a constructive alliance and better outcomes.

Although it is only recently that writers (for example, Greenberg and Pavio, 1997; Kennedy-Moore and Watson, 1999; Saunders, 1999) have begun to emphasize the importance of eliciting emotion during therapy, in the early 1980s researchers had already shown that therapists who were emotionally responsive to their clients had far better outcomes than did those who were unresponsive (Cooley and Lajoy, 1980; Orlinsky and Howard, 1986). Flexibility by the therapist in response to their clients has also been shown to be essential to generating positive benefits from treatment (Ringler, 1977; Schaap *et al.*, 1993). This demand for flexibility is almost identical to what Andrews (2001) described as the "specific responsivity principle" which likewise refers to the need to adjust the delivery of treatment to the unique features of each client. All these observations of careful research have been replicated in studies examining the views of clients (Saunders, 1999).

Of course some therapist characteristics impede the achievement of treatment goals. For example, Lieberman, Yalom and Miles (1973) showed that a confrontational style by the therapist prevented clients from deriving benefits from treatment. This use of the term "confrontation," and the way we will use the term in this chapter, refers to an aggressive, demanding and somewhat demeaning way of challenging the client's view of various issues. Not surprisingly these same researchers found that angry responses by the therapist and behaviors indicating rejection of the client or his/her views also blocked the achievement of treatment goals (Lieberman, Yalom and Miles, 1973).

The above-mentioned therapist characteristics that facilitate benefits being derived from treatment, also significantly reduce drop-outs and minimize the number of clients who fail to comply with treatment requirements (Bennun *et al.*, 1986; Heppner and Clairborn, 1989; Horvath, 2000; Saunders, 1999). These are important observations because sexual offender treatment drop-outs (Abel *et al.*, 1988; Browne, Foreman and Middleton, 1998; Marques *et al.*, 1994) and those offenders who fail to attain the goals of therapy as a result of noncompliance (Marques *et al.*, 2005) have either the same poor outcome as untreated offenders, or in some cases a worse outcome.

Therapeutic relationship

As we noted, the formation of an effective alliance between the therapist and the client is largely a function of the display of the appropriate characteristics by the therapist. However, the attainment of the goals of treatment is facilitated primarily by the quality of the alliance (Martin, Garske and Davis, 2000). The findings reported in the previous section, where research was focused on the qualities of the treatment provider, were likely the result of these qualities producing an effective alliance. As we saw, clients do not always identify the qualities in their therapists that the therapists believe they are displaying. In the majority of the above studies, judgments about the therapist' qualities were made by independent judges. It appears that when these judgments are made independently and they identify positive qualities, then the alliance is very likely to be good and treatment will be effective (Horvath and Symonds, 1991).

The recent focus of research has been more on the client–therapist relationship than on the qualities of the therapist (Martin, Garske and Davis, 2000: Norcross, 2002; Samstag *et al.*, 1998; Tyron and Kane, 1990, 1993). These studies all show that it is the quality of the therapeutic relationship that predicts positive outcomes. Indeed it has been argued that this relationship is far more important (and thus so are the therapist characteristics) than are the procedures used to change behaviors and cognitions (McLeod, 1990). In confirmation of this suggestion, Norcross (2002) found that the alliance accounted for 30% of the benefits derived from treatment while the use of specific techniques generated only 15% of these positive changes. Others have found similar superior effects resulting from the alliance than from procedures (Martin, Garske and Davis, 2000; Morgan *et al.*, 1982). Several studies have also shown that a good quality alliance reduces drop-out rates (Beckham, 1992; Piper *et al.*, 1999; Samstag *et al.*, 1998; Tyron and Kane, 1990, 1993) which, as noted, is a particularly important benefit.

Group climate

Although most treatment approaches with the majority of Axis 1 and Axis 2 disorders involve individual therapy, there is evidence suggesting that group treatment for these disorders may be more effective (Bednar and Kaul, 1994; McRoberts, Burlingame and Hoag, 1998). Yalom (1995), for example, claims that the evidence on the benefits of group therapy is so compelling that researchers should focus on determining the factors that maximize its effectiveness rather than continue to employ and evaluate individual therapy. Just as we saw in our review of the influence of the therapeutic alliance, research on group treatment indicates that the quality of the group climate accounts for more of the derived benefits than does the implementation of any set of procedures.

Earlier we suggested that it was the presence of positive therapist characteristics that resulted in an effective alliance. The same appears to be true in the creation of the most effective group climate. Both Karterud (1988) and Nichols and Taylor (1975) demonstrated that highly effective treatment groups had leaders with the characteristics identified earlier as those that facilitated the achievement of a good alliance and that generated the best results. Studies using Moos's (1986) scale for measuring the aspects of group treatment, have found that the quality of the group climate is essential to achieving the desired treatment changes. Braaten (1989), for example, found that it was only when groups scored high on Moos's subscale of "cohesiveness" that they produced benefits, and Budman *et al.* (1993) showed that the cohesion of groups significantly influenced the degree of participation and predicted the degree to which clients completed between-sessions practice.

Results with sexual offenders

The responsivity principle derived by Andrews, Bonta and Hoge (1990) from an extensive meta-analysis of treatment for offenders has, as we saw, two components: first, general responsivity which not only requires treatment providers to employ demonstrably powerful change strategies but also that therapists must be selected for having, and being trained in, the qualities described in the previous section; and second, specificity responsivity which demands that treatment be adjusted to each client's unique features. Hanson *et al.* (2009) showed that the principles derived by Andrews, Bonta and Hoge from their meta-analysis, also applied to the treatment of sexual offenders. Adjusting treatment delivery to meet the needs of specific responsivity clearly requires a skilled and sensitive therapist. In addition, Dowden and Andrews (2004) demonstrated that treatment benefits with offenders were only apparent in those offender programs where therapists had these requisite skills. Consistent with this, Hanson *et al.* (2009) found that with sexual offenders, the responsivity principle accounted for most of the observed benefits from treatment. From these various studies it is clear that a skilled therapist, with the qualities identified in our review of the general clinical literature (for example, empathy, warmth, rewardingness, genuineness and respect), is required to maximize treatment gains as well as to increase compliance and reduce drop-outs. We now turn to what the evidence with sexual offenders tells us about these issues.

Results from the Sexual Offender Literature

Therapist qualities

We mentioned earlier that judgments of treatment providers about their own therapeutic style are not always matched by appraisals of their clients (Free *et al.*, 1985). Therefore, research addressing therapist features that influence outcome should be based either on evaluations by the clients or on evaluations by independent judges. Drapeau and his colleagues (Drapeau, 2005; Drapeau *et al.*, 2004) had sexual offenders indicate what they believed were the most helpful elements of the treatment in which they were involved. These offenders stated quite clearly that the way the therapist delivered the program was the crucial factor, although they did say the specific procedures employed in treatment were also helpful. Qualities such as empathy, warmth and genuineness were viewed by the offenders as the most significantly helpful features of the therapists' style and they said that the alliance the therapist formed with them was critical. When the offenders perceived the therapist as lacking these skills, or when they saw him/her as being unsupportive, they disengaged from active participation in treatment.

In two studies of sexual offender treatment, Marshall and colleagues (Marshall *et al.*, 2003b, 2002) rated the presence of various therapist qualities from videotapes made in treatment programs run in various English prisons. First, Marshall *et al.* (2003b) established that ratings conducted independently by three trained researchers met criteria for interrater reliability, a determination that was repeated throughout these studies to ensure consistency. Marshall *et al.* (2002) then examined the relationship between ratings of the therapist qualities and changes evident on a large battery of pre- and post-treatment tests. What they found was that the presence of four therapist qualities was powerfully predictive of changes on all of the tests measuring treatment gains. These four qualities were empathy, warmth, directiveness and rewardingness. Empathy was defined as the capacity to identify emotional issues in others, to be able to adopt the other person's perspective, and to convey sympathy for the other person. Warmth identified a calm, friendly and compassionate response toward others, while directiveness was deemed to be evident when the therapist offered suggestions for change or provided guidance to clients in moving toward the goals of treatment. To be judged as rewarding the therapist had to encourage participation and reward each small step toward the targets of treatment.

These four therapist features were found to account for between 30% and 60% of the magnitude of changes on the various measures in the battery evaluating treatment benefits. In fact in most cases the presence of the four identified therapist qualities explained over 40% of the positive changes. Note that this reveals a greater influence of therapist characteristics on the benefits derived from sexual offender treatment than is true for the treatment of other Axis 1 and Axis 2 disorders. Presumably this is because sexual offenders, unlike other clients, typically present as reluctant and somewhat suspicious. Thus therapists providing treatment for sexual offenders need to be more motivational in their approach. As Miller and Rollnick (1991, 2002) point out in their classic texts, to be motivational, therapists must display the features identified as crucial in Marshall *et al.*'s studies.

Marshall *et al.* (2003b) also showed that a confrontational style on the part of the therapist resulted in either no gains or, in some cases, poorer performance on the tests after treatment. The general clinical literature indicates the same effects for a confrontational style. In addition, in Drapeau's studies (Drapeau, 2005; Drapeau *et al.*, 2004) sexual offenders said they disengaged from active participation in treatment when they perceived the therapist as confrontational. Interestingly, Drapeau's clients said they wished to be challenged, so it was not that they wanted to avoid examining difficult issues, but rather that they wanted to be challenged in a respectful and supportive manner. Other studies examining sexual offenders in treatment have similarly found negative effects (typically reduced participation and reduced treatment gains) when the therapist was confrontational in his/her challenges (Beech and Fordham, 1997; Harkins and Beech, 2007; Hudson, 2005; Williams, 2004). There is, therefore, substantial evidence indicating that therapists should avoid a confrontational style with sexual offenders.

Group climate

Beech has led the way in evaluating the group climate of sexual offender treatment. He and his colleagues (Beech and Fordham, 1997; Beech and Hamilton-Giachritsis, 2005) applied Moos's (1986) Group Climate Scale (GCS) to seven prison-based sexual offender group programs and 12 community-based group programs. In both studies they found that scores on two of the GCS subscales were significantly correlated with changes on a variety of measures of the targets of treatment. Scores on both the Cohesiveness subscale and the subscale assessing Expressiveness predicted treatment gains. Cohesiveness describes how well group participants bond with each other and how well they work together and support one another. Expressiveness is evident when group members are actively involved in discussions about themselves or others, and when they are emotionally expressive. On this latter point, Pfäfflin *et al.* (2005) also showed that treatment gains with sexual offenders were only initiated when sexual offenders expressed an understanding of the issues that was accompanied by emotional expressiveness.

Clark and Erooga (1994) have also demonstrated that establishing a cohesive group results in greater engagement in treatment among sexual offenders and leads them to be more hopeful about their future. There is clear evidence from the general clinical literature that engendering hope in clients during treatment results in significant reductions in their problematic behaviors (Snyder, 1994; Snyder, Rand and Sigmon, 2005) and we have shown that increases in hope among sexual offenders as a result of treatment are associated with reductions in re-offending (Marshall *et al.*, 2008). Thus, therapists who engender cohesiveness and expressiveness in their group will generate greater engagement in treatment and increase hope for the future, resulting in more positive changes in sexual offenders.

Other process factors

There are no doubt many other factors involved in the delivery of treatment that influence outcome, but we cannot cover them all. We will discuss just two strategies that treatment providers should adopt if they are to ensure that sexual offenders are fully engaged and thereby reduce their chances of re-offending: first, therapists should be motivational, and second, they should focus on the offenders' strengths. A motivational style of delivering treatment has been outlined by Miller and Rollnick (1991, 2002). They point out that motivation is not a fixed feature of a person but rather fluctuates according to a variety of internal and external influences. Miller, Benefield and Tonigan (1993) have shown this motivational approach to be effective with substance abusers and it has been suggested (Garland and Dougher, 1991; Kear-Colwell and Pollack, 1997) that such an approach is particularly suitable for sexual offenders since they characteristically present as unmotivated or hesitant about entering treatment.

Mann (1996; Mann and Rollnick, 1996) has demonstrated the value of a motivational style with sexual offenders, both in engaging them and in reducing their future risk. She (Mann and Webster, 2002) observed that many sexual offenders refused an offer of treatment despite acknowledging that they had a problem. Her examination of these men revealed that it was their belief about what treatment involved that resulted in their refusal. These offenders said they believed treatment would attack them about their past and would focus exclusively on an analysis of their crimes; what they wanted, these offenders said, was treatment that would give them a better life. The first phase of our treatment program (Marshall *et al.*, 2011) is entirely directed toward motivating the clients to engage effectively in treatment. In this initial phase we indicate to the offenders that the goals of treatment are to equip them with the skills, attitudes and self-confidence necessary to help them build a better life. We tell them that successfully achieving the goal of a better life will necessarily reduce their risk to re-offend. Our outcome data reported in our book (Marshall *et al.*, 2011) support this view.

Miller's motivational approach involves working collaboratively with clients. In Drapeau's (2005) study the sexual offenders indicated that they worked more effectively when the therapist involved them in all the decisions about treatment. Mann and Shingler (2006) have outlined the ways in which therapists can work collaboratively with sexual offenders not only in treatment but also when scoring risk assessment instruments. Working collaboratively indicates a respect for the client that is not apparent when programs are simply imposed on sexual offenders; as noted earlier, these offenders wish to be treated with respect (Drapeau, 2005) and respectful therapists more effectively achieve the goals of treatment (Strupp, 1980).

Finally, we (Marshall *et al.*, 2011) have attempted to persuade therapists working with sexual offenders to adopt the strategies embodied in the nascent "positive psychology" approach to treatment (Linley and Joseph, 2004; Snyder and Lopez, 2005) which is essentially strength-based. Positive psychology rejects the deficit model that was prevalent until recently in the assessment and treatment of psychological problems (for a clear statement of, and criticisms of, the deficit model, see Seligman, 2002; Seligman and Csikszentmihalyi, 2000). The change in emphasis adopted by advocates of positive psychology is to focus on the client's current strengths in order to facilitate building new strengths in the areas of present dysfunctions (Hodges and Clifton, 2004).

Acknowledging strengths in clients runs counter to the practice of most current treatment programs for sexual offenders where there is an almost exclusive focus on deficiencies and unnecessary attention to the details of the offense, and where pre- and post-treatment assessments target only deficits. Unfortunately research with sexual offenders has mostly ignored an examination of their possible strengths. Even the ability of sexual offenders to resist opportunities to offend has been ignored and yet child molesters, for example, must necessarily be exposed to numerous opportunities to offend that they apparently do not act on. Why they are able on some occasions to resist these opportunities has not been investigated but if researchers were to change their concerns from deficits to strengths, then questions such as these might be answered to the benefit of designing more effective treatment.

Conclusions

There are many ways in which the delivery of treatment for sexual offenders can be made maximally effective. Clearly the way in which treatment is delivered is a critical factor, as is the cohesiveness and expressiveness of the groups. The focus of treatment on motivating offenders, working collaboratively with them, and concentrating on current strengths and on building other strengths, is also, we would argue, crucial to generating treatment benefits. Since there is evidence that all these features of treatment enhance effectiveness by soliciting the full engagement of offenders throughout the course of treatment, then ethically responsible therapists should adopt all these strategies. We have attempted to integrate all these features into our strength-based program and our (Marshall *et al.*, 2011) follow-up data encourage the belief that such an approach maximizes positive treatment outcomes. The examination of re-offense data on 535 sexual offenders treated in our program and released for 8.4 years (minimum five years, maximum 17 years) revealed a sexual re-offense rate of 5.6% against an expected rate (based on actuarial assessments) of 23.8%. Our motivational approach resulted in 96.2% of all available sexual offenders entering treatment from which only 4.2% dropped out. The majority of drop-outs resulted from factors beyond their or our control (such as death, deportation, parole release, or expiry of sentence). Clearly on all relevant issues our motivational, strength-based approach is successful. Other authors (Ayland and West, 2006; Beech and Print, 2008; Bremer, 2006; Ward, Mann and Gannon, 2007) have also advocated a change in sexual offender treatment to emphasize clients' strengths.

We encourage therapists dealing with sexual offenders similarly to adopt a motivational, collaborative and strength-based approach and to be warm, empathic, directive and rewarding towards their clients. Treatment is best done in groups, where it is essential to create a cohesive and expressive group climate. We look forward to future evaluations of such programs, but in the meantime ethical considerations, and the available evidence, strongly suggest that such an approach will maximize reductions in re-offending and save many people from suffering at the hands of known sexual offenders.

References

Abel, G.G., Mittelman, M., Becker, J.V. *et al.* (1988) "Predicting child molesters' response to treatment," *Annals of the New York Academy of Sciences* 528, 223–234.

Alexander, J.F., Barton, C., Schiavo, S. and Parsons, B.V. (1976) "Systems-behavioral intervention with families of delinquents: therapist characteristics, family behavior and outcome," *Journal of Consulting and Clinical Psychology* 44, 656–664.

Andrews, D.A. (2001) "Principles of effective correctional programs," in L.L. Motiuk and R.C. Serin (eds), *Compendium 2000 on Effective Correctional Programming*. Ottawa: Correctional Services of Canada, pp. 9–17.

Andrews, D.A. and Bonta, J. (2006) *The Psychology of Criminal Conduct*, 4th edn. Newark, NJ: LexisNexis/Anderson.

Andrews, D.A., Bonta, J. and Hoge, R.D. (1990) "Classification for effective rehabilitation: rediscovering psychology," *Criminal Justice and Behavior* 17, 19–52.

Ayland, L. and West, B. (2006) "The Good Way model: a strengths-based approach for working with young people, especially those with intellectual difficulties, who have sexually abusive behaviour," *Journal of Sexual Aggression* 12, 189–201.

Beckham, E.E. (1992) "Predicting dropout in psychotherapy," *Psychotherapy* 29, 177–182.

Bednar, R., and Kaul, T. (1994) "Experiential group research: can the canon fire?," in A.E. Bergen and S.L. Garfield (eds), *Handbook of Psychotherapy and Behavior Change*. New York: John Wiley & Sons, Inc, pp. 631–663.

Beech, A.R. and Fordham, A.S. (1997) "Therapeutic climate of sexual offender treatment programs," *Sexual Abuse: A Journal of Research and Treatment* 9, 219–237.

Beech, A.R. and Hamilton-Giachritsis, C.E. (2005) "Relationship between therapeutic climate and treatment outcome in group-based sexual offender treatment programs," *Sexual Abuse: A Journal of Research and Treatment* 17, 127–140.

Beech, A.R. and Print, B. (2008) Strengths-based approaches to working with those who sexually abuse: a new paradigm? Paper presented at the 18th Annual Conference of the National Organization for the Treatment of Sexual Abusers, Cardiff, UK, September 15.

Bennun, I., Hahlweg, K., Schindler, L. and Langlotz, M. (1986) "Therapist's and client's perceptions in behaviour therapy: the development and cross-cultural analysis of an assessment instrument," *British Journal of Clinical Psychology* 27, 145–150.

Braaten, L.J. (1989) "Predicting positive goal attainment and symptom reduction from early group climate dimensions," *International Journal of Group Psychotherapy* 39, 377–387.

Bremer, J. (2006) "Building resilience: an ally in assessment and treatment," in D.S. Prescott (ed.), *Risk Assessment of Youth Who Have Sexually Abused: Theory, Controversy, and Emerging Issues*. Oklahoma City, OK: Wood'n'Barnes, pp. 222–238.

Browne, K.D., Foreman, L. and Middleton, D. (1998) "Predicting treatment dropout in sex offenders," *Child Abuse Review* 7, 402–419.

Budman, S.H., Soldz, S., Demby, A. *et al.* (1993) "What is cohesiveness? An empirical examination," *Small Group Research* 24, 199–216.

Burns, D.D. and Auerback, A. (1996) "Therapeutic empathy in cognitive-behavioral therapy: does it really make a difference?," in P. Salkovskis (ed.), *Frontiers of Cognitive Therapy*. New York: Guilford Press, pp. 135–164.

Clark, P. and Erooga, M. (1994) "Groupwork with men who sexually abuse children," in T. Morrison, M. Erooga and R.C. Becket (eds), *Sexual Offending Against Children: Assessment and Treatment of Male Abusers*. New York: Routledge, pp. 102–128.

Conte, J.R. and Schuerman, J.R. (1987) "The effects of sexual abuse on children: a multidimensional view," *Journal of Interpersonal Violence* 2, 380–390.

Cooley, E.J. and LaJoy, R. (1980) "Therapeutic relationship and improvements as perceived by clients and therapists," *Journal of Clinical Psychology* 36, 562–570.

de Ruiter, C., Garssen, B., Rijken, H. and Kraaimaat, F. (1989) "De therapeutische relatie bij kortdurende gedrags-therapeutische behandeling voor agorafobie (Therapeutic relationship in short-term behavioral treatment of agoraphobia)," *Gedragstherapie* 22, 313–322.

Dowden, C. and Andrews, D.A. (2004) "The importance of staff practice in delivering effective correctional treatment: a meta-analysis review of core correctional practice," *International Journal of Offender Therapy and Comparative Criminology* 48, 203–214.

Drapeau, M. (2005) "Research on the processes involved in treating sexual offenders," *Sexual Abuse: A Journal of Research and Treatment* 17, 117–125.

Drapeau, M., Körner, C.A., Brunet, L. and Granger, L. (2004) "Treatment at La Macaza Clinic: a qualitative study of the sexual offenders' perspective," *Canadian Journal of Criminology and Criminal Justice* 46, 27–44.

Egan, G. (1998) *The Skilled Helper: A Problem-Management Approach to Helping*. Pacific Grove, CA: Brooks/Cole.

Elliott, R. (1985) "Helpful and non-helpful events in brief counseling interviews: an empirical taxonomy," *Journal of Counseling Psychology* 32, 307–322.

Frank, J.D. (1971) "Therapeutic factors in psychotherapy," *American Journal of Psychotherapy* 25, 350–361.

Frank, J.D. (1973) *Persuasion and Healing*, 2nd edn. Baltimore: Johns Hopkins University Press.

Frankl, V.E. (1978) *The Unheard Cry for Meaning: Psychotherapy and Humanism*. New York: Simon and Schuster.

Free, N.K., Green, B.L., Grace, M.D. *et al.* (1985) "Empathy and outcome in brief focal dynamic therapy," *American Journal of Psychiatry* 142, 917–921.

Garland, R.J. and Dougher, M.H. (1991) "Motivational intervention in the treatment of sex offenders," in W.R. Miller and S. Rollnick (eds), *Motivational Interviewing: Preparing People to Change Addictive Behavior*. New York: Guilford Press, pp. 303–313.

Greenberg, L.S. and Pavio, S. (1997) *Working with Emotions in Psychotherapy*. New York: Guilford Press.

Hanson, R.K., Bourgon, G., Helmus, L. and Hodgson, S. (2009) "The principles of effective correctional treatment also apply to sexual offenders: a meta-analysis," *Criminal Justice and Behavior* 36, 865–891.

Hanson, R.K., Gordon, A., Harris, A.J.R. *et al.* (2002) "First report of the collaborative outcome data project on the effectiveness of psychological treatment for sex offenders," *Sexual Abuse: A Journal of Research and Treatment* 14, 167–192.

Harkins, L. and Beech, A.R. (2007) "Measurement of the effectiveness of sex offender treatment," *Aggression and Violent Behavior* 12, 36–44.

Heppner, P.P. and Clairborn, C.D. (1989) "Social influence research in counseling: a review and critique," *Journal of Counseling Psychology* 36, 365–387.

Hodges, T.D. and Clifton, D.O. (2004) "Strengths-based development in practice," in P.A. Linley and S. Joseph (eds), *Positive Psychology in Practice*. Hoboken, NJ: John Wiley & Sons, Inc, pp. 256–268.

Horvath, A.O. (2000) "The therapeutic relationship: from transference to alliance," *Journal of Counseling Psychology/In Session: Psychotherapy in Practice* 56, 163–173.

Horvath, A.O. and Symonds, B.D. (1991) "Relation between working alliance and outcome in psychotherapy: a meta-analysis," *Journal of Counseling Psychology* 38, 139–149.

Hudson, K. (2005) *Offending Identities: Sex Offenders' Perspectives of Their Treatment and Management*. Portland, OR: Willan Publishing.

Kanfer, F.H. and Goldstein, A.P. (1991) *Helping People Change*. New York: Pergamon.

Karterud, S. (1988) "The influence of task definition, leadership and therapeutic style on inpatient group cultures," *International Journal of Therapeutic Communities* 9, 231–247.

Kazdin, A.E. (1978) *History of Behavior Modification: Experimental Foundations of Contemporary Research*. Baltimore: University Park Press.

Kear-Colwell, J. and Pollack, P. (1997) "Motivation or confrontation: which approach to the child sex offender?," *Criminal Justice and Behavior* 24, 20–33.

Keijsers, G.P.J., Schaap, C.P. and Hoogduin, C.A.L. (2000) "The impact of interpersonal patient and therapist behavior on outcome in cognitive-behavior therapy," *Behavior Modification* 24, 264–297.

Kennedy-Moore, E. and Watson, J.C. (1999) *Expressing Emotion: Myths, Realities, and Therapeutic Strategies*. New York: Guilford Press.

Kohut, H. (1990) "The role of empathy in psychoanalytic cure," in R. Langs (ed.), *Classics in Psychoanalytic Techniques*. Northvale, NJ: Aronson, pp. 463–473.

Koss, M.P. and Harvey, M.R. (1991) *The Rape Victim: Clinical and Community Interventions*, 2nd edn. Newbury Park, CA: Sage Publications.

Lambert, M.J. (1983) "Comment on 'A case study of the process and outcome of time-limited counseling'," *Journal of Counseling Psychology* 30, 22–25.

Lieberman, M.A., Yalom, I.D. and Miles, M.B. (1973) *Encounter Groups: First Facts*. New York: Basic Books.

Linley, P.A. and Joseph, S. (eds) (2004) *Positive Psychology in Practice*. Hoboken, NJ: John Wiley & Sons, Inc.

Lösel, F. and Schmucker, M. (2005) "The effectiveness of treatment for sexual offenders: a comprehensive meta-analysis," *Journal of Experimental Criminology* 1, 1–29.

Luborsky, L., Barber, J.P. and Crits-Christoph, P. (1990) "Theory-based research for understanding the process of dynamic psychotherapy," *Journal of Consulting and Clinical Psychology* 58, 281–287.

Mann, R.E. (1996) *Motivational Interviewing with Sex Offenders: A Practice Manual*. Hull: NOTA.

Mann, R.E. and Rollnick, S. (1996) "Motivational interviewing with a sex offender who believed he was innocent," *Behavioural and Cognitive Psychotherapy* 24, 127–134.

Mann, R.E. and Shingler, J. (2006) "Schema-driven cognition in sexual offenders: theory, assessment and treatment," in W.L. Marshall, Y.M. Fernandez, L.E. Marshall and G.A. Serran (eds), *Sexual Offender Treatment: Controversial Issues*. Chichester: John Wiley & Sons, Ltd, pp. 173–185.

Mann, R.E. and Webster, S. (2002) Understanding resistance and denial. Paper presented at the 21st Annual Research and Treatment Conference of the Association for the Treatment of Sexual Abusers, Montreal, October 30.

Marques, J.K., Day, D.M., Nelson, C. and West, M.A. (1994) "Effects of cognitive-behavioral treatment of sex offender recidivism: preliminary results of a longitudinal study," *Criminal Justice and Behavior* 21, 28–54.

Marques, J.K., Weideranders, M., Day, D.M. *et al.* (2005) "Effects of a relapse prevention program on sexual recidivism: final results from California's Sex Offender Treatment and Evaluation Project (SOTEP)," *Sexual Abuse: A Journal of Research and Treatment* 17, 79–107.

Marshall, W.L., Fernandez, Y.M., Serran, G.A. *et al.* (2003a) "Process variables in the treatment of sexual offenders: a review of the relevant literature," *Aggression and Violent Behavior* 8, 205–234.

Marshall, L.E., Marshall, W.L., Fernandez, Y.M. *et al.* (2008) "The Rockwood Preparatory Program for sexual offenders: description and preliminary appraisal," *Sexual Abuse: A Journal of Research and Treatment* 20, 25–42.

Marshall, W.L., Marshall, L.E., Serran, G.A. and O'Brien, M.D. (2011) *The Rehabilitation of Sexual Offenders: A Strengths-Based Approach*. Washington, DC: American Psychological Association.

Marshall, W.L., Serran, G.A., Fernandez, Y.M. *et al.* (2003b) "Therapist characteristics in the treatment of sexual offenders: tentative data on their relationship with indices of behavior change," *Journal of Sexual Aggression* 8, 25–30.

Marshall, W.L., Serran, G.A., Moulden, H. *et al.* (2002) "Therapist features in sexual offender treatment: their reliable identification and influence on behaviour change," *Clinical Psychology and Psychotherapy* 9, 395–405.

Martin, D.J., Garske, J.P. and Davis, M.K. (2000) "Relation of the therapeutic alliance with outcome and other variables: a meta-analytic review," *Journal of Consulting and Clinical Psychology* 68, 438–450.

Marziali, E. and Alexander, L. (1991) "The power of the therapeutic relationship," *American Journal of Orthopsychiatry* 61, 383–391.

McGuff, R., Gitlin, D. and Enderlin, D. (1996) "Clients' and therapists' confidence and attendance at planned individual therapy sessions," *Psychological Reports* 79, 537–538.

McLeod, J. (1990) "The client's experience of counseling and psychotherapy: a review of the research literature," in D. Mearns and W. Dryden (eds), *Experiences of Counseling in Action*. London: Sage Publications, pp. 66–79.

McRoberts, C., Burlingame, G.M. and Hoag, M.J. (1998) "Comparative efficacy of individual and group psychotherapy: a meta-analytic perspective," *Groups Dynamics: Theory, Research and Practice* 2, 101–117.

Miller, W.R., Benefield, R.G. and Tonigan, J.S. (1993) "Enhancing motivation for change in problem drinking: a controlled comparison of two therapist styles," *Journal of Consulting and Clinical Psychology* 61, 455–461.

Miller, W.R. and Rollnick, S. (1991) *Motivational Interviewing: Preparing People for Change*. New York: Guilford Press.

Miller, W.R. and Rollnick, S. (2002) *Motivational Interviewing: Preparing People for Change*, 2nd edn. New York: Guilford Press.

Mintz, J., Luborsky, L. and Auerbach, A.H. (1971) "Dimensions of psychotherapy: a factor-analytic study of ratings of psychotherapy sessions," *Journal of Consulting and Clinical Psychology* 36, 106–120.

Moos, R.H. (1986) *Group Environment Scale Manual*, 2nd edn. Palo Alto, CA: Consulting Psychologists' Press.

Morgan, R., Luborsky, L., Crits-Christoph, P., *et al.* (1982) "Predicting outcomes of psychotherapy by the Penn Helping Alliance Rating Method," *Archives of General Psychiatry* 39, 397–402.

Nichols, M.P. and Taylor, T.Y. (1975) "Impact of therapist interventions on early sessions of group therapy," *Journal of Consulting and Clinical Psychology* 31, 726–729.

Norcross, J.C. (2002) *Psychotherapy Relationships that Work*. New York: Oxford University Press.

Orlinsky, D.E., Grawe, K. and Parks, B.K. (1994) "Process and outcome in psychotherapy – noch einmal," in E. Garfield and S.L. Garfield (eds), *Handbook of Psychotherapy and Behavior Change*, 4th edn. New York: John Wiley & Sons, Inc, pp. 270–376.

Orlinsky, D.E. and Howard, K.I. (1986) "Process and outcome in psychotherapy," in S. L. Garfield and A.E. Bergin (eds), *Handbook of Psychotherapy and Behavior Change*, 3rd edn. New York: John Wiley & Sons, Inc, pp. 311–384.

Pfäfflin, F., Böhmer, M., Cornehl, S. and Mergenthaler, F. (2005) "What happens in therapy with sexual offenders? A model of process research," *Sexual Abuse: A Journal of Research and Treatment* 17, 141–151.

Piper, W.E., Ogrodniczuk, J.S., Joyce, A.S., *et al.* (1999) "Prediction of dropping out in time-limited interpretive individual psychotherapy," *Psychotherapy: Theory, Research and Practice* 36, 114–122.

Ringler, M. (1977) "The effect of democratic versus authoritarian therapist behaviour on success, success-expectation and self-attribution in desensitization of examination anxiety," *Zeitschrift für Klinische Psychologie* 6, 40–58.

Rogers, C.R. (1957) "The necessary and sufficient conditions of therapeutic personality change," *Journal of Consulting Psychology* 21, 95–103.

Rogers, C.R. (1961) *On Becoming a Person*. Boston: Houghton Mifflin.

Samstag, L.W., Batchelder, S.T., Muran, J.C. *et al.* (1998) "Early identification of treatment failures in short-term psychotherapy: an assessment of therapeutic alliance and interpersonal behavior," *Journal of Psychotherapy Practice and Research* 7, 126–143.

Saunders, M. (1999) "Clients' assessments of the affective environment of the psychotherapy session: relationship to session quality and treatment effectiveness," *Journal of Clinical Psychology* 55, 597–605.

Schaap, C., Bennun, I., Schindler, L. and Hoogduin, K. (1993) *The Therapeutic Relationship in Behavioural Psychotherapy*. Chichester: John Wiley & Sons, Ltd.

Seligman, M.E.P. (2002) *Authentic Happiness: Using the New Positive Psychology to Realize Your Potential for Lasting Fulfillment*. New York: Free Press.

Seligman, M.E.P. and Csikszentmihalyi, M. (2000) "Positive psychology: an introduction," *American Psychologist* 55, 5–14.

Snyder, C.R. (1994) *The Psychology of Hope: You Can Get There from Here*. New York: Free Press.

Snyder, C.R. and Lopez, S.J. (eds) (2005) *Handbook of Positive Psychology*. New York: Oxford University Press.

Snyder, C.R., Rand, K.L. and Sigmon, D.R. (2005) "Hope theory: a member of the positive psychology family," in C.R. Snyder and S.J. Lopez (eds), *Handbook of Positive Psychology*. New York: Oxford University Press, pp. 257–276.

Sterba, R. (1934) "The fate of the ego in analytic therapy," *International Journal of Psychoanalysis* 15, 117–126.

Strupp, H.H. (1980) "Success and failure in time-limited psychotherapy: a systematic comparison of two cases," *Archives of General Psychiatry* 37, 595–603.

Strupp, H.H. (1982) "The outcome problem in psychotherapy: contemporary perspectives," in J.H. Harvey and M.M. Parks (eds), *The Master Lecture Series: Psychotherapy Research and Behavior Change*, Vol. I. Washington, DC: American Psychological Association, pp. 43–71.

Strupp, H.H. and Hadley, S.W. (1979) "Specific vs. nonspecific factors in psychotherapy," *Archives of General Psychiatry* 36, 1125–1136.

Tyron, G.S. and Kane, A.S. (1990) "The helping alliance and premature termination," *Counseling Psychology Quarterly* 3, 233–238.

Tyron, G.S. and Kane, A.S. (1993) "Relationship of working alliance to mutual and unilateral termination," *Journal of Counseling Psychology* 40, 33–36.

Ullmann, L.P. and Krasner, L. (eds) (1965) *Case Studies in Behavior Modification*. New York: Holt, Rinehart and Winston.

Ward, T., Mann, R.E. and Gannon, T.A. (2007) "The good lives model of rehabilitation: clinical implications," *Aggression and Violent Behavior: A Review Journal* 12, 87–107.

Williams, D.J. (2004) "Sexual offenders' perceptions of correctional therapy: what can we learn?," *Sexual Addiction and Compulsivity* 11, 145–162.

Yalom, I.D. (1980) *Existential Psychotherapy*. New York: Basic Books.

Yalom, I.D. (1995) *The Theory and Practice of Group Psychotherapy*, 4th edn. New York: Basic Books.

15

A Forensic Psychologist's Involvement in Working with Sex Offenders

Daniel T. Wilcox

Introduction

Like many of my colleagues, I did not begin my career with any predetermined plan to work with sex offenders. Rather, this journey can best be explained in terms of a convergence of identified clinical needs in my work and practice opportunities that presented in my professional life. Initially, I worked with intellectually disabled individuals living in the community or in residential facilities and later with psychiatric patients in various settings. While undertaking these clinical roles as a psychologist working for the State of New York in the early 1980s, I became more aware of forensic issues and, among them, sexual offending. I subsequently moved to the United Kingdom and by the early 1990s had taken up similar employment responsibilities within the National Health Service (NHS) in central England, providing clinical psychological support to GPs (General Practitioners), as well as specialist mental illness and intellectual disabilities service provision. In this latter role, as principal psychologist responsible for Intellectual Disability Services, I began doing assessment and intervention work with intellectually disabled men who had convictions for sexual offenses.

Unfortunately, at that time, there was limited expertise and few specialist resources allocated to addressing inappropriate or abusive sexual behaviors in individuals with Intellectual Disabilities. However, owing to their criminal involvement, some of these men within secure health service facilities had Court-allocated probation officers and, relatedly, in 1994, I spoke with a probation-based treatment facilitator from the Regional Sex Offender Unit. This led to a sharing of ideas about available skills and culminated in my involvement in an innovative multi-agency treatment program for intellectually disabled men. These offenders were from the wider community,

The Wiley-Blackwell Handbook of Legal and Ethical Aspects of Sex Offender Treatment and Management, First Edition. Edited by Karen Harrison and Bernadette Rainey.
© 2013 John Wiley & Sons, Ltd. Published 2013 by John Wiley & Sons, Ltd.

including men on probation across the West Midlands, as well as from the regional forensic mental health service, and men with Intellectual Disabilities from the local health service area. All of these men had cognitive impairments that would have made mainstream sex offender groupwork involvement an inappropriate choice for them.

Over the years following this initial collaboration, I became more extensively involved in providing forensic psychological services and subsequently achieved Chartership with the British Psychological Society in forensic as well as clinical practice. Having worked with a number of NHS clinical psychology departments up until that time, I substantially changed direction and, over the past 17 years, have provided consultancy forensic psychology services to the National Probation Service across much of central England. This work has involved supervising psychology staff, individual interventions, group work, assessments and monitoring offender behavior. I had the good fortune of playing a role in the development of various regional probation initiatives including programs focusing on the needs of intellectually disabled offenders (Leyland *et al.*, 1995; Wilcox, 2004a, 2004b), young sex offenders (Gregory, 2004), offenders with challenging victim experiences (McEwan, Leyland and Wilcox, 1995) and mainstream sex offender groupwork (West Midlands Probation Service Sex Offender Unit, 1995/2000). Another key area of involvement was the employment of the polygraph with sexual offenders (Wilcox, 2000; Wilcox, Sosnowski and Middleton, 1999; Wilcox and Sosnowski, 2005).

Importantly, while this chapter focuses on my experiences as a forensic psychologist working with sex offenders, it also attempts to take account of the balance to be struck by my colleagues and me in our efforts to develop more effective assessment, treatment and supervision tools within what we considered to be an ethical framework. Nevertheless, the ardor of individuals spearheading change and innovation to benefit society, coupled with the pressure to place community protection above offender rights, has, in my opinion, impacted upon the objective assessment of risk in this population of offenders. Clearly, the significantly risk-averse circumstances that have existed over recent years have dictated that there has been decreased concern about proportionality and fairness in punishment, about treatment and rehabilitation, and even about reduction in recidivism. Instead, the primary aim appears frequently to be the achievement of public safety by controlling, incapacitating and containing the behavior, that is, the community involvement, of offenders. While these implicit goals, perhaps on some level, may be understandable, as practicing professionals in this field we have a responsibility to be scrupulously accurate and as even-handed as possible when conveying information, in particular when advising the Courts or other statutory services.

Importantly, the prevailing attitude about sexual offenders and their management is such that imposing more restrictive sanctions, whether founded on good science or not, will likely be received more positively by the wider public than a less viscerally-guided and tempered opinion which comprehensively conveys the strengths and weaknesses of one's professional views (see Chapter 8). It is against this backdrop that I will briefly examine my early professional experiences and discuss my involvement over time in working with sex offenders as a forensic psychologist.

Early Professional Influences and
Personal Values Development

At Bachelor's and Master's level my psychology training had a clinical and behavioral orientation. I had my own "lab rat" I named Corrina (after the Bob Dylan song) and I employed operant conditioning techniques to explore her learning behavior in T-Mazes and Skinner boxes. The research on learning theory, in those days, centered around the study of rodents (Calhoun, 1962; Skinner, 1974), birds (Guttman and Kalish, 1956; Fidura and Gray, 1966), monkeys (Brady, 1958; Harlow and Harlow, 1969), dogs (Pavlov, 1927; Solomon, Kamin and Wynne, 1953), and so on, and focused on developing an understanding of human behaviors, drives and, ultimately, how we relate to one another, with ongoing advice not to anthropomorphize, that is, ascribe human attributes or intentions to an animal's behavior. Notably, this period of my education appeared to have pre-dated much of the modern animal rights movement (Singer, 1975) and I note that at that time in the 1970s, a Master's level course was offered in the psychology department called, "Small Animal Surgery," wherein it was possible directly to evaluate the behavior of animals by systematically stimulating or ablating areas of their brain functioning and carefully recording the behavioral changes. Notably however, before I decided to study psychology, I had thought about majoring in philosophy, but was advised by my older brother that this was unlikely to be any more lucrative as a career option than my earlier childhood fantasy of becoming an archeologist, about which he said, "Don't bother, you have to be rich to start with." In any event, perhaps influenced by two terms of philosophy at university, including an ethics course, I concluded that "unless I was going into medicine in my future work, I could not find a way to justify cutting up small animals."

Nonetheless, though somewhat uncomfortable with some research, for example, that of Harlow and Harlow (1969), that frightened, baffled and deeply undermined the attachment potentials of baby rhesus monkeys (am I anthropomorphizing?), I experienced little personal disquiet about most of the experiments I read about. Rather, I accepted them as justified by an imperative – the pursuit of scientific knowledge. Clinical and social psychological research on humans, at that time, evidenced marginally greater levels of experimenter restraint as human rights were somewhat better established than those of animals. Nonetheless, researchers like Asch (1951), and more particularly Milgram (1974) and Zimbardo, Ebbesen and Maslach (1977), appeared to have "slipped in under the ethical radar" during the early second half of the twentieth century in carrying out important landmark research that, nonetheless, has since been viewed as morally questionable and unsupportable by modern ethics committees. Notably, Asch (1951) manipulated and deceived the participants in his study on conformity by systematically and clandestinely applying group pressure in order to influence and distort the participant's judgment and expressed perceptions. Milgram's (1974) subsequent research on obedience to authority again involved deceiving participants, though this time into believing they were acting as support staff to the experimenter and, as such, required to deliver electric shocks of increasing intensity to other subjects when their learning efforts failed within the context of a contrived experimental setting. This study gave indications that many individuals were willing to suspend or override their own judgment in circumstances where they were directed to do so by an individual presenting in an authoritative manner and directed them to do so. The participants also demonstrated a notable ability to suspend empathy.

Zimbardo, Ebbesen and Maslach (1977) explored this phenomenon further in their systematic research on attitude change, wherein they randomly selected individuals to play the roles of prisoners or prison guards and subsequently abandoned the experiment when the parties assumed their roles with such zeal that actual risk of harm to the parties was perceived as becoming too substantial. I also note in reflecting back to the early twentieth century, John Watson, the "father of behaviorism" (Watson and Rayner, 1920) conditioned a young child, Albert, to be fearful of white fluffy objects, such as rabbits and similar inanimate materials by coupling their presentation with an aversive stimuli, an unanticipated loud noise. Though Watson reported subsequently treating and reversing this experimentally induced phobia, this research would, by current standards, be judged as fatally flawed from a moral perspective.

Early Employment Experiences after Leaving Higher Education

My work in institutions put me in contact with many individuals who had experienced long-term neurological damage (tardive dyskinesia) as a result of the medication they had been prescribed over the years to control their behavior (Gelder *et al.*, 1996). As a novice psychologist, it seemed all too apparent to me that these "vacant souls" may likely have been over-treated with medication and that more active consideration of cost-benefit in relation to employing such medication would probably have been in their best interests during the preceding years. I also noted that those less empowered individuals with serious mental health problems or significant cognitive impairments (especially those who had patterns of criminal or antisocial behavior) enjoyed less protection and ethical treatment from society. Relatedly, I undertook a Master's thesis (Wilcox, 1982) reporting on the closure of Willowbrook, the largest state-run institution for the intellectually disabled in the United States. Notably, I observed that the vast majority of the individuals residing in this facility had not required such severe curtailing of their civil liberties as to be impelled to live in an institution all of their lives.

In other settings, social control efforts were being applied to populations such as the intellectually disabled; for example, the token economy system of Ayllon and Azrin (1968). Although these programs were often effective and well-intentioned, this could not so readily be asserted about other individualized interventions including a proliferation of electroconvulsive therapy (ECT) usage in psychiatric centers (APA, 1978) and the more extreme mid-twentieth-century patient management efforts including lobotomization (Valenstein, 1980). Notably, Dr Walter Freeman drove around the United States in his "lobotomobile" (Freeman and Watts, 1942), performing his frontal lobe cortical destruction practice with relative impunity, extolling the virtues of the "ice pick method" to control agitated and aggressive patients by inserting these instruments along the pathways of the optic nerves and separating the frontal lobe of the brain from the thalamus. In fact, Dr Freeman enjoyed a kind of celebrity status in his day, much the way that "Dr Death," Dr James P. Grigson (Wells and Quash, 2010), has over more recent years through his assessment of the psychopathy levels of convicted murderers in the United States to inform Court decisions as to whether these individuals should receive the death penalty or not.

In my experience of working in institutions in the last quarter of the twentieth century, there continued to be a custodial or "herding" approach to much of the "care" that was afforded to the intellectually disabled, with more able residents often "encouraged" to act as intermediaries in imposing control, if not structure, to an environment managed by too few residential staff. As in my work with community and hospitalized long-term psychiatric patients, I considered that there was a relative acceptance of the patient's disenfranchised status. Further, on reflection, I would judge that what appeared to be "normal," by virtue of being "accepted practice," suppressed self-questioning in me about any moral or ethical responsibilities I held in relation to these individuals, except in atypical circumstances. For example, in the late 1970s I was asked to address the challenging behavior of a young intellectually disabled man. In reviewing his clinical file, I found that, at the age of 13, he had been lobotomized in an attempt to manage his behavior more effectively. I reflected that, as a more challenged intellectually disabled adult with significant life-threatening issues, such as pica (APA, 2000) (an uncontrollable urge to eat inedible material including cigarettes, lit or unlit), he presented with no evidence of personality disorder or any helpful executive functioning abilities (Saunders and Summers, 2011) that might have assisted me in terms of developing more effective behavior management strategies with him.

My psychology Master's thesis (Wilcox, 1978) involved the use of abbreviated behavioral strategies for treating obesity. This followed on from what Skinner (1974) came to view as "radical behaviorism" and led to the acceptance and development of "self-control" techniques (Mahoney, Maura and Wade, 1973) and the subsequent recognition of cognitive behavioral therapy as a valid and powerful psychological intervention strategy (Beck, 1975; Ellis, 1973). In part, my interest in behavioral self-control developed through working with an extremely obese boy who had Prader–Willi syndrome (Holm *et al.*, 1993), giving rise to significant intellectual limitations and a lack of self-control, wherein any environmental cues of a visual, auditory, olfactory or gustatory nature would invariably trigger an urge in this youngster to consume as much food as possible. He was obese to a life-threatening degree and, indeed, at times, his poor self-control put him in immediate danger of choking. At other times, his behavior jeopardized the safety of others as well, when, for example, he would remove his seat belt and try to take control of the moving client transport and steer the vehicle in the direction of the "golden arches," that is, McDonalds. Importantly, it was noted during our engagement with him, that owing to his highly externalized locus of control (Rotter, 1954), when his living environment was modified into one that did not readily evidence cues for eating, then his ability to contend with a weight loss regime (which was critical to his health) was not only relatively straightforward but proved to be easier than for individuals who have more normal, internalized drives to eat.

Practicing in the United Kingdom

Working as a psychologist in the United Kingdom, my interest in learning theory, behavior modification and cognitive behavioral therapy continued to grow and when I moved to the United Kingdom and began working as a psychologist in the early 1990s, I began looking at how these tools could be brought to bear through the medium of group engagement to address antisocial and sexually inappropriate behaviors in intellectually disabled individuals (Wilcox, 1993). Shortly thereafter, I began working collaboratively with the regional NHS Forensic Service and the National Probation Service's West Midlands-based Sex Offender Unit to provide intervention work with intellectually disabled men. This collaboration across agencies enabled a helpful mix to be achieved for providing therapeutic support to intellectually disabled men who required skilled groupwork, underpinned by a sound knowledge of Intellectual Disabilities and concomitant issues that can arise with this population, including dual diagnoses. By 1995, I had begun transitioning from the NHS to working with the Probation Service, as well as providing forensic/clinical Court reports. In collaborative work with the Regional Sex Offender Unit, significant training and service development efforts followed in relation to working with intellectually disabled sexual offenders (Wilcox, 2004a, 2004b; Wilcox *et al.*, 2009) and mainstream offenders (Buschman *et al.*, 2008), and in introducing treatment and assessment innovations (Allam, 2000; Middleton and Wilcox, 1999/2000). These various initiatives gave rise to the first Home Office accredited Sex Offender Treatment Program (SOTP) in the United Kingdom in 2000, as well as the first polygraph trials employed with sex offenders on probation in the United Kingdom in 1999/2000 (Wilcox, 2002) (see Chapter 23). Relatedly, I have provided consultancy to the police in relation to sex offender management and risk assessment, offered support to services for young people who displayed sexually inappropriate behavior and regularly produced reports and given Court evidence in relation to the treatment, assessment and management of sexual offenders. In these settings, in particular where new developments are being implemented, reflection has played an important role. Nonetheless, while good intentions and ethical practice may overlap to some degree, they are not coterminous and one does not guarantee the other.

Clinical v. Forensic Psychology: Ethical Issues

In transitioning into forensic psychology work, I immediately became aware of marked differences in the demand characteristics of each setting. For example, individuals referred in primary care settings exercised self-determination, demonstrating choice and, usually, open engagement. Nevertheless, I note that my work with people in institutions, in particular those with significant intellectual limitations and poor behavioral adjustment, did offer me some insights into the challenges of working with those who did not actively wish to change or lacked insight into this process. Notably, the individuals I subsequently began working with at probation were compelled to undergo treatment, though they were often closed, resentful and resistive to engaging in work relating to their sexual offending. Indeed, I found that addressing sexually deviant and abusive behaviors seemed to present a new level of difficulty as regards the degree of misrepresentation, concealment and denial, both in individuals of normal intelligence and those with intellectual limitations. However, as an accepted, validated and proven program of treatment for sex offenders had not yet been established in the United Kingdom, we moved forward with as much confidence as we could muster, employing good intentions and the best practice notions available to us. Further, without research evidence, there was insufficient clarity as to whether treatment worked. In addition, through an evolving perception about how to assess treatment change (Beckett *et al.*, 1994), it became apparent that clinical judgment was not very reliable on its own and that a structured approach to assessment provided greater accuracy in predicting recidivism as well as treatment success.

Risk assessment gradually began to take shape with a layered or multi-level approach, incorporating the assessment of static, dynamic and acute factors contributing to risk of recidivism. While static or actuarial risk measures prove to be a fundamental building platform upon which more thorough risk assessment could occur, difficulties were noted in relation to reliance on this approach, with some practitioners and researchers (Berlin *et al.*, 2003; Quinsey *et al.*, 1998; Vess, 2011) highlighting its limitations as well as its benefits. Nevertheless, the introduction of structured risk assessment (Craig, Beech and Browne, 2006; Hanson and Thornton, 1999) has had an enormous impact on working with sex offenders, as has the subsequent introduction of accredited and carefully evaluated intervention programs, demonstrating positive treatment effect (Allam, 2000; Hanson, Broom and Stephenson, 2004; Marshall, Anderson and Fernandez, 1999).

The Development of Structured Risk Assessment

Historically, individual intervention work with sex offenders has proven to be very challenging. Deceitful, incomplete and self-serving views expressed by offenders have often been "the order of the day." Further, professionals have appeared to be no less vulnerable to grooming and manipulation (Salter, 1997) than are non-professionals. Notably, individual interventions provided up until the 1980s gave testimony to this vulnerability in psychiatrists, psychologists, and so on, where descriptions were given at times, by these professionals, of men being lured by coquettish girls who were determined to manipulate unsuspecting and vulnerable men into sexual activity (Salter, 1988). For example, Revitch and Weiss (1962: 78) wrote that: "The majority of pedophiles are harmless individuals and their victims are usually known to be aggressive and seductive children." While it would suit many people to believe that these misguided notions do not exist in the minds of professionals any more, this unfortunately is not the case. In my own experience, I recall completing an assessment of sexual risk in the mid-1990s wherein a man just over 20 years of age had coerced and manipulated an eight-year-old girl to fellate him. With a sense of incredulity and profound professional discomfort, another expert (at doctoral level) had expressed the opinion in his report to the Court that this incident simply reflected "mutual sexual exploratory behavior." While such contentions may seem naïve, untenable and offensive today, it is important to remember that these professionals were well-educated, though seemingly less well equipped in the prevailing circumstances of that time, and working then without important protective tools that currently exist to assist professionals in retaining an objective, though still open attitude about an offender's behavior and treatment potential. It is also perhaps not surprising that these situations occurred at times in the past given that many sexual offenders prove to be exceptionally skilled in grooming children, "responsible" adults and environments in order to meet their own pro-offending needs.

Today, structured risk assessment has largely replaced the past, very often, inadequate clinical judgment approach to evaluating an offender's potential for recidivating (Lindsay and Beail, 2004). Professionals recognize that many seemingly "model" sex offender groupwork attendees continue to engage in high risk behaviors, while producing "safe soundbites" (Burrell, 1999) within therapy and supervision sessions. This highlights the benefits of careful collaboration among various professionals working with offenders, including psychologists, therapists, group facilitators, supervising officers, polygraph examiners, police personnel, social services staff, health visitors, education professionals, family members and all other individuals who may have some support and "surveillance" role in helping to manage and reduce the risk of further offending. In my experience, coordinated external control is critical in offender work as a precursor and adjunct to the development of internal control whenever this additional step is achievable.

Static or actuarial risk assessment provides a helpful and objective starting point for more accurate assessment of risk. While it does not directly give an indication of the probability that an individual offender will re-offend, it assists in establishing categories of offenders who share similar characteristics associated with their age, relationship status and past history of sexual and non-sexual offending. Based on this information, individuals have been assigned into Very High, High, Medium and Low risk groupings and re-conviction rates established for convicted sexual offenders in research by Thornton (2007) and Hanson, Steffy and Gauthier (1993). This is accomplished by combining features considered to be relevant to assess risk in much the same way that life insurance assessors employ actuarial tables based on lifestyle data to make life expectancy estimates. As such, in Thornton's sample, within the Medium risk banding, 30% of the men included recidivated over a period of 15 years. Importantly, while it is justifiable to say that three out of 10 men within this group with these demographic and criminogenic characteristics re-offended (and indeed to extrapolate that, in general, offenders with these characteristics are likely to re-offend at a similar rate), this calculation does not, in itself, assist us in identifying which three out of 10 men within the group will re-offend. Nonetheless, accurate static risk assessment, confirmed by a review of an up-to-date Police National Computer (PNC), is a very helpful and hitherto unavailable tool that, in my opinion, must be employed at the beginning of any responsible, professional risk assessment. From the outset this reduces the professional's vulnerability to being manipulated into considering that the offender may be less risky, perhaps on the basis of a persuasive manner or agreeable interaction style. Indeed work by Hart and Hare (1994) has confirmed that such interpersonal factors, including superficial charm and a facility for manipulating, are, at times, with the benefit of structured assessment (employing the PCL-R), indications of heightened risk.

Bearing in mind the above concerns, treatment workers and psychology staff must review dynamic risk factors to ensure a fuller and more robust appreciation of an offender's risk. Importantly, the psychometric measures employed at the outset and completion of treatment evaluate and re-evaluate important factors that are subject to therapeutic change, whereas the static measures referenced above are not. These features, which can be influenced by treatment, are assessed through psychometric testing and focused upon within-group and individual intervention work. The dynamic risk factors (Beech, Fisher and Thornton, 2003) fall into four broad categories: offense-related cognitive distortions, sexual interests/deviant arousal, socio-affective functioning and self-management. Through the evaluation of these dynamic risk features, offenders are determined to be in the High or Low deviance category and the therapeutic focus of the work conducted to address these deficits, while strengthening protective features that may already exist. This assessment battery also incorporates validity measures to determine whether the respondent is intentionally misrepresenting himself for personal advantage or, as in some instances, there is also evidence of a degree of self-deception. These validity indices reduce the opportunity for offenders to misrepresent themselves successfully and intentionally for purposes of concealing their true thoughts, behaviors and characteristics as they relate to dynamic risk and the likelihood of future sexual offending. Bonta (1996) reported that dynamic risk assessment, in combination with the evaluation of static risk, proved more accurate and took account of individual, treatable criminogenic features. Notably, he found that dynamic risk played an important interactive role, augmenting the power of static risk assessment and providing professionals with further improved risk analysis upon which to consider the offender's treatment and supervision needs more objectively.

Collaborative Professional Working

As a forensic psychologist in this field, I have found that liaising with staff who conduct the risk assessments and provide the treatment intervention is of key importance in developing any individualized treatment intervention that is requested (Wilcox, Foss and Donathy, 2005). Further, in my opinion, ongoing assessment refinement occurs during groupwork and in many forensic and clinical situations such as one-to-one work. As an example, other group members can be more direct and challenging at times than the group facilitator would be and, while this needs to be responsibly and sensitively managed, it sometimes evokes information disclosure that would not otherwise occur. Further, where offenders in the group share similar deviant sexual interests, based on their known offense histories, but one is in denial, body language may present in ways that assist the facilitators in encouraging the denying offender to acknowledge atypical sexual interests and past deviant behaviors. As an example, I recall a group situation where a man accepting of his exhibitionistic interests reported upon the sense of excitement that he experienced in advance of sexually exposing himself. He then expressed the belief that the other group members would understand his thoughts and feelings at that time, though only one of his peers was nodding in agreement with the offender's comments (the other individual in the group who had also been convicted of indecent exposure, though he had previously been refusing to acknowledge his offense). Notably, observation of this man's reactions in group, together with subsequent individual discussions, served to assist in reversing this man's denial of having any interest in indecent exposure. Notably, these disclosures enabled a more robust and interactive treatment plan to be developed, along with enhanced self-management strategies.

The combination of improved risk assessment and more effective, accredited treatment programs has provided a much-needed structure for working with sex offenders. Importantly, from this operational base, the evaluation of acute risk factors, including response to supervision, access to potential victims and relevant lifestyle change issues, can also be factored in with the assessment of static and dynamic risk, and weighed up more meaningfully within the context of more effectively managing community safety.

In spite of the benefits of these various advances in sex offender treatment, individual work with offenders remains an important aspect of offender management and public protection. In relation to this, it is largely the responsibility of the supervising probation officer to assess acute concerns that may increase or decrease risk. This includes a careful evaluation of the offender's behavior in relation to supervision and any changes that may occur over time. Lifestyle changes are also important to monitor, taking account of employment, relationships, social involvements and personal behavior. Relatedly, there are indications that during periods of personal life disruption, offending behavior is more likely to re-occur (Beech, Fisher and Thornton, 2003) and that maladaptive coping strategies may emerge, including alcohol or substance misuse, as well as reckless behavior that may have a short-term, self-serving or risky, escapist focus. Access to potential victims is also an acute risk factor that should continuously be monitored and may require coordinated engagement with other professionals including social services.

Other Assessment Approaches

Other biological and physiological measures are also increasingly being employed to assist sex offender workers in understanding risk issues among offenders. These include polygraphy (Wilcox, 2009), penile plethysmography (Freund, 1963) and visual reaction time (Abel *et al.*, 1998). The polygraph monitors and records changes in an individual's physiological responses to stimuli presented by the polygraph examiner. The instrument collects and records physiological data in relation to respiratory activity, blood pressure and perspiration, contiguously with asking the individual questions in order to investigate sexual risk (see Chapter 23).

The penile plethysmograph (PPG), also referred to as phallometric testing, measures penile tumescence in response to various stimuli, of an auditory or visual nature, contrasting the individual's reaction to different types of sexual materials and themes presented. This type of testing is undertaken through employment of an apparatus placed around the offender's penis and the data recorded relate to the relative level of arousal the individual produces in response to various stimuli which may include child images, abuse themes, and so on. Research by Hanson and Bussiere (1998) indicates that physiological responding to child sexual themes on the PPG, was a significant predictor of risk as compared with the wide range of other factors that they examined within this landmark meta-analysis of risk factors. The visual reaction time measure explores pupillary response to various visual stimuli and there is evidence that this correlates well with sexual interest. Kalmus and Beech (2005) reviewed the forensic assessment of sexual interest in detail, describing these measures as well as a range of other approaches to evaluation in this area.

Whether for assessment, treatment or supervision of sexual offenders, information from a wide range of sources can be useful to develop more person-focused plans that support a non-offending and productive future lifestyle for individuals convicted of sexual crimes. This may include detailed records of past criminal activity, social services reports, medical records and relevant information in relation to occupational, educational or community activities. Whether working individually or within a group context as a forensic psychologist (or any other professional with a responsibility to protect the public from sexual offenders), it is recognized that while we all have a right to privacy and self-determination, there is significant research evidence that sexual offenders often have multiple deviant sexual interests (Abel and Rouleau, 1990; Heil, Ahlmeyer and Simons, 2003; O'Connell, 1998). As such, more thorough background information may reveal further risk factors that could impact on the likelihood that the individual will commit additional sexual offenses. Care and attention should be focused on these issues, allowing the individual to make personal choices while also endeavoring to assure reasonable levels of protection to the public.

Treatment Variations

Often offenders requiring individual interventions have specific challenges that cannot be addressed within mainstream offender treatment. This may include severe personality disturbances such as Borderline Personality Disorder or psychopathic personality. Further, significant cognitive or affective difficulties, as well as major mental illness (Garrett and Thomas-Peter, 2009), may impede an individual's ability to engage successfully in group treatment. At times, these conditions are reasonably well documented, though with other referrals, the key concern is often one of an inability to engage the individual in groupwork to a degree that provides demonstrable treatment benefits and avoids any significant disruption to the group process. Liaison with the referring probation officer and group facilitator is therefore an important starting point, together with conducting a mental status screening at the first appointment scheduled with the offender. Such a screening would include a review of key cognitive and affective features, though perhaps not a full examination as might occur through a psychiatric or clinical psychological evaluation.

Offenders are referred for individual assessment and/or intervention work for various reasons. They may be aggressive, disruptive, distracted, detached, overtly disturbed, dysregulated (cognitively, emotionally or behaviorally), lacking in insight, disinhibited, cognitively limited, emotionally unavailable, and so on. Sometimes, work undertaken may allow them to be reintegrated into group or to participate in certain modules while undertaking work in some specific and more challenging areas on an individual basis. These various steps are necessary to formulate responsive and informed plans for carrying out forensic psychological interventions with sexual offenders.

Ethical Considerations in the Treatment of Sexual Offenders

Developing accurate sex offender risk assessment, effective treatment and ways to measure progress in this regard have been an ongoing challenge since I began working in this field. Assessment has become more refined and there has been a growing recognition that the tools we employ must take sufficient account of the specific characteristics of the individual being assessed (see Chapter 4). While it is recognized that mainstream risk assessment tools such as the Static-99 (Hanson and Thornton, 1999) and RM2000 (Thornton, 2007) enable more accurate framing of individual risk assessment for mainstream offenders, their applicability to other types of sexual offenders including individuals with Intellectual Disabilities is less helpful. Beech, Craig and Browne (2009) and Craig, Lindsay and Browne (2010) noted that tailored instruments such as the ARMIDILO (Boer, Tough and Haaven, 2004) offer a greater opportunity to assess risk accurately in individuals with significant intellectual limitations (Blacker *et al.*, 2011). Similarly, measures have been developed for evaluating risk in young offenders (Prentky *et al.*, 2000; Worling and Curwen, 2001) though developments of this kind in relation to female offenders and non-contact internet offenders does not appear to have made as much progress (Buschman *et al.*, 2010; Wilcox and Buschman, 2010) (see Chapter 19). There have also been suggestions that risk assessment may be informed by the use of the polygraph (Gannon, Beech and Ward, 2009).

Treatment has also moved on, with the confrontational approaches employed in the 1980s and early 1990s giving way to more collaborative (though still compulsory) groupwork, following evidence by Beckett *et al.* (1994) that the latter approach yields better treatment outcomes. Fisher and Beech (1998) offered a framework for treatment that subsequently provided a model for the first accredited sex offender groupwork program in the United Kingdom. Beech and Fordham (1997) examined the salient features that enhance the treatment environment, noting that the "therapeutic climate" is an important aspect for group success. Garrett *et al.* (2003) examined the attitudes held by offenders about the sex offender groupwork program and, more recently, the perspectives of offenders have been taken more substantially into account within the context of their participation in various aspects of treatment, assessment and monitoring. Championed by Tony Ward and his colleagues, the language of offender treatment has changed and offenders can now be treated while in denial (Roberts and Baim, 1999; Ware and Marshall, 2008).

Different pathways to offending are now taken into account, with the recognition that some types of offenders are less likely to profit from current intervention programs. The more aggressive "hot seat" approach to eliciting disclosures from offenders in group has given way to less confrontational approaches to engagement and even "relapse prevention" is viewed now from the perspective of acquiring offense-free habits, employing the Better Lives model (Ward and Gannon, 2006) (see Chapter 17) and the Risk, Need, Responsivity ("RNR") approach (Andrews, Bonta and Hoge, 1990). The RNR model is based on the results of meta-analyses, which have consistently suggested that the intensity and duration of treatment should be proportionate to the assessed level of risk (largely reliant on a combination of static risk assessment and the evaluation of the individual's deviance levels). Further, the program targets the individual's criminogenic needs, with most sexual offenders attending the mainstream program, while those with cognitive impairments attend an adapted program, designed to take account of their learning difficulties. Similarly, female offenders, adolescent abusers and those convicted of internet sexual crimes will attend cognitive behavioral treatment programs, with these interventions giving due consideration to their individual characteristics and criminogenic needs. The model is tailored to the individual's learning style, motivation, abilities and strengths.

The responsivity principle highlights that the methods used to approach offender treatment will be matched to the perceived best style of engagement and the assessed characteristics of the offender. This enables facilitators in most groups to choose from different approaches to maximize the participant's capacity for engaging and making positive change. Similarly, the language employed in treatment has changed. For example, when the sex offender groupwork program was introduced in the West Midlands, offense disclosures were obtained during the foundation week by undertaking detailed offense accounts with each group member, employing vigorous efforts gradually to introduce greater acceptance of the group member's sexual offense, the planning stages and the impact it had on him and his victim thereafter. While out of necessity, this focus on obtaining offense accounts continues, the "hot seat" notion is no longer supported. However, a benefit of groupwork is that some individuals will be more amenable to engaging openly, and through reinforcing their efforts in the early offense account work, those attendees who are more closed may recognize the merits of more open engagement in group. Indeed, a common theme throughout my time working in sex offender treatment has been that while viewing the sexual crime as legally and morally unacceptable, efforts to make positive life changes, in cooperation with the facilitators, are actively supported, along with any willingness demonstrated on the part of the offender to acknowledge and recognize all of his thoughts, feelings and behaviors that underpinned his offending.

Importantly, in terms of learning theory, it is more helpful to focus on building protective factors in an individual's social repertoire to help them to lead healthy lives, wherein they respect the rights of others, rather than trying to prevent risky behavior from occurring. Indeed, a basic behavioral principle would dictate that when individuals make positive choices that are incompatible with targeted problem behaviors and these choices are reinforced, their ability to sustain these gains is greater than when they are simply punished for misbehaving.

Unfortunately, the public perception, at least in western society, appears to favor increasing sanctions for sex offenders, to reduce their freedom of movement and limit their rights, such that the community is better protected. There is also a limited general public belief that treatment works and, as such, offenders are often viewed as only worthy of punishment and unlikely to respond to therapy, irrespective of their subsequent criminal histories following their conviction for a sexual offense.

Over time, I consider that professionals in the field have acquired tools to improve risk assessment, demonstrate a positive treatment effect and reduce recidivism. Against this backdrop, there has been ongoing debate about the ethics of engaging sexual offenders in compulsory treatment. Concerns continue to be raised about the accuracy of assessment and the effectiveness of interventions, with some considering that it is appropriate to regard sex offender treatment as punishment (Glaser, 2005) and others asserting that this is not the case (Prescott and Levenson, 2010; Ward, 2010). The employment of tagging, compulsory polygraph testing, indefinite commitment, extended community supervision, compulsory sex offender registration and community notification all severely curtail the offender's rights generally in the hope of enhancing public protection (see Chapter 2). Ethical issues also arise in relation to matters of self-incrimination within individual or group treatment settings. In relation to this, responsible practice would dictate that the aim of intervention is not to trick the offender, but rather to assist the offender in achieving an offense-free lifestyle. As such, while it is necessary in treatment to gain information about past patterns of offending in order to develop more effective strategies in the future for the offender to remain offense-free, psychologists and other professionals have a responsibility to clarify to offenders that if they disclose specific information about their past offending that can be identified with a traceable criminal act, then this information will be reported. If offenders report such information intentionally, for example in relation to a sexual offense that preceded the index offense for which they have been convicted, then the treatment facilitator will support the offender's openness throughout this process of disclosure and investigation.

In my experience, individuals who have committed similar offenses to their index offense, prior to conviction, and make disclosures about these events, may well continue with their Court mandated community treatment, though further prosecution may lead the Court to a different view about disposition and, at times, individuals in this situation are incarcerated. Since the aim of the forensic psychologist or treatment worker is to work with the offender to avoid further sexual abuse, the honesty of the professional is important and it should be clarified that while the offender may disclose the details of previous sexual offenses committed, they may choose rather to discuss the type of offense and the offense circumstances in order to cooperate with the treatment worker and create better strategies to achieve offense-free lives in the future.

In some circumstances, psychologists may undertake different roles. They may, for example, have undertaken treatment work with an offender and then subsequently be required to act in the role of an appointed expert within Court proceedings. Importantly, in such circumstances, there is not necessarily an irresolvable conflict, though both roles require objectivity in assessment as well as respect for the integrity of the offender and honesty in reporting (Heltzel, 2007) (see Chapter 5).

Conclusions

Ethical practice has been a matter of concern to me for a number of years and in the early 2000s I was a member of the ethics sub-committee of the National Organization for the Treatment of Abusers (NOTA). I have subsequently become a member of the International Advisory Board for the *Journal of Sexual Aggression*, NOTA's designated professional publication. Within this context, as well as within my roles as Editorial Board Member with the *Child Abuse Review* and the *European Polygraph Journal*, issues of ethical conduct have had an ongoing presence. Further, as an Honorary Research Fellow, lecturer and longstanding placement supervisor for doctoral students in the forensic psychology program at the University of Birmingham, reflection in practice and the requirement of ongoing professional integrity are regularly impressed upon young psychologists in training. In relation to working with sexual offenders there are, in my opinion, significant demands if we are to work effectively and maintain a positive and enabling ethical perspective. I recall the "moral compass" employed at times by a past co-worker who would consider when reflecting on the actions of sexual offenders "I hate what you did but I respect all your efforts to change" (S. McEwan, personal communication, 1997) and consider that this was an honest and enabling appraisal by a skilled and resilient therapist.

In my work as a forensic psychologist with sex offenders, I would judge that I hold a similar perspective to many of my colleagues in this field. Specifically, I consider that assessing, treating and supervising sexual offenders who are mandated by the Court to engage in this process takes precedence over the offender's individual rights. If sexual offenders choose not to engage, then further Court ordered sanctions will be applied, possibly including incarceration or longer custodial sentences for sexual offenders who are already imprisoned. This position is not, however, synonymous with the assertion that sexual offenders do not have basic human rights, though clearly in these circumstances their rights are curtailed. In my opinion, sex offender treatment is increasingly moving towards a more intrinsically moral framework that recognizes that while offenders may not respect the rights of others, they nonetheless retain some fundamental rights to be treated in a way that reflects dignity, fairness and the intention not to cause harm. Further, I would judge that forensic psychologists and other treatment workers can confidently hold the view that besides doing good in relation to community safety, treatment plays a beneficial role in relation to attempting to safeguard the offender from the commission of future sexual offenses and that this is in the best interests of both the individual and those close to him.

While engaging in sex offender treatment, concerns for the social and emotional support and development of offenders are also a significant matter, as enhancing skills in these areas has clear protective features (Beech, Craig and Brown, 2009). Relatedly, law-abiding self-determination is encouraged, as well as positive and reciprocal relationship building. It is recognized that secure relations and stable employment often serve to mitigate against criminal actions, including sexual offending, although these issues are best assessed taking account of individual offender features and criminogenic factors. Further, although compelled to address significant offense-related issues, it is recognized that an individual's offending behavior represents only one aspect of his life and a recognition by professionals of his right to be treated in a fair and honest manner is an expectation he should hold and a responsibility we must bear.

References

Abel, G.G., Huffman, J., Warberg, B. and Holland, C.L. (1998) "Visual reaction time and plethysmography as measures of sexual interest in child molesters," *Sexual Abuse: A Journal of Research and Treatment* 10, 81–95.

Abel, G.G. and Rouleau, J.L. (1990) "The nature and extent of sexual assault," in W.L. Marshall, D.R. Laws and H.E. Barbaree (eds), *Handbook of Sexual Assault: Issues, Theories, and Treatment of the Offender*. New York: Plenum Press, pp. 9–12.

Allam, J. (2000) *Sex Offender Groupwork Program: Evaluation Manual Accredited Program*. Submitted for Home Office Accreditation: WMPS, Birmingham.

Andrews, D.A., Bonta, J. and Hoge, R.D. (1990) "Classification for effective rehabilitation: rediscovering psychology," *Criminal Justice and Behavior* 17, 19–52.

APA (American Psychiatric Association) (1978) *Electroconvulsive Therapy*. Washington, DC: APA.

APA (American Psychiatric Association) (2000) *Diagnostic and Statistical Manual of Mental Disorders – Fourth Edition – Text Revision*. Washington, DC: APA.

Asch, S.E. (1951) "Effects of group pressure upon the modification and distortion of judgement," in H. Guetzkon (ed.), *Groups, Leadership and Men*. Pittsburgh: Carnegie, pp. 177–190.

Ayllon, T. and Azrin, N. (1968) *The Token Economy*. Englewood Cliffs, NJ: Prentice-Hall.

Beck, A.T. (1975) *Cognitive Therapy and the Emotional Disorders*. New York: International Universities Press.

Beckett, R., Beech, A., Fisher, D. and Fordham, A.S. (1994) *Community-Based Treatment for Sex Offenders: An Evaluation of Seven Treatment Programs*. London: Home Office.

Beech, A.R., Craig, L.A. and Browne, K.D. (2009) *Assessment and Treatment of Sex Offenders: A Handbook*. Chichester: John Wiley & Sons, Ltd.

Beech, A.R., Fisher, D.D. and Thornton, D. (2003) "Risk assessment of sex offenders," *Professional Psychology: Research and Practice* 34, 4, 339–352.

Beech, A.R. and Fordham, A.S. (1997) "Therapeutic climate of sex offender treatment programs," *Sexual Abuse: A Journal of Research and Treatment* 9, 219–237.

Berlin, F.S., Galbreath, N.W., Geary, B. and McGlone, G. (2003) "The use of actuarial at civil commitment hearings to predict the likelihood of future sexual violence," *Sexual Abuse: Journal of Research and Treatment* 15, 4, 377–382.

Blacker, J., Beech, A.R., Wilcox, D.T. and Boer, D.P. (2011) "The assessment of dynamic risk and recidivism in a sample of special needs sexual offenders," *Psychology, Crime and Law* 17, 1, 75–92.

Boer, D.P., Tough, S. and Haaven, J. (2004) "Assessment of risk of manageability of intellectually disabled sex offenders," *Journal of Applied Research in Intellectual Disabilities* 17, 4, 275–283.

Bonta, J. (1996) "Risk-needs assessment and treatment," in A.T. Harland (ed.), *Choosing Correctional Options that Work: Defining the Demand and Evaluating the Supply*. Thousand Oaks, CA: Sage, pp. 18–32.

Brady, J.V. (1958) "Ulcers in 'executive' monkeys," *Scientific American* 199, 95–100.

Burrell, I. (1999) "Lie detectors are used to confront sex offenders: Britain set to follow US example and use polygraph tests for criminals in spite of international concern over their results," *Independent*, October 11.

Buschman, J., Wilcox, D.T., Krapohl, D.J., *et al.* (2010) "Cybersex offender risk assessment: an explorative study," *Journal of Sexual Aggression* 16, 2, 197–209.

Buschman, J., Wilcox, D.T., Spreen, M. *et al.* (2008) "Victim ranking among sex offenders," *Journal of Sexual Aggression* 14, 1, 45–52.

Calhoun, J.B. (1962) "Population density and social pathology," *Scientific American* 206, 139–146.

Craig, L.A., Beech, A.R. and Browne, K.D. (2006) "Cross-validation of the risk matrix 2000 sexual and violent scales," *Journal of Interpersonal Violence* 21, 5, 612–633.

Craig, L.A., Lindsay, W.R. and Browne, K.D. (2010) *Assessment and Treatment of Sexual Offenders with Intellectual Disabilities: A Handbook.* Chichester: John Wiley & Sons, Ltd.

Ellis, A. (1973) *Humanistic Psychotherapy: The Rational Emotive Approach.* New York: Julian Press.

Fidura, F.G. and Gray, J.A. (1966) "Visual discrimination of color, pattern and form in the Japanese quail (Coturnix coturnix japonica)," *Psychonomic Science* 11, 427–228.

Fisher, D. and Beech, A.R. (1998) "Reconstructing families after sexual abuse: the offender's perspective," *Child Abuse Review* 7, 6, 420–434.

Freeman, W. and Watts. J.W. (1942) *Psychosurgery. Intelligence, Emotion and Social Behavior Following Prefrontal Lobotomy for Mental Disorders.* Springfield: Charles C. Thomas.

Freund, K. (1963) "A laboratory method for diagnosing predominance of homo- and hetero-erotic interest in the male," *Behavior Research and Therapy* 1, 85–93.

Gannon, T.A., Beech, A.R. and Ward, T. (2009) "Risk assessment and the polygraph," in D.T. Wilcox (ed.), *The Use of the Polygraph in Assessing, Treating and Supervising Sex Offenders: A Practitioner's Guide.* Oxford: Wiley-Blackwell, pp. 129–154.

Garrett, T., Oliver, C., Wilcox, D.T. and Middleton, D. (2003) "Who cares? The views of sexual offenders about the group treatment they receive," *Sexual Abuse: A Journal of Research and Treatment* 15, 4, 323–338.

Garrett, T. and Thomas-Peter, B. (2009) "Interventions with sex offenders with mental illness," in A.R. Beech, L.A. Craig and K.D. Brown (eds), *Assessment and Treatment of Sex Offenders: A Handbook.* Chichester: John Wiley & Sons, Ltd.

Gelder, M., Gath, D., Mayou, R. and Cowen, P. (1996) *Oxford Textbook of Psychiatry.* Oxford: Oxford University Press.

Glaser, B. (2005) "An ethical paradigm for sex offender treatment," *Western Criminology Review* 6, 1, 154–160.

Gregory, G. (2004) A retrospective evaluation into the initial psychometric profiles of individuals who participate in a young adult sex offender treatment program. Master thesis, University of Birmingham.

Guttman, N. and Kalish, H.I. (1956) "Discriminability and stimulus generalization," *Journal of Experimental Psychology* 51, 71–88.

Hanson, R.K., Broom, I. and Stephenson, M. (2004) "Evaluating community sex offender treatment programs: a 12-year follow-up of 724 offenders," *Canadian Journal of Behavioral Science* 36, 2, 87–96.

Hanson, R.K. and Bussiere, M.T. (1998) "Predicting relapse: a meta-analysis of sexual offender recidivism studies," *Journal of Consulting and Clinical Psychology* 66, 2, 348–362.

Hanson, R.K., Steffy, R.A. and Gauthier, R. (1993) "Long-term recidivism of child molesters," *Journal of Consulting and Clinical Psychology* 61, 4, 646–652.

Hanson, R.K. and Thornton, D. (1999) *Static-99: Improving Actuarial Risk Assessments for Sex Offenders.* User Report 99-02. Ottawa: Department of the Solicitor General of Canada.

Harlow, H.F. and Harlow, M. (1969) "Effects of various mother-infant relationships on Rhesus monkey behaviors," in B.M. Foss (ed.), *Determinants of Infant Behavior*, Vol. 4. London: Methuen, pp. 15–36.

Hart, S.D. and Hare, R.D. (1994) "Psychopathy and the big 5: correlations between observers' ratings of normal and pathological personality," *Journal of Personality Disorders* 8, 32–40.

Heil, P., Ahlmeyer, S. and Simons, D. (2003) "Crossover sexual offenses," *Sexual Abuse: A Journal of Research and Treatment* 15, 4, 221–236.

Heltzel, T. (2007) "Compatibility of therapeutic and forensic roles," *Professional Psychology – Research and Practice* 38, 2, 122–128.

Holm, V.A., Cassidy, S.B., Butler, M.G. *et al.* (1993) "Prader-Willi syndrome: consensus, diagnostic criteria," *Pediatrics* 91, 2, 398–402.

Kalmus, E. and Beech, A.R. (2005) "Forensic assessment of sexual interest: a review," *Aggression and Violent Behavior* 10, 193–217.

Leyland, M., Wilcox, D.T., Stait, C. and Geach, M. (1995) Group Techniques with Learning Disabled Offenders. International Conference Presentation for the National Organization for the Treatment of Abusers (UK)/Association for Treatment of Sexual Abusers (USA), Cambridge, September.

Lindsay, W.R. and Beail, N. (2004) "Risk assessment: actuarial prediction and clinical judgment of offending incidents and behavior for intellectual disability services," *Journal of Applied Research in Intellectual Disabilities* 17, 4, 229–234.

Mahoney, M., Maura, N. and Wade, T. (1973) "The relative efficacy of self-reward, self-punishment, self-monitoring techniques," *Journal of Consulting and Clinical Psychology* 40, 404–407.

Marshall, W.L., Anderson, D. and Fernandez, Y. (1999) *Cognitive Behavioral Treatment of Sexual Offenders.* Chichester: John Wiley & Sons, Ltd.

McEwan, S., Leyland, M. and Wilcox, D.T. (1995) Victim to Victimiser: Group Work. International Conference Presentation for the National Organization for the Treatment of Abusers (UK)/Association for Treatment of Sexual Abusers (USA). Cambridge, September.

Middleton, D. and Wilcox, D.T. (1999/2000) Managing Rapists in the Community. Presentation for Senior West Midlands Probation Officers. Birmingham.

Milgram, S. (1974) *Obedience to Authority.* New York: Harper and Row Publishers.

O'Connell, M.A. (1998) "Using polygraph testing to assess deviant sexual history of sex offenders," *Dissertation Abstracts International* 58, 3023.

Pavlov, I.P. (1927) *Conditioned Reflexes,* trans. G.V. Anrep. London: Oxford University Press.

Prentky, R., Harris, B., Frizzell, K. and Rightland, S. (2000) "An actuarial procedure for assessing risk with juvenile sex offenders," *Sexual Abuse: A Journal of Research and Treatment* 12, 2, 71–93.

Prescott, D.S. and Levenson, J.S. (2010) "Sex offender treatment is not punishment," *Journal of Sexual Aggression* 16, 3, 275–285.

Quinsey, V.L., Harris, G.T., Rice, M.E. and Cormier, A. (1998) *Violent Offenders: Appraising and Managing Risk.* Washington, DC: American Psychological Association.

Revitch, E. and Weiss, R.G. (1962) "The pedophiliac offender," *Diseases of the Nervous System* 23, 73–78.

Roberts, B. and Baim, C. (1999) "A community based programme for sex offenders who deny their offending behaviour," *Probation Journal* 46, 4, 225–233.

Rotter, J.B. (1954) *Social Learning and Clinical Psychology.* New York: Prentice-Hall.

Salter, A. (1988) *Treating Child Sex Offenders and Victims: A Practical Guide.* Newbury Park, CA: Sage Publications Inc.

Salter, A. (1997) Sex Offender Assessment and Risk Management Issues. National Organization for the Treatment of Abusers (NOTA) Annual Conference. Southampton, England, September.

Saunders, N.L. and Summers, M.J. (2011) "Longitudinal deficits to attention, executive, and working memory in subtypes of mild cognitive impairment," *Neuropsychology* 25, 2, 237–248.

Singer, P. (1975) *Animal Liberation*. Wellingborough: Thorsons Publishers Limited.

Skinner, B.F. (1974) *About Behaviorism*. New York: Knopf.

Solomon, R.L., Kamin, L.J. and Wynne, L.C. (1953) "Traumatic avoidance learning: the outcomes of several extinction procedures with dogs," *Journal of Abnormal and Social Psychology* 48, 291–302.

Thornton, D. (2007) Scoring Guide for Risk Matrix 2000.9/SVC. Unpublished manuscript.

Valenstein, E.S. (1980) "Historical perspective," in E.S. Valenstein, *The Psychosurgery Debate*. San Francisco: Freeman, pp. 35–45.

Vess, J. (2011) "Ethical practice in sex offender assessment: consideration of actuarial and polygraph methods," *Sexual Abuse: Journal of Research and Treatment* 23, 3, 381–396.

Ward, T. (2010) "Punishment or therapy? The ethics of sexual offending treatment," *Journal of Sexual Aggression* 16, 3, 286–295.

Ward, T. and Gannon, T. (2006) "Rehabilitation, etiology, and self-regulation: the Good Lives Model of sexual offender treatment," *Aggression and Violent Behavior* 11, 770–794.

Ware, J. and Marshall, W.L. (2008) "Treatment engagement with a sexual offender who denies committing the offense," *Clinical Case Studies* 7, 6, 592–603.

Watson, J.B. and Rayner, R. (1920) "Conditioned emotional reactions," *Journal of Experimental Psychology* 3, 1–14.

Wells, S. and Quash, B. (2010) *Introducing Christian Ethics*. Chichester: John Wiley & Sons, Ltd.

West Midlands Probation Service, Sex Offender Unit (1995/2000) *Community Sex Offender Groupwork Program – Manual*. West Midlands Probation Service, Birmingham (subsequently accredited by the Home Office).

Wilcox, D.T. (1978) Abbreviated behavioral treatments of obesity: a comparative analysis. Master thesis, State University of New York at Geneseo, New York.

Wilcox, D.T. (1982) Deinstitutionalization of Willowbrook. Master thesis, State University of New York at Brockport, New York.

Wilcox, D.T. (1993) Group Therapy for People with Challenging Behaviors and Sexual Problems. Psychotherapy – Clinical Training for People with Learning Disability, West Midlands Psychiatry Regional Seminar. University of Birmingham, School of Medicine, June.

Wilcox, D.T. (2000) "Application of the clinical polygraph examination to the assessment, treatment and monitoring of sex offenders," *Journal of Sexual Aggression* 5, 2, 134–152.

Wilcox, D.T. (2002) The application of the clinical polygraph examination to the assessment, treatment and monitoring of sex offenders. PhD thesis, University of Surrey.

Wilcox, D.T. (2004a) Treatment of intellectually disabled men who have committed sexual offenses. Keynote presentation for Scottish National Organization for the Treatment of Abusers (NOTA) Annual Conference. Stirling, Scotland, October.

Wilcox, D.T. (2004b) "Treatment of intellectually disabled individuals who have committed sexual offenses: a review of the literature," *Journal of Sexual Aggression* 10, 1, 85–100.

Wilcox, D.T. (2009) *The Use of the Polygraph in Assessing, Treating and Supervising Sex Offenders*. Oxford: Wiley-Blackwell.

Wilcox, D.T., Beech, A.R., Markall, H. and Blacker, J. (2009) "Actuarial risk assessment and recidivism in a sample of UK intellectually disabled sexual offenders," *Journal of Sexual Aggression* 15, 1, 97–106.

Wilcox, D.T. and Buschman, J. (2010) "Polygraph testing internet offenders," *Forensic Update* 101, 30–35.

Wilcox, D.T., Foss, C.M. and Donathy, M.L. (2005) "A case study of a male sex offender with zoosexual interests and behaviors," *Journal of Sexual Aggression* 11, 3, 305–317.

Wilcox, D.T. and Sosnowski, D. (2005) "Polygraph examination of British sexual offenders: a pilot study on sexual history disclosure testing," *Journal of Sexual Aggression* 11, 1, 3–25.

Wilcox, D.T., Sosnowski, D. and Middleton, D. (1999) "The use of the polygraph in the community supervision of sex offenders," *Probation Journal* 46, 4, 234–240.

Worling, I.R. and Curwen, T. (2001) "Estimate of risk of adolescent offense recidivism (ERASOR; Version 2.0)," in M.C. Calder (ed.), *Juveniles and Children who Sexually Abuse: Frameworks for Assessment*. Dorset: Russell House, pp. 372–397.

Zimbardo, P.G., Ebbesen, E. and Maslach, C. (1977) *Influencing Attitudes and Changing Behavior*, 2nd edn. Reading, MA: Addison-Wesley.

16

Punishment and the Rehabilitation of Sex Offenders

An Ethical Maelstrom

Tony Ward and Chelsea Rose

Introduction

Psychologists and other practitioners working therapeutically with clients are confronted with normative or value based issues in every aspect of their work. Diagnosing mental disorders or problems, deciding what measures to use in assessment, and specifying the aims of therapy all contain an irreducible normative (value based) dimension (Brinkmann, 2011). For example, the fact that psychological problems cause distress in the lives of people suffering from them directly evokes the issue of harmful dysfunction, a value based concept. Just what part of the mind is malfunctioning, and why does this result in suffering and problems with living? The relationship between values and therapeutic interventions is even more apparent. Typically, the intention is to reduce persons' pain and to enhance their ability to deal effectively with their symptoms and live happier lives. Martin (2006) has argued that ethical values are evident in mental health practices in at least three major ways: (1) ethical behavior is likely to result in better levels of well-being and psychological health (for example, compassion deepens relationships); (2) clients are expected to take at least some degree of responsibility for their treatment; and (3) many mental disorders such as personality disorders and the paraphilias are in part defined by the values that the community holds about certain behaviors. Professional ethical codes have been developed explicitly to assist those involved in psychological assessment and treatment to make better normative and ethical decisions in their day-to-day work (Cooper, 2004; Day and Ward, 2010).

But just what is the normative dimension? What are values? In brief, values reflect individuals' judgments about what kind of activities and experiences are worth pursuing in their lives and likely to meet their core and related interests. The normativeness

The Wiley-Blackwell Handbook of Legal and Ethical Aspects of Sex Offender Treatment and Management, First Edition. Edited by Karen Harrison and Bernadette Rainey. © 2013 John Wiley & Sons, Ltd. Published 2013 by John Wiley & Sons, Ltd.

of values resides in their prescriptive nature: certain experiences or objects are thought to be worthwhile pursuing and therefore *ought* to be sought. They are thought to bring benefits to people and to improve the quality of their lives. There are different types of values each type associated with a distinct arena of human functioning, although for our purposes, two kinds are particularly relevant: prudential and ethical. *Prudential* values are those activities and outcomes that are likely to increase individuals' level of well-being or personal happiness, for example, health, relationships or work. Prudential values reside at the heart of psychological practice where the aim is to ease people's suffering and to restore or improve their capacity to live enjoyable and pain-free lives. While *ethical* values are those associated with the concepts of right and wrong, good and bad, they function to regulate relationships between people and to help coordinate competing or conflicting interests. In therapeutic contexts, ethical norms (principles and standards embodying values) are typically present in the form of codes of conduct that specify what constitutes acceptable (right/good) and unacceptable (wrong/bad) professional behavior. Thus ethical values in the form of principles and standards delineate the boundaries of permissible behaviors, while prudential values are more closely associated with the aims of therapeutic practice.

In the domain of forensic and correctional practice the relevance and influence of values, especially ethical values, is even more pronounced (Day and Ward, 2010). Criminal justice institutions such as the courts, police and prisons are necessarily involved with the phenomenon of crime and the way it is responded to and managed. Crimes are typically viewed as wrongful acts that have significantly harmful effects on individual citizens or important social institutions, for example, assault, theft, corruption or sexual violation. Thus, crimes are viewed as both unethical and illegal by the state because of the degree of harm they cause others and because this harm is thought to warrant sanctions of some kind (Duff and Green, 2011). It is clear that the boundary between harmful and harmless actions is in part a value distinction, as is the further distinction between what is ethically wrong and what is illegal. While prudential values exert an important influence on the way offenders are treated, and also in particular types of correctional programs, ethical values loom large and take center stage. The prominence of ethical values is due to two distinct issues: (1) the judgment that offenders have committed serious transgressions against members of the community, and the state, and (2) the decision to inflict sanctions, or legally justified harms, on these individuals. The infliction of harms on offenders by the state is known as legal punishment, and it creates significant ethical problems: can the intentional imposition of penalties upon an individual be ethically justified? And if so, how? For practitioners there are also further problems concerning the impact of such justifications of punishment on their practice and professional roles; are these acceptable or do they lead to other ethical problems (Ward and Salmon, 2009)? Also, where should the boundaries between practitioners' status as agents of the criminal justice system, and as mental health practitioners be drawn? Does one role trump the other, and if so, how can this be justified? Disappointingly, such matters have not been dealt with in any depth. Instead the focus has been on issues such as duty to warn, conflict of interests and protection of the community, rather than problems like human rights conflict or how to address practitioners' deep value commitments (Bush, Connell and Denny, 2006; Haag, 2006; Ward and Salmon, 2009).

In this chapter we explore ethical questions emerging from the institution of legal punishment for practitioners involved with sex offender rehabilitation. First, we outline the ethical problem of punishment in greater detail. Second, we analyze the concept of punishment and arrive at a specification of its core features. Third, three popular justifications of punishment are described. Fourth, four ethical problems related to the legal institution of punishment that arise for practitioners are outlined and discussed: the implications of working in correctional environments relying on certain conceptions of punishment; the issue of overlapping normative frameworks; the way punishment conceptions can define or constrain practitioners' roles; and finally, whether therapy for sex offenders should be viewed as a form of punishment or whether it constitutes therapy in the usual sense of that term.

The Problem of Punishment

Worrying about sentencing sex offenders to terms of imprisonment followed by strict parole conditions might seem to many people senseless. Surely, they claim, if individuals have committed serious crimes they should forfeit their freedom and associated rights? Furthermore, it may seem obvious that locking sex offenders away can only serve the greater good of the community, and also possibly deter them from committing further crimes. That is, punishment by imprisonment is deemed valuable because it is deserved, protects the community, rehabilitates offenders and, overall, encourages citizens to obey the law. So where is the problem? Unfortunately matters are not so simple, at least from an ethical perspective (Vess, 2009). The costs of punishment to the offender and his or her family are often extremely high and the intentional infliction of harm on another person needs a strong ethical justification. As Tadros (2011: 1) states:

> Punishment is probably the most awful thing that modern democratic states systematically do to their own citizens. Every modern democratic state imprisons thousands of offenders every year, depriving them of their liberty, causing them a great deal of psychological and sometimes physical harm. Relationships are destroyed, jobs are lost, the risk of the offender being harmed by other offenders is increased, and all at great expense to the state . . . Punishment is one rare example where intentionally harming others is deemed acceptable.

The problem of punishment arises from the need for ethical justification for intentionally harming another human being, when normally such actions are deemed unacceptable. It is not enough to state that criminal actions are deserved, or that punishment is likely to result in a reduction in crime or the reformation of an offender's character. What are required are reasons justifying the infliction of harm on others. Thus, it is necessary to provide an argument to justify the state acting in ways that impose harms on those who break the law. In addition to the suffering experienced by offenders and their families there is the question of the financial cost to the state of building and running prisons rather than putting the money to alternative uses such as creating better health care services or providing free high quality education and vocational training for everyone. However, before we turn to the justification of punishment it is first necessary to define this term and also that of treatment or rehabilitation.

What is Punishment?

State-inflicted punishment in the criminal justice system involves the intentional imposition of pain (sanction, burden) on an individual following his or her violation of important social norms that are intended to protect significant common interests of members of the political community (Bennett, 2008; Duff, 2001; Dolinko, 2011). Arriving at a comprehensive definition that contains strict, necessary and sufficient conditions of punishment has proved somewhat elusive. However, it is commonly accepted by philosophers and theorists of law that the institution of punishment has at least six essential elements (Boonin, 2008; Dolinko, 2011). In brief, the actions constituting punishment follow an offense against legal rules; are imposed and implemented by individuals authorized by the state; are intentional (directed toward a particular end or action outcome); are reprobative (express disapproval or censure); are retributive (follow an actual wrongful act committed by the offender); and are harmful (result in suffering, a burden or deprivation to the offender). According to this analysis the intention of an individual administering punishment is crucial when it comes to deciding whether punishment is being administered. The infliction of harm that follows from an action not intended to harm someone is *not* punishment. Relatedly, harmful consequences that follow an action that is intended to be beneficial, or not harmful, is not punishment either. An example of the latter is when therapy causes a person to become distressed as a result of being reminded of a painful earlier event; the suffering is a byproduct of a therapeutic encounter and is not the object of the therapist's intentions.

The terms *treatment* or offender *rehabilitation* are often not defined comprehensively, although Prescott and Levenson (2010: 276) state that:

> Rehabilitation is defined as restoring an individual to good health or a useful life through therapy and education. Punishment and rehabilitation are distinct goals of criminal justice, though they may both be facilitated through a sentence pronounced after conviction of a crime.

Treatment can mean simply action or conduct intended to advance someone's goals; for example: "I treated him with respect when administering punishment." In this sense of the term, treatment is entirely consistent with punishment. The more relevant sense of the term refers to its use in administering interventions intended to heal or manage a person's (physical or psychological) disorder or affliction. According to this sense of the term, the primary reason for treating someone is to restore him or her to a state of well-being and thus enable him or her to live a functionally better life. Treating an offender is thought to be in his or her own interests, and any benefits for the greater community are secondary. There may be borderline cases in which the interests of both the community and the person being treated are equally important. In the case of someone suffering from a contagious disease, quarantining him or her will protect others from infection and treatment during this period of imposed isolation will benefit directly the individuals concerned. It could be argued that sex offender therapy is like this, in that successful treatment will have positive effects for the wider community and also for a person participating in a therapy program. The associated terms of rehabilitation and therapy have similar meanings, except that in the case of the former it has been applied more widely to offenders. As we will see later, some theorists argue that there is no such thing as sex offender treatment at all, rather it is more accurately described as punishment.

Justification of Punishment

The literature on punishment is huge and a large number of theories or justifications have been proposed by moral philosophers and law theorists (see Boonin, 2008). However, a closer look at this writing reveals the existence of two main kinds of theories: retributive and consequential. In addition, a promising recent development has been the emergence of communicative theories with their reference to moral communities and the restorative function of punishment. In this section, we will describe these three types of punishment justification. Our intention is to outline each theory in its most basic form and we will not be engaging in critical analysis (for this see Boonin, 2008; Ward and Salmon, 2009).

Retributive justification

Retributive theories are backward-looking and justify punishment in terms of "its intrinsic justice as a response to crime" (Duff, 2001: 19). The primary aim of punishment is to hold offenders accountable for crimes by inflicting burdens that are roughly equal in harm to those inflicted on their victims. According to retributive theorists a key relationship is the one between past crimes and the present punishment as opposed to the consequential claim that punishment is justified by its beneficial consequences (see below). The state is thought to be ethically obligated to punish offenders because of the nature of the wrongful act and not for any other reasons. Therefore, the fact that punishment does not reduce crime is not of major concern to retributive theorists; it is fitting and just to punish in order to balance the moral ledger. In answer to the question why punish, retributive justifications typically utilize the notion of just deserts: offenders deserve to suffer for the wrongful acts they have committed.

Retributive theories are typically based on the Kantian idea that offenders are moral agents whose violation of moral norms requires a respectful and measured response. In the case of serious crimes the kind of reaction warranted is one that takes seriously the fact that the offender intentionally and knowingly committed a wrongful act and therefore is responsible for what he or she did. Punishment acknowledges the autonomy and responsibility of offenders and the significance of the norms violated by holding offenders accountable. Failure to hold offenders accountable and to punish can be seen as an unacceptable form of paternalism where individuals are viewed as morally deficient and lacking an understanding of what they did.

Consequential justification

Consequential theories of punishment locate their justification in the consequences of the practice; they are forward-looking theories (Bennett, 2008; Kleinig, 2008). Basically, consequential theories of punishment argue that there is a contingent relationship between the overall goal of crime reduction and the practice of punishment. The claim is that punishment functions to deter, incapacitate or reform offenders and that these effects in turn reduce the overall crime rate. Consequential theorists assert that punishment is more likely than other types of crime reduction practices to produce an overall aggregate effect of crime reduction and that this is what justifies them. Thus it is argued that a threat of punishment may deter individuals from committing crimes in the first place or stop offenders from committing further crimes because they want to avoid additional suffering. It is accepted that infliction of suffering is ordinarily a bad thing but that in the case of state inflicted punishment any harmful effects of punishment on offenders and their families are outweighed by the greater reduction of suffering to victims, potential victims and the wider community. The relationship is called a contingent one because it is based on the actual effects punishment has on crime rates rather than reflecting an intrinsic aspect of wrongful acts. That is, if other ways of reducing the crime rate such as situational crime control, education, persuasion and so on result in larger overall reductions in offending, then, according to consequential theorists, they should be implemented in its place.

The justification of consequential theories of punishment resides in the postulated aggregate reduction in crime rates compared to other crime-reducing strategies that do not involve the deliberate infliction of harm on an offender. While it is accepted that individuals undergoing punishment will suffer, sometimes considerably, this bad thing is on balance thought to be acceptable because of the greater good done, or the amount of harm avoided.

Communicative justification

A relatively recent innovation in the punishment literature has been the development of mixed or hybrid theories, which contain both consequential and retributive elements. One promising approach is the communicative theory of punishment of Antony Duff (2001). According to Duff, it is important to pay attention to the rights of all stakeholders in the criminal justice system including offenders because of their equal moral status; thus communicative theories of punishment have a *relationship* focus. From this perspective, offenders are viewed as members of a normative community (that is, "one of us") and therefore are bound and protected by the community's public values: autonomy, freedom, privacy and pluralism. A major assumption of such a viewpoint is that any punishment should be inclusive of offenders rather than exclusive. That is, while individuals who have committed public wrongs should be held to account because they have committed harmful actions against others, they ought to be approached as beings of value and dignity and treated with respect in the process of administering punishment. The notion of equal moral status means that punishment should seek to persuade rather than force offenders to take responsibility for their crimes. Furthermore, because offenders are viewed as fellow members of the moral community it is taken for granted that the aim of punishment is to communicate the wrongness of their actions in order to give them an opportunity to redeem themselves and ultimately be reconciled to the community. Duff argues that hard treatment such as imprisonment is obligatory because it draws offenders' attention to the seriousness of the wrongs they have committed and appropriately expresses social disapproval. Crimes are viewed as violations of important community norms that the offender is assumed to endorse as well.

A key difference between communicative and general retributive theories of punishment is that offenders are viewed as valued members of the community rather than as simply individuals who are held responsible. Thus the aim is to repair or restore offenders' relationships with victims (if possible), and the broader community. Duff argues that there are three aims integral to the institution of punishment: secular repentance, reform and reconciliation through the imposition of sanctions. More specifically, he argues that punishment is: "a burden imposed on an offender for his crime, through which, it is hoped, he will come to repent his crime, to begin to reform himself, and thus reconcile himself with those he has wronged" (Duff, 2001: 106).

Practice Ethical Issues Related to Punishment

Working in unethical environments

It could be argued that practitioners are immune from any ethical fall-out associated with punishment because their roles center around actions that are intended to benefit offenders directly and are not in any sense intentionally harmful or designed to express censure. In our view this is mistaken. For one thing, the daily professional actions of psychologists, social workers, therapists and program staff are embedded within criminal justice contexts. They work in prisons or community justice settings that have their rationale firmly grounded in the punishment of individuals who have been found guilty of breaking the law. If the external environment is characterized by the infliction of unjustified harms on offenders, then staff have an ethical obligation to seek to end such injustices. Failure to do so would arguably make practitioners complicit in unacceptable practices (Lazarus, 2004). The segregation of sex offenders for their protection may have the unintended result that they have little or no access to prison-supported leisure activities or vocational training opportunities (Ward and Birgden, 2007). In part, this measure could be due to excessive concern with security matters and an underplaying of sex offenders' legitimate claims for health and educational entitlements. Either way, it is unjust and, at the very least, ought to be explicitly addressed rather than simply be allowed to proceed unquestioned. It is easier to endorse these kinds of restrictive practices, or at least not to object to them, if the justification of punishment underlying penal policies is consequential or retributive in nature. By way of contrast, a communicative justification has at its center the aim of restoring offenders to their citizenship status and looks to engage them as moral equals, albeit as individuals who are obligated to make amends for their past harmful actions. From this perspective, denying offenders the opportunity to engage in activities that they are entitled to is unethical.

Thus, practitioners have an ethical responsibility critically to scrutinize the broader living environment and conditions of sex offenders and to ascertain whether or not they are being treated fairly and respectfully. Part of this responsibility involves articulating and evaluating the conceptions of punishment underpinning penal and correctional practices.

Overlapping normative frameworks

Practitioners working with offenders are subject to at least two distinct, although partially overlapping, sets of normative requirements: as criminal justice employees and as mental health professionals. It is helpful to construe these role expectations and their respective ethical requirements as normative frameworks that stipulate the type of tasks practitioners ought to engage in, and the duties and entitlements associated with such roles. As employees authorized by the state to work with offenders, a major concern is to monitor their risk levels, as the level of risk concerns the likelihood an offender will re-offend, in order to ensure the community is protected. In addition, they are likely to evaluate the degree to which offenders accept responsibility for their past criminal actions and display contrition. These are both value laden tasks with a strong ethical overlay, as ultimately there is a responsibility to ensure that the community is safe from further predation by dangerous individuals. From the perspective of the criminal justice system, the major responsibility of practitioners is to the community, and the state. The institution of punishment constitutes a normative backdrop for criminal justice practitioners and in part constrains and shapes their roles within correctional agencies. What we mean by this is that because offenders are subject to state-authorized sanctions the conception(s) of punishment underlying their policies will in part dictate how practitioners go about fulfilling their roles as criminal justice employees (we will discuss this in greater depth below). But an essential element will involve viewing offenders through a conceptual lens partially determined by concerns for the protection of the community. Thus the major values will be ethical in nature and concerned with the rightness or wrongness of offenders' actions, and the "goodness" or "badness" of their characters. In our experience practitioners rarely use these terms (they may use the language of dynamic risk factors such as offense supportive beliefs and attitudes) but it does seem that these distinctions capture their ethical aims very well.

However, as psychologists or clinicians working with offenders therapeutically, practitioners' actions are also constrained by their respective ethical codes. Typically professional ethical codes contain a set of foundational principles that stipulate they should be respectful of clients' autonomy, promote their well-being, avoid engaging in harmful and deceitful practices, and act in a just and fair manner (Ward and Syversen, 2009). The values in question are primarily prudential in nature and practices based on these values oriented towards reducing individuals' suffering and increasing their level of well-being, or, if you like, happiness. Attention to clients' propensity to act in harmful ways towards themselves and others is certainly prescribed but the primary focus is on the good of the client from a prudential perspective.

The major ethical problem arising from the presence of the two normative frameworks of community protection and client well-being is that it can make it difficult for clinicians to decide how to act in certain contexts and also result in overlooking or dismissing the interests of offenders. It seems to us that the communicative justification of punishment can help to reduce the conflict because of its requirement that offenders are treated with dignity and are members of the moral community. Punishment is delivered in ways that are respectful and the aim is ultimately to facilitate their reintegration into the community. By contrast, consequential justifications with their emphasis on the greater good, and retributive approaches with their stress on desert, are much more likely to overlook the legitimate concerns of offenders in favor of the interests of members of the community (see Ward and Salmon, 2009).

Regardless of what conception of punishment underlies penal policies at any point in time, one thing is clear: practitioners' work in the criminal justice system is regulated by distinct sets of normative concerns. There are at least two, not mutually exclusive, ways to approach this problem. The first is to compile a hybrid ethical code that contains components that speak to the distinct ethical duties of criminal justice practitioners. For example, there will be sections addressing issues of punishment and community protection *and* others more directly dealing with therapeutic actions and contexts. The second is to create a comprehensive ethical framework that can provide the resources to resolve competing demands, or at least makes a reasonable attempt to do so. For example, the key argument of a recent article by Ward and Syversen (2009) is that researchers and practitioners ought to justify their ethical decisions in a stepwise process, typically first relying on their commonsense everyday reasoning and then in successive steps appealing to the standards of ethical codes, principles underling ethical codes (such as beneficence, autonomy, justice and integrity), ethical concepts and theory and, ultimately, the concept of human dignity (see Chapter 2). The concept of human dignity is an old ethical idea that has at its core the claim that every human being has intrinsic worth and is equal in this respect (Waldron, 2009; Beyleveld and Brownsword, 2001). Thus, because of their inherent dignity, human beings are assumed to possess equal moral status and therefore are expected to receive due consideration in matters that directly affect their core interests. Dignity functions as a foundational concept for practitioners and reminds them that a dignified human life requires certain well-being and empowerment goods.

Punishment and professional roles

As stated earlier, assumptions concerning punishment are likely to be reflected in the specific penal policies and practices embedded in the criminal justice system and constrain or even directly shape the professional tasks constituting the roles of psychologists and other types of correctional practitioners (Ward and Syversen, 2009). We will now briefly consider the practice implications of the three justifications of punishment outlined above.

Retributive justifications   A major implication is that less attention is given to the question of how to intervene therapeutically in offenders' lives and more to holding them accountable. That is, overall, retributive theories are associated with correctional policies and practices that are responsibility-focused. The reason for the accent on responsibility rather than crime reduction and/or offender reintegration is that punishment is thought to be intrinsically related to wrongful acts rather than to future beneficial consequences. Relatedly, an emphasis on offender accountability means that victims' rights and the community's views will be given priority in the sentencing process and subsequent correctional interventions. Because retributive reactions to crime are essentially backward-looking, punishment allows victims to express their anger and to have their experiences taken into account in the sentencing process. Accountability, from a retributive perspective, encourages offenders to face up to the nature of the harm inflicted and to make amends through accepting the burdens associated with hard treatment. In some retributive contexts, the inherent dignity and moral agency of offenders may get swamped in the press for just deserts, and overly severe sentences can be imposed alongside harsh punishment conditions, for example, in prison (Golash, 2005). The ethical challenge for practitioners is that there may be threats to offenders' human rights and also correspondingly restricted funding for treatment and reintegration programs (Griffin, 2008). The lack of funding is connected to a greater concern with accountability and redress as opposed to prudential concerns such as enhanced offender functioning and reintegration. The reduced interest in treatment programs and post-release planning is to be expected because offenders are considered to be moral agents and therefore responsible for their crimes. The significant issues confronting correctional personnel are thought to be rooted in matters of accountability and redress rather than rehabilitation. In fact rehabilitative interventions are looked at with suspicion because of a fear they imply a lack of autonomy and responsibility in offenders. A danger of highlighting moral accountability is that ethical considerations will be elevated over prudential or psychological ones and areas of psychological or social need will be overlooked. Because offenders are presumed to be competent there is no reason to inquire into their level of social and psychological functioning. To do so can be viewed as disrespectful and as stripping individuals of their status as moral equals.

As stated above, a worry for practitioners is that legitimate psychological problems such as impulsivity will be characterized as simple failures of the will rather than as significant self-regulation impairments. In the determination to respect offenders' rights to punishment there is a real possibility that their proclivity to re-offending will be framed in terms of intentionality and willpower, to an exclusion of questions of psychological vulnerability (Andrews and Bonta, 2006). That is, ethical concerns are seen as typically trumping psychological issues and, despite the presence of problems that merit psychosocial interventions, offenders will be expected to make their own way without potentially valuable therapeutic help. Given the interest that retributive theories of punishment have in moral agency as opposed to psychological functioning, one possibility is that there will be considerable effort put into determining the psychological conditions and parameters of responsible behavior. This could be evident in the conceptualization and management of disorders such as psychopathy primarily in terms of moral deficits rather than psychiatric symptoms. The identification of disorders that undermine agency would be viewed as relevant and given priority, but care would be taken to make sure that the boundaries of such cases are tightly drawn. This is in order to prevent the medicalization of the criminal justice system and a subsequent tendency to see offenders as victims rather than responsible moral agents. The majority of offenders, including violent and sexual offenders will be held accountable, and it would be anticipated that punishment will result in acceptance of responsibility, remorse and a reform of character. The question of offender reform is considered to be an individual matter and it is unlikely that a large role for community reintegration programs or recognition of the community's obligation actively to scaffold individuals' reintegration efforts will be accepted.

Consequential justifications   We will now briefly examine the practice implications of a consequential justification of punishment in the correctional arena. What are the implications likely to be for practitioners? A first comment is that an emphasis on deterrence, incapacitation or reformation is liable to create a practice environment where there is significant pressure on staff to detect and manage risk variables in individual offenders and within correctional contexts. The primary focus will be technical and revolve around the development of procedures designed to measure dynamic and static risk factors reliably. That is, there will be a stress on estimating the degree to which individuals constitute a threat to the community and then putting procedures in place to reduce or minimize these risk factors in the most cost-efficient manner. From this viewpoint, individuals who have committed crimes will be viewed as bearers of risk, potential agents of harm, or hazards, resulting in secondary attention to therapeutic relationship factors and offenders' personal goals and aspirations. Security concerns and the rights of victims and the community are likely to trump those of offenders. Second, an exclusive focus on crime reduction by way of deterrence, incapacitation, or reformation points to offenders being regarded as simply a means through which the community's aims for safety are pursued rather than as independent moral agents who ought to be reasoned with, not coerced. The lack of recognition of offenders as beings with inherent dignity, and whose autonomy and equal standing should be acknowledged, reflects an overly objective rather than involved perspective towards them (Bennett, 2008; Beyleveld and Brownsword, 2001). Objectivity in this sense is a mode of analysis that concentrates on causal factors generating behavior as opposed to grasping offenders' understanding of the world and their reasons for acting. By way of contrast, an involved perspective yields an analysis of offenders' sense of meaning and their reasons for doing what they did. In light of a reductionistic, objective attitude toward offenders it is probable that interventions intended to enhance a person's abilities and well-being will be less prominent and that there will be a porous boundary between ethical and prudential values evident in programs. In other words, risk reduction programs might appear to be extensions of punishment because of their strong emphasis on community safety and close monitoring of offenders. It is also to be expected that measures such as civil commitment (see Chapter 24), extended supervision orders, geographical restrictions (see Chapter 25) and community notification (see Chapter 21) will feature prominently because of their risk detection and management functions. We further anticipate that assessment and treatment will concentrate on individual offenders as opposed to interventions that include families and the community.

Communicative justifications   In brief, the implications for clinical practice in the correctional domain following from a communicative theory of punishment are best summed up by the concepts of inclusiveness and mutual respect (Darwell, 2006). Offenders are regarded as fellow travelers, members of the political and moral community who share the same entitlements and obligations as everyone else. Offenders are held to account when they violate moral and legal norms because these norms are binding on everyone and judged to protect the core interests of all citizens. However, because of their equal moral standing in the political sense, community punishment is administered in a respectful manner. According to the communicative theory, criminal sanctions aim to communicate to offenders the wrongness of their actions and to express the hope that they will prompt repentance, self-reform and reconciliation. Rehabilitation implications arising from this theory of punishment are likely to build on the values of respect, autonomy, dignity and mutuality. In our view, a strength-based and community-oriented treatment approach is more consistent with this approach to punishment than risk-oriented interventions. One reason for this judgment is that strength-based approaches such as the Good Lives Model take seriously offenders' deep commitments while also being aware of the necessity to respect the rights to safety of the rest of the community (Maruna, 2001; Ward and Maruna, 2007). By way of contrast, the usual implementations of the risk management are typically preoccupied with threat detection and its management and give less priority to offenders' own interests and preferences.

Is therapy punishment?   It is hopefully apparent from our earlier discussion of normative frameworks and professional roles that the boundaries between therapy and punishment with sex offenders are not that clear. In fact, some researchers have argued they do not exist and what we call sex offender treatment is simply an aspect of punishment, and therefore traditional codes of ethics are ill-suited to the task of guiding therapists working with this group (Glaser, 2010). However, this view has been hotly contested by others who assert that sex offender treatment does meet the requirements of treatment and therefore traditional ethical codes ought to be used to guide the actions of therapists (Prescott and Levenson, 2010). It is useful to look at a recent debate on this topic because it illustrates the problems we highlighted earlier in this chapter. Mainly, there has been a failure to appreciate the problems of role boundaries and conflicting normative frameworks confronting sex offender therapists.

In his recent paper, Glaser (2010; and see Chapter 17) argued that because sex offender treatment occurs within a criminal justice context it contains aspects of punishment, and therefore traditional ethical codes cannot hope to guide practitioners. He asserted that a lack of consent (that is, indirectly or indirectly coercive treatment), the intentional infliction of harm apparent in some treatment modules (such as cognitive restructuring), disregard of confidentiality and, most significantly, the fact that the aim of treatment is to protect the public, and not to restore or enhance the functional capacity and well-being of offenders, are all deeply ethically problematic. Glaser concluded that overall sex offender treatment was more consistent with the definition of punishment than that of treatment. Furthermore, he asserted that relying on standard practitioner ethical codes will most likely result in deceitful and duplicitous behavior on the part of therapists, which will ultimately erode their ethical integrity. According to Glaser, this kind of unethical behavior is likely to occur because of the ignored coercive and punishment-oriented nature of standard sex offender treatment. He proposed that if sex offender practitioners grasp the nettle, so to speak, and come to terms with the fact that sex offender treatment contains aspects of punishment, they would accept that only a justified theory of punishment could provide the necessary ethical guidance. Glaser argued that therapists should be honest with offenders and tell them that treatment is an aspect of punishment, but also reassure them that punishment will be delivered in ways that are consistent with human rights and the maximization of liberty of all concerned (including offenders). Furthermore, he asserted that a (justified) punishment-oriented intervention approach would be more ethical. This is because punishment would lead to more respectful attitudes towards offenders, have greater transparency concerning the aims of treatment, and be less likely to result in abuses of power within a therapeutic context.

In their response to Glaser, Prescott and Levenson (2010) argued that, in general, traditional codes of ethics (for example, social workers' and psychologists' ethical codes) do address the issue of balancing the rights of clients with those of others and, further, that Glaser is incorrect to state that they do not. Prescott and Levenson asserted that because offenders' rights have to be considered by therapists, they are not simply agents of social control. They point out that mental health ethical codes allow for the breaking of confidentiality in specific circumstances, that this is not a "routine" occurrence, and that not all breaches arise from the neglect of clients' well-being. Relatedly, their view is that a crude juxtaposition of offenders versus the rights of others amounts to a false dichotomy, one that does not do justice to the ethical complexities of current sex offender practice. Prescott and Levenson stated that there are aspects of sex offender treatment that seek to improve the well-being of sex offenders and that, therefore, a purely punishment-oriented ethical code would not be well fitted to the task of regulating practice.

In our view, the picture is much more complex than that portrayed by either of the above positions. If we examine sex offender treatment carefully it becomes apparent that it contains aspects of both punishment and treatment; or at least incorporates some elements of punishment. Insufficient care is taken to analyze the key concepts of treatment and punishment, and to reflect thoroughly on the practices evident in current sex offender treatment. For example, Prescott and Levenson criticize Glaser for not appreciating treatment as it is understood traditionally within the sexual offending domain, while Glaser, rightly in our view, states that some aspects of what have been regarded as sex offender treatment meet the definition of punishment. An informative example of a treatment module that possesses some aspect of punishment is what has been termed cognitive restructuring. In cognitive restructuring therapists explicitly aim to induce in offenders a feeling of responsibility and some degree of guilt. Guilt is viewed as a marker of an acknowledgement that what the offender did was wrong and that he acted in ways that were unethical and damaging to his victim. This seems like an ethical response to us, one attuned to Duff's (2001) requirement that punishment should express to the offender a need to express remorse and actively invest in the process of behavioral and psychological reform.

But does cognitive restructuring with its dual (often implicit) aims of inducing guilt and acknowledgement of responsibility meet the criteria of punishment? In our opinion, it appears to do so. The actions that constitute cognitive restructuring (or at least some of them) are (1) authorized by the state or agency; (2) intentional, as practitioners are aiming to encourage the offender to accept responsibility and experience guilt; (3) reprobative, in that therapeutic practices express disapproval of an individual's sexually abusive actions; (4) retributive, because the interventions follow wrongful acts that were (5) committed by offenders; and (6) harmful, in that the person experiences considerable distress as a consequence of the intended interventions. In fact, an aim of the intervention is to induce guilt. It could be argued that the guilt is merely a byproduct of accepting responsibility. However, in our view this is incorrect because one of the constituent features of accepting responsibility *is* the experience of guilt; it is hardly a byproduct. Another treatment module that is consistent with the analysis of punishment is empathy training, where one of the stated aims is for the offender to grasp the fact he has severely harmed another person, and furthermore, to imagine what the victim might have experienced him- or herself.

However, by way of contrast, it is clear that there are components of sexual offending treatment that do not meet the (rough) definition of punishment and that therefore should not be viewed as punishment. A good example of such interventions are those associated with increasing sex offenders' repertoire of social and intimacy building skills and their level of personal well-being. More specifically, therapeutic actions in an intimacy module are (1) authorized by the state or an agency; (2) intended to promote an offender's level of functioning and well-being; (3) not reprobative, because they are not intended to express disapproval, at least not directly; (4) retributive, as they follow from the fact of sexual offending (5) committed by the individual in question; and finally (6) well-being-enhancing rather than harm-creating. The failure to meet criteria (3) and (6) indicates that such actions are not examples of punishment and therefore Prescott and Levenson (2010) are correct in asserting that at least some parts of sex offender treatment cannot be conceptualized accurately as punishment. We suggest that other modules that fit this description are problem solving, sexual education and emotional regulation training.

What can we conclude from the debate concerning sex offender treatment status? In our view there are elements of sex offender treatment that directly aim to enhance the level of an individual's functioning rather than intentionally to inflict pain (authorized sanction) on him. Conversely, there are aspects of treatment that look very much like punishment. What this suggests is that working with sex offenders (and indeed all offenders) is ethically complex and demands high levels of ethical reasoning and sophistication. Classifying punishment-related tasks as treatment may well lead to a paternalistic, somewhat demeaning response towards offenders. While mistaking treatment tasks for punishment is likely to leave offenders bereft of the psychological resources they require to lead prudentially and ethically better lives.

Conclusions

In conclusion, working therapeutically with sex offenders is a value laden enterprise and calls for psychological and ethical competence. A challenge for practitioners employed in the criminal justice sectors is that they frequently have competing normative demands placed on them. Their practice is embedded in quite distinct sets of values that orientate them to different goals and responsibilities. In our view, the lesson to be learned is to be mindful of the inherent complexity of this work and not to strain for simplicity or clarity when neither is warranted or even possible. Practitioners are both moral agents with duties to the state and the community, and therapists working side by side with quite damaged individuals in order to help them lead personally more fulfilling, and socially more responsible, lives.

Acknowledgment

Parts of this chapter have been published previously in T. Ward and K. Salmon (2009) "The ethics of punishment: implications for correctional practice." *Aggression and Violent Behavior*, 14, 239–247. We would like to thank Elsevier Science for permission to use this material.

References

Andrews, D.A. and Bonta, J. (2006) *The Psychology of Criminal Conduct*, 4th edn. Cincinnati, OH: Anderson Publishing.

Bennett, C. (2008) *The Apology Ritual: A Philosophical Theory of Punishment*. Cambridge: Cambridge University Press.

Beyleveld, D. and Brownsword, R. (2001) *Human Dignity in Bioethics and Law*. New York: Oxford University Press.

Boonin, D. (2008) *The Problem of Punishment*. New York: Cambridge University Press.

Brinkmann, S. (2011) *Psychology as a Moral Science: Perspectives on Normativity*. New York: Springer.

Bush, S.S., Connell, M.A. and Denny, R.L. (2006) *Ethical Practice in Forensic Psychology: A Systematic Model for Decision Making*. Washington, DC: American Psychological Association.

Cooper, D.E. (2004) *Ethics for Professionals in a Multicultural World*. Upper Saddle River, NJ: Pearson Prentice Hall.

Darwell, S. (2006) *The Second-Person Standpoint: Morality, Respect, and Accountability*. Cambridge, MA: Harvard University Press.

Day, A. and Ward, T. (2010) "Offender rehabilitation as a value laden process," *International Journal of Offender Therapy and Comparative Criminology* 54, 289–306.

Dolinko, D. (2011) "Punishment," in J. Deigh and D. Dolinko (eds), *The Oxford Handbook of Philosophy of Criminal Law*. Oxford: Oxford University Press, pp. 403–440.

Duff, R.A. (2001) *Punishment, Communication, and Community*. New York: Oxford University Press.

Duff, R.A. and Green, S.P. (eds) (2011) *Philosophical Foundations of Criminal Law*. Oxford: Oxford University Press.

Glaser, B. (2010) "Sex offender programs: new technology coping with old ethics," *Journal of Sexual Aggression* 16, 261–274.

Golash, D. (2005) *The Case against Punishment: Retribution, Crime Prevention, and the Law*. New York: New York University Press.

Griffin, J. (2008) *On Human Rights*. Oxford: Oxford University Press.

Haag, A.D. (2006) "Ethical dilemmas faced by correctional psychologists in Canada," *Criminal Justice and Behavior* 33, 93–109.

Kleinig, J. 2008. *Ethics and criminal justice: An introduction*. Cambridge: Cambridge University Press.

Lazarus, L. (2004) *Contrasting Prisoners' Rights: A Comparative Examination of England and Germany*. New York: Oxford University Press.

Martin, M. (2006) *From Morality to Mental Health: Virtue and Vice in a Therapeutic Culture*. New York: Oxford University Press.

Maruna, S. (2001) *Making Good: How Ex-Convicts Reform and Rebuild Their Lives*. Washington, DC: American Psychological Association.

Prescott, D. and Levenson, J. (2010) "Sex offender treatment is not punishment," *Journal of Sexual Aggression* 16, 275–285.

Tadros, V. (2011) *The Ends of Harm: The Moral Foundations of the Criminal Law*. Oxford: Oxford University Press.

Vess, J. (2009) "Fear and loathing in public policy: ethical issues in laws for sex offenders," *Aggression and Violent Behavior* 14, 264–272.

Waldron, J. (2009) *Dignity, Rank, and Rights: The 2009 Tanner Lectures at UC Berkeley*. New York: New York University of Law.

Ward, T. and Birgden, A. (2007) "Human rights and correctional clinical practice," *Aggression and Violent Behavior* 12, 628–643.

Ward, T. and Maruna, S. (2007) *Rehabilitation: Beyond the Risk Paradigm*. London: Routledge.

Ward, T. and Salmon, K. (2009) "The ethics of punishment: correctional practice implications," *Aggression and Violent Behavior* 14, 239–247.

Ward, T. and Syversen, K. (2009) "Vulnerable agency and human dignity: an ethical framework for forensic practice," *Aggression and Violent Behavior* 14, 94–105.

17

Distinguishing Moral and Clinical Decisions in Sex Offender Programs
The Good Lives Model and Virtue Ethics
Bill Glaser

Introduction

The Good Lives Model (GLM) of sex offender rehabilitation has captured the hearts and minds of therapists and program designers throughout the world. It offers an alternative not only to the punitive approaches which dominated correctional environments for many years after Martinson's (1974) gloomy conclusion that "Nothing Works," but also to the seemingly mechanistic risk-avoidance strategies of the risk–needs–responsivity (RNR) model which replaced them. By contrast, the GLM is optimistic and holistic, encouraging an offender to believe that they can achieve an offense-free life by building up their own strengths and capabilities, rather than simply enduring a lifetime of continuing restrictions and avoidance (Ward and Gannon, 2006; Wilson and Yates, 2009). Indeed, the GLM now is one of the top three theories guiding treatment approaches in a recent survey of sex offender programs in the United States and Canada (McGrath *et al.*, 2010).

The popularity of the GLM seems to be very much a product of its appeal to a positive view of human nature, far more in keeping with clinicians' ethical values of caring, benevolence and respect for autonomy. We want to regard our offender clients as (at least potentially) worthwhile human beings who can be taught to use their own skills and abilities to become pro-social rather than as dogs which need to be trained to control their inherent viciousness. But this view is not, as yet, based on sound empirical evidence: we know, for example, that offenders who adopt law-abiding lifestyles tend to have happier and more fulfilling lives but we do not yet know whether the reverse is true; that is, the pursuit of a more fulfilling life may simply make offenders happier criminals (Andrews, Bonta and Wormith, 2011; Glaser, 2011).

For the time being, therefore, the GLM needs moral as well as clinical justifications for its approach. For example, it explicitly states that we must value offenders as fellow

The Wiley-Blackwell Handbook of Legal and Ethical Aspects of Sex Offender Treatment and Management,
First Edition. Edited by Karen Harrison and Bernadette Rainey.
© 2013 John Wiley & Sons, Ltd. Published 2013 by John Wiley & Sons, Ltd.

human beings who have in particular the same goals and dreams as the rest of us and must be respected as autonomous agents trying to achieve such "goods" (Ward and Gannon, 2006). It goes on to describe, largely in moral terms, what is "good" in human life and how to achieve such "goods." From this description, the GLM then draws a number of inferences which have an important influence on the design and implementation of offender rehabilitation programs.

Thus it is these moral considerations, rather than clinical factors, which may determine assessments and interventions carried out using the GLM even though they are seemingly clinical in nature. In broad terms, these seemingly clinical procedures include the clarification of an offender's life-goals, selecting the skills and capacities needed to achieve them by non-criminal means, judging when they have been achieved, and so forth. But the confusion of clinically and ethically based decisions carries risks: biased assessments, inappropriate treatment and threats to the integrity of the treatment program.

This chapter uses the GLM as an example of how moral and clinical decisions in offender rehabilitation programs may be difficult to distinguish. It first provides a brief overview of some moral theories commonly used as the ethical bases of human service models. From among the available candidates, virtue ethics seems to fit best with the assumptions and practices of the GLM. The shortcomings of this framework are then described, particularly those which might impact on the decisions made by clinicians using a GLM approach, and some ways of overcoming these, using ethical rather than clinical responses, are suggested. The chapter concludes that, however difficult they may be to attain, the GLM's aspirations of achieving a meaningful and worthwhile life for even the most despised members of our community may result in policy and attitude changes that will be of enormous benefit to society as a whole.

Some Moral Theories

All clinicians involved in human service delivery, at least implicitly, practice according to ethical norms which, most of the time, are fairly self-evident; for example, avoid harm to the client, offer the best available treatment, and so forth. These norms often take the form of codes of ethics governing the conduct of particular health service professionals, such as social workers, doctors and psychologists, and, using them, the clinician generally has no difficulty in deciding how to act morally (Beauchamp, 2009). In contentious areas of practice, however (and offender rehabilitation is certainly one of these), ethical codes of practice may not provide enough, or any, guidance. For example, in sex offender programs, where the clinician often has to serve twin goals of both promoting an offender's best interests and protecting the community, principles of traditional ethical codes guiding health professionals may give very little guidance for using interventions that are standard for such programs; for example, limiting confidentiality, restricting choice of treatment, and so forth (Glaser, 2003, 2009). In such cases, the interventions need to be justified by reference to more general moral theories (Beauchamp, 2009). There are several such theories, derived from thousands of years of philosophical tradition: all have their limitations and none will be likely to provide a complete justification for a particular practice (Ward and Salmon, 2011).

Utilitarian theories regard an action or practice as right if it leads to the maximal balance of "good" over "bad" consequences for the affected parties. Whether "good" and "bad" consequences can be quantified and balanced in this fashion is problematic (can we increase the good in a community by denying offenders their human rights so that the rest of the community sleeps more peacefully?). "Rule utilitarians" partly solve the quantification problem by formulating moral rules which usually maximize "good"; we can more easily live by these rather than going to the trouble and expense of calculating the consequences for each act. Moral worthiness is still, however, only attached to the consequences of a deed or a rule, not to the motive which inspires it: it does not matter whether a practitioner treats an offender fairly because he/she has a duty to do so or because he/she wants a pay-rise: the consequences of the fair treatment are all that count morally (Beauchamp, 2009; Blackburn, 2001).

Kantian theories (also known as deontological theories), by contrast, are very much concerned with motives: an act cannot be morally praiseworthy if it is not performed out of a sense of duty. Thus, in the example above, the therapist wanting a pay-rise could not be praised for his/her fair treatment of the offender. Duty is morally praiseworthy because it is the one force, free of other more ignoble motives, that enables us to follow moral principles which are rational and universal. These principles are defined by their consistency. For example, I have a duty to tell the truth, because if I followed a moral "rule" allowing me to lie, that could not be universalized: we would be in a world where nobody could believe anyone else. Another expression of this consistency is the principle that we should always treat people as ends rather than as means: this is because morality must respect its foundation, reason, wherever it is found, including the capacity of others (including offenders) to reason about their situation (Beauchamp, 2009; Blackburn, 2001). But Kantian theories give us little guidance on what to do when moral principles conflict; for example, our truth-telling duty obliges us to reveal a victim's personal details to an offender though this conflicts with our duty to protect the victim.

Rights theory in one sense is based on both utilitarian and Kantian theories because it often links rights with rules or principles generated by each of them. Rights can be seen as justified claims based on, or expressed by, these rules. These claims are made by individuals or groups of others or society; they usually imply obligations on those against whom the claim is made, but sometimes may be over-ridden (Beauchamp and Childress, 2009). Respect for offender rights is an important moral value for proponents of positively focused rehabilitation theories such as the GLM: offenders should only have to forfeit the rights, such as freedom rights, directly restricted by their punishment but they still retain the rights essential to their functioning as autonomous human agents; for example, the rights to material subsistence, equal treatment in their environment and personal security. As discussed below, the human rights perspective is fundamental for guiding and structuring the assessment, treatment and monitoring of offenders, but it is only part of the moral underpinning of the GLM approach (Ward and Birgden, 2007; Connolly and Ward, 2008).

Virtue ethics, although first expounded by Aristotle, arose in its modern form as a reaction to the cynical view that contemporary context-free morality was nothing more than an elaborate way of justifying acts based on personal likes and dislikes. Therapists have colluded with this version of morality by encouraging their clients to pursue their personal preferences without regard for seemingly arbitrary moral rules (Stewart-Sicking, 2008). By contrast, virtue ethics de-emphasizes the importance of *acting* on rules and stresses *being* a moral person. The purpose of morality is to live as fulfilling a life as possible by cultivating virtues which, for an offender, might include kindness, honesty and integrity. These virtues are more likely than rules to motivate a person's good actions and they can and should be learned throughout life in a practical fashion; for example, an offender who has learned and practiced kindness, and who understands how cultivating kindness achieves particular kinds of moral goods, is more likely to act kindly rather than one who is kind purely out of a sense of duty or obligation (Beauchamp, 2009; Blackburn, 2001). Virtue ethics as the basis of the GLM is discussed more fully below.

To complete this survey, two more recently developed moral theories will be briefly mentioned. The *ethics of care* can be seen as a version of virtue ethics emphasizing caring as a virtue. It is of special significance for practitioners in the health and welfare fields because, rather than focusing on moral principles or rules (for example, avoid harm to clients, maintain confidentiality), it draws out the ethical implications of relationships, emotions, context, and so forth, which make up the subtle and complex network of human interactions (Beauchamp, 2009). Thus clinicians treating sex offenders are in a caring relationship with them, whatever the punishment they are undergoing, and hence should carefully cultivate caring virtues such as attentiveness, responsiveness and respectfulness by, for example, empathically understanding offenders' unique life-histories (Ward and Salmon, 2011).

Finally, *casuistry* is a moral theory which questions the usefulness of the grand theories described above and advocates reliance on moral narratives, paradigm cases and precedents. These become a body of knowledge, reflecting the moral consensus in society, which guides subsequent moral decision-making (Beauchamp, 2009). For those involved in sex offender programs, however, the use of this sort of moral method may be perilous: consider the moral value (if any) of the sensationalist "narrative" which has inspired the human rights violations characterizing recent sex offender legislation (Vess, 2009; see Chapter 9).

To summarize, the clinician working in a sex offender program can choose from a variety of theories for ethical justification of their practice. None provides the perfect answer to the many moral dilemmas which face such programs; many complement each other's approaches. Some, like human rights theory, provide important "baseline" perspectives which a practitioner is obliged to consider first before embarking on the complex and morally perilous processes of assessment, treatment and outcome evaluation. The GLM, however, which makes its moral aims much more explicit than other rehabilitation approaches, seems to conform closely in its moral aims to one of the theories discussed above: virtue ethics. We now turn to a discussion of the relationship between them.

The GLM and Its Moral Underpinnings

The GLM has been described in greater detail elsewhere, particularly in the extensive contributions by Ward and his colleagues (Ward and Gannon, 2006; Ward and

Stewart, 2003; Wilson and Yates, 2009). For the purposes of the present chapter, it can be said that it espouses very specific ideas about human nature and the meaning of human existence. Offenders, it argues, are like the rest of humanity, with the same goals, dreams and aspirations. In particular, they, like the rest of us, seek out primary goods such as healthy living and functioning, knowledge, excellence in work and play, inner peace, happiness, and so on, which (as empirical studies seem to suggest) are sought by all human beings both for their own sake and because they are likely to enhance human psychological well-being. Different people will give priority to different goods and different ways of achieving them (so-called secondary goods, such as obtaining a job to achieve excellence in work, maintaining a relationship to achieve friendship); these differences produce the rich variety of personal identities we find in society (Ward and Stewart, 2003; Ward and Gannon, 2006).

Criminal behavior occurs when various obstacles (also called criminogenic needs) block or frustrate the pursuit of primary goods by pro-social means. Such obstacles are the product of biological (for example, brain development), psychological (for example, motivation) and social learning (for example, social and cultural) factors and may be manifest in a variety of ways, such as the use of inappropriate means to obtain primary goods, a lack of capacity to achieve them, and so on. The model thus explicitly states that criminal behavior is not intrinsically bad or blameworthy but rather a *maladaptive* attempt to achieve otherwise worthy goals. All humans (including offenders) must still be respected as autonomous individuals who flourish when they can make decisions for themselves. Thus rehabilitation interventions must provide an offender with the skills and capabilities which they can use, together with their pre-existing strengths and preferences to devise and implement non-offending life plans, rather than simply dictating to them a list of "dos and don'ts."

The GLM seemingly avoids moral judgments of an offender or of the goods they seek: as we have just seen, criminal behavior is "maladaptive" rather than "bad" and, furthermore, the goods themselves, such as healthy living, may not have any particular moral significance. But it recognizes that:

> rehabilitation as a process aiming to promote achievement is highly value-laden. That is to say it involves a variety of different types of values including, but not limited to, prudential values (what is in the best interest of individual clients), utilitarian values (what is in the best interests of the community), and epistemic or knowledge-based values (what are our methods of best practice). (Siegert *et al.*, 2007: 1609)

These values, as has been pointed out by Ward and Stewart (2003), are an integral part of the responses to the questions implicitly asked by offenders when they begin a rehabilitation program: "How can I live my life differently?" and "How can I be a different kind of person?" The skills, attitudes and understanding, the ability to reason about them, and most importantly, the motivation to achieve them, inculcated by the GLM in offenders, are not merely strategies to achieve a more appropriate lifestyle but are also ways of enabling offenders to achieve their full potential and consistently "do the right thing." They have a moral status as virtues, dispositions to act in morally valued ways which are permanent and consistent. Philosophers will label these capabilities differently from clinicians; for example, the traditional virtue of temperance may be re-labeled by the GLM approach as the cultivation of sexual self-regulation; that of courage as the ability to resist strong urges, emotions and the demands of criminal peers; and that of wisdom as the abandonment of offense-supportive cognitions (Ward *et al.*, 2006). But whatever the label used, the concept of virtue usefully encapsulates what an offender needs to become in order to deal with the maladaptive criminal behavior they use to obtain primary goods.

The GLM closely parallels virtue theory in specifying the nature and development of the moral actions to which we all (often unconsciously) need to be committed:

> There are certain types of action that one will never perform, whatever the consequences, unless one has already gone badly wrong – unless one has become the kind of human being who is unwittingly or perversely frustrating himself in developing those relationships needed to achieve his good or goods. [The theory] also enables us to understand how and why it is that our desires, as they develop through and from early childhood, need to be transformed so that we acquire the virtues. (MacIntyre, 2009: 117–118)

Virtue theory would agree that the moral purpose of offender rehabilitation is not merely the avoidance of immoral or illegal acts or the slavish obedience to rules for doing so. Indeed, the GLM does not label the capabilities it inculcates as obligations or duties (although they can legitimately be seen as such). Rather, rehabilitation should see the deliberate acquisition of capabilities as achieving a rich, fulfilling and morally valuable life (Frankena, 1973; Ward *et al.*, 2006).

When Virtue Theory Is Problematic: Pitfalls for the GLM

Determining when behaviors are "maladaptive"

The recognition of the GLM as an ethical theory has important consequences. The key danger is that of confusing clinical and ethical dilemmas; for example, if a child molester insists that children are not harmed by his activities, is this because he lacks skills to pursue a common human good of intimacy or is he asserting a moral stance which is consistent with the ethical ideals and the "good life" goals of the social or cultural group of which he is a part? In the latter case, labeling his attitudes and behaviors as "maladaptive" inevitably results in the retort of "By whose standards?," particularly if the offender is otherwise leading a productive and fulfilling lifestyle. The offender (possibly rightly) may perceive encouragement to adopt other ways of pursuing his presumed goal of intimacy, as being "brain-washing" or some other unwarranted attempt to force him to adopt beliefs and practices which are alien or even repugnant to him.

There is an enormous variety of well-documented cases of societies and cultures in which behavior regarded by conventional morality as evil or immoral is seen as perfectly normal and consistent with the achievement of a worthwhile life. Goldhagen (1996) has documented in chilling detail how, in Nazi Germany, huge numbers who killed and tortured Jews, whether by gassing them in death camps, shooting them while serving police battalions, or in grueling and horrendous death marches, were ordinary middle-class citizens, very few of whom had affiliations to the Nazi party or were forced to do these grisly duties. They discussed their deeds publicly, even carrying them out in full view of family and loved ones. Accepting a centuries-old tradition of virulent anti-Semitism as an integral part of their beliefs, they saw nothing wrong or immoral in what they had done, even the tiny minority who faced legal inquiries at the end of the war. Indeed they had no need to do so: these beliefs did not prevent them from living productive and satisfying lives and achieving all they wanted to achieve (Goldhagen, 1996, especially ch. 16).

Similarly, sex offending can be condoned by entire cultures and societies. Rape-supportive societies have common characteristics: male deities are preferred, warfare is glorified, the political and economic power of women is limited, the sexes are rigidly segregated, and child-care as an occupation is denigrated (Sanday, 1981). It is not surprising, therefore, that in societies such as our own, which demonstrate a number of these characteristics, a significant proportion of young men perpetrate, or at least approve of, rape, but are otherwise "normal" members of the community (Hermann, 1990). In some cultures, adult–child sexual relationships are, or have been, routinely encouraged, with apparently no detriment to the growth and development of either perpetrators or child participants (Currier, 1981). Such examples have been used to justify the advocacy of groups such as the Paedophile Information Exchange and the North American Man-Boy Love Association (NAMBLA) for "children's rights" and, in particular, the rights of children to do whatever they wish with their own bodies (O'Carroll, 1982, especially chs. 5 and 7). In other words, adult–child sexual activity, in the eyes of these organizations, is not only permissible but is necessary to achieve such good lives goals as autonomy, relatedness and happiness.

This problem of culture-specific virtues is not easily resolved. Seemingly we should espouse some sort of moral relativism: we have no right to judge the moral worth of good lives goals set by another culture, if they enable the goal-seeker to live an adaptive and fulfilling life, even if they involve practices that would be labeled as maladaptive in our own. We might engage in "practical discourse" about differing cultural versions of morality to assess practices such as genocide or child–adult sexual activity; at the very least, themes such as freedom of choice and consent can be explored (Lukes, 2008; MacIntyre, 2006). Perhaps such discourse might even result in agreement about human goods or human capabilities which "exert a moral claim that they should be developed" and applied universally (Nussbaum, 2000: 69). However, empirical attempts to derive a list of such goods have had only limited success, despite the optimistic assessments of GLM theorists (Ward and Gannon, 2006). A major problem here is that virtues that are common to many cultures may not have the same significance in each culture that values them (Stewart-Sicking, 2008).

The emphasis placed by the GLM on the human rights of offenders (Connolly and Ward, 2008; Ward and Birgden, 2007) does, indirectly, recognize the existence of a universal, non-culturally-specific, set of virtues, that is, those which will result in the preservation of the rights of individuals, as set out in universally applicable agreements such as the Universal Declaration of Human Rights (United Nations, 1948). In particular, offenders are encouraged to respect the rights of others (as well as insisting that their own rights be enforced), in order to achieve primary goods such as relatedness (Connolly and Ward, 2008). Yet, in the case of the child molester adduced above, this still leaves us with the problem of differentiating clinical from moral judgments. We could well say to the offender that he was infringing on the rights of the child he had victimized, but it is doubtful that we could conclude that his behavior in doing so was "maladaptive," even if he agreed to define the "rights" of children in a conventional fashion (that is, avoiding the interpretations offered by the Paedophile Information Exchange or NAMBLA). Human goods, in many cases, can be achieved more easily and effectively by resorting to criminal behavior than by pro-social means. Our child molester could well argue that he achieved primary goods such as mastery through multiple completed offenses, friendship through association with other child molesters and creativity through planning and implementing increasingly devious ways of offending (Andrews, Bonta and Wormith, 2011).

There are a number of implications of these dilemmas for those using the GLM in treatment programs. The first is that offending behaviors clearly are often not maladaptive. It is understandable that a therapist may want to preserve an appearance of impartiality or avoid alienating the client by not using value-laden terms such as "bad" for offending behavior. But the therapist may then be helping the offender to avoid responsibility for their behavior by excusing it as "maladaptive." The approach needs to be pragmatic: the fact that the offender has been convicted and punished is proof that they are at risk of future conflict with the criminal justice system if they continue to use offending behaviors (whether or not they are adaptive) and it is the therapist's task to help them find alternatives to such behaviors. This approach, of course, is perilously close to that of the seemingly soul-less RNR model, but it seems to be one of the few alternatives realistically of use to offenders who are otherwise achieving their goals successfully using criminal means.

The second implication is that the GLM's ideal of giving offenders the opportunity to define their good lives goals will be limited for offenders from cultures or societies that condone sexual aggression. In our society such offenders, unfortunately, are common; that is, young men among us who, despite the advances of feminism in the last half-century, still value misogyny and male domination, which, as we have seen above, they do not consider obstacles to the achievement of primary goods such as intimacy and happiness. Here the therapist may need to be less focused on goods. Thus (for example) reinforcing bans on substance abuse may mean, at least in the short term, an inability to obtain goods such as friendship (through camaraderie at pubs), mastery (defeating other young males in drunken brawls) and sexual satisfaction (through alcohol-fuelled sexual assaults). It could be argued that such paternalistic measures remain morally praiseworthy because they ultimately achieve long-term goals which are in the offender's best interest, such as health or intimacy, but whether offenders actually want their lives to pursue this course is debatable (Glaser, 2011).

The problem of motivation

Virtue-based ethical theories judge actions by their motives rather than their consequences: a person may be praised for their bravery even though their brave actions result in defeat. There are various kinds of virtue-based ethical systems, differentiated by the goods that motivate the virtues concerned: egoism (resulting in virtues of prudence and others focused on a concern for one's own interests), the general good of society (resulting in virtues such as benevolence), and duty (resulting in virtues which are considered good for their own sake, such as honesty or justice) (Frankena, 1973). These ethical systems may recognize the existence of one primary virtue (on which all others are based) or many distinctive ones, and the same virtues (for example, kindness) may be motivated by self-interest, the general good, and its recognition as an admirable virtue in and of itself.

What distinguishes the GLM as a virtue-theory is that it relies heavily on self-interest as a motivator: one's primary goods are acquired to ensure one's life goals and any benefit for others (for example, through kindness to others) is significant only as a way to achieve satisfaction for oneself (for example, relatedness). This is troublesome for two reasons. First, the paradoxical conclusion is reached that, unless everybody in a community has exactly the same goals in life, a particular individual cannot benefit from pursuing their own self-interest if all other members of the community are ethically committed to pursuing *their* unique self-interests. Conflict must inevitably arise (Frankena, 1973) and, in the special case of offenders, that conflict will involve therapists who advocate not only for the interests of the community but also their own self-interest, for example, professional success, security when dealing with challenging clients, and so on.

Second, the GLM seems to down-play the role of other virtues other than prudence (motivated by self-interest) as a basis for ethical living (see Frankena, 1973). For example, it seems to have little to say about altruism, although it does acknowledge that rehabilitation is a value-laden process which must take into account non-prudential values such as the interests of the community and the use of best practice models and methods (Ward and Gannon, 2006). Even so, it would seem that benevolence, and associated virtues such as altruism, are important to cultivate in an offender in order to achieve rehabilitation aims such as non-recidivism, even though they may not be important in achieving that offender's primary goods.

One way of resolving these issues is to cease making moral judgments about motives and simply judge actual deeds instead. Utilitarian thinkers such as Singer (1980: 209) urge that we judge acts by their consequences:

> People might give money to famine relief because their friends will think better of them, or they might give the same amount because they think it their duty. Those saved from starvation by the gift will benefit to the same extent either way.

According to Singer, praising motives is useful because it emphasizes the ethical values that promote the doing of good deeds. But this should not prevent us from assigning moral worth to the deeds themselves, whatever the motive that prompts them.

This is a useful pragmatic approach because, for example, it allows a clinician to praise an offender for complying with a relapse prevention plan, even though such compliance may be the product of a desire to avoid police contact, a wish to please the therapist, or a lack of opportunity to offend, rather than any motive derived from their good lives plan. Indeed one suspects that these less noble motives are the predominant drivers of pro-social lifestyles in most offenders, especially during the early phases of rehabilitation. Thus praising pro-social deeds, in and of itself, can be a useful start for the rehabilitation process.

Yet, for the GLM, motivation is important. Defining and achieving good lives goals as motivators may be a more effective long-term strategy to promote desistance from offending than simply eradicating, controlling or managing risk (Ward *et al.*, 2006). While exogenous factors such as age, marriage and employment all influence cessation of offending, an important factor seems to be the offender's own ability to reconstruct their identity as non-criminal and by learning how to achieve their primary goods by non-criminal means. In turn, this requires the motivation to develop certain personal qualities such as adequate self-control, reflexivity and confidence in one's effectiveness as an autonomous agent (Ward and Laws, 2010).

We do not yet have the empirical evidence to assess whether, in fact, the GLM contributes to desistance independently of the other factors just noted (Ward and Laws, 2010). However, as the next section shows, the hypothesis that the GLM can produce a better outcome for offender rehabilitation than other rehabilitation methods challenges us to justify ethically the aims of rehabilitation and how we evaluate them.

The aims of offender rehabilitation and how we know it is working

What does offender rehabilitation hope to achieve? Presumably the primary aim is the protection and safety of the community. But the GLM's focus extends far beyond this. We need to question whether the state's power to manage and impose criminal penalties should be used to force offenders to live fulfilling lives, particularly seeing that the criminal justice system does not have the resources to achieve this. Such an aim would be better addressed by non-coercive agencies, from the areas of health, mental health, education and welfare, devoting more of their skills and resources to crime prevention (Andrews, Bonta and Wormith, 2011).

Limitations on the scope of all offender rehabilitation programs are ethically essential because such programs are part of a regime of punishment. No matter how well-intentioned an offender rehabilitation program is and no matter how successfully it works to promote an offender's best interests, it cannot intervene in an offender's life more than to the extent minimally necessary to achieve the aim of the punishment imposed. That aim is primarily the protection of the community; any punishments aiming at more than this need to be justified ethically, even if they produce enormous benefits for the offender (Glaser, 2003, 2011; see Chapter 16).

The GLM, as we have seen, requires a comprehensive and demanding set of interventions which may be disproportionate to the punishment imposed. Rather than, for example, simple risk-avoidance, because of its moral underpinning, the GLM requires an offender to recognize their life-goals, formulate plans to achieve them, behave in a fashion consistent with them and display virtues such as prudence to demonstrate that they are being influenced by the "right" motives. Such "punishment for an offender's own good" can possibly be justified by paternalistic considerations, but the therapist needs to be constantly wary of ethical pitfalls such as coercively inflicting their own attitudes and values on the offender and misrepresenting the purpose of an intervention as being that of the offender's well-being even though it may be primarily aimed at other goals such as the protection of society (Glaser, 2011).

Furthermore, as we have seen, there is still no good evidence that a more rewarding life for an offender will help them to desist from re-offending more than less intrusive measures such as marriage or employment.

It is not only difficult to use the GLM to define the aims of rehabilitation, it also becomes harder to determine when rehabilitation is to be concluded, or at least when enough interventions have been provided to an offender to increase appreciably the chance of a successful outcome. For the GLM a successful outcome includes not only the reduction of re-offending risk (by, for example, enhancing an offender's empathy and coping skills) but also the creation of "social supports and opportunities and . . . ways of living that follow from a personally significant and ethically accept-able (redemptive) practical identity" (Ward and Laws, 2010: 21; see Chapter 22).

There are clearly enormous practical and ethical problems in measuring such out-comes. For example, rehabilitation programs conducted in a custodial setting face huge difficulties in accessing "social supports and opportunities" for their clients: does this mean that discharge from the program (and release from custody) must be delayed for long periods until such supports can be located? What are the character-istics of a "personally significant" identity? Many sex offenders (including many who are rarely detected) do not identify themselves as sex offenders and manage to lead "personally significant" fulfilling and productive lives as respected members of the community, despite their continuing high risk (Glaser, 2011). And, finally, what sorts of identities are "ethically acceptable"? Many offenders, as we have seen above, comply seemingly conscientiously with rehabilitation interventions but are motivated by desires to avoid police contact, finish the program as quickly as possible, and so on, rather than ethically "purer" motives such as good lives goals. Does this mean that they have to continue rehabilitation until they acquire the "right" motives? And, apart from asking them (and running the risk of encouraging some very creative lying), how will we know when they do?

The GLM and punishment The GLM literature so far has had very little to say on its role in the punishment of offenders, although there has been some discussion on the ethics of punishment and how this might affect offender rehabilitation gener-ally (Ward and Salmon, 2009). However, the GLM has important implications for the criminal law: it is a punishment option which is much more broad-ranging and (possibly) more intrusive than more traditional ones. Sentencing courts and correc-tional services need to develop an understanding of its foundation in virtue ethics, and one way of doing so is to start with the general influence of this ethical theory on legal practice and principles.

Writers on virtue ethics have only recently begun to consider its place in criminal jurisprudence. Its great advantage is that it provides a richer and more thoughtful moral account of the aims of the law than the more traditional (and overly simplistic) ones of (for example) punishing non-conformity with moral principles or preventing threats to the well-being of society. Instead, virtue jurisprudence contends that the goal of the criminal law is to promote human flourishing by inculcating moral virtues, encouraging practical reasoning in pursuit of them and punishing characteristics (vice) that subvert the virtues (Huigens, 2007; Yankah, 2004).

To do this, the law, at least in some instances, judges character as well as deeds. Character judgments become especially important when decisions regarding punishment are being made (sentencing). Thus, historically, prison conditions became an attempt to reform a criminal's character by, for example, solitary confinement, strict separation of prisoners and enforced silence, giving the offender the opportunity to contemplate his misdeeds and discover the right principles to guide his life (McGowen, 1995). Even now, a first-time offender will usually be treated more leniently than an offender with an extensive criminal history, at least in part because the latter is thought to be more predisposed to vice. Other modern legal sanctions aimed at punishing an offender's "bad" character may include being deprived of the right to vote, being precluded from certain types of professional employment or government appointments, and so on (Yankah, 2004).

But the ambitious goals of virtue jurisprudence are in danger of being corrupted into justifications for the abandonment of traditional legal protections of offenders and the abuse of their rights (Yankah, 2004). This is seen clearly in the case of sex offenders where legally mandated restrictions on their liberties effectively become character-based punishments. The use, in many jurisdictions, of compulsory community notification (see Chapter 21), civil commitment (see Chapter 24), post-sentence extended supervision and indeterminate sentences (see Chapter 9) is usually justified by the offender's estimated high risk of re-offending. Yet the shortcomings of risk assessment instruments (for example, extrapolating the risk for an individual offender from group norms) are not widely known or understood, particularly by legal professionals (Vess, 2009). "Risk" thus becomes not a statement about the similarity of a particular offender to other recidivist individuals but rather an assumption about the individual predisposition to vice of the offender concerned. It becomes easy to blur the distinction between an empirical judgment of "high risk" and the moral one of being "incorrigibly bad."

The proponents of the GLM model are well aware of this danger, and have rightly placed a considerable emphasis on the preservation of an offender's human rights throughout the rehabilitation process. An offender cannot achieve a fulfilling life without receiving proper respect for their autonomy and dignity (Ward and Birgden, 2007; Ward and Salmon, 2009; see Chapter 2). Yet, as we have already seen, the GLM, as a form of punishment based on virtue ethics, broadens the aims of punishment substantially. The restrictions particularly aimed at sex offenders listed above all can be enforced for prolonged or indeterminate periods. Without the limits imposed by, say, a fixed term of imprisonment or a finite period for a community-based corrections order, the danger now is that the extent of the rehabilitation required, based on risk assessment, will come to determine the extent of the "punishment" imposed; this already seems to be occurring when Australian courts impose extended supervision orders (Ogloff and Doyle, 2009).

What does this mean for offender rehabilitation programs using a GLM approach? For example, an offender might continue to be detained or placed under some sort of supervision because they have an inappropriate or incomplete good lives plan, even if they have otherwise complied with program requirements. Whether and when GLM values such as respect for an offender's autonomy and dignity outweigh such considerations is still unclear.

Good Lives and a Flourishing Society

In the current state of knowledge, one suspects that the aims of the GLM, for most offenders, will remain aspirational rather than attainable. Quite apart from the difficulties of verifying the GLM's claims empirically, there are important moral dilemmas raised by the approach. As we have seen, much criminal behavior is not maladaptive and does not prevent the offender from leading a fulfilling life; offense-free lifestyles can be maintained by otherwise morally dubious motives; moral considerations make it difficult to define and measure rehabilitation outcomes; and this lack of clarity is worsened by the tendency of virtue jurisprudence to punish predispositions to vice rather than evil deeds.

Yet, the GLM, as grudgingly acknowledged even by its detractors, remains attractive. In the not-so-distant past, the fear of sex offenders justified the public shaming of exhibitionists, electric shock aversion for rapists and surgical castration of hundreds of offenders. At least the GLM has provided therapists horrified by these degrading procedures, "something positive to hold on to" (Andrews, Bonta and Wormith, 2011: 748). Moreover, the positive approach of the GLM seems to have a lot to offer non-sex-offender populations: it is guiding the treatment of those with mental health problems in a forensic setting (Barnao, Robertson and Ward, 2010) and interventions with clients of general medical rehabilitation programs (Siegert *et al.*, 2007).

More generally, the GLM's concepts can help in formulating more integrated and comprehensive responses to the enormous public policy challenges of dealing with sex offenders. The replacement of the stereotype of the incorrigible monster with that of the fellow human being who wants to lead a fulfilling life could do much to influence thinking in areas such as public education about offenders; cooperation among clinical, law enforcement and correctional practitioners; governments' responsibility for coordination and policy development; community reintegration of offenders; heeding the voices of victims; and more careful analyses of the consequences of strategies such as community notification and post-sentence detention of sex offenders (Robinson, 2003).

Finally, the GLM's vision can guide us: those who have to deal with sex offenders and their deeds, whether as therapists, victim advocates or people involved in the detection and control of offenders. There was a time when these seemingly disparate groups were allies, with the common aim of raising awareness of, and mounting a comprehensive approach to, an enormous social problem. Now, irrational fears of allegedly high recidivism rates and mutual accusations of bias and hysteria, punitive harshness and dangerous leniency have driven us into opposing camps (Berliner, 2003). It is hopefully not too late to humanize both offenders and victims and the GLM may be an important way of doing this.

There is still much for the GLM to do. At the very least it will have to refine its description of its expected outcomes and make them more coherent with the legal system's views of the aims of punishment. In the meantime, however, if an offender, as part of his/her punishment, develops a vague awareness that there are alternatives to a criminal lifestyle and that he/she may have a role in determining them, then that in itself will be a considerable achievement.

References

Andrews, D.A., Bonta, J. and Wormith, J.S. (2011) "The risk-need-responsivity model: Does adding the good lives model contribute to effective crime prevention?," *Criminal Justice and Behaviour* 38, 7, 735–755.

Barnao, M., Robertson, P. and Ward, T. (2010) "Good lives model applied to a forensic population," *Psychiatry, Psychology and Law* 17, 2, 202–217.

Beauchamp, T.L. (2009) "The philosophical basis of psychiatric ethics," in S. Bloch and S.A. Green (eds) *Psychiatric Ethics*, 4th edn. Oxford: Oxford University Press, pp. 229–250.

Beauchamp, T.L. and Childress, J.F. (2009) *Principles of Biomedical Ethics*, 6th edn. New York: Oxford University Press.

Berliner, L. (2003) "Victim and citizen perspectives on sex offender policy," in R.A. Prentky, E.S. Janus and M.C. Seto (eds), *Sexually Coercive Behavior: Understanding and Management*. New York: New York Academy of Sciences, pp. 464–473.

Blackburn, S. (2001) *Being Good: A Short Introduction to Ethics*. Oxford: Oxford University Press.

Connolly, M. and Ward, T. (2008) *Morals, Rights and Practice in the Human Services: Effective and Fair Decision-Making in Health, Social Care and Criminal Justice*. London: Jessica Kingsley.

Currier, R.L. (1981) "Juvenile sexuality in global perspective," in L.L. Constantine and F.M. Martinson (eds), *Children and Sex: New Findings, New Perspectives*. Boston: Little Brown and Company, pp. 9–19.

Frankena, W.K. (1973) *Ethics*, 2nd edn. Englewood Cliffs, NJ: Prentice-Hall Inc.

Glaser, B. (2003) "Therapeutic jurisprudence: an ethical paradigm for therapists in sex offender treatment programs," *Western Criminology Review* 4, 2, 143–154.

Glaser, B. (2009) "Treaters or punishers? The ethical role of mental health clinicians in sex offender programs," *Aggression and Violent Behaviour* 14, 248–225.

Glaser, B. (2011) "Paternalism and the good lives model of sex offender rehabilitation," *Sexual Abuse: A Journal of Research and Treatment* 23, 3, 329–345.

Goldhagen, D.J. (1996) *Hitler's Willing Executioners*. London: Abacus.

Hermann, J.L. (1990) "Sex offenders: a feminist perspective," in W.L. Marshall, D.R. Laws and H.E. Barbaree (eds), *Handbook of Sexual Assault: Issues, Theories and Treatment of the Offender*. New York: Plenum Press, pp. 177–193.

Huigens, K. (2007) "Law and morality: the jurisprudence of punishment," *William and Mary Law Review* 48, 1793–1821.

Lukes, S. (2008) *Moral Relativism*. London: Profile Books.

Martinson, R. (1974) "What works? Questions and answers about prison reform," *Public Interest* 35, 22–54.

McGowen, R. (1995) "The well-ordered prison: England, 1780–1865," in N. Morris and D.J. Rothman (eds), *The Oxford History of the Prison: The Practice of Punishment in Western Society*. Oxford: Oxford University Press, pp. 71–99.

McGrath, R.J., Cumming, G.F., Burchard, B.I., *et al.* (2010) *Current Practices and Emerging Trends in Sexual Abuser Management: The Safer Society (2009 North American Survey)*. Brandon, Vermont: Safer Society Press.

MacIntyre, A. (2006) "Moral relativism, truth and justification," in A. MacIntyre (ed.), *The Tasks of Philosophy: Selected Essays*. Cambridge: Cambridge University Press, pp. 52–73.

MacIntyre, A. (2009. "The illusion of self- sufficiency," In *Conversations On Ethics*. edited by A. Voorhoeve, 111–131. Oxford: University Press.

Nussbaum, M.C. (2000) *Women and Human Development: The Capabilities Approach*. Cambridge: Cambridge University Press.

O'Carroll, T. (1982) *Paedophilia: The Radical Case.* Boston: Alyson Publications.

Ogloff, J.R.P. and Doyle, D.J. (2009) "A clarion call: caution and humility must be the theme when assessing risk for sexual violence under post-sentence laws," *Sexual Abuse in Australia and New Zealand* 2, 59–69.

Robinson, L.O. (2003) "Sex offender management: the public policy challenges," in R.A. Prentky, E.S. Janus and M.C. Seto (eds), *Sexually Coercive Behavior: Understanding and Management.* New York: New York Academy of Sciences, pp. 1–7.

Sanday, P.R. (1981) "The socio-cultural context of rape: a cross-cultural study," *Journal of Social Issues* 37, 5–27.

Siegert, R.J., Ward, T., Levack, W.M. and McPherson, K.M. (2007) "A good lives model of clinical and community rehabilitation," *Disability and Rehabilitation* 29, 20–21, 1604–1615.

Singer, P. (1980) *Practical Ethics.* Cambridge: Cambridge University Press.

Stewart-Sicking, J.A. (2008) "Virtues, values and the good life: Alasdair MacIntyre's virtue ethics and its implications for counselling," *Counselling and Values* 52, 156–171.

United Nations (1948) Universal Declaration of Human Rights, http://www.un.org/en/documents/udhr (accessed August 25, 2012).

Vess, J. (2009) "Fear and loathing in public policy: ethical issues in laws for sex offenders," *Aggression and Violent Behaviour* 14, 264–272.

Ward, T. and Birgden, A. (2007) "Human rights and clinical correctional practice," *Aggression and Violent Behavior* 12, 6, 628–643.

Ward, T. and Gannon, T.A. (2006) "Rehabilitation, etiology and self-regulation: the good lives model of sex offender treatment," *Aggression and Violent Behaviour* 11, 77–94.

Ward, T. and Laws, D.R. (2010) "Desistance from Sex Offending: Motivating Change, Enriching Practice," *International Journal of Forensic Mental Health* 9, 1, 11–23.

Ward, T. and Salmon, K. (2009) "The ethics of punishment: correctional practice implications," *Aggression and Violent Behavior* 14, 239–247.

Ward, T. and Salmon, K. (2011. "The ethics of care and the treatment of sex offenders," *Sexual Abuse: A Journal of Research and Treatment* 23, 3, 397–413.

Ward, T. and Stewart, C.A. (2003) "Good lives and the rehabilitation of sex offenders," in T. Ward, D.R. Laws and S.M. Hudson (eds), *Sexual Deviance: Issues and Controversies.* Thousand Oaks, CA: Sage, pp. 21–44.

Ward, T., Vess, J., Collie, R.M. and Gannon, T.A. (2006) "Risk management or goods promotion: the relationship between approach and avoidance goals in treatment for sex offenders," *Aggression and Violent Behaviour* 14, 378–393.

Wilson, R.J. and Yates, P.M. (2009) "Effective interventions and the good lives model: maximizing treatment gains for sex offenders," *Aggression and Violent Behaviour* 14, 157–161.

Yankah, E.N. (2004) "Good guys and bad guys: punishing character, equality and the irrelevance of moral character to criminal punishment," *Cardozo Law Review* 25, 1019–1056.

18

Pharmacological Treatment of Sexual Offenders and Its Legal and Ethical Aspects

Raphaela Basdekis-Jozsa, Daniel Turner and Peer Briken

Introduction

For more than 40 years paraphilic patients and sexual offenders have been treated with androgen lowering medications. Nevertheless, empirical evidence concerning the reduction of relapses with sexual offenses following androgen lowering treatment is still very small according to the high standards of evidence-based medicine. This might also be due to the fact that there is still a lack of comprehensive knowledge about the role of sexual hormones in the development and course of paraphilias.

First attempts to treat paraphilic patients pharmacologically were made in the 1940s through the use of estrogens (Foote, 1944; Golla and Hodge, 1949; Whittaker, 1959), a treatment method that was abandoned shortly afterwards due to the severe side effects observed when used on a regular basis (Symmers, 1968). This was followed, in the 1970s, with the development of pharmacological treatments of paraphilic patients created from the idea that levels of testosterone could be lowered by administering androgen lowering agents such as progesterone, for example Medroxyprogesterone Acetate (MPA) or Cyproterone Acetate (CPA). Due to the severe side effects, however, other substances with similar levels of effectiveness but with fewer side effects have also been sought. In the 1990s, therefore, androgen lowering treatment was further promoted through research conducted on breast and prostate cancer therapy (Vance and Smith, 1984; Smith, 1986; Guay, 2009), with the introduction of Gonadotropin-Releasing Hormone (GnRH) agonists which lower serum testosterone levels below the usual castration level, that is, serum concentrations of under 50 nanograms per deciliter or 1.735 millimoles per liter.

The Wiley-Blackwell Handbook of Legal and Ethical Aspects of Sex Offender Treatment and Management,
First Edition. Edited by Karen Harrison and Bernadette Rainey.
© 2013 John Wiley & Sons, Ltd. Published 2013 by John Wiley & Sons, Ltd.

Effects of Androgen Lowering Treatments

The element which all androgen lowering agents have in common is that they reduce plasma testosterone levels. The first substance used with sex offenders that had this effect was CPA, which has three modes of action:

1. it competes with testosterone at receptor-binding sites in different organs;
2. it blocks testosterone and estrogen synthesis;
3. it inhibits the secretion of GnRH in the hypothalamus (Guay, 2009).

MPA has more progesterogenic than anti-androgenic effects and thus inhibits the secretion of GnRH in the hypothalamus, resulting in a faster reduction of testosterone serum levels within a period of only two weeks (Guay, 2009; Hebebrand, Hebebrand and Remschmidt, 2002).

GnRH analogues are the third group of androgen lowering agents which are in use (Belchetz *et al.*, 1978; Allolio *et al.*, 1985; Kendrick and Dixson, 1985; Moss and Dudley, 1989; McEvoy, 1999; Guay, 2009; Thibaut *et al.*, 2010). By stimulating the pituitary cells to release luteinizing hormone (LH), the use of GnRH analogues will initially result in an increase of serum testosterone, known as the *flare-up effect*. This effect should be counteracted in the treatment of patients with severe paraphilias through the use of an additional application of CPA within the first weeks of treatment. Following continued use of GnRH analogues, a desensitization of GnRH receptors can be observed, which results in a decrease of LH and subsequently of serum testosterone to castration levels. This can therefore be seen as an indirect way of lowering serum testosterone levels (Belchetz *et al.*, 1978; McEvoy, 1999). Because GnRH analogues also influence other cerebral areas like the olfactory bulb or the amygdala, GnRH is believed to act as a neuromodulator, which might also cause observable effects on sexual behavior (Kendrick and Dixson, 1985; Moss and Dudley, 1989; Schmidt *et al.*, 2004; Bloch *et al.*, 2006).

Conversely, CPA and MPA show an anti-libidinal effect by blocking androgen receptors (Heller, Laidlaw and Harvey, 1958; Money, 1968; Laschet and Laschet, 1975; Hucker, Langevin and Bain, 1988; Cooper *et al.*, 1992; Bradford and Pawlak, 1993; Meyer and Cole, 1997; Maletzky, Tolan and McFarland, 2006) and thus reduce sexual drive as well as sexual functioning. GnRH analogues (available through the products triptorelin, leuprorelin and goserelin) might lead to a sufficient reduction of sex-drive in offenders with sexual deviations including deviant sexual fantasies and behavior (Czerny, Briken and Berner, 2002), and furthermore, may be even more potent than CPA or MPA.

Side Effects of Androgen Lowering Treatments

All androgen lowering agents carry the risk of severe side effects, such as thromboembolic phenomena (blood clots), osteoporosis (Smith, 2002; Walsh, 2005), diabetes, weight gain, hypertonus (having an excessive level of skeletal muscle tension or activity), hyperlipoproteinemia (high cholesterol) (see Laaksonen *et al.*, 2004; Keating, O'Malley and Smith, 2006), gynecomastia (breast growth), feminization, hot flushes, night sweating (Rösler and Witztum, 1998; Sharifi, Gulley and Dahut, 2005) and hepatocellular (liver) damage. Other effects include emotional disturbances, depression, anxiety, fatigue, malaise, memory difficulties, lack of drive and listlessness, with these collectively known as the androgen-deprivation syndrome (Neumann and Kalmus, 1991; Shahinian *et al.*, 2006; Giltay and Gooren, 2009). While effects may be less severe than those listed above, they can reduce the patient's quality of life (Rösler and Witztum, 1998).

While CPA and MPA have a higher risk for liver damage than GnRH agonists, both substance groups can cause the above-mentioned side effects as well as a number of sexual dysfunctions, including erectile dysfunction, impotence, reduction of libido, partial azoospermia (low sperm count) and, depending on the duration of treatment, possible infertility.

GnRH analogues, however, often show fewer side effects, particularly regarding the amount of weight gain, gynecomastia, depressive symptoms and thromboembolism; but have a similar or even higher risk for osteoporosis, hot flushes and blood pressure variations (Czerny, Briken and Berner, 2002). Therefore regular assessments, especially of bone mineral density, blood levels and hormone levels, are necessary (Thibaut *et al.*, 2010). Although GnRH analogues seem to be promising substances in the treatment of paraphilias, recent research, however, does not completely confirm these assumptions. Different meta-analyses and reviews have created a picture of uncertainty, with inconsistent treatment effects noted (Briken, Hill and Berner, 2003; Briken and Kafka, 2007; Lösel and Schmucker, 2005; Eher *et al.*, 2007; Schmucker and Lösel, 2008; Guay, 2009; Jordan *et al.*, 2011b). Furthermore, many of these studies also did not reach the necessary methodological quality required (Thibaut *et al.*, 2010).

As actions of testosterone are manifold in the adult male, so too are its side effects (Kaufman and Vermeulen, 2005). Normal levels of androgens are necessary for the development of bones, different metabolic aspects, erythropoiesis (production of red blood cells), skin, mood, and several other functions. A decline of testosterone through androgen lowering agents in male patients will also result in a decline of estradiol, which plays an important role in the development of osteoporosis. Bone mineral density starts to decrease within the first year of treatment, and can lead to osteoporosis and a high risk of fractures. Other changes include weight gain and a decrease in muscle mass and strength. A decrease in muscle strength is often directly correlated to a decrease in bone mass, and any weight gain may consequently further increase the risk of falls and therefore of fractures as well (Smith, 2002).

Weight gain is also related to an increased risk of cardiovascular diseases, metabolic syndromes and the development of diabetes as a consequence of hyperinsulinemia (excess levels of insulin in the blood), hyperglycemia (excess levels of glucose in the blood) and insulin resistance (Keating, O'Malley and Smith, 2006). Androgen lowering agents also increase levels of low density lipoprotein, total cholesterol and triglycerides, all important risk factors for cardio- and cerebrovascular (brain) diseases (Sharifi, Gulley and Dahut, 2005). The observed weight gain following androgen lowering treatment is also related to an elevation of blood pressure, which is another risk factor for cardio- and cerebrovascular diseases. Changes within the hematopoietic (organs and tissues) system may cause thromboembolic complications like deep vein thrombosis, and are also connected to the increase of plasma lipoproteins. Beside these severe side effects, low plasma testosterone levels are also related to an increase in migraines, muscle cramps, phlebitis (inflammation of veins caused by blood clots), vertigo, gallbladder stones and gastrointestinal complications. In addition, low testosterone levels might also be responsible for memory difficulties (Cherrier, Aubin and Higano, 2009; Mottet *et al.*, 2006).

Considering the different effects and side effects of androgen lowering agents in the treatment of sexual offenders with severe paraphilias, we can summarize that this treatment is far from without risks. An interdisciplinary team of psychiatrists, psychotherapists, doctors and endocrinologists should therefore closely monitor such treatment. A comprehensive treatment plan, including risk assessment (prior fractures, cardiovascular events, family history of osteoporosis and cardiovascular disease, alcohol consumption and smoking habits), laboratory controls and measures of bone mineral density, should be compiled before starting therapy and reviewed on an annual basis. Concurrent administration of calcium and vitamin D should also occur. In patients with documented osteoporosis, augmented treatment with biphosphonates should be considered in consultation with an osteologist. Additionally, lifestyle interventions like diet (including smoking cessation) and exercises should also be considered to counteract the detrimental effects of androgen lowering agents.

Who Might Benefit from Treatment?

While discussing effects and side effects of androgen lowering therapy we have to consider who should be treated and why. First of all, treatment of sexual offenders is more influenced by considerations of risk and public protection than of the well-being of the potential patient himself. This is often aggravated by the fact that a large percentage of offenders are incarcerated or hospitalized in forensic settings. In some cases the decision about androgen lowering treatment may be influenced by irrational anxiety on the side of therapists as well as offenders, too. To determine suitability for androgen lowering treatment, three important issues must first be considered:

1. there is a considerable number of sexual offenders who do not fulfill the diagnostic criteria for paraphilias;
2. there is a considerable number of paraphilic patients who cannot be considered as sexual offenders and are not at risk of sexual offending;
3. there is a considerable number of sexual offenders and paraphilic patients who have relevant co-morbid psychiatric disorders (Briken, Hill and Berner, 2011).

Most experts agree that androgen lowering therapy is recommended only for patients with *severe* paraphilias. For that reason, it is necessary first to define what is meant by the term "severe."

According to Briken *et al.* (2006), a useful criterion for assessing the severity of a paraphilia includes an addictive-like or progressive course of paraphilic symptomatology, such as an increase in the frequency of acting out the paraphilic behavior accompanied by a decrease in satisfaction. Another aspect is the combination of a paraphilia with any form of sadism (Berger *et al.*, 1999; Berner, Berger and Hill, 2003; Nitschke, Osterheider and Mokros, 2009) in terms of co-morbidity, which means sexual sadism as well as sadistic personality pathology or signs of sadism at the crime scene (Knight and Prentky, 1990). However, notwithstanding the fact that we can find ways of describing the severity of paraphilias, there is still a problem in the poor conceptualization of different paraphilias themselves within the Diagnostic and Statistical Manual of Mental Disorders (DSM-IV-TR) and the International Classification of Diseases (ICD-10),[1] where the "definitions are dominated by notions of the unconventional nature of drive, rather than its psychological or physical characteristics" (Grubin and Beech, 2010: 434). To further aid with treatment selection, Maletzky, Tolan and McFarland (2006) have also proposed a scale to determine clinical and risk factors, which can lead to a recommendation for androgen lowering treatment for high-risk sex offenders with severe paraphilias. Factors included in this scale are: multiple victims, multiple paraphilias, deviant sexual interests, use of force, male victims, age under 30 at the time of release, central nervous system dysfunction, psychiatric illness, sexual violence under institutional conditions, and a history of treatment failure. Risk assessment instruments such as the Static-99 (Hanson and Thornton, 1999), the Stable-2007 (Hanson *et al.*, 2007), and the Sexual Violence Risk Scale (Boer *et al.*, 1997) are also useful when measuring severity in terms of risk.

With regard to treatment selection, the first step must therefore be a thorough diagnostic and prognostic assessment with respect to the principles of risk, need and responsivity (Andrews, Bonta and Hodge, 1990). On this basis, the second step is to develop a treatment plan, which should include treatment of co-morbid psychiatric disorders, with a focus on symptoms like impulsivity and antisocial behavior as well as on paraphilic urges, fantasies and behavior. Any treatment plan should also focus on the resources of the offender. The complexity of needs within the treatment of sexual offenders therefore clarifies that pharmacological treatment can only be one part of the treatment plan, accompanied by an additional and specialized psychotherapeutical approach.

Taking these factors into consideration, Briken, Hill and Berner (2003) proposed an algorithm for determining the suitability of pharmacological treatment with paraphilic sexual offenders. This is guided by the degree and severity of the diagnosed paraphilia and includes the following five points.

First, in sexual offenders with mild paraphilic symptomatology without prior hands-on delinquency (that is, those classified as low risk), who mostly suffer themselves, a psychotherapeutical treatment of the paraphilia is the first line treatment, augmented by treatment of co-morbid psychiatric disorders, including psychopharmacological treatment with neuroleptics, mood stabilizers, and so on. An additional pharmacological treatment with selective serotonin reuptake inhibitors (SSRIs) is recommended in patients with a risk for hands-on delinquency and/or strong paraphilic urges. Briken, Hill and Berner (2003) also recommend SSRIs if additional symptoms such as anxiety, social phobia, obsessive-compulsive behavior and depression are present.

Second, in sexual offenders with a moderate to high risk for hands-on offenses (for example, impulsive, aggressive and psychopathic patients) and an insufficient improvement under SSRI treatment, treatment with CPA (or MPA in the United States) is recommended. In patients where there is a history of unreliable compliance, intramuscular application of CPA could be considered. However, due to the (severe) side effects regarding liver function, treatment is inadvisable for patients with pre-existing liver damage or who develop liver dysfunction during treatment. For these cases, treatment with GnRH agonists should be considered.[2]

Third, in sexual offenders with a moderate to high risk of re-offending and who show no improvement under CPA, treatment with GnRH agonists should be considered. This may also be suitable for those sexual offenders with a high risk for re-offending who have been non-compliant with CPA medication. In these circumstances GnRH agonists could be an advantage, because it only needs to be administered once every three months.

Fourth, in sexual offenders showing an insufficient improvement under CPA or a GnRH agonist alone, the combination of an anti-androgen agent with a SSRI could be considered; especially if there are co-morbid symptoms of depression, anxiety or obsessive-compulsive behavior.

Fifth, in sexual offenders with a high risk of re-offending, especially those with a high score of psychopathy and who may counteract anti-androgen treatment by secret self-application of testosterone, a combination of CPA and GnRH agonists could be a possible option.

When discussing legal and ethical aspects of androgen lowering treatment in sexual offenders it is important to note that it should only be used with moderate to high risk sexual offenders who have not benefited from other kinds of treatment.

The Rationale for Treatment

The effect of androgens include the many and very different aspects of cerebral structures and functions as well as the gonads, the cardiovascular system, the immune system, neurotransmitters and the musculoskeletal system (Rahman and Christian, 2007; Bain, 2007; Li and Al Azzawi, 2009; Jordan *et al.*, 2011a). It is clear that testosterone in males is strongly related to sexual interest, thoughts, motivation, desire, arousal, spermatogenesis (sperm development), erection and ejaculation. Increasing plasma levels of testosterone in puberty leads to increased sexual activity, while decreasing plasma levels in older age often leads to a decline in sexual interest (Bancroft, 2005; Gooren and Bunck, 2004). Although this relation seems to be quite simple, the mechanism of action is very sophisticated. Testosterone has an impact on dopaminergic, cholinergic and serotonergic systems, which for their part have an influence on some aspects of our behavior including impulsivity, disinhibition, compulsivity and obsession. It is also worth noting that there is often a stronger effect of androgens in men with lower plasma testosterone concentrations when compared to men with normal plasma testosterone concentrations (Schmidt *et al.*, 2009). That can lead to a higher risk of illicit testosterone abuse in sexual offenders, who are being treated anti-hormonally. Furthermore, sexual activity itself is also able to change levels of sex hormones (Christiansen, 2004; Corona *et al.*, 2010), even though no differences regarding the kind of sexual activity mentioned have been found including orgasmic frequency or sexual stimuli such as erotic movies.

Based on this knowledge of associations between neurobiological functioning and sexual behavior, androgen lowering treatment in sexual offenders seems to have some rationale regarding the described effects on sexual urges in the treatment of patients with paraphilias when coupled together with a psychotherapeutical approach (Berlin, 2008; Codispoti, 2008). This is especially so for those patients whose paraphilic urges bring them into conflict with others (for example, sexual sadism or pedophilia); here sufficient treatment plays a key role in reintegration and (secondary) prevention. Despite this knowledge, the key question is how reliable the relationship is between decreased plasma testosterone levels and decreased rates of recidivism.

Androgen Lowering Treatment and Recidivism Rates

The major goal of androgen lowering treatment in sexual offenders is a substantial reduction in sexual arousability and desire, in order to increase the possibility of controlling sexual (especially paraphilic) thoughts, impulses, urges and behavior. This might be helpful in sexual offenders with severe paraphilias (such as sexual sadism), where psychotherapy alone is not enough to increase control over these urges, and where other pharmacological options like anti-depressants (SSRIs) are insufficient in their effects. For these sexual offenders an anti-androgenic treatment can be a starting point, enabling the offender to engage in psychotherapeutical interventions which should increase voluntary control over sexual arousal and sex drive, and teach the offender self-management and relapse prevention skills, which should lead to a reduced recidivism risk (Fedoroff, 2009; Hanson *et al.*, 2009; Ward and Gannon, 2006; Stinson, Sales and Becker, 2008).

Nevertheless, therapists should be aware that androgen lowering agents may only influence the intensity of sexual interest and/or desire, but not necessarily the preference itself (Thibaut *et al.*, 2010). Psychotherapeutical interventions can address self-control mechanisms helping offenders to avoid acting upon their sexual urges and impulses, although because sexual arousal is not completely traceable to neural, hormonal or genetic factors, but rather must be viewed within the complexity of cultural and sociosexual influences (Bancroft, 2009; Schober and Pfaff, 2007), a complete "cure" of paraphilias is doubtful.

As different reviews within the last few years have stated, the effects of androgen lowering agents on relapse prevention are controversial (Eher *et al.*, 2007; Thibaut *et al.*, 2010; Jordan *et al.*, 2011a, 2011b), since almost all existing studies do not meet the high quality criteria of evidence-based medicine. At the same time one has to keep in mind that double-blind, placebo-controlled studies are virtually absent due to the ethically questionable act of withholding a potentially effective medication from a treatment group. This is especially pertinent when successful therapy can lead to early releases and other adjustments to penal penalties. Despite this, the Institute for Sex Research and Forensic Psychiatry in Hamburg, Germany, is currently planning a randomized placebo controlled trial to test the efficacy of GnRH agonists in men with severe pedophilia in a forensic setting (see Briken and Berner, in press).

Legal and Ethical Aspects of Androgen Lowering Treatment for Sexual Offenders

Legal prerequisites

When assessing the legal context of androgen lowering treatment for sexual offenders, the human rights perspective in general and the clinical treatment in particular have to be considered. Pharmacological treatment of sexual offenders with androgen lowering agents takes place between relapse prevention and physical injury. On the one hand it is seen as a guarantor of public safety – especially by criminal law and political agents. On the other hand it is seen as a treatment, which infringes with its effects and especially side effects upon the patient's physical integrity, his ability for a life with sexuality (Koller, 2008). In Germany, as elsewhere, medical intervention is considered to constitute a physical injury, unless the written informed consent of the patient is present. This particularly applies for androgen lowering treatment with its aforementioned severe side effects.

The legal requirement for such treatment, in Germany, is defined by the German castration law of 1969 and is of a high standard. Information regarding the effects and side effects of the treatment is required, as too are the conditions for suitability. This information is important so that the patient is able to understand what he is giving informed consent to and thus enabling him to make an independent decision. The issue of informed consent within this group of patients is therefore crucial (see Chapter 3). For years, punishment, risk assessment and community protection have been the major issues with this offender group. Periods of long incarceration were the reality for many sexual offenders, with this only being reduced if the offender consented to androgen lowering treatment. There is therefore the ethical and legal problem of whether consent in this situation is voluntary informed consent; patients who fear extensive incarceration may easily consent to almost any kind of treatment, if it would result in the possibility of a shorter term of imprisonment. Within a retrospective study at a forensic psychiatric hospital Briken *et al.* (2009) assessed 79 sexual offenders, nearly half of whom had been treated with androgen lowering agents. Patients who were subject to androgen lowering treatment not only had more and higher levels of freedom while in the institution, but also had more home-leave opportunities. Fedoroff (1995) interestingly notes that sexual offenders who have the choice between treatment with SSRIs or androgen lowering agents choose almost exclusively SSRIs.

When considering the legal aspects of androgen lowering treatment of sexual offenders, therapists also have to consider the European Convention on Human Rights (ECHR), especially Articles 8 and 14, and the Declaration of Human Rights of the United Nations, especially Articles 16 and 25. This is because restricting somebody's ability to have sexual relations fulfills the circumstance of trespassing upon someone's human rights. The concept of human rights includes the basic understanding that rights are "viewed as entitlements to non-interference from others in the agent's affairs and/or to the provision of goods that are seen as being owed to the person concerned" (Ward and Birgden, 2007: 198). This definition clarifies that human rights involve duties and obligations; in other words, every agent has to accept that s/he has rights concerning the core values of well-being and freedom. At the same time s/he has to accept that other people have the same rights to freedom and well-being (Gewirth, 1981, 1996, 1998). From this point of view sexual offenders are both holders and violators of human rights. In the treatment of those who have violated the rights of others the crucial aspect lies within this duality. Both rights, those of the offender and those of the victim, should therefore be acknowledged and incorporated into the decision-making process concerning treatment (Ward and Birgden, 2007; see Chapter 2).

While it is clear that certain rights should be curtailed as a consequence of sexual offenders violating the rights of others by committing sexual offenses, sexual offenders do not forfeit their human rights in general because of the crimes they have committed (Ward and Birgden, 2007). For practitioners this implicates a therapeutic approach including respect and dignity towards the offenders to encourage their appreciation of the rights and interests of their victims, which is an important step forward in minimizing risks of re-offending. Furthermore this ethical therapeutic approach enables the offender autonomously to make informed voluntary decisions, the only basis on which the decision to partake in androgen lowering therapy should be founded.

According to Article 3 of the ECHR a state must protect its citizens from inhuman or degrading treatment, regardless of competing interests such as national security or public protection. The question here is therefore whether androgen lowering treatment is capable of causing the intense physical and mental suffering and acute psychiatric disturbances which can amount to torture, or inhuman or degrading treatment. Unlike surgical castration (most) effects of androgen lowering treatment are reversible or can be treated with co-medications without leaving permanent stigmas like scars. However, there is still a lack of knowledge concerning possible long-lasting side effects, especially regarding the long-term effects on fertility. Side effects such as hot flushes, lethargy, decrease of muscle mass, bone loss, and so on, which also occur in surgical castration, could also be judged as humiliating and/or degrading; although with termination of the treatment, these effects will fade away. Bearing this in mind Article 8, which proclaims the individual's ability to have sexual relations, restricts both kinds of androgen lowering treatments, but again within the pharmacological alternative the possibility for sexual relations is greater and limitations are reversible. Finally, Article 12 proclaims the right of marriage and to raise a family, the latter being surely curtailed. This article in particular clarifies that not only the offenders but also their partners in life are affected by androgen lowering treatment since their (human) rights are restricted as well (for more information on androgen lowering treatment and human rights, see Harrison and Rainey, 2009).

With regard to these specific aspects of restricting the human rights of sexual offenders, once more the possibility of obtaining truly informed consent to androgen lowering treatment has to be determined thoroughly. The validity of the given informed consent has to be proven by assessing the sufficient understanding of the nature and the effects of this treatment by the offender, including all potential side effects, and making sure that the written consent is provided without any kind of coercion (Harrison, 2010).

The legality of androgen lowering treatment of sexual offenders differs throughout Europe, and even between different states in the United States. Voluntary "chemical castration" is practiced in many countries in Europe, including the United Kingdom, France, Belgium, Germany, the Czech Republic, Denmark, Sweden, Hungary and Italy (Harrison, 2007). Mandatory "chemical castration" (combined with psychotherapy) came into effect in Poland on June 9, 2010, and is applicable to anyone guilty of raping a child under the age of 15 (Baczynska, 2009). In July 2011, South Korea enacted a law for mandatory chemical castration of child molesters whose victims are under the age of 16 (Shim, 2011) and a similar law came into effect in Russia in October 2011 (Pitalev, 2011). The French National Assembly is considering legislation for mandatory chemical castration as well (Grubin and Beech, 2010). When discussing the issues of androgen lowering treatment for sexual offenders in an international perspective, it is therefore necessary to take these different conditions into account.

The crucial legal aspect for androgen lowering treatment in sexual offenders is therefore the validity of the offender's informed consent, which has to be assessed by therapists thoroughly. This can be done by using the following procedure.

First, the four legal standards of competence to consent must be obtained:

i.   to understand information relevant to the decision about treatment;
ii. to rationally prepare the information (or reason about it) in a manner that allows everyone to make comparisons and weigh options;
iii. to appreciate the significance for one's own situation of the information disclosed about the illness and possible treatments; and
iv. to express a choice (Grisso and Appelbaum, 1995).

The therapist can use special instruments for this assessment like the MacArthur Competence Assessment Tool-Treatment (Grisso, Appelbaum and Hill-Fotouhi, 1997).

Second, consideration should be given to the legal background of treatment (for example, treatment in prison, in a forensic psychiatric hospital, in an outpatient setting) and its implications for the informed consent. This issue could be solved by the assessment of two different therapists, who separately form their own recommendation for treatment.

Third, the issue of independence must be addressed: therapists who give recommendations about possible androgen lowering treatment should not be involved in the process of recommending higher grades of home leave or probation.

Fourth, in cases of cognitively impaired, mentally impaired or juvenile sexual offenders, where the ability to give informed consent is diminished, the legal guardian has to be completely informed about the planned treatment; the guardian's ability to consent has to be proven as well.

Fifth, potential patients have to be informed comprehensively about the reasons, relevance and consequences of treatment as well as alternative treatments and their possible effects. Therapists have to be cautious and should try to be objective. They should avoid any attitude towards possible promises regarding parole or home leave since that could be understood as badgering. Suggestive statements should also be avoided.

Ethical aspects

In a discussion concerning the ethical issues of androgen lowering treatment with sexual offenders, their values, emotions, attitudes and (religious) beliefs must be considered in addition to medical ethics. Sexual offenders who refuse androgen lowering treatment may be kept in prison or in a forensic hospital without the possibility of parole. On the other hand, if they agree to treatment against their best judgment, there is a high risk of non-compliance (for example, either by not taking the medication or with the parallel use of testosterone from the black market). It must also be considered that withholding a possible efficient medication from sexual offenders is ethically problematic. This matter is even more complicated by the fact that a substantial number of sexual offenders also suffer from psychiatric disorders (such as psychosis or intellectual disabilities; see Raymond *et al.*, 1999; Kafka and Hennen, 2002; Dunsieth *et al.*, 2004; Fazel *et al.*, 2007; Sajith, Morgan and Clarke, 2008) besides the paraphilia, which might affect their ability to understand fully the complexity of androgen lowering treatment and their capacity to give informed consent.

In order to establish an ethical approach to androgen lowering treatment, we have to be clear about the major aims of treatment. As we have learned, rehabilitation is an important part of secondary prevention, with specialized therapeutic programs being developed to address behavior modifications (Mann, Hanson and Thornton, 2010; Andrews and Bonta, 2010). All interventions are thus designed to increase voluntary control over sexual arousal, and to teach self-management and relapse-prevention skills. Androgen lowering therapy might increase these effects by reducing sexual drive and urges, which might only then enable some sexual offenders to participate in psychotherapeutical interventions. This is important for those groups of sexual offenders who meet the above-mentioned criteria for androgen lowering treatment (moderate to high risk of re-offending; non-responding to other forms of treatment, such as psychotherapy alone, or augmented by pharmacotherapy with, for example, SSRIs). Another ethical issue which must be considered by therapists is the use of off-label drugs. SSRIs as well as most GnRH analogues have no proven indication for the treatment of paraphilias. Although this is not an obstacle for treatment, the advantages and disadvantages of their use must be weighed continuously during the course of treatment, and the patient must be informed about this circumstance.

Due to the fact that sexual offending is the kind of crime that society is understandably particularly concerned about, the treatment of sexual offenders is never a private business between therapist and patient, but takes place in the middle of the political arena under the spotlight of the media. Therefore there is a substantial need for more studies with greater methodological quality regarding effectiveness and efficiency of GnRH agonist treatment, to learn more about the function of testosterone in paraphilias and to create guidelines for treatment methods based on these findings. If treatment cannot be proven to work, then it is ethically questionable whether it should be used. Until such guidelines are published, the following statements could lead decisions for androgen lowering treatment:

- There is no ethically justifiable reason for surgical castration.
- Androgen lowering treatment should not be administered within compulsory treatment.
- Androgen lowering treatment should not be withheld due to dogmatic reasons.
- Therapists should ensure that informed consent, despite any difficulties in achieving it, is given voluntarily. This is especially so with patients who have cognitive disabilities or psychiatric co-morbidities.
- Patient information should be easily comprehensible.
- Before starting androgen lowering therapy, possible reasons for termination of treatment should be considered carefully.
- With the start of androgen lowering therapy patients should be encouraged to lead a healthy lifestyle (for example, sports, nutritional regime) to prevent long-term consequences. Medication dosage must be reviewed on a regular basis, with the algorithm of medication (1. SSRI, 2. CPA, 3. GnRH, 4. GnRH + CPA) also being usable in reverse order. A reasonable interruption of medication might also lower side effects.
- Androgen lowering treatment should not influence home leave. Androgen lowering treatment should not be started at the end of therapy in a forensic hospital, but earlier, so as to monitor effects and side effects.
- Androgen lowering therapy is not the optimal solution for all problems and should therefore not be overestimated.
- Androgen lowering therapy should be embedded into a complex treatment plan, consisting of psychotherapy, ergotherapy (the use of physical activity and exercise in the treatment of disease), social skills training, and offense-specific treatment programs.

Public Protection and Human Rights

Judicial and political systems are obliged to prosecute those who violate the rights of others in an attempt to protect society. Historically, the main focus of such systems has been on punishment, risk assessment and relapse prevention to reach these aims. Reduction of recidivism rates in the sense of a rehabilitative strength-based approach has not therefore been primarily addressed (Ward and Birgden, 2007; Marshall *et al.*, 2011). With this background in mind, therapists working with sexual offenders often find themselves in a difficult position. They offer support to their patients while creating an atmosphere of confidence, but they also have to make sufficient risk assessments, inform their patients about every aspect of treatment (positive and negative), ensure truly informed consent to treatment is given, and make recommendations for home leave or release on parole. The treatment of sexual offenders has always been problematic. On the one hand therapists have to face the need for public safety, but on the other they must consider the best interest of the patient (Gooren, 2011). Therapists should be aware of the fact that as long as paraphilias are regarded as a disorder, sexual offenders with paraphilias have to be seen as patients first and not (only) as perpetrators. Depending on severity, risk and setting, only sexual offenders with (severe) paraphilias should be treated with androgen lowering medications. Studies have shown that between 10 and 15% of all sexual offenders in German forensic psychiatric institutions fulfill these criteria and thus are treated with androgen lowering agents (Czerny, Briken and Berner, 2002). In another survey Turner and Briken (in press) have also shown that 11% of all sexual offenders within forensic-psychiatric hospitals (in- and out-patient) have been treated with GnRH and 5% with CPA.

With any kind of (medical) treatment the physician or therapist has to balance expected use and expected side effects, in order to follow the Hippocratic oath of "to do good or to do no harm" (Smith, 2005). The same is applicable to androgen lowering treatment in sexual offenders, but has to be extended by certain security aspects. In this special case the physician or therapist also has to consider the need to protect society, which leads to a shift of the treatment focus from the best interests of the patient to public safety (Grubin and Beech, 2010). So the physician or therapist finds himself caught in a mesh of challenges, which have to be satisfied in an ethically clear manner considering human rights, medical ethics, legal principles and medically proven efficacy.

To take all of the above-mentioned aspects into account therapists have to consider different perspectives concerning the treatment of sexual offenders. They have to:

- face the sex offender with dignity and respect (the *human rights perspective*);
- ensure that only sexual offenders with severe paraphilias will be treated with anti-androgens (the *psychiatric/sexual medicine perspective*);
- validate the informed consent given for androgen lowering treatment (the *legal and ethical perspective*);
- entrench pharmacological treatment within a context of psychotherapy (the *psychotherapeutic perspective*).

A sophisticated policy of treatment is therefore needed, where sexual offenders should be seen primarily as human beings who need support. Respect, unprejudiced attitudes and compassion are the fundamental pillars of any offender therapy. Only then will offenders be in the situation to make an informed voluntary decision, which will ensure that treatment is taking place on an ethical basis (Ward and Birgden, 2007; Birgden and Perlin, 2009). Treatment based on this human rights perspective views sexual offenders both as rights-holders *and* duty bearers (Ward and Birgden, 2007). Furthermore, this perspective addresses the needs of both the offender and society by reducing criminogenic factors as well as maximizing different coping skills to enable the offender to make his own decisions and follow his plans, and to develop understanding for the interests of others. Treatment on this basis allows offenders to live a life that is both personally meaningful to them and offense-free (Ward and Birgden, 2007).

Notes

1 Definitions of paraphilias in the DSM-IV-TR as well as in the ICD-10 describe only the unconventional nature of these dispositions, for example for DSM-IV-TR: "recurrent, intense sexually arousing fantasies, sexual urges or behaviours generally involving (1) non-human objects, (2) the suffering or humiliation of oneself or one's partner, or (3) children or other non-consenting persons that occur over a period of 6 months" (Criterion A), which "cause clinically significant distress or impairment in social, occupational, or other important areas of functioning" (Criterion B). In this definition the specific psychological conditions are not mentioned; rather we can find a differentiation between paraphilias and paraphilic disorders, which leads to labeling of non-normative sexual behavior. Within the development of DSM-V a clearer distinction between paraphilias and paraphilic disorders has been made.

2 In Germany the GnRH agonist Salvacyl® (triptorelin) is approved for "severe sexual abnormalities," and is registered in seven other European countries (France, the United Kingdom, Sweden, Norway, Denmark, the Netherlands and Finland).

References

Allolio, B., Keffel, D., Deuss, U. and Winkelmann, W. (1985) "Treatment of sex behavior disorders with LH-RH superagonists [Behandlung sexueller Verhaltensstörungen mit LH-RH Superagonisten]," *Deutsche Medizinische Wochenschrift* 110, 50, 1952.

Andrews, D.A. and Bonta, J. (2010) *The Psychology of Criminal Conduct*, 5th edn. New Providence: LexisNexis Matthew Bender.

Andrews, D.A., Bonta, J. and Hodge, R.D. (1990) "Classification for effective rehabilitation: rediscovering psychology," *Criminal Justice and Behavior*, 17, 19–52.

Baczynska, G. (2009) Poland Okays Forcible Castration for Paedophiles, http://www.reuters.com/article/2009/09/25/us-castration-idUSTRE58O4LE20090925 (accessed August 25, 2012).

Bain, J. (2007) "The many faces of testosterone," *Clinical Interventions in Aging* 2, 567–576.

Bancroft, J. (2005) "The endocrinology of sexual arousal," *Journal of Endocrinology* 186, 411–427.

Bancroft, J. (2009) *Human Sexuality and Its Problems*, 3rd edn. New York: Churchill Livingstone.

Belchetz, P.E., Plant, T.M., Nakai, Y., *et al.* (1978) "Hypophysial responses to continuous and intermittent delivery of hypothalamic gonadotropin releasing hormone," *Science* 202(4368), 631–633.

Berger, P., Berner, W., Bolterauer, J. *et al.* (1999) "Sadistic personality disorder in sex offenders: relationship to antisocial personality disorder and sexual sadism," *Journal of Personality Disorders* 13, 2, 175–186.

Berlin, F.S. (2008) "Basic science and neurobiological research: potential relevance to sexual compulsivity," *Psychiatric Clinics of North America* 31, 623–642.

Berner, W., Berger, P. and Hill, A. (2003) "Sexual sadism," *International Journal of Offender Therapy and Comparative Criminology* 47, 383–395.

Birgden, A. and Perlin, M.L. (2009) "Where the home in the valley meets the damp dirty prison: a human rights perspective on therapeutic jurisprudence and the role of forensic psychologists in correctional settings," *Aggression and Violent Behavior* 14, 4, 256–263.

Bloch, M., Rubinow, D.R., Berlin, K. *et al.* (2006) "Monoamines and neurosteroids in sexual function during induced hypogonadism in healthy men," *Archives of General Psychiatry* 63, 4, 450–456.

Boer, D.P., Hart, S.D., Kropp, P.R. and Webster, C.D. (1997) *Manual for the Sexual Violence Risk*. Burnaby, Canada: Simon Fraser University.

Bradford, J.M. and Pawlak, A. (1993) "Double-blind placebo crossover study of cyproterone acetate in the treatment of the paraphilias," *Archives of Sexual Behavior* 22, 5, 383–402.

Briken, P. and Berner, W. (in press) "Double-blind, controlled, clinical trial planned in Germany to investigate the efficacy of psychotherapy combined with triptorelin in adult male patients with severe pedophilic disorders: presentation of the study protocol," *Israeli Journal of Psychiatry and Related Sciences*.

Briken, P., Habermann, N., Kafka, M.P., *et al.* (2006) "The paraphilia-related disorders: an investigation of the relevance of the concept in sexual murderers," *Journal of Forensic Sciences* 51, 683–688.

Briken, P., Hill, A. and Berner, W. (2003) "Pharmacotherapy of paraphilias with long-acting agonists of luteinizing hormone-releasing hormone: a systematic review," *Journal of Clinical Psychiatry* 64, 890–897.

Briken, P., Hill, A. and Berner, W. (2011) "Pharmacotherapy of sexual offenders and men who are at risk of sexual offending," in D. Boer, R. Eher, M.H. Miner, F. Pfäfflin and L.A. Craig (eds), *International Perspectives on the Assessment and Treatment of Sexual Offenders: Theory, Practice and Research*. Chichester: John Wiley & Sons, Ltd, pp. 419–431.

Briken, P. and Kafka, M.P. (2007) "Pharmacological treatments for paraphilic patients and sexual offenders," *Current Opinion in Psychiatry* 20, 609–613.

Briken, P., Wetzel, K., Habermann, N. *et al.* (2009) "Antiandrogenic pharmacotherapy of sexual offenders and home leave steps in the forensic psychiatric hospital Berlin, [Antiandrogene Therapie und Lockerungen bei Sexualstraftätern im Maßregelvollzug Berlin]." *Psychiatrische Praxis* 36, 5, 232–237.

Cherrier, M.M., Aubin, S. and Higano, C.S. (2009) "Cognitive and mood changes in men undergoing intermittent combined androgen blockade for non-metastatic prostate cancer," *Psychooncology* 18, 237–247.

Christiansen, K. (2004) "Behavioral correlates of testosterone," in E. Nieschlag and H.M. Behre (eds), *Testosterone: Action, Deficiency, Substitution*, 3rd edn. Cambridge: Cambridge University Press, pp. 125–172.

Codispoti, V.L. (2008) "Pharmacology of sexually compulsive behaviour," *Psychiatric Clinics of North America* 31, 4, 671–679.

Cooper, A.J., Sandhu, S., Losztyn, S. and Cernovsky, Z. (1992) "A double-blind placebo controlled trial of medroxyprogesterone acetate and cyproterone acetate with seven pae-dophiles," *Canadian Journal of Psychiatry* 37, 10, 687–693.

Corona, G., Ricca, V., Boddi, V. *et al.* (2010) "Autoerotism, mental health, and organic distur-bances in patients with erectile dysfunction," *Journal of Sexual Medicine* 7, 182–191.

Czerny, J.P., Briken, P. and Berner, W. (2002) "Antihormonal treatment of paraphilic patients in German forensic psychiatric clinics," *European Psychiatry* 17, 2, 104–106.

Dunsieth, N.W. Jr., Nelson, E.B., Brusman-Lovins, L.A. *et al.* (2004) "Psychiatric and legal features of 113 men convicted of sexual offences," *Journal of Clinical Psychiatry* 65, 293–300.

Eher, R., Gnoth, A., Birklbauer, A. and Pfäfflin, F. (2007) "The effects of antiandrogenic medication on relapse rates of sex offenders: a review [Antiandrogene Medikation zur Senkung der Rückfälligkeit von Sexualstraftätern: Ein kritischer Überblick]," *Recht und Psychiatrie* 25, 103–111.

Fazel, S., Sjostedt, G., Langstrom, N. and Grann, M. (2007) "Severe mental illness and risk of sexual offending in men: a case-control study based on Swedish national register," *Journal of Clinical Psychiatry* 68, 588–596.

Fedoroff, J.P. (1995) "Antiandrogenes vs. serotonergic medications in the treatment of sex offenders: a preliminary compliance study," *Canadian Journal of Human Sexuality* 4, 111–122.

Fedoroff, J.P. (2009) "The paraphilias," in M. G. Gelder (ed.), *New Oxford Textbook of Psychiatry*, 2nd edn. Oxford: Oxford University Press, pp. 832–842.

Foote, R. (1944) "Hormone treatment of sex offenders," *Journal of Nervous and Mental Disorders* 99, 928–929.

Gewirth, A. (1981) *Reason and Morality*. Chicago, IL: University of Chicago Press.

Gewirth, A. (1996) *The Community of Rights*. Chicago, IL: University of Chicago Press.

Gewirth, A. (1998) *Self-fulfilment*. Princeton, NJ: Princeton University Press.

Giltay, E.J. and Gooren, L.J. (2009) "Potential side effects of androgen deprivation treatment in sex offenders," *Journal of the American Academy of Psychiatry and the Law* 37, 1, 53–58.

Golla, F.L. and Hodge, S.R. (1949) "Hormone treatment of sexual offenders," *Lancet* I (6563), 1006–1007.

Gooren, L.J. (2011) "Ethical and medical considerations of androgen deprivation treatment of sex offenders," *Journal of Clinical Endocrinology and Metabolism* 96, 12, 3628–3637.

Gooren, L.J. and Bunck, M.C. (2004) "Androgen replacement therapy: present and future," *Drugs* 64, 17, 1861–1891.

Grisso, T. and Appelbaum, P. (1995) "Comparison of standards for assessing patients' capacities to make treatment decisions," *American Journal of Psychiatry* 152, 1033–1037.

Grisso, T., Appelbaum, P. and Hill-Fotouhi, C. (1997) "The MacCAT-T: a clinical tool to assess patients' capacities to give informed consent," *Psychiatry Services* 48, 11, 1415–1419.

Grubin, D. and Beech, A. (2010) "Chemical castration for sex offenders," *British Medical Journal* 340, c74, 433–434.

Guay, D.R.P. (2009) "Drug treatment of paraphilic and nonparaphilic sexual disorders," *Clinical Therapeutics* 31, 1–31.

Hanson, R.K., Harris, A.J., Scott, T.L. and Helmus, L. (2007) Assessing the risk of sexual offenders on community supervision: the Dynamic Supervision Project, http://www.publicsafety.gc.ca/res/cor/rep/_fl/crp2007-05-en.pdf (accessed August 25, 2012).

Hanson, R.K., Bourgon, G., Helmus, L. and Hodgson, S. (2009) "The principles of effective correctional treatment also apply to sexual offenders. A meta-analysis," *Criminal Justice and Behavior* 36, 865–891.

Hanson, R.K. and Thornton, D. (1999) *Static-99: Improving Actuarial Risk Assessment for Sex Offenders*. Ottawa: Department of the Solicitor General of Canada.

Harrison, K. (2007) "The castration cure," *Prison Service Journal* 175, 13–18.

Harrison, K. (2010) "The use of pharmacotherapy with high-risk sex offenders," in K. Harrison (ed.), *Managing High Risk Sex Offenders in the Community: Risk Management, Treatment and Social Responsibility*. Cullompton: Willan Publishing, pp. 105–132.

Harrison, K. and Rainey, B. (2009) "Suppressing human rights? A rights-based approach to the use of pharmacotherapy with sex offender," *Legal Studies* 29, 1, 47–74.

Hebebrand, K., Hebebrand, J. and Remschmidt, H. (2002) "Pharmacological agents for treatment of paraphilias and hypersexual disorders [Medikamente in der Behandlung von Paraphilien und hypersexuellen Störungen]," *Fortschritte der Neurologie Psychiatrie* 70, 462–475.

Heller, C.G., Laidlaw, W.M. and Harvey, H.T. (1958) "Effects of progestational compounds on the reproductive process of the human male," *Annals of the New York Academy of Sciences* 71, 649–655.

Hucker, S., Langevin, R. and Bain, J. (1988) "A double-blind trial of sex drive reducing medication in paedophiles," *Sexual Abuse: A Journal of Research and Treatment* 1, 2, 227–242.

Jordan, K., Fromberger, P., Stolpmann, G. and Müller, J.L. (2011a) "The role of testosterone in sexuality and paraphilia – a neurobiological approach. Part I: testosterone and sexuality," *Journal of Sexual Medicine* 8, 2993–3007.

Jordan, K., Fromberger, P., Stolpmann, G. and Müller, J.L. (2011b) "The role of testosterone in sexuality and paraphilia – a neurobiological approach. Part II: testosterone and paraphilia," *Journal of Sexual Medicine* 8, 3008–3029.

Kafka, M.P. and Hennen, J. (2002) "A DSM-IV Axis I comorbidity study of males (n = 120) with paraphilias and paraphilia-related disorders," *Sex Abuse* 14, 349–366.

Kaufman, J.M. and Vermeulen, A. (2005) "The decline of androgen levels in elderly men and its clinical and therapeutic implications," *Endocrine Reviews* 26, 6, 833–876.

Keating, N.L., O'Malley, A.J. and Smith, M.R. (2006) "Diabetes and cardiovascular disease during androgen deprivation therapy for prostate cancer," *Journal of Clinical Oncology* 24, 4448–4456.

Kendrick, K.M. and Dixson, A.F. (1985) "Luteinizing hormone releasing hormone enhances proceptivity in a primate," *Neuroendocrinology* 41, 449–453.

Knight, R.A. and Prentky, R.A. (1990) "Classifying sexual offenders: the development of corroboration of taxonomic models," in W.L. Marshall, D.R. Laws and H.E. Barbaree (eds), *Handbook of Sexual Assault: Issues, Theories, and Treatment of the Offender. Applied Clinical Psychology*. New York: Plenum Press, pp. 23–52.

Koller, M. (2008) "Antiandrogen treatment – relapse prevention or assault [Triebdämpfende Medikation zwischen Rückfallprophylaxe und Körperverletzung]," *Recht and Psychiatrie* 26, 187–199.

Laaksonen, D.E., Niskanen, L., Punnonen, K. *et al.* (2004) "Testosterone and sex hormone-binding globulin predict the metabolic syndrome and diabetes in middle-aged men," *Diabetes Care* 27, 5, 1036–1041.

Laschet, U. and Laschet, L. (1975) "Antiandrogens in the treatment of sexual deviations of men," *Journal of Steroid Biochemistry* 6, 6, 821–826.

Li, J. and Al Azzawi, F. (2009) "Mechanism of androgen receptor action," *Maturitas* 63, 142–148.

Lösel, F. and Schmucker, M. (2005) "The effectiveness of treatment for sexual offenders: a comprehensive meta-analysis," *Journal of Experimental Criminology* 1, 117–146.

Maletzky, B.M., Tolan, A. and McFarland, B. (2006) "The Oregon depo-Provera program: a five-year follow-up," *Sex Abuse* 18, 3, 206–216.

Mann, R.E., Hanson, R.K. and Thornton, D. (2010) "Assessing risk for sexual recidivism: some proposals on the nature of psychologically meaningful risk factors," *Sex Abuse* 22, 191–217.

Marshall, W.L., Marshall, L.E., Serran, G.E. and O'Brien, M.D. (2011) *Rehabilitating Sexual Offenders. A Strength-Based Approach*. Washington, DC: American Psychological Association.

McEvoy, G. (1999) *AHFS Drug Information*. Bethesda, MD: American Society of Health System Pharmacists.

Meyer, J.W. and Cole, C.M. (1997) "Physical and chemical castration of sex offenders: a review," *Journal of Offender Rehabilitation* 25, 3–4, 1–18.

Money, J. (1968) "Discussion on hormonal inhibition of libido in male sex offenders," in R.P. Michael (ed.), *Endocrinology and Human Behaviour*. London: Oxford University Press, p. 169.

Moss, R.L. and Dudley, C.A. (1989) "Luteinizing hormone releasing hormone (LHRH) peptidergic signals in the neural integration of female reproductive behaviour," in J.M. Lakovski, J.R. Perez-Polo and D.K. Rassin, *Neural Control of Reproductive Function*. New York: Liss, pp. 485–499.

Mottet, N., Prayer-Galetti, T., Hammerer, P. *et al.* (2006) "Optimizing outcomes and quality of life in the hormonal treatment of prostate cancer," *BJU International* 98, 20–27.

Neumann, F. and Kalmus, J. (1991) "Cyproterone acetate in the treatment of sexual disorders: pharmacological base and clinical experience," *Experimental and Clinical Endocrinology* 98, 2, 71–80.

Nitschke, J., Osterheider, M. and Mokros, A. (2009) "A cumulative scale of severe sexual sadism," *Sex Abuse* 21, 262–278.

Pitalev, I. (2011) Russian deputies approve chemical castration for pedophiles, http://en.rian.ru/russia/20111004/167381251.html (accessed August 25, 2012).

Rahman, F. and Christian, H.C. (2007 "Non-classical actions of testosterone: an update," *Trends in Endocrinology and Metabolism* 18, 10, 371–378.

Raymond, N.C., Coleman, E., Ohlerking, F. *et al.* (1999) "Psychiatric comorbidity in pedophilic sex offenders," *American Journal of Psychiatry* 156, 786–788.

Rösler, A. and Witztum, E. (1998) "Treatment of men with paraphilia with a long-acting analogue of gonadotropin-releasing hormone," *New England Journal of Medicine* 338, 7, 416–422.

Sajith, S.G., Morgan, C. and Clarke, D. (2008) "Pharmacological management of inappropriate sexual behaviours: a review of its evidence, rationale and scope in relation to men with intellectual disabilities," *Journal of Intellectual Disability Research* 52, 12, 1078–1090.

Schmidt, P.J., Berlin, K.L., Danaceau, M.A. *et al.* (2004) "The effects of pharmacologically induced hypogonadism on mood in healthy men," *Archives of General Psychiatry* 61, 10, 997–1004.

Schmidt, P.J., Steinberg, E.M., Negro, P.P. *et al.* (2009) "Pharmacologically induced hypogonadism and sexual function in healthy young women and men," *Neuropsychopharmacology* 34, 565–576.

Schmucker, M. and Lösel, F. (2008) "Does sexual offender treatment work? A systematic review of outcome evaluations," *Psicothema* 20, 1, 10–19.

Schober, J.M. and Pfaff, D. (2007) "The neurophysiology of sexual arousal," *Best Practice and Research. Clinical Endocrinology and Metabolism* 21, 3, 445–461.

Shahinian, V.B., Kuo, Y.F., Freeman, J.L. and Goodwin, J.S. (2006) "Risk of the 'androgen deprivation syndrome' in men receiving androgen deprivation for prostate cancer," *Archives of Internal Medicine* 166, 4, 465–471.

Sharifi, N., Gulley, J.L. and Dahut, W.L. (2005) "Androgen deprivation therapy for prostate cancer," *Journal of the American Medical Association* 294, 238–244.

Shim, S-W. (2011) "S. Korea enacts 'chemical castration' law to punish paedophiles," Reuters, http://in.reuters.com/article/2011/07/24/idINIndia–58423020110724 (accessed August 25, 2012).

Smith, C.M. (2005) "Origin and use of primum non nocere – above all, do no harm!," *Journal of Clinical Pharmacology* 45, 4, 371–377.

Smith, M.R. (2002) "Osteoporosis during androgen deprivation therapy for prostate cancer," *Urology* 60, 79–86.

Smith, J.A. Jr. (1986) "Luteinizing hormone-releasing hormone (LH-RH) analogues in treatment of prostatic cancer," *Urology* 27, 9–15.

Stinson, J.D., Sales, B.D. and Becker, J.V. (2008) *Sex Offending. Causal Theories to Inform Research, Prevention, and Treatment. American Psychological Association.* Washington, DC: Sage.

Symmers, W.S.C. (1968) "Carcinoma of the breast in transsexual individuals after surgical and hormonal interference with primary and secondary sex characteristics," *British Medical Journal* 2(5597), 83–85.

Thibaut, F., De La Barra, F., Gordon, H. *et al.* (2010) "The World Federation of Societies of Biological Psychiatry (WFSBP) Guidelines for the biological treatment of paraphilias," *World Journal of Biological Psychiatry* 11, 604–655.

Turner, D. and Briken, P. (in press) "Prescription of testosterone lowering agents in sexual offender treatment in German forensic psychiatric institutions," *Journal of Sexual Medicine.*

Vance, M.A. and Smith, J.A. (1984) "Endocrine and clinical effects of leuprolide in prostate cancer," *Clinical Pharmacology and Therapeutics* 36, 3, 350–354.

Walsh, P.C. (2005) "Risk of fracture after androgen deprivation for prostate cancer," *Journal of Urology* 174, 3, 929–930.

Ward, T. and Birgden, A. (2007) "Human rights and correctional clinical practice," *Aggression and Violent Behavior* 12, 628–643.

Ward, T. and Gannon, T.A. (2006) "Rehabilitation, etiology, and self-regulation: the comprehensive good lives model of treatment for sexual offenders," *Aggression and Violent Behavior* 11, 77–94.

Whittaker, L.H. (1959) "Oestrogen and psychosexual disorders," *Medical Journal of Australia* 46, 2, 547–549.

19

Female Sexual Offenders
The Need for a Gender-Responsive Approach

Sherry Ashfield, Sheila Brotherston,
Hilary Eldridge and Ian Elliott

Introduction

Historically, sexual offending has been perceived to be a form of behavior largely associated with men. The prevailing view that women identified as engaging in sexual offending must be inherently similar to their male counterparts led to little attention being given to the potential significance of gender. However, as the body of empirical information on women who sexually offend has developed, it has become apparent that a blanket application of research knowledge based on *male* sexual offenders to the understanding of sexual offending by females is not a viable option. In sexual offending, as in general offending, gender matters. Although women may engage in similar acts to men, their pathways to offending remain uniquely female and so demand separate explanations to those of their male counterparts (Harris, 2010). This chapter will therefore review the developments that have occurred in the understanding of female sexual offending and the significance of a gender-responsive approach to this population. It will then explore how gender-responsiveness can inform understanding of good practice in the assessment and treatment of female sex offenders.

Although the involvement of females in the sexual abuse of children can be identified in literature from as early as 27AD (Saradjian, 2010), professionals have consistently struggled to accept that such behaviors can be attributed to women (Denov, 2001, 2003; Saradjian, 2010). Bunting (2005) suggests that the apparent invisibility of female sex offenders in comparison with their male counterparts has been influenced by the low rates of sex offenses attributed to women within criminal justice and research statistics. She illustrates how prevalence rates for female sexual abuse of children ranges from 1%, identified through child protection agencies, to 50% of a

The Wiley-Blackwell Handbook of Legal and Ethical Aspects of Sex Offender Treatment and Management,
First Edition. Edited by Karen Harrison and Bernadette Rainey.
© 2013 John Wiley & Sons, Ltd. Published 2013 by John Wiley & Sons, Ltd.

child care sample, depending on the research method and the nature of the population under investigation, and recommends that changes should be made to a range of governmental systems to facilitate the development of baseline information on cases where female sexual abuse has occurred. There is now a general acceptance by professionals working in this field that sexual abuse perpetrated by females is likely to be underestimated (Bunting, 2005; Cortoni, 2010).

The relationship between poor information gathering and professional attitudes to female sexual offenders has traditionally been symbiotic in nature, with low prevalence rates cited as "mitigating against resources being prioritized in this area of work" (Bunting, 2005: 74). This attitude can also be seen in relation to training provision for staff, with Bunting commenting in her review of national provision in the United Kingdom that many of the training courses offered appeared to make "only a passing reference to this issue" (Bunting, 2005: 83).

Against this background it is perhaps not surprising that historically understanding of female sexual offending has been limited. Miller (2003) describes how two frames of reference have traditionally dominated attitudes to female sex offenders: a gender-biased approach which focuses on the women's own victimization to the exclusion of any work around the harm they had inflicted on others, and a gender-blind approach which views all abusers as similar, with gender being irrelevant. The influence of the latter approach is still apparent in the language used by some professionals who continue to describe female sex offenders in terms associated with male sex offender assessment tools and the persistence by many in seeking to define levels of risk by females as "high," "medium" and "low" despite the lack of empirical evidence regarding female sexual offending patterns and characteristics with which to support each classification.

However, over the past two decades interest in this group of women has begun to grow and develop (Cortoni, 2010). The impetus behind this emerging interest is unclear. It may be that cases were brought into the public arena via media coverage, as was demonstrated in the United Kingdom, or that professionals became more aware of the lack of treatment provision for women within the criminal justice system. Whatever the reason, the result has been a positive increase in the body of empirical research available. Although this is welcome and, some might argue, long overdue, it remains important to place these developments in context and to recognize that the body of research relating to female sex offenders, in comparison with their male counterparts, is limited and that many questions still remain unanswered.

Overview of Recent Developments

A review of the research that has emerged over the past two decades demonstrates the degree to which research relating to male sex offenders remained the benchmark by which female sex offenders continued to be viewed. One of the key themes of this research is the degree to which female sex offenders remained similar to or different from their male counterparts. Consequently, although research focused on issues relating to recidivism, treatment needs, typologies and deviant sexual interests, an acknowledgement of the potential significance of gender remained elusive. The lack of gender awareness during this period can be understood as a reflection of the social perception of crime generally being viewed as largely a male phenomenon (Harris, 2010) with historically little attention being given to the development of classification systems for generic female offending populations (Blanchette and Brown, 2006). In the absence of other models it is perhaps not surprising that researchers found themselves relating back to what was known about male sex offenders. Fortunately this is now beginning to change as research emerges that is based around what is known about other female populations or is structured to build on information provided directly from the narratives of female sex offenders; for example, Gannon's use of Grounded Theory methodology in the development of her Descriptive Model of Female Sexual Offending (Gannon and Rose, 2008). However, leaving to one side the wisdom or otherwise of using male sex offender knowledge as the baseline, the contribution made by comparative studies of male and female sex offenders to the current body of knowledge cannot be overlooked.

Reviewing the progress achieved, it is possible to identify key areas where the significance of gender is now acknowledged (Gannon, 2010). These include: reconviction rates, deviant sexual arousal patterns, offense supportive cognitions and typologies and theories of sexual offending. This chapter will review each of these in turn.

Reconviction data

One of the areas of particular interest has been comparison of reconviction data of males and females. The underreporting of sexual abuse by females has been highlighted in a range of studies (Ford, 2006; Denov, 2003; Mendel, 1995) and it is anticipated that the factors associated with the underreporting of abuse may continue to have relevance for the underreporting of repeat offending. It is also recognized that reconviction rates for sexual offending are generally lower than for other forms of offending and may not accurately reflect the rate of sexual harm that occurs within society. Nevertheless the fact that significant differences between the genders have been identified cannot be overlooked, with male sex offenders identified as having a recidivism rate of 13.5% (Hanson and Morton-Bourgon, 2005) and females identified as having a considerably lower rate of recidivism, at 1 to 3% (Cortoni, 2010).

This is of particular importance in relation to risk assessment measures, as it suggests that most female sex offenders identified are unlikely to be reconvicted at some future date. It also suggests that attempts to use research methods based on recidivism characteristics as predicators of risk are likely to have little veracity, due to the paucity of the available sample. For example, Sandler and Freeman (2009) project from their data of a New York State sample that of 90 females who might be convicted annually of sexual offending only two would be expected to recidivate; while Muskens *et al.*'s (2011) study found no sexual recidivism among their sample of 52 women.

This highlights not only the lack of value that male tools based on reconviction data will hold for females, but their potential to overestimate the risks associated with female sex offenders (Sandler and Freeman, 2009). Although some speculation has occurred regarding possible differences between sole and co-offender recidivism rates, large samples will be needed before it will be possible to validate recidivism-based risk markers for female sex offenders (Cortoni and Hanson, 2005). It is necessary to recognize and avoid the potential dangers for professionals of including generalized statements regarding risk in assessment processes which are not supported by empirical evidence in relation to female sex offenders. All too often the desire to quantify the level of risk associated with a female sex offender in terms of risk assessment models that are already established in criminal justice systems leads to the application of unhelpful and potentially inaccurate labeling. Until empirical research on female sex offenders is able to identify significant recidivism risk markers which can be used to develop generic risk assessment models, good practice supports the completion of individualized assessments which seek to identify factors of particular relevance to the individual woman. As Wijkman, Bijleveld and Hendricks (2010: 19) conclude in their study of characteristics and female sex offender types, "*the* female sex offender probably does not exist."

Offense supportive cognitions

One of the areas of general agreement in the research relating to female sex offenders is the degree to which their life histories are characterized by abuse, both in childhood and in their intimate adult relationships (Saradjian, 1996; Giguere and Bumby, 2007; Gannon and Rose, 2008; Eldridge, Elliott and Ashfield, 2010). Although past victimization in not related to future recidivism among female offenders per se (Blanchette and Brown, 2006) and should not be viewed as having a causative link with female offending (Cortoni, 2010), Eldridge and Saradjian (2000) hypothesize that through her abusive life experiences a woman may have learned to fulfill unmet needs by sexual abuse of a child or adult. They suggest that understanding the individual woman's abuse history will provide a context in which to understand the development of the women's cognitions and belief systems. This view is supported by Frey (2010), in relation to adolescent females who engage in sexual harm; she emphasizes the need to consider the impact of maltreatment on the development of a range of factors associated with sexual offending for females, including cognition, self-regulation and identity development. Reviewing the individual abuse history may also lead to the identification of trauma symptoms which may need support or treatment before other elements of assessment are investigated. This demonstrates the need for theoretical approaches and practice to work in tandem, as assessment does not occur in a vacuum and needs to adapt to the realities of the woman's current circumstances and challenges.

Much of the work with male sex offenders in the past decade has been influenced by the application of the Implicit Theory approach (Ward and Keenan, 1999). This suggests that male sex offenders who abuse children hold generalized beliefs that are supportive of sexual offending. It is suggested that these can be broken down into five implicit theories or motivational cognitions which influence their abusive behaviors. These include: *children as sexual objects* (a belief that children desire sexual contact with adults and can give consent), *nature of harm* (a belief that sexual activity with an adult is not harmful to a child), *entitlement* (a belief that the offender is superior and deserving of special treatment), *dangerous world* (a belief that the world is inherently a hostile place) and *uncontrollability* (a belief that the world is unmanageable and the offender has little control over his or her behavior); all of which can lead the offender to "misinterpret" victim behavior. The first attempts at reviewing female cognitions in line with these categories (Beech *et al.*, 2009) suggested that, with the exception of the entitlement theory, female sex offenders shared similar cognitions to their male counterparts. This raised questions for clinicians with experience working with female sex offenders, as their clinical experience was that the women's cognitions did not mirror those of their male counterparts, but rather demonstrated distinct female-specific variations influenced by their life experiences as women.

This observation appeared to be supported by research evidence following the analysis of a matched comparison study between female sex offenders and a general female non-offending cohort which set out to explore the extent to which the cognitions of the female sex offenders differed from their non-offending female counterparts (Gannon and Rose, 2009). This study indicated that female sex offenders were more likely than other women in society to view ambivalent male behaviors as potentially threatening and harmful. Gannon and Rose (2009) concluded that female sex offenders are less likely to view *the world* as a dangerous place, in keeping with their male counterparts, but are in fact disposed to identify *men* as dangerous. Although acknowledging the small sample size (19) and recommending caution regarding the relevance for wider populations, they hypothesize that female sex offenders' abusive developmental histories lead them to link abusive and powerful behaviors with males, and passivity, harmlessness and helplessness with women. They suggest it is these sex role stereotypes that play a significant part in female sex offender offense supportive cognitions. For example, it may be that sex role stereotypes regarding men as harmful influence some women to regard younger males and children as more attractive sexual partners, presenting in the women's reasoning a dynamic where they perceive themselves as more in control. This explanation may have some validity. However, the bias in this sample towards co-abusing women may also have significance and it is possible that solo abusers may not share this cognition. The fact that female sex offenders can also target and harm adult female victims suggests that this hypothesis may not have relevance for all. Ward and Beech's (2006) discussion of the role of the ecological niche (the role of the individual within the social and cultural environment in which they operate) in relation to male sex offenders suggests that attention also needs to be given to the influence on female sex offenders' cognitions of living in an environment that views males as perpetrators and females as victims, views female sexual harm as less harmful than male sex offending, and views victimization of adolescent males by adult women as "status enhancing" (Elliott *et al.*, 2012).

Based on the outcome of their previous research regarding cognitions, Gannon and Rose replicated Beech *et al.*'s (2009) original study. Again, the small sample size of 16 needs to be acknowledged, but by replicating Beech's methods Gannon suggests that although it is possible to categorize female sex offenders' cognitions using the five Implicit Theory headings, the actual content of the women's cognitions is female-specific. This study suggests that the content of the woman's cognitions indicate a belief that the *victim* is sexual, rather than a more global perception of children as sexual; a belief that sexual abuse by *men* is harmful, with abuse by women being not harmful or less harmful; *men* are dangerous, not women; *men* control the actions of women; and finally, *men* have entitlement to sexually abuse.

An early construct of the nature of entitlement which has been largely overlooked is the degree to which entitlement may fit with social norms relating to motherhood (Eldridge and Saradjian, 2000). It is proposed that some female sex offenders, specifically those who target their own children, associate giving birth with a sense of entitlement to use the child for their own purposes. Victims of enmeshed relationships with mothers speak of a sense of being a commodity with no intrinsic worth in their own right and no right to a separate identity (Saradjian, 2010). This suggests that there may be benefit in reviewing the construct of entitlement from a wider theoretical field. It may seem counterintuitive to explore female sex offender implicit thinking alongside constructs of motherhood, yet research indicates that a significant number of female sex offenders are mothers (Wijkman, Bijleveld and Hendricks, 2010). It also suggests that female sex offenders can and do experience parenting difficulties prior to or alongside their offending (Eldridge, Elliott and Ashfield, 2010). To date, few attempts have been made to consider the impact of the ecological niche of motherhood on cognitions relating to women who abuse children, sexually or in other ways.

Building on Eldridge and Saradjian's work (2000), Elliott *et al.* (2012) put forward the hypothesis that the concept of entitlement, rather than being based on a sex role belief that men have entitlement to sexually abuse, actually reflects a belief regarding prioritizing of needs. So, for example, the lone female sex offender may place her own needs (for intimacy, power and sex) before those of a child victim, while the co-abusing female may place her partner's needs before those of the child. This hypothesis perhaps reflects the difference in the sample group available to Elliott *et al.*, whose clinical work covers both women with convictions and women who have come to the attention of social care agencies but have not appeared in the criminal justice system, in contrast to the prison-based sample available to Gannon and Rose (2008, 2009).

Returning to the reality of motherhood and its associations with sexual offending, Elliott *et al.* (2012) suggest that as many female sex offenders are primary and often lone parents, a potential bias towards the entitlement of partners may also continue to have implications for their ability to protect children from harm, even after previous abusive partners have left or been removed from the family home. Elliott and Ashfield (2011) outline examples of how some women's desire to meet their partner's entitlement may also increase the possibility of involvement in abuse linked to online technology. Even when the male offender is only known to the woman through a cyber-relationship, her desire to maintain his interest and his needs may lead her to acquiesce in or become involved in the sexual abuse of her children.

Deviant sexual interests

As well as the research pattern of indiscriminately applying male theories of sexual offending to female sexual offending, it is interesting to see the degree to which the term "pedophile" has become a term widely used in society at large to describe anyone convicted of sexual offending, regardless of gender. The assumption is that all sex offenders share the same deviant sexual interests and arousal patterns. Cortoni

(2010) highlights the intrinsic bias that may exist in the diagnostic criteria in the Diagnostic and Statistical Manual of Mental Disorders (DSM) IV against its use with females, but suggests that from a clinical perspective women are more likely to display sexual attraction to both adults and children rather than the more exclusive sexual attraction to children often identified in males. Although Lambert and O'Halloran (2008) identified a group of women who were contributing to and accessing a female pro-pedophilic website, it is unclear as to the degree to which their cyber activities were representative of the totality of their sexual interests or arousal. Following an extensive review of sexual arousal within a non-offending female population, Chivers *et al.* (2004), in their initial comparative study between males, females and transsexuals, question the relationship between self-reported preferences and sexual arousal patterns in women per se. They also suggest that sexual arousal patterns play a fundamentally different role in male and female sexuality and highlight the degree to which conclusions about females have been influenced by what is known in relation to males. Given this situation, it is imperative that caution is exercised in relation to conclusions drawn regarding small sample studies of females who engage in sexual harm. However, it remains important to acknowledge research that is available at present and the developments that have occurred.

Research relating to the arousal patterns of female sex offenders is limited, with early studies focusing either on individual cases (Chow and Choy, 2002) or on small samples (Mathews, Matthews and Speltz, 1989; Hunter *et al.*, 1993). Nathan and Ward's (2002) study indicated that 41% of their sample of 12 women was found to have some level of deviant sexual arousal. This would appear to suggest that deviant sexual arousal may, as with some male offenders, increase the risk associated with their behavior. However, this also suggests that 59% (that is, the majority of their sample) did not appear to have a level of deviant sexual arousal. Saradjian (1996) observed that female sex offenders who were initially coerced by their male partners did not exhibit significant levels of masturbatory fantasy, and Ford (2006) suggests that sexual arousal as a motivating factor may have increased significance for specific types of female sex offenders; for example, women who are offending alone or those who treat the child victim as a surrogate partner.

Chivers (2009) in her later study demonstrated that although male physiological sexual arousal patterns reflect their sexual preferences, women's arousal patterns are more fluid. This suggests that arousal patterns are not gender-neutral but gender-specific. They also speculate that female sexuality may be more motivated by a desire to be wanted by someone else and more closely linked to notions of romance than sexual arousal. This indicates that Miller's (1976) constructs of relational theory and the significance of connectedness with others may also have significance for female sexual arousal in a way that has previously been overlooked. It may be that some female sex offenders seek to meet needs more closely linked to intimacy than sexual gratification. Although it is likely that some female sex offenders do experience deviant arousal patterns, the lack of general understanding in relation to female sexual arousal per se suggests that, in keeping with other elements of female sex offending, exploration of female sex offenders' arousal levels should be carried out on an individual basis.

Typologies and theories of female sex offending

Harris (2010) suggests that although men and women who commit similar offenses display similar behaviors they do so for very different reasons. Explanations given for one gender cannot simply be transferred across to the other. Although typologies for male sex offenders have now been established with some degree of empirical basis, typologies in relation to female sex offenders continue to be largely descriptive in nature, and there remains a lack of unity in both research methods and populations. Nevertheless some patterns are apparent and four specific areas or categories have emerged. These are identified as follows.

Women who abuse adolescents   Although comments on this typology often appear to suggest that young males are victims, it is important to remember that some women will choose young females. This type of offender will typically act from a position of power, achieved either through a professional relationship (teacher, residential worker) or through dynamics with other family members (friend's mother, family friend). These offenders often elevate the victim to adult status and in cases of abuse of male victims their behavior is often condoned by wider society as potentially a positive learning experience for the young male in question. Public and media responses following the sentencing of female teachers who have offended against male pupils demonstrate the ambivalence society may feel regarding this form of behavior (Ellen, 2009) and once again raises the issue of the impact of the ecological niche in which female sex offenders exist in their core thinking.

Women who abuse young children   This may be one of the smaller groups of female sex offenders, or it may be that the very young age of some of their victims (pre-verbal) makes their behaviors even more difficult to detect. These women typically act alone and usually abuse their own birth children but may target children outside the home also. The level and severity of their childhood histories is likely to be more extensive than other female sex offenders and may also have been replicated in their adult peer relationships.

Women who have co-offenders   The presence of a co-offender is one of the significant differences identified between male and female sex offenders (Bunting, 2005). Women may be described as "accompanied" and actively participate in the abuse, possibly moving on to solo abuse in their own right (Atkinson, 1996) or "coerced/emotionally dependent" (Saradjian, 1996; Cortoni, 2009) and more likely to abuse only in the company of their male partner (Atkinson, 1996; Saradjian, 1996). This category is viewed as representing most female sex offenders who come to attention (Atkinson, 1996; Grayston and De Luca, 1999; Bunting, 2005) and perhaps fits most comfortably into perceived norms of female behavior, that is, the male is the aggressor and the female is the victim. As such, professionals may be over-zealous in their willingness to place a woman into this category without sufficient exploration of the information available, particularly from child victims. Many aspects of the dynamic of the relationship between the female and her male co-offender require further research. However, the manner by which some women can be drawn into sexual offending by partners can demonstrate similar patterns to those described by partners of sadistic offenders.

Women who abuse adults   This category represents the group of female sex offenders about whom least is known. Schwartz and Cellini (1995) suggest that these women are much less likely to come to the attention of the authorities but do not give explanations as to why this might be the case. Vandiver and Kercher (2004) identified a small number in their sample of 471 women and suggested that they were likely to be older and have almost exclusively female victims. Clinical experience at the Lucy Faithfull Foundation also suggests that these women may offend in a group context with both male and female co-offenders.

Harris (2010) suggests that theories relating to female sex offenders may fall into three classifications: multifactor theories, with comprehensive, multiple perspectives; single factor theories, which focus on specific variables believed to be particularly relevant to the offending; and micro-level theories, incorporating cognitive, affective and contextual variables taken from offense narratives. As greater emphasis is now turning to theoretical concepts in relation to more generic female offenders, it may be that future work in relation to female sex offenders will begin to review these women in line with what is known about other women with complex lives and traumatic histories, rather than simply what is known about male sex offenders.

One area where progress has been made in micro-level theory is a model based on the narratives of 22 incarcerated female sex offenders (Gannon, Rose and Ward, 2008; Gannon, 2010). However, this developmental model also suffers from the limitations of a small sample and a very distinct population. Nevertheless it represents the first model that is based on the narratives of female sex offenders rather than research relating to their male counterparts. The model divides into three stages. The first stage covers background factors including family environment, abusive experiences, lifestyle outcomes, vulnerability factors and major life stresses. The second stage covers the pre-offense period and examines how the vulnerability factors identified in stage one develops into risk factors in the period preceding the offending. The third stage covers the offense period and examines the approaches the woman took to facilitate her offending. One of the difficulties that may exist with this model, in its current form, is the effort that will be required to translate it into a practical form which can support assessment and treatment services. The diagrams associated with the model are complex and detailed and as such are likely to challenge practitioners seeking to use it without any prior knowledge of female sexual offending research. It is anticipated that this will be addressed over time and a more practice-based model may emerge.

Building on this model, Gannon (2010) turned her attention to the identification of what she considered to be three distinct pathways evidenced in the pre-offense and offenses phases by 82% of the sample population, and suggested that this pathway model may be key in assisting practitioners to assess the treatment needs of their clients. As with previous research the sample size suggests caution, as the individual pathways are based on behaviors relating to small numbers, that is, nine, five and four women. These three pathways are: an Explicit Approach pathway, characterized by high levels of planning and a range of motivations; a Directed Avoidant pathway, characterized by a desire not to offend and evidence of male planning and fear/ intimacy goals and motivations; and an Implicit Disorganized pathway, with minimal planning, high levels of impulsivity and no clear goals or motivations. Although this model once again reflects similar models identified in relation to male sex offenders and so is more revisionist than developmental in nature, one of its obvious strengths is the degree to which it requires professionals to acknowledge the reality that there are some women who actively choose to sexually harm children in their own right without external influence by male partners. The pathways approach is an interesting one and it is hoped that additions to the sample size and attention to associated cognitions within each pathway will confirm its validity for assessment and treatment.

Gender Responsiveness and Practice Issues

Although the reconviction rates for female sex offenders remains low, women can still harm children without re-arrest or reconviction. Consequently it is imperative that the safety of children remains a primary consideration during any period of practical engagement with the woman by professionals, regardless of their background. Government-published guidance for the Safeguarding of Children in the United Kingdom (HM Government, 2006) reminds all agencies of their responsibility to protect children from abuse and neglect. Yet this responsibility can create tensions for organizations who view their responsibilities as solely towards the well-being of the woman. Denov (2001) suggests that professionals struggle to accept the harm associated with female sexual offending and try to define behaviors in terms of more acceptable cultural norms relating to women. Failure to accept that a female sex offender may hold dual status as victim and perpetrator may cloud professional judgment and result in potential risks to children and young people going unrecognized.

The sexual nature of the behaviors demonstrated by female sex offenders means that many professionals continue to refer back to what is perceived to be acceptable practice in relation to the management of male sex offenders. Giguere and Bumby (2007) highlight the need for management strategies that are gender-responsive to the needs of this specific population. Yet despite the strides made in the development of theories relating to female sex offenders and their behaviors, little attention has been given as to what good practice in relation to the management of female sex offenders might be. Ashfield *et al.* (2010) suggest that good practice with female sex offenders requires professionals to be able to recognize the woman as a *woman* who has engaged in sexual offending rather than simply a sex offender who is not male, and to respond to her in a manner that is gender-responsive. In order to do this it is important to draw on what is perceived to be gender-responsive practice in relation to other groups of female offenders and seek to apply this in relation to this specific client group.

Bloom (2006: 4) defines gender-responsiveness as responses that reflect the "realities of the lives of women and girls and that addresses and responds to their strengths and challenges." Bloom and Covington (2000) identify the five core elements of a gender-responsive approach to female offenders as recognition of the importance of relationships; recognition of the trauma and mental health needs; recognition of the significance of children; recognition of the need for community reintegration and belonging; and recognition of strengths and the potential to acquire self-efficacy (Covington, 2012). It is proposed that awareness of these core elements will facilitate good practice with female sex offenders by informing decision making in relation to the following areas: the women and their lives, intervention and reintegration.

The women and their lives

Although females who engage in sexual offending are not a homogeneous group and a female sex offender can be of any age, class or intellectual ability (Bunting, 2005), research suggests that many female offenders experience lives that include severe physical, sexual and emotional abuse (Travin, Cullen and Protter, 1990; Matthews, Mathews and Speltz, 1991; Saradjian, 1996; Eldridge, Elliott and Ashfield, 2010). Experiences of parenting are also often chaotic (Ford, 2006) and disrupted (Harper, 1993), and result in poor attachment patterns (Eldridge, Elliott and Ashfield, 2010; Saradjian, 1996; Allen, 1991). Salter (1995) in her chapter, "Footprints on the Heart," observes how adult survivors of child sexual abuse have a high incidence of being revictimized as adults (Briere and Runtz, 1988; Herman, 1981; Wyatt, Guthrie and Notgrass, 1992), so it is not surprising that Saradjian (1996) found that all of the women in her sample reported being abused in their adult relationships. Eldridge, Elliott and Ashfield (2010) also report 74% of their sample experiencing exploitative or abusive relationships. Like Lewis and Stanley (2000) they also note that these relationships may still be ongoing at the point at which the woman is identified as a sexual offender. Saradjian (1996) draws correlations between the impact of multiple and repeated abuse with the poor self-concepts and low self-esteem demonstrated by the women in her sample and highlights the women's perceptions regarding their lack of power and ability to affect change. She also notes their lack of positive female peer friendships and social isolation.

Given these developmental and relationship factors, Ford (2006) suggests that it is perhaps not surprising that some female abusers show symptoms of psychiatric disorder, particularly Post Traumatic Stress Disorder. Depression was frequently reported by Eldridge, Elliott and Ashfield (2010), with 42% of their sample prescribed anti-depressant medication at the time of their offense. Fazel *et al.* (2008) suggest that routine psychiatric screening at court or on reception into custody could be helpful. As Ford and Cortoni suggest (2008), the presence of mental health problems can interfere with any attempt to address the sexual nature of the woman's offending, so good practice would suggest the importance of developing a clearer understanding of the impact of any mental health issues that may be impacting on an individual woman's life as well as on her offending behavior. Research suggests it is only in quite rare cases that psychiatric issues will be directly related to female offending behavior (Blanchette and Brown, 2006; Bonta, Law and Hanson, 1997), so it is important that this issue is not allowed to overshadow work on cognitions, problematic relationships and other offense-related issues. A holistic approach should address victimization without allowing it to become an excuse not to engage in more specific offense-related work designed to facilitate the woman to gain a greater understanding of the decisions she made to involve herself in the sexual abuse of a child (Ford, 2006; Hunter, Becker and Lexier, 2006).

An aspect of the women's lives that is often overlooked is their role as a parent. Wijkman, Bijleveld and Hendricks (2010) noted that two-thirds of their sample had children, and Eldridge, Elliott and Ashfield (2010) noted how 44% of their sample reported an inability to cope with their children which predated their offending. Over one-third had also been the subject of concerns in relation to their parenting, including neglect and physical and emotional abuse of their children. Given the models of care often experienced by female sex offenders in their life histories, it is possible that they have little knowledge of positive parenting skills or the emotional resilience necessary to form strong positive attachments to their children. Additionally the circumstances in which they conceive children, for example, through rape or abusive intimate relationships, may also have implications for the psychological meanings they attach to the individual child. Good practice would suggest that, as well as assessing the impact of the woman's offending on her individual victim, attention should also be given to the nature of her parenting as a whole to identify deficits and strengths which may affect any child with whom she has contact.

Intervention

The key to intervention is to identify the needs or goals the women were seeking to meet through the abusive behaviors and to help them find non-abusive ways to meet those needs (Eldridge and Saradjian, 2000). Eldridge, Elliott and Ashfield (2010) suggest that when faced with painful situations most humans will revert to previous patterns used to make themselves feel better, and in the case of sexual offending this can lead to re-offending.

In order to assist a woman to stop sexually offending it is important to assist her to understand why and how she came to do what she did. There is no single reason why females sexually offend, so it is necessary for any assessment model used to have flexibility and a capacity to account for individual differences. Each woman will also display a number of protective factors or strengths that should also be identified through the assessment process. Eldridge, Elliott and Ashfield (2010) suggest from their sample that female sex offenders do exhibit a range of social, self-management and interpersonal skills which they can utilize to good effect in working towards a life which is free from abuse for them and others. Although this would seem to conflict with earlier discussions regarding low self-worth and self-efficacy, they suggest that the issue may be less about skills deficits and more regarding external circumstances and stress factors. When the women were in a safe, therapeutic environment with a trusted worker, they could demonstrate a range of positive strengths which they did not feel able to utilize in their day-to-day lives when faced with the presence of controlling or violent partners.

This highlights the significance of the relationship that develops between the worker and the woman and the degree to which a positive therapeutic relationship can facilitate significant growth and development for the women and suggest optimism regarding hope of positive change in the woman's behaviors. However, it is not unusual for female sex offenders to describe the dynamic of their relationship with their allocated worker as less than positive, with professionals viewed as not listening to or hearing the emotional content the women are seeking to convey (Ashfield *et al.*, 2010). In order to create change in their lives women need to experience relationships which do not repeat their histories of abuse and loss. Bloom (2006) suggests that it is important for women to learn and experience healthy relationships with staff as part of the intervention process. To do this professionals need to be able to utilize empathy to demonstrate a willingness to engage with the woman in a manner which is collaborative and seeks to establish her intrinsic worth, rather than reinforce her previous experiences of hostility and powerlessness (van Wormer, 2001; Ford, 2006; Ashfield *et al.*, 2010).

Reintegration

Covington (2012) suggests that the relational nature of women's lives is particularly important when considering the continuum of care required to connect female offenders back into the community after custody. She suggests that recognition of the importance of community reintegration as early as possible in the intervention process will ensure that appropriate services are identified to support the woman to enable her to re-establish links with her family and her community. Given the significance afforded to reintegration back into families and communities for the generic female offender's sense of well-being and purpose, Saradjian's (1996) comments regarding the lack of supports available to female sex offenders should not be overlooked. As the economic stresses and changes in criminal justice policies focus increasingly on third sector provision of services, the potential for female sex offenders to become the forgotten few is likely to increase. Community-based services that focus on the needs of female offenders are often reluctant to accept female sex offenders into their projects, citing concerns regarding the safety of children or the potential impact of adverse publicity in the event that their role is made public. However, discussions with staff within these services suggests that the decision-making process may also be influenced by an unwillingness to accept the reality of the female sexual abuser's status as both a victim and a perpetrator. Service provision in relation to accommodation, trauma, parenting skills, relationships, financial management and employment and training should form an integral part of the reintegration plan for female sex offenders, yet this is rarely found to be the case. Howells and Day (2003) highlight the interplay between internal and external factors in determining a client's readiness to engage with treatment. Treatment does not sit outside the reality of the woman's day-to-day experience, so until she can see evidence that her basic needs for security, safety and connectiveness with others are achievable, her readiness to engage is likely to be limited.

Conclusion

The growth in research in relation to female sexual offending in recent years is a positive development, but many questions still remain unanswered. The focus on revisionist approaches to this client group means that the influence of male sex offending theory and knowledge continues to dominate both organizational and individual responses. Yet it is possible to sense that the wind of change is blowing, with theorists now beginning to accept that female sex offenders are first and foremost women and that gender holds significance for risk factors, treatment factors and reintegration. However, the challenge now remains to ensure that these women are afforded the same level of service provision as their more generic female offending peers. Until this is achieved, female sex offenders will continue to experience significant levels of disadvantage and discrimination, not because they are females (and by definition not males) but because they continue to challenge our core beliefs and expectations of female behavior.

References

Allen, C.M. (1991) *Women and Men Who Sexually Abuse Children: A Comparative Analysis.* Brandon, VT: Safer Society Press.

Ashfield, S., Brotherston, S., Eldridge, H. and Elliott, I.A. (2010) "Working with female sexual offenders: therapeutic process issues," in T.A. Gannon and F. Cortoni (eds), *Female Sexual Offenders: Theory, Assessment And Treatment.* Chichester: John Wiley & Sons, Ltd, pp. 161–180.

Atkinson, J.L. (1996) "Female sex offenders: a literature review," *Forum on Corrections Research* 8, 39–42.

Beech, A.R., Parrett, N., Ward, T. and Fisher, D. (2009) "Assessing female sexual offenders motivations and cognitions, an exploratory study," *Psychology Crime and Law* 15, 201–216.

Blanchette, K. and Brown, S.L. (2006) *The Assessment and Treatment of Women Offenders: An Integrated Perspective.* Chichester: John Wiley & Sons, Ltd.

Bloom, B.E. (2006) Gender responsive strategies: research, practice and guiding principles for women offenders. Keynote presentation at the Excellence in Justice symposium of Ohio State University, Columbus, November 17, http://www.drc.state.oh.us/web/iej_files/200702_KeynotePresentation_BarbaraBloom.pdf (accessed September 6, 2012).

Bloom. B.E. and Covington, S. (2000) Gendered justice: programming for women in correctional settings. Paper presented at the 52nd Annual Meeting of the American Society of Criminology, San Francisco, CA, November, http://www.stephaniecovington.com/pdfs/11.pdf (accessed September 6, 2012).

Bonta, J., Law, M. and Hanson, R.K. (1997) "The prediction of criminal and violent recidivism among mentally disordered offenders: a meta-analysis," *Psychological Bulletin* 123, 123–142.

Briere, J.N. and Runtz, M. (1988) "Post sexual abuse trauma," in E. Wyatt and G.J. Powell (eds), *Lasting Effects of Child Sexual Abuse.* Thousand Oaks, CA: Sage, pp. 85–99.

Bunting, L. (2005) *Females who Sexually Offend against Children: Responses of the Child Protection and Criminal Justice Systems.* NSPCC Policy Practice Research Series. London: NSPCC Inform.

Chivers, M.L. (2009) "Arousing questions about female sexuality," *Queen's University Journal* 136, http://queensjournal.ca/story/2009-02-09/features/arousing-questions-about-female-sexuality/ (accessed September 6, 2012).

Chivers, M.L., Rieger, G., Latty, E. and Bailey, J.M. (2004) "A sex difference in the specificity of sexual arousal," *Psychological Science* 15, 736–744.

Chow, E.W.C. and Choy, A.L. (2002) "Clinical characteristics and treatment response to SSRI in a female paedophile," *Archives of Sexual Behaviour* 31, 211–215.

Cortoni, F. (2009) "Violence and women offenders," in J. Barker (ed.), *Women and the Criminal Justice System: A Canadian Perspective.* Toronto: Emond Montgomery Publications, pp. 175–199.

Cortoni, F. (2010) "The assessment of female sexual offenders," in T.A. Gannon and F. Cortoni (eds), *Female Sexual Offenders: Theory, Assessment And Treatment.* Chichester: John Wiley & Sons, Ltd, pp. 87–100.

Cortoni, F. and Hanson, R.K. (2005) *A Review of the Recidivism Rates of Adult Female Sex Offenders (Research Report R–169).* Ottawa: Correctional Service Canada.

Covington, S. (2012) Trauma matters: creating services for women. Paper presented at the Women, Crime and Criminal Justice Conference, Cambridge, January 10–12.

Denov, M.S. (2001) "A culture of denial: exploring professional perspectives on female sex offending," *Canadian Journal of Criminology* 43, 303–329.

Denov, M.S. (2003) "The myth of innocence: sexual scripts and the recognition of child sexual abuse by female perpetrators," *Journal of Sex Research* 40, 303–314.

Eldridge, H.J., Elliott, I.A. and Ashfield, S. (2010) "Assessment of women who sexually abuse children," in M.C. Calder (ed.), *Sexual Abuse Assessments.* Lyme Regis: Russell House, pp. 213–227.

Eldridge, H.J. and Saradjian, J. (2000) "Replacing the function of abusive behaviours for the offender: remaking relapse prevention in working with women who sexually abuse children," in D.R. Laws, S.M. Hudson and T. Ward (eds), *Remaking Relapse Prevention with Sex Offenders: A Sourcebook.* Thousand Oaks, CA: Sage, pp. 402–426.

Ellen, B. (2009) This shameful liaison does not deserve prison. *Observer* (Nov 29), http://www.guardian.co.uk/commentisfree/2009/nov/29/barbara-ellen-madeleine-martin-comment (accessed September 6, 2012).

Elliott, I.A. and Ashfield, S.A. (2011) "The use of online technology in the offence processes of female child molesters," *Journal of Sexual Aggression* 17, 92–104.

Elliott, I.A., Beech, A.R., Eldridge, H. and Ashfield, S. (2012) "Assessing female child molesters' motivations and cognitions," in B.K. Schwartz (ed.), *The Sex Offender, Current Trends in Policy and Treatment Practice*, Vol. 7. Kingston, NJ: Civic Research Institute, pp. 15–115.

Fazel, S., Sjostedt, G., Grann, M. and Langstrom, N. (2008) "Sexual offending in women and psychiatric disorder: a national case-control study," *Archives of Sexual Behaviour* 39, 1, 161–167.

Ford, H. (2006) *Women who Sexually Abuse Children.* Chichester: John Wiley & Sons, Ltd.

Ford, H. and Cortoni, F. (2008) "Sexual deviance in females: assessment and treatment," in D.R. Laws and W.T. O'Donohue (eds), *Sexual Deviance: Theory, Assessment and Treatment.* New York: Guilford Press, pp. 508–526.

Frey, L.L. (2010) "The juvenile female sexual offender: characteristics, treatment and research," in T.A. Gannon and F. Cortoni (eds), *Female Sexual Offenders: Theory, Assessment And Treatment.* Chichester: John Wiley & Sons, Ltd, pp. 53–71.

Gannon, T.A. (2010) Female sexual offenders: key developments over the past two decades. Paper presented at the Annual Conference of the National Organisation for the Treatment of Abuser (NOTA), Belfast, September 21–23.

Gannon, T.A. and Rose, M.R. (2008) "Female child sexual abusers: towards integrating theory and practice," *Aggression and Violent Behaviour* 21, 194–207.

Gannon, T.A. and Rose, M.R. (2009) "Offence-related interpretative bias in female child molesters: a preliminary study," *Sexual Abuse: A Journal of Research and Treatment* 21, 194–208.

Gannon, T.A., Rose, M.R. and Ward, T. (2008) "A descriptive model of the offence process for female sexual offenders," *Sexual Abuse: A Journal of Research and Treatment* 20, 352–374.

Giguere, R. and Bumby, K. (2007) Female Sex Offenders (Policy and Practice Brief), Center for Sex Offender Management, US Department of Justice, http://www.csom.org/pubs/female_sex_offenders_brief.pdf (accessed September 6, 2012).

Grayston, A.D. and de Luca, R.V. (1999) "Female perpetrators of child sexual abuse: a review of the clinical and empirical literature," *Aggression and Violent Behaviour* 4, 93–106.

Hanson, R.K. and Morton-Bourgon, K.E. (2005) "The characteristics of persistent sexual offenders: a meta-analysis of recidivism studies," *Journal of Consulting and Clinical Psychology* 73, 1154–1163.

Harper, J. (1993) "Prepubertal male victims of incest: a clinical study," *Child Abuse and Neglect* 17, 419–421.

Harris, D.A. (2010) "Theories of female sexual offending," in T.A. Gannon and F. Cortoni (eds), *Female Sexual Offenders: Theory, Assessment And Treatment*. Chichester: John Wiley & Sons, Ltd, pp. 31–51.

Herman, J.L. (1981) *Father-Daughter Incest*. Cambridge, MA: Harvard University Press.

HM Government (2006) *Working Together to Safeguard Children: A Guide to Inter-Agency Working to Safeguard and Promote the Welfare of Children*. London: HM Government.

Howells, K. and Day, A. (2003) "Readiness for anger management: clinical and theoretical issues," *Clinical Psychology Review* 23, 2, 319–337.

Hunter, J.A., Becker, J.V. and Lexier, L.J. (2006) "The female juvenile sex offender," in H.E. Barbaree and W.L. Marshall (eds), *The Juvenile Sex Offender*, 2nd edn. New York: Guilford Press, pp. 148–165.

Hunter, J.A., Lexier, L.J., Goodwin, D.W. *et al.* (1993) "Psychosexual, attitudinal and developmental characteristics of juvenile female perpetrators in a residential treatment setting," *Journal of Child and Family Studies* 2, 317–326.

Lambert, S. and O'Halloran, E. (2008) "Deductive thematic analysis of a female paedophile website," *Psychiatry, Psychology & Law* 15, 284–300.

Lewis, C.F. and Stanley, C.R. (2000) "Women accused of sexual offenses," *Behavioural Sciences and the Law* 18, 73–81.

Mathews, R., Matthews, J.K. and Speltz, K. (1989) *Female Sexual Offenders: An Exploratory Study*. Orwell, VT: Safer Society Press.

Matthews, J.K., Mathews, R. and Speltz, K. (1991) "Female sex offenders: a typology," in M.Q. Patton (ed.), *Family Sexual Abuse: Frontline Research and Evaluation*. Thousand Oaks, CA: Sage, pp. 199–219.

Mendel, M.P. (1995) *The Male Survivor: The Impact of Sexual Abuse*. Thousand Oaks, CA: Sage.

Miller, D.L. (2003) Research approaches and treatment protocols with female sexual perpetrators: going beyond gender-biased and gender-blind approaches. Paper presented at the 22nd Annual Conference of the Association for the Treatment of Sexual Abusers (ATSA), St Louis, MO, October.

Miller, J .B. (1976) *Towards a New Psychology of Women*. Boston, MA: Beacon Press.

Muskens, M., Bogaerts, S., van Casteren, M. and Labrijn, S. (2011) "Adult female sexual offending: a comparison between co-offenders and solo offenders in a Dutch sample," *Journal of Sexual Aggression* 17, 46–60.

Nathan, P. and Ward, T. (2002) "Female sex offenders: clinical and demographic features," *Journal of Sexual Aggression* 8, 5–21.

Salter, A.C. (1995) *Transforming Trauma*. Thousand Oaks, CA: Sage.

Sandler, J.C. and Freeman, N.J. (2009) "Female sex offender recidivism: a large-scale empirical analysis," *Sexual Abuse: A Journal of Research and Treatment* 21, 455–473.

Saradjian, J. (1996) *Women who Sexually Abuse Children: From Research to Clinical Practice.* Chichester: John Wiley & Sons, Ltd.

Saradjian, J. (2010) "Understanding the prevalence of female-perpetrated sexual abuse and the impact of that abuse on victims," in T.A. Gannon and F. Cortoni (eds), *Female Sexual Offenders: Theory, Assessment And Treatment.* Chichester: John Wiley & Sons, Ltd, pp. 9–30.

Schwartz, B.K. and Cellini, H.R. (1995) *The Sex Offender: Corrections, Treatment and Legal Practice.* New York: Civic Research Institute.

Travin, S., Cullen, K. and Protter, B. (1990) "Female sex offenders: severe victims and victims and victimisers," *Journal of Forensic Sciences* 35, 140–150.

Vandiver, D.M. and Kercher, G. (2004) "Offender and victim characteristics of registered female sexual offenders in Texas: a proposed typology of female sexual offenders," *Sexual Abuse: A Journal of Research and Treatment* 16, 121–137.

Van Wormer, K. (2001) *Counselling Female Offenders and Victims: A Strengths-Restorative Justice Approach.* New York: Springer.

Ward, T. and Beech, A.R. (2006) "An integrated theory of sexual offending," Aggression and Violent *Behaviour* 11, 44–63.

Ward, T. and Keenan, T. (1999) "Child molesters' implicit theories," *Journal of Interpersonal Violence* 14, 821–838.

Wijkman, M., Bijleveld, C. and Hendricks, J. (2010) "Women don't do such things! Characteristics of female sex offenders and offender types," *Sexual Abuse: A Journal of Research and Treatment* 22, 135–156.

Wyatt, G.E., Guthrie, D. and Notgrass, C.M. (1992) "Differential effects of women's child sexual abuse and subsequent sexual revictimisation," *Journal of Consulting and Clinical Psychology* 60, 167–173.

Part Three
Legal and Ethical Issues in Risk Management

20

A Convergent Approach to Sex Offender Risk Assessment

Jeffrey C. Singer, Douglas P. Boer and
Martin Rettenberger

Introduction

Although Lanyon (2001) provides a useful framework for conducting psychological evaluations with sex offenders, there is more than one general method or approach to conducting sex offender risk evaluations. These approaches can be broadly defined as either actuarial assessment or structured professional judgment. Some other terms have been used to describe hybrid methods such as empirical actuarial. To date, no one particular method or approach to sexual offense risk assessment has a distinct advantage over the others to purport a "best practice" model. Indeed, it appears that Boer's (2006) conclusion that there was no convergence of opinion regarding the risk assessment of sex offenders at that time is still the case today.

Thankfully, one approach that can be fully retired without controversy in this discussion has been referred to as unguided clinical judgment. Unguided clinical judgment (UCJ) has been referred to as "subjective and impressionistic" (Grove and Meehl, 1996) as well as "unrestrained" (Wollert, 2007). UCJ occurs when the evaluator formulates a clinical hypothesis or applies an idiosyncratic and unverifiable criterion for basing conclusions. Such an approach is typically based exclusively on a review of records and an unstructured clinical interview. Sometimes UCJ is offered without the articulation of rationale. UCJ has the advantage of convenience and feels intuitively good through relying on basic common sense.

Evaluators relying on UCJ often produce reports that contain material similar to the following: he was too unempathic and showed no remorse; too rehearsed or not rehearsed enough; too emotional or not emotional enough; did not know his crime cycle or knew his crime cycle by rote; wore a Bruce Lee shirt and is therefore violent; has stared at female therapists and therefore has "rapism"; had group sex and is

The Wiley-Blackwell Handbook of Legal and Ethical Aspects of Sex Offender Treatment and Management, First Edition. Edited by Karen Harrison and Bernadette Rainey.
© 2013 John Wiley & Sons, Ltd. Published 2013 by John Wiley & Sons, Ltd.

therefore deviant; minimized, denied, and blamed others, sees self as a victim of the system; and, the best example of the worst behavior that gets subjected to UCJ that is erroneously interpreted to mean the examinee is at high risk to sexually re-offend, "He walked out of the interview." Other examples of UCJ errors include noting that inconsistency, prevaricating, having access to willing partners yet sexually offending, insufficient treatment, needing treatment, being antisocial, being angry, intimacy deficits, having cognitive distortions, and substance abuse all are indicative of high sexual re-offense risk. The aforementioned variables are greatly context dependent on the evaluation circumstance. Research has either not supported the above factors as being directly associated with sexual re-offense, or are indicative of being merely a typical recidivist (for example, by being antisocial), or the constructs are so vague that they are unfalsifiable, meaning untestable.

Bad ideas apparently die very slowly, perhaps in part owing to the availability cascade heuristic, which posits that if something is said enough times, it must be true (Kuran and Sunstein, 1999). Yet as far back as 1986, Meehl concluded that when compared to a mechanical algorithmic assessment approach, unaided clinical judgment is inferior. Meehl (1986: 373–374) concluded, "There is no controversy in social science that shows such a large body of qualitatively diverse studies coming out so uniformly in the same direction as this one." For the past 40 years, unstructured, or unguided, clinical judgment has been shown to be an inaccurate method for making diagnoses or judgments, and typically creates false positive results (Janus and Meehl, 1997). A false positive is concluding that a condition exists when it does not. Such approaches are vulnerable to numerous sources of error, including the fundamental attribution error (Ross, 1977) as well as various forms of cognitive heuristics (Kahneman, 2011, 2003; Kahneman and Tversky, 1973, 1984, 1996; Tversky and Kahneman, 1974; 1983), that is, the tendency to use thinking short-cuts when faced with complex tasks. Aside from being an inaccurate method, not surprisingly, UCJ has poor inter-rater reliability (Grove *et al.*, 2000; Monahan and Steadman, 1994), yet continues to be used even in basic clinical practice (Vrieze and Grove, 2009).

The problems with UCJ came into sharp focus with the landmark ruling of the Supreme Court of the United States in *Barefoot* v. *Estelle,* 463 U.S. 880 (1983), noting "that psychiatrists are always wrong with respect to future dangerousness, only most of the time." In that case one of the experts cited Monahan's classic book *Predicting Violent Behavior: An Assessment of Clinical Techniques,* highlighting that the:

> "best" clinical research currently in existence indicates that psychiatrists and psychologists are accurate in no more than one out of three predictions of violent behavior over a several-year period among institutionalized populations that had both committed violence in the past . . . and who were diagnosed as mentally ill. (Monahan, 1981: 77)

Yet Monahan (1981: 19) began his monograph by highlighting that "there may be circumstances in which prediction is both empirically possible and ethically appropriate ." Around the same time, much research on the prediction of violence was being done in the maximum-security treatment program in the Oak Ridge Division of the Mental Health Centre in Penetanguishene, Ontario, Canada. The aggregate of this important work can be found in *Violent Offenders: Appraising and Managing Risk* (Quinsey *et al.*, 1998). These events heralded the second generation of risk assessment measures (Monahan, 1984; Otto 1992), driven by enthusiasm over actuarial, static factor assessment.

Actuarial Assessment

The allure of actuarial assessment is understandable. This approach considers a small number of variables with the application of explicit statistical rules for combining and weighing a few variables into a total risk tally. In addition to empirically based norms, true actuarial assessment eliminates the potential error and bias of human judgment. The elimination of human error is enhanced by the focus in actuarial assessment on static, or historical, variables that cannot be altered. Sexual recidivism actuarial risk assessment instruments (Janus and Prentky, 2003; Prentky *et al.*, 2006), also called actuarial risk assessment instruments (Vrieze and Grove, 2008), are also based on regression equations between predictor and outcome variables, decision trees, or arithmetic algorithms and have explicit rules for scoring. Actuarial tests are based on the idea that practitioners can tally the number of pre-defined risk factors and see the observed rate of sexual recidivism with other sexual recidivists who share the same historical pre-determined risk factors. The clear advantage of actuarial risk assessment is the elimination of subjective human judgment. Actuarial tests yield ranges of risk such as low, medium and high, with percentages of those sexual recidivists who share the common historical risk characteristics. The most recognized sexual recidivism actuarial risk assessment instrument is the Static-99 (Hanson and Thornton, 1999). Subsequent measures to the Static-99 include the Static-99R and the Static-2002R (all downloadable from the Static-99 website, www.static99.org) and the Sex Offender Risk Appraisal Guide (SORAG) (Quinsey *et al.*, 1998). New promising actuarial tests are the well-researched Multisample Age-stratified Table of Sexual recidivism rates (MATS-1) (Wollert *et al.*, 2010) and the Minnesota Sex Offender Screening Tool-3 (MnSOST-3) (Duwe and Freske, 2012).

Assuming the empirical validation studies of actuarial tests are psychometrically sound, actuarial assessment can potentially be a relevant source of information regarding risk assessment (for example, Barbaree *et al.*, 2001). However, actuarial instruments do not yield information regarding recognized diagnoses of any form of psychopathology, mental disorders, mental conditions, personality disorders, or mental illnesses, nor do such instruments provide any information on risk-relevant symptomology of the client being assessed. The use of actuarial instruments under diagnostic conditions can be likened to a cardiologist applying a life insurance actuarial table to make a diagnosis of cardiac disease. However, since one might argue that actuarial results can be a proxy to impaired sexual behavioral control, several issues regarding actuarial assessment need to be addressed.

All forms of assessment require an understanding of the base rate issue. The base rate is simply the frequency of any event of interest occurring. For example, if 0.5% of the general public were ophthalmologists and 99.5% of the public were not ophthalmologists, then the base rate of being an ophthalmologist is simply 0.5%. A difficult concept to accept is that sexual re-offense rates among convicted sex offenders are low (Sandler, Freeman and Socia, 2008; Wollert and Waggoner, 2009) and subsequent analyses using Static-99 shows that recidivism rates are decreasing, resulting in reduced percentage risk levels (Helmus, Hanson and Thornton, 2009) and reduced certainty in assessed risk levels (Wollert, 2006). So, considering the low base rate of sexual re-offense, the question becomes this: are actuarial tests able to detect a counterintuitively low frequency event without creating too many false positives?

Another problem with actuarial assessment is the applicability of nomothetic data to the individual case. The analogy between actuarial assessments in the insurance industry to this type of assessment clouds an important difference between the two situations. The insurance actuary has no interest in when a particular death will occur but only how to maximize profits based on group data. The current circumstance does not call for an aggregate norm but case-specific information. The authors of the Static-99 echo this caution:

> The recidivism estimates provided by the Static-99 are group estimates based upon reconvictions and were derived from groups of individuals with these characteristics. As such, these estimates do not directly correspond to the recidivism risk of an individual offender. (Harris *et al.*, 2003, Appendix 7: 71)

Mossman (2006, 2008) and Mossman and Sellke (2007) have published a series of articles noting that this issue can be overcome, while not surprisingly others disagree (Cooke and Michie, 2010; Hart, Michie and Cooke, 2007; Vrieze and Grove, 2008). However, Donaldson and Abbott (2011) offer explicit advice on how to address this challenge. Nonetheless, there is no shortage of understandable criticisms to level at the actuarial approach in sex offense evaluations; for example, that they offer the mere illusion of precision (Cooke, 2010) or that such instruments do not adequately account for age (Waggoner, Wollert and Cramer, 2008).

Concerns about the accuracy of the Static-99 appear to have been borne out. Table 20.1 highlights the results of three studies of sexual re-offense rates, which are lower than predicted by the Static-99 (also reflected in the table from Harris *et al.*, 2003). One of authors of the Static-99 noted:

> In applying these actuarial instruments, there are, however, a number of important points that practitioners must keep in mind. First, the prediction level of all the instruments is low . . . Such levels do not warrant high confidence in decisions. Second, typically the instruments are applied to situations in which the base rate of recidivism is low, making it difficult to increase the overall hit rate over simply using the base rates. (Knight and Thornton, 2007: 83)

In spite of the relatively recent introduction of the Static-99R with the hope of increased actuarial accuracy, problems remain. The scoring of the Static-99R requires human judgment to decide which is the correct reference group to apply. The introduction of such judgment obviates the very point of actuarial assessment. Furthermore, the reference group themselves have not been adequately examined regarding group exclusivity (Abbott, 2009, 2011; Donaldson and Abbott, 2011; Campbell and DeClue, 2010a, 2010b).

Table 20.1 Variability of recidivism percentages for sexual offenders with Static-99 scores of ≥6.

Research study	No. of men with score ≥ 6	"Recidivism" defined as	5-year recidivism percentage	10-year recidivism percentage	15-year recidivism percentage
Static-99 developmental sample (Harris *et al.*, 2003)	129	Arrests or convictions for sexual offenses (not necessarily violent)	38.8	45	52
Helmus (2008)	556	Arrests or convictions for sexual offenses (not necessarily violent)	27	33.5	–
Abracen and Looman (2006)	133	Convictions for sexual offenses (not necessarily violent)	13.5	–	–
Austin, Peyton and Johnson (2003)	59	Arrests or convictions for *any* offenses (not necessarily sexual or violent)	23.7 (6-year follow-up)	–	–

Static-99R troubles notwithstanding, reviews of the performance of sexual recidivism actuarial risk assessment instruments have been mediocre (Eher *et al.*, 2008; Kroner, Mills and Reddon, 2005; Langton *et al.*, 2007; Mokros *et al.*, 2010; Vrieze and Grove, 2010; Yang, Wong and Coid, 2010) except for ruling out the risk of sexual re-offense (Campbell, 2011).

Another approach combines actuarial with clinical judgment. Research by Hanson and Morton-Bourgon (2009) has borne out that this is not an acceptable method, as it creates error from the mixing of two completely different approaches of assessment. The effects of anchoring, a cognitive heuristic (thinking short-cut), further compounds the error rate with the adjusted-actuarial approach, and is addressed more comprehensively in the following section of this chapter. New research examining clinical overrides with the outdated Static-99 highlights this error (Storey *et al.*, 2012). Basically, Storey *et al.* (2012) found that when clinicians used their discretion to override risk ratings derived using the Static-99, the accuracy of their risk ratings decreased. Other studies on this issue have been reviewed by Hanson and Morton-Bourgon (2009) and by Campbell and DeClue (2010b), and the findings of these authors are not convincing that clinically adjusted actuarial scores have greater predictive accuracy.

Structured Professional Judgment

The other major method, known as structured professional judgment (SPJ; Douglas, Skeem and Deavers, 2005), has been called guided professional judgment (Lieberman, Krauss and Kyger, 2007) as well. This method assesses risk factors and symptom variables that have been found repeatedly in the empirical literature extant to be associated with sexual re-offense risk and diagnostic accuracy. SPJ allows the examiner to integrate and synthesize a multitude of variables in a structured manner with the goal of deciphering the empirically supported relevant diagnostic or risk factors along the continuums of frequency, intensity, duration, likelihood, imminence and salience. This approach is more flexible than an actuarial approach and allows for the consideration of case-specific considerations. The relevant risk factor variables are combined accordingly in the present, to make a systematic, professional opinion about the respondents' diagnosis and/or risk depending on the referral question.

The Sexual Violence Risk-20 (SVR-20) (Boer *et al.*, 1997) is a structured clinical checklist designed for the risk assessment of sexual violence in sex offenders. The SVR-20 authors refer to it as an "aide memoire" or a means to structure one's clinical thinking about the case at hand. This procedure reflects the application of what was called an empirically guided approach, or guided professional judgment, and is presently referred to as SPJ. The items are based on sexual offense recidivism risk factors gathered from reviews of the empirical literature extant. The final risk judgment can be indicated in terms of low, moderate or high in terms of need for treatment and level of supervision intensity. For many sex offender evaluations the SVR-20 can add useful information (Boer *et al.*, 1997: 26–27).

Limitations to using this approach are the absence of actual empirically derived scoring norms and cut-off scores, the presumption that the presence of more risk factors automatically means greater risk, the assumption that the list is exhaustive, and that this type of risk assessment approach leaves the weighting of each risk factor to each individual examiner. It is also worth noting that seeing a large number of risk factors can unduly bias the perception of risk just as easily as seeing a small number of risk factors as an artifact of cognitive heuristics, that is, availability and representativeness heuristics.

Among the strengths of SPJ risk assessment is that the risk items have an empirical basis for consideration and that "case-specific" factors can be considered, which in such evaluations seems prudent. The SVR-20 also helps organize the myriad of variables in such evaluations. While this approach allows for the consideration of either higher, or lower, sexual recidivism risk than fixed actuarial scoring rules allow, merely to tally SVR-20 factors to adjust an actuarial score is not acceptable practice. It would be the haphazard (that is, untested) mixing of two assessment models plus the error created by anchoring effects.

Anchoring

The issue of anchoring deserves some special attention in this chapter as it is seen as one possible means of providing a risk assessment that incorporates actuarial data with either SPJ data or, more loosely termed, "psychologically meaningful risk factors" (Mann, Hanson and Thornton, 2010). The term risk assessment is defined by Boer *et al.* (1997: 1) as "the process of evaluating individuals to (1) characterize the risk that they will commit violence in the future, and (2) develop interventions to manage or reduce that risk." Given that such risk characterizations would be different for each individual, risk assessment necessarily occurs under conditions of uncertainty. When people are tasked with making decisions under conditions of uncertainty, Tversky and Kahneman (1974) demonstrated that people would resort to thinking short-cuts, also called "cognitive heuristics." Despite the function of cognitive heuristics to economize complex judgments, these short-cuts can lead to systematic and substantial severe errors. One reliable heuristic occurs when people are given identical information in various orders and make significantly different judgments when an initial estimate is adjusted as new information is added. Tversky and Kahneman (1974: 1128) noted, "different starting points yield different estimates, which are biased toward the initial values." In other words, when people are tasked to make judgments under conditions of uncertainty, such as risk assessments, they are greatly influenced, or "anchored," by their starting point in the analysis. That the anchoring bias is still being discussed more than 35 years later (Kahneman, 2011: 119–128) highlights the importance of this bias.

Adjusting actuarial results within any type of assessment method appears to be an exemplar of the anchoring bias. For example, regarding pure actuarial results:

> This strategy is not that of taking an actuarial estimate as an additional piece of information to combine with a clinical appraisal of dangerousness, but rather to *anchor* clinical judgment by having the clinician start with an actuarial estimate of risk and then to alter it by examining dynamic variables, such as treatment outcome, treatment intensity, and supervision quality. (Quinsey, Rice and Harris, 1995: 100; emphasis added)

That advice defines the anchoring bias. In a well-known article on risk communication, actuarial data is again laden with this term: "Actuarial data to *anchor* clinical risk assessments have been reported both for inpatient violence (McNeil and Binder, 1994) and for violence in the open community (Harris, Rice and Quinsey, 1993)" (Monahan and Steadman, 1996: 931; emphasis added). Adjusting actuarial data not only causes inaccurate findings as a result on the anchoring heuristic, but from the compounding error variance created from data that co-vary. Whatever accurate yield has been already gleaned will be diminished by double counting this information from an adjustment. In conclusion, we clearly do not see adjusting actuarial test data using SPJ information, however conceived, as a valid approach to risk assessment.

Incremental Validity

Recently it has been suggested that using more than one type of test (for example, more than one type of actuarial test, one based on static factors and the other on dynamic factors) might provide a psychometrical basis for a convergent approach to risk assessment.

Incremental validity is defined as the degree to which a measure explains or predicts a phenomenon of interest, relative to other measures (Haynes and Lench, 2003). In more comprehensive terms, Hunsley (2003) noticed various different ways of defining incremental validity, including psychological measures to improve base rate measures, increasing predictive efficiency, and improving predictions in comparison with other sources of data. Despite the high potential for psychological research and clinical practice, until now there has been only little systematic effort in most areas of applied psychology to evaluate the incremental validity of measures and assessment procedures (Hunsley and Meyer, 2003).[1]

In forensic psychology, the concept of incremental validity has arisen in reference to the field of risk assessment research and practice. In simple words, the incremental validity raises the question whether a particular risk assessment instrument adds to the prediction of recidivism beyond what is captured by other risk assessment instruments.

The concept of incremental validity is of interest for both forensic prediction research and practice. First, as already mentioned above, surveys of forensic clinicians involved in sexual offender risk assessment and civil commitment proceedings demonstrate that most evaluators use different kinds of clinical and predictive data sources (Seto, 2005; Archer *et al.*, 2006). Second, if used independently of each other, different risk assessment methods reach satisfying predictive validity indices (Hanson and Morton-Bourgon, 2009). For instance, Hanson and Morton-Bourgon (2009) showed that actuarial tests as well as SPJ methods yielded effect sizes which were classified as moderate to good for the prediction of violent and sexual recidivism for different sexual offender populations. Third, even if different risk assessment instruments showed independently predictive validity, upon closer inspection of the results, different risk assessment instruments for sexual offenders could produce different risk rankings and the risk judgments derived from different instruments could also differ significantly, respectively (Craig *et al.*, 2004; Barbaree, Langton, and Peacock, 2006a,

2006b). Therefore, studies about the incremental validity of forensic risk assessment instruments could help to guide the selection, application and combination of different risk prediction measures for sexual offenders.

Although these findings from previous studies indicate the need for research on incremental validity, up to this point there have been very few research papers on this topic.[2] Even if some results provide support for the combination of different clinical and risk assessment instruments (for example, Olver, Wong and Nicholaichuk, 2009; Hanson *et al.*, 2007; Eher *et al.*, 2011), other researchers presented empirical evidence for the opposite point of view. Seto (2005), for instance, addressed the issue of whether combining multiple actuarial risk tools increases accuracy in predicting sexual offender recidivism and concluded that such combinations would not provide a consistent advantage over the predictive accuracy of the best single scale.

The concept of incremental validity could be especially relevant for the discussion about a convergent risk assessment approach, because if someone is able to examine the additional value of a particular measure (such as a risk assessment instrument that measures clinical, therapeutic relevant and dynamic risk factors) beyond what is captured by another measure (such as an actuarial tool that only uses static and historical risk factors in order to estimate the base rate for recidivism), one could argue that the best practice recommendation is to use both measures and to combine the results in a convergent approach (see Boer, 2006). Taking into account the existing research about incremental validity in forensic risk assessment instruments, there are at least two reasons to assume that SPJ instruments are incrementally valid beyond the classical actuarial risk assessment instruments (ARAIs) like the Static-99 or the Sex Offender Risk Appraisal Guide (SORAG). First, the above-mentioned research papers indicated that risk assessment instruments that contain predominantly dynamic risk factors show a significant improvement in predictive accuracy beyond the static risk factors as captured by, for instance, Static-99 or SORAG (for example, Hanson *et al.*, 2007; Eher *et al.*, 2011). Given the fact that SPJ instruments usually consist of a substantial number of dynamic items, one could further assume that SPJ instruments are also incrementally valid. Second, the incremental validity cannot only be assessed by predictive accuracy but must also consider other issues of risk assessment and management. SPJ instruments have a clear focus not only on risk prediction per se but also on strategies that would most effectively manage this risk (Hart and Boer, 2009). Therefore, probably the most important "incremental" improvement of SPJ instruments beyond ARAIs could be the consideration of the characteristics of each individual case in order to prevent future violence in the most effective way. However, up to this point there have been only very few studies about the incremental validity of SPJ instruments, so at the moment the concept of incremental validity provides hypotheses for future research rather than clear empirical evidence.

Conclusions

The idea of a "convergent" approach to risk is not to be confused with anchoring actuarial findings with SPJ findings or "psychologically meaningful risk factors" (Mann, Hanson and Thornton, 2010). Nor is the use of actuarial test data as an anchor for SPJ findings or other risk factors a valid approach. There are no data that provide any empirical support for either approach. Indeed, even if some empirical validation were to be found showing the incremental validity of using both actuarial and SPJ strategies, the end result may have better predictive accuracy, but would probably be no more useful than using the two types of tests independently.

The convergent approach simply means using a variety of tests that "converge" on the issue at hand. Medical doctors, when diagnosing an illness, often order blood tests (or other physical tests), take the patient's temperature and blood pressure and observe the patient to come to an initial hypothesis of what might be ailing the patient. Some of these data are actuarial (for example, temperature readings), others more SPJ in nature, all leading or converging on a potential diagnosis. The value of the diagnosis is to provide a starting point for treatment. The analogy to risk assessment and risk management is clear: we carry out a variety of tests to find out the risk issues and levels to intervene appropriately and manage risk.

Actuarial tests are valuable in that such instruments give us an idea of the person's risk from a group perspective – the characteristics he shares in common with a validation group gives us a baseline idea of the risk he poses within certain time frames (providing the validation study is from a relevant population). SPJs provide an individualized case analysis of risk issues that are unique to that individual. The combination of the findings is not to be carried out in any numerical fashion, but should be reported in isolation and then discussed in combination. Thus, Mr Doe was assessed using the Static-99R (for example), indicating a risk level of X. He was also assessed with the SVR-20 (for example), indicating a risk level of Y. If these risk levels are similar (for example, both high), it is a matter of prescribing risk management measures appropriate to his risk level. If the risk levels are different, then an explanation as to why this might be the case would be useful. For example, if the Static-99 finding were lower than the SVR-20 finding of risk, there may be factors on the SVR-20 that resulted in the higher risk level (for example, features of sexual deviancy).

In sum, we recommend the independent reporting of findings from risk assessment tests and the integration of these findings in the discussion section of risk assessment reports. As noted by Skeem and Monahan (2011: 38), there is still a lack of evidence for the supremacy of one sort of test over another and it is time to shift our attention from "predicting violence to understanding its causes and preventing its (re)occurrence." Finally, we support the use of actuarial tests primarily as a risk baseline which will show the risk group most closely matched by the client. However, for better understanding of the clients being assessed, the use of an appropriate SPJ is suggested (for example, Boer, 2006; Hanson and Morton-Bourgon, 2007).

Notes

1   Therefore in 2003 *Psychological Assessment* addressed the problem of incremental validity in a special section on incremental validity and utility in clinical assessment (Hunsley, 2003).

2   An exception is the concept of psychopathy defined by Hare (2003) and his *Psychopathy Checklist-Revised* (PCL-R). Originally conceptualized as a personality disorder, the PCL-R

is mostly used as a risk assessment instrument. However, because of the fact that the PCL-R has its seeds in the general personality research, the PCL-R is the only risk assessment instrument within forensic psychology for which at least a few studies about the incremental validity of the measure exist (Garb, 2003).

References

Abbott, B. (2011) "Is the Static-99R preselected high risk group appropriate to compare the risk performance of individuals undergoing sexually violent predator risk assessments?" Unpublished paper.

Abbott, B. (2009) "Applicability of the new Static-99 experience tables in sexually violent predator risk assessments," *Sexual Offender Treatment*, 4, 1.

Abracen, J. and Looman, J. (2006) "Evaluation of civil commitment criteria in high risk sample of sexual offenders," *Journal of Sexual Offender Civil Commitment: Science and the Law* 1, 124–140.

Archer, R.P., Buffington-Vollum, J.K., Stredny, R.V. and Handel, R.W. (2006) "A survey of psychological test use patterns among forensic psychologists," *Journal of Personality Assessment* 87, 84–94.

Austin, J., Peyton, J. and Johnson, K.D. (2003) Reliability and validity study of the Static-99/RRASOR sex offender risk assessment instruments, https://www.ncjrs.gov/App/Publications/abstract.aspx?ID=243142 (accessed September 15, 2012).

Barbaree, H.E., Langton, C.M. and Peacock, E.J. (2006a) "The factor structure of static actuarial items: its relation to prediction," *Sexual Abuse: A Journal of Research and Treatment* 18, 207–226.

Barbaree, H.E., Langton, C.M. and Peacock, E.J. (2006b) "Different actuarial risk measures produce different risk rankings for sexual offenders," *Sexual Abuse: Journal of Research and Treatment* 18, 4, 423–440.

Barbaree, H.E., Seto, M.C., Langton, C.M. and Peacock, E.J. (2001) "Evaluating the predictive accuracy of six risk assessment instruments for adult sex offenders," *Criminal Justice and Behavior* 28, 490–521.

Boer, D.P. (2006) "Sexual offender risk assessment strategies: is there a convergence of opinion yet?" *Sexual Offender Treatment* 1, 1–4.

Boer, D.P., Hart, S.D., Kropp, P.R. and Webster, C.D. (1997) *Manual for the Sexual Violence Risk – 20: Professional Guidelines for Assessing Risk of Sexual Violence*. Vancouver, BC: The Mental Health, Law, and Policy Institute.

Campbell, T.W. (2011) "Predictive accuracy of Static-99R and Static-2002R," *Open Access Journal of Forensic Psychology* 3, 82–106.

Campbell, T.W. and DeClue, G. (2010a) "Flying blind with naked factors: problems and pitfalls in adjusted actuarial sex offender risk assessment," *Open Access Journal of Forensic Psychology* 2, 75–101.

Campbell, T.W. and DeClue, G. (2010b) "Maximizing predictive accuracy in Sexually Violent Predator evaluations," *Open Access Journal of Forensic Psychology* 2, 148–232.

Cooke, D.J. (2010) "More prejudicial than probative? A critique of violence risk assessment of offenders using actuarial tools, due to their limitations in predicting the future behaviour of individual," Law Society of Scotland, *The Journal Online*, http://www.journalonline.co.uk/Extras/1007494.aspx (accessed September 15, 2012).

Cooke, D.J. and Michie, C. (2010) "Limitations of diagnostic precision and predictive utility in the individual case: a challenge for forensic practice," *Law and Human Behavior* 34, 4, 259–274.

Craig, L.A., Browne, K.D., Stringer, I. and Beech, A. (2004) "Limitations in actuarial risk assessment of sexual offenders: a methodological note," *British Journal of Forensic Practice* 6, 16–32.

Donaldson, T.S. and Abbott, B.R. (2011) "Prediction in the individual case: an explanation and application of its use with the Static-99r in sexually violent predator risk assessments," *American Journal of Forensic Psychology* 1, 5–35.

Douglas, K.S., Skeem, J. and Deavers, L. (2005) "Violence risk assessment: getting specific about being dynamic," *Psychology, Public Policy, and Law* 11, 3, 347–383.

Duwe, G. and Freske, P.J. (2012) "Using logistic regression modeling to predict sexual recidivism: the Minnesota Sex Offender Screening Tool–3 (MnSOST–3)," *Sexual Abuse: A Journal of Research and Treatment* 24, 4, 350–377.

Eher, R., Matthes, A., Schilling, F. *et al.* (2011) "Dynamic risk assessment in sexual offenders using STABLE–2000 and the STABLE–2007: an investigation of predictive and incremental validity," *Sexual Abuse: A Journal of Research and Treatment.* DOI:10.1177/1079063211403164.

Eher, R., Rettenberger, M., Schilling, F. and Friedemann, P. (2008) "Failure of Static–99 and SORAG to predict relevant reoffense categories in relevant sexual offender," *Sexual Offender Treatment* 3, 1.

Garb, H.N. (2003) "Incremental validity and the assessment of psychopathology in adults," *Psychological Assessment* 15, 508–520.

Grove, W.M., Zald, D.H., Lebow, B.S. *et al.* (2000) "Clinical versus mechanical prediction: a meta-analysis," *Psychological Assessment* 12, 19–30.

Grove, W.M. and Meehl, P.E. (1996) "Comparative efficiency of informal (subjective, impressionistic) and formal (mechanical, algorithmic) prediction procedures: the clinical-statistical controversy," *Psychology, Public Policy, & Law* 2, 2, 293–323.

Hanson, R.K., Harris, A.J.R., Scott, T. and Helmus, L. (2007) *Assessing the Risk of Sexual Offenders on Community Supervision: The Dynamic Supervision Project. (User Report No. 2007-05.* Ottawa: Public Safety Canada.

Hanson, R.K. and Morton-Bourgon, K. (2007) *The Accuracy of Recidivism Risk Assessments for Sexual Offenders: A Meta-analysis. Corrections User Report No. 2007-01.* Ottawa: Public Safety and Emergency Preparedness Canada, Corrections Research.

Hanson, R.K. and Morton-Bourgon, K. (2009) "The accuracy of recidivism risk assessments for sexual offenders: a meta-analysis of 118 prediction studies," *Psychological Assessment* 21, 1–21.

Hanson, R.K. and Thornton, D. (1999) *Static 99: Improving Actuarial Risk Assessments for Sex Offenders (User Report 1999-02).* Ottawa: Department of the Solicitor General of Canada.

Hare, R.D. (2003) *Manual for the Psychopathy Checklist–Revised*, 2nd edn. Toronto: Multi Health Systems.

Harris, A., Phenix, A., Hanson, R.K. and Thornton, D. (2003) *Static-99 Coding Rules Revised – 2003.* Ottawa: Department of the Solicitor General of Canada.

Harris, G.T., Rice, M.E. and Quinsey, V.L. (1993) "Violent recidivism of mentally disordered offenders: the development of a statistical prediction instrument," *Criminal Justice and Behavior* 20, 315–335.

Hart, S.D. and Boer, D.P. (2009) "Structured professional judgement guidelines for sexual violence risk assessment: The Sexual Violence Risk–20 (SVR–20) and Risk for Sexual Violence Protocol (RSVP)," in R.K. Otto and K.S. Douglas, *Handbook of Violence Risk Assessment.* Oxford: Routledge, pp. 269–294.

Hart, S.D., Michie, C. and Cooke, D.J. (2007) "Precision of actuarial risk assessment instruments: evaluating the 'margins of error' of group v. individual predictions of violence," *British Journal of Psychiatry* 190(suppl. 49), 60–65.

Haynes, S.N. and Lench, H.C. (2003) "Incremental validity of new clinical assessment measures," *Psychological Assessment* 15, 456–466.

Helmus, L. (2008) Static-99 recidivism percentages by risk level, http://www.static99.org/pdfdocs/october2008estimates.pdf (accessed September 20, 2012). Supplemental data from L. Helmus (2007) A multi-site comparison of the validity and utility of the Static-99 and Static-2002 for risk assessment with sexual offenders. BA thesis, Carleton University, Ottawa, Ontario, Canada.

Helmus, L., Hanson, R.K. and Thornton, D. (2009) "Reporting Static-99 in light of new research on recidivism norms," *ATSA Forum* 21, 1, 38–45.

Hunsley, J. (2003) "Introduction to the special section on incremental validity and utility in clinical assessment," *Psychological Assessment* 15, 443–4465.

Hunsley, J. and Meyer, G.J. (2003) "The incremental validity of psychological testing and assessment: conceptual, methodological, and statistical issues," *Psychological Assessment* 15, 446–455.

Janus, E.S. and Meehl, P.E. (1997) "Assessing the legal standard for predictions of dangerousness in sex offender commitment proceedings," *Psychology, Public Policy, and Law* 3, 1, 33–64.

Janus, E.S. and Prentky, R.A. (2003) "Forensic use of actuarial risk assessment with sex offenders: accuracy, admissibility, and accountability," *American Criminal Law Review* 40, 1143, 1–59.

Kahneman, D. (2003) "A perspective on judgment and choice: mapping bounded rationality," *American Psychologist* 58, 9, 697–720.

Kahneman, D. (2011) *Thinking Fast and Slow.* New York: Farrar, Straus & Giroux.

Kahneman, D. and Tversky, A. (1973) "On the psychology of prediction," *Psychological Review* 80, 237–251.

Kahneman, D. and Tversky, A. (1984) "Choices, values and frames," *American Psychologist* 39, 341–350.

Kahneman, D. and Tversky, A. (1996) "On the reality of cognitive illusions," *Psychological Review* 103, 3, 582–591.

Knight, R.A. and Thornton, D. (2007) Evaluating and improving risk assessment schemes for sexual recidivism: a long-term follow-up of convicted sexual offenders, http://www.ncjrs.gov/pdffiles1/nij/grants/217618.pdf (accessed September 6, 2012).

Kroner, D.G., Mills, J.F. and Reddon, J.R. (2005) "A coffee can, factor analysis, and prediction of antisocial behavior: the structure of criminal risk," *International Journal of Law and Psychiatry* 28, 360–374.

Kuran, T. and Sunstein, C.R. (1999) "Availability cascades and risk regulation," *Stanford Law Review* 51, 4, 683–768.

Langton, C.M., Barbaree, H.E., Seto, M.C. *et al.* (2007) "Actuarial assessment of risk for reoffense among adult sexual offenders: evaluating the predictive accuracy of the Static-2002 and five other instruments," *Criminal Justice and Behavior* 34, 1, 37–59.

Lanyon, R.I. (2001) "Psychological assessment procedures in sex offending," *Professional Psychology: Research and Practice* 32, 3, 252–260.

Lieberman, J.D., Krauss, D.A. and Kyger, M. (2007) "Determining dangerousness in sexually violent predator evaluations: cognitive-experiential self-theory and juror judgments of expert testimony," *Behavioral Sciences and the Law* 25, 4, 507–526.

Mann, R.E., Hanson, R.K. and Thornton, D. (2010) "Assessing risk for sexual recidivism: some proposals on the nature of psychologically meaningful risk factors," *Sexual Abuse: A Journal of Research and Treatment* 22, 2, 191–217.

McNeil, D.E. and Binder, R.L. (1994) "Screening for risk of inpatient violence: validation of an actuarial tool," *Law and Human Behavior* 18, 579–586.

Meehl, P.E. (1986) "Causes and effects of my disturbing little book," *Journal of Personality Assessment* 50, 370–375.

Mokros, A., Stadtland, C., Osterheider, M. and Nedopil, N. (2010) "Assessment of risk for violent recidivism through multivariate Bayesian classification," *Psychology, Public Policy, and Law* 16, 4, 418–450.

Monahan, J. (1981) *Predicting Violent Behavior: An Assessment of Clinical Techniques.* Beverly Hills, CA: Sage.

Monahan, J. (1984) "The prediction of violent behavior: toward a second generation of theory and policy," *American Journal of Psychiatry* 141, 10–15.

Monahan, J. and Steadman, H. (eds) (1994) *Violence and Mental Disorder: Developments in Risk Assessment.* Chicago: University of Chicago Press.

Monahan, J. and Steadman, H.J. (1996) "Violent storms and violent people: how meteorology can inform risk communication in mental health law," *American Psychologist* 51, 9, 931–938.

Mossman, D. (2006) "Another look at interpreting risk categories," *Sexual Abuse: A Journal of Research and Treatment* 18, 1, 41–63.

Mossman, D. and Sellke, T. (2007) "Avoiding errors about 'margins of error'." *British Journal of Psychiatry* 191, 6, 561.

Mossman, D. (2008) "Analyzing the performance of risk assessment instruments: a response to Vrieze and Grove (2007)," *Law and Human Behavior* 32, 3, 279–291.

Olver, M.E., Wong, S.C.P. and Nicholaichuk, T.P. (2009) "Outcome evaluation of a high-intensity inpatient sex offender treatment program," *Journal of Interpersonal Violence* 24, 522–536.

Otto, R.K. (1992) "Prediction of dangerous behavior: a review and analysis of 'second generation' research," *Forensic Reports* 5, 103–133.

Prentky, R.A., Janus, E., Barbaree, H. *et al.* (2006) "Sexually violent predators in the courtroom: science on trial," *Psychology, Public Policy, and Law* 12, 357–393.

Quinsey, V.L., Harris, G.T., Rice, M.E. and Cormier, C.A. (1998) *Violent Offenders: Appraising and Managing Risk.* Washington, DC: American Psychological Association.

Quinsey, V., Rice, M. and Harris, G. (1995) "Actuarial prediction of sexual recidivism," *Journal of Interpersonal Violence* 10, 85–105.

Ross, L. (1977) "The intuitive psychologist and his shortcomings: distortions in the attribution process," in L. Berkowitz (ed.), *Advances in Experimental Social Psychology*, vol. 10. New York: Academic Press, pp. 173–220.

Sandler, J.C., Freeman, N. and Socia, K.M. (2008) "Does a watched pot boil?: A time-series analysis of New York State's sex offender registration and notification law," *Psychology, Public Policy, and Law* 14, 4, 284–302.

Seto, M.C. (2005) "Is more better? Combining actuarial risk scales to predict recidivism among adult sex offenders," *Psychological Assessment* 17, 156–167.

Skeem, J.L. and Monahan, J. (2011) "Current directions in violence risk assessment," *Current Directions in Psychological Science* 20, 1, 38–42.

Storey, J.E., Watt, K.A., Jackson, K.J. and Hart, S.D. (2012) "Utilization and implications of the Static-99 in practice," *Sexual Abuse: A Journal of Research and Treatment.* Advance online publication. DOI:10.1177/1079063211423943.

Tversky, A. and Kahneman, D. (1974) "Judgment under uncertainty: heuristics and biases," *Science* 185, 4157, 1124–1131.

Tversky, A. and Kahneman, D. (1983) "Extensional versus intuitive reasoning: the conjunction fallacy in probability judgment," *Psychological Review* 90, 4, 293–315.

Vrieze, S.L. and Grove, W.M. (2008) "Predicting sex offenders recidivism. I. Correcting for item overselection and accuracy overestimation in scale development. II. Sampling error-induced attenuation of predictive validity over base rate information," *Law and Human Behavior* 32, 3, 266–278.

Vrieze, S.L. and Grove, W.M. (2009) "Survey on the use of clinical and mechanical prediction methods in clinical psychology," *Professional Psychology: Research and Practice* 40, 5, 525–531.

Vrieze, S.L. and Grove, W.M. (2010) "Multidimensional assessment of criminal recidivism: problems, pitfalls, and proposed solutions," *Psychological Assessment* 22, 2, 382–395.

Waggoner, J., Wollert, R. and Cramer, E. (2008) "A re-specification of Hanson's 2006 Static-99 experience table that controls for the effects of age in a sample of 552 young sex offenders," *Law, Probability, and Risk* 7, 305–312.

Wollert, R. (2007) "Poor diagnostic reliability, the Null-Bayes logic model, and their implications for sexually violent predator evaluations," *Psychology, Public Policy, & Law* 13, 3, 167–203.

Wollert, R. (2006) "Low base rates limit expert certainty when current actuarials are used to identify sexually violent predators: an application of Bayes's Theorem," *Psychology, Public Policy, and Law* 12, 1, 56–85.

Wollert, R and Waggoner, J. (2009) "Bayesian computations protect sexually violent predator evaluations from the degrading effects of confirmatory bias and illusions of certainty: a reply to Doren and Levenson," *Sexual Offender Treatment* 1, 1–23.

Wollert, R., Cramer, E., Waggoner, J. *et al.* (2010) "Recent research (n = 9,305) underscores the importance of using age-stratified actuarial tables in sex offender risk assessments," *Sexual Abuse: A Journal of Research and Treatment* 22, 4, 471–490.

Yang, M., Wong, S.C.P. and Coid, J. (2010) "The efficacy of violence prediction: a meta-analytic comparison of nine risk assessment tool," *Psychological Bulletin* 136, 740–767.

21

Sex Offender Registration in the United States and the United Kingdom
Emerging Legal and Ethical Debates
Terry Thomas

Introduction

The registration of convicted sex offenders in the interests of better public protection is a policy that has been adopted in an increasing number of jurisdictions around the world. The United States and the United Kingdom set the template for others to follow in Canada, France, Australia, the Republic of South Africa, the Republic of Ireland and elsewhere (Thomas, 2011); Germany has a localized *Lander*-based register (Obergfell-Fuchs, 2011). Questions about the viability and efficacy of sex offender registers (or registries as they are known in the United States) have been raised and legal and ethical challenges have become more frequent as registers, and the registration process, appear to become more sophisticated and more onerous, as well as now including forms of public access to them.

This chapter gives a brief background to the rise of sex offender registers over the last 20 to 30 years in the United States and the United Kingdom, before looking at legal challenges and the most recent response and developments in the light of those challenges and the questions that they pose.

What Is a Sex Offender Register?

The principles of sex offender registration are that anyone convicted of a designated sexual offense should, in addition to being punished, be required to notify a law enforcement agency of any changes to their home address or any other details about themselves and their circumstances for a given period of time and sometimes for the remainder of their lives. The "requirement to notify" is an attempt to improve

The Wiley-Blackwell Handbook of Legal and Ethical Aspects of Sex Offender Treatment and Management, First Edition. Edited by Karen Harrison and Bernadette Rainey.
© 2013 John Wiley & Sons, Ltd. Published 2013 by John Wiley & Sons, Ltd.

the quality of data held by law enforcement authorities on the whereabouts of sex offenders in their local communities. The overall aim is that an improved knowledge base of this nature, for the police, should lend itself to better approaches to public protection, and could also deter and prevent the offender from committing further offenses. The "requirement to notify" has become known as complying with the sex offender register. A person who is "required to notify" and who fails to comply has committed a new offense, usually punishable by a fine or custodial sentence.

Sex offender registration is for purposes of public protection and is not part of the punishment of an offender for his/her original offense. In practice such a clear and simple distinction may not be appreciated by the person required to register. As register requirements have been strengthened, the experience of registration could increasingly be seen as punitive and mean "the community's protection is in effect the sex offender's punishment" (Kemshall, 2008: 21).

Having compiled registers of people convicted for sex offenses, some jurisdictions have gone further with policies of public access to the register or "community notification." In the United States there is a universal right of access and in the United Kingdom a more limited version of information disclosure has evolved.

Sex offender registration is premised on the belief that sex offenders are invariably going to re-offend and be persistent serial offenders and that therefore the public has an added need to impose these "requirements" on them in the interests of public protection and community safety. As one parliamentarian forcefully stated during discussions on the UK register, "Once a paedophile always a paedophile is a much more certain saying than once a burglar, always a burglar, or even once a rapist, always a rapist" (*Hansard*, HC Deb, January 27, 1997, vol. 289, col. 41).

In practice not all sex offenses are sexual offenses against children by people who might be called "pedophiles" although it is those offenses that invariably cause most public concern and bring down most opprobrium on the offenders concerned. Also in practice there is research to show that sex offenders in fact often do *not* re-offend in any repeated pattern of offending. The opening sentence of one UK inspection of police and probation work on the management of sexual offenders in the community made it quite clear that "statistically sexual offenders are reconvicted less frequently than most other offenders" (Criminal Justice Joint Inspection, 2010: 2).

The Association for the Treatment of Sexual Abusers (ATSA) in the United States similarly states on its website that "Sexual offence recidivism rates are much lower than commonly believed; averaging 14 and 20% over five year follow up periods" (ATSA, 2010), and, on the subject of treatment, that "recent, statistically sophisticated studies with extremely large combined samples have found that contemporary cognitive-behavioural treatment does help to reduce rates of sexual re-offending by as much as 40%" (ATSA, 2010).(However, see Chapter 13.) To that extent it might be argued that registers are somewhat flawed from the outset. Some sex offenders will re-offend but many will not.

Further concerns with registers arise when the question is asked as to whether they make any difference; that is, do they actually contribute to greater public protection and safer communities? These questions have been largely unanswered by researchers and for now we might just question whether registers have been an example of "enact first, question later." In the United States, for example, Logan (2009: 115), having examined the available research, has pointed out that "it is unclear whether registration and notification actually reduce crime."

Sex Offender Registers in the United States

Origins and development

The United States is generally considered as the place where sex offender registers originated, with California being the first jurisdiction to be credited with starting a register in 1947. A small number of other states followed until there was a lull in interest between the 1960s and the mid-1970s (Jenkins, 1998). Social workers "discovered" child sexual abuse in the 1980s (Jenkins, 1998) but it was to be Washington State which really rekindled interest in 1990 following a high profile attack on a seven-year-old boy. The perpetrator was a previously convicted and "known" sex offender and an accompanying public outcry demanded that something must be done. Washington's response was not only to have a register but to make that register open and accessible to the public (Boerner, 1992). This innovation created much public and media interest as registers had previously only been available to the police and other professionals.

The State of Minnesota followed Washington by introducing their register in 1991. This policy development also followed the high-profile abduction of a child – Jacob Wetterling aged 11 years (Logan, 2003). Jacob's mother Patty Wetterling organized a national campaign to have registers across the whole country and in 1994 the federal Jacob Wetterling Crimes against Children and Sexually Violent Offender Registration Act was passed requiring every US state to have a sex offender register. States which did not create a register risked losing federal funding for criminal justice matters known as Byrne Funding.[1] In 1996 Massachusetts became the last state to put a sex offender register in place.

Two years after the Wetterling Act in 1996 the federal laws were strengthened by the passing of a national version of a New Jersey state law known as Megan's Law requiring some form of public access to all the registers now in place in the 50 US states (see below). Federal guidance was published on how both the registers and Megan's Law should be implemented; the guidelines were said to be just a starting point and "a floor not a ceiling" (*Federal Register*, 1997: 139). In addition a new federal law was passed to enable the development of a national sex offender register drawing from all the individual state registers (Pam Lychner Act 1996). A further strengthening of the Jacob Wetterling Act came through the 1998 Jacob Wetterling Improvements Act with updated guidance on implementation from the Attorney General (*Federal Register*, 1999; for a full history of US sex offender laws at this time, see Logan, 2009; Hebenton, 2009).

Community notification

The question of public access to sex offender registers was not taken up in Minnesota or in the 1994 federal Jacob Wetterling Act and the policy of access was left to the discretion of the individual states. Louisiana, for example, required registrants actually to visit and notify their neighbors personally (Louisiana Revised Statutes 15:540 *et seq.*), and New Jersey introduced their Megan's Law allowing access and mandating law enforcement agencies to proactively publicize the whereabouts of sex offenders in a policy of what now became known as "community notification." The New Jersey Megan's Law was named after seven-year-old Megan Kanka, assaulted and killed by a previously convicted sex offender living in the same street as the Kanka family but unknown to them.

The 1996 federal Megan's Law took the principles of the New Jersey law and requested that all US states now introduce a form of public access. The exact form of community notification was still left to the states. Some gave universal access while others made risk assessments and only disclosed information on offenders assessed as high risk. The means of dissemination had variations from pro-active leafleting, flyers and public meetings through to the more discrete enquiries that could be made by individuals at a police station. Within a few years states started to use the internet and web sites as a form of disseminating information on sex offenders (see Thomas, 2003).

Some states saw the opportunity to tie "community notification" in with education of the public on the nature of sexual offending. A two-hour meeting attended by the author in Minnesota consisted of an hour of general points being made about sexual offending and the relevant law on registers and public protection (education) followed by an hour on the identity of the new sex offender in the neighborhood (community notification) and the arrangements made for his supervision by probation.

Legal challenges

The legalities of the US registers introduced in the 1990s were challenged in the courts at state level and federal level. The courts invariably supported the intentions of the legislators. The two most important challenges reached the Supreme Court in 2003 in the cases of *Smith* v. *Doe* (538 US 84 (2003)) and *Connecticut Department of Public Safety* v. *Doe* (538 US 1 (2003)); both were decided on the same day.

The *Smith* v. *Doe* case was a challenge to the sex offender register in Alaska that its retrospective nature put it in breach of the US Constitution's *ex post facto clause* (Article 1, ss9 and 10), that laws could not "make more burdensome the punishment for a crime after its commission." The Supreme Court rejected the arguments on the basis that the register was not a punishment but a form of public protection and therefore a law that was simply regulatory in nature (for a critique of this judgment, see Logan, 2009: 136–141).

In Connecticut the challenge was that the community notification of people on the state register was being made without any procedural due process allowing those people to put their case against community notification and the clear burden and stigma that it imposed on them. The Supreme Court again rejected the challenge because the Connecticut Department of Public Safety as custodians of the register had made the disclaimer that disclosure was based solely on the existence of a conviction. There had been no risk assessments made and therefore no requirement for any due process. Connecticut had based its registration and community notification arrangements on a "conviction based regime" and any opportunities for due process had been fully met within the criminal court proceedings (for a critique of this judgment, see Logan, 2009: 141–147).

These two Supreme Court cases were seen as giving a ringing endorsement to the use of registers to improve public protection from sex offenders. Registers and community notification were regulatory and not a form of punishment and could therefore be retrospective. An emboldened federal legislature now decided to update all the 1990s laws in a new all-encompassing law to be known as the Adam Walsh Act 2006.

The legislative response

The Adam Walsh Child Protection and Safety Act 2006 is named in memory of six-year-old Adam Walsh, abducted from a Florida shopping mall in 1981; his remains were found a few weeks later. Adams parents, John and Reve Walsh, became national campaigners for better child protection arrangements over the intervening 25 years, with John Walsh achieving a certain celebrity status as the presenter of the national television show *Americas Most Wanted*.

The Adam Walsh Act (AWA) repealed all of the old federal registration laws. It was divided into seven separate Sub Titles, but it was Title 1, called the Sex Offender Registration and Notification Act or SORNA, that would have the greatest impact on sex offender registration in the United States. SORNA was designed to improve the quality of individual state registers, to create more consistency between them and to avoid any loopholes. The unspoken aim was to achieve a level playing field that offered no "havens" of escape for sex offender registrants by allowing them to have lesser restrictions on them in one state than in other states. The AWA and SORNA were a major federal exercise in trying to achieve state compliance on matters of sex offender registration that had been determined in Washington DC.

> The AWA . . . compels massive changes to existing state registration and notification systems . . . state laws will become broader and more onerous in numerous respects, including the scope of offences covered; duration of registration; frequency and methods that registration and updates must occur (in person); and extent of registrants subject to community notification (based on conviction, not individual risk). (Logan, 2009: 65–66)

The new law and arrangements took their lead from the Supreme Court decisions of 2003 and in particular the "permissions" now granted to allow for "conviction based regimes" and for regulatory laws to be "retrospective." Sex offenders were to be categorized by their convictions as tier 1, 2 or 3 from the least serious offenses (tier 1) to the most serious (tier 3). This categorization determined the time periods for registration from 15 years (tier 1), to 25 years (tier 2) and indefinite lifetime registration for tier 3 registrants. Registers were to be retrospective and include all those currently "in the system" but also anyone with old sexual offenses that had pre-dated the registers who now re-entered the system, whether for new sexual crimes or any other crimes.

Registration requirements also became more burdensome. People were going to be required to register at home and at work or college if these places were in different areas, teenagers as young as 14 were to register, more information was to be provided to law enforcement agencies, and penalties for non-compliance were increased. Community notification now had to be available through the internet, if not already arranged, and new national arrangements were put in place allowing public access to the national register devised originally under the Pam Lychner Act and now referred to as the Dru Sjodin National Sex Offender Public Web Site (accessible at www.nsopw.gov; Department of Justice, 2008).

The Act introduced the federal SMART office (Sex Offender Sentencing, Monitoring, Apprehending, Registering and Tracking) to assist the states in implementing the Act. The SMART office started work in December 2006 and is located in the Department of Justice Office of Justice Programs (SORNA, s146). More federal help became available because the Act required the federal US Marshals Service to be involved in tracking the non-compliant registrant who was now to be referred to as a "fugitive" (SORNA, s141).

As with previous federal laws the Attorney General produced guidelines on how the law should work, including regulations that confirmed the retrospective nature of SORNA (*Federal Register*, 2007; *Federal Register*, 2008). As before the National Guidelines were said to be just a starting point and "a floor not a ceiling," but the new arrangements had to be in place by July 27, 2009, with Byrne funding again being dependent on a substantial degree of compliance.

In the years following the passing of the AWA, states worked to implement the new stronger registration provisions. As the July 2009 deadline for implementation approached it became clear that the states were struggling to meet it. In March 2009, with just four months to go before the July deadline, the Congressional Sub Committee on Crime, Terrorism and Homeland Security was convened to specifically look at the problems states were encountering in implementing SORNA. The Sub Committee's chair Robert Scott opened proceedings by reporting "not a single state, tribe, territory or the District of Columbia has [been] found to be in compliance with the provisions of SORNA" (US House of Representatives, 2009). Even the popular nationwide television program the *Oprah Winfrey Show* (2009) pitched in with a plea for help for the Act.

The July 27, 2009 deadline came and went with still not one state having achieved compliance with SORNA. The first state actually to do so was Ohio in September 2009, some two months past the deadline (Department of Justice, 2009), followed by Delaware and then Florida in May 2010 (Department of Justice, 2010). All the other registration jurisdictions had requested and been granted extensions to July 27, 2011 but even by that deadline only 14 states out of the 50 had implemented the SORNA requirements along with nine Native American tribes and the territory of Guam (Department of Justice, 2011).

There has been one US Supreme Court ruling to date on SORNA and that concerned its retrospective nature. Thomas Carr appealed against his conviction under SORNA for failing to re-register when he moved from Alabama to Indiana because his movement took place before the enactment of SORNA. The Supreme Court ruled in his favor but avoided the question of whether or not the law was *ex post facto* by focusing on the wording of "travels" as opposed to "had travelled" in the past (*Carr v. US*, No 08-1301, 2010).

The Sex Offender Register in the United Kingdom

Origins and development

The Sex Offender Act 1997 was the legal underpinning for the UK sex offender register which was implemented from September 1, 1997. Unlike the United States, there had been no great public demand for such a measure and the demand, if any, came more from the professionals working in this area and the willingness of government simply to transplant a US policy to the United Kingdom. The parliamentary discussions on the Bill were held within months of a general election and no doubt some of these discussions were political posturing in order to look "tough" on crime; any real opposition to the new law was decidedly muted. For the government Timothy Kirkhope said he wanted the Act to be "draconian" even though it was not part of the offender's punishment (*Hansard*, HC Deb, Standing Committee D, February 4, 1997, col. 8) and for the opposition Alun Michael said he was only too happy "to get [this Bill] through as quickly as possible" (*Hansard*, HC Deb, January 27, 1997, vol. 289, col. 33).

The 1997 Act covered England, Wales, Scotland and Northern Ireland and therefore had to account for the variations in laws between these component parts of the United Kingdom (see Schedule 1 of the Act for lists of the different laws). The different jurisdictions also allowed for minor variations in the idea of the register itself. In England, Wales and Northern Ireland, for example, registration was automatic on conviction for certain offenses, but in Scotland the law allowed for a small element of judicial discretion (Sexual Offences Act 2003, Schedule 3, para. 60).

The 1997 Act was later supplemented by the Criminal Justice and Court Services Act 2000, introducing the localized Multi-Agency Public Protection Arrangements (MAPPA) to effectively manage the register. These arrangements included the police, probation service and later the prison service as the "core" "responsible authorities" and the social care services, health services and others as authorities under a duty to cooperate (see Bryan and Doyle, 2003; National Offender Management Service, 2009). This was an example of local level sex offender management and is a form of intervention that has never really been implemented in the United States in any comparable way.

Following a formal review of the registration process in 2001 attempts were made to strengthen the register. The review made direct reference to the Sarah Payne case and its "unprecedented media coverage" (Home Office/Scottish Executive, 2001: 3) but it added a note of caution declaring that any strengthening had to be balanced and proportionate and should the registration requirements become too onerous the law might be challenged under the European Convention on Human Rights and the recently enacted Human Rights Act 1998 (Home Office/Scottish Executive, 2001). Sarah Payne was an eight-year-old girl who was sexually assaulted and killed in Sussex during the summer of 2000.

The registration laws were updated in sections 80 to 93 of the Sexual Offences Act 2003. The basic principles remained the same but the opportunity was taken to strengthen the register and close perceived "loopholes." The White Paper preceding the 2003 Act remained mindful of the Sarah Payne case and was unequivocal about the impact of the media coverage the case had received:

> recent high profile cases have caused widespread public concern about the dangers that some sex offenders pose . . . [and] . . . an obligation rests on Government to respond to this concern, to do what it can to make people feel secure, and to ensure they are better protected . . . the . . . new legislation [was] to further strengthen measures against sex offenders across the United Kingdom. (Home Office/Scottish Executive, 2001: 7)

In terms of these "strengthening measures" the government now seemed to ignore its own 2001 note of caution about the register becoming too onerous and liable to challenge. The 2003 Act reduced the time period for reporting, introduced annual verification reporting and added more offenses to those designated as leading to registration. Section 58 of the Violent Crime Reduction Act 2006 (introducing a new s96B into the Sexual Offences Act 2003) gave the police greater powers of entry to the homes of registered sex offenders, and yet more offenses were designated as leading to registration in 2007 (Sexual Offences Act 2007 (Amendments of Schedules 3 and 5) Order 2007 no. 296). Furthermore, in Scotland, registered sex offenders were required to provide the police with more information about their bank accounts and credit cards (Sexual Offences Act 2003 (Notification Requirements) (Scotland) Regulations 2007 no. 246) (see also Thomas, 2010, Table 4.3, for more details of these strengthening exercises).

All of these activities to "close loopholes" continued throughout this period, leading some observers to question whether the register was now in danger of becoming so onerous that it not only infringed human rights but became more of a punishment than a measure of public protection (see, for example, Thomas, 2008, 2010). In 2011 two registered sex offenders successfully challenged the Home Office in the UK Supreme Court, and parts of the Sexual Offences Act 2003 concerned with registration were declared incompatible with the European Convention on Human Rights (see below).

Community notification

The United Kingdom did not, and does not, allow any general public access to its sex offender register or any overt form of "community notification" comparable to that in the United States. A newspaper-led campaign in the summer of 2000 had called for a form of "community notification" in the United Kingdom following the abduction and murder of Sarah Payne. Despite the widespread reporting of the murder and the campaign and despite it later being revealed that the man eventually convicted for the child's murder was already on the register, the government was not persuaded (Bennetto, 2000).

What the United Kingdom did allow, however, was a more limited system of "discretionary disclosure" carried out by the police. The police make these "discretionary disclosures" to individual members of the public if they believe it will prevent a crime or safeguard children. The courts have upheld their right to make these disclosures (*R* v. *Devon CC ex p L* [1991] 2FLR; *R* v. *Chief Constable of North Wales Police ex parte AB* [1997] 3WLR and *R* v. *Chief Constable of North Wales Police and Others ex parte Thorpe and Another, The Times Law Report*, March 23, 1998) and guidance on how the policy should be implemented has been provided (Home Office, 1999; National Offender Management Service, 2009, Section Six). Evaluation of the "discretionary disclosure" system has generally been favorable (Cann, 2007).

In 2007 proposals were made to strengthen these arrangements. The Home Office *Review of the Protection of Children from Sex Offenders* had first put forward the idea of new laws in this area (Home Office, 2007) and a government Action Plan said the idea would be taken forward and be the subject of trials in four pilot areas (HM Government, 2008).

The new laws were in s140 of the Criminal Justice and Immigration Act 2008, which amended the Criminal Justice Act 2003, inserting s327A and s327B and Schedule 34A. The law now added to the "discretionary disclosure" process by placing a duty on the "responsible authorities" to consider disclosure of records on any child sex offender they currently manage with a "presumption that they should disclose" to "any particular member of the public" if they decided that there was a risk of "serious harm" to a particular child or children and disclosure was considered necessary to protect that child or children (Criminal Justice Act 2003, s327A).

Who exactly a "particular member of the public" might be is not defined, but in the Action Plan it was suggested that it would be "parents or legal guardians of children under 18" (HM Government, 2008: 27) and in the parliamentary debate Vernon Coaker for the Home Office said it could include "girlfriends, friends or family members" (*Hansard*, HC Deb, Standing Committee, November 29, 2007). Home Office guidance would later say the information was for the person able to use it to safeguard the child or children, usually "the parent, guardian or carer of the child" (Home Office, 2010: paras. 4.2 and 4.8).

The original Bill had referred only to a "risk of harm" and the addition of the word "serious" to make it "serious harm" was made after suggestions in parliament that the whole process of disclosure was to be exceptional rather than routine. The "responsible authority" should only disclose that information which it considers relevant and is under no duty to disclose at all if it considers it unnecessary. The authority may also impose conditions on recipients of information to prevent them passing it on to others (Criminal Justice Act 2003, s327A(5)). Interestingly, in parliament, opposition spokespersons had said it would be impossible to maintain any confidentiality (*Hansard*, HC Deb, Standing Committee, November 29, 2007, col. 705). No sanctions are referred to in the Act should an individual ignore any conditions.

A "child sex offender" was now defined as anyone committing one of the offenses against a child now listed in a new Schedule 34A added to the Criminal Justice Act 2003 and the information to be disclosed can include convictions, cautions, final warnings and reprimands (s327A(5) and (9)). According to the Act, this meant that "soft" information such as suspicions or police intelligence should *not* be disclosed, but the Home Office guidance to the police was more expansive and said that such "soft" information could be disclosed under the pre-existing "discretionary disclosure" scheme, although the "presumption to disclose" in the Act itself would not cover such soft information (Home Office, 2010: paras. 2.5–2.6).

The evaluation reports from the pilot schemes were published in March 2010 for England and Wales and October 2010 for Scotland and both were favorably disposed to the new arrangements. The authors found the number of enquiries being made for information was lower than had been anticipated, but in cases where enquiries had been made, the applicants had been satisfied with the process. Police and offender managers thought the new procedures clarified and endorsed what had previously been seen as "good practice" and no significant changes were found in the behavior of registered sex offenders who knew about the scheme; the evaluators in England and Wales had been unable to interview any sex offenders who had actually had information on them disclosed (Kemshall *et al.*, 2010); in Scotland eight registrants were interviewed but most were non-committal about the exercise (Chan *et al.*, 2010).

Legal challenges

Angus Thompson from Newcastle had been one of the first people in the United Kingdom to become registered for life in the late 1990s, and in 2008 he argued that his offenses were isolated and that he posed no long-term risk to anyone. On that basis he did not need to be registered any longer. The problem was that there was no judicial mechanism open to him to appeal against his continued registration. Indefinite registration was a part of the legislation and having no appeal tribunal had always been the government's intention (for a full parliamentary discussion, see *Hansard*, HC Deb, Standing Committee D, February 4, 1997 cols. 20–29; Thomas, 2009).

Thompson challenged this lack of a forum to discuss continued registration and the possibility of deregistration in the context of Article 8 of the European Convention on Human Rights, the right to privacy. He argued that the need to continually report to the police and give information long after his original offense, and when he believed he posed no threat to anyone, was invading his right to privacy. It was accepted that some people might need to be registered for life but equally some people could change, with or without treatment programs, and did not need such indefinite registration periods. Thompson's challenge was joined to that of a young person referred to in the courts as "F" who was in the same position and making the same argument.

The appeals of Thompson and "F" were heard at all three levels of the UK judicial system:

- The Divisional Court initially granted the respondents' claims and made a declaration of incompatibility with the Convention in December 2008 (*F and Angus Aubrey Thompson* v. *Secretary of State for the Home Department* [2008] EWHC 3170).
- The Court of Appeal dismissed the Home Office appeal against the Divisional Court decision. The UK Supreme Court dismissed the second Home Office

appeal (*F and Angus Aubrey Thompson* v. *Secretary of State for the Home Department* 23 July 2009 [2010] 1WLR 29).)

• The Supreme Court found registration to be proportionate (within the parameters of Article 8) but agreed that there should be some form of appeal available in order to review the position and to end the requirement to notify should the time come when that was appropriate (*R (on the application of F (by his litigation friend F)) and Thompson (FC) (Respondents)* v. *Secretary of State for the Home Department (Appellant)* [2010] UKSC 17).

The legislative response

Most of the legal challenges to the UK register have not required the British government to make any response, but the case of *F and Thompson* was of a different quality and proposals for change were required.

Scotland responded to the ruling in October 2010 and Northern Ireland, England and Wales did so in February 2011. Scotland proposed an automatic review of all lifetime registrants by the police after 15 years; the person on the register would be informed whether or not they were no longer considered a risk and were being relieved of all obligations to continue notifying the police of their circumstances. If the police informed them that they could not be safely deregistered the person concerned could appeal to a Sheriff's court for a review of the police decision. This idea was put out for consultation and then duly enacted through the Sexual Offences Act 2003 (Remedial) (Scotland) Order 2011 (a summary of the responses to the original consultation is available at http://origin-www.legislation.gov.uk/ssi/2011/45/pdfs/ssien_20110045_en.pdf).

The response from England and Wales was more limited. The Home Secretary made it clear she resented having to do anything on this matter of reviews and prefaced her parliamentary announcement with comments that she was "disappointed and appalled" at the court ruling and "will deliberately set the bar for those reviews as high as possible" (*Hansard*, HC Deb, February 16, 2011, cols. 959–969). The proposal was to offer lifetime registrants a decision from the police concerning the need for continued registration; this would not be done automatically as in Scotland and the individual concerned would have to make an application and could do so after 15 years of release from custody. There was to be no further right of appeal other than possibly a judicial review of the police decision (Home Office, 2011a); the 2003 Act required a Remedial Order to introduce the reviews, and this was laid before parliament on June 14, 2011.

The parliamentary Joint Committee on Human Rights examined the proposed Remedial Order in October 2011 and found it to be somewhat wanting; the Committee "express[ed] concern about the Government's approach in this case" (House of Lords/House of Commons, 2011: 4). The Committee criticized in particular the lack of an independent element in the review and stated the need for a "proportionality test" and for any review guidance produced to be statutory guidance rather than just the administrative guidance that had been proposed (House of Lords/House of Commons, 2011) (see Chapter 2).

The Northern Ireland Department of Justice published a consultation document in July 2011 asking for views on their proposals. These were very similar to those announced in England and Wales but with the addition of allowing an appeal against the police decision to the Crown Court rather than only the recourse to a judicial review as in England and Wales (Department of Justice (Northern Ireland), 2011; a summary of responses can be accessed at http://www.dojni.gov.uk/index/public-consultations/archive-consultations/summary_of_responses_to_consultation_on_sex_offender_notification_and_violent_offender_orders.pdf). At the time of writing (December 2011) no further action has been taken in Northern Ireland.

Discussion

The United States and the United Kingdom appear to be on roughly parallel lines when it comes to sex offender registration. The US arrangements appear to be more onerous and the United Kingdom has not attempted any universal right of access to the register or any form of "community notification," but it has developed its own forms of selective disclosure. Both jurisdictions are experiencing the difficulties of focusing a growing bureaucratic public protection system on to the wide and varied patterns of behavior of those people we call sex offenders; unintended consequences are almost inevitable. In the United Kingdom the legislators have run into the constraining influence of the European Convention on Human Rights, and in the United States problems are being experienced in the implementing of a federal law at state level. These difficulties are all taking place within a hostile climate of press and public opinion directed at sex offenders and of which legislators feel obliged to take note.

On the same day that the UK Home Secretary announced the new proposals to "review" lifetime registrants in February 2011, she had also proposed a further tightening and strengthening of the sex offender register. The timing was clearly designed to reinforce the message that the government was not happy to have to introduce the reviews demanded by the Supreme Court and was therefore compensating by making the register yet more robust. The new proposals were that in future people on the register would have to notify the police of *all* foreign travel and not just travel lasting more than three days, provide more personal information about bank and credit card details, and notify the presence of any children living in the same household. Homeless people on the register would be asked to report weekly to the police (Home Office, 2011b). The existing restrictions on travel had already been cited by the courts as one of the reasons for ruling the current arrangements incompatible with the European Convention and yet further restrictions were now being proposed (see Chapter 26).

In the United States other bureaucratic restrictions have been added to make communities safer. The use of "sex offender residency restrictions" have been introduced by many states which prevent registered sex offenders living close to schools or child care facilities (see Chapter 25). Distances of 1,000 to 2,500 feet have been invoked as the safety margin. This has led to people having to move home and having their family lives disrupted, despite the fact that there is little evidence that these restrictions make much difference; as one offender commented:

> It doesn't matter where a sex offender lives if he sets his mind on re-offending . . . he just gets closer by walking or driving. I never noticed how many schools and parks there were until I had to stay away from them. (Levenson and Cotter, 2005: 174)

The residency restrictions have also led to homelessness and in an extreme case in Florida to sex offenders creating their own shanty town of tents and cardboard boxes under the Julia Tuttle Causeway Bridge (Allen, 2009). The United Kingdom has been more selective with its imposition of restrictions, using Sex Offender Prevention Orders as customized orders for individuals (see Lieb, Kemshall and Thomas, 2011).

Making registration more than just a paper exercise has required the involvement of the police in the management of those on the register to ensure their compliance. Policing has traditionally been about crime prevention and crime investigation but now as custodians of the sex offender register there is a requirement that they risk assess and manage sex offenders in the community. Management means supervision and monitoring and these are arguably new roles for the police and ones with which they are not immediately familiar. Reports in the United Kingdom suggest that the police are working well with other agencies in exchanging information but less well in actually acting on that information, making clear risk assessments and having clearly defined lead agencies in the management process (Criminal Justice Joint Inspection, 2011).

In the United Kingdom there have been cases of the police not fully knowing the law on registration and having to pay compensation to people falling foul of their lack of knowledge (*Yorkshire Post*, 2009). Conversely people on the sex offender register have continued to offend (see, for example, IPCC, 2009, 2011).

Elsewhere it has been argued that sex offender registers are:

> [a] policy made in a research vacuum, with ill-defined and hesitant aims, which is then left "hanging in the air" to be adjusted and amended by politicians listening to the practitioners and specialist lobby groups as well as the public reactions to the latest high-profile crime against a child. (Thomas, 2010: 72)

The result has been a policy without an evidence base that shows that registers make any difference at all, that has nonetheless become ever more punitive and hawkish with only limited restraining influences. Sex offenders are the one group it is acceptable to hate (Spencer, 2009). While the US federal authorities wait to see if all the states can comply with the AWA and the UK government considers the changes to their review proposals put forward by the Joint Committee on Human Rights, other difficulties will doubtless continue to arise for those trying to implement sex offender registers.

Note

1   Byrne Funding is a mechanism allowing the federal government to help fund local state criminal justice programs; it is administered by the federal Bureau of Justice Assistance and named in memory of police officer Edward Byrne, killed at the age of 22 while on duty in New York City in 1988.

References

Allen, G. (2009) Sex offenders forced to live under Miami bridge, May 20, http://www.npr.org/templates/story/story.php?storyId=104150499 (accessed September 7, 2012).

ATSA (Association for the Treatment of Sexual Abusers) (2010) Facts about Adult Sex Offenders, http://www.gimeweb.com/index.php?option=com_content&view=article&id=214:atsa-facts-about-sexual-abusers&catid=157:facts&Itemid=25 (accessed June 28, 2011).

Bennetto, J. (2000) "Straw refuses to grant the public access to sex offenders register but proposes stricter laws," *Independent*, September 16, p. 1.

Boerner, D. (1992) "Confronting violence: in the act and in the word," *University of Puget Sound Law Review* 15, 3, 525–577.

Bryan, T. and Doyle, P. (2003) "Developing multi agency public protection panels," in A. Matravers (ed.), *Sex Offenders in the Community*. Cullompton: Willan Publishing, pp. 189–206.

Cann, J. (2007) *Assessing the Extent of Discretionary Disclosure under the Multi-Agency Public Protection Arrangements (MAPPA). Home Office On-line Report 13/07*, http://webarchive.nationalarchives.gov.uk/20110218135832/http://rds.homeoffice.gov.uk/rds/pdfs07/rdsolr1307.pdf (accessed September 15, 2012).

Chan, V., Homes, A., Murray, L. and Treanor, S. (2010) Evaluation of the sex offender community disclosure pilot, http://www.scotland.gov.uk/Publications/2010/10/25093915/0 (accessed September 15, 2012).

Criminal Justice Joint Inspection (2010) *Restriction and Rehabilitation: Getting the Right Mix – An Inspection of the Management of Sexual Offenders in the Community*. London: HM Inspectorate Probation and HM Inspectorate Constabulary.

Criminal Justice Joint Inspection (2011) *Putting the Pieces Together: An Inspection of Multi Agency Public Protection Arrangements*. London: HM Inspectorate Probation and HM Inspectorate Constabulary.

Department of Justice (2008) Department of Justice announces improvements and name change for Dru Sjodin Sex Offender Public Web Site, http://www.ojp.gov/newsroom/pressreleases/2008/smart09009.htm (accessed September 7, 2012).

Department of Justice (2009) Justice Department announces first two jurisdictions to implement Sex Offender Registration and Notification Act, http://www.ojp.usdoj.gov/newsroom/pressreleases/2009/SMART09154.htm (accessed September 7, 2012).

Department of Justice (2010) Justice Department announces fifth jurisdiction to implement Sex Offender Registration and Notification Act, http://www.ojp.usdoj.gov/newsroom/pressreleases/2010/SMART10072.htm (accessed September 7, 2012).

Department of Justice (2011) Justice Department finds 24 jurisdictions have substantially implemented SORNA requirements, http://www.ojp.usdoj.gov/newsroom/pressreleases/2011/SMART_PR-072811.htm (accessed September 7, 2012).

Department of Justice (Northern Ireland) (2011) *Consultation on Sex Offender Notification and Violent Offender Orders – Proposals for Legislation: A Consultation Paper*. Belfast: Public Protection Unit.

Federal Register (1997) "Final guidelines for Megan's Law and the Jacob Wetterling Crimes against Children and Sexually Violent Offender Registration Act," 62 (139): 39009–39020, July 21.

Federal Register (1999) "Megan's Law: final guidelines for the Jacob Wetterling Crimes against Children and Sexually Violent Offender Registration Act as amended," 64 (2): 572–587, January 5.

Federal Register (2007) "Office of the Attorney General: applicability of the Sex Offender Registration and Notification Act," 72 (39): 8894–8897, February 28.

Federal Register (2008) "Office of the Attorney General: the National Guidelines for Sex Offender Registration and Notification," 73 (128): 38030–38070, July 2.

Hebenton, B. (2009) "Comparative analysis of the management of sexual offenders in the USA and UK," in J.L. Ireland, C.A. Ireland and P. Birch (eds), *Violent and Sexual Offenders: Assessment, Treatment and Management*. Cullompton: Willan Publishing, pp. 257–283.

HM Government (2008) *Saving Lives. Reducing Harm. Protecting the Public. An Action Plan for Tackling Violence 2008–11*. London: Home Office.

Home Office (1999) *Draft Guidance on the Disclosure of Information about Sex Offenders who May Present a Risk to Children and Vulnerable Adults*. London: Police Science and Technology Unit.

Home Office (2007) *Review of the Protection of Children from Sex Offenders*. London: Home Office.

Home Office (2010) *The Child Sex Offender (CSO) Disclosure Scheme Guidance Document 1*, Circular 007/2010. London: Home Office.

Home Office (2011a) *Impact Assessment: Reviewing Offenders Subject to Indefinite Notification Requirements (Part 2 of Sexual Offences Act 2003)*. London: Home Office.

Home Office (2011b) *Reforming the Notification Requirements of Registered Sex Offenders (Part 2 of the Sexual Offences Act 2003): A Targeted Consultation*. London: Home Office.

Home Office/Scottish Executive (2001) *Consultation Paper on the Review of Part 1 of the Sex Offenders Act 1997*. London: Home Office/Scottish Executive.

House of Lords/House of Commons (2011) *Proposal for the Sexual Offences Act 2003 (Remedial) Order 2011*, Joint Committee on Human Rights 19th Report of Session 2010–12, HL paper 200/HC 1549, October. London: The Stationery Office.

IPCC (Independent Police Complaints Commission) (2009) IPCC investigation finds organisational failing with Gwent police, http://www.ipcc.gov.uk/news/Pages/pr180509_hewitt.aspx?auto=True&l1link=pages%2Fnews.aspx&l1title=News%20and%20press&l2link=news%2FPages%2Fdefault.aspx&l2title=Press%20Releases (accessed September 7, 2012).

IPCC (Independent Police Complaints Commission) (2011) *Report on the Investigation into the Management of a Registered Sex Offender by Merseyside Police Sex Offender Unit, 24 August*. London: IPCC.

Jenkins, P. (1998) *Moral Panic: Changing Concepts of the Child Molester in Modern America*. London and New Haven: Yale University Press.

Kemshall, H. (2008) *Understanding the Community Management of High Risk Offenders*. Maidenhead: McGraw Hill/Open University Press.

Kemshall, H. and Wood, J. with Westwood, S. *et al.* (2010) *Research Report 32: Child Sex Offender Review (CSOR) Public Disclosure Pilots: A Process Evaluation*. London: Home Office.

Levenson, J. and Cotter, R. (2005) "The impact of sex offender restrictions: 1000 feet from danger or one step from absurd," *International Journal of Offender Therapy and Comparative Criminology* 49, 168–177.

Lieb, R., Kemshall, H. and Thomas, T. (2011) "Post-release controls for sex offenders in the US and UK," *International Journal of Law and Psychiatry* 34, 226–232.

Logan, W. (2003) "Jacob's legacy: sex offender registration and community notification laws, practice and procedure in Minnesota," *William Mitchell Law Review* 29, 4, 1287–1341.

Logan, W. (2009) *Knowledge as Power: Criminal Registration and Community Notification Laws in America*. California: Stanford University Press.

National Offender Management Service (2009) *MAPPA Guidance 2009 Version 3.0.* London: Public Protection Unit.

Obergfell-Fuchs, J. (2011) Experiences with sex offender registration in Germany. Paper presented at the annual meeting of the American Society of Criminology, Washington DC, November 19.

Oprah Winfrey Show (2009) Help get funding for the Adam Walsh Child Protection and Safety Act, April 15, www.oprah.com/world/Adam-Walsh-Child-Protection-and-Safety-Act/print/1 (accessed September 7, 2012).

Spencer, D. (2009) "Sex offender as homo sacer," *Punishment and Society* 11, 2, 219–40.

Thomas, T. (2003) "Sex offender community notification: the American experience," *Howard Journal of Criminal Justice* 42, 3, 217–228.

Thomas, T. (2008) "The Sex Offender Register: a case study in function creep," *Howard Journal of Criminal Justice* 47, 3, 227–237.

Thomas, T. (2009) "The Sex Offender Register: some observations on the time periods for registration," *Howard Journal of Criminal Justice* 48, 3, 257–266.

Thomas, T. (2010) "The Sex Offender Register, community notification and some reflections on privacy," in K. Harrison (ed.), *Managing High-Risk Sex Offenders in the Community: Risk Management, Treatment and Social Responsibility.* Cullompton: Willan Publishing, pp. 61–78.

Thomas, T. (2011) *The Registration and Monitoring of Sex Offenders: A Comparative Study.* London: Routledge.

US House of Representatives (2009) *Sex Offender Notification and Registration Act (SORNA): Barriers to Timely Compliance by States,* Sub Committee on Crime, Terrorism and Homeland Security, of the Committee on the Judiciary, March 10, Serial No. 111–21G.

Yorkshire Post (2009) "Taxpayers pick up £23,000 bill after sex offender sues police for wrongful arrest," July 20, p. 1.

22

A More Ethical Way
of Working
Circles of Support and Accountability
Stephen Hanvey and Mechtild Höing

Introduction

The return to society of an offender after a prolonged prison sentence for serious sexual assault presents a complex challenge for more than just that individual. Justice has been seen to have been done, although victims of such crimes may live with devastating consequences long beyond the sentence itself. Statutory agencies will do their best to meet the legal obligations of monitoring and managing the risks still posed, and the wider community, by and large, will be happy to leave it all to the law enforcement agencies; unless of course they happen to discover their street now houses one such returnee. Any volunteer-based program, therefore, which purports to assist and support the reintegration of those with sexual convictions back into society might seem to be either dangerously naive, willfully irresponsible or a combination of both. Its advocates, however, would argue that it is a more ethically desirable way of responding; highly successful in reducing sexual re-offending; and, fully in tune with sex offender treatment programs, which increasingly draw on the "Good Lives" principles of achieving the "human goods" viewed as integral to effective offender rehabilitation (Ward and Stewart, 2003). This chapter will describe the objectives and process of the rapidly growing Circles of Support and Accountability (COSA) program now embedded in Canada, some US states, England, Wales, Scotland, the Netherlands and a few other European countries. It will also explore the ethical questions and theoretical principles, effectiveness and scope for future developments. The heart of the COSA program is perhaps most simply conveyed in the words of the German poet Goethe: "If you treat an individual as he is, he will stay as he is, but if you treat him as if he were what he ought to be and could be, he will become what he ought to be and could be."

The Wiley-Blackwell Handbook of Legal and Ethical Aspects of Sex Offender Treatment and Management,
First Edition. Edited by Karen Harrison and Bernadette Rainey.
© 2013 John Wiley & Sons, Ltd. Published 2013 by John Wiley & Sons, Ltd.

Differing Community Responses

Before describing how COSA operate as a community-based program, it may be valuable to remind ourselves of the usual social context and response to those who have committed the most repellent of offenses against children and young people. This will quickly route us to some of the ethical challenges around retributive and rehabilitative approaches to those with such serious convictions. One influential part of this wider social context is the role and function of the press (see Chapter 8). Nevertheless, the serendipity of the *News of the World*'s "name and shame" campaign in 2000 with the arrival of COSA in the United Kingdom from Canada that very year, merits a revisiting of some of the interplay and further sharpens questions raised. By what right does any institution – for example, a tabloid newspaper or indeed a well-intentioned group of local individuals – claim a moral authority to protect the public in its chosen manner? Whose "community" is it exactly that such claims are being made for, with such markedly opposing strategic intentions of social exclusion or inclusion? It would appear that the questions originate at a local level, and in this there may be some indication as to where they can be addressed most effectively. Philpot for instance (Hanvey, Philpot and Wilson, 2011: 177) refers to the evidence of other writers that national press campaigns, such as "naming and shaming began with local and regional newspapers campaigns and only later was adopted by the national press." The drive to remove, to exclude, and thereby to continue the punishment of those who have committed these offenses, in a manner it must be recognized that finds no matching hostility for any other offending group, is entirely contrary to the community-based rehabilitative imperative proposed by some. Tim Newell, a former prison governor and early encourager of COSA in the United Kingdom, frames rehabilitation as a mutually dependent process, and one certainly not to be left solely to the statutory agencies. In *Forgiving Justice: A Quaker Vision for Criminal Justice*, he states:

> The offender has obligations, but so has the community: to respond to the criminal not just as someone who should be condemned or ostracised for the crime, but as someone who must be urged and helped to repent the crime and restore himself or herself to the community. (Newell, 2007: 87)

As representatives of an offended against community, much in the way of a Crown Court jury, COSA volunteers assume one side of this responsibility, by both supporting and also holding to account the ex-offender now committed to an offense-free life. As is explored below, there are clearly connections of principle and purpose between COSA and the broader approach of restorative justice, as rehabilitative rather than retributive, and "community-owned." A marked difference, however, is that whereas restorative justice programs, at least those working largely with young offenders in the United Kingdom, bring together victim and offender, COSA includes no such element of face-to-face contact. A proportion of Core Members will have abused family members and all contact with dependents is likely to have been terminated around the time of conviction. There have been instances however, over time, of tentative connections being re-established with grown-up offspring, once any license restrictions have come to an end; COSA volunteers would certainly be expected to provide feedback in their supervision meetings with their Coordinator their perceptions as to the motivation and risks in such possible reconnections.

The Origins, Operation and Development of COSA

It was in Ontario, Canada in 1994 that a Mennonite fellowship accepted into its midst a notoriously high risk sex offender, Charlie Taylor, as he left prison, friendless, unwanted anywhere, and, unsurprisingly, much to the resistance, fear and anger of the local Hamilton community. The small group of church volunteers or "Circle," set around Charlie Taylor and coordinated by their Pastor, Harry Nigh, were there to go out with him when he needed to go out, to ensure he both had some degree of safe social contact, but was also kept focused on the task of not getting back into re-offending ways or opportunities. As months and indeed years passed with no re-offending by Charlie, the success of this eminently simple, albeit labor-intensive approach was noted by prison authorities across Canada who were looking to release others who presented similar risks post-incarceration. Very quickly the concept of "Circles of Support and Accountability" was developed and taken up by other Mennonite fellowships across Canada. Both functions, "support" and "accountability," are critical to the model; COSA have never been about simply providing such individuals with unconditional and unquestioning support. Part of their attraction was, and continues to be, given the volunteer-base of the service, the relatively low cost compared with the considerable expense of further custody, treatment programs and so on. One police public protection officer has commented to one of the authors how he appreciates the local, additional surveillance COSA can provide: " I know I've got a another four or five pairs of eyes keeping a look out on this guy and what he's up to" (M. Ashthorpe, personal communication, 2009). The key expenses of COSA are the salary of the professionally qualified coordinator who selects, trains and supervises the local volunteers and the expenses of the volunteers themselves, in travel, further training and so on.

The heart of COSA is these locally recruited, carefully screened and trained volunteers who commit, for a minimum of one year, serving in groups of four or five, to giving practical and social support to someone with convictions for serious sexual offenses, and who otherwise would be totally isolated in the community and at a high risk of re-offending. This individual, however, known in the Circle as the "Core Member," is just as much a volunteer, crucially recognizing the risk he or she still poses, and expressly not wanting to re-offend.[1] Their participation in a Circle is not part of their license conditions, thereby avoiding any risk of "plea-bargaining" when release from prison is being considered. On a weekly basis, moving to fortnightly over time, in a discreet and confidential setting such as a community center room, church facility or similar, the Circle will meet for an hour or so and the conversation will focus on what the Core Member has been doing to keep to his relapse prevention plan and avoid re-offending. The regular meeting is not some form of treatment-manqué, or therapy, but focused on the here and now of practical adjustment to living again in society. Social events will be arranged between one or two volunteers and the Core Member from time to time, going to see a film in a risk-managed manner, meeting up for a cup of coffee on a Saturday morning, and marking occasions which otherwise can of themselves become alienating and depressing reminders of isolation and loneliness; that is, birthdays, festivals and community events. A designated mobile phone is given to volunteers, for the contacts with the Core Member between meetings, protecting family privacy and marking the boundaries essential to COSA practice.

The training COSA volunteers undertake stresses that the objective is not to become "friends" with the Core Member but rather to model, and to help the individual develop, those pro-social skills that will enhance his ability to develop appropriate adult relationships. This is of itself supportive, but together with this objective goes the parallel attention to accountability. A written contract, agreed before commencement of the Circle between the Core Member and the volunteers, serves to remove one of the most dangerous ploys of control and grooming through which previous offending has often been made more possible: the enforcement of "secrets." In essence the volunteers will know the broad nature of the sexual offending history of their Core Member and crucially he will know that they know.

Fundamental to the "contract" between the Core Member and their particular COSA volunteers is the notification for the Core Member that if the volunteers, who are supervised by the professionally qualified coordinator, have any concerns as to his attitudes, his behavior or a failure to commit and engage with the process, this will be immediately fed back to the offender manager. This may result in a recall to custody ensuing, if the nature of the concerns raised by the volunteers is felt by statutory partners to signify an unacceptable increase in risk. Critically around this "inner" Circle of trained and supervised volunteers is an "outer" ring or "external Circle" which is made up of partner agencies also involved in the management of the Core Member; police, the probation service, mental health specialists and so on. In England and Wales, Circles intentionally complement the work of the Multi-Agency Public Protection Arrangement (MAPPA) partners, providing further valuable data as to the "ups and downs" of the Core Member's life back in the community. Thus the Circle volunteers can provide an additional early warning system, including more positive feedback, as to any hopeful developments in the individual's known and perceived personal circumstances which might support a reduction in the statutory agencies' assessment of dynamic risk factors.

Written accounts of the weekly meetings with the Core Member, as volunteers work to keep him focused on all that he can be doing to avoid falling back into reoffending patterns and situations, contribute to the essential information bank for better management needed by statutory partners. Indeed a somewhat counterintuitive aspect of COSA is the willing participation of ex-offenders in a scheme that is quite overt about reporting concerns to the agencies, reports which may trigger further incarceration. The answer may be in the underlying commitment not to reoffend, variable though that may be from one day to the next for the Core Member, and, as time goes by, in the respect he develops for the volunteers who give so freely of their own time, helping him to complete housing application forms, accompanying him on hospital visits, meeting for social events and so on. Feedback from Core Members repeatedly stresses how nowhere else in their lives do they have this very basic human support, and often it is the first ever real sense of acceptance of them as individuals greater than the sum of their offending past, rather than the "monster" often portrayed in the media. One Core Member has expressed this in terms of the invaluable ordinariness of the service:

> They're ordinary things, but extremely precious because that's somebody that's not giving up their time because they have to; they're giving up their time because they want to. That's incredible for them to actually sort of say, "I wanna spend time with you." (Hanvey, Philpot and Wilson, 2011: 85)

Having been introduced to the COSA model, a number of probation authorities and police forces in the United Kingdom became reassured of their validity and cost-effectiveness over time, particularly with the arrival of a national "code of practice," introduced and applied by the national charity, Circles UK, in 2009. By 2011 the original two key pilot COSA projects funded by the Home Office, originally three before a merging of two of them, had grown. At the time of writing (December 2011) there are 11 local programs, running over 70 Circles across England and Wales, with 400 volunteers. Interest in Circles by the probation services of the Netherlands, encouraged and facilitated by academics from Avans University of Applied Sciences who work closely with the probation services, resulted in COSA developments in pilot schemes in the southern part of the Netherlands and a joint, successful application to the European Commission from Avans, Circles UK and Justitiehuis Antwerpen (Antwerp House of Justice, the local probation service). This application was for two-year funding to enable the further roll-out of Circles and to develop a European COSA Handbook which has now been produced to encourage and facilitate the establishment of the model, with vital consistency of operational standards, across any other European state interested, and which is described below. Throughout the Netherlands there are now 16 Circles in operation, while in Belgium, due to implementation problems as a result of political problems, there is now one Circle on its way. The European COSA Handbook can be accessed through the web sites www.cosanederland.nl/research and www.circles-uk.org.uk.

Evaluation and Research

For any new model, and especially one which appropriates elements of a highly professionalized sphere of work into a more community-based arena, the need to evidence effectiveness is pronounced. Given the longer establishment of COSA in Canada, the key research so far has been undertaken there, with reassuring and impressive findings. Two matched control studies have been able to compare male sex offenders who have had substantial time in a Circle with those who have not. In Wilson, Picheca and Prinzo's study (2007b) and a replication study (Wilson, Cortoni and McWhinnie, 2009), reductions in sexual re-offending of up to 83% were demonstrated in the COSA groups. The first part of the 2007 study (Wilson, Picheca and Prinzo, 2007a), which involved a COSA group of 60 men and a matched control cohort of the same number, had also researched the perspectives of Core Members, volunteers and statutory partners on COSA. Of the professionals interviewed (n = 17), 70% reported that what they liked most about COSA was that they increase offender responsibility and accountability, and 63% reported that community safety was the focus.

More recently in England, one of the original two COSA pilot projects, Hampshire and Thames Valley Circles Project, has reviewed their first 60 Core Members, after nine years of Circles provision. Having double-checked their own reconviction data against the Police National Computer record, just one reconviction was identified for a sexual offense by this group of medium and high risk offenders (Bates *et al.*, 2011). This small-scale study, while having no matched comparison group, is also illuminating in highlighting a number of pro-social achievements made by Core Members, in terms of developing more stable relationships outside the Circle and progress in relation to better management of challenges related to drug and alcohol dependency. During their time in the Circle, for instance, nearly 50% of Core Members were supported and encouraged by their volunteers to access employment and education. The study also identified that 13% of the Core Members surveyed had support for drug or alcohol problems from the Circle that they felt were beneficial, and nearly 50% had improved their links with their families and increased their support networks, other than the Circle itself. While in any ideal, and perhaps hermetically sealed, world of research, a randomized control study would be desirable for most accurately examining the identifiable and attributable impact of COSA in reducing sexual re-offending, ethical considerations render this impossible. The motivation of Core Members is of course central to the model and could be factored in to any such study, although, as anyone who has ever tried to give up anything can attest, a fervent intention to desist is not of itself a guaranteed elixir. Meanwhile COSA remain committed to developing matched control studies as numbers of Circles grow and render this at least an ever more fruitful avenue for evaluation. However, it is also gratifying to recognize that where COSA have been in operation in England and Wales since 2002 for instance, not one of the 21 probation trusts, nor one of a similar number of police forces, who refer and often support their local project financially, have withdrawn their engagement, citing any reservations as to COSA's process, integrity or effectiveness.

COSA in the Field of Restorative Justice

As COSA become more and more an accepted and appreciated part of effective sex offender management in the community, there is also a growing need for a normative positioning of this approach within the field of restorative justice (see Chapter 7), and a need to account for the ideological roots of its mission statements and the changes they have gone through while the concept has been implemented in other jurisdictions. In contemporary sex offender rehabilitation, three tendencies influence policies and practice. First, there is a punitive, restrictive, excluding tendency (actuarial justice) which is focused on public protection and retribution (La Fond, 2008;

Vess, 2009). Examples of this approach are long detention policies, preventive deten-tion (see Chapter 9) and specific sex offender laws about notification (see Chapter 21) and housing restrictions (see Chapter 25). A more inclusive, restorative approach focuses on community peace and reconciliation between offender and victim(s) by restoration of damage done to victims (restorative justice) (Ward, 2009; Ward and Langlands, 2009). Examples of this approach are initiatives like peace conferences, offender–victim encounters and community services. A third tendency is an inclusive communitarian approach, focusing on community safety, offender reintegration and reconciliation between offender and the community (Raynor and Robinson, 2009; McNeill, 2009). This approach is often also called "restorative" justice, because of the restorative element in the main goal, with the offender ultimately leading a responsible life and contributing to the community. Restoration here is a two-sided process; not only is the offender expected to restore damage done to the victim and society, by acknowledging responsibility and changing his behavior, but the com-munity is also restoring the harm which is done to the offender's resources and opportunities through detention and punishment by getting involved with and actively supporting his re-entry into society (Raynor and Robinson, 2009; Duff, 2001). The restorative approaches to rehabilitation are attempts to overcome the dichotomy underneath the actuarial justice which positions the concerns of the offender opposite to the concerns of the victim and the community. Duff (2001) outlines a communicative theory of punishment for these restorative approaches, stating that all parties involved are members of a normative community and are bound and protected by liberal democratic values of autonomy, freedom, privacy and plural-ism. Human rights and human dignity are basic concepts and values to be respected (see Chapter 2). Offenders need to be included and at the same time need to be held accountable and take responsibility for their crimes. Repentance, reform (of behavior) and reconciliation are the main goals of rehabilitation in this view.

COSA are an example of this restorative justice approach with a strong emphasis on inclusion and community involvement based on shared values of a normative community. At the beginning, the ethical values of the COSA model were rooted in the faith-based and redemptive view of sex offender rehabilitation of a particular Mennonite church, and for many COSA volunteers and project staff, especially in Canada, this is still the case. The founders of the model, Nigh and Kirkegaard, both chaplains, believed firmly in the Christian concept of redemption and the benefits of restorative justice. They also were highly influenced by René Girard's sociological theory about the function and effects of social exclusion and scapegoating and John McKnight's (1995) views on the eroding effects of individualism on society. At the same time they were also influenced by strong supporters of community involvement like Jean Vanier, Wolf Wolvensberger, Shalom Schwartz, Jerome Miller and Rudolf Steiner (Petrunik, 2007). With the proliferation and professionalization of the COSA model through Canada and Europe, the normative basis shifted into a more rational-legal view (Petrunik, 2007).

Concepts like restorative justice, civil renewal and social inclusion are now used to describe what lies at the core of the model and have replaced the Christian termi-nology (Bates, Saunders and Wilson, 2007). More secular ways to express the three basic assumptions which are still in place are shown below:

1. Core Members are believed to be able to make significant changes in their attitudes and behavior or at least learn to control deviant impulses, and to be able
   to desist from their former criminal lifestyle (no more victims).
2. Core Members are believed to be entitled to membership of the society (no one
   is disposable).
3. Society is believed to be responsible for its own safety and to be able to take care
   of it (Petrunik, 2007; Bates, Saunders and Wilson, 2007; Wilson, McWhinnie
   and Wilson, 2008; Kirkwood and Richley, 2008).

These developments ask for a more scientific approach to COSA. Research into the
effectiveness as described earlier (Wilson, Picheca and Prinzo, 2007a, 2007b; Bates,
Saunders and Wilson, 2007; Bates *et al.*, 2011) and the development of a theoretical
model of change as described below are examples of this rationalization of COSA.

The COSA Model of Change

Ever since the first Circle in Canada dealt with a Core Member with a 100% risk of
recidivism, calmed down community upheaval at his re-entrance, and allowed him
to lead a safe and responsible life, Circles have proven to be able to meet these aims
in the great majority of cases. How is this achieved? Accounts of effective factors and
mechanisms in the COSA literature reflect three distinct perspectives: an ecological
perspective, a social learning perspective and a motivational perspective.

From the ecological perspective the key feature for effectiveness is the surrogate
social network a Circle delivers and the support, monitoring capacity and accountability it provides (Saunders and Wilson, 2003). Circles provide a healthy environment
for a Core Member by offering moral support in times of crises and by celebrating
successes and milestones. Practical support in issues of housing, work and income and
leisure activities enhance the chances of real social integration (Wilson, Picheca
and Prinzo, 2007a; Brown and Dandurand, 2007; Petrunik, 2007). Monitoring
capacity is built by close cooperation between the Circle and professional agencies
involved in sex offender after-care, as signals of changes in risk or problem behavior
are communicated to the professionals in the outer Circle. Accountability is realized
by confronting the Core Member about inadequate behavior and attitudes and by
encouraging the use of adequate coping strategies. From a social learning perspective,
a key factor for effectiveness is the fact that the volunteers encourage a healthy lifestyle
by modeling behavior, decrease social isolation by teaching the Core Member how
to make friends and to build and sustain a trusting relationship with adults, and
enlarge his self-efficacy by expressing their belief in his ability to change (Wilson,
Picheca and Prinzo, 2007a).

Finally, from the motivational perspective, the quality of the relationship between
Core Member and volunteers and the active involvement of the Core Member in the
goal setting of the Circle is essential. The voluntary commitment of members of
the society, a shared and meaningful agreement to the general aim ("no more
victims") and openness ("no secrets") through a written covenant (Brown and
Dandurand, 2007; Petrunik, 2007) are key features that support a moral bond

and increase the motivation to not disappoint the Circle. To achieve this, a perceived reciprocity in the relationship between Core Member and volunteers is necessary (Höing and Vogelvang, 2011). The voluntary commitment by the Core Member is based on intrinsic motivation through deeply felt social needs and on the fact that the intervention targets are defined in cooperation with the Core Member (Wilson, Picheca and Prinzo, 2007b; Höing and Vogelvang, 2011).

Important preconditions for the effectiveness of COSA are model integrity and program integrity. Model integrity is achieved when the Circle is able to build a trusting relationship and when monitoring, support and accountability processes in the Circle are balanced and meet the specific needs of the core member. Also good working alliances between the inner and outer Circle and a high level of cooperation between professionals in the organizations involved in sex offender after-care are needed to achieve model integrity (Höing and Vogelvang, 2011). Program integrity (integrity to quality standards of deliverance) is essential with regard to selection, training, coaching and supervision of volunteers and the selection of Core Members. Personal characteristics of individual volunteers (knowledge, skills and personality) contribute to the Circle dynamics and the level of model integrity (balanced execution of support, monitoring and accountability), while personal characteristics of the Core Member (level of risk, need for support and responsivity) determine the possible range of change in dynamic risk and protective factors. The role of the Circle coordinator is crucial in safeguarding the quality of Circles.

Theoretical Support

In the past decades theories on effective sex offender rehabilitation and relapse prevention have shifted from models that concentrate on mere risk reduction, like the Relapse Prevention model (Pithers *et al.*, 1983) and the Risk, Needs, Responsivity (RNR) model (Andrews and Bonta, 2003), on to more comprehensive models, that include the perspective of the offender and his personal needs and biography, like the Good Lives/self-regulation model (Ward and Stewart, 2003; Ward and Gannon, 2006) and the literature on desistance (Maruna and Toch, 2003; Farral and Calverley, 2006; McNeill, 2009). These models are all at least partly supported by empirical evidence. The COSA approach is comprehensive and incorporates several effective aspects of these models of change. The key ideas of relapse prevention theory are incorporated into the functions of the inner Circle: to offer support, especially in stressful circumstances, monitor behavior, but also emotional deterioration, and hold the Core Member accountable for exercising adequate relapse prevention strategies.

The COSA model is in line with the Risk and Needs principles in the RNR model, which state that the intensity of the intervention should match the level of risk and criminogenic needs. Circles are reserved for medium to high risk sex offenders with a high need for social support, which is apparent in a tendency to isolate themselves, further increasing risk. The responsivity principle of the RNR model states that the intervention should match the learning abilities and learning style of the offender (see Chapter 14). In COSA, this principle is met by the careful selection of volunteers and through the matching of volunteers with the sex offender and his specific needs.

Quarterly evaluations of the Circle process using a standardized scoring instrument are held to monitor the progress of the Core Member.

The holistic and strength-based approach of the Good Lives/self-regulation model is represented in COSA both in the humanistic view of sex offender reintegration and in the fact that Circles work with the sex offender as a whole person (see Chapter 17). He is not only supported in managing risk and risk factors, but also encouraged and supported by the Circle volunteers to develop adequate skills and strategies to achieve goals that are instrumental to primary needs such as autonomy, intimacy, mastery and so on. Within the Circle, the specific needs of the offender are assessed and action plans are made. The Circle advises, assists and models adequate strategies, skills and behavior to target these needs.

Finally, the model is consistent with desistance theory, which places the offender's behavior in a biographical context. The absence of recidivism is described not as an outcome of treatment or intervention, but as a result of an individual process of a former offender. The motors of these processes, according to McNeill (2009), are three characteristics of the offender and his environment: his human capital (skills and social competences); his social capital (the quality of his social network – in terms of bonding within intimate relationships, linking him to external resources and bridging diverse lifestyles and life experiences); and the transitions in his narrative identity (the cognitions he holds about himself). The building of a positive narrative identity is a key feature of desistance. Circles help the Core Member to build social and human capital, and support and encourage the development of a positive narrative identity. Social capital is increased by offering a surrogate social network, by supporting the Core Member in his efforts to develop a social network of his own and to improve the quality of relationships within his existing social network. Human capital (social skills, adequate coping strategies and self-regulation skills) is increased by offering modeling behavior, by holding the Core Member accountable for his actions and by encouraging him to practice and enforce the skills and strategies he has learned in sex offender therapy. The Circle supports the Core Member in his efforts to build a positive narrative identity by offering him a safe space to incorporate his offense history into the narrative about himself. In the Circle, the Core Member experiences that disclosure does not lead to exclusion and rejection, as long as he accepts responsibility and allows himself to be held accountable. The unique monitoring role of the Circle addresses the fact that desistance is not a linear process. Critical incidents and life events may occur and may bring about emotional stress, raising the level of risk of re-offending. Not all Core Members are at all times able to show appropriate coping strategies. The limited monitoring capacity of professional organizations like police and probation services is supported and extended by the Circle. Frequent contact and explicit discussions about the emotional state of the Core Member, confronting him with signals of emotional setbacks, reduce the opportunity for him to isolate himself and fall back into problem behavior without anyone noticing. The exchange of this kind of information with professionals in the outer Circle allows immediate and adequate intervention if risk levels are unacceptably high. Finally, COSA acknowledge the fact that sustainable desistance is a process that not only takes time but is sometimes not a realistic option– therefore Circles are able to offer long-term support. The first Canadian Circles (and many after them) offered their very high risk Core Members lifelong support, which resulted in no recidivism.

Community Support

While empirical and theoretical evidence of effectiveness regarding relapse prevention is of primary concern to professionals and researchers, policy makers and politicians are also concerned with the broader effects on public safety and on the community. Public safety is not only a matter of crime statistics, but is also a subjective variable, dominating the political agenda more and more. Research into the community effects of COSA show their potential to increase subjective feelings of public safety (Wilson, Picheca and Prinzo, 2007a). An explanation for this effect is probably that in restorative justice approaches like COSA, it is not only the sex offender who has to change; the community itself goes through transitions. Through a Circle, the local community takes responsibility for the safe re-socialization of sex offenders and offers opportunities for real reintegration, thereby increasing the agency and empowerment of local members of society. In the past decades, Western societies have gone through significant transitions. Traditional moral institutions and values, such as well-established faith communities, trade unions and family, have been eroded and there is a space for new organizing frameworks for community survival and peaceful cohabitation. While moral standards and values have become highly individualized, the boundaries of individual freedom have been collectively chosen as the grid that needs to be secured in order to maintain social cohesion. The need for safety has become a growing concern and Western sociologists speak of "fear driven societies" (for example, Bauman, 2007). Punitive systems in this context transcend their original function to canalize revenge into proportionate vindication, to prevent new crimes and to rehabilitate the offender, and now also function to express the moral standards of society. Safety (and also "security") has become an organizing principle for society – or at least is presented as a reasonable option by those who believe in a "safe new world" (Boutellier, 2011). While the need for safety seems to grow in our age of uncertainties (Bauman, 2007), trust in the power and competency of politicians and governments to meet this need has declined. There is a growing call for civil commitment and participation of members of society in order to make safety a shared responsibility. In the opinion of Andrew McWhinnie (2011), one of the first Circles advocates in the professional field, the unique involvement of volunteers in sex offender rehabilitation through Circles is a way of community building that in the past decades has been compromised by the professionalization of justice and probation. In line with Christie's (1977) theory on community building through resolving conflict, McWhinnie states that through Circles the community reclaims the conflict and by this activates its innate capacity to preserve order and to make peace.

Of course the willingness of volunteers to step into this process of change cannot be taken for granted, and an important part of COSA project development is informing the public and recruiting volunteers. Experiences in the United Kingdom and the Netherlands show that it is important to invest in good public relations and that media attention for COSA, even if negative, is an effective way to recruit volunteers who want to contribute to a safer community. In the Netherlands, serious media coverage is generally in favor of Circle projects and offers opportunities to inform the public about effective sex offender management in the community. The careful preparation of Circle projects takes time – nine to 12 months is not exceptional, and sufficient financial support is essential to guarantee quality deliverance and sustainability. In Canada, the United Kingdom and the Netherlands, the government supports the COSA model through sustainable financing of COSA projects, or at least parts of it, thereby also expressing the view that safe rehabilitation of sex offenders is a task for the whole community.

Professional Support

While the punitive political context which is currently dominant in many Western societies may be, in a paradoxical way, supportive of community involvement, professionals in the field of sex offender research, treatment and risk management are increasingly and more openly supportive of restorative and inclusive practices like COSA (for example, Blackwell, 2011). COSA combine the call for crime control with individual responsibility in a context of restoration and social inclusion. According to Nellis (2008), at least in the United Kingdom, this combination generates support from professional organizations such as probation services, and increasingly it even generates support from politicians, who view COSA as an answer to the media pressure and general anxiety about sex offenders re-entering society. Speaking at a church conference in October 2011, a British government justice minister alluded most positively to COSA and to their work with "the most excluded and despised group of offenders" and applauded the way in which "carrying out this valuable job in conjunction with the public sector agencies of the criminal justice sector elevates volunteers to being real agents of change in the rehabilitation revolution" (Circles UK, 2011). First evaluations of the implementation of COSA in the Netherlands show positive effects on the cooperation between local professionals in the field of sex offender after-care and increased monitoring capacity (Höing and Vogelvang, 2011). While professionals (especially therapists) at first may be suspicious of the volunteers' capacities to deal with high risk sex offenders, they become more and more aware of the potential of Circles and the value of their focus on daily needs, rather than the criminogenic needs which are dealt with in sex offender therapy (Höing and Vogelvang, 2011).

What Needs to Be in Place?

Starting a COSA initiative is not a simple task and should be carefully anticipated and prepared for. Like all innovations in the field of probation and community involvement the feasibility of COSA is dependent on the legal, institutional and cultural context (Canton, 2009). In the United States, COSA projects have been established by a variety of organizations and use a variety of models (Ruth-Heffelbower, 2011). In Europe, however, through a joint effort funded by the

European Commission (Daphne III program for the prevention of violence against women and children), COSA organizations in the United Kingdom, the Netherlands and Belgium have developed a European model for COSA. In this model some basic requirements have been described:

1. Government acknowledgement of and responsibility for the problem of sexual offending should be visible in the availability of victim services and professional offender treatment.
2. Sustainable funding of Circle projects should be guaranteed (for at least two years).
3. Sex offender legislation should be able to provide a legal context for the monitoring and supportive function of Circles.
4. Professional organizations in the field of sex offender after-care must be willing to cooperate with Circles and with each other.
5. Information-sharing protocols must be in place or must be developed.
6. Structured risk assessment of Core Members should be available to COSA staff.
7. COSA projects must be willing to comply with general quality standards (outlined in a code of practice) and seek (inter)national cooperation with other Circle projects to guarantee peer support and to enhance program integrity (Höing *et al.*, 2011).

The Wider European Potential and the Future

European interest in Circles is growing. New projects are being developed in Spain and Latvia, and organizations in France, Bulgaria, Romania, Germany and Sweden have also shown interest in COSA. International cooperation is encouraged by national Circle organizations in the United Kingdom and the Netherlands and by the European Organisation for Probation. There are plans for forming a European Platform that offers materials and support for high quality COSA implementation and research in European countries. However, the three partner countries (the United Kingdom, the Netherlands and Belgium) which have developed the European Handbook are mindful that certain protections need to be in place to safeguard the integrity and reputation of the essential COSA model. These protections are laid down in a Code of Practice. There are also other essential requirements regarding levels of sex offender management that must be in place, in order to be able to operate Circle projects in line with the Code of Practice; for example, availability of specific sex offender treatment and probation service engagement.

The objectives of any such European Platform, to oversee take-up and development in other member states, might be conceptualized as follows:

1. to establish an internationally agreed description of COSA, their principles, values and process;
2. to develop and provide means through which the agreed description can be shared with those seeking to introduce COSA into their national context;
3. to register the national contextual factors which may necessitate an acceptable adapted version of the COSA model;

4. to provide a collaborative network of acknowledged practitioners for the provision of training, guidance and support to new and developing national programs;
5. to apply common and agreed standards and criteria of membership for the purpose of quality assurance and "brand-protection" in the interests of all such national programs;
6. to develop learning and improve practice through the sharing and joint commission of research and evaluation;
7. To disseminate the value, benefits and potential of COSA though academic avenues and international forums and events (B. Vogelvang, personal communication, 2011).

Such potential developments underline a growing appreciation of the wider applicability of this innovative model, beyond its expansive original Canadian home.

Conclusion

Driving the development of COSA is an over-riding intention to prevent further sexual re-offending and the ongoing hurt and trauma that can stay for so long with those abused in childhood or their teenage years. It is the dependency upon volunteers, ordinary members of the community, to provide the transformational experience for someone with sexual convictions, from being the demonized social outcast to a safely functioning, albeit wary member of society, which is perhaps the elixir at the heart of COSA. The humanity of individuals who can see beyond the awful past to a possible future is conveyed in the words of Seona, one such volunteer, to whom rightly belongs the last word of this chapter:

> I believe that if someone has committed these horrendous offences – and they really are awful – and they've, for example, been to prison and served their time and perhaps done a sex offender treatment programme, come out and said they want to try to reintegrate, to rehabilitate and not to offend again, then we are doing them a disservice if we don't help them to do just that. It's no good isolating them as if they're a leper in the community, because all they do is offend again. (Hanvey, Philpot and Wilson, 2011: 149)

Note

1 While most COSA are provided for men with sexual convictions, a small number have been run for women.

References

Andrews, D.A. and Bonta, J. (2003) *The Psychology of Criminal Conduct*, 3rd edn. Cincinnati: Anderson.

Bates, A., Macrae, R., Williams, D. and Webb, C. (2011) "Ever increasing circles: a descriptive study of Hampshire and Thames Valley Circles of Support and Accountability 2002–09,"

Journal of Sexual Aggression, http://www.tandfonline.com/doi/abs/10.1080/13552600.
2010.544415 (accessed September 7, 2012).

Bates, A., Saunders, R. and Wilson, C. (2007) "Doing something about it. A follow-up study of sex offenders participating in Thames Valley Circles of Support and Accountability," *British Journal of Community Justice* 5, 21, 29–38.

Bauman, Z. (2007) *Liquid Times: Living in an Age of Uncertainty*. Cambridge: Polity Press.

Blackwell, T. (2011) "Sex abuse researcher tout rehab, no prison," *National Post*, November 4, http://www.bishop-accountability.org/news2011/11_12/2011_11_03_Blackwell_SexAbuse.htm (accessed September 15, 2007).

Boutellier, H. (2011) *De improvisatiemaatschappij [The Improvisation Society]*. Den Haag: Boom.

Brown, R. and Dandurand, Y. (2007) Successful strategies that contribute to safer communities. Paper presented at the 16th United Nations Commission on Crime Prevention and Criminal Justice, Vienna, Austria, April 23–27.

Canton, R. (2009) "Taking probation abroad," *European Journal of Probation* 1, 1, 66–78.

Christie, N. (1977) "Conflicts as property," *British Journal of Criminology* 17, 1, 1–15.

Circles UK (2011) *Business Plan 2011–14*. Reading: Circles UK.

Duff, A. (2001) "Punishment, communication and community," in D. Matravers and J. Pike (eds), *Debates in Contemporary Political Philosophy, an Anthology*. London/New York: Routledge, pp. 387–407.

Farral, S. and Calverley, A. (2006) *Understanding Desistance from Crime. Theoretical Directions in Resettlement and Rehabilitation*. Cullompton: Willan Publishing.

Hanvey, S., Philpot, T. and Wilson, C. (2011) *A Community-Based Approach to the Reduction of Sexual Reoffending*. London: Jessica Kingsley.

Höing, M., Bates, A., Caspers, J. *et al.* (2011) *European Handbook. Circles of Support and Accountability*. 's-Hertogenbosch: Circles Together for Safety.

Höing, M. and Vogelvang, B. (2011) *COSA in Nederland. Implementatiestudie. [COSA in the Netherlands. Implementation Study]*. 's-Hertogenbosch: Circles NL.

Kirkwood, S. and Richley, T. (2008) "Circles of Support and Accountability: the case for their use in Scotland to assist in the community reintegration and risk management of sexual offenders," *SCOLAG Legal Journal* 372, 236–239.

La Fond, J. (2008) "Sexually violent predator laws and the liberal state: an ominous threat to individual liberty," *International Journal of Law and Psychiatry* 31, 158–171.

Maruna, S. and Toch, H. (2003) *Making Good: How Ex-Convicts Reform and Rebuild Their Lives*. Washington, DC: American Psychological Association.

McKnight, J. (1995) *The Careless Society: Community and Its Counterfeits*. New York: Basic Books.

McNeill, F. (2009) "What works and what's just?," *European Journal of Probation* 1, 1, 21–40.

McWhinnie, A. (2011) Circles of Support and Accountability comes home. Paper presented at ATSA conference, Toronto, November 1–4.

Nellis, M. (2008) *Circles of Support and Accountability for Sex Offenders in England and Wales: Their Origins and Implementation between 1999–2005*. Unpublished: Circles UK.

Newell, T. (2007) *Forgiving Justice. A Quaker Vision for Criminal Justice*. London: Quaker Books.

Petrunik, M. (2007) "Circles of Support and Accountability: tensions between faith based and rational utilitarian responses to moral panic over high risk sex offenders," *International Journal of Restorative Justice* 3, 1, 66–89.

Pithers, W.D., Marques, J.K., Gibat, C.C. and Marlatt, G.A. (1983) "Relapse prevention with sexual aggressives: a self-control model of treatment and maintenance of change," in J.G. Greer and I.R. Stuart (eds), *The Sexual Aggressor: Current Perspectives on Treatment*. New York: Van Nostrand Reinhold, pp. 214–239.

Raynor, P. and Robinson, G. (2009) "Why help offenders? Arguments for rehabilitation as a penal strategy," *European Journal of Probation* 1, 1, 3–20.

Ruth-Heffelbower, A-C. (2011) Into the future. Expansion of Circles of Support and Accountability (COSA) in the US. Paper presented at ATSA conference, Toronto, November 1–4.

Saunders, R. and Wilson, C. (2003) *Circles of Support and Accountability in the Thames Valley – Interim Report*. London: Quaker Communications.

Vess, J. (2009) "Fear and loathing in public policy: ethical issues in laws for sex offenders," *Aggression and Violent Behavior* 14, 264–272.

Ward, T. (2009) "Dignity and human rights in correctional practice," *European Journal of Probation* 1, 2, 110–123.

Ward, T. and Gannon, T.A. (2006) "Rehabilitation, etiologic, and self-regulation: the comprehensive good lives model of treatment for sexual offenders," *Aggression and Violent Behavior* 11, 77–94.

Ward, T. and Langlands, R. (2009) "Repairing the rupture: restorative justice and the rehabilitation of offenders," *Aggression and Violent Behavior* 14, 205–214.

Ward, T. and Stewart, C. (2003) "Criminogenic needs and human needs: a theoretical model," *Psychology, Crime and Law* 9, 125–143.

Wilson, R., Cortoni, F. and McWhinnie, A. (2009) "Circles of support and accountability: a Canadian national replication of outcome findings," *Sexual Abuse: A Journal of Research and Treatment* 21, 412–430.

Wilson, R., McWhinnie, A. and Wilson, C. (2008) "Circles of Support and Accountability: an international partnership in reducing sexual offender recidivism," *HM Prison Service Journal* 178, 26–36.

Wilson, R., Picheca, J. and Prinzo, M. (2007a) "Evaluating the effectiveness of professionally facilitated volunteerism in the community-based management of high-risk sex offenders: part one – effects on participants and stakeholders," *Howard Journal* 46, 3, 289–302.

Wilson, R., Picheca, J. and Prinzo, M. (2007b) "Evaluating the effectiveness of professionally facilitated volunteerism in the community-based management of high-risk sex offenders: part two – a comparison of recidivism rates," *Howard Journal* 46, 4, 327–337.

23

Ethical Practice and the Use of the Polygraph in Working with Sex Offenders

Daniel T. Wilcox

Introduction

There is a major divide in the great polygraph debate, with researchers from an academic perspective tending to be on one side and professionals who have a practitioner orientation on the other. This chapter examines the application of the polygraph in working with sex offenders and explores the related ethical implications. Notably, the author is a psychologist working within the forensic field and not a polygraph examiner. However, as an experienced practitioner and researcher, with knowledge of the use of the polygraph, it is hoped that this perspective may assist the reader in achieving a broader understanding of these issues. Further, as a psychologist qualified to practice in the United Kingdom and Europe, I recognize that there may be an ethnocentric slant to my observations, owing, in part, to the relative recency of polygraph's employment in sex offender work on the Eastern side of the Atlantic. Nonetheless, I consider that the issue of human rights, in particular, in the post-9/11 world in which we live, represents a universal theme in Western society and I believe that the British perspective is likely to resonate with other nations that are now struggling to achieve a balance between individual rights and public safety (Vess, 2011).

It seems to me that detailed analysis of polygraphy, with regards to information gathered, scoring and data interpretation, exceeds the scope of this chapter and may also tax the patience and knowledge base of readers who would wish to consult this volume. For those who may desire a greater understanding of polygraphy in general, I would recommend a review of Abrams (1989), Matte (1996), Kleiner (2001), US Government (2006) and Wilcox (2009). Nonetheless, an overview of polygraphy theory, practice and history is provided in the following sections, to enable the reader to consider the ethical issues explored within a more meaningful context.

The Wiley-Blackwell Handbook of Legal and Ethical Aspects of Sex Offender Treatment and Management, First Edition. Edited by Karen Harrison and Bernadette Rainey.
© 2013 John Wiley & Sons, Ltd. Published 2013 by John Wiley & Sons, Ltd.

What Is the Polygraph, and How Does It Work?

Wilcox, Sosnowski and Middleton (1999: 234) provide descriptive information about what the polygraph is and how it works:

> A polygraph instrument collects physiological data from at least three systems within the human body. Convoluted rubber tubes are placed over the examinee's chest and abdominal area, to record respiratory activity. Two small metal plates are attached to the fingers to record sweat gland activity and a blood pressure cuff, or similar device, records cardiovascular activity. A typical polygraph examination will include a period referred to as a pre-test interview, a chart collection phase and a test data analysis.

In the pre-test phase, the polygraph examiner will acquaint the examinee with the polygraph procedure and the equipment to be employed. During this period, the examiner and examinee will discuss and confirm the test questions to be asked, employing a "yes or no" response format. Notably, when conducting post-conviction sex offender (polygraph) testing (PCSOT), it is quite common for examinees to make relevant disclosures about offense issues, at this early stage (Grubin *et al.*, 2004; Heil, Ahlmeyer and Simons, 2003; Wilcox, O'Keeffe and Oliver, 2009). The control or comparison question technique is the type of polygraph examination normally used in assessing sex offenders. Employing this approach, the examinee is polygraphed during the chart collection phase, when the agreed questions (relevant, irrelevant and comparison) are asked, while physiological changes in the offender are simultaneously recorded. When subsequently analyzing the data, it is the relationship between the question responses and these indices that informs the polygraphist's judgment as to whether it is considered that the examinee has been truthful or deceptive. At the conclusion of testing, based on the analysis, the polygraphist gives one of three opinions: pass, fail or, much less frequently, inconclusive results. The subsequent post-test interview is designed to gain further information, from the offender's point of view, about the test results. Often, additional disclosures are obtained at this stage from the examinee in explaining the test results, in particular, in circumstances where the test has been failed.

The Polygraph Accuracy Debate

While estimates of polygraph accuracy vary depending upon the kind of examination administered and the practitioner/researcher involved, there is a substantial general consensus that employment of the polygraph affords better assessment of deceitfulness than professional interviewers can achieve without employing this technology (English *et al.*, 2000; Grubin, 2008, 2010a; Wilcox, 2000, 2009).

Ansley (1990) asserted that when a trained polygraph examiner appropriately utilizes established test procedures, the information gathered in relation to these physiological indices can inform the examiner's decision making to levels of 90% accuracy, or above. However, the accuracy figures given are often not easy to confirm, as comparisons between laboratory and field studies are difficult to make.

The challenge arises, since the former situation is more controlled and artificial, often exploring issues of little material consequence to the examinee, while the latter conditions, though considerably more important to the examinee, are much less subject to the establishment of ground truth as a means of determining accuracy.

In the United States, the US National Research Council (2003) undertook a comprehensive assessment of the polygraph. They concluded that polygraph accuracy ranged from 81–91%. They further asserted that, while polygraph results are not infallible, they are well above chance, though falling short of perfection. In the circumstances, it was considered that the polygraph would have less utility in circumstances where likely deception rates were less than 10%; for example, in areas such as security vetting or employment selection. However, in the forensic area of sex offender treatment, its helpfulness seems much more apparent, in particular to practitioners in the field. Relatedly, Ahlmeyer *et al.* (2000: 123) noted that "sexual offenders are extremely reluctant to disclose their offending histories," and based on wide-ranging research exploring polygraphy (Buschman *et al.*, 2008, 2010; English *et al.*, 2000, 2003; Grubin, 2006; Grubin *et al.*, 2004; O'Connell, 1998; Wilcox, 2002; Wilcox and Sosnowski, 2005) as well as clinical interviews where immunity from prosecution was granted (Abel and Roleau, 1990), rates of deception were found to be very high. Notably, Grubin (2010b) found that polygraph testing increased offense-related disclosures among the sex offenders in this study by a factor of 14, with 40% of these individuals acknowledging medium to high levels of risk in their polygraph disclosures. In this post-conviction setting, the polygraph may be most appropriately viewed as a tool to assist in investigating offender behavior but not employed for evidentiary purposes.

Madsen (2009) has noted that, while the level of accuracy of polygraphy remains a subject of debate, its recognized utility in sex offender work and capacity for obtaining additional offense-related information, makes the polygraph an instrument of choice in areas where it has been introduced as a means of improving intervention work with sex offenders. However, concerns have also been raised that it may be possible to beat the polygraph, though research by Honts, Hodes and Raskin (1985) has suggested that success in doing so is unlikely, unless an individual has an opportunity to practice countermeasures while undergoing a polygraph and observing their physiological tracings. In the absence of such practice, Honts, Hodes and Raskin (1985) formed the view that successful faking was improbable. Further, it is considered that while access to such technology and training would not be impossible, it nonetheless seems unlikely in relation to most individuals involved in PCSOT.

Proponents of the polygraph assert that the involuntary nature of the examinee's physiological reactions detected by the polygraph can give valuable information relating to their autonomic arousal levels. This part of the nervous system is associated with the recognized "fight or flight" response that individuals produce under conditions of perceived threat. It is posited that when a subject is attempting to deceive the examiner, their physiological reactions will differ from times when information is being provided in an open and honest way. Importantly, though the polygraph is regarded as a lie detector, there are, in fact, no known physiological correlates with lying that cannot be attributed to other factors. As such, substantial efforts need to be made to eliminate other possible causes of physiological change when the examiner interprets the activity produced by the autonomic nervous system during testing. However, it is theorized that the greater the perception of threat, the more it may be anticipated that changes in respiration, heart rate and galvanic skin response will be apparent. On this basis, it is hypothesized that producing deceitful responses to questions of marked significance to the respondent will lead to greater levels of physiological reactivity, than the physiological responses that would derive from responding to irrelevant, neutral questions or from responding honestly. Importantly, individualized baselines of reactivity can be established, taking into account an offender's general level of test anxiety and through comparison of item responses. This enables the examiner to factor out generalized anxiety or emotional arousal and focus directly on the key test issues (Grubin, 2010b; Wilcox, 2002). Nonetheless, critics continue to assert that there is no physiological response that is exclusively related to deception (Iacono, 2008a, 2008b; Lykken, 1998), and the British Psychological Society (2004: 29) concluded that:

> although polygraph equipment does accurately measure a number of physiological activities, these activities do not reflect a single underlying process. Furthermore, these activities are not necessarily in concord, either within or across individuals.

A Brief History of Polygraphy

The development of polygraphy dates back well over a hundred years. Notably, in 1908 Munsterberger became a major proponent of research to determine physiological correlates associated with deception. Prior to this time, Italian researchers, such as Lombroso (1895), had already begun to explore this issue. However, the most notable polygraph development occurred within the United States, with Munsterberger's protégé, Marston, taking the lead. Marston's confidence and charismatic style moved the polygraph onto the national scene quite quickly, when, in 1923, Marston was the first person to submit his lie detector test as evidence in a court case (Marston, 1938). The equipment he used at that time was crude by comparison with modern polygraph instruments and, indeed, involved only the evaluation of systolic blood pressure changes in relation to the questioning he undertook as his basis for the evidence he reported. Further, the equipment he was able to employ at that time necessitated intermittent, rather than continuous, blood pressure measurement, and did not involve the direct monitoring of any other physiological indices. In Marston's efforts to have this procedure accepted for evidentiary purposes, the case ultimately went to the Supreme Court where it was ruled that polygraphy did not meet the prevailing standards for scientific acceptability. Nonetheless, polygraphy developed over the years through Marston's efforts and those of a number of polygraph practitioners and proponents who followed him, including Larson (1932), Keeler (Harrelson, Gerow and Gerow, 1998), Reid (1947), Backster (1963) and Matte (1996).

Larson was a forensic psychiatrist whose interest in the polygraph led him to develop the first polygraph that simultaneously recorded the three physiological indices incorporated into modern polygraph testing. Subsequently, Keeler developed the first portable polygraph instrument and, indeed, his contribution was such that he is now regarded as the father of modern polygraphy. Keeler also worked with the police, establishing the first polygraph unit in Chicago, where this technology was used to curb the criminal activity of notorious gangsters, such as Al Capone and Bugsy Malone. In competition with Keeler, Reid, a Chicago lawyer, also impacted on the development of polygraphy and the two of them established the first known polygraph training schools. Increasingly, this gave rise to the establishment of more standardized questioning and scoring protocols. In the 1960s, Backster made further significant contributions to the professional development of polygraph practice and, with continuing refinement through the work of Matte (1996) and others (Abrams, 1989; Kleiner, 2001), polygraph testing procedures became progressively more rigorous. Further, as the profession moved into the twenty-first century, the polygraph instruments became modernized, such that the traditional polygraphs with multiple pens recording physiological changes on paper unraveling from a cylinder were replaced with laptop units, improving the efficiency and effectiveness of the data collection.

As it developed, the polygraph began to be employed for police enquiries, criminal proceedings, security vetting, employment selection and as wide a range of applications as people concerned about determining "truthfulness" could imagine. It may be noted, for example, that the polygraph has been employed in relation to fidelity issues (Madsen and Wilcox, 2009), and in the officiation of fishing contests (S. Sosnowski, personal communication, 2000) and, more recently, has even been considered to determine the honesty of sportsmen, including cricketers (BBC, 2011). The polygraph is also used for investigative purposes to assist with case assessment and decisions about formalizing charges within various agencies and security services around the world. Notably, it was considered to assist greatly in decision making and resource deployment in a recent UK police pilot (Hamilton, 2011). The polygraph's scientific and legal standing grew over time, but it was not until the early 1990s that the Supreme Court in the United States began to take a different view on its use (*Daubert* v. *Merrell Dow Pharmaceuticals* 509 US 579 (1993)). By 2003, polygraph evidence was admissible in court in 19 US states. A more comprehensive history of polygraph development may be found in Wilcox and Madsen (2009).

Post-Conviction Sex Offender Polygraph Testing

The earliest post-conviction use of the polygraph within the criminal justice system is noted in the work of two US judges. In 1969, Judge Tuttle used the polygraph to identify those offenders who had violated the conditions of their probation and reportedly he believed that periodic polygraph examination could reduce the likelihood that an offender would engage in further criminal activity. Relatedly, Schmidt, Solomon and Johnson (1973), when reporting on Tuttle's work, proposed that the polygraph acted as an artificial conscience. In 1975, Judge Partee also employed the polygraph in decision making with regard to applications for probation (Abrams and Abrams, 1993) and formed the view that polygraphy showed much merit in this regard.

While these early polygraph investigations had been adopted for the surveillance and management of various types of offender, predominantly those considered high risk, as time passed this post-conviction application began to be used increasingly in sex offender work. Notably, PCSOT was described as effective in monitoring and reducing recidivism rates among convicted sex offenders. Early research by Abrams and Ogard (1986) reported that 69% of the men in their study who received periodic polygraph examinations were not convicted of re-offending, compared to 26% of men who were subject to supervision alone.

Over time, the acceptance of the polygraph, particularly in relation to sex offender work, has grown, such that it is an integral part of many sex offender assessment and treatment programs internationally (Wilcox, 2009; Wilcox and Gray, 2012). Holden (2009) reported that in 2007, 46 of the 50 US states employed PCSOT for treating, assessing and supervising sex offenders. He noted that the other four states were reviewing their positions with regard to integrating the polygraph into their treatment programs on a regular basis. Continuing research has consistently noted increases in offense disclosures by convicted sexual offenders who are subject to polygraph testing, with evidence of earlier onset of offending, significantly more offenses and victims reported, as well as indications of substantial crossover from one kind of sexually abusive involvement to another; for example, from adults to children, females to males, intrafamilial to extrafamilial and non-contact to contact offending (Ahlmeyer *et al.*, 2000; Heil, Ahlmeyer and Simons, 2003; O'Connell, 1998; Wilcox *et al.*, 2005). Relatedly, the perception of sex offender workers has been that the polygraph can significantly assist in the management of offenders, increasing an understanding of areas of risk and contributing to the development of more robust relapse prevention strategies (Grubin, 2010a). Notably, in 2007 legislation was passed in the United Kingdom (the Offender Management Act 2007) introducing the mandatory employment of the polygraph with convicted sex offenders upon release into the community after serving sentences of one year or more in prison for certain sexual offenses. In addition, Gannon, Beech and Ward (2008), in their discussion of risk prediction, considered that there was reasonable evidence to support polygraph use in some areas of risk assessment with sex offenders.

Post-Conviction Polygraph Testing Formats

There are four basic formats for PCSOT.

Sexual History Disclosure Examinations

Sexual History Disclosure Examinations (SHDE) explore the offender's past sexual behavior and interests broadly through a systematic and detailed review of sexual behavior over the duration of the individual's life prior to their sexual conviction for their index offense. In circumstances where an individual has made reasonable progress in treatment, the SHDE may be a helpful test to administer, enabling a fuller understanding of sexual risk issues that will enable treatment workers to develop more robust and comprehensive relapse prevention strategies.

Specific Issues Tests

In relation to Specific Issues Tests, Trepper and Barrett (1989) reported that, among sex offenders, there were four basic types of denial: denial of facts, denial of responsibility, denial of awareness and denial of impact. A Specific Issue Test is a very focused examination, designed to address denial issues, that can present in various ways; for example, "I didn't commit the sexual offense," "I didn't know she was under age," "I was completely drunk, don't remember," "she's done it with all my friends, it didn't cause her any harm." In general, Specific Issue Denial Tests, if deemed necessary, are administered at an earlier stage. This is because treatment progress can be substantially reduced in intervention work where an offender is comprehensively in denial. Further, this attitude, if strongly voiced by the offender, can have a negative impact on the group process.

Maintenance Examination

A third type of PCSOT is the Maintenance Examination, which focuses on an offender's adherence to requirements mandated by the courts. It often concerns the level of cooperation the individual is demonstrating with regard to treatment and rehabilitation requirements. The maintenance examinations, like the monitoring tests (described below), are often subject to periodic re-administration focusing on issues arising further to the offender's index offense, normally over the previous six months.

Monitoring Polygraph Examinations

Monitoring Polygraph Examinations focus directly upon specific issues about possible new offenses or breaches. This type of examination has significant relevance for supervising officers as it concerns the offender's ongoing compliance with probation requirements.

Assessment Protocol for PCSOT

When questions are asked of the subject during polygraph testing, physiological responses are simultaneously recorded in relation to question items posed that are a mixture of irrelevant (for example, involving known factual information like name, age, and so on), relevant (for example, directly associated with the offense-related area of concern being examined) and comparison questions that are designed to evoke some doubt or self-questioning but are not central to the assessment enquiry. The offender is considered to have passed his polygraph examination if his response to relevant questions is not considered to be significantly at variance with his response to comparison items. Failing the polygraph would occur where there was evidence of significantly stronger responding on the relevant items and passing occurs when differences are minimal. For detailed information concerning PCSOT, the reader is advised to see Sosnowski and Wilcox (2009).

The Ethical Debate

There have been ongoing ethical and legal disputes as to whether an individual who does not wish to be polygraphed should be compelled to do so. Arguments against its use have centered on the assertion that this is an infringement of the offenders' human rights. However, polygraph supporters would assert that individuals under Court Orders will, by virtue of these circumstances, naturally have fewer rights and that the relevant polygraph questions relate only to sexual offense issues. They would further judge that while offenders have rights just as everyone else does in society, with regard to general privacy, dignity and choice, they have no right to commit sexual offenses and, as such, monitoring these issues is appropriate and justified. Polygraph advocates would state that with this responsibility to society in mind, the professional's duty to protect the public outweighs the individual's right in this specific area of enquiry, and the efficacy of this technology has, in their view, been demonstrated (Grubin, 2010a). Advocates of PCSOT would also assert that the polygraph can serve to enhance internal self-control efforts as well as modifying external risk features (Edson, 1991; English, 2002; Teuscher, 1978; Wilcox and Donathy, 2008; Wilcox, O'Keeffe and Oliver, 2009). Notably, Harrison and Kirkpatrick (2000) reported that 72% of the sex offenders in their study indicated that the polygraph increased their compliance, openness and engagement in treatment and supervision.

One key concern about the use of polygraphy with sexual offenders is that an element of deception is often described as an inherent feature of polygraphy (Vess, 2011). It is entailed in the acquaintance test, wherein the examiner takes steps to impress upon the examinee that the polygraph is virtually infallible. Holden (2000) describes this as part of the necessary process of establishing a psychological set asserting that in the absence of focusing the offender squarely on the imperative of being truthful and recognizing the seriousness of the examination results, accuracy rates will be reduced. During this exercise the examinee is instructed to deny the number on a card he has chosen from a deck, while being polygraphed. Following this acquaintance test the examiner identifies the deception and explains to the offender the differences in the psychological responses produced for the deceitful response in comparison with the truthful responses to clarify how an accurate assessment of honesty can be made based on an interpretation of these tracings. In testing, this exercise may be facilitated by the use of a marked set of cards from which the examiner will be able to identify the number chosen by the examinee. Grubin (2010b) noted that in the UK trials, this ploy was not used, asserting that it was unnecessary owing to the high levels of accuracy achievable through polygraph employment. Polygraphists report that it can be helpful to employ this strategy, noting that it affords the polygraphist an opportunity to judge whether the offender is attempting to use any cognitive or behavioral counter-measures in order to deceive the examiner. Sosnowski (personal communication, 2000) offered the analogy that knowing the number of the card is equivalent to "walking a tightrope with a safety net," asserting that the safety net does not diminish the skill of the tightrope walker any more than the use of this strategy reduces the polygraph examiner's ability to interpret the tracings accurately.

It is also described that the development of comparison questions requires the polygraphist to encourage the offender openly to endorse a probable lie about their own past behavior. As an example, the examinee might be asked if he has ever engaged in any transgression or minor illegality, such as taking something from the workplace that did not belong to him. The polygraphist impresses upon the examinee the importance of being honest as a prerequisite for passing the polygraph test. This discussion serves to pressure the examinee into confirming their general honesty, such that, while the examinee might defensively say that he has, for example, inadvertently taken paperclips from the workplace, subject to additional questioning he may be more likely than in other circumstances to say "nothing else" prematurely, rather than experience evident disapproval from the polygraphist for past dishonest or questionable behavior. This area of discussion forms the basis for developing comparison questions and, for the purposes of PCSOT, the polygraphist may confidently ask the question, "Other than paperclips, have you ever taken anything from the workplace that did not belong to you?" and anticipate that the examinee will respond, "No." Notably, an element of deceitfulness or uncertainty may likely exist in the examinee's mind about responding "no" to this question and the physiological reactivity to these comparison questions would be weighed against those produced in response to relevant questions such as "Have you touched a child for sexual reasons?" or "Have you been alone with a child for sexual reasons, since your last polygraph examination?"

The polygraphist anticipates that the examinee's responses to the comparison questions will likely produce a degree of emotional discomfort and heightened physiological reactivity. However, it would also be expected that the tracings recorded will be greater in response to the relevant questions than the comparison questions if the examinee is being deceitful about the key issues of concern that are being addressed. As such, it is the difference in responding to relevant and comparison questions that informs the polygraphist's judgment. Among individuals being polygraphed, it is widely reported that, further to completion of the acquaintance test, those who were genuinely fearful that they would be falsely accused, due to their high levels of generalized anxiety, begin to relax and feel comfortable that the examiner can distinguish between nervous responding and guilt. However, individuals with significant information that they are hoping to hide from the examiner will generally begin to display more worry at this point as they feel more concerned that their deceitfulness will be detected.

A possible exception to the above has been suggested in relation to the psychopath or compulsive liar, who may consider the acquaintance test a challenge and as such simply decide to increase their efforts to deceive the polygraphist more successfully. Such individuals are considered likely to fail initial periodic polygraph examinations, though they tend to open up more over the course of undertaking periodic tests as indications of their deceitfulness become more evident (Sosnowski, personal communication, 2002).

Notably, the purpose of the polygraph is to get the offender to pass (English *et al.*, 2000) since failing may suggest a need for more resources to monitor, treat and manage the offender. However, passing the examination reflects that the offender is being sufficiently open such that their offending is reasonably well understood and they therefore demonstrate a better potential for working with professionals to avoid re-offending. In relation to this, polygraph testing often gives indications of significantly more offending and deviant activity than has been previously reported.

Reports of significant increases in disclosures are well established, together with a broadly positive view from sex offender treatment workers. Kokish, Levenson and Blasingame (2005) found that the majority of their 95 offenders, who took 333 polygraph tests, reported that this was a helpful part of treatment and they agreed with the polygraphist's conclusions 90% of the time. Kokish, Levenson and Blasingame (2005) considered that the relatively low numbers of false indications, for both deception and truthfulness, reflected favorably on the responsible employment of polygraphs in sex offender work and tended to concur with the accuracy levels previously reported by the US National Research Council (2003).

Recidivism reduction remains the key aim in sex offender work. In relation to this, as referenced previously, Abrams and Ogard (1986) described significant decreases in re-offending in their study of offenders who were subject to polygraph testing as compared with those who were not. Edson (1991) reported on the influence of polygraph testing in his sample of 173 sex offenders who underwent periodic PCSOT, describing that 95% of these individuals were not reconvicted of sexual offenses over a period of nine years, although he did not have a control group. Grubin (2006) reported that his voluntarily assessed offenders engaged in reduced numbers of further offenses that were also less serious, further to polygraph testing. Notably, McGrath *et al.* (2007) did not find that sexual recidivism was reduced through polygraph testing. However, in their study, the polygraph was employed at unusually infrequent intervals, with an average of 22 months between assessments among these 104 sex offenders, matched against offenders in the program who were not polygraphed. Nevertheless, the polygraphed group had committed significantly fewer non-sexual violent offenses at the time of a five-year follow-up. It is observed that standard employment of periodic polygraph testing would dictate that intervals of approximately six months are advisable (American Polygraph Association, 2007; ATSA, 2001) between examinations, and question whether the significantly increased length of time between tests has influenced assessed sexual recidivism. However, it is noteworthy that, even in these circumstances, there was a significant reduction in violent offending in the polygraphed group. In numerous case studies (Grubin, 2006; Wilcox and Buschman, 2011; Wilcox, O'Keeffe and Oliver, 2009) offenders described that they have a greater capacity for managing deviant sexual behaviors and interests when engaging in periodic polygraph tests and indeed they request such monitoring.

Concerns have been raised that compulsory polygraph testing will impede the therapeutic process. Grubin (2008) asserts that the polygraph is misrepresented as an interrogative tool within the PCSOT setting, describing that it enables examinees to engage more fully in the therapeutic process and that its focus is on facilitating truth telling more than exposing lies as when employed in many other settings. Importantly, polygraph-acquired disclosures provide helpful treatment and supervision guidance to be taken into account along with other information sources. However, English *et al.* (2003), Grubin (2010b) and Wilcox (2000, 2009) advise that case management decisions should not be made independent of other corroborating evidence. Rather, in conjunction with other professionals, information obtained during polygraph testing might impact on both supervision and treatment issues. Relatedly, there are also reports that false disclosures occur at times. Kokish, Levenson and Blasingame (2005) found this to be in the region of 5%.

Impact on Treatment

Considering that, arguably, polygraph administration entails a degree of misrepresentation and a potential for intimidation and threat, one may question whether it is consistent with a positive treatment ethos (Beech and Fordham, 1997; Garrett *et al.*, 2003) based on collaboration, honesty and open engagement. In relation to this, it may be noted that the polygraphist's role, though linked closely with the other professionals working with the offender, is to undertake periodic polygraph examinations while liaising with treatment workers and case managers, to support the development of more focused intervention and supervision. Further, this facilitative role is largely endorsed by staff and group attendees (Grubin, 2010a; Kokish, Levenson and Blasingame, 2005; Wilcox and Donathy, 2008).

There are, however, further difficulties with the application of the polygraph, in that individuals tested, who are more disclosing about their offending histories, may be considered by those supervising them as more risky than those who continue to withhold relevant information about their offense backgrounds when polygraphed or engaging in treatment work. This is perhaps a natural reaction among professionals who have a responsibility to protect the public, though this kneejerk response should be guarded against and professionals who have access to polygraph testing would benefit from guidance (Gannon, Beech and Ward, 2008) to ensure that they do not overreact to new disclosures in their assessment of the relative risk of such as individual, in comparison with someone else who has not been so open. Gannon, Beech and Ward (2009) reported that while there is evidence that the polygraph significantly increases disclosures concerning historical and current risk factors, it presently has no role in actuarial risk assessment.

In further considering the polygraph's future role in sex offender work, treatment facilitators recognize that some offenders tend to produce safe soundbites within group but may have aspects to their private lives about which the police, probation and other professionals recognize that they have little knowledge but some underlying sense of concern. In the formal assessment of risk (Hanson and Thornton, 2000), convictions and the nature of known offenses are considered to form a significant part of actuarial/static risk assessment. As such, the mere disclosure of other offenses, however disturbing to the professionals involved, should not naturally lead to any augmentation of perceived risk. Indeed, more openness might rather reflect greater cooperation and perhaps an opportunity to consider lessening the level of supervision needed for this individual.

In a formal assessment of risk, convictions and appearances (but not numbers of offenses) are considered in determining actuarial or static risk levels. In relation to this, the polygraph can serve as a risk screening tool, providing additional information to support static risk assessment, in particular, in relation to gaining clarification about recognized aggravating factors associated with offending, including relationship status and types of past victims. Further, the polygraph can assist in exploring acute risk factors concerning lifestyle and self-management issues associated with victim access, supervision and involvement in offense-related behaviors (Buschman *et al.*, 2010). These factors do not change the current risk management approaches (such as RM2000 or Static-99) though they may inform clinical judgment and assist in fine-tuning treatment as well as suggesting guidance for supervision/monitoring (Gannon, Beech and Ward, 2008). As with many other issues in the consideration of ethical practice, while some might conclude that the use of the polygraph is an unreasonable infringement on the rights of sexual offenders, others might persuasively argue that it would be irresponsible not to use the polygraph when information so pertinent to public safety might otherwise be much less readily obtainable (Salter, 1997).

Initially, the polygraph was employed in the United Kingdom on a voluntary basis and many professionals described that the individuals they most wanted to polygraph refused to participate in these trials, while those who did participate were free to disengage at any point they chose. Nonetheless, and in spite of low polygraph pass rates, significant amounts of information were obtained about the offending behavior of the individuals who participated. Some of these individuals wanted to prove that they were innocent and some wanted to demonstrate their ability to deceive the criminal justice system. Some also considered it a challenge to see if they could beat the polygraph. One could argue that it would be more ethical to polygraph people who volunteered, though this would exclude a significant group of individuals who remain a risk to the community and continue to engage in activities about which the authorities have only limited knowledge. Polygraph critics would suggest that the successful results of the voluntary research trials may be the result of a more cooperative and participative group of subjects than compulsorily tested sex offenders might prove to be (Grubin, 2008; Ben-Shakhar, 2008; Meijer *et al.*, 2008). Nonetheless, while the current UK trials involving mandatory PCSOT have not yet been evaluated, indications in the United States (Heil and English, 2009) suggest similar results using PCSOT, whether conducted voluntarily or involuntarily, or with offenders on probation or in prison.

Conclusions

The legality of polygraph use varies from country to country and differs according to its various applications. On the basis of its assessed accuracy levels, I consider that its merits in some areas may be greater than in others. Further, I note that the US National Research Council's (2003) findings suggested that its effectiveness in assessing deceitfulness is considerably better than that of the average individual or even trained professionals who do not employ this technology. As such, it is observed that the assessed 10 to 20% error rate noted in polygraph testing by the US National Research Council (2003) would raise questions about the use of the polygraph in areas where the likelihood of deception is low; for example, in relation to security vetting. Further, I would judge that its application for investigative as opposed to evidentiary purposes, where more significant levels of deceitfulness are likely (for example, in sexual offender assessment), ought to be viewed as sufficiently different as to be considered on its own merit and distinct from the polygraph's other asserted uses. In addition, the growth in use of the polygraph in sex offender work should, in my opinion, be a subject of some reflection in advance of criticism, since experienced practitioners in this field appear, in the great majority, to accept its utility and efficacy. However, issues of informed consent and possible self-incrimination should be considered on a case by case basis. Chaffin (2011) expressed clinical and ethical concerns with regard to polygraph testing juveniles and relatedly referenced that it may be inappropriate to assess other vulnerable individuals, such as those who have mental ill health or intellectual disabilities, in this way. Clearly, vulnerability and capacity are important considerations when using PCSOT, and careful judgment, as well as advanced training for polygraph examiners, would be appropriate to ensure best practice, with careful consideration given to the ethical issues involved. In the United Kingdom the polygraph is not employed with individuals under the age of 18 for PCSOT purposes. Perhaps relatedly, the author recognizes a need for specialized PCSOT training to take account of the possible effects of recollecting traumatic experiences, in particular among individuals being polygraphed who are psychologically more vulnerable. It is advised that working in an integrated way with the rest of the supervision and intervention staff will afford greater protection in this regard and also reflects responsible practice. It is also noted that in the United States, offenders are often obliged to pay for their own periodic polygraph examinations and, in circumstances where they fail, the frequency of retesting is greater, such that they may feel more impelled to pass their examinations in order to avoid increasing costs to them and their families. Such conditions may pressure offenders to be more open, though they may also introduce extraneous variables affecting the quality and accuracy of information conveyed. This practice is not employed in the United Kingdom, though comparison of disclosures does not suggest that paying personally for polygraph tests notably changes the range and type of information proffered by offenders. Finally, while it is legal to impel offenders to pay for their own polygraphs in parts of the United States, the ethical aspect of this practice continues to be the subject of debate.

Offenders involved in treatment have a right to privacy in areas unconcerned with their offending behaviors, though by virtue of their convicted status, their rights are limited and they must face identified consequences for non-compliance with the conditions of their court orders. This applies to treatment involvement, psychometric assessment, supervision, restrictions imposed on their freedom of movement and their capacity for making various independent choices. In this sense, the polygraph is not different from other court mandated requirements and, while considered invasive, if administered in accordance with strict professional standards, it could hardly be seen to be more intrusive than other accepted assessment and treatment strategies, including phallometric testing (Kalmus, Beech and Warberg, 2009), the use of which is accepted by the European Court of Justice.

The US National Research Council (2003) concluded that the polygraph was substantially better than chance, though short of perfection in its capacity for assessing deceitfulness. The British Psychological Society (2004) also expressed concerns about polygraph validity and accuracy, though the investigating committee did report that there was a developing body of evidence to suggest that the polygraph can encourage sex offenders to disclose their deviant thoughts and behaviors in ways that may assist those responsible for their supervision and treatment. The author would concur with these views and advise the reader to differentiate more carefully between the contexts within which polygraphy may be debated (Grubin, 2010b). Within the field of sex offender work, the polygraph should, in my view, be regarded as one of a number of tools that may, in concert, be employed to improve assessment, treatment and offender monitoring. While it is certainly not infallible, this charge may equally be leveled in relation to professional judgment, psychometric evaluation and offender treatment based on observations and assessed results in terms of our work in this field (Blacker *et al.*, 2011; Hanson *et al.*, 2002; Thornton *et al.*, 2003; Wilcox *et al.*, 2009). Though safeguards are in order, the capacity of polygraphy to contribute in an integrated way to better offense understanding, treatment engagement and supervision are such that, while being mindful of sound ethical practice, its rejection would, in my opinion, ultimately reduce public protection. Taking full account of the rights of convicted individuals is an important consideration in any democratic society and, notably, steps can and should be taken to minimize the risk of self-incrimination by asking questions that relate to offending behavior without seeking specific information that might directly lead to further criminal investigation. Importantly, offenders may nonetheless choose to give detailed disclosures about past offending behavior and such self-reports should be supported and respected by the professionals involved.

Where disclosures occur, it is clear that they will need to be followed up if this is in the interest of protecting vulnerable individuals, though this same challenge occurs within group work or individual supervision. As a society we must safeguard the rights of all of our citizens to the degree achievable, taking steps to enable offenders to hold themselves more accountable, as per the conditions of their court orders and gaining necessary information to assist them in developing more robust and tailored future plans for offense-free lives. Ultimately, the polygraph is only one of a number of tools that professionals can employ in the work that they undertake and, as with other interventions, it can be subject to misuse. This, however, reflects a need for vigilance and sound ethical standards. Nevertheless, the risk that polygraphy may be misused or the argument that it is not 100% accurate should not compel us to conclude that therefore polygraphy should be disused. Indeed, taking these two criteria into account, if this were the case, as a practicing forensic psychologist, I should in good faith consider finding other work.

References

Abel, G.G. and Roleau, J.L. (1990) "The nature and extent of sexual assault," in W.L. Marshall, D.R. Laws and H.E. Barbaree (eds), *Handbook of Sexual Assault: Issues, Theories, and Treatment of the Offender.* New York: Plenum, pp. 9–21.

Abrams, S. (1989) *The Complete Polygraph Handbook.* Lexington, MA: Lexington Books.

Abrams, S. and Abrams, J.B. (1993) *Polygraph Testing of the Pedophile.* Portland, OR: Ryan Gwinner Press.

Abrams, S. and Ogard, E. (1986) "Polygraph surveillance of probationers," *Polygraph* 13, 3, 174–182.

Ahlmeyer, S., Heil, P., McKee, B. and English, K. (2000) "The impact of polygraphy on admissions of victims and offences in adult sex offenders," *Sexual Abuse: A Journal of Research and Treatment* 12, 123–138.

American Polygraph Association (2007) "Model policy for post conviction sex offender testing," *American Polygraph Association* 36, 2, 112–116.

Ansley, N. (1990) "The validity and reliability of polygraph decisions in real cases," *Polygraph* 19, 3, 169–181.

ATSA (Association for the Treatment of Sexual Abusers) (2001) *Practice Standards and Guidelines for the Members of the Association for the Treatment of Sexual Abusers.* Beaverton, OR: ATSA.

Backster, C. (1963) "New standards in polygraph chart interpretation: do the charts speak for themselves?," *Law and Order* 11, 6, 67–68.

BBC (2011) "Steve Waugh calls for lie detector tests in cricket," *BBC News Online*, July 20, http://www.bbc.co.uk/sport/0/cricket/14208703 (accessed September 7, 2012).

Beech, A.R. and Fordham, A.S. (1997) "Therapeutic climate of sex offender treatment programs," *Sexual Abuse: A Journal of Research and Treatment* 9, 219–237.

Ben-Shakhar, G. (2008) "The case against the use of polygraph examinations to monitor post-conviction sex offenders," *Legal and Criminological Psychology* 13, 191–207.

Blacker, J., Beech, A.R., Wilcox, D.T. and Boer, D.P. (2011) "The assessment of dynamic risk and recidivism in a sample of special needs sexual offenders," *Psychology, Crime and Law* 17, 75–92.

British Psychological Society (2004) *A Review of Current Scientific Status and Fields of Application of Polygraph Deception Detection: Final Report from the Working Party.* Leicester: British Psychological Society.

Buschman, J., Wilcox, D.T., Foulger, S.A. *et al.* (2008) "Sexual history disclosure polygraph examinations among a group of 25 Dutch men who downloaded child pornography," *Panopticon* 2, 36–48.

Buschman, J., Wilcox, D.T., Krapohl, M.D. *et al.* (2010) "Cybersex offender risk assessment. An explorative study," *Journal of Sexual Aggression* 16, 2, 197–209.

Chaffin, M. (2011) "The case of juvenile polygraphy as a clinical ethics dilemma," *Sexual Abuse: A Journal of Research and Treatment* 23, 3, 314–328.

Edson, C. (1991) *Sex Offender Treatment.* Medford, OR: Department of Corrections.

English, K. (2002) The containment approach for managing sexual offenders. Keynote presentation, National Organisation for the Treatment of Abusers, Cardiff, UK, September.

English, K., Jones, L., Pasini-Hill, D. *et al.* (2000) *The Value of Polygraph Testing in Sex Offender Management: Research Report Submitted to the National Institute of Justice.* Denver, CO: Office of Research and Statistics.

English, K., Jones, L., Patrick, D. and Pasini-Hill, D. (2003) "Sexual offender containment. Use of post-conviction polygraph," *New York Academy of Sciences* 989, 411–427.

Gannon, T.A., Beech, A.R. and Ward, T. (2008) "Does the polygraph lead to better risk prediction for sexual offenders?," *Aggression and Violent Behavior* 13, 1, 29–44.

Gannon, T.A., Beech, A.R. and Ward, T. (2009) "Risk assessment and the polygraph," in D.T. Wilcox (ed.), *The Use of the Polygraph in Assessing, Treating and Supervising Sex Offenders: A Practitioner's Guide.* Oxford: Wiley-Blackwell, pp. 129–154.

Garrett, T., Oliver, C., Wilcox, D.T. and Middleton, D. (2003) "Who cares? The views of sexual offenders about the group treatment they receive," *Sexual Abuse: A Journal of Research and Treatment* 15, 4, 323–338.

Grubin, D. (2006) *Polygraph Pilot Study: Final Report.* London: Home Office.

Grubin, D. (2008) "The case for polygraph testing of sex offenders," *Legal and Criminological Psychology* 13, 177–189.

Grubin, D. (2010a) "A trial of voluntary polygraphy testing in 10 English probation areas," *Sexual Abuse: A Journal of Research and Treatment* 22, 3, 266–278.

Grubin, D. (2010b) "The polygraph and forensic psychiatry," *Journal of the American Academy of Psychiatry and the Law* 38, 446–451.

Grubin, D., Madsen, L., Parsons, S. *et al.* (2004) "A prospective study of the impact of polygraphy on high risk behaviors in adult sex offenders," *Sexual Abuse: A Journal of Research and Treatment* 16, 209–222.

Hamilton, F. (2011) "Suspects to face police lie detector for first time," *The Times*, December 31, http://www.lccsa.org.uk/news.asp?ItemID=17720&pcid=2&cid=15&mid=71&archive=yes (accessed September 7, 2012).

Hanson, R.K., Gordon, A., Harris, A.J. *et al.* (2002) "First report of the collaborative outcome data project on the effectiveness of psychological treatment for sex offenders," *Sexual Abuse: A Journal of Research and Treatment* 14, 2, 169–194.

Hanson, R.K. and Thornton, D. (2000) "Improving risk assessments for sex offenders: a comparison of three actuarial scales," *Law and Human Behaviour* 24, 1, 119–136.

Harrelson, L.H., Gerow, N.S. and Gerow, J.R. (1998) *Lie Test: Deception, Truth and the Polygraph.* Fort Wayne, IN: Jonas Publishing.

Harrison, J.S. and Kirkpatrick, B. (2000) "Polygraph testing and behavioural change with sex offenders in an outpatient setting: an exploratory study," *Polygraph* 29, 20–26.

Heil, P., Ahlmeyer, S. and Simons, D. (2003) "Crossover sexual offences," *Sexual Abuse: A Journal of Research and Treatment* 15, 221–236.

Heil, P. and English, K. (2009) "Sex offender polygraph testing in the United States: trends and controversies," in D.T. Wilcox (ed.), *The Use of the Polygraph in Assessing, Treating and Supervising Sex Offenders: A Practitioner's Guide.* Oxford: Wiley-Blackwell, pp. 181–216.

Holden, E.J. (2000) "Pre and post conviction polygraph: building blocks for the future – procedures, principles and practices," *Polygraph* 29, 69–97.

Holden, E. J. (2009) "Foreword," in D.T. Wilcox (ed.), *The Use of the Polygraph in Assessing, Treating and Supervising Sex Offenders: A Practitioner's Guide.* Oxford: Wiley-Blackwell, pp. xxiii–xxvi.

Honts, C.R., Hodes, R.L. and Raskin, D.C. (1985) "Effects of physical countermeasures on the physiological detection of deception," *Journal of Applied Psychology* 70, 177–187.

Iacono, W.G. (2008a) "Accuracy of polygraph techniques: problems using confession to determine ground truth," *Physiology and Behaviour* 95, 24–26.

Iacono, W.G. (2008b) "Effective policing: understanding how polygraph tests work and are used," *Criminal Justice and Behaviour* 35, 10, 1295–1308.

Kalmus, E., Beech, A.R. and Warberg, B. (2009) "Forensic assessment of sexual interest: a review," in D.T. Wilcox (ed.), *The Use of the Polygraph in Assessing, Treating and Supervising Sex Offenders: A Practitioner's Guide.* Oxford: Wiley-Blackwell, pp. 297–322.

Kleiner, M. (ed.) (2001) *Handbook of Polygraph Testing.* San Diego, CA: Academic Press.

Kokish, R., Levenson, J.S. and Blasingame, G.D. (2005) "Post-conviction sex offender polygraph examination: client reported perceptions of utility and accuracy," *Sexual Abuse: A Journal of Research and Treatment* 17, 2, 211–221.

Larson, J.A. (1932) *Lying and Its Detection: A Study of Deception and Deception Tests.* Chicago, IL: University of Chicago Press.

Lombroso, C. (1895) *L'Hommecriminel*, 2nd edn. Paris, France: Felix Alcan.

Lykken, D.T. (1998) *A Tremor in the Blood: Uses and Abuses of the Lie Detector*, 2nd edn. New York: Plenum.

Matte, J.A. (1996) *Forensic Psychophysiology Using the Polygraph: Scientific Truth Verification – Lie Detection*. New York: JAM Publications.

Madsen, L. (2009) "The accuracy of polygraphy in the treatment and supervision of sex offenders," in D.T. Wilcox (ed.), *The Use of the Polygraph in Assessing, Treating and Supervising Sex Offenders: A Practitioner's Guide*. Oxford: Wiley-Blackwell, pp. 155–180.

Madsen, L. and Wilcox, D.T. (2009) "The empirical evidence for the value of post-conviction polygraph in the treatment and supervision of sex offenders," in D.T. Wilcox (ed.), *The Use of the Polygraph in Assessing, Treating and Supervising Sex Offenders: A Practitioner's Guide*. Oxford: Wiley-Blackwell, pp. 49–64.

Marston, W.M. (1938) *The Lie Detector Test*. New York: Richard R. Smith.

McGrath, R.J., Cumming, G.F., Hoke, S.E. and Bonn-Miller, M.O. (2007) "Outcomes in a community sex offender treatment program: a comparison between polygraphed and matched non-polygraphed offenders," *Sexual Abuse: A Journal of Research and Treatment* 19, 381–393.

Meijer, E.H., Verschuere, B., Merckelbach, H.L.G.J. and Crombez, G. (2008) "Sex offender management using the polygraph: a critical review," *International Journal of Law and Psychiatry* 31, 423–429.

O'Connell, M.A. (1998) "Using polygraph testing to assess deviant sexual history of sex offenders," *Dissertation Abstracts International* 58, 3023.

Reid, J.E. (1947) "A revised questioning technique in lie detector tests," *Journal of Criminal Law and Criminology* 37, 6, 542–547.

Salter, A. (1997) Sex offender assessment and risk management issues. National Organisation for the Treatment of Abusers (NOTA) Annual Conference, Southampton, UK, September.

Schmidt, H.K., Solomon, G.F. and Johnson, H. (1973) "The artificial conscience," *Corrective and Social Psychology* 23, 93–100.

Sosnowski, S. and Wilcox, D.T. (2009) "Basics of post-conviction sex offender polygraph testing," in D.T. Wilcox (ed.), *The Use of the Polygraph in Assessing, Treating and Supervising Sex Offenders: A Practitioner's Guide*. Oxford: Wiley-Blackwell, pp. 65–91.

Teuscher, T. (1978) "The polygraph and probation," *Polygraph* 7, 1–4.

Thornton, D., Mann, R.E., Webster, S.D. *et al.* (2003) "Distinguishing and combining risks for sexual and violent recidivism," *Annals of New York Academy of Science* 989, 225–235.

Trepper, T.S. and Barrett, M.J. (1989) *Systemic Treatment of Incest: A Therapeutic Handbook*. New York: Brunner/Mazel.

US Government (2006) *Federal Polygraph Handbook*. Washington: Department of Defence, Polygraph Program.

US National Research Council (2003) *The Polygraph and Lie Detection: Committee to Review the Scientific Evidence on the Polygraph*. Washington, DC: National Academic Press.

Vess, J. (2011) "Ethical practice in sex offender assessment: consideration of actuarial and polygraph methods," *Sexual Abuse: A Journal of Research and Treatment* 23, 3, 381–396.

Wilcox, D.T. (2000) "Application of the clinical polygraph examination to the assessment, treatment and monitoring of sex offenders," *Journal of Sexual Aggression* 5, 134–152.

Wilcox, D.T. (2002) Polygraph examination of British sexual offenders: a pilot study on sexual history disclosure testing. Doctoral dissertation. University of Surrey, Guildford, UK.

Wilcox, D.T. (ed.) (2009) *The Use of the Polygraph in Assessing, Treating and Supervising Sex Offenders: A Practitioner's Guide*. Oxford: Wiley-Blackwell.

Wilcox, D., Beech, A.R., Markall, H. and Blacker, J. (2009) "Actuarial risk assessment and recidivism in a sample of UK intellectually disabled sexual offenders," *Journal of Sexual Aggression* 15, 97–106.

Wilcox, D.T. and Buschman, J. (2011) "Case studies in the utility of the polygraph," *Sexual Offender Treatment* 6, 1.

Wilcox, D.T. and Donathy, M.L. (2008) "The utility of the polygraph with sex offenders in England," *Conference Permanente Europeenne de la Probation,* http://www.cep-probation.org/news/65/46/the-utility-of-the-polygraph-with-sex-offenders-in-england (accessed September 15, 2012).

Wilcox, D.T. and Gray, R. (2012) "The use of the polygraph with sex offenders in the UK," *European Polygraph* 6, 19, 55–68.

Wilcox, D.T. and Madsen, L. (2009) "Pre-conviction and post-conviction polygraph testing: A brief history," in D.T. Wilcox (ed.), *The Use of the Polygraph in Assessing, Treating and Supervising Sex Offenders: A Practitioner's Guide.* Oxford: Wiley-Blackwell, pp. 31–48.

Wilcox, D.T., O'Keeffe, Z. and Oliver, C. (2009) "Case study in the utility of the polygraph," in D.T. Wilcox (ed.), *The Use of the Polygraph in Assessing, Treating and Supervising Sex Offenders: A Practitioner's Guide.* Oxford: Wiley-Blackwell, pp. 97–113.

Wilcox, D.T. and Sosnowski, D.E. (2005) "Polygraph examination of British sexual offenders: a pilot study on sexual history disclosure testing," *Journal of Sexual Aggression* 11, 1, 3–25.

Wilcox, D.T., Sosnowski, D. and Middleton, D. (1999) "The use of the polygraph in the community supervision of sex offenders," *Probation Journal* 46, 4, 234–240.

Wilcox, D.T., Sosnowski, D., Warberg, B. and Beech, A.R. (2005) "Sexual history disclosure using the polygraph in a sample of British sex offenders in treatment," *Polygraph* 34, 171–181.

24

Sex Offender Civil Commitment
Legal and Ethical Issues
Rebecca L. Jackson and Christmas N. Covell

Introduction

Few issues in forensic psychology and psychiatry are as divisive as the civil commitment of sexual offenders. Contemporary sex offender civil commitment statutes allow for the indefinite commitment of individuals who have been charged or convicted of a statutorily defined "sexually violent offense" and are at an elevated risk to re-offend sexually due to a mental abnormality or personality disorder. Because sex offender civil commitment statutes place two fundamental values in opposition (personal liberty versus public safety), ethics, morals and values often overlap and underlie any related discussion. Proponents of these statutes frame them as necessary public safety measures, while some critics have characterized these statutes as "witch hunts" (Good and Burstein, 2010: 61).

The purpose of this chapter is not to persuade the reader regarding the ethics or morality of sex offender civil commitment. Instead, we will provide an overview of the laws, their history, and legal challenges in the United States (for a consideration of the policies and laws used in Australia, England and Wales, Germany and South Africa, see Chapter 9). Following the discussion of legal challenges, we will shift our focus to the ethical application of these statutes in terms of evaluating, treating and managing those individuals who are subject to them. Sex offender civil commitment remains controversial, legally, ethically and morally. The following chapter reviews some of the more common areas of debate.

The Wiley-Blackwell Handbook of Legal and Ethical Aspects of Sex Offender Treatment and Management,
First Edition. Edited by Karen Harrison and Bernadette Rainey.
© 2013 John Wiley & Sons, Ltd. Published 2013 by John Wiley & Sons, Ltd.

Legal Issues in Sex Offender Civil Commitment

The re-emergence of sex offender civil commitment

Contemporary sex offender civil commitment laws, sometimes called Sexually Violent Predator (SVP) or Sexually Dangerous Person laws, have existed in the United States since 1990.[1] The notion of civil commitment for sexual offenders dates back to at least 1939, when Minnesota passed a sexual psychopath statute, which allowed for the civil commitment of sexual offenders in lieu of incarceration. The theory behind the earlier statutes was similar to the foundation of criminal responsibility standards. That is, if a person's mental illness was responsible for the crime, the offender deserved treatment for the mental disorder, not punishment for the crime. The early sexual psychopath laws were enacted to help society deal with sexual offenders who were too mentally ill to deserve punishment (Janus, 2000). Support for this type of civil commitment for sexual offenders flagged as skepticism regarding the effectiveness of sex offender treatment rose (see Chapter 13).

The new generation of sex offender civil commitment began in Washington State following brutal, and widely publicized, offenses by known sexual offenders. Public outrage regarding mandatory release of high risk sexual offenders led to the creation of a Gubernatorial Task Force on Community Protection that was charged with making recommendations to change the existing laws pertaining to sex offenders. During this period of time, Westley Allen Dodd, a confessed killer of young boys, was apprehended trying to abduct a six-year-old boy. The need to alter current laws, with an eye toward both harsher penalties for sex offenses as well as their prevention, met with great public support. The Task Force's findings and recommendations were included in a comprehensive bill addressing sex offenses. Included in this bill were the state's sex offender registry and community notification program as well as the civil commitment law for SVPs. Washington State's Community Protection Act was passed in 1990. In this new model of sex offender civil commitment, treatment followed punishment.

Following Washington's passage of the Community Protection Act, several additional states passed similar civil commitment statutes. Kansas has the most well-known of the second-generation commitment laws, due largely to the US Supreme Court's decisions in *Kansas* v. *Hendricks* (521 U.S. 346 (1997)) and *Kansas* v. *Crane* (534 U.S. 407 (2002)). Hendricks challenged the constitutionality of the Kansas law claiming *ex post facto* and double jeopardy violations. Hendricks was a convicted child molester serving a sentence in a Kansas state penal institution. Shortly before his release in 1994, the state petitioned to have Hendricks civilly committed under a newly enacted SVP law (see Kan. Stat. Ann. 59–29[a], 1994). Because Hendricks had already served a criminal sentence for these crimes, he argued that the civil statute violated his constitutional right not to be tried or punished for the same crime twice. The Kansas statute allows for the commitment of:

> any person who has been convicted of or charged with a sexually violent offense and who suffers from a mental abnormality which predisposes the person to commit sexually violent offenses in a degree constituting such person a menace to the health and safety of others. (Kan. Stat. Ann. 59–29[a], 1994)

In upholding the statute, the Supreme Court upheld the state's police power rights and legitimized the constitutionality of SVP commitment laws. Importantly, the Court pointed to the existence of a treatment program in its finding that the purpose of the statute was not punitive, but instead that it existed to treat the individual's mental disorder. According to Vlahakis (2010) the *Hendricks* decision all but put to rest constitutional challenges based on double jeopardy and *ex post facto* claims.

The issue of sex offender civil commitment was again addressed by the Supreme Court in *Kansas* v. *Crane* (534 U.S. 407 (2002)). Michael Crane, a convicted sex offender, argued that as *Hendricks* required a complete lack of control of sexual impulses and behavior, since he retained some control, he was ineligible for civil commitment. The Supreme Court disagreed and found that "serious," but not complete, volitional impairment was required for commitment. The Court did not articulate an operational definition of "serious difficulty," instead stating that "safeguards of human liberty in the area of mental illness and the law are not always best enforced through precise bright-line rules" (*Kansas* v. *Crane* 534 U.S. 868 (2002)).

The final avenue for direct statutory attacks on state civil commitment laws was closed by *Seling* v. *Young* (531 U.S. 250 (2001); Vlahakis, 2010). In *Seling*, Young argued that, despite the constitutionality of sex offender civil commitment laws in general (as determined by *Hendricks*), Washington's law as applied to him was unconstitutional (a so-called "as applied challenge"). The Court rejected the claim. Although Vlahakis (2010: 2–5) characterized the *Seling* decision as the end to statutory challenges against sex offender civil commitment, he notes that it "open[ed] the door to indirect attacks," based on civil rights violations, such as conditions of confinement, use of seclusions and restraints, and adequacy of treatment.

The US Supreme Court once again ruled on the issue of sex offender civil commitment in 2010 in *US* v. *Comstock* (560 U.S. (2010)). Unlike the previous cases, Comstock questioned the constitutionality of the federal sex offender civil commitment statute. The five respondents in Comstock challenged the statute on several grounds. Similar to challenges brought against state statutes, the respondents claimed that the statute was punitive (that is, criminal) and not civil in nature and therefore violated the double jeopardy and *ex post facto* clauses and the Sixth and Eighth Amendments of the US Constitution. They further claimed that the statute denied them substantive due process and equal protection and violated procedural due process because a standard less stringent than beyond a reasonable doubt was applied (clear and convincing evidence was the standard of proof adopted by the federal statute). The final challenge claimed that the Act exceeded the powers granted to Congress by Article I, Section 8 of the Constitution, namely the Necessary and Proper Clause. The Necessary and Proper Clause allows Congress:

> To make all Laws which shall be necessary and proper for carrying into Execution the [enumerated] Powers, and all other Powers vested by this Constitution in the Government of the United States, or in any Department or Officer thereof. (US Constitution, Article I, Section 8, Clause 18)

Because civil commitment has been a power granted to the states, the respondents claimed that Congress overstepped their authority by implementing a civil commitment statute. The District Court had accepted arguments that the standard of proof should have been beyond a reasonable doubt and also agreed that Congress exceeded its powers by passing such a statute. The Court of Appeals upheld the decision, agreeing that Congress had overstepped its legislative authority. The Court did not address the standard of proof question, nor did it address the other constitutional challenges.

Then Solicitor General Elena Kagan (now Justice Kagan) argued on behalf of the US government to the US Supreme Court that civilly committing sexual offenders was a necessary and proper act in order to protect society from dangerous individuals. The US Supreme Court found on a number of grounds that Congress had not exceeded its powers and the US government could legitimately enact the statute. Importantly, the statute as written does preserve the state's authority in the civil commitment process. The federal statute requires that the Attorney General inform the state that it may seek to civilly commit one of its citizens (or inform the state where the initial trial was held) and encourage the state to take jurisdiction over the individual. It also requires the federal government to release the individual to state custody when that state accepts responsibility for the individual. Only when that avenue fails will the federal government move to commit the individual.

Management of sex offender civil commitment programs

The management and administration of sex offender civil commitment programs has also been the subject of legal scrutiny. Currently, 21 jurisdictions (20 states and the federal government) have sex offender civil commitment, or SVP, laws. All but one program (Texas) operate using secure residential facilities. The Texas statute provides for civil commitment on an outpatient basis, with several conditions and restrictions on their behavior. Likewise, all programs offer sex offender treatment. In the majority of programs, participation in the treatment program is voluntary. In contrast, failure to participate in outpatient sex offender treatment in Texas is a violation of an offender's conditional release and constitutes a third degree felony. Individuals who violate the conditions of the civil commitment are returned to prison. Challenges to SVP programs themselves are typically aimed at the adequacy of the treatment programs, conditions of confinement and security measures.

A common theme in the majority of cases regarding sex offender civil commitment programs is the deference given to professional judgment in making decisions regarding clinical and security matters. The Courts have not attempted to legislate best practice, but instead weigh the evidence available concerning practice standards and judge programs against that existing standard. Programs, therefore, must ensure they are maintaining current practice and are abreast of advances in the field. It is incumbent upon program administrators and clinicians constantly to monitor their program against progress in the field at large.

A common complaint from opponents and residents of civil commitment programs (individuals housed in sex offender civil commitment facilities are often called residents) is that the conditions are more prison-like than hospital-like and are therefore punitive in nature. Individuals subject to these statutes are neither prisoners nor traditional mental health patients. The hybrid nature of the population results in hybrid facilities that are neither prisons nor typical psychiatric hospitals. The Courts have repeatedly recognized that this population has safety and security needs that must be met, even in the context of a treatment setting. However, no definitive ruling has been issued regarding conditions of confinement for this population. For example, the Seventh Circuit has ruled that SVPs are entitled to treatment equal to prisoners, but the Ninth Circuit has determined that SVPs are entitled to more considerate treatment than that provided to prisoners. Until and unless the Supreme Court rules on this issue, programs must follow the guidelines established in their jurisdiction.

Treatment programs

Although commitment to a sex offender civil commitment program is involuntary, the choice to participate in treatment is typically voluntary. Many programs have chosen to implement incentives to encourage individuals to participate in treatment. For example, programs may grant additional privileges to those involved in treatment. Critics have suggested that this practice essentially punishes individuals who do not participate in treatment. Despite the claims, this practice has withstood legal challenge on multiple occasions (*Capello* v. *Seling* 02 SV 05242 (W.D. Washington Aug 30, 2002); *Hargett* v. *Adams* 2005 WL 399300 (N.D. III. 2005); *Spicer* v. *Richards* WL 4561101 W.D. Washington (2007)). Failure to participate in treatment carries the natural consequence of reducing one's prospects of being released. Additional consequences such as fewer privileges or less access to recreation has resulted in claims of coercion (*Hargett* v. *Adams* 2005 WL 399300 (N.D. III. 2005); *Hydrick* v. *Hunter* 500 F.3d 978 984 992–993 (2007); *Spicer* v. *Richards* WL 4561101 W.D. Washington (2007)) and has called into question the "voluntary" nature of treatment participation.

Regarding the delivery of treatment itself, several legal challenges have resulted in broad parameters for treatment implementation. Importantly, the Courts have consistently deferred to professional judgment in the majority of treatment-related matters. The Supreme Court in *Hendricks* established that "states enjoy wide latitude in developing treatment regimens" (*Kansas* v. *Hendricks* 521 U.S. 501 (1997)). Nonetheless, the Courts have provided guidance on the matter. For example, in *Turay* v. *Seling* (108 F. Supp. 2d 1148 (W.D. Washington 2000)), the Washington State sex offender civil commitment program was instructed to modify their treatment program in the following ways:

(i)   provide for initial and ongoing training and hiring of competent therapists;
(ii)   implement strategies to improve trust and rapport between residents and treatment providers;
(iii) implement a therapy program that includes all professionally recognized therapy components;
(iv)   develop and maintain individualized treatment plans that include objective benchmarks of improvement;
(v)   provide a psychologist or psychiatrist expert in diagnosis and treatment of sex offenders to supervise and consult with the treatment staff.

Additional cases, such as *Canupp* v. *Liberty Behavioral Health Corporation* (04-CV-00260 (M.D. Fla. March 2, 2007)) have established additional safeguards for treating civilly committed sex offenders with developmental disabilities or severe psychiatric disorders.

As demonstrated above, sex offender civil commitment or SVP statutes have undergone, and typically withstood, legal scrutiny on a number of grounds. The issue of whether we *can* as a society civilly commit sex offenders has been answered in the affirmative. The administrators and clinicians responsible for these programs have been granted much latitude to implement programs that conform to the requirements of the statutes and subsequent case law. Despite the legal validation of these laws and their administrative practices, scholars and practitioners alike continue to ask: *should* we as a society civilly commit sex offenders? Perhaps more specifically to our purpose in this chapter, the question posed is: should mental health professionals participate in any aspect of their implementation?

Ethical Issues in Sex Offender Civil Commitment

Behavioral health professionals have assumed several roles in the evaluation and treatment of persons involved in the civil commitment process. In negotiating the complexities of the legislation and its implementation, practitioners have voiced a number of concerns regarding the ethics of participating or performing certain functions within the process. Now more than 20 years after the initial development and implementation of SVP legislation and practices, the field has become more familiar with the practical realities, implications and unique challenges that come with SVP legislation and management programs. At the same time, the state of knowledge and science utilized by behavioral health practitioners in the field has drastically expanded and advanced. Coinciding with these developments, practitioners have begun increasingly to debate the appropriateness of the nature and degree of their participation in the civil commitment process.

At the center of the debate are concerns that the concept and practice of civil commitment is fundamentally at odds with foundational ethical principles of behavioral health disciplines. Controversial from their inception, it has been contended that SVP laws deprive individuals of fundamental rights to freedom and procedural fairness. Specifically, it has been argued that the requirements and implementation of the laws circumvent procedural safeguards and protections inherent in the constitution (and codified into law), and, as they subject individuals to indeterminate periods of confinement for crimes they *might* commit, are punitive in nature, rather than therapeutic. As such, many practitioners view participation in SVP work as representing complicity in the suppression of individual rights to liberty and fairness, and participation in a retributional and punitive process (rather than one that is rehabilitative or therapeutic). These views are therefore at odds with ethical principles underlying behavioral science disciplines that call for practitioners to respect and safeguard individual rights and to do no harm to clients in their applications of behavioral science. For instance, the Ethical Principles of Psychologists and Code of Conduct (EPPCC) emphasize these expectations in the principle of "Beneficence and Nonmaleficence" in which psychologists are expected to "seek to safeguard the welfare and rights of those with whom they interact professionally" and to "take care to do no harm" (American Psychological Association, 2002: 1062).

These concerns, and the ensuing debate in the field, has intensified as SVP legislation and confinement programs have matured, and a trend towards very long periods of post-incarceration confinement and low discharge rates has been observed. Also highlighting concerns regarding restriction of liberties and the punitive nature of SVP laws, confinement programs were noted to lack systems, procedures and resources for the release/transition of residents in their facilities into the community. Further, practitioners began to identify new concerns regarding the paucity of research demonstrating the effectiveness of SVP legislation in preventing or substantially reducing rates of sex crimes in the community. Adding to this concern is the rising, exorbitant costs of SVP laws to communities, and whether the benefit obtained from these programs justifies their cost. This latter issue has been a particular point of contention among practitioners, due to fears that "SVP programs will draw more and more resources away from programs that address the great bulk of sexual violence in the community" (Janus, 2004: 1237).

Another area of contention represents the ways in which clinicians must attempt to balance their responsibilities to safeguard the rights of individuals with that of the safety of communities, which is highlighted in various ethical guidelines. For instance, the preamble to the EPPCC makes it clear that psychologists have responsibilities both to society and to the individual, to "improve the condition of individuals, organizations, and society" (American Psychological Association, 2002: 1062). Indeed one justification for SVP legislation is predicated on the legal principle of "police power," allowing states with the responsibility of protecting its citizens "the right to write statutes for the benefit of society at large, even when providing this benefit may come at the cost of restricting the liberties of certain individuals" (Testa and West, 2010: 35). However, this argument, used as justification for restricting the rights and liberties of an identified subgroup, is thought by many to represent a "slippery slope"; ultimately allowing for a gradual expansion of the applicability of such restrictions to other subgroups of individuals deemed "undesirable" through the inappropriate pathologizing of their behaviors. The American Psychiatric Association raised an additional professional objection, describing SVP legislation as an abuse of psychiatric principles and practices in order to affect social policy and shortcomings of the criminal justice system (Brief for the American Psychiatric Association, 1997). Finally, there is growing concern regarding the unclear benefits of SVP programs to the community at large – benefits that are used to justify the harm or liberties taken from the individuals in these cases.

Forensic/psycho-legal evaluations of SVPs

Ethical concerns regarding the participation of forensic mental health experts in SVP evaluation center on the state of the science in the field, and its applicability to psycho-legal concepts in SVP statutes. Several elements are required to civilly detain an individual in jurisdictions with SVP legislation: a history of conviction of a sexually violent offense (as defined by that jurisdiction), a high likelihood of future sexual re-offense, and the presence of a mental disorder that predisposes an individual to engage in acts of sexual violence. Given the central features of identifying the presence of a mental disorder and determining risk for future re-offense in SVP determinations, the expertise of forensic psychiatrists and psychologists in the areas of identification and classification of mental disorders and the understanding and prediction of human behavior, can uniquely contribute to the Court's understanding of these areas. Further, because of the importance of these issues in the determination of SVP status, the opinions of experts can have considerable influence on outcomes in the commitment process (Sreenivasan, Weinberger and Garrick, 2003). However, there are limitations to the scientific knowledge in the field, as well as disagreements in the conceptualization, application and practices in determining mental abnormality, re-offense risk and predisposition, leading to debates within the field about the implications of these limitations. Specifically, many contend that we cannot perform diagnostic classification and risk assessment with enough consistency or accuracy to ethically justify or allow use of the science in SVP determinations, particularly given the gravity of determinations made with these data.

Diagnosis in the context of SVP legislation   A central area of disagreement and debate involves the practice of clinical diagnosis, and the applicability of psychiatric diagnostic categories to civil commitment criteria. Civil Commitment Statutes require the presence of a "mental disorder," "mental abnormality" or "personality disorder" (with a connection to sexual re-offense risk), as part of the requirement for determining whether a particular offender meets the criteria as an SVP. These statues, as well as subsequent case law (*Kansas* v. *Hendricks* 521 U.S. 346 (1997); *State* v. *Post* 197 Wis. 2d 279, 301, 541 N.W.2d 115, 121 (1995)) rely on the *Diagnostic and Statistical Manual of Mental Disorders*, now in its fourth edition (DSM-IV-TR; American Psychiatric Association, 2000) to identify and define these disorders.

Independent of SVP evaluations, critical debate regarding reliability and validity issues with the DSM classification system and diagnostic criteria, along with their applicability in "real world" situations, have been long raised (and recently intensified with the anticipated development of the DSM-5). Issues about validity center on whether DSM diagnostic classifications and criteria represent distinct, identifiable clinical conditions that are scientifically well grounded, relevant and meaningful in "real world" contexts; that is, that can be identified and understood outside theoretical paradigms and laboratory conditions. Next, reliability is concerned about the extent to which clinicians can consistently identify a condition in different individuals and across professionals.

The most common DSM-IV-TR diagnoses utilized in civil commitment proceedings involve the paraphilias (such as pedophilia), and personality disorders (such as antisocial personality disorder). Conflicts and debate regarding diagnoses utilized in SVP determinations typically center around validity of diagnoses (particularly "not otherwise specified" diagnoses, and proposed paraphilia diagnoses/criteria for the DSM-5); reliability of identifying diagnoses; sensitivity/specificity of diagnostic criteria (with the ability to select a subset of offenders); and the empirical connection between diagnostic conditions and re-offense "predisposition" (for example, in the case of antisocial personality disorder). As many of the diagnoses commonly seen in

SVP evaluations rely almost exclusively on observed behaviors to meet diagnostic criteria, many practitioners have also raised concerns regarding the pathologizing of simply undesirable or illicit behavior (particularly the paraphilias and Antisocial Personality Disorder) allegedly to support the medicalization of a questionable preventive detention procedure. Criticism of frequently utilized diagnoses of paraphilia, not otherwise specified (no consent) and personality disorder, not otherwise specified with antisocial features are also prominent, citing questionable validity and medicalization of criminal behavior, and pressure to create or over-fit diagnoses to support recommendations for civil commitment. In particular, there is growing concern with the proposed development of the diagnostic criteria for paraphilias in the DSM-5, in that the suggestions for revisions and identification of new disorders and their proposed definitions have been politicized and reflect undue influence from the SVP management industry, rather than the state of the science. Particular controversy has arisen over the proposed hebephilic and pedohebephilic subtypes for pedophilic disorder (Fabian, 2011; Frances and First, 2011), paraphilic coercive disorder (Zonana, 2011) and hypersexual disorder (Kafka, 2009), with the latter two now only being considered for inclusion in the appendix (American Psychiatric Association, 2012). These concerns stem, once again, from aspirational principles of Beneficence and Nonmaleficence, which includes the expectation that practitioners actively guard against undue influence and inappropriate use of their work (American Psychological Association, 2002).

Differences in understanding and use of the "predisposed" criteria in SVP legislation have also raised concerns among forensic practitioners. There are those that contend only paraphilias demonstrate a sufficient theoretical and empirical basis to "predispose" an individual to engage in future acts of sexual violence (Vognsen and Phenix, 2004), and while other disorders may be associated with or increase the likelihood of sexual offense behavior (for example, antisocial personality disorder), the association is insufficient to meet the legal definition of "predispose." Despite professional concerns about the validity and reliability of personality disorder diagnoses (particularly antisocial personality disorder), the courts have established this class of disorders as an acceptable basis for civil commitment (*In re Det. of Barnes*, 689 N.W.2d 455, 458 (Iowa 2004); *Martin et al.* v. *Reinstein* 987 P.2d 779 (Ariz. Ct. App. 1999)). However, diagnosis alone is insufficient to establish or infer predisposition to engage in sexual offense behavior (First and Halon, 2008).

Diagnostic classifications whose criteria can be met exclusively by observed behavior can also be problematic in that subsequent analyses of predisposition are "circular" (Elwood, 2009). Specifically, the very behavior used to diagnose mental abnormality (such as pedophilia) is the same behavior that the individual is predisposed to engage in based on that diagnosis (such as sexual contact with children). There are concerns that the current science is too limited to establish an adequate causal connection between diagnostic criteria and features, and a predisposition for engaging in future illegal sex acts, both in general and for a specific individual. This is consistent with general ethical concerns that the available science cannot, in good faith, be used reliably and accurately to inform triers of fact on key issues to assist them in their determinations, given the importance of the concept of "predisposition" to the process and criteria for civil commitment.

Risk assessment in SVP cases The state of the science in the area of risk assessment has seen significant advances since the initial development of SVP statues (see Chapter 20). The most significant advances include the development of actuarial tools for assessing risk, and the demonstration of the superiority of these instruments in predicting risk of recidivism to unstructured clinical judgment (Hanson and Bussière, 1998; Bonta, Law and Hanson, 1998; Monahan *et al.*, 2001). In brief, current concerns center around the accuracy and reliability of existing actuarial tools, appropriate use/misuse of actuarial instruments, the applicability of group estimates to an individual, the sufficiency of actuarial tools in predicting risk, and the application of risk estimates to legal definitions of "likelihood" for re-offense. Assessments of re-offense risk address central criteria of SVP determinations, highlighting the importance of ethical practice in this arena, particularly given the seriousness of the implications (that is, long-term, indefinite detention) for opinions regarding future offense risk.

A major area of contention for the practice of risk assessment in SVP cases involves the applicability of group-based estimates to an individual. Determinations of risk probabilities rely on comparisons of an individual to a reference group, and the known statistical relationship between specific characteristics of that group and sexual recidivism. This can result in several difficulties in applying the instrument and the degree to which the results can be relied upon. The first issue is the outcome measure, as the behaviors utilized in the development of the actuarial tool may not be relevant or consistent with those behaviors for which the clinician is interested in generating a risk estimate (for example, non-contact offenses). In addition, risk probabilities for a given category of risk represent an aggregate of the risk level in that cohort, though each individual within that group likely has a different "true risk" estimate. Risk estimates using actuarial data applied to individuals in SVP proceedings may therefore be limited, as forensic clinicians are only able to determine relative risk, and with some degree of error, while being unable to determine "true risk" rates for an offender, and triers of fact may have conceptual difficulty with this distinction. Practitioners have raised the question as to whether these estimates, and other related error rates, are therefore of sufficient accuracy to be applied to SVP proceedings, in which the outcomes can have serious repercussions in terms of deprivation of liberty for an individual on the one hand, or increased threats to public safety for the community on the other.

Actuarial tools do not purport to cover all possible factors with a relevant relationship to sexual recidivism. This has led to some debate about what other factors forensic evaluators should assess, as well as what approach should be used to conduct a comprehensive risk appraisal. Advocates for a "pure actuarial" approach contend that accurate, reliable risk assessments must eliminate clinical judgment altogether and rely solely on empirically derived risk tools, noting their limitations and highlighting the importance of ethical concepts of "transparency" and accountability for the work of clinicians (Abbott, 2011; Campbell, 2010). Others contend that such evaluations are incomplete, and possibly unethical for failing to consider all available risk-relevant information (Sreenivasan *et al.*, 2000). They argue that a comprehensive approach must involve inclusion of a structured clinical approach to a comprehensive risk assessment (in which other factors with statistical association to risk that do not appear in actuarial tools should also be considered). This dovetails with other concerns regarding the ability in the field to assess only a limited aspect of risk; namely likelihood of re-offense, and no other features that may be relevant to SVP determinations, such as "the possible nature, severity, imminence, or frequency" (Hart, Michie and Cooke, 2007: s60) of future sexual violence. Further, though it has been argued in the literature that predominant use of actuarial instruments is most appropriate for evaluations of long-term risk with applications to dichotomous decisions (to commit or not to commit) in SVP proceedings, the impact of factors such as treatment participation/completion and management level may be of increasing interest to the Courts (*In re Valdez*, No. 99-000045CI, at 6 (Fla. Cir. Ct. Aug 21, 2000)).

In recent years, there has been a growing body of research identifying additional factors relevant to sexual offense risk determinations, particularly dynamic risk factors (that is, risk factors that change, such as intimacy, self-regulation or social influences), along with preliminary data suggesting that inclusion of these additional risk factors in actuarial assessments of static risk may improve predictive accuracy (Hanson *et al.*, 2007; Eher *et al.*, 2011). However, this research remains in its early stages, as does the relevance of these factors to determinations of risk in psycho-legal contexts such as SVP proceedings.

Beginning in the early 1990s, a decline in national rates of sexual violence has been observed in the United States and Canada. Helmus, Hanson and Thornton (2009) subsequently determined that the base rates of the original development sample of the Static-99, one of the most widely used tools for estimating recidivism in SVP cases, significantly differed from the current recorded rates, requiring that the instrument be re-normed. Near the same time, it was determined that age also had a statistical impact on risk estimates (particularly for older offenders), leading to further modification of the instrument. These changes, in the context of prior concerns regarding inter-rater reliability and external validity (Abbott, 2011; Sreenivasan, Weinberger and Garrick, 2003), have led to increasing attention being paid to the ethical obligations of forensic clinicians to understand and convey the limits of actuarial instruments in their reports and testimony. In addition, these recent developments have highlighted broader ethical considerations regarding the sufficiency of the instrument in the high-stakes context of SVP evaluations.

Concerns regarding the application of risk assessment procedures and tools to the legal criteria in the various state statutes have also been raised. This basically concerns the degree to which information provided by the procedures and instruments utilized in a risk appraisal assess the precise standard being required by the legal system in SVP proceedings; such as whether statistical probabilities for re-offense address the legal definition of "likely"; that risk determinations provide estimates relevant to the context sought by a particular statute (such as re-offense risk with treatment, under supervision, short-term risk, long-term risk, etc.), or matches the "outcome" as defined by the statute (type/nature of sexual violence). Further, current risk schemes and tools do not directly address these issues, and experts are asked to "bridge the gap" and apply risk assessment data to the psycho-legal context, which can arguably be accomplished at varying levels of competency, accuracy and ethical practice, failing to highlight limits of data or to be "transparent" in the process.

As is evident even in the brief discussion here, risk appraisals are fairly complex, particularly in the context of SVP proceedings, and require considerable experience and knowledge of the development, application and limitations of risk assessment principles, procedures and instruments to complete competently. A number of concerns have been raised regarding the ability of forensic clinicians in SVP cases to conduct accurate assessments and utilize actuarial risk tools appropriately. Identified problems include ignorance of risk assessment principles and lack of training and familiarity with the application and scoring of risk tools, as well as interpretation and integration of the resulting probability estimates into a larger evaluation, and awareness and communication of these limitations of the instruments to triers of fact. As poorly done risk assessments are not simply useless, but actually cause harm (Janus and Prentky, 2003), serious ethical concerns regarding the performance of risk assessments by forensic evaluators in SVP proceedings have been raised.

The concerns regarding limitations in the science and practice of risk assessment summarized here further emphasize the ethical difficulty faced by forensic practitioners working in the SVP arena. With clinicians working to balance the weighty issues of individual liberties of offenders with public safety concerns, questions regarding the sufficiency of risk assessment paradigms and tools, as well as the potential consequences of limitations in scientific knowledge and clinical practice, are sobering.

Role of forensic experts in SVP cases Forensic mental health experts are uniquely positioned to make significant contributions in assisting triers of fact in applying psychological science and principles to civil commitment criteria, given their expertise in behavioral principles, diagnosis, risk assessment and analysis and research in the SVP field. With the current state of the science and conflicting opinions regarding matters such as diagnostic formulations, determinations of predisposition, and apparent use and application of actuarial risk instruments, experts testifying in SVP cases typically provide fairly complex and lengthy information on these issues. Having expertise in matters of law, rather than behavioral science, it has been suggested that judges (as well as juries) may have difficulty in accurately assessing the quality and accuracy of expert testimony (Appelbaum, 2002; Sreenivasan, Weinberger and Garrick, 2003) in SVP cases. As such, substantial weight, perhaps undue weight, may be given to the opinions of testifying experts and actuarial findings informing judicial decisions (Sreenvasian, Weinberger and Garrick, 2003; Janus and Prentky, 2003), threatening expectations that practitioners avoid "misuse of their influence" (American Psychological Association, 2002: 1062) and ensure that others understand the nature and implications of the "limitations of their expertise" (American Psychological Association, 2002: 1063). This is compounded by the assertion that by proving testimony in that vein (particularly ultimate issue testimony), experts are "serving as an agent of the state's punitive apparatus" (Bonnie, 1998: 7), in ethical conflict with their role as an impartial professional imparting expert scientific knowledge (Specialty Guidelines for Forensic Psychology, 2011; see Chapter 5).

Treatment of SVPs

For clinicians providing treatment services to individuals subject to SVP laws, the principles of effective therapy in general equally apply to the specialty area of treatment of this population (Levenson *et al.*, 2009; Marshall *et al.*, 2003; Marshall, 2005). In general, behavioral health clinicians must have a strong theoretical framework from which they formulate and deliver treatment; they must establish therapeutic rapport, foster a therapeutic alliance, and work collaboratively with their therapy clients or residents (Beech and Hamilton-Giachritsis, 2005; Beech and Fordham, 1997). Without the application of these basic principles of effective therapy, there is no reason to believe that any treatment approach would be very effective at facilitating change in individuals. In essence, the role of the sexual offense therapist is to help protect the community by helping SVP clients make pro-social changes in their thoughts, feelings and behaviors, and thus reduce their risk of re-offending. To be effective, therapists must apply the same principles of ethical and effective treatment to their SVP clients as they would with any other therapy client.

However, participation in treatment activities with SVP clients or within SVP processes also presents unique ethical challenges for clinicians. Indefinite terms of confinement, and therefore treatment, place clinicians in the difficult position of continuing to work with some residents long after substantial treatment gains and progress have been made, though practical barriers (such as inadequate community transition programming and legal restrictions) inhibit release and opportunities for further rehabilitation. Clinicians may also struggle with the notion of probable lifetime confinement for residents with substantial, intractable difficulties, for which our current knowledge and science, so far, has little to offer in terms of effective interventions and treatment.

Settings for confinement programs are often correctional in nature, where facilities, personnel and practices have a primary goal of community safety and security, rather than the well-being or therapeutic management of its residents (for a discussion of these issues, see Weinberger and Sreenivasan, 1994). Institutional policies and procedures may significantly conflict with the ethical principles and practices of behavioral health clinicians, particularly principles pertaining to multiple-role conflicts and resident rights to autonomy, privacy and confidentiality. In addition, by the very nature of SVP laws, clinicians are often working with individuals whose initial and ongoing participation is coerced to some degree, and in which certain treatment goals are not developed collaboratively between the therapist and client, but dictated by virtue of the client's circumstance (for example, participation in antiandrogenic pharmacotherapy in some jurisdictions (Harrison, 2008)). Further, clinicians in these settings may often be in the position of enforcing policies and facilitating institutional or system rules and practices that are punitive rather than rehabilitative or therapeutic, or that serve the function of justice, under the guise of "treatment." Most of these circumstances are in direct opposition to professional ethics principles and standards for behavioral health professionals, who have ethical responsibilities to avoid multiple relationships, and ensure the confidentiality of the client's information and promote rights to dignity, fair treatment and self-determination. These circumstances are also very disruptive to the establishment of therapeutic or working relationships between clinicians and residents, considered essential to promoting behavioral change in the field and representative of the ethical principle of "fidelity" in which practitioners aspire to "establish relationships of trust with those with whom they work" (American Psychological Association, 2002: 1062). Clinicians working with individuals designated as SVPs in community settings share many of these same challenges and often face intense, sometimes invasive oversight and direction of their work with residents.

Given these distinct challenges to ethical clinical practice, opponents of SVP legislation have argued that behavioral health professionals should not participate in treatment or management efforts with residents.

Agents of change or agents of justice?   Clinicians must often walk a tightrope between working in the best interests of their clients, and working to maintain the safety of individuals in the community. Behavioral health practitioners working within SVP facilities are participating in a hybrid justice and therapeutic process that readily lends itself to the blurring of professional role boundaries between these two processes, placing practitioners in the ethically uncomfortable arena of being in dual or multiple roles with their clients, or confusing their clients about the nature of their role (that is, forensic vs. correctional vs. therapeutic). As noted previously, practitioners are often asked, or even required, to perform a myriad of functions aimed at population control and security measures in the contexts of these settings, that have the effect of subtly (or even clearly) impacting the actual or perceived role of practitioners in these settings. In essence, poor role definitions and role conflicts are problematic as they can lead to impairments in professional judgment and treatment relationship, impact therapeutic goals and effectiveness, and exploit and harm clients, and as such, clinicians are expected to avoid such circumstances (American Psychological Association, 2002; Specialty Guidelines for Forensic Psychology, 2011). These consequences are particularly problematic in the SVP arena, as poor treatment outcomes can lead to risks to the community.

One of the more noted examples of role dilemmas faced by practitioners involves resident participation in therapeutic programming itself. Documentation generated in the course of treatment is often utilized later in forensic evaluations and legal processes pertaining to the ongoing detention (or initial detention in the case of detainees) of a resident and can be used to support their continued detention (with the argument that had the resident not participated in treatment, this information would not have been gathered, recorded and used in this manner). Indeed, in some programs, clinicians may be directed or even trained to focus on specific information in their documentation that would facilitate the goals of decision makers and other third parties (such as forensic evaluators) in their functions. Many feel this places the clinician in the position of serving in an investigative role for these other purposes, threatening their primary role as a therapist or agent of change, as well as their ethical responsibilities to ensure the well-being of their client, and to avoid deception or misrepresentation of information or their role to their clients (Winick, 1998). In fact, the Specialty Guidelines for Forensic Psychology (2011: 8) specifically warn:

> Therapeutic services can have significant effects on current or future legal proceedings. Forensic practitioners are encouraged to consider these effects and minimize any unintended or negative effects on such proceedings or therapy when they provide therapeutic services in forensic contexts.

A vested interest in civil detention of SVPs?

Throughout the controversy, proponents have held that the intent behind SVP legislation, to detain, and ideally rehabilitate a very small subset of highly dangerous individuals – who, if left to their own devices, would engage in a disproportionate amount of crime, and do real harm to communities through additional victimization of others – remains worthwhile, both as a social policy and as a legitimate venue for clinicians to apply their unique skills and training. Though threatening to professional ideals of autonomy and fairness, the concept of preventative detention for the protection of the community is not new or foreign to the mental health field. In countering a number of identified concerns of professionals outlined previously in this chapter, it has been argued that clinicians have a long history of regularly participating in processes to civilly commit individuals on the grounds that they represent a danger to others, based on an underlying mental illness (though typically psychoses, and severe cognitive and mood disorders). Commitments can become quiet lengthy as well, in part for legal and politicized reasons (for example, some Not Guilty by Reason of Insanity cases), and due to serious, intractable symptoms that exceed our scientific ability to effectively treat and restore functioning to a degree that would allow that individual to live safely in the community. Next (with some variation in social policy over time), detention of persons with sexual behavior problems, both for their rehabilitation and the safety of the community, is also not novel to the mental health field; "sexual psychopath" legislation was initiated in the 1930s (Sreenivasan, Frances and Weinberger, 2010).

Another contention is that SVP legislation places additional ethical demands on behavioral health practitioners. Practitioners specializing in working with sexual behavior problems have a wealth of knowledge, training and skills in the areas of human behavior, sexual functioning and deviance, statistical analysis and investigation, risk assessment and management, evaluation, diagnosis and case conceptualization, and therapeutic intervention. Such expertise can be of tremendous value in the SVP arena, and practitioners may accordingly have ethical demands to offer and apply that knowledge and expertise in service to the public. Specifically, aspirational guidelines expect that practitioners strive to be:

> committed to increasing scientific and professional knowledge of behavior and people's understanding of themselves and others and to the use of such knowledge to improve the condition of individuals, organizations, and society . . . [and to] help the public in developing informed judgments and choices concerning human behaviour. (American Psychological Association, 2002: 1062)

The expertise of practitioners in the field can inform policy, decision makers and the public; effect behavioral changes in individuals to reduce their risk of committing future acts that harm communities; ensure that other forms of community management of sexual offense behaviors are considered; and that decisions made are based on science, rather than other factors that may encourage poor outcomes.

A number of scientific advances have occurred in the field of sex offense management over the past two decades, and ongoing legislation and scrutiny of the knowledge in the field, development tools and interventions, and their application will likely spur these efforts forward, and assist the field in addressing gaps that not only improve the quality and accuracy of our assessments, testimony and interventions, but also help reduce some of the ethical quandaries that face the field with the implementation of SVP legislation.

Note

1   For the sake of convenience the term Sexually Violent Predator (SVP) will be used throughout this chapter.

References

Abbott, B. (2011) "Throwing the baby out with the bath water: is it time for clinical judgment to supplement actuarial risk assessment?," *Journal of the American Academy of Psychiatry and the Law* 39, 2, 222–230.

American Psychiatric Association (2000) *Diagnostic and Statistical Manual of Mental Disorders*, 4th edn., text rev. Washington, DC: American Psychiatric Association.

American Psychiatric Association (2012) DSM–5 Development: Paraphilias, http://www. dsm5.org/proposedrevision/Pages/ParaphilicDisorders.aspx (accessed September 18, 2012).

American Psychological Association (2002) "Ethical principles of psychologists and code of conduct," *American Psychologist* 57, 1060–1073.

Appelbaum, P. (2002) "Policing expert testimony: the role of professional organizations," *Psychiatric Services* 53, 389–390.

Beech, A. and Fordham, A. (1997) "Therapeutic climate of sexual offender programs," *Sexual Abuse: A Journal of Research and Treatment* 9, 3, 219–238.

Beech, A. and Hamilton-Giachritsis, C.E. (2005) "Relationship between therapeutic climate and treatment outcome in group-based sexual offender treatment programs," *Sexual Abuse: A Journal of Research and Treatment* 17, 2, 127–140.

Bonnie, R. (1998) "Forum – psychiatrists and the death penalty: some ethical dilemmas: comments," *Current Opinion in Psychiatry* 11, 3–11.

Bonta, J., Law, M. and Hanson, K. (1998) "The prediction of criminal and violent recidivism among mentally disordered offenders: a meta-analysis," *Psychological Bulletin* 123, 2, 123–142.

Brief for the American Psychiatric Association (1997) Brief for the American Psychiatric Association as Amicus Curiae, *Kansas* v. *Crane*, 521 U.S. 346 (1997).

Campbell, T. (2010) "Maximizing accuracy and welcoming scrutiny in SVP evaluations: an additional response to Wilson and Looman," *Open Access Journal of Forensic Psychology* 2, 337–346, http://www.forensicpsychologyunbound.ws/OAJFP/Sex_Offenders_files/ Campbell3%202010.pdf (accessed September 18, 2012).

Eher, R., Matthes, A., Schilling, F., *et al.* (2011) "Dynamic risk assessment in sexual offenders using STABLE–2000 and the STABLE–2007: an investigation of predictive and incremental validity," *Sexual Abuse: A Journal of Research and Treatment*. DOI: 10.1177/ 1079063211403164.

Elwood, R. (2009) "Mental disorder, predisposition, prediction, and ability to control: evaluating sex offenders for civil commitment," *Sexual Abuse: A Journal of Research and Treatment* 21, 4, 395–411.

Fabian, J. (2011) "Diagnosing and litigating hebephilia in sexually violent predator civil commitment proceedings," *Journal of the American Academy of Psychiatry and the Law* 39, 496–505.

First, M. and Halon, R. (2008) "Use of DSM paraphilia diagnoses in sexually violent predator commitment cases," *Journal of the American Academy of Psychiatry and the Law* 36, 443–454.

Frances, A. and First, M.B. (2011) "Hebephilia is not a mental disorder in DSM-IV-TR and should not become one in DSM-5," *Journal of the American Academy of Psychiatry and the Law* 39, 78–85.

Good, P. and Burstein, J. (2010) "A modern day witch hunt: the troubling role of psychologists in sexual predator laws," *American Journal of Forensic Psychology* 28, 23–47.

Hanson, R.K. and Bussière, M.T. (1998) "Predicting relapse: a meta-analysis of sexual offender recidivism studies," *Journal of Consulting and Clinical Psychology* 66, 348–362.

Hanson, R.K., Harris, A.J.R., Scott, T.-L. and Helmus, L. (2007) *Assessing the Risk of Sexual Offenders on Community Supervision: The Dynamic Supervision Project (User Report 2007-05)*. Ottawa: Public Safety Canada.

Harrison, K. (2008) "Legal and ethical issues when using antiandrogenic pharmacotherapy with sex offenders," *Sexual Offender Treatment* 3, 2, accessed 12 February 2012. http://www.sexual-offender-treatment.org/2-2008_01.html (accessed September 7, 2012).

Hart, S., Michie, C. and Cooke, D. (2007) "Precision of actuarial risk assessment instruments," *British Journal of Psychiatry* 190, s60–s64.

Janus, E. (2000) "Sexual predator commitment laws: lessons for law and the behavioral sciences," *Behavioral Sciences and the Law* 18, 5–21.

Janus, E. (2004) "Closing Pandora's box: sexual predators and the politics of sexual violence," *Seton Hall Law Review* 34, 4, 1233–1253.

Janus, E. and Prentky, R. (2003) "Forensic use of actuarial risk assessment with sex offenders: accuracy, admissibility and accountability," *American Criminal Law Review* 1443, 1–59.

Kafka, M. (2009) "Hypersexual disorder: a proposed diagnosis for DSM-V," *Archives of Sexual Behavior* 39, 377–400.

Levenson, J.S., Macgowan, M.J., Morin, J.W. and Cotter, L.P. (2009) "Perceptions of sex offenders about treatment: satisfaction and engagement in group therapy," *Sexual Abuse: A Journal of Research and Treatment* 21, 1, 35–56.

Marshall, W.L. (2005) "Therapist style in sexual offender treatment: influence on indices of change," *Sexual Abuse: A Journal of Research and Treatment* 17, 2, 109–116.

Marshall, W.L., Fernandez, Y.M., Serran, G.A. *et al.* (2003) "Process variables in the treatment of sexual offenders: a review of the relevant literature," *Aggression and Violent Behavior* 8, 205–234.

Monahan, J., Steadman, H., Silver, E. *et al.* (2001) *Rethinking Risk Assessment: The Macarthur Study of Mental Disorder and Violence*. New York: Oxford University Press.

Specialty Guidelines for Forensic Psychology (2011) http://www.ap-ls.org/aboutpsychlaw/SGFP_Final_Approved_2011.pdf (accessed September 7, 2012).

Sreenivasan, S., Frances, A. and Weinberger, L. (2010) "Normative versus consequential ethics in sexually violent predator laws: an ethics conundrum for psychiatry," *Journal of the American Academy of Psychiatry and the Law* 38, 386–391.

Sreenivasan, S., Kirkish, P., Garrick, T. *et al.* (2000) "Actuarial risk assessment models: a review of critical issues related to violence and sex-offender recidivism assessments," *Journal of the American Academy of Psychiatry and the Law* 28, 438–448.

Sreenivasan, S., Weinberger, L. and Garrick, T. (2003) "Expert testimony in sexually violent predator commitments: conceptualizing legal standards of 'mental disorder' and 'likely to reoffend'," *Journal of the American Academy of Psychiatry and the Law* 31, 471–485.

Testa, M. and West, S. (2010) "Civil commitment in the United States," *Innovations in Clinical Neuroscience* 7, 10, 30–40.

Vlahakis, J.C. (2010) "Legal issues involving sexually violent persons," in A. Schlank (ed.), *The Sexual Predator*, vol. IV. Kingston, NJ: Civic Research Institute, pp. 212–230.

Vognsen, J. and Phenix, A. (2004) "Antisocial personality disorder is not enough: a reply to Sreenivasan, Weinberger, and Garrick," *Journal of the American Academy of Psychiatry and the Law* 32, 440–442.

Weinberger, L.E. and Sreenivasan, S. (1994) "Ethical and professional conflicts in correctional psychology," *Professional Psychology: Research and Practice* 25, 2, 161–167.

Winick, B. (1998) "Sex offender law in the 1990s: a therapeutic jurisprudence analysis," *Psychology, Public Policy, and Law* 4, 1/2, 505–570.

Zonana, H. (2011) "Sexual disorders: new and expanded proposals for the DSM–5 – do we need them?," *Journal of the American Academy of Psychiatry and the Law* 39, 245–249.

25

Sex Offender Residence Restrictions
A Systematic Review of the Literature
Daniel Pacheco and J.C. Barnes

Introduction

Historically, one type of offender has generated contempt and loathing like no other: the sex offender (Chaffin, 2008). Though the reasons for these strong reactions are varied, the mere mention of the words "sex offender" tends to draw mental images of the nude, lifeless body of a helpless child along with images of a predatory-looking male being escorted by law-enforcement as the alleged attacker. Because of real events that reflect these images and the public's outrage that such a heinous crime is possible in modern society, legislators have taken up the mantle of doing everything within their power to curtail similar offenses from happening in the future (Leon, 2011). The result has been a propagation of laws specifically targeting sex offenders, affecting nearly every aspect of their lives (Mulford, Wilson and Parmley, 2009).

Though sex offender policies have been on the books for decades, a recent acceleration in the passing of new statutes has been observed. This recent surge of legislation can be attributed primarily to the Jacob Wetterling Act 1994, which established sex offender registries, and Megan's Law 1996, which established community notification (Center for Sex Offender Management, 2008; see Chapter 21). One particular legislative mandate specifically targeting sex offenders that has gained recent momentum is residency restriction(s) (Barnes, 2011). A residency restriction typically has two acceptations: (1) a specific location or venue from which an offender is prohibited from approaching (such as a school, park or playground); and (2) the perimeter or margin that circumnavigates a prohibited location (for example, an (arbitrarily) legislatively prescribed zone around a school, park or playground). Expressly, residency restrictions prohibit sex offenders from residing within a certain geographic margin

The Wiley-Blackwell Handbook of Legal and Ethical Aspects of Sex Offender Treatment and Management,
First Edition. Edited by Karen Harrison and Bernadette Rainey.
© 2013 John Wiley & Sons, Ltd. Published 2013 by John Wiley & Sons, Ltd.

of any place where children might congregate (Nieto and Jung, 2006). Although such places usually include schools, daycare centers, parks, shopping malls and sports facilities, prohibited venues can be extended to include churches, zoos, theme parks and certain restaurants (such as Chuck E. Cheese Pizza in the United States), among others (Maguire and Singer, 2011). Sex offenders can also be barred from residing in certain neighborhoods and apartment complexes. The idea is to create a buffer or aegis between the otherwise unsuspecting public and the offender.

There is a nascent body of literature emerging on the topic of sex offender residency restrictions. This body of academic scholarship, however, appears fractured and tends to come in one of two forms: (1) law-review articles found in legal journals as well as opinion and commentary pieces, and (2) empirical-based research. The law-review and commentary papers tend to focus on the (un)constitutionality of residency restrictions (Hobson, 2005; Janicki, 2006; Logan, 2006; West, 2007), *ex post facto* challenges (Bains, 2007; Loudon-Brown, 2007; Agudo, 2008; Saxer, 2008) and punitiveness (Logan, 2006; Bains, 2007; Agudo, 2008; Wright, 2008; Mancini, 2009; Mancini and Mears, 2010), usually in the larger context of sex offender registration and community notification requirements. Although much of the work within this stream of literature is important and relevant, this chapter will focus exclusively on the second line of scholarship: the empirical-based research. The objective of the chapter is systematically to review the empirical literature with an eye towards summarizing "what we know" about sex offender residence restrictions.

The chapter will therefore comprehensively review the current empirical literature on sex offender residency restrictions. It begins by identifying the two most prominent theoretical traditions that appear to be the basis for sex offender residence restrictions: deterrence or rational choice theory (Apel and Nagin, 2011; Nagin, 1998; Pratt *et al.*, 2008; Stafford and Warr, 1993) and routine activities theory (Cohen and Felson, 1979). Sex offender residency restrictions are then considered through the prism of these theories in an attempt to understand the justification or rational basis for the enactment of these laws. This is then followed by a systematic review of the empirical literature, the primary focus of the current work.

Theoretical Background

In general, there are two theoretical frameworks that can help illuminate the logic and/or the goals of sex offender residence restrictions. First is deterrence or rational choice theory (Apel and Nagin, 2011; Nagin, 1998; Pratt *et al.*, 2008; see also Stafford and Warr, 1993). Three aspects of deterrence/rational choice theory must be explicated: first, the idea of specific deterrence; second, the idea of general deterrence; and third, the idea that deterrence serves not only to explain crime but also to provide a meaningful policy response to crime (Jacobs, 2010). Specific deterrence refers to the way an already punished offender elects to avoid further criminal involvement because of the threat of additional punishment for subsequent acts. In other words, individuals are specifically deterred if after they have been punished they resist future criminal activity. General deterrence refers to the vicariously encoded perceptions of the larger community that result from punishments meted out to others in the individual's social group or community. An individual can be generally deterred by the knowledge of the punishment of another person. The third idea, that deterrence serves as a viable policy response, has the most direct connection to sex offender residence restriction laws. Broadly stated, deterrence is based on the perceptions of the would-be offender, specifically as to how (s)he perceives punishment for the criminal act. Individuals who refrain and/or desist from criminal conduct because the risk or threat of punishment are considered to have been deterred. Below, we will link sex offender residence restrictions with deterrence/rational choice theory. Before moving to this discussion, however, the second theoretical framework that informs the current task will be introduced.

The second theory is routine activities theory (Cohen and Felson, 1979). Routine activities theory posits that crime occurs at the intersection in time and space of (1) the presence of a motivated offender; (2) the absence of a capable guardian; and (3) the presence of a suitable target. In most cases, the motivated offender is always assumed to exist (that is, would-be offenders are always available). With that in mind, the theory suggests that the probability of the convergence of the three elements is affected by a would-be victim's regular habits. For example, an individual (or suitable target) who regularly uses cocaine places him/herself at risk of victimization by having contact with drug sellers (Jacobs, 1999; see also Cullen and Agnew, 2006). The balance of the probability that a crime will occur changes congruently with the nature of the activity so that individuals whose daily routines exclude contact with risk-dense situations are less likely (compared to individuals whose daily routines include contact with risk-dense situations) to be victimized.

Drawing on these two theoretical traditions sets the stage for the presumed rationale that is used to codify and enforce residency restrictions on sex offenders. The first, deterrence theory, can be applied at both the specific and general level where the intent of the policy is to deter sexual offending. For an offender to be subject to a residency restriction, (s)he would have been subject to some form of punishment. Consequently, because of that prior punishment and the threat of "new" punishment if residency restrictions are violated, specific deterrence is assumed to be at work.

General deterrence can also be applied because of the public manner in which residence restrictions are enforced. The community at large is profoundly aware of the residency restrictions imposed on sex offenders, among a litany of other requirements. This vicarious acknowledgement and encoding of the punishment imposed on others can dissuade a would-be sex offender from engaging in sexually criminal conduct to avoid punishment under the rubric of deterrence.

Similarly, the intent of sex offender residency restrictions can be viewed through the prism of routine activities theory. Potentially "motivated offenders" are removed from the equation by residence restrictions (Barnes, 2011). Inasmuch as a sex offender would be prohibited from residing within a certain proximity or margin from where children congregate, (s)he is extracted from the time and space within which a sexual offense would occur. Therefore, the convergence of the requisite criteria (the presence of a motivated offender and suitable target, and the absence of a capable guardian) is disrupted and the opportunity for the motivated offender to offend is obstructed.

Sex Offender Management and Residency Restrictions

Having provided a theoretical backdrop for sex offender residence restrictions, the empirical literature that has analyzed these laws will now be considered. This section offers a brief overview of the empirical literature surrounding sex offender policies generally. In doing so, sex offender residency restrictions will be highlighted as an element of the overall sex offender management apparatus. This section will provide a platform upon which the remainder of the study, the systematic literature review, will be built.

Sex offender residency restrictions are, fundamentally, a form of offender management that has become manifest in legislative policy. Beginning with the Jacob Wetterling Act of 1994 and Megan's Law of 1996 (Center for Sex Offender Management, 2008), concerted efforts have been made to impose substantial requirements on sexual offenders. These efforts include requirements such as broad-based registration, regardless of the facts of the offense; community notification; residency restrictions, as showcased in the current chapter; and avoiding places where children gather; as well as ancillary things such as submitting DNA; driver's license flagging; and acquiescing to intermittent polygraph testing (Mancini, Barnes and Mears, 2011; for polygraph testing, see Chapter 23). The intended purpose behind the imposition of such requirements is commonly stated as being public safety and, more specifically, the safety of children (see Levenson and D'Amora, 2007).

Some of the research that examines sex offender residency restrictions includes them as one element of the overall sex offender management apparatus in an effort to evaluate the impact of legislation such as the Jacob Wetterling Act and Megan's Law. For example, Sandler, Freeman and Socia (2008) used time-series analysis to evaluate the impact of New York's sex offender registration and notification law. These authors, drawing on data from over 170,000 sexual offense arrests in New York between 1986 and 2006, sought to determine whether the enactment of the law, which included residency restrictions, resulted in: (1) decreased sexual offender recidivism, and (2) deterrence of "nonregistered offenders from committing registerable sexual offenses" (Sandler, Freeman and Socia, 2008: 297). The researchers concluded that enactment of the law did *not* reduce sexual offender recidivism or deter sexual offending. Reduced sexual offender recidivism is one of the main reasons for the enactment of residency restrictions. Research by Willis and Grace (2009) focused on the risk factors associated with recidivism and the importance of reintegrative planning for sex offenders. The success of reintegrative planning is predicated on being reconnected to prosocial and supportive family networks (Willis and Grace, 2008). Residency restrictions translate into increased social isolation and the preclusion of sex offenders to reside with supportive family members, ultimately leading to an increased risk of recidivism. In the words of Willis and Grace (2009: 509), sex offender residency restrictions "increase the same risk they intend to deter."

The role of the public's perceptions regarding sex offender residency restrictions is not trivial. Public opinion polls illuminate the way people feel about the policies that govern the management of sex offenders. For example, a small survey of 115 individuals collected from a US-wide online community message board suggested that although most people support Megan's Law, they also did not believe sex offender management policies, including residency restrictions, reduce recidivism (Schiavone and Jeglic, 2009). Interestingly, in some cases, individuals want to see offender registries expanded to include other types of crime (Craun, Kernsmith and Butler, 2011). Although there appears to be broad-based public support for punitive-based sex offender policy, there is substantially less support for the execution (that is, capital punishment) of sex offenders than there is for the execution of murderers (Mancini and Mears, 2010). The work by Mancini and Mears (2010) also indicated that support for the execution of sex offenders depended on whether the victim was a child.

Other work has focused on the negative effects of sex offender policies on the offenders themselves. Not only must offenders contend with the secondary punishments that arise from having a felony conviction (such as ineligibility to vote; denial of professional licenses), sex offenders in particular must also negotiate a myriad of other unofficial, secondary penalties because of their status as a sex offender. These can include difficulties with family (Tewksbury and Levenson, 2009); obtaining employment and the inherent stress that comes with being unemployed and stigmatized (Levenson and Tewksbury, 2009; Tewksbury and Zgoba, 2010); as well as housing (Herendeen, 2010; Suresh *et al.*, 2010). In fact, some investigations have found that sex offender registration and notification requirements result in difficulty assimilating into prosocial support networks (Willis and Grace, 2008; Lasher and McGrath, 2012); concentrations of offenders in socially disorganized neighborhoods (Hipp, Turner and Jannetta, 2010; Suresh *et al.*, 2010); and, ultimately, sex offenders being pushed or funneled into areas with many other offenders where demand for needed services taxes capacity (Hipp *et al.*, 2009). Consequently, sex offenders are effectively routed into areas where residents are least likely to be deterred from criminal conduct, as well as being least subject to the supervision of capable guardians. Ultimately, these effects may result in failed reintegration (Wakefield, 2006).

The Current Study

Scholars have analyzed the impact of residence restrictions by using a myriad of outcomes. Some examinations have focused on the impact of residency restrictions on recidivism, while others have analyzed the impact of these laws on the local community, the offender's contact with family, and the offender's access to treatment. Scholars have typically anchored their research in two broad theoretical backgrounds: deterrence/rational choice theory; and routine activities theory. This research has illuminated the rationale underlying the enactment as well as the anticipated implications and effects of these policies. The lacuna that remains is a broad-based assessment of the residence restriction literature.

Although prior works have provided cursory summaries of the effects of sex offender residency restrictions (Barnes, 2011; Burchfield, 2011; Socia, 2011a, 2011b; Tewksbury, 2011), a systematic review of the empirical scholarship has not yet been published (but see Nieto and Jung, 2006, for a comprehensive review of the research focused on sex offender management and correctional practices). Consequently, the current research synthesizes the scholarship on sex offender residency restrictions by providing a comprehensive and systematic review of the literature.

Methods

Data retrieval

In order to comprehensively evaluate the empirical status of sex offender residency restrictions it was necessary to obtain all scholarly works published and accessible through conventional databases. The initial search began by utilizing three databases: (1) Google Scholar; (2) the National Criminal Justice Reference Service; and (3) Web of Knowledge (formerly Web of Science). In order to pull articles from these three databases, several keyword searches were performed. To be specific, the following four search terms were used to target eligible articles: (1) "residence restriction"; (2) "residency restriction"; (3) "sex offender residence restriction"; and (4) "sex offender residency restriction." All articles/papers available in at least one of these databases as of May 25, 2011 were included in this review.

During the data retrieval process, 625 "hits" were returned based on the search terms that were entered. A hit is simply a matched result for the specific search term(s) entered for the database being queried. Several hits were duplicates, either because the target article was in multiple databases or the retrieval algorithm identified the same article across the different search terms. Importantly, the database search identified a number of articles that were not contextually salient (for example, because the article covered a topic other than residency restrictions within the purview of sex offender policy). Each hit was scrutinized and assessed for inclusion into the study resulting in a "usable target." A large number of hits were initially returned for each database and search term; however, the number of hits iteratively decreased as the search term string increased. As a result, the number of unique hits decreased to zero in the last six searches because the universe of eligible target articles had already been detected and returned in antecedent searches. The results of the search procedure are documented in Table 25.1.

The initial search netted a sample of 113 *possible* eligible articles. Not all articles included in the initial sample, however, were eligible for inclusion in the review. To identify eligible articles systematically, we followed three inclusion criteria. First, the article must have been published between 1994 and 2011. This criterion was included because it was important to account for the surge of sex offender legislation that occurred immediately after the passage of the Jacob Wetterling Act of 1994. The Jacob Wetterling Act required states to establish registries for sex offenders, starting a succession of increasingly restrictive statutes aimed at sex offenders (Mancini, Barnes and Mears, 2011).

The second inclusion criterion was that the article be a substantive analysis rather than an opinion or commentary piece. One of the universal principles of credible academic scholarship found in an analysis is the neutral, unbiased nature of the work. Thus, we only included papers that presented some type of analysis of sex offender

Table 25.1 Database article search "hit" and "unique target article" counts.

Search term	Google Scholar		National Criminal Justice Reference Service		Web of Science	
	Hits	*Unique targets*	*Hits*	*Unique targets*	*Hits*	*Unique targets*
Residence restriction	113	36	2	1	134	0
Residency restriction	236	49	4	2	44	0
Sex offender residence restriction	10	1	0	0	3	0
Sex offender residency restriction	76	1	2	0	1	0

residence restriction laws. Opinion papers and commentary pieces were omitted because they do not present new, objective information. For example, several of the articles obtained were law-review articles that would not necessarily constitute an analysis with the same definition as expected in an empirical sense. Law-review articles were consequently not included in the main analysis. It was only important that the work present an analysis; the type of analysis, whether quantitative, qualitative or a review, was assessed later as a means to further classify target articles.

Finally, the third eligibility criterion restricted the sample to academic or scholarly works. This criterion was set in place because of the quality standard inherent in the peer-review process for publication in academic and scholarly journals. Technical documents and white papers are not subject to the rigors of peer review and were thus not included in this review. Because the topic of sex offender statutes can sometimes evolve into ideologically driven discussions (for a consideration of this point, see Mancini, 2009), we limited our analysis to peer-reviewed papers which (ostensibly, at least) should eliminate this problem (Cooper, 1998). This inclusion criterion is unlikely to have had any effect on the substantive results because only four articles were omitted for this reason.

After carrying out the inclusion process, the final sample consisted of 32 articles. The final analytic sample consisted of a variety of papers dealing with residency restrictions in some capacity. As will be seen momentarily, the studies were published across a range of outlets, and the analytic strategies, the initial research questions and the ultimate conclusions differed from study to study.

Data organization

Once all accessible articles were obtained, the analysis proceeded in two steps. The first step was to evaluate each article and determine whether it presented a new analysis. The second step consisted of indexing all analytic articles by documenting relevant elements from each study. This step, in other words, was organizational. During this step each article was reduced to a case (i.e., row) in the data file. Variables (i.e., columns) for each case (i.e., article) represent unique information taken from each article in the same way that the values for variables differ among cases in standard, empirical research (Cooper, 1998).

The result of using the two-step synthesis was a summary of the articles using 10 different variables. The variables included the year the article was published; the author name(s); analysis type (that is, qualitative, quantitative or policy review); data source; research question(s); sample size; venue (data location); unit of analysis used in the study; analytic approach (for example, Geographic Information Systems, survey); and the main research findings. The first two variables are used to identify the article. The analysis type variable was used to classify the articles based on the kind of analysis that was conducted. The data source, sample size and venue describe the data used in the analysis. The research question(s) variable was important to ensure that each article analyzed sex offender residence restrictions in some way. The unit of analysis identifies the level of aggregation used in the study and the analytic approach (type of analysis) summarizes the methodological technique used to analyze the data. The main finding is a variable that explains the results from each paper. The findings from the current study are presented in the following section.

Results

Sex offender residency restrictions have been studied in a variety of ways, using different units of analysis, analyzing different hypotheses, and employing assorted approaches to conceptualizing different phenomena such as the distance between a child safety zone and an offender's address. Table 25.2 provides the information gleaned from the current review. It is important to note that the articles included in Table 25.2 are sorted (descending) by publication date and author surname.

As can be seen in Table 25.2, each article was first classified by the type of analysis that was conducted, resulting in 24 quantitative studies, one qualitative study, and seven policy reviews. Studies were classified as quantitative if they had a decidedly computational approach to the analysis and manner in which the research questions were answered. The single study that was classified as qualitative (Meloy, Miller and Curtis, 2008) was a comprehensive content analysis of sex offender residency restriction policies in 30 states. The seven policy reviews focused on the concept of residency restrictions from a general perspective, debating the efficacy of deploying such restrictions while the empirical evidence may be contraindicated.

The majority of articles (n = 18) utilized data from a law enforcement agency. Slightly fewer than half of these articles analyzed data from a state sex offender public notification registry or database. Other articles utilized data from property tax authorities (n = 3) so that geographic land parcels could be identified by Geographic Information Systems (GIS) applications. One study used a survey of Florida residents aged 18 and older through a Computer Assisted Telephone Interview. Of course, the type of analysis and source of the data were dependent on the type of research question being considered. In some cases, the analysis concerned geography, meaning that the data used in the analysis may have come from a government taxing authority.

Table 25.2 Overview of articles.

Year	Author(s)	Type	Data source	Research question(s)	Sample size	Venue (state)	Unit of analysis	Type of analysis	Main finding
2006	Zandbergen and Hart	Quantitative	Orange Co. Property Appraisers Office	What are the housing options for RSOs?	332,859	FL	Parcel	GIS	Imposition of SORR severely restricts housing options
2007	Levenson and Hern	Quantitative	Primary, SO counseling centers	What are the unintended consequences of RR?	148	IN	Offender	Survey	SORR disrupts stability
2007	Levenson et al.	Policy review						Lit review	Highlights unintended consequences
2007	Tewksbury and Levenson	Policy review						Other	Enumerates flaws with policy; not evidence-based
2007	Walker	Policy review						Lit review	Unintended consequences
2008	Briley	Quantitative	Nebraska State SO Registry	What is the impact of imposing RR on housing?	256	NE	Offender	GIS	Enactment of SORR would force many to relocate
2008	Mercado et al.	Quantitative	Primary, New Jersey SO Internet Registry	Do SORR affect re-entry?	137	NJ	Offender	Survey	SOs perceive RR has negative effects on employment, housing and social relations
2008	Duwe et al.	Quantitative	Minnesota Dept. of Corrections	Do SORR reduce recidivism?	224	MN	Offender	GIS	No support that SORR reduce recidivism
2008	Grubesic and Murray	Quantitative	Hamilton Co. Sheriff's Office	How can the spatial distribution of SO be influenced?	1,095	OH	Offender address	GIS	Makes the case for using a GIS methodology to promote the idea of spatial equity

Year	Author			N	State	Unit	Method	Findings
2008	Grubesic et al.	Quantitative	Hamilton Co. Sheriff's Office	Are there demographic and socioeconomic differences inside/ outside SRZs?	1,095	OH	Offender address	GIS	Results contradict other findings – unrestricted areas possess a more favorable demographic
2008	Hughes and Burchfield	Quantitative	Illinois State Police	Are SORR efficacious and fair?	3,105	IL	Offender	GIS	Chicago's 500-foot margin has greater implications for disadvantaged neighborhoods than affluent ones
2008	Knoll	Quantitative	South Carolina Dept. of Probation, Parole and Pardon Services	What is the impact of a one-mile buffer; how many SOs would have to relocate; is distance a risk factor?		SC	Residential parcels	GIS	Residential land is restricted; 48 to 66% of SOs would have to relocate; distance was not a risk factor
2008	Levenson	Quantitative	Primary, SO in outpatient treatment	What is the impact of SORR on offenders?	109	FL	Offender	Survey	SOs report less housing available; greater homelessness/transience/ financial hardship
2008	Meloy et al.	Qualitative	Government documents	How effective are SO laws?	30	US	State	Content Analysis of SORR policy	SORR tend to be politically motivated and not evidence-based
2008	Wunneburger et al.	Quantitative				TX	Incident/ event/ address	Spatial Analysis	No relationship between location of crime and SO residence
2009	Barnes et al.	Quantitative	South Carolina Dept. of Probation, Parole and Pardon Services	Do SORR impact housing and treatment opportunities?	246	SC	Offender address	GIS	Increased distance to treatment facilities; large % have to move

(Continued)

Table 25.2 (Continued)

Year	Author(s)	Type	Data source	Research question(s)	Sample size	Venue (state)	Unit of analysis	Type of analysis	Main finding
2009	Chajewski and Mercado	Quantitative	New Jersey SO Registry	Do SORR impact housing availability?	268	NJ	Offender	GIS	Imposing RR would require the relocation of several offenders
2009	Colombino et al.	Quantitative	New Jersey Dept. of Corrections	Do SOs seek out their victims in public locations?	405	NJ	Offender	Descriptive	Most offenders do not victimize in public areas or places where children congregate
2009a	Zandbergen and Hart	Quantitative	FL SO Registry (2003)	Is street geocoding appropriate for assessing SORR violations?	744	FL	Offender address	GIS	Street geocoding was found to have substantial errors
2009b	Zandbergen and Hart	Quantitative	Miami-Dade Co. tax assessment authority	What is the availability and spatial distribution of affordable housing in Miami-Dade Co.?	927,647	FL	Housing units	GIS	Housing options are significantly reduced with SORR
2009	Zgoba et al.	Quantitative	New Jersey SO Registry	Is housing availability impacted by SORR?	211	NJ	Offender	GIS	If SORR were in place, majority of SOs would be unable to remain in current residence
2010	Grubesic	Quantitative	Illinois SO Registry	Where are RSOs clustering in Illinois?	10,700	IL	Offender address	GIS	GIS statistical approaches can be used to ID SO clustering
2010	Mack and Grubesic	Quantitative	Hamilton Co., OH; Jefferson Co., KY	Can SO residence location be predicted?	2,024	OH/ KY	Offender	GIS	SO residence selection correctly predicted 75% of time using index of social disorganization

Year	Author	Method	Source	Research Question	N	State	Unit	Analysis	Finding
2010	Mancini et al.	Quantitative	Random sample of FL residents 18+	Do people support SORR policies?	1,308	FL	Respondent	Survey	Florida residents support SORR
2010	Zandbergen et al.	Quantitative	Florida Dept. of Law Enforcement	Are SOs who live closer to schools/daycares more likely to recidivate sexually than those who are farther away?	330	FL	Offender	GIS	No statistically significant difference between re-offending and proximity
2011	Barnes	Policy review						Lit Review	SORR built on weak theoretical and logical foundations
2011	Berenson and Appelbaum	Quantitative	New York SO Registry	What is the impact of SORR on residential availability?	518	NY	Offender	GIS	Substantial area off limits to RSOs
2011	Burchfield	Policy review						Lit Review	Unintended consequences
2011	Colombino et al.	Quantitative	New Jersey Dept. of Corrections	Do sex crime locations differ between child offenders vs. adult offenders?	1,557	NJ	Offender	Comparison	Offense location matters; inverse of public expectations
2011	Socia	Quantitative	New York Co. property tax authority	What are the housing options under different SORR scenarios?	5,520	NY	Block group	GIS	Housing options are severely limited under SORR policies
2011	Zgoba	Policy review						Lit review	SORR are not logical or sensible

Notes: GIS: geographic information system. RR: residence restrictions. RSO: registered sex offender. SO: sex offender. SORR: sex offender residence restrictions. SRZ: spatial restriction zone.

Two predominant approaches to investigating the impact of sex offender residency restrictions resulted: (1) examining the sex offender's address (n = 7); and (2) analyzing the policy governing the management of sex offenders (n = 7). The remaining studies employed variants of GIS spatial analysis using parcels or neighborhood-level data.

Geographically, all data came from the Midwest or Eastern part of the United States. Florida and New Jersey were represented in 10 studies, and New York and South Carolina were analyzed in two articles each; the 14 studies from these four Eastern states comprised more than a third of the articles used in the current analysis. The Midwest states were represented in nine studies and included Illinois (n = 2), Indiana (n = 1), Minnesota (n = 1), Nebraska (n = 1) and Ohio (n = 3). Kentucky was represented in a study that also used Ohio data. Texas, a large, central-southern state, was represented in a single study.

The majority of articles (n = 19) used an individual-level unit of analysis (such as the offender or the offender's address). In other words, most articles analyzed micro-level data of sex offenders. Across all studies, the sample sizes ranged from 109 to 10,700, with a mean of 1,288 and a standard deviation of 2,411. The studies that used a unit of analysis such as housing units (n = 1) or geographic parcels (n = 3) tended to have larger sample sizes than studies using offenders or offender addresses.

In that the current work is a systematic review of the literature on sex offender residency restrictions, the methodological approach – specifically, the type of analysis that was undertaken by the original study author(s) – was also assessed. For example, over half of the articles (n = 18) used a GIS application to analyze data. Surveys were used (n = 4) as well as literature reviews (n = 7), but in disproportionately fewer instances when compared to GIS. It is easy to understand why GIS applications dominate this line of inquiry since most scholars have been interested in understanding the actual boundaries that are set in place by residence restrictions.

A broad range of outcomes is represented by the main findings; however, some fairly consistent themes are evident. Perhaps most importantly, two studies specifically analyzed the impact of residence restrictions on recidivism (Duwe, Donnay and Tewksbury, 2008; Zandbergen, Levenson and Hart, 2010). No evidence was found, by Duwe and colleagues, to suggest that sex offender residency restrictions reduce recidivism. Similarly, Zandbergen *et al.* examined whether sex offenders who resided in closer proximity to school and day care centers were more likely to recidivate than sex offenders who lived further away from such restricted areas. They found no statistically significant difference between re-offending and residential proximity to the restricted areas in the study. As previously stated, sex offender residency restriction has become an integral element of the broader sex offender management apparatus. Speculatively, the objective of having residency restrictions as a part of sex offender management policy is to curtail sexual offense recidivism. However, there is no evidence, to date, that suggests that sex offender residency restrictions have a favorable impact on recidivism.

Outcomes other than recidivism were also analyzed. For instance, 11 studies found that residency restrictions had a deleterious effect on housing, the most common being a reduction in eligible/permissible housing. Similarly, four of the studies used in the analysis found that the imposition of residency restrictions, even at a fairly permissive margin of 500 feet, would require the offender to relocate from their current domicile. Moreover, and in keeping with the obvious problem of housing, the work by Levenson and Hearn (2007) found that residency restrictions are disruptive to an offender's residential stability, sometimes resulting in homelessness and transience (Levenson, 2008). Similar findings are reported in two additional articles (Mercado, Alvarez and Levenson, 2008; Zandbergen and Hart, 2009b).

Another significant theme that emerged from this analysis was the notion that residency restrictions carried many unintended consequences. Under the rubric of sex offender residence restrictions, unintended consequences tend to be negative occurrences (that is, recidivism and residential instability) that result from the application of a policy that are contradictory to the policy's intended purpose. For example, a sex offender's reintegration into a community may be adversely affected by a residency restriction policy if the restrictions are so severe or restrictive that the offender's residential stability is compromised. In four of the six works classified as literature reviews, unintended consequences were a substantial finding.

Several articles emphasized the lacuna between the evidence and how residency restriction policies are formulated (Levenson, Zgoba and Tewksbury, 2007; Meloy, Miller and Curtis, 2008; Barnes, 2011; Zgoba, 2011) and demonstrated that sex offender residency restriction policy is not evidence-based and is largely constructed on weak theoretical and logical arguments. In fact, four quantitative articles found a poor relationship between the geographic proximity of the offense location and the offender's residence. Similarly, Colombino, Mercado and Jeglic (2011) reported that the location where a sex offender is most likely to commit a sexual offense is in a private residence; contradicting the general public perception that sexual offending is most likely to occur in public areas where children congregate.

In the following discussion section, the authors advance an interpretation of the research and analyses conducted on sex offender residency restrictions. Although there were several methodological approaches undertaken to increase insight into the impact of residence restrictions (for example, GIS offers a level of spatial measurement sophistication that cannot otherwise be captured through standard statistical techniques), the results suggest that sex offender policy regarding residence restrictions is misinformed and weakly founded. Below, we consider these issues in greater detail.

Discussion

In many jurisdictions, sex offender residency restrictions have become an integral element of the overall sex offender management apparatus. The obvious intention of residency restrictions is to deter sex offenders from further sexual offending, while assuming that they comprise a homogenous population (Malesky, 2010). Sex offender management, and more specifically residency restrictions, has become the *sine qua non* response of public policy and legislative mandates for at least 30 states and the federal government (Socia and Stamatel, 2010; Leon, 2011; Mancini, Barnes and Mears, 2011). Interestingly, though, there is no empirical evidence that residency restrictions reduce recidivism (Duwe, Donnay, and Tewksbury 2008; but see our discussion of future research needs below). In fact, even when sex offenders fail to register as legislatively mandated, they do not recidivate with any more celerity or frequency than those who have registered as directed (Levenson *et al.*, 2010). The fact that residency restrictions are becoming more prevalent in spite of the accumulating evidence questioning their efficacy suggests that such policy is based on flawed perceptions (Merriam, 2008), political pressures (Meloy, Miller and Curtis, 2008) and public insistence (Mancini *et al.*, 2010; Tewksbury, 2011).

Though residency restrictions appear to have little impact on recidivism risks, they may impact on other aspects of the re-entry process and these are issues worth considering. Prescribing residence restrictions may have considerable implications, not only for the offenders subject to the restrictions, but for law enforcement, communities and the criminal justice system (Bonnar-Kidd, 2010; Mulford, Wilson and Parmley, 2009). As noted by previous scholars, residence restriction laws can lead to homelessness (Herendeen, 2010), unemployment (Levenson and Tewksbury, 2009; Lasher and McGrath, 2012) and displacement to socially disorganized areas (Hipp, Turner and Jannetta, 2010), among a variety of other things (Tewksbury and Levenson, 2009). For the community at large, one of the most profound implications is the false sense of security that can be experienced from the general awareness of the restrictions imposed on sex offenders (Shoop, 2010). Moreover, at least one unacknowledged implication, hence far, is that most research has utilized samples of offenders from sex offender registries, suggesting that those offenders are in compliance with registration and notification mandates. Whether these research findings would also apply to non-compliant (that is, non-registered) sex offenders remains an open empirical question.

By definition, residency restrictions limit available housing for sex offenders. The limitation is primarily based on a potential residence's proximity to venues where children are most likely to congregate, such as schools and parks (Barnes, 2011). However, with margins that can extend up to 2,500 feet, or even a mile (5,280 feet) in some cases, the eligibility of available housing is particularly limited for sex offenders, potentially funneling them into more disadvantaged or rural areas, away from family support networks, employment opportunities and resources such as counseling. This in itself is counterintuitive to the notion of rehabilitation and reintegration with the objective of becoming stable, functioning and prosocial members of society (Levenson and Hearn, 2007; Mercado, Alvarez and Levenson, 2008; Zandbergen and Hart, 2009b).

Sex offenders are not a homogenous subpopulation (Malesky, 2010) and do not recidivate with greater celerity or frequency than non-sexual offenders (Caldwell, 2007). In fact, there are a number of misconceptions concerning sex offenders, including the notion that their residential proximity to schools and parks places those attending the school and those using the parks at greater risk of victimization than an offender's social or relationship proximity (Merriam, 2008; Casady, 2009; Chajewski and Mercado, 2009). Consequently, the policies that prescribe the manner in which sex offenders should be managed are based on misconceptions of an offender subpopulation and are not grounded in solid adherence to theoretical tenets or empirical evidence (Mancini, 2009).

The nascent literature on sex offender residency restrictions is broad, revealing varied consequences of the policy focused on the offender. Two studies of those reviewed examined sex offender residency restriction policy through the prism of recidivism. The principal rationale subserving sex offender management policy is to reduce sexual offense recidivism among those with a proclivity toward that behavior; however, most of the work on sex offender residency restrictions has not focused on the impact such policy has on sex offender recidivism. Future research should focus on whether the enactment of sex offender residency restrictions has a favorable effect on sexual offense recidivism. To date, however, there is too limited evidence to say definitively that sex offender residence restrictions do not work.

The current study is not without its limitations. It is a systematic review of the published work on sex offender residency restrictions. However, because of the inconsistencies in the unit of analysis across studies, among other things such as the various methodological approaches used in the analyses, the current work was more accurately called a systematic review of the sex offender residency restriction literature as opposed to a formal meta-analysis. It is important to understand the distinction between the two because, for one, a systematic review cannot be subjected to the same statistical tests as a meta-analysis. Additionally, objective measures such as effect sizes are not part of a systematic review.

Another limitation that proceeds from not undertaking a formal meta-analysis is the inability to generalize the findings because of the lack of objective measures and the application of probability theory. The results offered in this article have a distinctively qualitative-like nature that proceeds from the observations made of prior work on sex offender residency restrictions. Although the end result is a rich composition of various aspects of sex offender residency restrictions, it does fail to meet a certain scientific standard usually inherent in quantitative analyses (Tewksbury, 2009).

Despite these limitations, sex offender residency restrictions nevertheless appear to be based on contradictory evidence, weak logic and poor theoretical support (Erooga, 2008). For example, Wunneburger, Olivares and Maghelal (2008), in a study of sex offenders in Texas, found no relationship between crime location and the offender's residence. Moreover, the evidence regarding offense location suggests sex offenses are more likely to occur in a familiar place with a familiar person (Colombino, Mercado and Jeglic, 2011), thus calling into question the need for laws such as residence restrictions. The prevailing strategy that is used to enact sex offender management policy is to assert that it promotes public safety, and especially the safety of children. Although the tenor of such rhetoric has an inherent "feel good" quality, presumably because of the severity of the restrictions, the reality is that they are merely perceptions (Shoop, 2010). The problem that can potentially arise is that the places where the risks actually exist may be ignored, and one's sensitivity to actual risks may be attenuated. Alternatively, hypersensitivity to sex offenders residing within certain areas has the potential to cause a maelstrom among neighborhood residents, regardless of whether the offender satisfies the requisite boundary requirements, promoting the principle of "Not in My Back Yard" (Burchfield and Mingus, 2008; Dallas, 2008). Stigmatizing and labeling sex offenders does less for the promotion of public safety from a policy perspective than an intrepid examination of the difference between the intended and actual outcomes from enacting residency restrictions.

The imposition of residency restrictions on sex offenders offers a visible example of the chasm between empirical evidence (that is, good research) and public policy.

It appears that regardless of the evidentiary foundations laid down by scientific research, the general population continues to support such policies (Mancini *et al.*, 2010). Although their rationale is flawed, the general population and its elected representatives are convinced that sex offender residency restrictions are a "good idea." The challenge for the future is to educate the general population by using the available evidence and to encourage representatives to consider evidence-based policies (Clear, 2010). In so doing, the general population can have greater confidence that policy will actually bolster their safety rather than simply provide the perception of safety.

References

Agudo, S.E. (2008) "Irregular passion: the unconstitutionality and inefficacy of sex offender residency laws," *Northwestern University Law Review* 102, 1, 307–341.

Apel, R. and Nagin, D.S. (2011) "General deterrence: a review of recent evidence," in J.Q. Wilson and J. Petersilia (eds), *Crime and Public Policy.* New York: Oxford, pp. 411–436.

Bains, C. (2007) "Next generation sex offender statutes: constitutional challenges to residency, work, and loitering restrictions," *Harvard Civil Rights-Civil Liberties Law Review* 42, 483–499.

Barnes, J.C. (2011) "Place a moratorium on the passage of sex offender residence restriction laws," *Criminology and Public Policy* 10, 2, 401–409.

Barnes, J.C., Dukes, T., Tewksbury, R. and De Troye, T.M. (2009) "Analyzing the impact of a statewide residence restriction law on South Carolina sex offenders," *Criminal Justice Policy Review* 20, 1, 21–43.

Berenson, J.A. and Appelbaum, P.S. (2011) "A geospatial analysis of the impact of sex offender residency restrictions in two New York counties," *Law and Human Behavior* 35, 3, 235–246.

Bonnar-Kidd, K.K. (2010) "Sexual offender laws and prevention of sexual violence or recidivism," *American Journal of Public Health* 100, 3, 412–419.

Briley, A.D. (2008) Residency restrictions in Nebraska: the potential consequences of LB 1199 for registered sex offender in Omaha and its surrounding communities. Master thesis, Graduate College at the University of Nebraska, Omaha, NE. Retrieved from Google Scholar. UMI No. 145672.

Burchfield, K.B. (2011) "Residence restrictions," *Criminology and Public Policy* 10, 2, 411–419.

Burchfield, K.B. and Mingus, W. (2008) "Not in my neighborhood: assessing registered sex offenders' experiences with local social capital and social control," *Criminal Justice and Behavior* 35, 3, 356–374.

Caldwell, M.F. (2007) "Sexual offense adjudication and sexual recidivism among juvenile offenders," *Sex Abuse* 19, 2, 107–113.

Casady, T. (2009) "A police chief's viewpoint: geographic aspects of sex offender residency restrictions," *Criminal Justice Policy Review* 20, 1, 16–20.

Center for Sex Offender Management (2008) *Legislative Trends in Sex Offender Management.* Washington, DC: Center for Sex Offender Management.

Chaffin, M. (2008) "Our minds are made up – don't confuse us with the facts: commentary on policies concerning children with sexual behavior problems and juvenile sex offenders," *Child Maltreatment* 13, 2, 110–121.

Chajewski, M. and Mercado, C.C. (2009) "An evaluation of sex offender residency restriction functioning in town, county, and city-wide jurisdictions," *Criminal Justice Policy Review* 20, 1, 44–61.

Clear, T.R. (2010) "Policy and evidence: the challenge to the American Society of Criminology: 2009 Presidential Address to the American Society of Criminology," *Criminology* 48, 1, 1–26.

Cohen, L.E. and Felson, M. (1979) "Social change and crime rate trends: a routine activity approach," *American Sociological Review* 44, 588–608.

Colombino, N., Mercado, C.C. and Jeglic, E.L. (2009) "Situational aspects of sexual offending: implications for residence restriction laws," *Justice Research and Policy* 11, 27–43.

Colombino, N., Mercado, C.C. and Jeglic, E.L. (2011) "Preventing sexual violence: can examination of offense location inform sex crime policy?," *International Journal of Law and Psychiatry* 34, 3, 160–167.

Cooper, H. (1998) *Synthesizing Research*. Thousand Oaks, CA: Sage.

Craun, S.W., Kernsmith, P.D. and Butler, N.K. (2011) "Anything that can be a danger to the public: desire to extend registries beyond sex offenses," *Criminal Justice Policy Review* 22, 3, 375–391.

Cullen, F.T. and Agnew, R. (eds) (2006) *Criminological Theory: Past to Present*. Los Angeles: Roxbury.

Dallas, C. (2008) "Not in my backyard; the implications of sex offender residency ordinances in Texas and beyond," *Texas Tech Law Review* 41, 1235–1274.

Duwe, G., Donnay, W. and Tewksbury, R. (2008) "Does residential proximity matter? A geographic analysis of sex offense recidivism," *Criminal Justice and Behavior* 35, 4, 484–504.

Erooga, M. (2008) "A human rights-based approach to sex offender management: the key to effective public protection," *Journal of Sexual Aggression* 14, 3, 171–183.

Grubesic, T.H. (2010) "Sex offender clusters," *Applied Geography* 30, 1, 2–18.

Grubesic, T.H. and Murray, A.T. (2008) "Sex offender residency and spatial equity," *Applied Spatial Analysis and Policy* 1, 3, 175–192.

Grubesic, T.H., Murray, A.T. and Mack, E.A. (2008) "Sex offenders, housing and spatial restriction zones," *GeoJournal* 73, 4, 255–269.

Herendeen, R. (2010) How much punishment do homeless sex offenders deserve? Residency registration requirements as punishment for acts derivative of status, http://works.bepress.com/rosalind_herendeen/1 (accessed September 7, 2012).

Hipp, J.R., Jannetta, J., Shah, R. and Turner, S. (2009) "Parolees' physical closeness to health service providers: a study of California parolees," *Health and Place* 15, 679–688.

Hipp, J.R., Turner, S. and Jannetta, J. (2010) "Are sex offenders moving into social disorganization? Analyzing the residential mobility of California parolees," *Journal of Research of Crime and Delinquency* 47, 4, 558–590.

Hobson, B.R. (2005) "Banishing acts: how far may states go to keep convicted sex offenders away from children," *Georgia Law Review* 40, 961–994.

Hughes, L.A. and Burchfield, K.B. (2008) "Sex offender residence restrictions in Chicago: an environmental injustice?," *Justice Quarterly* 25, 4, 647–673.

Jacobs, B.A. (1999) *Dealing Crack: The Social World of Streetcorner Selling*. Boston, MA: Northeastern University Press.

Jacobs, B.A. (2010) "Deterrence and deterrability," *Criminology* 48, 2, 417–441.

Janicki, M.A. (2006) "Better seen than herded: residency restrictions and global positioning system tracking laws for sex offenders," *Public Interest Law Journal* 16, 285–311.

Knoll, C.C. (2008) Geographic analysis of sex offender residency restriction legislation. Master thesis, University of South Carolina, Columbia, SC. Retrieved from Google Scholar. UMI No. 1460215.

Lasher, M.P. and McGrath, R.J. (2012) "The impact of community notification on sex offender reintegration: a quantitative review of the research literature," *International Journal of Offender Therapy and Comparative Criminology* 56, 1, 6–28.

Leon, C. (2011) "The contexts and politics of evidence-based sex offender policy," *Criminology and Public Policy* 10, 2, 421–430.

Levenson, J.S. (2008) "Collateral consequences of sex offender residence restrictions," *Criminal Justice Studies* 21, 2, 153–166.

Levenson, J.S. and D'Amora, D.A. (2007) "Social policies designed to prevent sexual violence: the emperor's new clothes," *Criminal Justice Policy Review* 18, 2, 168–199.

Levenson, J.S. and Hearn, A.L. (2007) "Sex offender residence restrictions: unintended consequences and community reentry," *Justice Research and Policy* 9, 1, 59–73.

Levenson, J. and Tewksbury, R. (2009) "Collateral damage: family members of registered sex offenders," *American Journal of Criminal Justice* 34, 54–68.

Levenson, J.S., Zgoba, K. and Tewksbury, R. (2007) "Sex offender residence restrictions: sensible crime policy or flawed logic?," *Federal Probation* 71, 3, 2–9.

Levenson, J., Letourneau, E., Armstrong, K. and Zgoba, K.M. (2010) "Failure to register as a sex offender: is it associated with recidivism?," *Justice Quarterly* 27, 3, 305–331.

Logan, W.A. (2006) "Constitutional collectivism and ex-offender residence exclusion laws," *Iowa Law Review* 92, 1–40.

Loudon-Brown, M. (2007) "'They sent him on a path where he's bound to get ill': why sex offender residency restrictions should be abandoned," *NYU Annual Survey of American Law* 62, 795–846.

Mack, E.A. and Grubesic, T.H. (2010) "Sex offenders and residential location: a predictive analytic framework." Working paper no. 2010-03. Phoenix: Arizona State University.

Maguire, M. and Singer, J.K. (2011) "A false sense of security: moral panic driven sex offender legislation," *Critical Criminology* 19, 4, 301–312.

Malesky Jr., L.A. (2010) "Sex offender laws: a critical analysis [Review of the book Sex Offender Laws: Failed Policies, New Directions, by R.G. Wright]," *Sex Roles* 63, 292–294.

Mancini, C. (2009) Sex crime in America: examining the emergence and effectiveness of sex offender laws. Doctoral dissertation, Florida State University, Tallahassee, FL. Retrieved from ProQuest (Publication no, 3385282).

Mancini, C., Barnes, J.C. and Mears. D. (2011) "It varies from state to state: an examination of sex crime laws nationally," *Criminal Justice Policy Review*, forthcoming.

Mancini, C. and Mears, D.P. (2010) "To execute or not to execute? Examining public support for capital punishment of sex offenders," *Journal of Criminal Justice* 38, 5, 959–968.

Mancini, C., Shields, R.T., Mears, D.P. and Beaver, K.M. (2010) "Sex offender residence restriction laws: parental perceptions and public policy," *Journal of Criminal Justice* 38, 5, 1022–1030.

Meloy, M.L., Miller, S.L. and Curtis, K.M. (2008) "Making sense out of nonsense: the deconstruction of state-level sex offender residence restrictions," *American Journal of Criminal Justice* 33, 2, 209–222.

Mercado, C.C., Alvarez, S. and Levenson, J. (2008) "The impact of specialized sex offender legislation on community reentry," *Sexual Abuse* 20, 2, 188–205.

Merriam, D.H. (2008) "Residency restrictions for sex offenders: a failure of public policy," *Planning and Environment Law* 60, 10, 3–13.

Mulford, C.F., Wilson, R.W. and Parmley, A.M. (2009) "Geographic aspects of sex offender residency restrictions: policy and research," *Criminal Justice Policy Review* 20, 1, 3–12.

Nagin, D. S. (1998) "Criminal deterrence research at the outset of the twenty-first century," *Crime and Justice* 23, 1–42.

Nieto, M. and Jung, D. (2006) *The Impact of Residency Restrictions on Sex Offenders and Correctional Management Practices: A Literature Review.* (CRB 06-008). Sacramento: California Research Bureau.

Pratt, T.C., Cullen, F.T., Blevins, K.R. *et al.* (2008) "The empirical status of deterrence theory: a meta-analysis," in F.T. Cullen, J.P. Wright, and K.R. Blevins (eds), *Taking Stock: The Status of Criminological Theory.* New Brunswick, NJ: Transaction, pp. 367–395.

Sandler, J.C., Freeman, N.F. and Socia, K.M. (2008) "Does a watched pot boil? A time-series analysis of New York state's sex offender registration and notification law," *Psychology, Public Policy, and Law* 14, 4, 284–302.

Saxer, S.R. (2008) "Banishment of sex offenders: liberty, protectionism, justice, and alternatives," *Washington University Law Review* 86, 1397–1446.

Schiavone, S.K. and Jeglic, E.L. (2009) "Public perception of sex offender social policies and the impact on sex offenders," *International Journal of Offender Therapy and Comparative Criminology* 53, 6, 679–695.

Shoop, D.E. (2010) Problem definition and agenda setting among Pennsylvania's municipal governments: sex offender residency restriction ordinances. Doctoral dissertation, Pennsylvania State University, University Park, PA. Available from ProQuest Dissertations and Theses database. UMI No. 3399707.

Socia, K.M. (2011a) "Overview of 'The policy implications of residence restrictions on sex offender housing in Upstate NY'," *Criminology and Public Policy* 10, 2, 349–350.

Socia, K.M. (2011b) "The policy implications of residence restrictions on sex offender housing in Upstate NY," *Criminology and Public Policy* 10, 2, 349–350.

Socia, K.M. and Stamatel, J.P. (2010) "Assumptions and evidence behind sex offender laws: registration, community notification, and residence restrictions," *Sociology Compass* 4, 1, 1–20.

Stafford, M.C. and Warr, M. (1993) "A reconceptualization of general and specific deterrence," *Journal of Research in Crime and Delinquency* 30, 2, 123–135.

Suresh, G., Mustaine, E.E., Tewksbury, R. and Higgins, G.E. (2010) "Social disorganization and registered sex offenders: an exploratory spatial analysis," *Southwest Journal of Criminal Justice* 7, 2, 180–213.

Tewksbury, R. (2009) "Qualitative versus quantitative methods: understanding why qualitative methods are superior for criminology and criminal justice," *Journal of Theoretical and Philosophical Criminology* 1, 1, 38–58.

Tewksbury, R. (2011) "Policy implications of sex offender residence restriction laws," *Criminology and Public Policy* 10, 2, 345–348.

Tewksbury, R. and Levenson, J. (2007) "When evidence is ignored: residential restrictions for sex offenders," *Corrections Today* 69, 54–57.

Tewksbury, R. and Levenson, J. (2009) "Stress experience of family members of registered sex offenders," *Behavioral Sciences and the Law* 27, 611–626.

Tewksbury, R. and Zgoba, K.M. (2010) "Perceptions and coping with punishment: how registered sex offenders respond to stress, internet restrictions, and the collateral consequences of registration," *International Journal of Offender Therapy and Comparative Criminology* 54, 4, 537–551.

Wakefield, H. (2006) "The vilification of sex offenders: do laws targeting sex offenders increase recidivism and sexual violence," *Journal of Sexual Offender Civil Commitment: Science and the Law* 1, 1, 141–149.

Walker, J.T. (2007) "Eliminate residency restrictions for sex offenders," *Criminology and Public Policy* 6, 4, 863–870.

West, A. (2007) "The Georgia legislature strikes with a vengeance! Sex offender residency restrictions and the deterioration of the ex post facto clause," *Catholic University Law Review* 57, 239–268.

Willis, G.M. and Grace, R.C. (2008) "The quality of community reintegration planning for child molesters: effects on sexual recidivism," *Sexual Abuse: A Journal of Research and Treatment* 20, 218–240.

Willis, G.M. and Grace, R.C. (2009) "Assessment of community reintegration planning for sex offenders: poor planning predicts recidivism," *Criminal Justice and Behavior* 36, 5, 494–512.

Wright, R.G. (2008) "Sex offender post-incarceration sanctions: are there any limits?," *Criminal and Civil Confinement* 34, 17–50.

Wunneburger, D.F., Olivares, M. and Maghelal, P. (2008) "Internal security for communities: a spatial analysis of the effectiveness of sex offender laws," in D. Sui (ed.), *Geospatial Technologies and Homeland Security*. Dordrecht: Springer, pp. 103–124.

Zandbergen, P.A. and Hart, T.C. (2006) "Reducing housing options for convicted sex offenders: investigating the impact of residency restriction laws using GIS," *Justice Research and Policy* 8, 2, 1–24.

Zandbergen, P.A. and Hart, T.C. (2009a) "Geocoding accuracy considerations in determining residency restrictions for sex offenders," *Criminal Justice Policy Review* 20, 1, 62–90.

Zandbergen, P.A. and Hart, T.C. (2009b) *Availability and Spatial Distribution of Affordable Housing in Miami-Dad County and Implications of Residency Restriction Zones for Registered Sex Offenders*. Miami: ACLU.

Zandbergen, P.A., Levenson, J.S. and Hart, T.C. (2010) "Residential proximity to school and daycares: an empirical analysis of sex offense recidivism," *Criminal Justice and Behavior* 37, 5, 482–502.

Zgoba, K.M. (2011) "Residence restriction buffer zones and the banishment of sex offenders," *Criminology and Public Policy* 10, 2, 391–400.

Zgoba, K.M., Levenson, J. and McKee, T. (2009) "Examining the impact of sex offender residence restrictions on housing availability," *Criminal Justice Policy Review* 20, 1, 91–110.

26

The Traveling Sex Offender
Monitoring Movements across International Borders
Terry Thomas

Introduction

As new laws and policies over the last 20 years have sought to improve public protection from sexual offenders at national levels, attention has increasingly been turned to the person who moves away from their local community and even crosses international borders in order to commit sexual offenses. The fear has been expressed that such international travel is intended to avoid the public protection restraints of registers, supervision, and so on, or to commit new offenses where the person concerned is not known. International travel is also believed to be undertaken in order to commercially sexually exploit children in countries where the laws and law enforcement may be less rigorous. Some people may even be motivated to travel in order to find employment in schools or child care facilities, giving them access to children and the opportunity to abuse those children.

The extensive publicity attending the disappearance in 2007 of the four-year-old English girl Madeleine McCann while on holiday with her parents in Portugal raised yet more awareness of crimes related to tourism and the potential international dimension to offending against children (BBC News, 2007; Botterill and Jones, 2010).

This chapter seeks to examine the movement of people, both as potential sexual offenders and as known and convicted sex offenders, across international borders and to look at the policies and measures being put in place to reduce the possibilities of them using their travel to sexually offend, re-offend or cause further sexual harm. The term "traveling sex offender" has been coined by the British police.[1]

The current domestic responses to convicted sex offenders in the United Kingdom and the United States are premised on the idea that the known sex offender will at some point re-offend and can never really be successfully treated or rehabilitated. National policies seek to "identify" and make the sex offender "visible" to the authorities and to prevent him or her from becoming "invisible" (see Chapter 21); policies to monitor the traveling sex offender are guided by similar ideas.

The Reasons for Travel

The concerns about international travel for purposes of sexual offending are focused on those who have already been convicted, and also those who are potential new sexual offenders, not as yet known to the authorities; these concerns fall broadly into four areas:

1. people engaging in "sexual tourism";
2. avoiding domestic public protection registration requirements;
3. being able to offend where they are not known; and
4. avoiding employment screening for work with children.

Engaging in "sexual tourism"

The term "sexual tourism" was first used in the 1990s to describe the behavior of men from economically developed countries traveling to the less well developed parts of the world in order to sexually exploit women and children. The narrative since the mid-1990s has been that these men are aware that they are traveling to parts of the world where poverty and deprivation has forced people, including children, into the practice of sexual prostitution. These same geographic areas often have less clearly defined laws on ages of consent and less rigorous law enforcement arrangements. The expectation was that men could travel to certain countries and more easily engage in sexual activities with children that would be illegal and subject to clear law enforcement in their own countries (Muntarbhorn, 1996; Kane, 1998; Levy, 1999).

As the problem became recognized, voluntary groups like ECPAT (End Child Prostitution, Child Pornography and the Trafficking of Children for Sexual Purposes) were established and started to campaign for wider awareness and appropriate laws to protect children in particular. The World Tourism Organization (1995) made a formal *Statement on the Prevention of Organized Sex Tourism* at its 1995 conference in Cairo producing a "Code of Conduct for the protection of children from sexual exploitation in travel and tourism," and the European Commission (1996) has also put its weight behind raising awareness.

The first World Congress against Commercial Sexual Exploitation of Children, held in Stockholm (August 27–31, 1996), was organized by ECPAT jointly with UNICEF (the UN Children's Fund) and the government of Sweden. Over 120 countries were represented there, along with delegates from Interpol (the International Criminal Police Organization), the International Association of Travel Agents, the European Union and others. On behalf of the British government Timothy Kirkhope told the Congress, "it is essential that there is effective action both nationally and internationally to combat the scourge of child exploitation and sex tourism" (Home

Office, 1996a; see also Alexander *et al.*, 2000). The Stockholm conference was followed by a further World Congress in Yokohama in 2001 and in Rio de Janeiro in 2008 (see UNICEF, 2008).

Just how much "sex tourism" was taking place was uncertain (see, for example, Karlen and Hagner, 1996; Barrett, Barrett and Mullenger, 2000). Where it was taking place was also uncertain. South East Asian countries, such as Thailand, the Philippines and Vietnam, were regularly cited but reports also came in from all over the world claiming new "destination countries" (see Burrell, 1998).

The imminent enlargement of the European Union from 15 to 25 countries (in May 2004) prompted reports of sex tourism taking place within the European area itself:

> Towns on the Czech border with Germany openly advertise child sex, with a teddy bear in the window indicating that paedophiles are welcome – blue curtains means a male child prostitute and pink curtains a girl. The Czech Republic will join the EU next year (Bright, 2003)

The EU responded with its Council Framework Decision 2004/68/JHA which called upon all Member States to take action against child abuse and the sexual exploitation of children, including child pornography.

The terms "sex tourism" and "sex tourist" have been criticized for being too narrow. Many of the people so defined were often not "tourists" but were travelers for business purposes, military forces working overseas, diplomats and governmental employees posted abroad and expatriates residing abroad. Some people may travel without the intent to commit offenses but still commit them on their arrival.

Avoiding domestic public protection registration requirements

Another reason for the international movement of convicted and registered sex offenders has been cited as their wish to avoid domestic sex offender registration and associated public protection "requirements" imposed by a given jurisdiction.

Within months of the UK sex offender register being implemented in September 1997, stories began to circulate that sex offenders in the Northern Ireland area of the United Kingdom were moving south across the border to the Republic of Ireland in order to avoid having to comply with their registration requirements (*Sunday Times*, 1997). The validity of such stories was hard to verify and the reports were formally discounted at the time in the Irish parliament (see House of Oireachtas – Official Report, December 9, 1997).

A few years later the chair of the UK House of Commons all-party parliamentary children's group outlined the potential problem when it came to known child sex offenders:

> We have always foreseen that as the laws became tighter, paedophiles would go to areas in the world where there was no control on them. It's essential that we do everything we can internationally to protect these children. (quoted in Gillan, 1999)

In practice an overwhelming 97% majority of UK registered sex offenders are reported to comply with their domestic registration requirements (Home Office/Scottish Executive, 2001: 12). The UK's Child Exploitation and On-Line Protection Centre (CEOP) have nonetheless noted that of those 3% of offenders who fail to comply, many are reported to have gone overseas. CEOP has estimated that "70% of missing registered and very high risk sex offenders subject to notification requirements and located by CEOP in 2007-8 had travelled abroad whilst missing" (cited in Association of Chief Police Officers, 2009: para. 46).

Being able to offend where they are not known

People traveling to areas where they are not known in order to resume offending is not a new phenomenon. The growth in the ownership and use of cars and the improved road systems of the 1950s and 1960s in Europe and the United States had required the police to respond to the newly mobile offender. The fear in the 1990s was that cheap international flights and ease of communication between countries was leading to a new generation of international offending and not least among those wishing to commit sexual offenses. The loss of borders between large tracts of the European Union in its development of "an area of freedom, security and justice," and the continuing enlargement of the European Union with the joining of new Member States, led a UK Association of Chief Police Officers (ACPO) spokesman to point out that:

> There will be people coming into this country with criminal records and sex offenders too – guaranteed. The reality is we don't know who they are and we should – no matter where they come from. (quoted in Parry, 2007)

Case studies rather than statistics were cited to support this view. The UK police were not informed of the arrival in the United Kingdom of Viktor Dembovskis, a convicted sex offender in Latvia who went on to commit serious sexual offenses and murder in the United Kingdom (Cowan, 2006). Josef Kurek from Poland was sentenced to two years' imprisonment for raping a woman near Llanelli in Wales; Kurek had previous convictions for sexual offenses and rape in Poland (Parry, 2007).

Avoiding employment screening for work with children

A fourth reason for convicted sex offenders to travel was reportedly to enable them to obtain employment giving them access to children in schools, play centers, nurseries, children's homes, health establishments and similar places. This access was then used as a base from which to abuse children.

Many countries now have employment screening arrangements to prevent unsuitable people from working with children (Loucks, Lyner and Sullivan, 1998). These arrangements usually include the disclosure to an employer of previous criminal records and data from a sex offender register. A decision is then made by the employer on the suitability of the applicant to work with children. The traveling sex offender is understood to be working on the premise that a different country might not have any screening arrangements in place and even if they did it might not have access to his criminal conviction or register record held in his home country. On that basis the offender might find employment in that country that would be denied to him at home.

A report for the European Commission in 1999 on people with convictions traveling to avoid employment screening had concluded that, in Europe at least, "anecdotal evidence and reports from countries with established Common Travel Areas suggest it is not a major problem" (Thomas, Katz and Wattam, 1999: para. 9.2.28). The case of Michel Fourniret was used to explain the risk posed. Michel Fourniret was a convicted child sex offender in France who on leaving prison moved to Belgium in the late 1980s and obtained work in a school where he continued his offending; the screening arrangements were inadequate and Fourniret had not been prevented from gaining employment with children (Castle, 2004; Fitch, Spencer Chapman and Hilton, 2007).

The 2004 Bichard Report in the United Kingdom was an enquiry into two child murders in Soham, Cambridgeshire. Although there was no international component to the crime, the man eventually convicted (Ian Huntley) had been known to the police but still obtained employment giving him access to children. The Bichard Report made recommendations on the better screening of workers in child care positions and took the opportunity to recommend the improved screening of overseas workers, stating that:

> Proposals should be brought forward as soon as possible to improve the checking of people from overseas who want to work with children and vulnerable adults. (Bichard Report, 2004, Recommendation 30: 147)

The UK National Society for the Prevention of Cruelty to Children (NSPCC) have cited figures from the UK Border Agency reporting a total of 17,013 people coming into the United Kingdom from other European countries in 2004 to work with children (Fitch, Spencer Chapman and Hilton, 2007: 2). The NSPCC also cited CEOP evidence that "people who have been convicted of sexual offences against children are increasingly travelling to other countries" and this was in part to "obtain employment with children and abuse again" (Fitch, Spencer Chapman and Hilton, 2007: 2).

These four rationales are put forward to explain why known sex offenders, and unknown potential sex offenders, engage in international travel. The four rationales have arguably been based more on anecdotal evidence and case studies with limited statistical evidence or serious research to support their claims; often they are based on the fear of possibilities that might happen if we take no precautions rather than any more substantive evidence. A policy response has nevertheless been mounted and can be framed as identification and interventions aimed at (1) the outbound international traveler and (2) the inbound traveler.

The Outbound Traveler

Organizing travel for the purpose of "sexual tourism"

In the 1970s and 1980s it was possible openly to organize travel for the purpose of easy access to prostitution. Australia was an early entrant into the field of policies to stop people organizing such travel for the purpose of child exploitation. The Crimes (Child Sex Tourism) Amendment Act 1994 made it an offense to engage in sexual activities with children in foreign countries or to encourage, benefit or profit from such activities. Custodial penalties of over 20 years in prison could be imposed.

The United Kingdom's first tentative move into the field of "sex tourism" was also to try and prevent UK individuals and agencies from openly organizing international travel for the purposes of buying sexual services. The Sexual Offences (Conspiracy and Incitement) Act 1996 was designed to prevent tour operators and travel agents from openly organizing and advertising travel arrangements based around sexual activities available in other countries. These organizing activities were to be regarded as "conspiracy" and "incitement" to commit sexual offending (see Home Office, 1996b).

In the United States similar arrangements to penalize organizers have been made through the 2003 Prosecutorial Remedies and Other Tools to End the Exploitation of Children Today Act 2003 (known as the PROTECT Act), where section 105 states that a person who for private financial gain:

> arranges, induces, procures or facilitates the travel of a person knowing that such a person is travelling in interstate commerce or foreign commerce for the purpose of engaging in illicit sexual conduct shall be fined under this title or imprisoned not more than 30 years or both.

The obvious deficit in these arrangements was the ability of those individuals intent on sexual offending to make their own travel arrangements, especially through the internet, without the need for facilitating agents and organizers.

Notification of travel

In 2001 the United Kingdom introduced arrangements whereby all registered sex offenders wishing to travel abroad for more than eight days had to notify the police in advance of their travel intentions (Sex Offenders (Notice Requirements) (Foreign Travel) Regulations 2001 SI 1846). The UK registrant must provide the name of the country they are going to, the date of departure, the carriers they intend to use and their specific point of arrival, the address of accommodation on the first night away, the date of their return and point of arrival back in the United Kingdom; they must also notify the police when they are back.

On initial receipt of the notified information the police had to decide if they were going to forward the information to their colleagues in the destination country or not. This could be done either directly, police force to police force, or through the channels of Interpol and its "green notices" system (see below). It is left to the discretion of the law enforcement agencies *receiving* the information as to whether they act upon it.

The time period of eight days abroad was agreed after discussions between the Home Office, police, probation service, social services representatives and children's charities and "the conclusion reached was that a qualifying period shorter than eight days would result in an unwieldy, unresponsive and consequently less effective system for the police to administer" (*Hansard*, HC Deb, February 12, 2002, vol. 280, col. 306-7W). "Unwieldy" and "less effective" it may have been but, nonetheless, the period of eight days abroad was soon reduced to three days (Sexual Offences Act 2003 (Travel Notification Requirements) Regulations 2004 SI 1220); the Regulations applied to England, Wales and Northern Ireland only, with Scotland having its own Regulations (Sexual Offences Act 2003 (Travel Notification Requirements) (Scotland) Regulations 2004 SSI 205).

The campaign group ECPAT UK argued that even three days was too long a period without notification and argued that travel abroad to sexually abuse children could take place within those three days. ECPAT (2011) wanted what they termed the "three day loophole" to be closed. The Home Office has accepted these arguments and in June 2011 made proposals to remove the specified period altogether and require notification of *any* travel overseas regardless of length of time (Home Office, 2011: para. 2.1).

In the United States, similar arrangements have been introduced requiring registered sex offenders to inform the police or other custodians of the register that they are going abroad (Sex Offender Registration and Notification Act 2006, s128).

These proposals inevitably only apply to the "known" and registered sexual offender and not to the "unknown" potential offender without a previous record.

Prevention of travel

Once notified of travel arrangements, some jurisdictions now have powers to prevent that travel from taking place.

The UK police can prevent a person who is a registered sex offender from traveling to another country by applying to a Magistrates' Court for a Foreign Travel Order (FTO). The FTO became operative on May 1, 2004 as a civil order that could be placed on a person thought necessary to protect children outside the United Kingdom from serious sexual harm. Once made, the Order prevents that person leaving the country. The FTO originally lasted for six months and failure to comply constituted an offense in itself (Sexual Offences Act 2003, ss114–122); the maximum time limit for the Order was later raised from six months to five years (see below).

Critics of FTOs soon drew attention to the fact that despite the legislation very few FTOs were actually being made. ECPAT UK estimated that only three Orders were made between 2004 and 2008 and contrasted this with the making of over 3,000 Football Banning Orders to prevent football hooligans from traveling abroad and causing trouble at football games and tournaments (ECPAT, 2008: 17–18). The official figures showed that six FTOs were made during the four years following their introduction in May 2004 (*Hansard*, HC Deb, July 19, 2010, WA col. 36W PQ 8564); 32,336 names were on the sex offender register at the end of 2009 (Criminal Justice Joint Inspection, 2010: 22).

These low figures could indicate an original overreaction and a degree of moral panic about a problem that was perhaps not as widespread as believed, or alternatively it could show a lack of resolve on the part of the police to apply for FTOs. The police have admitted that the number of high risk sex offenders traveling abroad is "likely to be measured in hundreds" although they admit "it is not possible to quantify precisely" (Association of Chief Police Officers, 2009: para. 51).

ECPAT UK coordinated publicity on their report *Return to Sender* (see above) (Lewis, 2008; ECPAT, 2008) to coincide with the return of Paul Gadd (the pop star "Gary Glitter") to the United Kingdom following a custodial sentence served in Vietnam for child sexual offenses. Home Secretary Jacqui Smith also chose August 20, 2008, the day Gadd landed at Heathrow airport, to announce her proposals which included strengthening the FTO by increasing the duration of the Order from a maximum of six months to a potential five years and requiring those subject to an Order to surrender their passports to the police for this period (Home Office, 2008). These proposals duly became law in sections 23 to 25 of the Policing and Crime Act 2009.

After the Glitter publicity the number of FTOs made by the courts increased marginally, with 12 being made in the period 2008–2009 (*Hansard*, HC Deb, July 19, 2010, WA col. 36W PQ 8564). The police have continued to argue for even stronger FTO laws, including the possibility of an indefinite lifetime ban rather than just five years (Association of Chief Police Officers, 2009: para. 5) and the power to apply for FTOs for people *without* convictions and presumably therefore not on the sex offender register (Association of Chief Police Officers, 2009: paras. 14–15). The police argued that the anti-grooming Risk of Sexual Harm Orders could be applied for people without previous convictions and FTOs should therefore be the same; exactly what arguments would be made and evidence laid in applying for Orders for people without convictions was left unsaid.

The Inbound Offender

If the outbound sex offender could be asked to notify the authorities before he or she left the country and in the United Kingdom could be stopped from traveling at all if an FTO was issued, the position of the inbound sex offender was more problematic. The problem starts with the police and immigration authorities' ability to identify the incoming sexual offender in the first place.

Notification of arrivals

The arrival of a person in a given jurisdiction who has convictions for sexual offenses is somewhat problematic. This is true if the person is a national of the host country returning home having been convicted abroad, or a foreign national with convictions arriving on legitimate business for the first time. It is also true of the registered sex offender who has left their country of registration and is returning to that country whether or not any new offenses were committed during the period away. The question for the police is just how they would know if an arrival to the United Kingdom is such an offender or is known to have been convicted for sexual offenses committed abroad.

There is no problem if the offender is a well-known person such as the professional boxer Mike Tyson (Schaeffer, 2000) or the pop singer "Garry Glitter" (see Taylor,

2006) who both have well-publicized convictions for sexual offenses. If the offender has been tracked through international police cooperation channels with a view to prosecution on his return then, again, the problem does not arise (see below). The difficulty is when the person is not in the public eye and the agencies are dependent on other sources of information.

The United Kingdom has considered the possibility of requiring all in-bound registered sex offenders to report themselves automatically to the authorities (Home Office/Scottish Executive, 2001: ch. 7) but has so far not implemented any such requirement. The Republic of Ireland, for example, requires just such automatic reporting (Sex Offenders Act 2001, s13).

The Home Office has advised the UK police forces that there are a number of other possible sources that might assist them to identify the sexual offender. This might include the UK diplomatic service who may have been involved with repatriation to the United Kingdom, or other police intelligence sources (Home Office, 2004: 33–34, 2010: 44). ECPAT UK has suggested that some returning British national offenders should be chaperoned by law enforcement agencies to ensure they are made subject to Notification Orders (see below) when they get here (ECPAT, 2008: 15).

If visa arrangements for non-British nationals are required, the existence of a conviction record may have to be declared, although there may not be international arrangements in place to ratify that declaration.

Interpol uses a series of color-coded "international notices" that circulate between police of different countries and the green-colored notice warns the receiving police that a person is inbound to their jurisdiction and that that person is a known offender, including sex offenders. Some 1,092 green notices were issued in 2007 (Interpol, 2011). The system is not used to its full extent and Kristin Kvigne, head of the child abuse unit at Interpol, has complained that:

> Green notices are being gravely underused by too many countries. We feel there is a responsibility to protect children in other countries and that is why they are a useful tool. (quoted in Townsend, 2008)

Anyone arriving in the United Kingdom with convictions for sex offenses committed overseas may be included on the national sex offender register. The people concerned may be UK nationals convicted in other countries or foreign nationals convicted in their home countries. The police must apply to a Magistrates' Court for a Notification Order that would effectively allow them to put the new arrival on the UK sex offender register (Sexual Offences Act 2003, ss97–103; the process is described in a Parliamentary Written Answer, *Hansard*, HC Deb, July 15, 2010, col. 824-5W).

The US Sex Offender Registration and Notification Act (SORNA) 2006 allows foreign convictions to be added to US registries as long as there is equivalence and robust judicial processes (SORNA 2006, s111(5)B) and directs the Attorney General to establish a federal system for informing domestic jurisdictions about persons entering the United States who require registration or re-registration (SORNA 2006, s128).

The identification of inbound sexual offenders is considered further below when we look at the international exchange of information on sexual offenders.

Prosecution on return from travel

The policing and prosecution of sex offenders when they are abroad has traditionally been left to the law enforcement agencies of the country they are in when the offenses are committed. In the mid-1990s the idea of "extraterritorial jurisdiction" was developed whereby people who committed sexual offenses abroad could be prosecuted on their return to their home country.

Sweden prosecuted one of their nationals, Bengt Bolin, in Sweden for offenses against children committed in Thailand in 1993 (Home Office, 1996c: Annex D). Australia amended its laws to enable prosecutions on return from overseas where the offense had been committed. As noted above, the Crimes (Child Sex Tourism) Amendment Act 1994 made it an offense to engage in sexual activities with children in foreign countries or to encourage, benefit or profit from such activities.

A UK Home Office report on how such "extraterritorial jurisdiction" might work drew on the Swedish experience as a model of how a new law might be drawn up (Home Office, 1996c). The Sex Offenders Act 1997 Part 2 duly introduced laws permitting such prosecutions of sex offenders committing offenses abroad (the law is now in section 72 of the Sexual Offences Act 2003 as amended by the Criminal Justice and Immigration Act 2008). The first time the new law was used was to prosecute Kenneth Biden for offenses committed on a campsite in France. Biden was arrested in Exeter in Devon on his return (Hopkins, 2000).

Such prosecutions have not been frequent events and the work to collate evidence from another country and bring it to the UK prosecuting authorities and court is not easy and at times is very complex (see, for example, Child Exploitation and Online Protection Centre, 2010a). In Gloucestershire the Crown Prosecution Service took over four years to bring Patrick Matthews to court for alleged sexual offenses against children in India, only to have the judge dismiss the case because of the time it had taken (Crown Prosecution Service South West, 2010). ECPAT UK said this was far more than an example of the work being complex and the "incompetence" of the prosecuting officers but reflected "the more general problem that the UK is reluctant to properly pursue extra-territorial offences" (ECPAT, 2011: 23; see also Montgomery, 2010).

In recent years some countries have become more proactive in terms of "extraterritorial jurisdiction" and law enforcement agents from the offender's home country have traveled out to other countries to help local officers enforce laws and protect children from the "sexual tourist."

The US PROTECT Act (see above) made it a crime for any US citizen to travel abroad, for the purpose of sex tourism involving children. The US Immigration and Customs Enforcement agency, known as ICE, was formed in 2003 as part of the Department of Homeland Security and part of its brief has been the implementation of the child protection sections of the PROTECT Act 2003. ICE has successfully prosecuted people on their return to the United States. On September 10, 2003, ICE agents in Seattle arrested Michael Clark, a US citizen, on charges of traveling to Cambodia to engage in sex with minors. Clark was extradited from Cambodia, upon the request of the United States, after he was arrested and charged by Cambodian police in June with "debauchery involving illicit sexual conduct" with boys approximately 10 and 13 years old (see statement by ICE Assistant Secretary Michael J. Garcia, March 4, 2004 to the House of Representatives Committee on the Judiciary, http://www.ice.gov/doclib/news/library/speeches/oppredator_030404.pdf).

ICE has also been proactive in sending its agents to other countries to track down US citizens committing sexual offenses abroad. These foreign attachés work in cooperation with local police in places such as Thailand, Cambodia and the Philippines, and the overall aim is stated as follows:

> To enhance our work in this area, ICE will use undercover operations and innovative approaches to identify child sex tourists and those who traffic minors and other victims. Essential to our success is coordinating with our national and international partners, both governmental and non-governmental. (ICE, 2010: 4)

The International Exchange of Information Held on Sex Offenders

Central to all these activities to contain and prevent sexual offending by people crossing international borders is the exchange of personal information on the "known" sex offender. Various mechanisms and specialist units have been devised by the police and other agencies to process this information and ensure that the right information reaches the right person at the right time to enable them to do their job.

Within the United Kingdom

In the United Kingdom, the centralized CEOP unit established in 2006 has created its Overseas Tracker Team to facilitate this level of monitoring (Child Exploitation and Online Protection Centre, 2009: 25–26); in their annual report of 2010 CEOP stated that the Team is "far more operational and proactive than ever before" (Child Exploitation and Online Protection Centre, 2010b: 29). CEOP has signed a Memorandum of Understanding with the Australian Federal Police with both agencies agreeing to adopt strategies to enhance current arrangements for sharing information and criminal intelligence (Child Exploitation and Online Protection Centre, 2011). CEOP also participates in the ACPO-led "Travelling Sex Offender Working Group," formed in 2010.

The United Kingdom's 250-mile land border between Northern Ireland and the Republic of Ireland has posed particular problems for monitoring the traveling sex offender. The close cultural affinities between the two countries mean the land border facilitates frequent and easy crossings. Both countries have their own version of a sex offender register and the authorities on both sides of the border have responded with a Memorandum of Understanding on the monitoring of sex offenders (Department of Justice, Equality and Law Reform, 2006; Home Office, 2006) and an Agreement on the policing and exchange of information on sex offenders (House of Commons, 2009).

The Northern Ireland authorities wishing to register a new arrival from the South who is on the Republic's sex offender register must apply to a court using the

Notification Order procedures (see above). No such court requirements exist for sex offenders traveling in the opposite direction because the registration law in the Republic simply places the onus on the inbound sex offender to report to the authorities within three days of arrival for the purpose of registration (Sex Offender Act 2001 Republic of Ireland, s13). The Department of Justice in Northern Ireland has proposed introducing a similar system for the North which would obviate the need to apply for a Notification Order (Department of Justice, 2010); at present the proposals remain as proposals.

In terms of employment screening, the UK Criminal Records Bureau (CRB), which services employers' needs for criminal record background checks, has long recognized the need for accurate and up-to-date criminal records from overseas. The CRB initially created an Overseas Information Service that simply provided information to UK employers on what they might expect from overseas jurisdictions (for more on this, see Thomas, 2007: 157–158, 169–172). Developments within the European Union are set to improve this picture and close what the UK NSPCC describes as an "information gap" (Fitch, Spencer Chapman and Hilton, 2007; see also below).

European initiatives

In 1959 Member States of the Council of Europe had agreed to exchange criminal conviction records on each other's nationals when they had appeared in court in another country (Council of Europe, 1959, Article 22); this arrangement was to apply to all offenders and not just sex offenders. The idea was to ensure that all these "Article 22 notifications" meant the offender's home country knew about any criminal record held in another Council of Europe country. In practice it did not always work particularly well.

The United Kingdom received 27,000 criminal conviction records from across Europe on its national citizens between 1995 and 2007 that had not been passed on to operational police forces but allowed literally to gather dust on a shelf in the Home Office. This figure included an estimated 540 serious crimes of rape, murder and robbery and the police did not know the offenders or their whereabouts (Amroliwala, 2007).

The European Union has sought to strengthen this position. A 2005 White Paper considered how all criminal records could be shared between the Member States whether they were records of sexual offenses or not (European Commission, 2005). An EU 2005 Framework Decision (2005/876/JHA) asked all Member States to exchange criminal records on their nationals offending in other Member States. Each country would nominate a Central Authority for the Exchange of Criminal Records to be the single point of contact for such exchanges (Jacobs and Blitsa, 2008). The 2005 Framework Decision has now been firmed up with a new Framework Decision (2009/315/JHA) *requiring* all Member States to exchange criminal records to be implemented in April 2012 and to be supported by new electronic hardware known as ECRIS (the European Criminal Records Information System).

The UK Central Authority for the Exchange of Criminal Records is located in Hampshire as part of the ACPO Criminal Record Office initiative (HM Inspectorate of Constabulary, 2010). The result should be a merging of domestic and foreign convictions for a more comprehensive list of antecedents that will assist the police, vetting agencies such as the CRB, and the courts. New laws have already been passed to facilitate the latter and to enable the new "combined" foreign and domestic criminal records to be admissible in UK courts (Coroners and Justice Act 2009, s144 and Schedule 17; see also Ministry of Justice, 2010).

There will be residual problems with the data quality of criminal records kept by some EU Member States and their respective commitment to ensuring information reaches those who need it, but the European Union already has in mind a system of incorporating criminal records from outside the European Union to form a third country national's index of criminal records (Council of the European Union, 2006).

North American initiatives

In the United States, following the passing of SORNA 2006, a new National Sex Offender Targeting Center has been established by the federal US Marshals Service which "will assist federal, state federal, state local *and foreign law enforcement agencies* by supplementing and coordinating state and local efforts to identify and arrest fugitive sex offenders" (US Department of Justice, 2008: 38, emphasis added). Furthermore, an International Tracking of Sex Offenders Working Group was formed in 2008 under the auspices of the Department of Justice SMART office (Sex Offender Sentencing, Monitoring, Apprehending, Registering, and Tracking). Work is well underway to develop a Registered Sex Offender International Tracking System working with the custodians of sex offender registers in other countries (see the International Tracking of Sex Offenders Working Group, 2010).

Discussion

There are currently in excess of 218 million passenger journeys made across the UK border each year; Heathrow airport alone facilitates over 60 million international passenger journeys a year (Cabinet Office, 2007: paras. 1.24–1.25). Identifying the convicted sex offender, or the potential sex offender, out of these numbers, whether inbound or outbound, is potentially an enormous task.

While no one would wish to stop attempts to prevent harm to children, there are still criticisms to be made of all these activities when it comes to interventions aimed at the traveling sex offender. Little differentiation is made, for example, between types of sexual offending or between convicted sex offenders and people with no criminal record who might offend.

Many of the measures now in place are extremely rigid and bureaucratic and do not have any real evidential basis that they make any difference to levels of offending. The evidence provided by ECPAT UK (2011), for example, to justify the reporting of *all* travel abroad by registered sex offenders has been questioned:

> Such a selection of information as "evidence" in support of changes to the current system of notification for foreign travel should cause immediate concern. Firstly, using tabloid

newspaper reports as the factual basis for a change of Government policy is completely irresponsible and would extend a worrying trend for the development of policy in Home Affairs on the basis of media pressure. Secondly, there is no evidence to suggest that the men in these case studies would have been prevented from committing the offences (or in one case alleged offences) described if a requirement to notify the police of all foreign travel was added to the notification requirements. (UNLOCK campaign group, http:// forum.unlock.org.uk/attach.aspx?a=160)

The rhetoric of politicians calling for an EU-wide sex offender register has been equally criticized as impractical. On November 23, 2007 the Parliamentary Assembly of the Council of Europe passed a Resolution calling for a Europe-wide sex offender register. Ms Marietta de Pourbaix-Lundin from Sweden was appointed as Rapporteur on the subject and her report appeared in May 2010 (Council of Europe, 2010).

The Report recommended that the Assembly did *not* support a Europe-wide sex offender register because of the logistical problems, but instead was in favor of individual countries creating their own sex offender registers. The Report did express the view that sex offenders travel to avoid conviction and that increased cooperation between European countries was important to prevent sex offenders from traveling from one country to another with ease. Rather than yet more grand policies, however, the Report wanted to see better use made of Interpol's existing international sex offender database held in Lyon, France.

On a specific level the UK courts have cited the existence of travel notification requirements as one of the prime reasons the UK sex offender register is not compatible with Article 8 of the European Convention of Human Rights, the right to privacy. Reporting restrictions caused Article 8 to be engaged and to cause intrusions on a person's private and family life (*JF and Angus Aubrey Thompson* v. *Home Office* [2009] EWCA Civ 792 Appendix); this case was later upheld in the UK Supreme Court (*R (on the application of F (by his litigation friend F)) and Thompson (FC) (Respondents)* v. *Secretary of State for the Home Department (Appellant)* [2010] UKSC 17). Even tighter restrictions now being proposed would only increase the incompatibility (see Chapter 2).

As with other parts of the law and policies on sexual offending, the need to contain the traveling sex offender needs to be based more on primary research and less on media reports, case studies and politicians playing to the public gallery.

Note

1 The Association of Chief Police Officers (ACPO) formed a "Travelling Sex Offender Working Group" in 2010 (Child Exploitation and Online Protection Centre, 2010b).

References

Alexander, S., Meuwese, S. and Wolthuis, A. (2000) "Policies and developments relating to the sexual exploitation of children: the legacy of the Stockholm Conference," *European Journal on Criminal Policy and Research* 8, 479–501.

Amroliwala, D. (2007) *Report of the Inquiry into the Handling by Home Office Officials of Notifications, by Other European Countries, of Criminal Convictions for UK Citizens.* London: Home Office.

Association of Chief Police Officers (2009) *Memorandum on the Policing and Crime Bill 2009 Part 2 Clauses 21–24 Submitted to House of Commons Policing and Crime Bill Committee Session 2008–9.* London: Association of Chief Police Officers.

Barrett, D., Barrett, E. and Mullenger, N. (eds) (2000) *Youth Prostitution in the New Europe: The Growth in Sex Work.* Lyme Regis: Russell House Publishing.

BBC News (2007) MEPs want EU sex offender list, http://news.bbc.co.uk/1/hi/uk/6958807.stm (accessed September 7, 2012).

Bichard Report (2004) *A public inquiry report on child protection procedures in Humberside police and Cambridgeshire constabulary, particularly the effectiveness of relevant intelligence-based record keeping, vetting practices since 1995 and information sharing with other agencies,* HC 653. London: The Stationery Office.

Botterill, D. and Jones, T. (eds) (2010. *Tourism and Crime: Key Themes.* Oxford: Goodfellow Publishers Ltd.

Bright, M. (2003) "Bid to curb paedophile sex tourists," Guardian, November 16.

Burrell, I. (1998) "Sex tourists turn to the Caribbean," Independent, October 13.

Cabinet Office (2007) *Security in a Global Hub: Establishing the UK's New Border Arrangements.* London: The Cabinet Office.

Castle, S. (2004) "Cross-border sex crimes spur EU countries to share criminal records," Independent, July 20.

Child Exploitation and Online Protection Centre (2009) *Annual Review 2008–2009.* London: Child Exploitation and Online Protection Centre.

Child Exploitation and Online Protection Centre (2010a) Guilty plea for overseas child abuser, http://ceop.police.uk/Media-Centre/Press-releases/2010/GUILTY-PLEA-FOR-OVERSEAS-CHILD-ABUSER/ (accessed September 7, 2012).

Child Exploitation and Online Protection Centre (2010b) *Annual Review 2009–2010.* London: Child Exploitation and Online Protection Centre.

Child Exploitation and Online Protection Centre (2011) CEOP and Australian Federal Police strengthen their partnership, http://ceop.police.uk/Media-Centre/Press-releases/2011/CEOP-and-Australian-Federal-Police-strengthen-their-partnership-/ (accessed September 7, 2012).

Criminal Justice Joint Inspection (2010) *Restriction and Rehabilitation: Getting the Right Mix.* London: Criminal Justice Joint Inspection.

Council of Europe (1959) *Convention on Mutual Assistance in Criminal Matters* (ETS 30). Strasbourg: Council of Europe.

Council of Europe (2010) *Reinforcing Measures against Sex Offenders,* Committee on Legal Affairs and Human Rights (Doc. 12243), May 4. Strasbourg: Council of Europe.

Council of the European Union (2006) *Commission Working Document on the Feasibility of an Index of Third-Country Nationals Convicted in the European Union,* COM (2006) 359 final. Brussels: Council of the European Union.

Cowan, R. (2006) "Three life sentences for Latvian who raped and killed girl, 17," Guardian, March 30.

Crown Prosecution Service South West (2010) Judge dismisses ground breaking sexual offences case, http://www.cps.gov.uk/southwest/cps_southwest_news/patrick_matthews/ (accessed September 7, 2012).

Department of Justice (2010) *Arrangements for Notification of Sex Offenders from Jurisdictions outside the UK: A Consultative Document,* Public Protection Unit. Belfast: Department of Justice.

Department of Justice, Equality and Law Reform (2006) New Memo of Understanding signed regarding sex offenders, www.justice.ie/en/JELR/Pages/PR07000339 (accessed September 7, 2012).

European Commission (1996) *Communication from the Commission on Combating Child Sex Tourism,* Com (96) 547. Brussels: European Commission.

European Commission (2005) *White Paper on Exchanges of Information on Convictions and the Effect of such Convictions in the European Union,* Com 2005 10 final. Brussels: European Commission.

ECPAT (End Child Prostitution, Child Pornography and Trafficking of Children for Sexual Purposes UK) (2008) *Return to Sender.* London: ECPAT.

ECPAT (End Child Prostitution, Child Pornography and Trafficking of Children for Sexual Purposes UK) (2011) *Off the Radar: Protecting Children from British Sex Offenders who Travel.* London: ECPAT.

Fitch, K., Spencer Chapman, K. and Hilton, Z. (2007) *Protecting Children from Sexual Abuse in Europe: Safer Recruitment of Workers in a Border-free Europe.* London: NSPCC.

Gillan, A. (1999) "Paedophile law change sought," Guardian, July 23.

HM Inspectorate of Constabulary (2010) *ACPO Criminal Record Office (ACRO) – Police National Computer Compliance Report.* London: HMIC.

Home Office (1996a) UK proposes three-point plan to combat child sex tourism, http://www.prnewswire.co.uk/cgi/news/release?id=19294 (accessed September 7, 2012).

Home Office (1996b) *Sexual Offences (Conspiracy and Incitement) Act 1996* (Circular ref. 44/1996). London: Home Office.

Home Office (1996c) *Review of Extra-Territorial Jurisdiction –Steering Committee Report* (Sentencing and Offences Unit). London: Home Office.

Home Office (2004) *Guidance on Part 2 of the Sexual Offences Act 2003,* 1st edn. London: Home Office.

Home Office (2006) *Memorandum of Understanding – Information Sharing Arrangements Relating to Sex Offenders (Circular no. 43/2006).* London: Home Office.

Home Office (2008) "Tightening rules for sex offenders" (press release), August 20. London: Home Office.

Home Office (2010) *Guidance on Part 2 of the Sexual Offences Act 2003,* 2nd edn. London: Home Office.

Home Office (2011) *Reforming the Notification Requirements of Registered Sex Offenders (Part 2 of the Sexual Offences Act 2003): A Targeted Consultation.* London: Home Office.

Home Office/Scottish Executive (2001) *Consultation Paper on the Review of Part 1 of the Sex Offenders Act 1997.* London: Home Office/Scottish Executive.

Hopkins, N. (2000) "Paedophile jailed for abuse of girls at French campsite," Guardian, January 22.

House of Commons (2009) *Northern Ireland Affairs Committee Cross Border Co-operation between the Governments of the United Kingdom and the Republic of Ireland* HC 78, 18 June, paras. 92–99. London: House of Commons.

ICE (2010) Strategic plan 2010 fiscal years 2010–2014, http://www.ice.gov/doclib/news/library/reports/strategic-plan/strategic-plan–2010.pdf (accessed September 7, 2012).

International Tracking of Sex Offenders Working Group (2010) White Paper, http://www.ojp.gov/smart/pdfs/InternationalTrackingofSexOffendersWorkingGroup.pdf (accessed September 15, 2012).

Interpol (2011) Key statistics, http://www.interpol.int/public/ICPO/multimedia/keyStatistics.asp (accessed June 23, 2011).

Jacobs, J. and Blitsa, D. (2008) "Major 'minor' progress under the Third Pillar: EU institution building in the sharing of criminal record information," *Chicago-Kent Journal of International and Comparative Law* 111–165.

Kane, J. (1998) *Sold for Sex*. Aldershot: Arena.

Karlen, H. and Hagner, C. (1996) *Commercial Exploitation of Children in Some Eastern European Countries*. London: ECPAT.

Levy, A. (1999) "Cross-border movement for abusive purposes: the adequacy of UK safeguards," *Childright* 159, 6–8.

Lewis, P. (2008) "Britain accused of turning a blind eye to child sex tourism," Guardian, August 18.

Loucks, N., Lyner, O. and Sullivan, T. (1998) "The employment of people with criminal records in the European Union," *European Journal on Criminal Policy and Research* 6, 2, 195–210.

Ministry of Justice (2010) *Implementation of Section 144 and Schedule 17 of the Coroners and Justice Act 2009* (Circular no. 2010/12). London: Ministry of Justice.

Montgomery, H. (2010) "Child sex tourism: is extra territorial legislation the answer?," in D. Botterrill and T. Jones (eds), *Tourism and Crime: Key Themes*. Oxford: Goodfellow Publishers Ltd, pp. 69–84.

Muntarbhorn, V. (1996) *Sexual Exploitation of Children*, Study Series No. 8, UN Centre for Human Rights. Geneva: United Nations.

Parry, P. (2007) Warning on migrant sex offenders, http://news.bbc.co.uk/1/hi/wales/6895621.stm (accessed September 15, 2012).

Schaeffer, S. (2000) "Anger as Tyson is granted visa for Glasgow fight,"Independent, May 19.

Sunday Times (1997) "Paedophiles go south to avoid sex offender register," Sunday Times, December 7.

Taylor, J. (2006) "Glitter gets three years in Vietnam jail for child sex,"Independent, March 4.

Thomas, T. (2007) *Criminal Records: A Data Base for the Criminal Justice System and Beyond*. London: Palgrave, Macmillan.

Thomas, T., Katz, I. and Wattam, C. (1999) *CUPICSO: The Collection and Use of Personal Information on Child Sex Offenders*. London: NSPCC.

Townsend, M. (2008) "Babies are new target, Met warns as paedophile threat spirals," Observer, August 24.

UNICEF (United Nations Children's Fund) (2008) World Congress against the Sexual Exploitation of Children and Adolescents comes to a close, http://www.unicef.org/media/media_46636.html (accessed September 7, 2012).

US Department of Justice (2008) *Review of the Department of Justice's Implementation of the Sex Offender Registration and Notification Act*, Office of the Inspector General – Evaluation and Inspections Division. Washington: US Department of Justice.

World Tourism Organization (1995) UNWTO Statement on the Prevention of Organized Sex Tourism, Resolution A/Res/338 (Xi), Cairo, Egypt, October 17–22, http://ethics.unwto.org/en/content/staements-policy-documents-child-protection (accessed September 15, 2012).

27

Hell is Other People
The Importance of Controlling Pedophilic Activity
Xanthè Mallett and Jann Karp

Introduction

"Hell is other people" are Garcin's words in Sartre's *Huis Clos* (Sartre, 1990: 95). The three key characters in this play "are in hell precisely because they are prevented by their own choices from establishing any proper relations with those around them" (Manser, 1967: 98). The notion of proper and improper relationships is central to the theme of this chapter – child sexual abuse, arguably the ultimate form of an improper relationship. The three "characters" of this paper are the people who are engaged in committing, reporting and controlling pedophilic activity. The community's and society's engagement with this crime involves a degree of fear, which can obstruct the development of preventative solutions. The community (in this discussion) are all people affected by the acts of the offender, such as victims and their family, friends, as well as police, lawyers, journalists and commentators.

Cases of child sexual abuse cause a significant degree of alarm for a number of reasons. Part of the panic arises from the range of social identities of those found guilty; generally speaking, offenders cover a broad demographic and they cannot be easily differentiated from other members of society. Another aspect of the fear is the lack of power felt by parents and society in general when trying to protect their children – a strong societal and familial impulse – as statistics demonstrate that in the majority of cases, children are not molested by strangers, but rather by family members and friends. These issues collide to cause an overwhelming and emotional response to cases of alleged child molestation, which often results in public demand for increased punishment and control of offenders, regardless of whether empirical evidence suggests that the sanctions proposed offer any additional safety to children.

The Wiley-Blackwell Handbook of Legal and Ethical Aspects of Sex Offender Treatment and Management,
First Edition. Edited by Karen Harrison and Bernadette Rainey.
© 2013 John Wiley & Sons, Ltd. Published 2013 by John Wiley & Sons, Ltd.

Part of the difficulty in dealing with cases of child abuse, and even more so child sexual abuse (CSA), is that this is a subject which many people would rather avoid. The topic of sexual abuse is uncomfortable. However, with a view to increasing child safety, we must achieve an improved understanding of how to respond to abused children, as well as how to protect them. Part of this discussion needs to be a debate as to how to successfully monitor and manage individuals who pose a risk to children.

Since the 1990s, sex offenders have been considered the ultimate dangerous criminal class (Lynch, 2002), and how best to protect children from abuse remains one of the long, dark questions at the intersection between sex and society; a key aspect of which is how to monitor the behavior of those convicted of CSA upon release. When considering the monitoring of pedophilic behavior, we must consider our three main stakeholders: the offender, the victim and the community. Balancing the requirements and rights of all three groups in such an emotive arena is a significant challenge. One recent suggestion that has been made is that electronic monitoring (EM) with associated global positioning system (GPS) capability may be a suitable method of supervising those found guilty of CSA upon release from prison. The question remains, however: given the complex nature of these crimes, can the electronic tagging of those convicted of CSA help protect children?

With a view to addressing this question, we will review offender demographics and the evaluation of the reliability and effectiveness of electronic tags currently in use. This discussion will be set within the global context. The problems associated with monitoring those found guilty of CSA will also be highlighted, as will the transnational nature of the crimes.

Child Sexual Abuse: The Facts

Using the correct terminology to describe the victims of these crimes is very important, not only culturally but also for legal reasons. CSA can generally be defined as contact between a child and an adult (or other person significantly older than the juvenile) in a position of power or control over the child, where the minor is being used for the sexual gratification of the other person or adult (Hersen and Gross, 2008). Furthermore, Interpol suggests that indecent images of children should not be referred to as "pornography," as these type of terms refer to adults engaging in consensual sexual acts distributed (in most cases) legally to the general public for their sexual pleasure (Interpol, n.d. a).

CSA exploits children's inability to make free and reasoned decisions, and is therefore non-consensual by definition (Frank, Camp and Boutcher, 2010). In terms of protecting children, Article 34 of the United Nations Convention on the Rights of the Child (UNCRC) provides that:

> States Parties undertake to protect the child from all forms of sexual exploitation and sexual abuse. For these purposes, States Parties shall in particular take all appropriate national, bilateral and multilateral measures to prevent:

(a)   The inducement or coercion of a child to engage in any unlawful sexual activity;
(b)   The exploitative use of children in prostitution or other unlawful sexual practices;
(c)   The exploitative use of children in pornographic performances and materials.

Since the adoption of the Convention in 1989, the UNCRC has been ratified by more governments than any other human rights instrument. Two optional protocols exist within this convention, one being the Optional Protocol to the Convention on the Rights of the Child on the Sale of Children, Child Prostitution and Child Pornography (United Nations Treaty Collection). The protocol was adopted by the UN General Assembly in 2000. As of August 2011, 119 states were party to the protocol, with a further 37 states having signed but not ratified the protocol. The second optional protocol relates to the involvement of children in armed conflict (United Nations Treaty Collection). Despite the notable efforts of many nations, CSA, including the dissemination of indecent material, remains a serious issue (Healy, 2004).

Crimes against children, including CSA, are committed in two primary ways. The first occurs at a local level, usually taking place in the home or within the circle of family and close friends. The other is international (Interpol, n.d. b), which has two distinct but inter-related aspects. The first consists of offenders from all over the world accessing and distributing indecent images of children via the internet, developing pedophile networks without ever having to leave their homes (Akdeniz, 2008). This can develop into child grooming (Martellozzo, Nehring and Taylor, 2010), a transnational problem (Gallagher *et al.*, 2006), where offenders visit chat rooms, and send indecent images of themselves to juveniles or influence children into performing sexually explicit acts in front of web-cameras, and sometimes encourage children to meet in person with the intent of sexually assaulting them (Ost, 2009). Other predators elect to travel to access children, often to developing nations. The relative wealth of the offender, together with the lack of understanding or effective legislation, means that the abuse of children can be easier in these countries. This type of crime is linked to child trafficking, organized crime and murder (Interpol, n.d. b). Known as "sex tourists," these individuals are commonly aware that the chances of being caught and prosecuted are reduced if the acts are not committed in the country in which they live – sometimes even believing that the same laws do not apply (see Chapter 26).

The literature indicates that 60 to 70% of child molesters target girls, approximately 20 to 33% boys, and around 10% children of either sex (Grubin, 1998). Obtaining reliable and accurate statistics on the incidence (number of new cases per annum) and prevalence (proportion of children in a population affected) of CSA is difficult due to the fact that this is essentially a hidden crime, the effects of which many victims will not disclose for years, if ever. The picture is further complicated by the fact that the child's age and gender will affect the likelihood and/or timing of disclosure by the child, as will environmental and cultural factors such as ethnicity and religion. Furthermore, cultural norms also influence whether an abused child's family will report the abuse to authorities (Fontes and Plummer, 2010). Consequently, determining the size of the problem is extremely difficult; from what information is available, it is widely accepted that this is a very significant, international problem across all cultural and socio-economic groups.

Child sex offenders, to gain access to children successfully, must be socially competent to some extent and capable of "normal" interactions: if pedophiles were not capable of gaining people's trust, they would not have the opportunity to perpetrate the abuse. One study suggests that although sexual attraction to children is clearly relevant to understanding the behavior of those who commit CSA, other social factors, in particular a general preoccupation with children, are probably of equal importance, both in terms of causation and in relation to assessing risk (Martellozzo, Nehring and Taylor, 2010). The flip side of this is the increasing social sensitivity which means there is the potential for misinterpretation of the motives of individuals who are very interested in but harbor no sexual desire towards children; they are, for example, simply dedicated teachers or care staff. The fear of child sexual abuse can raise concern in what are essentially perfectly normal and safe situations. Examples of this are common; one such case occurred in the United Kingdom where a Scottish Council Education Department banned parents from videoing their children during public performances. While accepting that protecting children must be at the forefront of policy making, there was cross-party support from Members of the House of Commons for the view that this was an over-reaction (UK Government, 2003).

We know that CSA occurs in all aspects of society. There are two types of offenders; intra-familial and extra-familial (Sullivan *et al.*, 2011). The vast majority of child sexual assaults are committed by someone the child knows. This includes assaults undertaken by youth offenders, with one study, comprising data from a large number of sex offender programs in the United States, suggesting that 39% of victims are related to the offender and live in the same household, while only 6% of victims are strangers (Ruan *et al.*, 1996).

The extra-familial category also includes those who use their profession or hobby as a means of accessing minors; schools and youth clubs are common contact points, as are day care centers (JSOnline, 2012; Colton, Roberts and Vanstone, 2010) and church groups (Parkinson, Oates and Jayakody, 2009). Teaching is one such profession, with potentially 20% of female students in the United States having been sexually harassed by their teachers (Winslow and Zhang, 2008). The problem appears to be even more widespread in other continents, particularly Africa. For example, a recent survey in South Africa indicated that school teachers were responsible for 32% of reported cases of child sexual assault (Krug *et al.*, 2002). Although these are extra-familial abusers, their work environments often place them *in loco parentis*; consequently, the grooming methods employed are more similar in nature to those of intra-familial abuse than those who engage in other forms of extra-familial abuse (Colton, Roberts and Vanstone, 2010).

Offender Demographics and the Scale of Child Sexual Abuse

The current understanding is that the majority of those who undertake CSA are men, and it is an act commonly associated with male sexual aggression (Martellozzo, Nehring and Taylor, 2010). Research conducted with online sexual offenders, as with other sex offenders, indicates that they represent a mixed and broad demographic

(Sheehan and Sullivan, 2010), and they cannot be easily differentiated from other members of society (Martellozzo, Nehring and Taylor, 2010) . As a result, authors focus on distinctive grooming behaviors (Grubin, 1998). In terms of strategy, there are a number of common mechanisms. As a generalization, males often use manipulation to isolate (physically and psychologically) the victim for a sexual relationship, in concurrence with coercive approaches to ensure the victim does not reveal the true nature of the relationship to others (Campbell, 2009).

Although the majority of CSA appears to be carried out by males, a number of recent cases in the United Kingdom have illustrated that women do exploit children, both in person and via the internet, although this area is currently under-researched (Martellozzo, Nehring and Taylor, 2010). Corby (1998) states that women account for approximately 4% of offenders, while another study suggests 5% (Grubin, 1998), with mothers accounting for 2% of the total. Women grooming a child for unlawful sexual activity is an increasingly taboo subject and this may reduce the disclosure rate (Elliott, 1993). Grooming by both males and females in schools is one significant problem, the scale of which is again difficult to determine as some researchers suggest low reporting rates, at around 6% (Knoll, 2010). Add to this the taboo of reporting women for sexual assault, and the disclosure against female teachers may be further reduced.

In addition, some women are passively involved in child abuse through lying to authorities for their male partners who are accused of holding indecent images of children; the female partners claim that they are represented in the images, and not a juvenile. This can be classed as perverting the course of justice and/or criminal conspiracy. It is unclear as to why relatively little attention has been paid to the female sex offender, in the case of either passive or active abuse, but the picture is complicated by the fact that evidence suggests (Denov, 2004) that female sex offenders are treated less seriously than males by all professionals with whom they come into contact, including the police and therapists.

Juvenile sex offenders appear to be as heterogeneous as the adult group, and the types of behavior they carry out are similar. Importantly, adolescent sex offenders are thought to account for around 33% of all sex crimes, and although many will commit offenses against children this is largely related to the fact that the age of the victim will be similar to the age of the offender; that is, their sexual interest is "age appropriate." Only a small proportion of juvenile sex offenders that target juveniles have a sexual interest in children specifically. A number of adults found guilty of CSA began molesting children in their teens (Vielmetti, 2010); however, only a small percentage continue to commit sex crimes as adults (Grubin, 1998).

GPS: International

Between 1980 and 2000 worldwide prison populations exploded (Austin, Irwin and Kubrin, 2003). In response to this unprecedented growth in numbers of incarcerated individuals and the associated costs,[1] a number of intermediate sanctions were endorsed as less expensive, but also effective and "tough" alternatives. The goal of these sanctions was to reduce prison populations (Payne and Gainey, 2000) while providing a greater level of offender accountability, as well as an increased level of surveillance than would be provided by traditional probation services (Payne and Gainey, 2000.) To date, however, little empirical evidence is available to demonstrate the extent to which these intermediate measures, including EM, have fulfilled the dual aims of reduced costs to the taxpayer with no compromise to public safety. Despite the lack of empirical evidence regarding the effectiveness of EM, this approach has received significant support and is being expanded as a mechanism for monitoring high risk offenders in the community (Padgett, Bales and Blomberg, 2006; George, 2006). The State of North Carolina (2005) also commented on the technical difficulties, stating that GPS can be an effective option under the correct circumstances, but is limited to areas with comprehensive mobile telephone coverage, and that therefore its use should be restricted to urban areas until the technology improves. It should be noted, however, that although GPS can be reliable down to one meter, it can usually only be relied upon to 15 meters on average (Michael and Michael, 2009), and extraneous artifacts may affect the reliability, including urban clutter such as skyscrapers, and even weather conditions.

EM is a term that applies to programs that use technological devices to help ensure that offenders remain in compliance with the terms of their sentences (Finn and Muirhead-Steves, 2002). There are two forms of EM. In its simplest form, radio frequency (RF) monitoring can determine if an individual is present or absent at a specific place (George, 2006). The second form, when the profile of the offender requires it, is a system in which a transmitter can be used in combination with GPS capability (Killias *et al.*, 2010), which uses satellite tracking to monitor movements outside of the home (Finn and Muirhead-Steves, 2002) as a means of monitoring the offender's access to certain banned geographical areas, as this will be recorded as a violation. These systems can be performed by either passive (intermittent) or active (constant) monitoring of an offender. Constant systems involve the attachment of a transmitter to an offender which omits a continuous signal to a receiver (Finn and Muirhead-Steves, 2002), whereas passive systems use a non-continuous signal. The basic belief is that the addition of EMGPS to parole supervision will either deter recidivist behavior and rehabilitate parolees, or at least minimize their potential access to individuals or activities (Finn and Muirhead-Steves, 2002).

Today, EM is used in almost every country in the world (Killias *et al.*, 2010). In the United States, adult and juvenile offenders (Raider, 1994; Roy, 1997) have been subject to EM orders for some time (Padgett, Bales and Blomberg, 2006). In the 1980s, when EM was in its growth phase in the United States, supporters claimed that it would be of significant value in controlling various types of offender, although this has not been supported by the research (George, 2006). Importantly, one study (Padgett, Bales and Blomberg, 2006) suggests that EM is being used for relatively serious offenders, and is thus likely to provide an alternative to custodial sentences.

The policy for EM varies between states, the legislation being heavily influenced in some instances by high-profile cases, particularly those that have been heavily publicized. For example, in Florida, the sexual battery and murder of nine-year-old Jessica Lunsford in 2005, allegedly at the hands of a registered sex offender, prompted legislation that required child sex offenders to wear GPS tracking devices for the rest of their lives following release from prison (Padgett, Bales and Blomberg, 2006). Whether driven by the Act which followed this case (the Jessica Lunsford Act 2005) or by the general increased awareness of the capabilities of GPS systems, legislation related to the monitoring of offenders in the community was proposed in at least 11 additional states, as well as at the federal level, in 2005 (Padgett, Bales and Blomberg, 2006).

Convicted sex offenders have been wearing electronic tags in Queensland, Australia, since 2007, with 21 offenders wearing electronic anklets or bracelets that were not fitted with GPS monitoring. However, following the arrest of convicted pedophile Graeme Paul Hancock at a park in Brisbane for allegedly taking photographs of a naked four-year-old girl, this technology was deemed inadequate as Hancock's monitor was not fitted with GPS. Consequently, the authorities knew that he was not at home, but were not aware of his specific location (news.com.au, 2009). In 2011 the Police Minister for Queensland, Neil Roberts, announced that GPS tracking would be introduced for sex offenders for the first time in Australia, following a newspaper campaign which began in 2011 (Fagan, 2011). Queensland Corrective Services aimed to subject 67 sex offenders to EM as part of their supervision orders, as part of which they would be fitted with a GPS device by early 2012 (Helbig, 2011), and stated that the technology forms the backbone of Queensland's sex offender supervision scheme. Although the opposition Deputy Leader, Tim Nicholls, welcomed the move, he said the government had acted as a result of public pressure (Wardill, 2011).

Current Attempts at Control

Denouncing those who commit sexual crimes against children is easy; understanding the psychology of the perpetrators is not. Because of the emotive nature of the crimes, society and the press continue to label them as monsters, evil, or worse. However, some authors suggest that labeling offenders may impede our ability to understand them, and, importantly, our ability to intervene effectively. The public frequency of negative and often ill-informed comments makes more challenging the need to treat offenders or influence future behavior (Walters, 2012) (see Chapter 8). When considering developments and changes to penal policy, society must remember that we are not simply deciding how to punish a marginal group of people – whether to deter, reform or incarcerate them (Shannon and Uggen, 2012). How we treat offenders is a reflection of society as whole, and the manner in which we choose to punish and control offenders may be central to our development as a society. Are we then choosing for surveillance to become a more central aspect of society?

This type of criminal activity has a high level of covert practice. The criminal elements of *mens rea* (the guilty thought) and *actus reus* (the guilty act) are carried out in private settings. According to widespread belief, sanctions vary in their undesirable effects, such as the deterioration of defendants' family and work lives. An example of a very serious sanction currently supported by German law permits some sex offenders to volunteer for surgical castration as part of their treatment, although there have been recent calls by the Strasbourg Council of Europe's anti-torture panel for this to be stopped, particularly as the surgery is irreversible and there is no evidence that it reduces recidivism rates (Reilhac and Thomas, 2012). Often the argument is postulated that electronic tagging as a sanction will reduce re-offending when compared to imprisonment, as this decreases the disintegrative effect on the offender (Hucklesby, 2008). The minimization of social disintegration of sexual offenders cannot be used as an argument for electronic tagging with GPS monitoring, however, as social integration is not a marker of psycho-sexual health – often those who undertake these crimes are very good at social interaction and heavily involved in community life, while undertaking the sexual abuse of children with whom they have contact. In fact, successful social integration which may be viewed as rehabilitation is often the mechanism by which some offenders will gain an advantage when accessing children such as those working in day care centers and schools (Knoll, 2010).

There are also pertinent philosophical implications for widening the use of EMGPS. Previous research has signified that there are six fundamental questions:

1. Why is the privacy invasion occurring?
2. Is the purpose both important and legitimate?
3. Is the invasion relevant to its justifying purpose?
4. Is the proposed method the only or least invasive one available?
5. What procedural restraints or restrictions have been placed on the privacy-invading methods?
6. How will the information be protected post-acquisition (Payne and Gainey, 2000)?

The answers can be endlessly debated. However, the determination of the use of electronic monitoring with GPS should not be based on the feasibility and implementation in the legal environment, but rather the question is a moral one: how is EM actually going to help protect children? At this point again pedophiles are subordinate, a minority in the hierarchy of criminal prevention and they will be subjected to different forms of control.

Communities agree that it is to everyone's advantage to protect children. High-profile cases of CSA result in cries for increased legislation to protect children within society, often driven by media attention. This has led to violence within community groups against the actual offender. The political and media commentary gains an advantage, as commentators appear to be protectors of vulnerable children. Even if this attention were to subside, and with it the public outcry for action, the EM of offenders appears set to continue (Padgett, Bales and Blomberg, 2006).

Access to Information and Associated Legalization

Over recent decades, countries all over the world have rewritten their criminal laws aimed at regulating sexual activity – including striking expansions in criminal regulation (Frank, Camp and Boutcher, 2010). Many of these changes came about after 1996, following the First World Congress against the Commercial Sexual Exploitation of Children, and, by 2007, 211 nation states had committed to the Stockholm Agenda for Action. This Agenda challenged states, societies and organizations to fight the commercial sexual exploitation of children (World Congress against the Commercial Sexual Exploitation of Children, 1996). The key question is whether any of the sweeping reforms have improved the safety of children.

Specifically, in 1996 there was a very significant increase in the number of reforms to law regarding CSA, peaking in 1998 at almost 14 reforms per year, before dropping back in 2004 (Frank, Camp and Boutcher, 2010). Many of the reforms removed distinctions between various kinds of penetration, increased the age of consent, and neutralized the gender difference, thereby protecting boys as well as girls. The same period saw a mirrored increase in the reform of laws regarding rape, demonstrating that in general sex laws defending the cardinal rule of consent were being extensively advanced (Frank, Camp and Boutcher, 2010).

A key aspect of monitoring those accused and found guilty of CSA is the recording of information such as offender location, and importantly who has access to this information. There are examples where members of the public, from anywhere in the world, can source information on offenders. For example, the US web site www.safekidzone.com allows visitors to view a map of the locations of sex offenders, some with associated photographs. To gain full access to the site's services you have to join and pay a monthly subscription. One of the services available allows a child to summon immediate help by using a "panic button" on their mobile phone and the child is then located by GPS. Another site (www.city-data.com/so/sexoffenders. html) provides lists of sex offenders subdivided by state. Once you select a region, a map appears which pinpoints the home address of each registered offender, together with details of the crime for which they were found guilty, their date of birth, and physical description. These web sites are in addition to the federal site (http:// www.nsopw.gov/Core/Portal.aspx?AspxAutoDetectCookieSupport=1) which also lists offenders by state, but you have to enter a first and last name of the person of interest to obtain information. This site also allows you to search a radius around a specific address. Importantly, a caveat declares that: "Unlawful use of sex offender registry information to threaten, intimidate, harass, or injure a registered sex offender or any other person is prohibited and will be prosecuted to the full extent of the law."

There are also applications, available on mobile phones, which can be downloaded free of charge to locate known sex offenders in the community. One such application, "Life360," plots your locations – using GPS tracking in your mobile phone – of you and your family in relation to registered sex offenders in your area. If your local and/ or national government has not facilitated this function, the map simply shows your position, together with the locations of police stations and hospitals, or "safe zones." Using this application, you can search the world map for sex offenders, and once located (shown as a tab on the map), you can click on any tab which displays and find the name, date of birth, home address, description and photograph of the offender. Currently, offender information only appears to be available for the United States.

The United Kingdom also has a register, the Violent and Sex Offender Register (ViSOR), which comprises a database of the records of those required to register with the police under the Sex Offenders Act 2003, which includes individuals jailed for over 12 months for violent offenses, as well as those considered at risk of offending. Access to the register is limited, however, to the police, the National Probation Service, Her Majesty's Service personnel, and private companies running prisons (see Chapter 21). In April 2010, lifelong registration on the list was successfully challenged and upheld by the Supreme Court. The basis for the ruling was that lifelong registration was incompatible with Article 8 of the European Convention on Human Rights (Kilkelly, 2003; Council of Europe, 2010) (see Chapter 2).

Political and Religious Aspects of Child Sexual Abuse Monitoring

There seems little doubt that criminal policy has been politicized (Shannon and Uggen, 2012). "Evil" is a deeply religio-moral concept, and when someone does something with which we vehemently disagree we may label this as evil (Walters, 2012). However, this type of religious terminology can cloud the issue, as there is little scientific foundation to the lay concept of "inherent evil," and it does not reflect much of what we know of offenders. Religious conviction of acting for the "common good" denies the very reality that pedophilic activity is located within all our communities. Theories and empirical research have demonstrated how political influence has shaped incarceration patterns. Punishment and imprisonment are fundamentally exercises in power, influenced by numerous factors including political forces, policy choices, public sentiment and the pressure applied by the media (Shannon and Uggen, 2012). The players in this power matrix represent that culmination of social, and subsequently political, influence, the result being social trends heavily impacting fiscal policy (as noted above).

Sex offenders will act in an objective manner while participating within the communities in which they live, and will often become active when they subjectively notice a personal advantage. Rarely, even in the situations that would be abhorrent to the majority, such as the sexual abuse of children, do perpetrators see their behavior as gratuitous or unjustified. Rather, they often view their acts as reasonable and justifiable (Walters, 2012; Baumeister, 1997; Martellozzo, Nehring and Taylor, 2010). Although we apply religio-moral judgment to sexual offenses involving children, there is another religious aspect of CSA, in that members of the church have been implicated in offenses. Since the mid-1980s, there have been a number of high-profile convictions and on-going investigations into alleged CSA committed by Catholic priests, and members of other religious orders (White and Terry, 2008; Parkinson, Oates and Jayakody; 2009, Gavrielides, 2012), known as clerical child sexual abuse (CCSA) (Donnelly and Inglis, 2009). Cases of this nature receive significant media and public attention, and have occurred in many countries including the United Kingdom, Ireland, Belgium, France, Germany, Australia, the United States, Canada, Mexico and elsewhere throughout the world. A serious aspect of these cases is that evidence exists which suggests that members of the Catholic hierarchy were aware of, and did not report, the allegations of abuse to the civil authorities. In a number of cases, the response was to reassign the accused to other locales, where they still had access to children, a practice for which the church has been heavily criticized (White and Terry, 2008).

Problems with Using EMGPS to Monitor and Control Child Sex Offenders in the Community

The proliferation of information technologies has facilitated the expansion of opportunities for the sexual abuse of children (Martellozzo, Nehring and Taylor, 2010). As a consequence, the internet is being used more and more by pedophiles and the associated networks which support them to distribute indecent images of children. The result is that images produced of abuse undertaken in Asia can be instantly sent to Europe, America and Australia. The perpetrators are difficult to identify, as the faces of the abusers are rarely shown in the images (Black *et al.*, 2009). As a result of this mechanism of distribution, CSA is a truly transnational crime (Healy, 2004). This causes significant problems in terms of investigating and identifying those actually undertaking the abuse, as well as controlling the networks to prevent further dissemination of indecent material. Collaboration between inter-disciplinary experts from international investigative agencies is required to police the internet in an attempt to reduce the amount of child abuse material worldwide. However, the term "transnational crime" has no judicial meaning; a person cannot be prosecuted for committing transnational crime (Davies, 2008).

Some authors suggest that many agencies using EM neither build rehabilitation aspects into the programs to work in association with the monitoring system, nor expect an enduring impact from its use (Padgett, Bales and Blomberg, 2006; Renzema and Mayo-Wilson, 2005). Further, the increased use of EMGPS is actually eroding the use of rehabilitation programs, with security being achieved predominantly through surveillance means. Rehabilitation is based on the premise that all but the most damaged of offenders are eventually reachable, if not redeemable; an altruistic standpoint (Nellis, 2006). To dispense with this service will ultimately impact on society as we become increasingly distrusting and fearful.

Conclusion

Readers at this point will anticipate a summation that includes a resolution to control pedophilic activity. The problem with providing conclusions previously presented in academic literature is the repetitive identification of a "demonic" creature that requires control. This type of analysis immediately leads to a particular reference to monitoring, regulating and in the main separating out of the "outsider" (Spencer, 2009). These offenders are outsiders in whatever community they are situated. The first step is to locate the offender within the criminal justice system, within the community, and within the familial or other type of setting within which they live. This also needs to occur within international legislative frameworks (Tagwireyi, 2011). The rule of law refers to the application of legal rules equally in all human situations. It should be unbiased and unaffected by emotion, politics, the media and all other external influences – the aim being universal fair treatment under the law as a routine mode of operating. However, socio-legal research confirms that legal decisions are made under inherent biases (Black, 1989) and social discrimination. Universalism therefore appears to be an unrealistic outcome. To reduce the inherent bias and protect all parties involved, perhaps the most appropriate manner to deal with a case, including those involving alleged CSA, would be to shift the attention from the social structure of the case to the process by which they are prosecuted. Much of the modern history within judgment research suggests that people's assessments of likelihood and risk do not conform with the laws of probability (Gilvovich and Griffin, 2002), which causes significant problems when considering the assessment of guilt or innocence in a jury trial, in a highly sensitive case such as one alleging CSA: Because of the emotive nature of CSA, it is even more imperative that we avoid letting ourselves apply a cognitive bias when analyzing the most appropriate way to protect children.

There is evidence to suggest that both radio frequency and GPS forms of EM can offer a level of control over an offender that conventional forms of probation supervision cannot (Nellis, 2006), and EM has been found to play an effective incapacitation and/or deterrence role in public safety (Padgett, Bales and Blomberg, 2006). However, as discussed, GPS is not as reliable as commonly assumed. It could be argued that EMGPS could be of use in reducing sex tourism of convicted offenders; however, many convicted pedophiles are subject to travel bans, so the effect will be reduced. Further, the same beneficial effect cannot necessarily be argued for in cases of CSA that do not include sex tourism as an element, as a very significant aspect of the abuse takes place at a physical distance from the victims via the internet, through the continuous cycle of distribution of indecent images. The problem is that the internet is so widely available in many diverse forms; home computers, tablets, via mobile telephone, through the television . . . the list appears endless. Whilst it is possible to reduce the access to internet-enabled devices in some cases, it is not possible to prevent other individuals facilitating offender access. Furthermore, anecdotal evidence suggests that images of CSA distributed across the Internet has led to increase in physical abuse worldwide (*Guardian*, 2004). There is no empirical evidence to suggest that EMGPS has any rehabilitative effect (Nellis, 2006); however, if rehabilitation programs were to be offered in conjunction with EMGPS monitoring, this may have an reductive effective in recidivist activity. EMGPS measures the offender's underlying criminality and the system's ability to detect that criminality and react to it. What the use of EM does not do is convey respect and concern: it merely fosters and encourages suspicion and anxiety on all sides (Nellis, 2006), and often offers society a false pretense of security and protection. As one author suggests (George, 2006), only when technologies are thoroughly entrenched in culture do the associated limitations begin to appear.

Child grooming, internet-based pedophile networks and sex tourism are all linked to other crimes such as child trafficking, organized crime and murder (Interpol, n.d. b; Winslow and Zhang, 2008). This demonstrates that CSA is a transnational crime. The EM with GPS of those found guilty of CSA on release from prison cannot adequately address all of the current issues, as a result of which it will have a limited effect in terms of improving child safety, and may simply foster a false sense of security within the populations directly affected. Consequently, because CSA is an international problem, and transnational in nature, universal legislation through bodies such as the United Nations and Interpol taking a global-institutionalized perspective appears the most appropriate way forward to improving the monitoring of child sex offenders with a view to protecting children. This should include regulation and legislature stating the suitable methods for treatment, control, supervision and management of those who pose a risk to children. Addressing different aspects of a complex issue with different recommendations only enhances the separateness of this criminal behavior.

Returning to the notion that hell is the "other," we acknowledge that the victim requires a high level of support and trust. Anyone who has been subjected to or has reported having been subjected to a pedophile's criminal interest in any form requires an appropriate response. The response need not be that we, as a community, castrate, electronically monitor or prevent any person suspected of pedophile activity from accessing the internet, or deny them any or all civil rights. The community response has to be one where the responsibility for a criminal's action is born within the group within which it occurs. Trust the victim and treat them with respect, regulate the offender and treat them as an individual, and make the community part of all responsibilities involving the detection and prevention of pedophilic activity. So hell can be the acts of an active pedophile, but hell must not be visited on the victim or the offender as then it is also visited on the community. Our relationships with pedophiles cannot be ones that strips that person of all humanity. The identification of a person as a "creature," "a demon," by attaching surveillance equipment to them allows the criminal justice system to function by the identifying that "outsider" as a "predator" without possibility of rehabilitation. Sartre concludes his play with Garcin saying, "OK, let us go on." So do we want to go on with the EM of people? We also ask: will the introduction of electronic tagging of criminals lead to a wider application of such surveillance technology? Possibly. As a society, is this what we would choose?

Acknowledgments

The authors wish to thank Alan Scott, Gail Hawkes and Peter Corrigan for their assistance during the preparation of this chapter.

Note

1   It costs $2.80 per day to electronically monitor a juvenile offender, as opposed to $160 to house the same offender in prison (State of North Carolina, 2005)

References

Akdeniz, Y. (2008) *Internet Child Pornography and the Law: National and International Responses*. Aldershot: Ashgate.

Austin, J., Irwin, J. and Kubrin, C.E. (2003) "It's about time: America's imprisonment binge," in T.G. Blomberg and S. Cohen (eds), *Punishment and Social Control*, 2nd edn. New York: Aldine de Gruyter, pp. 433–470.

Baumeister, R.F. (1997) *Evil: Inside Human Violence and Cruelty*. New York: Freeman.

Black, D. (1989) *Sociological Justice*. Oxford: Oxford University Press.

Black, S.M., Mallett, X., Rynn, C. and Duffield, N. (2009) "Case history: forensic hand image comparison as an aide for paedophile investigations," *Police Professional* 184, 21–24.

Campbell, A.M. (2009) "False faces and broken lives: an exploratory study of the interaction behaviors used by male sex offenders in relating to victims," *Journal of Language and Social Psychology* 28, 428–440.

Colton, M., Roberts, S. and Vanstone, M. (2010) "Sexual abuse by men who work with children," *Journal of Child Sexual Abuse* 19, 345–364.

Corby, B. (1998) *Managing Child Sexual Abuse Cases*. London: Jessica Kingsley.

Council of Europe (2010) European Convention on Human Rights, http://www.echr.coe.int/NR/rdonlyres/D5CC24A7-DC13-4318-B457-5C9014916D7A/0/CONVENTION_ENG_WEB.pdf (accessed May 2, 2012).

Davies, S.E. (2008) "Policing transnational crime: an introduction to police work in Australia," in R. Broadhurst and S.E. Davies (eds), *Policing in Context*. Australia: Oxford University Press, pp. 174–191.

Denov, M. (2004) *Perspectives on Female Sex Offending: A Culture of Denial*. Aldershot: Ashgate.

Donnelly, S. and Inglis, T. (2009) "The media and the Catholic Church in Ireland: reporting clerical child sex abuse," *Journal of Contemporary Religion* 25, 1–19.

Elliott, M. (1993) *Female Sexual Abuse of Children*. New York: Guildford Press.

Fagan, D. (2011) Show support for safety of our kids by signing petition for GPS tracking of sex offenders, *Courier-Mail*, http://www.couriermail.com.au/news/queensland/show-support-for-safety-of-our-kids/story-e6freoof-1226065179995 (accessed April 25, 2012).

Finn, M.A. and Muirhead-Steves, S. (2002) "The effectiveness of electronic monitoring with violent male parolees," *Justice Quarterly* 19, 293–312.

Fontes, L.A. and Plummer, C. (2010) "Cultural issues in disclosures of child sexual abuse," *Journal of Child Sexual Abuse* 19, 491–518.

Frank, D.J., Camp, B.J. and Boutcher, S.A. (2010) "Worldwide trends in the criminal regulation of sex, 1945–2005," *American Sociological Review* 75, 867–893.

Gallagher, B., Fraser, C., Christmann, K. and Hodgson, B. (2006) International and Internet Child Sexual Abuse and Exploitation. Project Report. University of Huddersfield, Huddersfield, UK, http://eprints.hud.ac.uk/461/1/1Gallagher2006.pdf (accessed September 7, 2012).

Gavrielides, T. (2012) "Clergy child sexual abuse and the restorative justice dialogue," *Oxford Journal of Law and Religion*, http://jcs.oxfordjournals.org/content/early/2012/04/23/jcs.css041.extract (accessed September 7, 2012).

George, M. (2006) "Electronic monitoring, effectiveness, and public policy," *Criminology and Public Policy* 5, 57–60.

Gilvovich, T. and Griffin, D. (2002) "Introduction – heuristics and biases: then and now," in T. Gilvovich, D. Griffin and D. Kahneman (eds), *Heuristics and Biases: The Psychology of Intuitive Judgement*. Cambridge: Cambridge University Press, pp. 1–18.

Grubin, D. (1998) Sex offending against children: understanding the risk, Police Research Series, http://library.npia.police.uk/docs/hopolicers/fprs99.pdf (accessed September 7, 2012).

Guardian (2004) "Internet porn 'increasing child abuse'," January 12, http://www.guardian.co.uk/technology/2004/jan/12/childprotection.childrensservices (accessed September 7, 2012).

Healy, M.A. (2004) Child pornography: an international perspective. Prepared as a working document for the World Congress against Commercial Sexual Exploitation, http://www.crime-research.org/articles/536/ (accessed September 7, 2012).

Helbig, K. (2011) GPS tracking for sex offenders soon, *Courier-Mail*, http://www.couriermail.com.au/ipad/gps-tracking-for-sex-offenders-soon/story-fn6ck51p-1226165122627 (accessed April 25, 2012).

Hersen, M. and Gross, A.M. (2008) *Handbook of Clinical Psychology, Volume 2: Children and Adolescents*. Chichester: John Wiley & Sons, Ltd.

Hucklesby, A. (2008) "Vehicles of desistance? The impact of electronically monitored curfew orders," *Criminology and Criminal Justice* 8, 51–71.

Interpol (n.d. a) Appropriate terminology, http://www.interpol.int/Crime-areas/Crimes-against-children/Appropriate-terminology (accessed September 7, 2012).

Interpol (n.d. b) Crimes against children, http://www.interpol.int/Crime-areas/Crimes-against-children/Crimes-against-children (accessed September 7, 2012).

JSOnline (2012) Dutch prosecutors demand 20-year sentence for man accused of molesting dozens of minors, *Journal Sentinel Online*, http://hosted.ap.org/fynamic/stories/E/EU_NETHERLANDS_PEDOPHILE_TRIAL?SITE=WIMIL%SECTION=HOMEand TEMPLATE+DEFAULT (accessed April 16, 2012.

Kilkelly, U. (2003) The right to respect for private and family life: a guide to the implementation of Article 8 of the European Convention on Human Rights, http://www.coe.int/t/dghl/publications/hrhandbooks/index_handbooks_en.asp (accessed September 7, 2012).

Killias, M., Gilliéron, G., Kissling, I. and Villettaz, P. (2010) "Community service versus electronic monitoring – what works better?," *British Journal of Criminology* 50, 1155–1170.

Knoll, J. (2010) "Teacher sexual misconduct: grooming patterns and female offenders," *Journal of Child Sexual Abuse* 19, 371–386.

Krug, E.G., Dahlberg, L.L., Mercy, J.A. *et al.* (2002) *World Report on Violence and Health*. Geneva: World Health Organization.

Lynch, M. (2002) "Pedophiles and cyber-predators as contaminating forces: the language of disgust, pollution, and boundary invasions in federal debates on sex offender legislation," *Law & Social Inquiry* 27, 529–566.

Manser, A. (1967) *Sartre: A Philosophical Study*. London: Athlone Press.

Martellozzo, E., Nehring, D. and Taylor, H. (2010) "Online child sexual abuse by female offenders: an exploratory study," *International Journal of Cyber Criminology* 4, 592–609.

Michael, M.G. and Michael, K. (2009) "Uberveillance: microchipping people and the assault on privacy," *Quadrant* LIII, 85–89.

Nellis, M. (2006) "Surveillance, rehabilitation, and electronic monitoring: getting the issues clear," *Criminology and Public Policy* 5, 103–108.

News.com.au (2009) Sex predators flout law through outdated technology, http://www.news.com.au/news/sex-predators-flout-law-through-outdated-technology/story-fna7dq6e-1225735937475 (accessed April 25, 2012).

Ost, S. (2009) *Child Pornography and Sexual Grooming: Legal and Societal Responses*. Cambridge: Cambridge University Press.

Padgett, K.G., Bales, W.D. and Blomberg, T.G. (2006) "Under surveillance: an empirical test of the effectiveness and consequences of electronic monitoring," *Criminology and Public Policy* 5, 61–92.

Parkinson, P., Oates, K. and Jayakody, A. (2009) Study of reported child sexual abuse in the Anglican Church, http://www.archive.anglican.org.au/docs/Study%20of%20Reported%20Child%20Sexual%20Abuse%20in%20the%20Anglican%20Church%20May%202009%20Full%20Report.pdf (accessed September 7, 2012).

Payne, B.K. and Gainey, R.R. (2000) "Electronic monitoring: philosophical, systemic, and political issues," *Journal of Offender Rehabilitation* 93–111.

Raider, M.C. (1994) "Juvenile electronic monitoring: a community based program to augment residential treatment," *Residential Treatment for Children and Youth* 12, 37–48.

Reilhac, G. and Thomas, L. (2012) Germany should stop the "degrading" practice of surgically castrating sex offenders, the anti-torture panel at Europe's top human rights watchdog said on Wednesday, http://in.reuters.com/article/2012/02/22/germany-castration-idINDEE81L0GL20120222 (accessed September 7, 2012).

Renzema, M. and Mayo-Wilson, E. (2005) "Can electronic monitoring reduce crime for moderate to high-risk offenders?," *Journal of Experimental Criminology* 1, 215–237.

Roy, S. (1997) "Five years of electronic monitoring of adults and juveniles in Lake County, Indiana: a comparative study of factors related to failure," *Journal of Crime and Justice* 20, 141–160.

Ruan, G., Miyoshi, T.J., Metzner, J.L. *et al.* (1996) "Trends in a national sample of sexually abusive youths," *Journal of the American Academy of Child and Adolescent Psychiatry* 35, 17–25.

Sartre, J. P. (1990) *Huis Clos*. London: Routledge.

Shannon, S. and Uggen, C. (2012) "Incarceration as a political institution," in E. Amenta, K. Nash and A. Scott (eds), *The Wiley-Blackwell Companion to Political Sociology*. Oxford: Wiley-Blackwell.

Sheehan, V. and Sullivan, J. (2010) "A qualitative analysis of child sex offenders involved in the manufacture of indecent images of children," *Journal of Sexual Aggression* 16, 143–167.

Spencer, D. (2009) "Sex offender as homo sacer," *Punishment and Society* 11, 219–240.

State of North Carolina, Department of Juvenile Justice and Delinquency Prevention (2005) Legislative Report on Electronic Monitoring of Juveniles: Calendar Year 2004, www.ncdjjdp.org/resources/statistics_legislative/04-05/EHALegislative04.doc (accessed September 15, 2012).

Sullivan, J., Beech, A.R., Craig, L.A. and Gannon, T.A. (2011) "Comparing intra-familial and extra-familial child sexual abusers with professionals who have sexually abused children with whom they work," *International Journal of Offender Therapy and Comparative Criminology* 55, 56–74.

Tagwireyi, G. (2011) Comprehensive legal approaches to combat child pornography: an international and regional perspective. Conference paper, http://www.commonwealthigf.org/wp-content/uploads/2011/03/ICIA-Conference-Paper-ICMEC-FINAL.pdf (accessed September 7, 2012).

UK Government (2003) Filming by parents of school nativity plays. House of Commons, Session 2002–2003, www.parliament.uk/edm/2002-03/390 (accessed September 7, 2012).

UN (United Nations) *United Nations Treaty Collection: Chapter IV Human Rights – Optional Protocol to the UN Convention on the Rights of the Child on the Involvement of Children in Armed Conflict*, http://treaties.un.org/Pages/ViewDetails.aspx?src=TREATYandmtdsg_no=IV-11-bandchapter=4andlang=en (accessed April 30, 2012).

Vielmetti, B. (2010) "Jury to decide fate of pedophile held at a mental health facility," *Journal Sentinel*, http://www.jsonline.com/news/crime/80762252.htm (accessed September 7, 2012).

Walters, G.D. (2012) *Crime in a Psychological Context: From Career Criminals to Criminal Careers*. London: Sage.

Wardill, S. (2011) "*Courier-Mail* campaign wins Bligh Pledge to fund GPS tracking for sex offenders," *Courier-Mail*, http://www.couriermail.com.au/news/queensland/

courier-mail-campaign-wins-bligh-pledge-to-fund-gps-tracking-for-sex-offenders/story-e6freoof–1226070220835 (accessed April 25, 2012).

White, M.D. and Terry, K.J. (2008) "Child sexual abuse in the Catholic Church: revisiting the rotten apples explanation," *Criminal Justice and Behavior* 35, 658–678.

Winslow, R.W. and Zhang, S.X. (2008) *Forcible Rape*. New Jersey: Pearson.

World Congress against Commercial Sexual Exploitation of Children (1996) 1st World Congress against the Commercial Sexual Exploitation of Children, http://www.csecworldcongress.org/en/stockholm/index.htm (accessed September 7, 2012).

Index

The Wiley-Blackwell Handbook of Legal and Ethical Aspects of Sex Offender Treatment and Management,
First Edition. Edited by Karen Harrison and Bernadette Rainey.
© 2013 John Wiley & Sons, Ltd. Published 2013 by John Wiley & Sons, Ltd.